DEADPOOL
CLASSIC

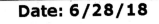

ALL THE REST

DEADPOOL

ALL THE REST

CAPTAIN AMERICA: WHO WON'T WIELD THE SHIELD?

"FORBUSH MAN: FORBUSH KILLS!"
WRITER: Jason Aaron
ARTIST & COLORIST:
Mirco Pierfederici

"DOCTOR AMERICA: OCCULT OPERATIVE OF LIBERTY"
WRITER: Matt Fraction
ARTIST: Brendan McCarthy
COLORIST: Howard Hallis

"THE GOLDEN AGE DEADPOOL"
WRITER: Stuart Moore
ARTIST: Joe Quinones
COLORIST: Javier Rodriguez

LETTERER: Todd Klein
COVER ART: Gerald Parel

CABLE #25
"TWO MUTANTS & A BABY"
WRITER: Duane Swierczynski
PENCILER: Paco Medina
INKER: Juan Vlasco
COLORIST: Edgar Delgado
LETTERER: VC's Joe Caramagna
COVER ART: Simone Bianchi, Andrea Silvestri & Simone Peruzzi

DEADPOOL & CABLE #26
WRITER: Duane Swierczynski
ARTIST: Leandro Fernandez
COLORIST: Steve Buccellato
LETTERER: Jeff Eckleberry
COVER ART: Dave Wilkins

AMAZING SPIDER-MAN ANNUAL #38
DEADPOOL ANNUAL #1
INCREDIBLE HULKS ANNUAL #1
"IDENTITY WARS"
PENCILERS: Lee Garbett (*Amazing Spider-Man*),
Juan Doe (*Deadpool*) & Al Barrionuevo (*Incredible Hulks*)
INKERS: Mark Pennington (*Amazing Spider-Man & Incredible Hulks*)
& Juan Doe (*Deadpool*)
COLORIST: Fabio D'Auria
LETTERER: VC's Clayton Cowles
COVER ART: Steve McNiven, Mark Morales & Marta Gracia

WOLVERINE/DEADPOOL: THE DECOY
WRITER: Stuart Moore
ARTIST: Shawn Crystal
COLORIST: John Rauch
LETTERER: Jeff Eckleberry
COVER ART: Skottie Young

FEAR ITSELF: DEADPOOL
"THE CHOSENEST"
"WALRUS BY NIGHT!"
"FROM TUSK TILL DAWN"
WRITER: Christopher Hastings
PENCILER: Bong Dazo
INKER: Joe Pimentel
COLORIST: Matt Milla
LETTERER: Simon Bowland
COVER ART: Ryan Stegman, Michael Babinski & John Rauch
Special Thanks to MC Hammer & Jeff Epstein

DEADPOOL CORPS: RANK AND FOUL
HEAD WRITER/COORDINATOR: Jeff Christiansen
WRITING/COORDINATION ASSISTANTS: Mike O'Sullivan,
Markus Raymond & Mike Fichera
WRITERS: Michael Hoskin, Ronald Byrd, Mike O'Sullivan,
Jacob Rougemont, Madison Carter, Markus Raymond,
Kevin Garcia, Stuart Vandal, Chris Biggs, Rob London,
Sean McQuaid, David Wiltfong, Eric J. Moreels & Mike Gagnon
SELECT CHARACTER ARTWORK: Gus Vazquez & Tom Chu
SELECT COLORING: Tom Smith
COPY EDITORS: Brian Overton & Ted Kutt
COVER ART: Humberto Ramos & Edgar Delgado

ASSISTANT EDITORS: Tom Brennan (*Captain America*), Sebastian Girner (*Cable*),
Ellie Pyle (*Identity Wars*) & Alex Starbuck (*Rank & Foul*)
ASSOCIATE EDITORS: Alejandro Arbona (*Amazing Spider-Man*)
& John Denning (*Rank & Foul*)
EDITORS: Stephen Wacker (*Captain America*), Axel Alonso (*Cable*),
Alejandro Arbona (*Origins, Identity Wars*), Sebastian Girner (*Decoy*),
Jordan D. White (*Fear Itself*) & Jeff Youngquist (*Rank & Foul*)

SENIOR EDITORS: Stephen Wacker (*Identity Wars*) &
Nick Lowe (*Fear Itself*) with Axel Alonso (*Origins*)

VP OF DIGITAL CONTENT & PROGRAMMING: John Cerilli
ASSOCIATE PRODUCER: Harry Go
DIGITAL PRODUCTION: Samantha Gallagher, Eric Bloom & Idette Winecoor
DIGITAL PRODUCTION MANAGER: Tim Smith 3

Deadpool created by **Rob Liefeld & Fabian Nicieza**

COLLECTION EDITOR: Mark D. Beazley
ASSISTANT EDITOR: Sarah Brunstad
ASSISTANT MANAGING EDITOR: Joe Hochstein
ASSOCIATE MANAGING EDITOR: Alex Starbuck
EDITOR, SPECIAL PROJECTS: Jennifer Grünwald

SENIOR EDITOR, SPECIAL PROJECTS: Jeff Youngquist
RESEARCH & LAYOUT: Jeph York
BOOK DESIGNER: Adam Del Re
SVP PRINT, SALES & MARKETING: David Gabriel

EDITOR IN CHIEF: Axel Alonso
CHIEF CREATIVE OFFICER: Joe Quesada
PUBLISHER: Dan Buckley
EXECUTIVE PRODUCER: Alan Fine

DEADPOOL CLASSIC VOL. 15: ALL THE REST. Contains material originally published in magazine form as CAPTAIN AMERICA: WHO WON'T WIELD THE SHIELD #1, CABLE #25, DEADPOOL & CABLE #26, AMAZING SPIDER-MAN ANNUAL #38, DEADPOOL ANNUAL #1, INCREDIBLE HULKS ANNUAL #1, WOLVERINE/DEADPOOL: THE DECOY #1, FEAR ITSELF: DEADPOOL #1-3 and DEADPOOL CORPS: RANK AND FOUL #1. First printing 2016. ISBN# 978-0-7851-9690-7. Published by MARVEL WORLDWIDE, INC., a subsidiary of MARVEL ENTERTAINMENT, LLC. OFFICE OF PUBLICATION: 135 West 50th Street, New York, NY 10020. Copyright © 2016 MARVEL No similarity between any of the names, characters, persons, or institutions in this magazine with those of any living or dead person or institution is intended, and any such similarity which may exist is purely coincidental. **Printed in the U.S.A.** ALAN FINE, President, Marvel Entertainment; DAN BUCKLEY, President, TV, Publishing and Brand Management; JOE QUESADA, Chief Creative Officer; TOM BREVOORT, SVP of Publishing; DAVID BOGART, SVP of Operations & Procurement, Publishing; C.B. CEBULSKI, VP of International Development & Brand Management; DAVID GABRIEL, SVP Print, Sales & Marketing; JIM O'KEEFE, VP of Operations & Logistics; DAN CARR, Executive Director of Publishing Technology; SUSAN CRESPI, Editorial Operations Manager; ALEX MORALES, Publishing Operations Manager; STAN LEE, Chairman Emeritus. For information regarding advertising in Marvel Comics or on Marvel.com, please contact Jonathan Rheingold, VP of Custom Solutions & Ad Sales, at jrheingold@marvel.com. For Marvel subscription inquiries, please call 800-217-9158. **Manufactured between** 1/1/2016 and 2/23/2016 by R.R. DONNELLEY, INC., SALEM, VA, USA.

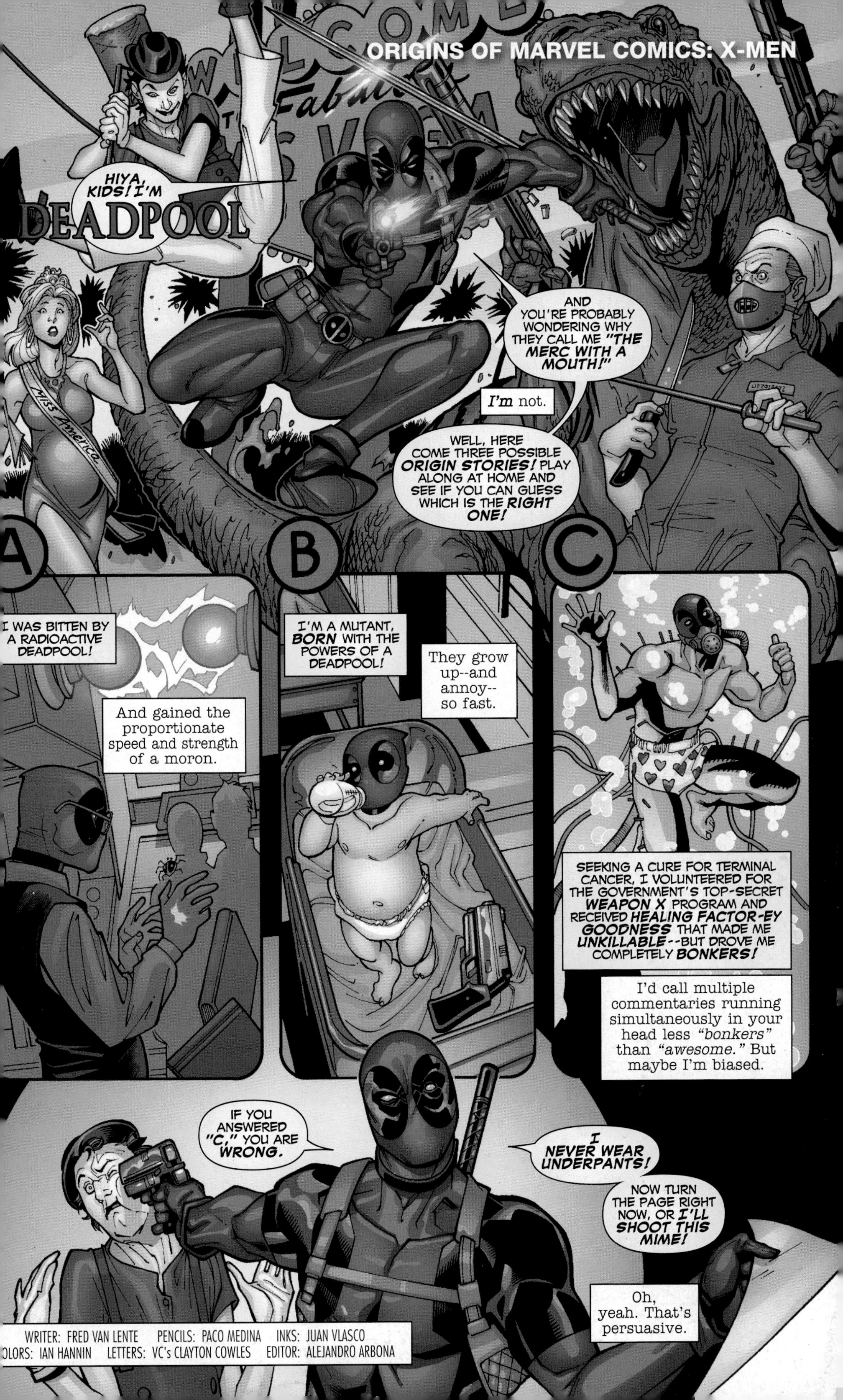

ORIGINS OF MARVEL COMICS: X-MEN
HIYA, KIDS! I'M DEADPOOL
AND YOU'RE PROBABLY WONDERING WHY THEY CALL ME "THE MERC WITH A MOUTH!"
I'm not.
WELL, HERE COME THREE POSSIBLE ORIGIN STORIES! PLAY ALONG AT HOME AND SEE IF YOU CAN GUESS WHICH IS THE RIGHT ONE!
A
I WAS BITTEN BY A RADIOACTIVE DEADPOOL!
And gained the proportionate speed and strength of a moron.
B
I'M A MUTANT, BORN WITH THE POWERS OF A DEADPOOL!
They grow up--and annoy--so fast.
C
SEEKING A CURE FOR TERMINAL CANCER, I VOLUNTEERED FOR THE GOVERNMENT'S TOP-SECRET WEAPON X PROGRAM AND RECEIVED HEALING FACTOR-EY GOODNESS THAT MADE ME UNKILLABLE--BUT DROVE ME COMPLETELY BONKERS!
I'd call multiple commentaries running simultaneously in your head less "bonkers" than "awesome." But maybe I'm biased.
IF YOU ANSWERED "C," YOU ARE WRONG.
I NEVER WEAR UNDERPANTS!
NOW TURN THE PAGE RIGHT NOW, OR I'LL SHOOT THIS MIME!
Oh, yeah. That's persuasive.
WRITER: FRED VAN LENTE PENCILS: PACO MEDINA INKS: JUAN VLASCO
OLORS: IAN HANNIN LETTERS: VC's CLAYTON COWLES EDITOR: ALEJANDRO ARBONA

CAPTAIN AMERICA:
WHO WON'T WIELD THE SHIELD

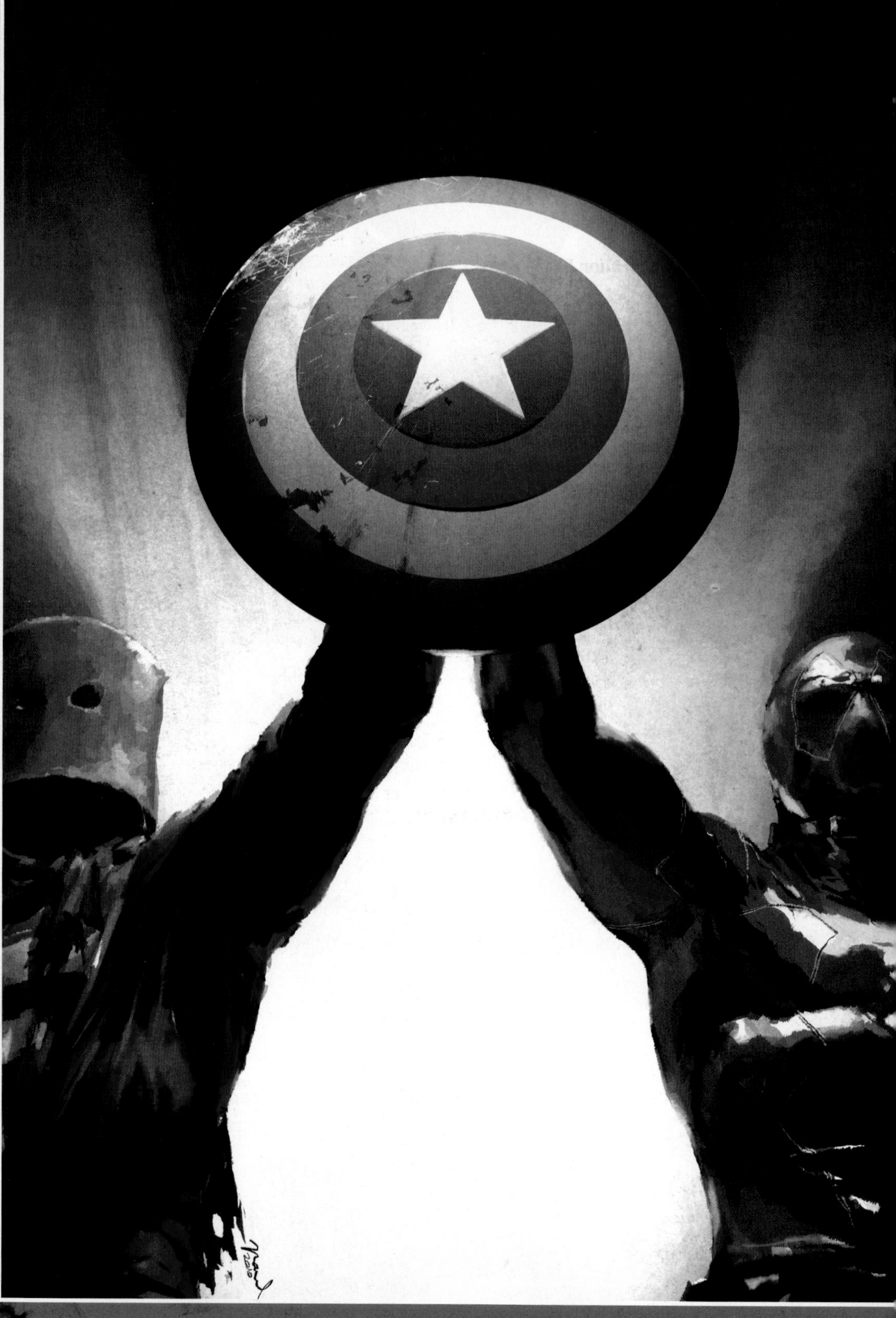

WON'T

CAPTAIN AMERICA
WHO (WILL) WIEL WIELD THE SHIELD?

This issue takes place AFTER the events of some comic on sale next month, completely blowing its ending.
And they still promoted Brevoort! The suckers.

MARVEL

To: Stephen Wacker, Senior Editor, Marvel Comics
From: Dave Althoff, Associate Counsel, Marvel Comics
Re: Captain America: Who Won't Wield the Shield

Steve,

We need to talk about this "Captain America: Who Won't Wield the Shield" nonsense. You can't be serious about publishing this book. I stopped by your office but Brennan says you're "in a meeting and won't come back until I leave you alone." How can you be in a meeting for sixteen days?! Is Brevoort leading a beard-trimming seminar or something?

I'm begging you – shelve the book. If not for me, then for my newborn twins. Look at them, Peter and Zachary – look at how happy they are. Now think of how they'll feel when this book gets us all canned. Think about it!

Look, I know you wanted me to name one of the kids Stephen. I'm prepared to do it – I'll get the birth certificate, change it up, and boom! Stephen Wacker Althoff. Just drop this book. Please? PLEASE?!

Regards,

Dave Althoff

Mr. Wacker,
when you wake
up, you should
probably read
this.

--Brennan

P.S. Spider-Man
stinks now!

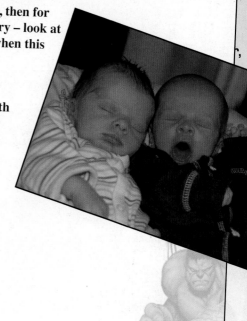

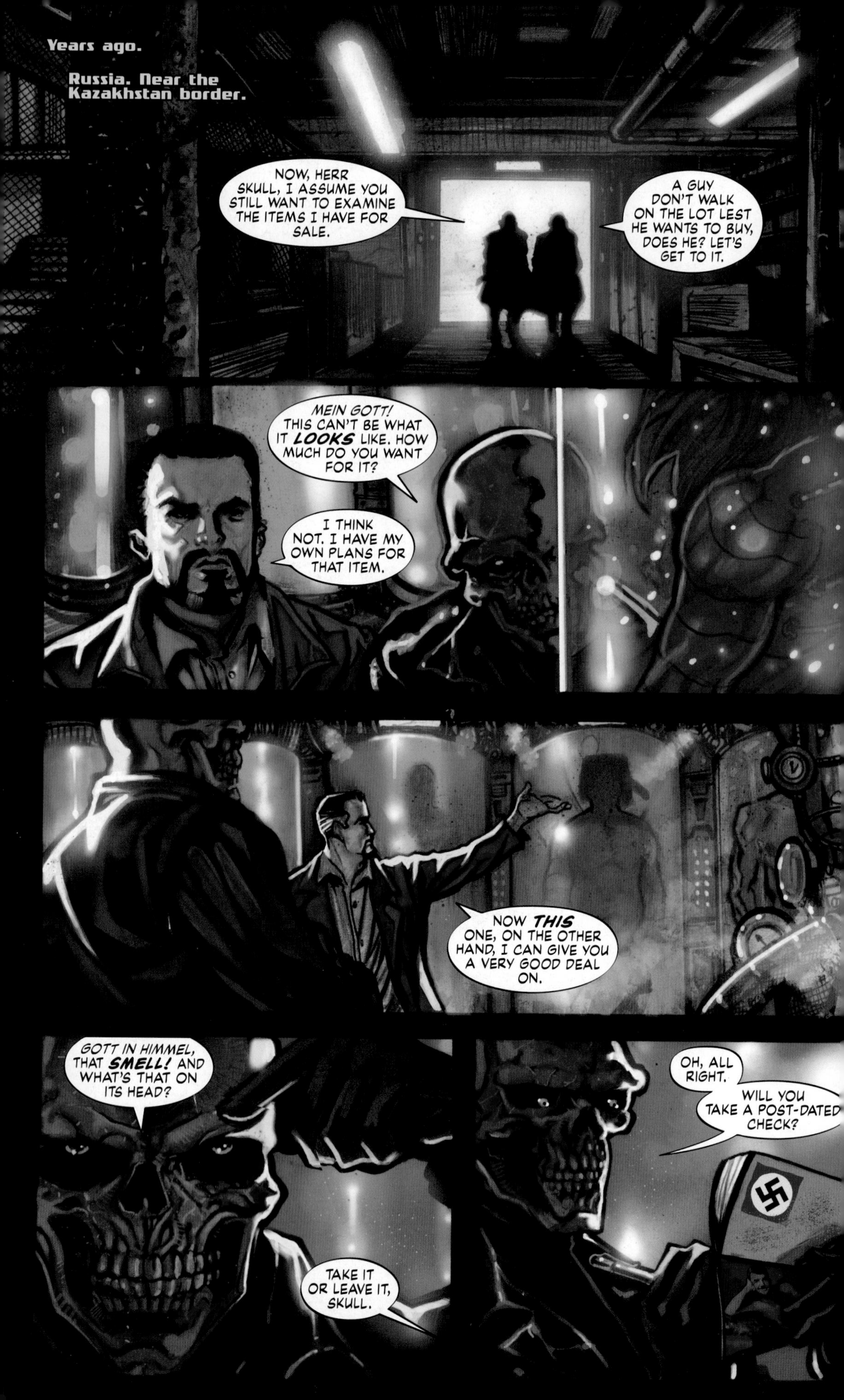
Years ago.
Russia. Near the Kazakhstan border.
NOW, HERR SKULL, I ASSUME YOU STILL WANT TO EXAMINE THE ITEMS I HAVE FOR SALE.
A GUY DON'T WALK ON THE LOT LEST HE WANTS TO BUY, DOES HE? LET'S GET TO IT.
MEIN GOTT! THIS CAN'T BE WHAT IT LOOKS LIKE. HOW MUCH DO YOU WANT FOR IT?
I THINK NOT. I HAVE MY OWN PLANS FOR THAT ITEM.
NOW THIS ONE, ON THE OTHER HAND, I CAN GIVE YOU A VERY GOOD DEAL ON.
GOTT IN HIMMEL, THAT SMELL! AND WHAT'S THAT ON ITS HEAD?
TAKE IT OR LEAVE IT, SKULL.
OH, ALL RIGHT.
WILL YOU TAKE A POST-DATED CHECK?

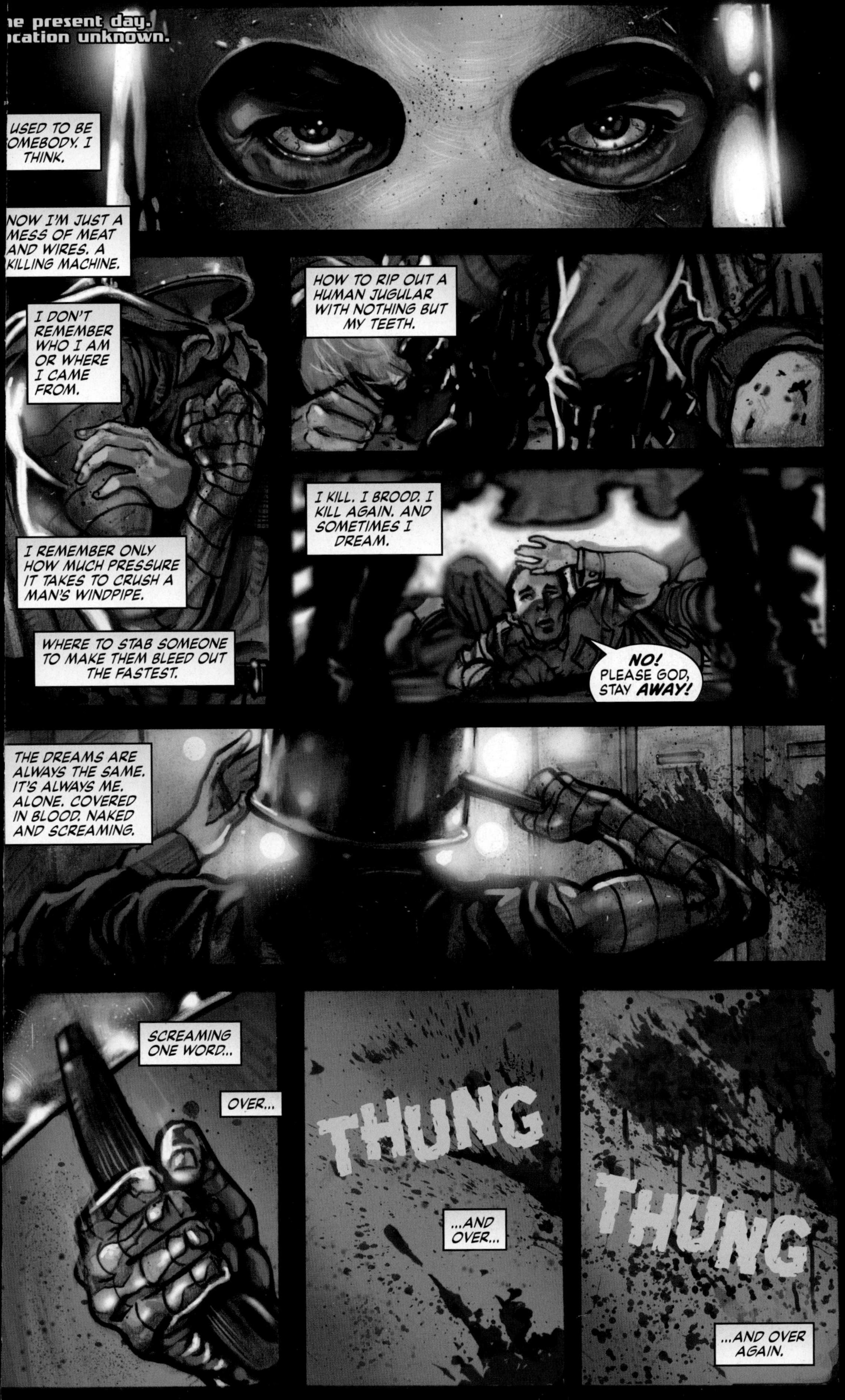

ne present day.
ocation unknown.
USED TO BE OMEBODY. I THINK.
NOW I'M JUST A MESS OF MEAT AND WIRES. A KILLING MACHINE.
I DON'T REMEMBER WHO I AM OR WHERE I CAME FROM.
HOW TO RIP OUT A HUMAN JUGULAR WITH NOTHING BUT MY TEETH.
I REMEMBER ONLY HOW MUCH PRESSURE IT TAKES TO CRUSH A MAN'S WINDPIPE.
WHERE TO STAB SOMEONE TO MAKE THEM BLEED OUT THE FASTEST.
I KILL. I BROOD. I KILL AGAIN. AND SOMETIMES I DREAM.
NO! PLEASE GOD, STAY AWAY!
THE DREAMS ARE ALWAYS THE SAME. IT'S ALWAYS ME. ALONE. COVERED IN BLOOD. NAKED AND SCREAMING.
SCREAMING ONE WORD...
OVER...
THUNG
...AND OVER...
THUNG
...AND OVER AGAIN.

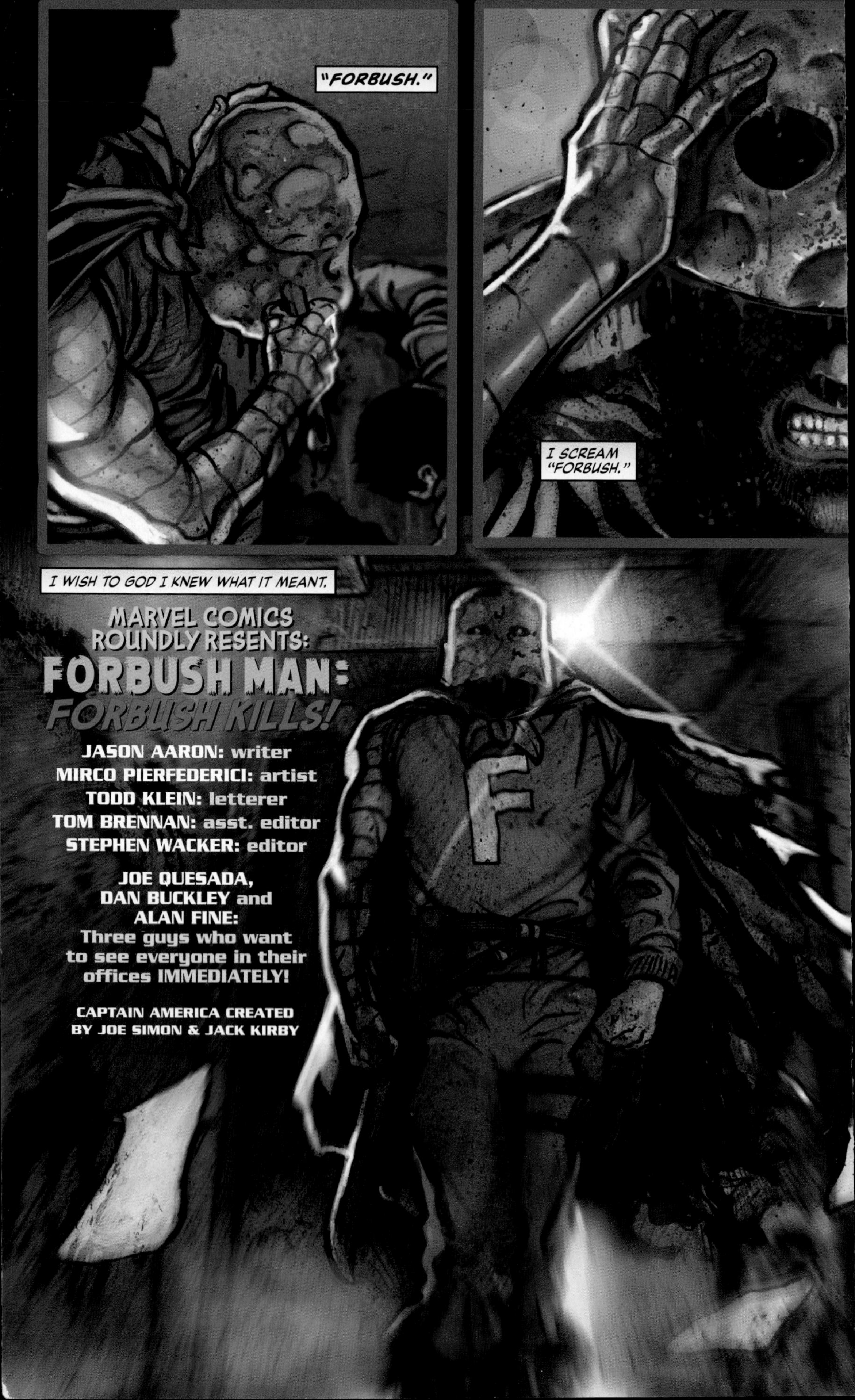
"FORBUSH."
I SCREAM "FORBUSH."
I WISH TO GOD I KNEW WHAT IT MEANT.
MARVEL COMICS ROUNDLY RESENTS:
FORBUSH MAN:
FORBUSH KILLS!
JASON AARON: writer
MIRCO PIERFEDERICI: artist
TODD KLEIN: letterer
TOM BRENNAN: asst. editor
STEPHEN WACKER: editor
JOE QUESADA, DAN BUCKLEY and ALAN FINE:
Three guys who want to see everyone in their offices IMMEDIATELY!
CAPTAIN AMERICA CREATED BY JOE SIMON & JACK KIRBY

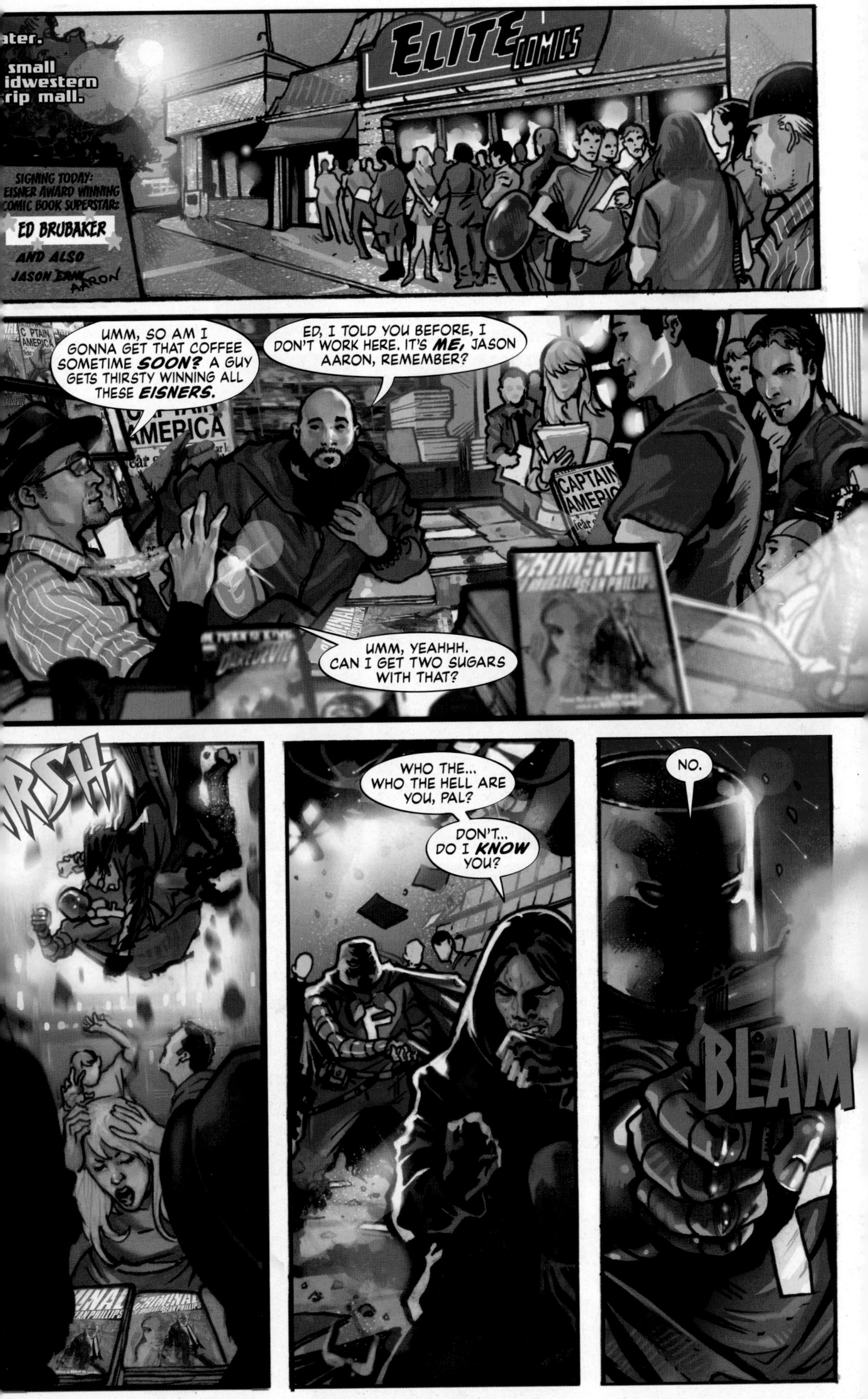

ater.
small
idwestern
rip mall.
ELITE COMICS
SIGNING TODAY: EISNER AWARD WINNING COMIC BOOK SUPERSTARz
ED BRUBAKER
AND ALSO
JASON AARON
UMM, SO AM I GONNA GET THAT COFFEE SOMETIME SOON? A GUY GETS THIRSTY WINNING ALL THESE EISNERS.
ED, I TOLD YOU BEFORE, I DON'T WORK HERE. IT'S ME, JASON AARON, REMEMBER?
UMM, YEAHHH. CAN I GET TWO SUGARS WITH THAT?
CAPTAIN AMERICA
RSH
WHO THE... WHO THE HELL ARE YOU, PAL?
DON'T... DO I KNOW YOU?
NO.
BLAM

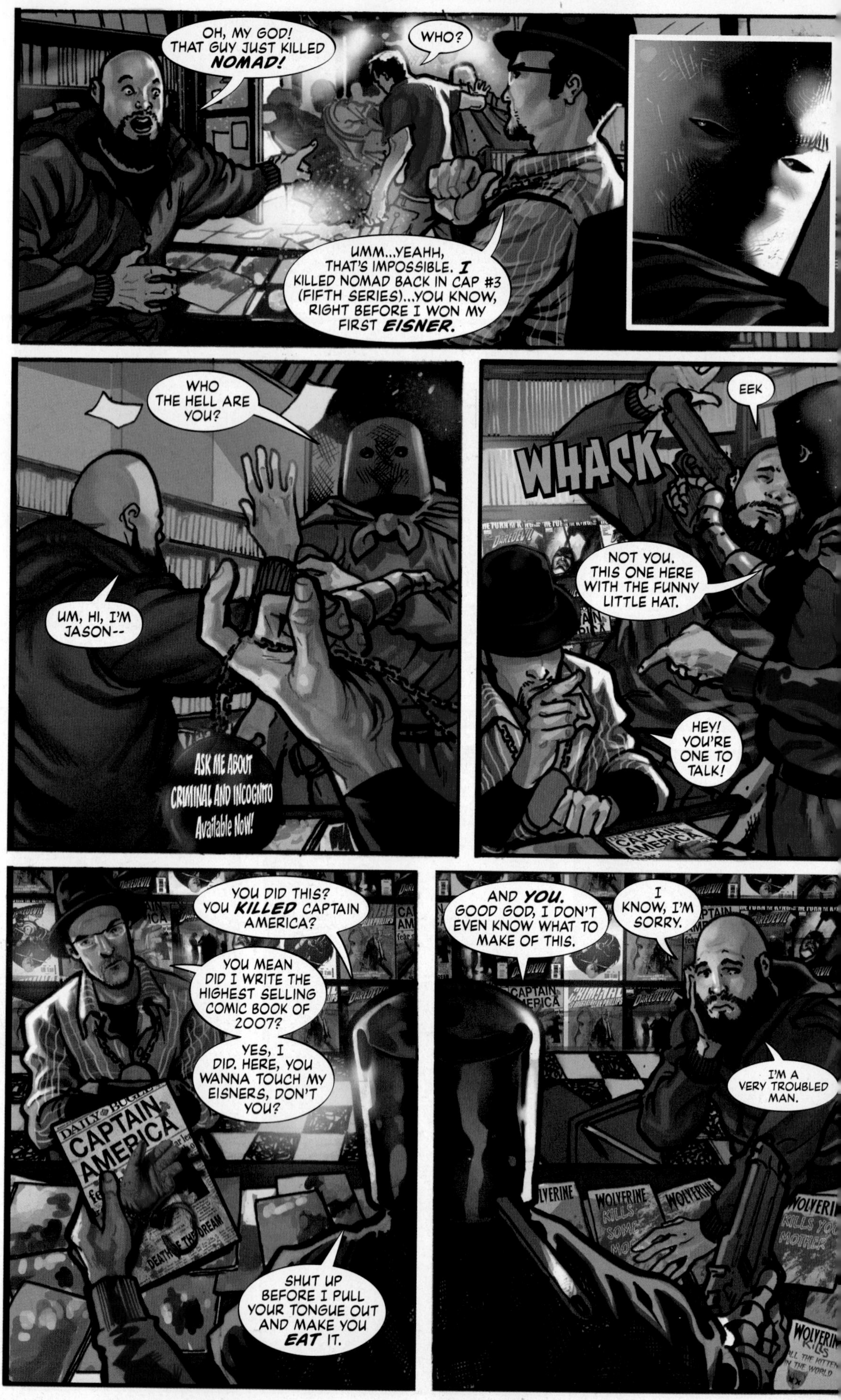

OH, MY GOD! THAT GUY JUST KILLED NOMAD!
WHO?
UMM...YEAHH, THAT'S IMPOSSIBLE. I KILLED NOMAD BACK IN CAP #3 (FIFTH SERIES)...YOU KNOW, RIGHT BEFORE I WON MY FIRST EISNER.
WHO THE HELL ARE YOU?
UM, HI, I'M JASON--
ASK ME ABOUT CRIMINAL AND INCOGNITO Available Now!
EEK
WHACK
NOT YOU. THIS ONE HERE WITH THE FUNNY LITTLE HAT.
HEY! YOU'RE ONE TO TALK!
CAPTAIN AMERICA
YOU DID THIS? YOU KILLED CAPTAIN AMERICA?
YOU MEAN DID I WRITE THE HIGHEST SELLING COMIC BOOK OF 2007?
YES, I DID. HERE, YOU WANNA TOUCH MY EISNERS, DON'T YOU?
DAILY BUGLE
CAPTAIN AMERICA
SHUT UP BEFORE I PULL YOUR TONGUE OUT AND MAKE YOU EAT IT.
AND YOU. GOOD GOD, I DON'T EVEN KNOW WHAT TO MAKE OF THIS.
I KNOW, I'M SORRY.
I'M A VERY TROUBLED MAN.
WOLVERINE
WOLVERINE KILLS SOME MO
WOLVERINE
WOLVERINE KILLS YOU MOTHER
WOLVERINE KILLS ALL THE KITTEN IN THE WORLD

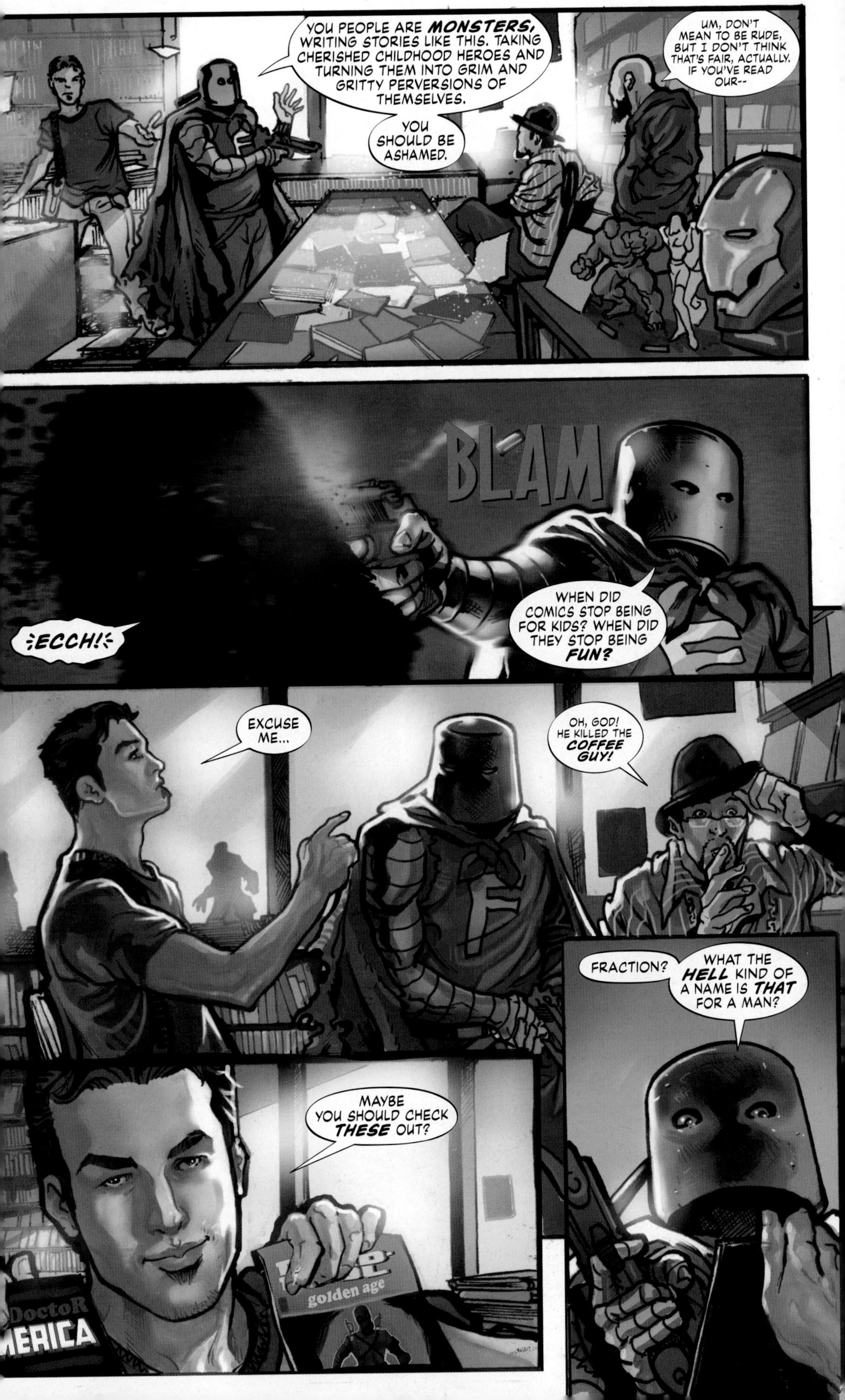

YOU PEOPLE ARE MONSTERS, WRITING STORIES LIKE THIS. TAKING CHERISHED CHILDHOOD HEROES AND TURNING THEM INTO GRIM AND GRITTY PERVERSIONS OF THEMSELVES.
YOU SHOULD BE ASHAMED.
UM, DON'T MEAN TO BE RUDE, BUT I DON'T THINK THAT'S FAIR, ACTUALLY. IF YOU'VE READ OUR--
BLAM
WHEN DID COMICS STOP BEING FOR KIDS? WHEN DID THEY STOP BEING FUN?
ECCH!
EXCUSE ME...
OH, GOD! HE KILLED THE COFFEE GUY!
FRACTION?
WHAT THE HELL KIND OF A NAME IS THAT FOR A MAN?
MAYBE YOU SHOULD CHECK THESE OUT?
golden age
DoctoR
MERICA

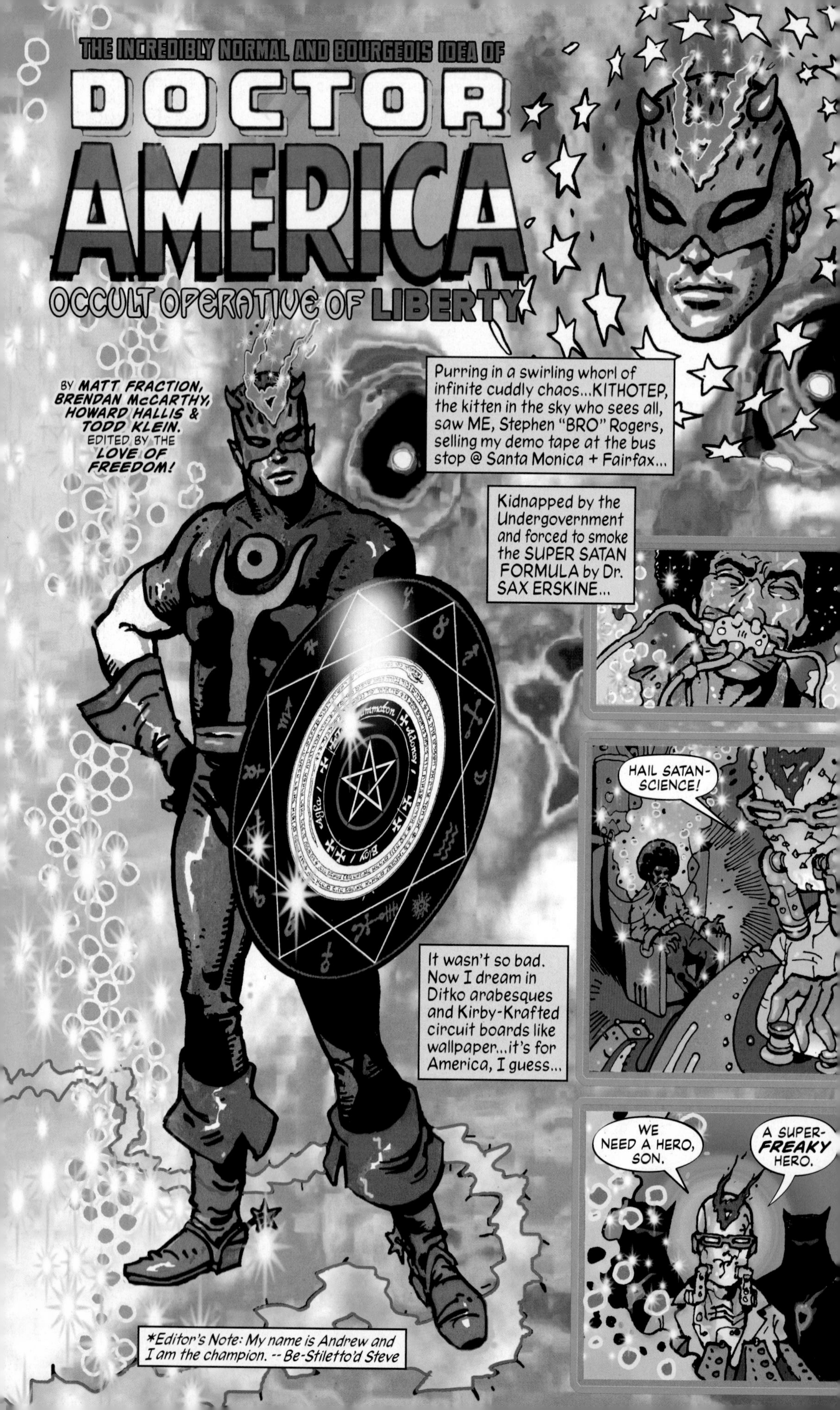

THE INCREDIBLY NORMAL AND BOURGEOIS IDEA OF
DOCTOR AMERICA
OCCULT OPERATIVE OF LIBERTY
BY MATT FRACTION, BRENDAN McCARTHY, HOWARD HALLIS & TODD KLEIN. EDITED BY THE LOVE OF FREEDOM!
Purring in a swirling whorl of infinite cuddly chaos...KITHOTEP, the kitten in the sky who sees all, saw ME, Stephen "BRO" Rogers, selling my demo tape at the bus stop @ Santa Monica + Fairfax...
Kidnapped by the Undergovernment and forced to smoke the SUPER SATAN FORMULA by Dr. SAX ERSKINE...
HAIL SATAN-SCIENCE!
It wasn't so bad. Now I dream in Ditko arabesques and Kirby-Krafted circuit boards like wallpaper...it's for America, I guess...
WE NEED A HERO, SON.
A SUPER-FREAKY HERO.
*Editor's Note: My name is Andrew and I am the champion. -- Be-Stiletto'd Steve

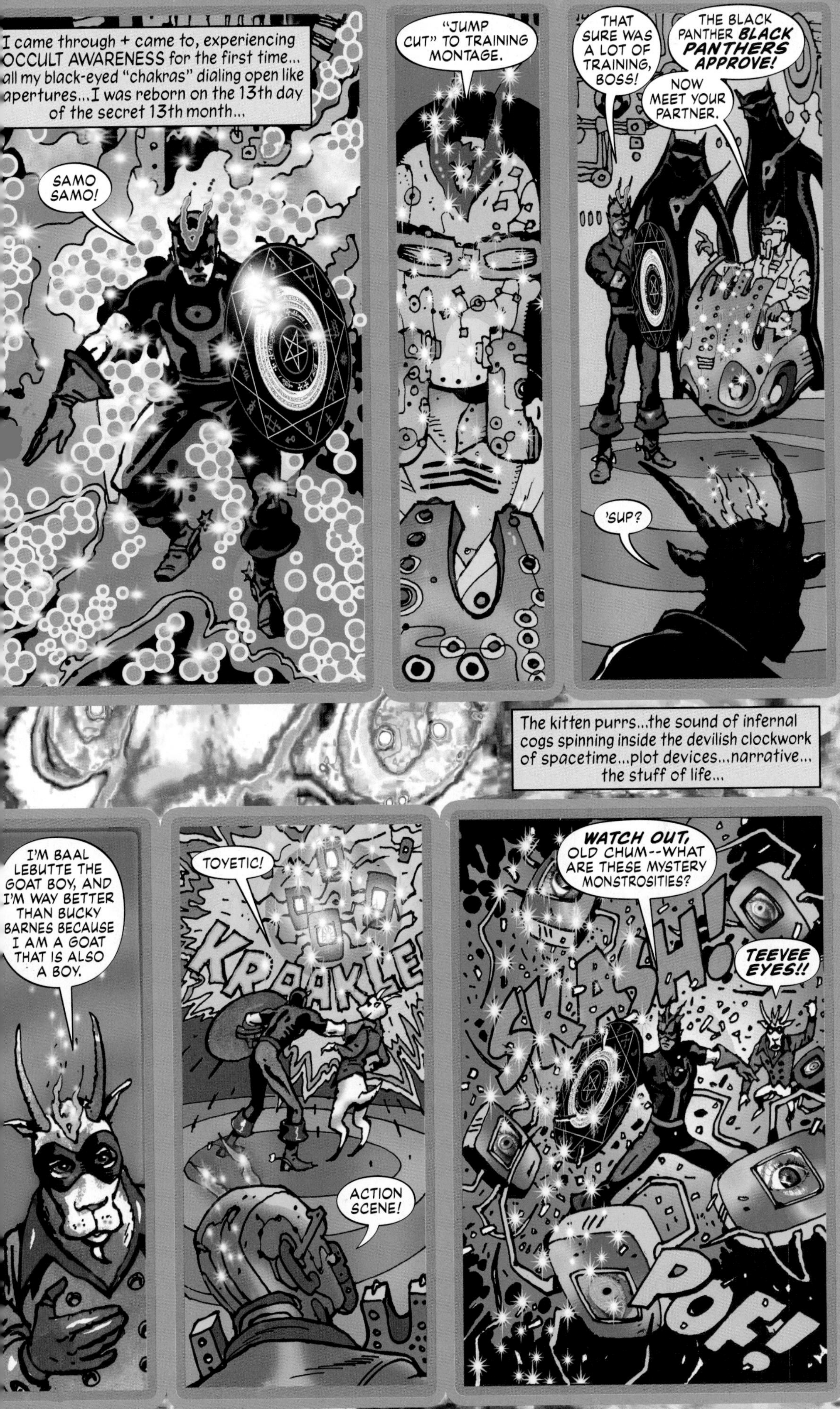
I came through + came to, experiencing OCCULT AWARENESS for the first time... all my black-eyed "chakras" dialing open like apertures...I was reborn on the 13th day of the secret 13th month...
SAMO SAMO!
"JUMP CUT" TO TRAINING MONTAGE.
THAT SURE WAS A LOT OF TRAINING, BOSS!
THE BLACK PANTHER **BLACK PANTHERS APPROVE!**
NOW MEET YOUR PARTNER.
'SUP?
The kitten purrs...the sound of infernal cogs spinning inside the devilish clockwork of spacetime...plot devices...narrative... the stuff of life...
I'M BAAL LEBUTTE THE GOAT BOY, AND I'M WAY BETTER THAN BUCKY BARNES BECAUSE I AM A GOAT THAT IS ALSO A BOY.
TOYETIC!
KRAAKLE
ACTION SCENE!
WATCH OUT, OLD CHUM--WHAT ARE THESE MYSTERY MONSTROSITIES?
TEEVEE EYES!!
POF!

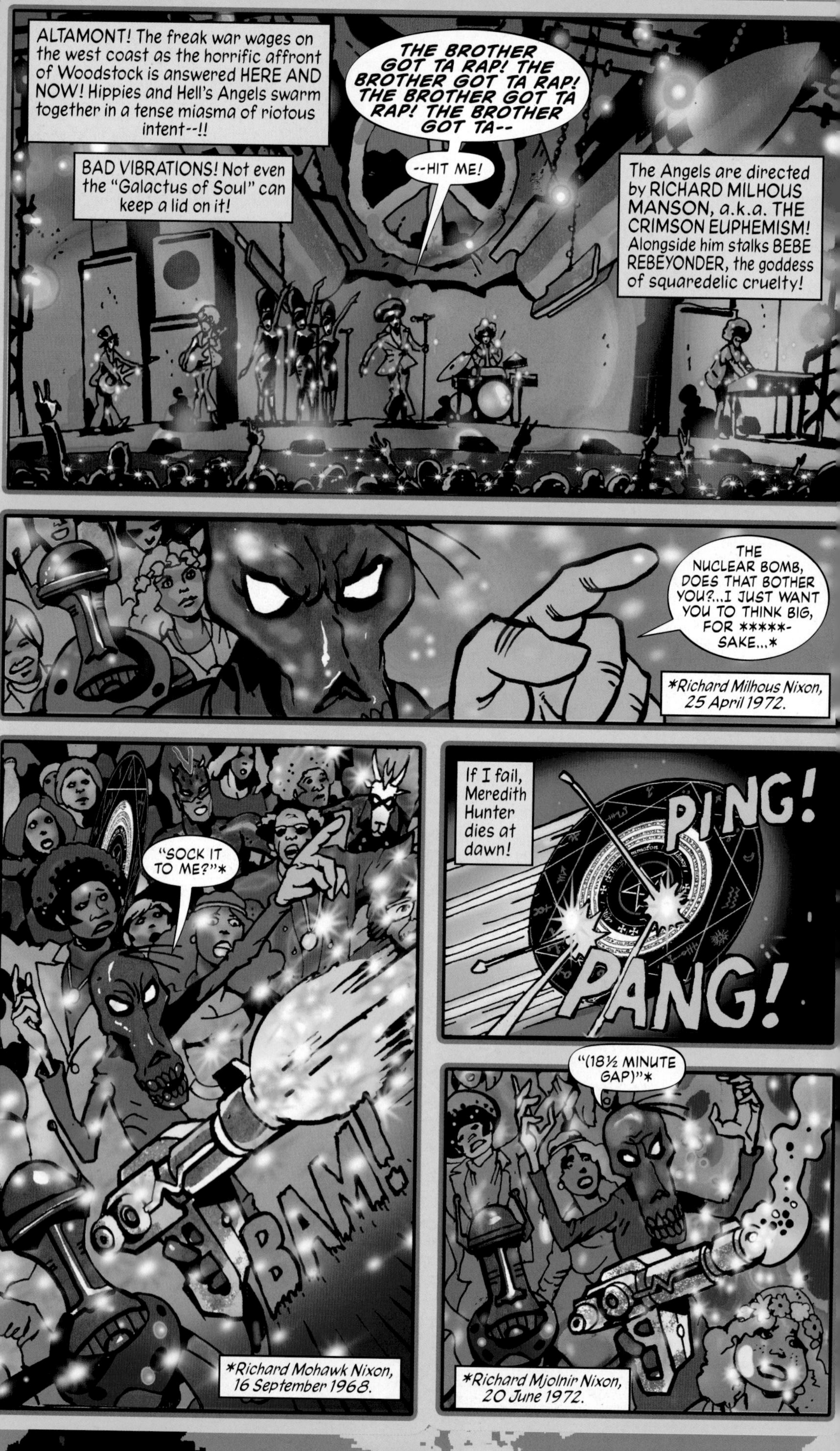
ALTAMONT! The freak war wages on the west coast as the horrific affront of Woodstock is answered HERE AND NOW! Hippies and Hell's Angels swarm together in a tense miasma of riotous intent--!!
THE BROTHER GOT TA RAP! THE BROTHER GOT TA RAP! THE BROTHER GOT TA RAP! THE BROTHER GOT TA--
--HIT ME!
BAD VIBRATIONS! Not even the "Galactus of Soul" can keep a lid on it!
The Angels are directed by RICHARD MILHOUS MANSON, a.k.a. THE CRIMSON EUPHEMISM! Alongside him stalks BEBE REBEYONDER, the goddess of squaredelic cruelty!
THE NUCLEAR BOMB, DOES THAT BOTHER YOU?...I JUST WANT YOU TO THINK BIG, FOR *****-SAKE...*
*Richard Milhous Nixon, 25 April 1972.
"SOCK IT TO ME?"*
BAM!
*Richard Mohawk Nixon, 16 September 1968.
If I fail, Meredith Hunter dies at dawn!
PING!
PANG!
"(18½ MINUTE GAP)"*
*Richard Mjolnir Nixon, 20 June 1972.

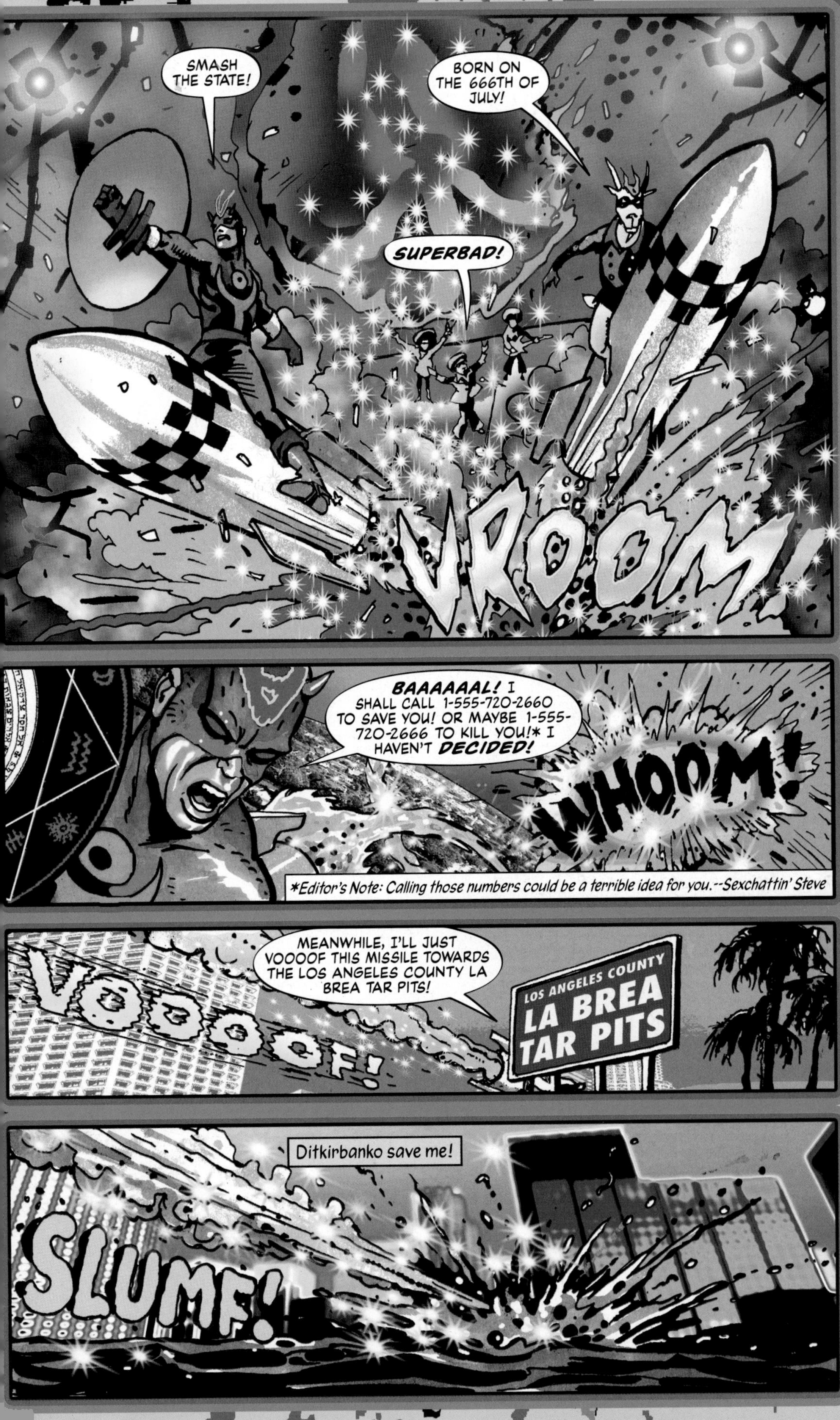
SMASH THE STATE!
BORN ON THE 666TH OF JULY!
SUPERBAD!
VROOM!
BAAAAAAL! I SHALL CALL 1-555-720-2660 TO SAVE YOU! OR MAYBE 1-555-720-2666 TO KILL YOU!* I HAVEN'T DECIDED!
WHOOM!
*Editor's Note: Calling those numbers could be a terrible idea for you.--Sexchattin' Steve
MEANWHILE, I'LL JUST VOOOOF THIS MISSILE TOWARDS THE LOS ANGELES COUNTY LA BREA TAR PITS!
VOOOOOF!
LOS ANGELES COUNTY
LA BREA TAR PITS
Ditkirbanko save me!
SLUMF!

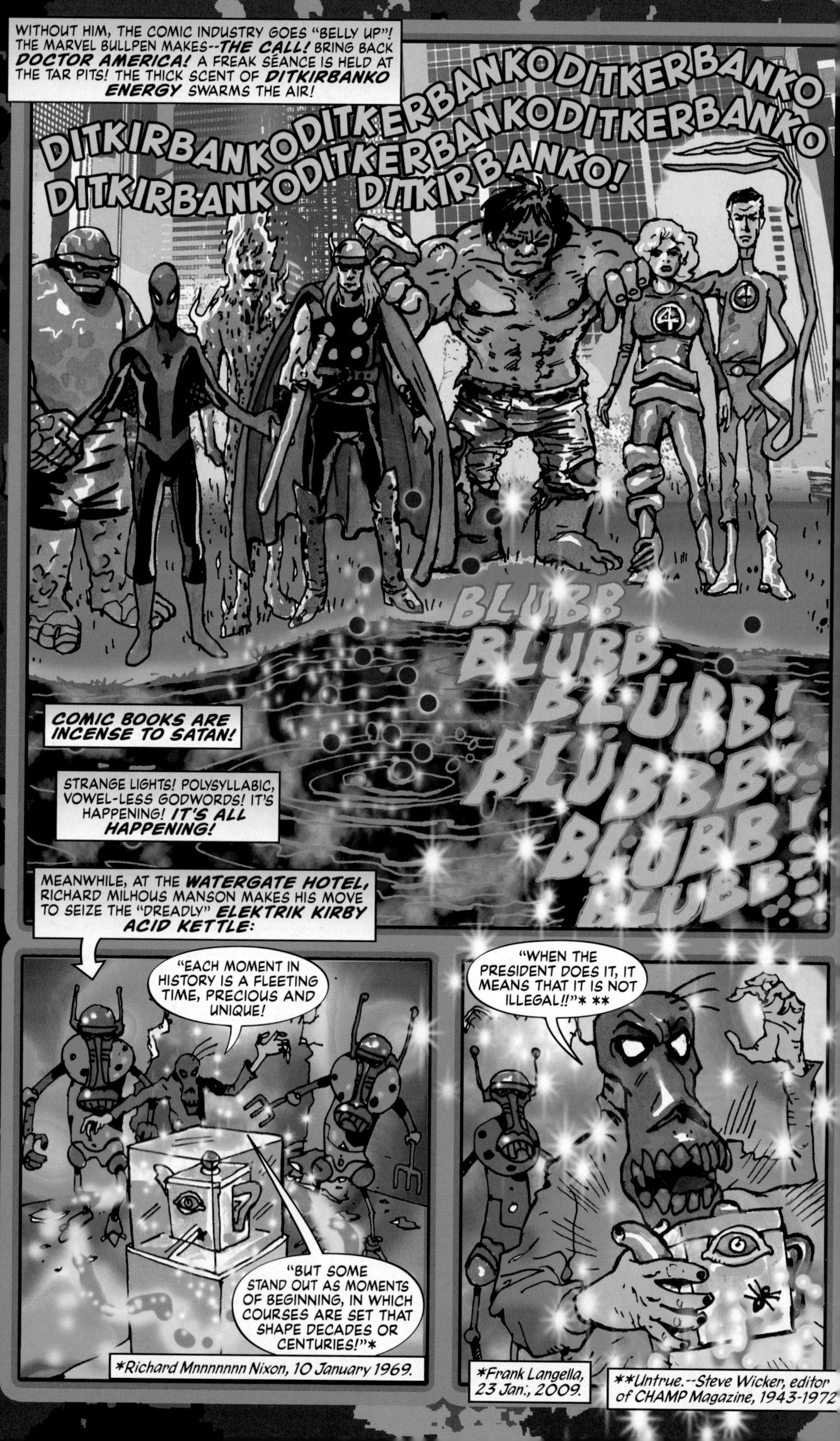
WITHOUT HIM, THE COMIC INDUSTRY GOES "BELLY UP"! THE MARVEL BULLPEN MAKES--THE CALL! BRING BACK DOCTOR AMERICA! A FREAK SÉANCE IS HELD AT THE TAR PITS! THE THICK SCENT OF DITKIRBANKO ENERGY SWARMS THE AIR!
DITKIRBANKODITKERBANKODITKERBANKO DITKIRBANKODITKERBANKODITKERBANKO DITKIRBANKODITKERBANKODITKERBANKO DITKIRBANKO!
BLUBB BLUBB BLUBB! BLUBBB BLUBB! BLUBB!
COMIC BOOKS ARE INCENSE TO SATAN!
STRANGE LIGHTS! POLYSYLLABIC, VOWEL-LESS GODWORDS! IT'S HAPPENING! IT'S ALL HAPPENING!
MEANWHILE, AT THE WATERGATE HOTEL, RICHARD MILHOUS MANSON MAKES HIS MOVE TO SEIZE THE "DREADLY" ELEKTRIK KIRBY ACID KETTLE:
"EACH MOMENT IN HISTORY IS A FLEETING TIME, PRECIOUS AND UNIQUE!
"BUT SOME STAND OUT AS MOMENTS OF BEGINNING, IN WHICH COURSES ARE SET THAT SHAPE DECADES OR CENTURIES!"*
*Richard Mnnnnnnn Nixon, 10 January 1969.
"WHEN THE PRESIDENT DOES IT, IT MEANS THAT IT IS NOT ILLEGAL!!"* **
*Frank Langella, 23 Jan., 2009.
**Untrue.--Steve Wicker, editor of CHAMP Magazine, 1943-1972

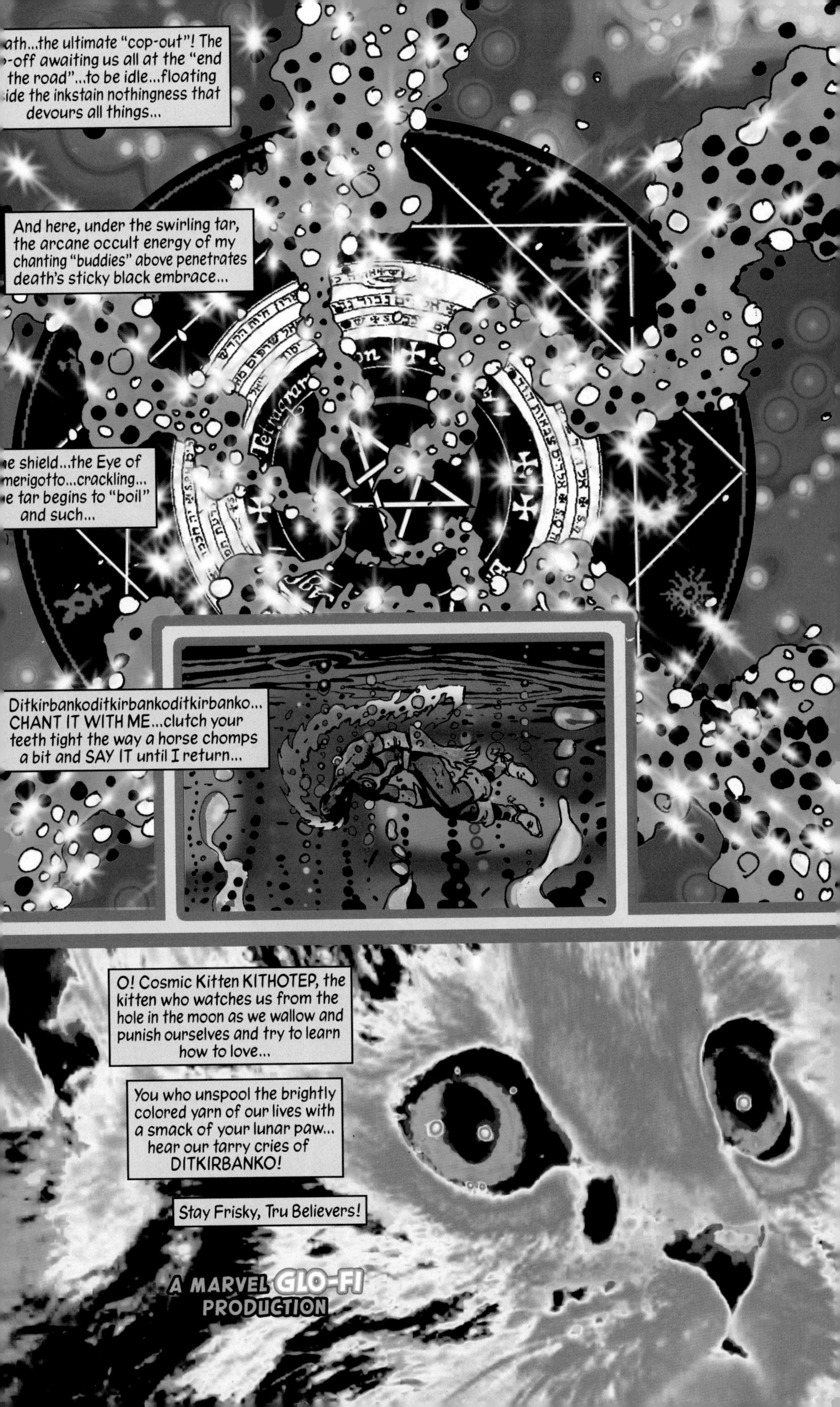

ath...the ultimate "cop-out"! The
-off awaiting us all at the "end
the road"...to be idle...floating
ide the inkstain nothingness that
devours all things...
And here, under the swirling tar, the arcane occult energy of my chanting "buddies" above penetrates death's sticky black embrace...
e shield...the Eye of
merigotto...crackling...
e tar begins to "boil"
and such...
Ditkirbankoditkirbankoditkirbanko... CHANT IT WITH ME...clutch your teeth tight the way a horse chomps a bit and SAY IT until I return...
O! Cosmic Kitten KITHOTEP, the kitten who watches us from the hole in the moon as we wallow and punish ourselves and try to learn how to love...
You who unspool the brightly colored yarn of our lives with a smack of your lunar paw... hear our tarry cries of DITKIRBANKO!
Stay Frisky, Tru Believers!
A MARVEL GLO-FI PRODUCTION

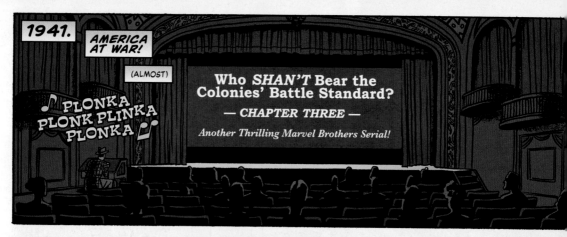

1941.

AMERICA AT WAR!

(ALMOST)

♪ PLONKA PLONK PLINKA PLONKA ♫

Who *SHAN'T* Bear the Colonies' Battle Standard?
— CHAPTER THREE —
Another Thrilling Marvel Brothers Serial!

IN A TOP SECRET GOVERNMENT LABORATORY, *DR. MYRON MACLAIN* DEDICATES ALL HIS ENERGY TO THE CAUSE OF LIBERTY!

BRAVELY, TIRELESSLY...DAY AFTER DAY HE LABORS, WITHOUT REST OR...OR...

Z

MACLAIN!!

UH! WHAT? I'M SORRY, KAISER!

GOD BLESS AMRRRICA!

HUH...THIS ALLOY OF VIBRANIUM AND STEEL. SOMEHOW, WHILE I WAS... RESTING MY *EYES*...IT ACHIEVED THE TENSILE STRENGTH I WAS HOPING FOR.

BETTER POUR IT INTO A MOLD BEFORE IT SETS...

THEN IT'S BACK TO THE...THE BUSINESS...

...OF FREEDOM...

OH, *COME ON!*

Z

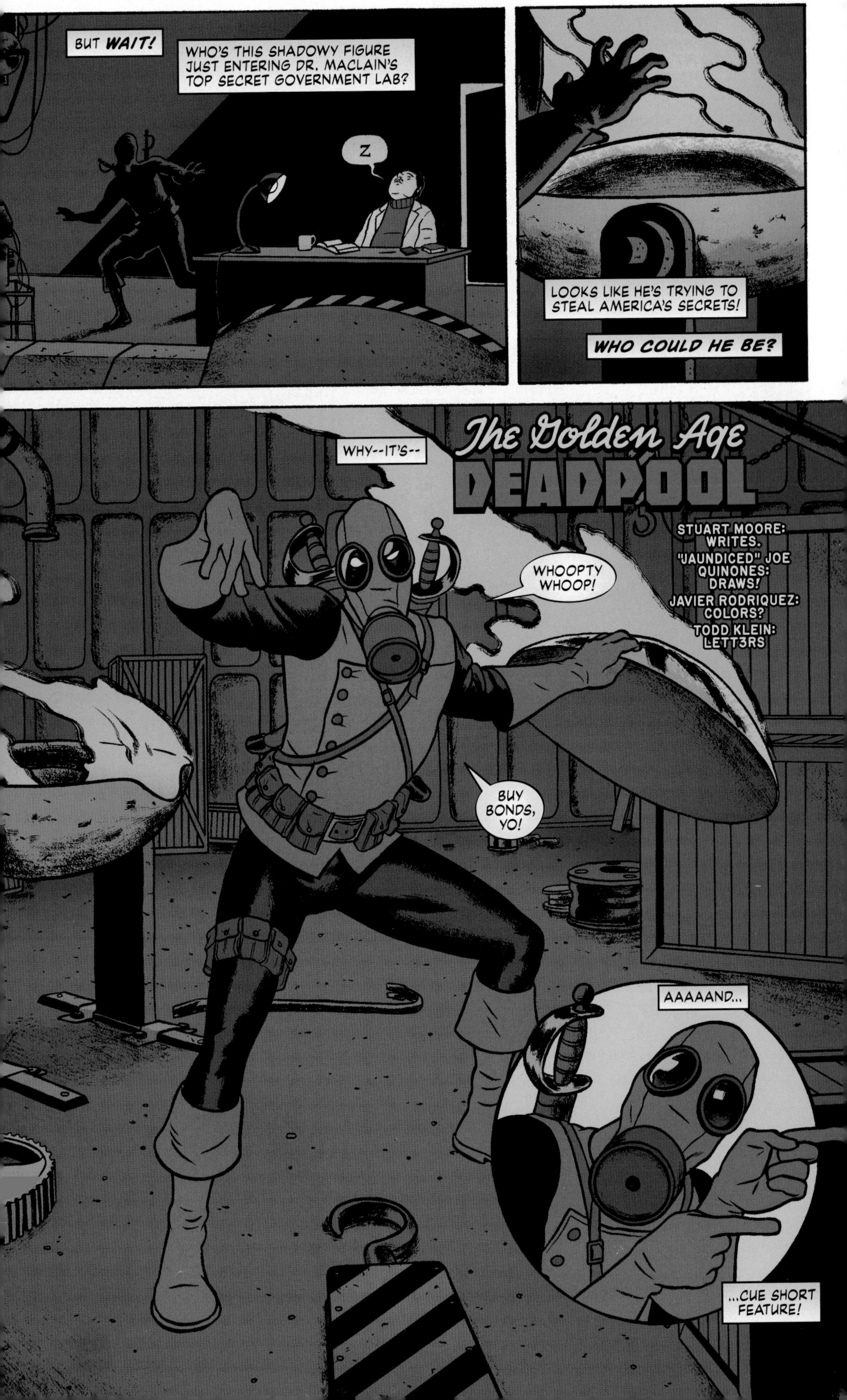

BUT WAIT!
WHO'S THIS SHADOWY FIGURE JUST ENTERING DR. MACLAIN'S TOP SECRET GOVERNMENT LAB?
Z
LOOKS LIKE HE'S TRYING TO STEAL AMERICA'S SECRETS!
WHO COULD HE BE?
WHY--IT'S--
The Golden Age DEADPOOL
STUART MOORE: WRITES.
"JAUNDICED" JOE QUINONES: DRAWS!
JAVIER RODRIQUEZ: COLORS?
TODD KLEIN: LETT3RS
WHOOPTY WHOOP!
BUY BONDS, YO!
AAAAAND...
...CUE SHORT FEATURE!

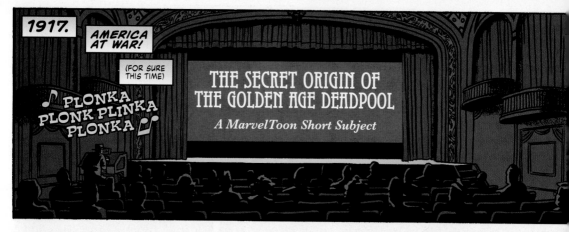

1917.

AMERICA AT WAR!

(FOR SURE THIS TIME)

♪ PLONKA PLONK PLINKA PLONKA ♫

THE SECRET ORIGIN OF THE GOLDEN AGE DEADPOOL

A MarvelToon Short Subject

AS THE U.S. ENTERS WORLD WAR I, PRESIDENT WOODROW WILSON SEES AN IDEAL CHANCE TO DISPOSE OF HIS EMBARRASSING NEPHEW...

...IT'LL BE GOOD P.R. FOR THE *FAMILY,* FREDDY.

DESPERATE TO ESCAPE THE FOXHOLES OF EUROPE, PRIVATE FREDERICK "WHEEZY" WILSON SEIZES ON A DARING PLAN: SMOKE HIS OWN WEIGHT IN CIGARS, THEN FAKE MUSTARD GAS POISONING. IN THE PROCESS, HE PERMANENTLY DAMAGES HIS LUNGS.

cough cough cough≑

TRY THIS ON, FREDDY.

THE MILITARY IS NOT FOOLED BY WILSON'S RUSE, BUT AGREES TO DISCHARGE HIM ANYWAY.

AND SO HE FINDS HIMSELF BACK IN THE STATES, PENNILESS, FORCED TO CARRY HIS GAS MASK AT ALL TIMES.

≑COUGH≑

AFTER A DECADE OF MENIAL JOBS, "WHEEZY" WILSON SPENDS MOST OF THE 1930S IN A STATE OF ABJECT POVERTY, WATCHING CARTOONS IN CUT-RATE THEATERS.

CUT OFF FROM ALL HUMAN CONTACT, HE STARES AT THE CRUDE, BIZARRE IMAGES DANCING ON THE SCREEN...

≑COUGH≑

...WHILE HIS MIND SLOWLY CRUMBLES.

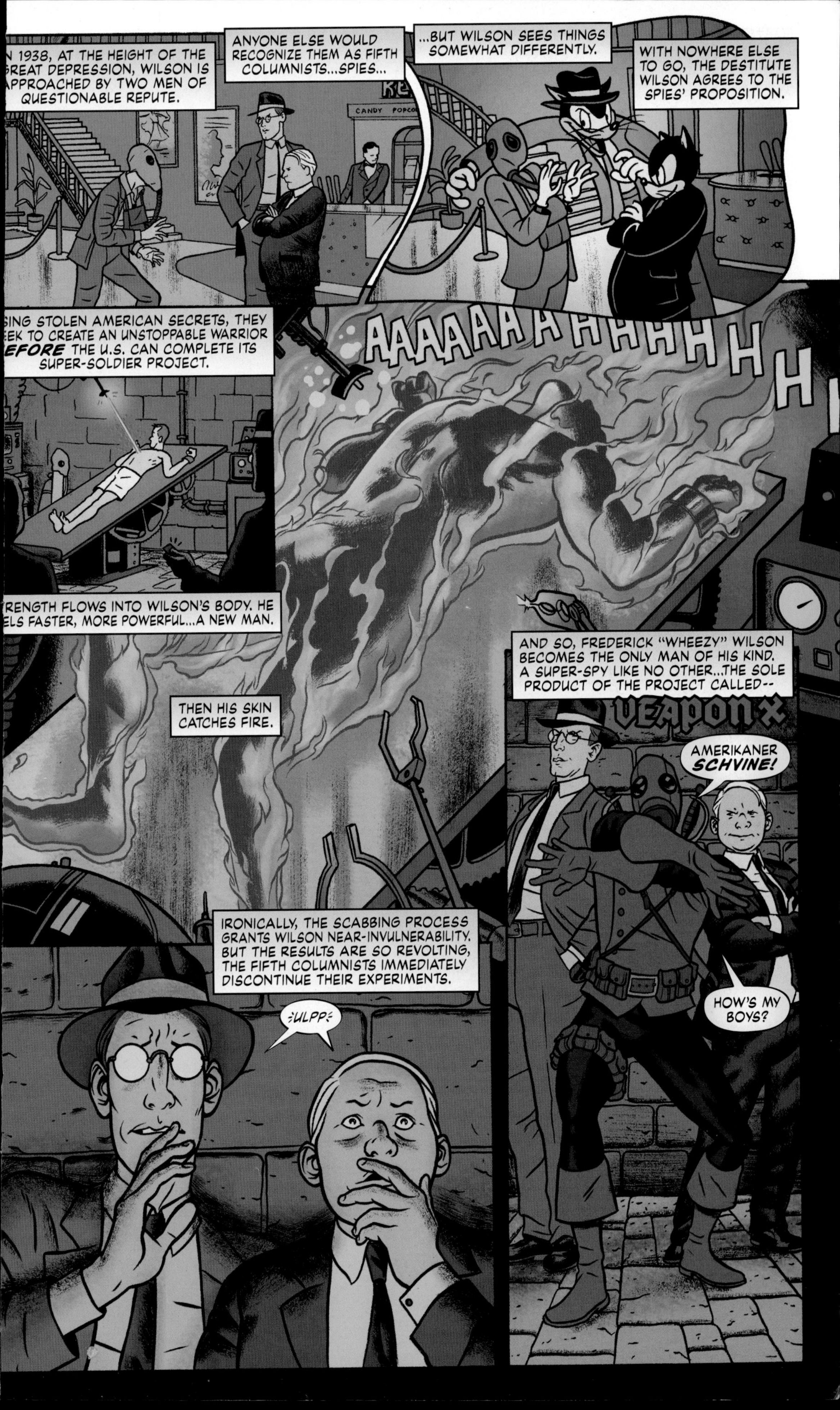

N 1938, AT THE HEIGHT OF THE GREAT DEPRESSION, WILSON IS APPROACHED BY TWO MEN OF QUESTIONABLE REPUTE.
ANYONE ELSE WOULD RECOGNIZE THEM AS FIFTH COLUMNISTS...SPIES...
...BUT WILSON SEES THINGS SOMEWHAT DIFFERENTLY.
WITH NOWHERE ELSE TO GO, THE DESTITUTE WILSON AGREES TO THE SPIES' PROPOSITION.
SING STOLEN AMERICAN SECRETS, THEY EEK TO CREATE AN UNSTOPPABLE WARRIOR EFORE THE U.S. CAN COMPLETE ITS SUPER-SOLDIER PROJECT.
AAAAAAAHHHHHHHH
RENGTH FLOWS INTO WILSON'S BODY. HE ELS FASTER, MORE POWERFUL...A NEW MAN.
THEN HIS SKIN CATCHES FIRE.
AND SO, FREDERICK "WHEEZY" WILSON BECOMES THE ONLY MAN OF HIS KIND. A SUPER-SPY LIKE NO OTHER...THE SOLE PRODUCT OF THE PROJECT CALLED--
WEAPON X
AMERIKANER SCHVINE!
IRONICALLY, THE SCABBING PROCESS GRANTS WILSON NEAR-INVULNERABILITY. BUT THE RESULTS ARE SO REVOLTING, THE FIFTH COLUMNISTS IMMEDIATELY DISCONTINUE THEIR EXPERIMENTS.
ULPP
HOW'S MY BOYS?

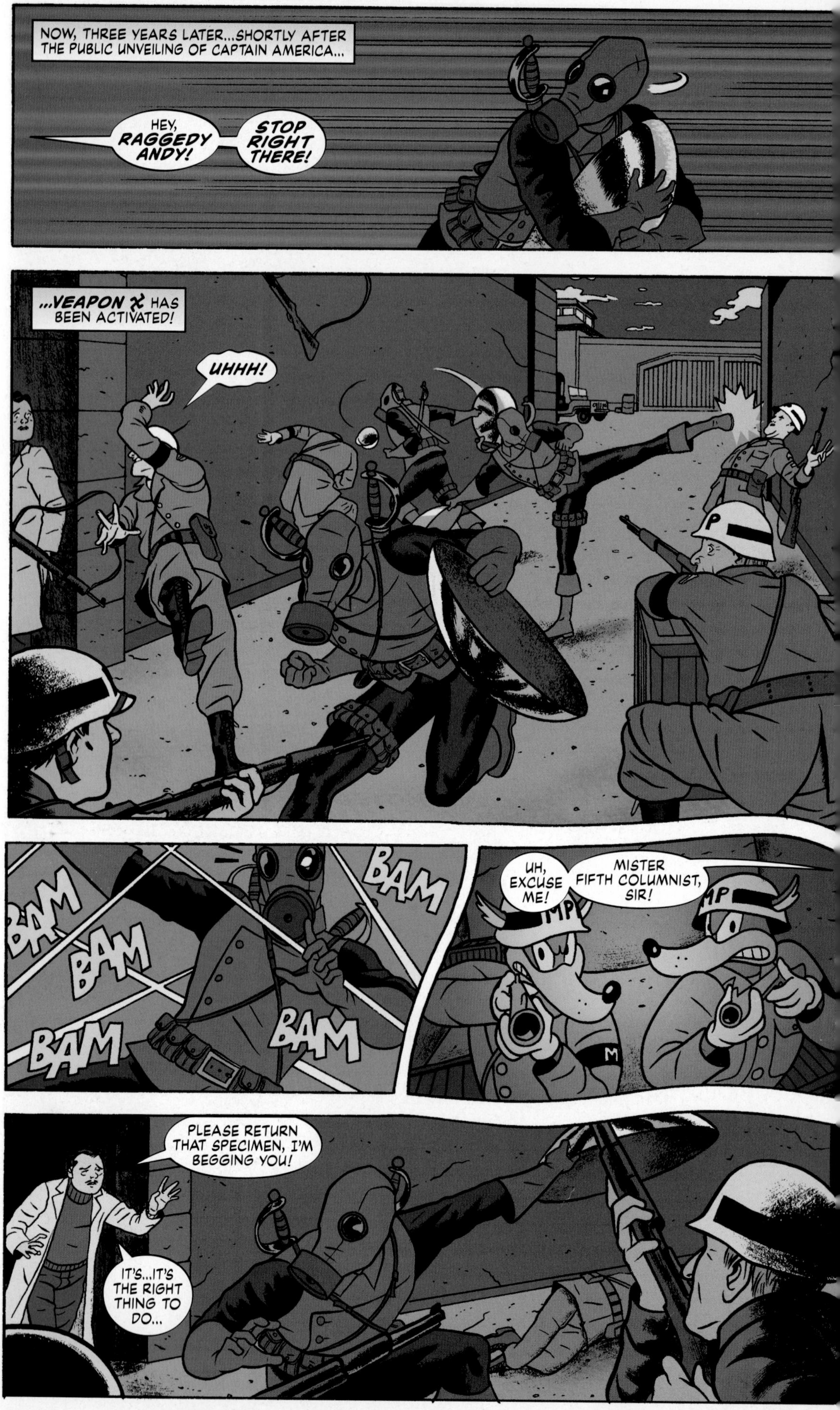

NOW, THREE YEARS LATER...SHORTLY AFTER THE PUBLIC UNVEILING OF CAPTAIN AMERICA...
HEY, RAGGEDY ANDY!
STOP RIGHT THERE!
...VEAPON X HAS BEEN ACTIVATED!
UHHH!
BAM
BAM
BAM
BAM
BAM
UH, EXCUSE ME!
MISTER FIFTH COLUMNIST, SIR!
PLEASE RETURN THAT SPECIMEN, I'M BEGGING YOU!
IT'S...IT'S THE RIGHT THING TO DO...

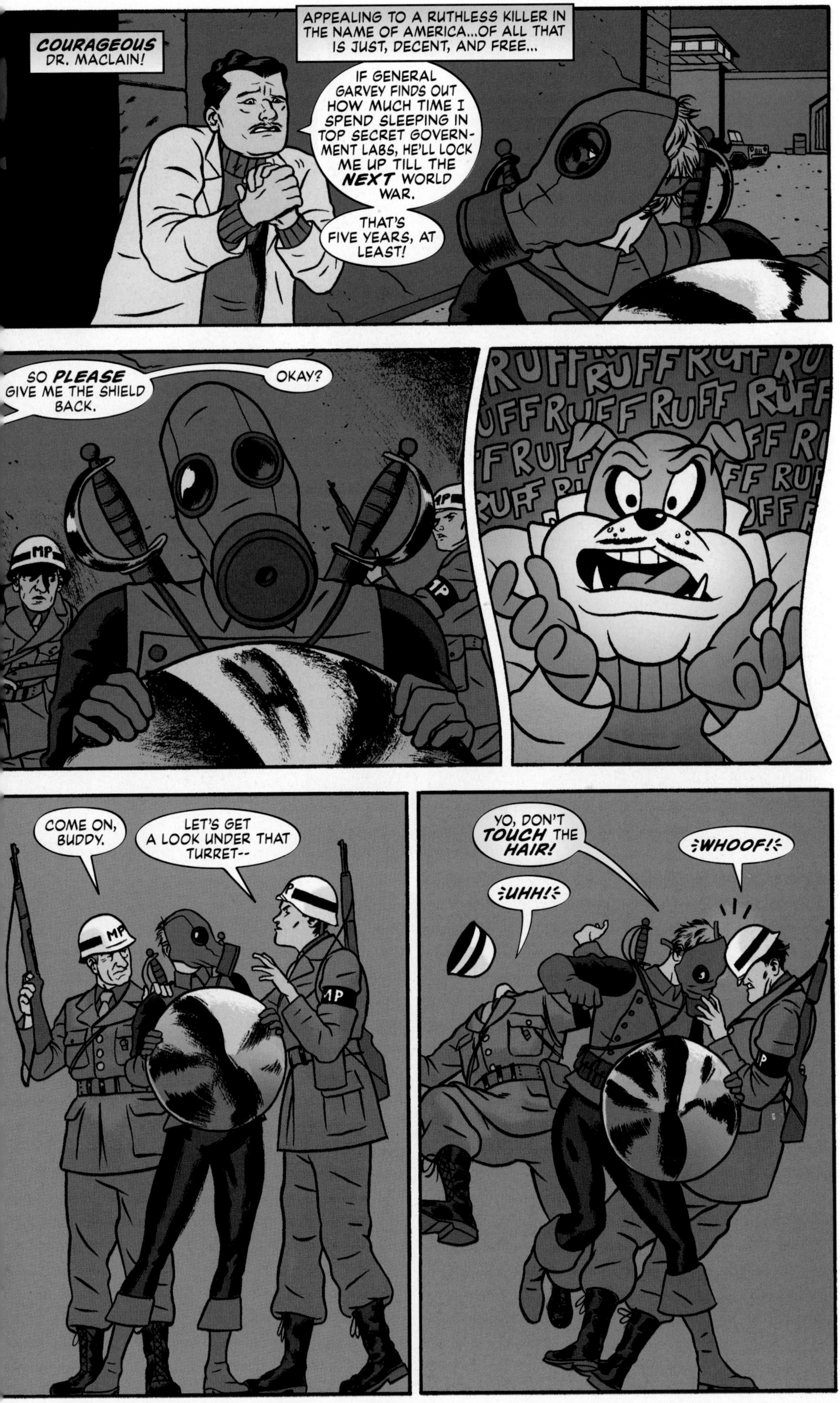

COURAGEOUS DR. MACLAIN!
APPEALING TO A RUTHLESS KILLER IN THE NAME OF AMERICA...OF ALL THAT IS JUST, DECENT, AND FREE...
IF GENERAL GARVEY FINDS OUT HOW MUCH TIME I SPEND SLEEPING IN TOP SECRET GOVERNMENT LABS, HE'LL LOCK ME UP TILL THE NEXT WORLD WAR.
THAT'S FIVE YEARS, AT LEAST!
SO PLEASE GIVE ME THE SHIELD BACK.
OKAY?
RUFF RUFF RUFF RUFF RUFF RUFF RUFF RUFF
COME ON, BUDDY.
LET'S GET A LOOK UNDER THAT TURRET--
YO, DON'T TOUCH THE HAIR!
WHOOF!
UHH!

OH, NO...

WHAT... WHAT... ⋇COUGH⋇

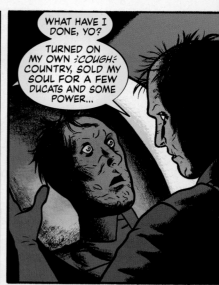

WHAT HAVE I DONE, YO?

TURNED ON MY OWN ⋇COUGH⋇ COUNTRY, SOLD MY SOUL FOR A FEW DUCATS AND SOME POWER...

WELL, NO MORE. **NO MORE!**

FROM NOW ON, I'LL BE A GOOD AMERICAN. I'LL RECYCLE SCRAP...SUPPORT THE DEVELOPMENT OF MAD-DESTRUCTIVE NUCLEAR WEAPONS. RIVET TILL I DROP...

⋇COUGH⋇

YES, GOOD. THAT ALL SOUNDS VERY NICE.

NOW MAY I HAVE THE--

I AM SORRY TO HEAR THAT, **VEAPON X.**

IT MEANS YOUR USEFULNESS IS ENDED.

BAM BAM BAM

BAM BAM

MP

BAM BAM

WHAT THE--

BAM BAM

BAM BAM

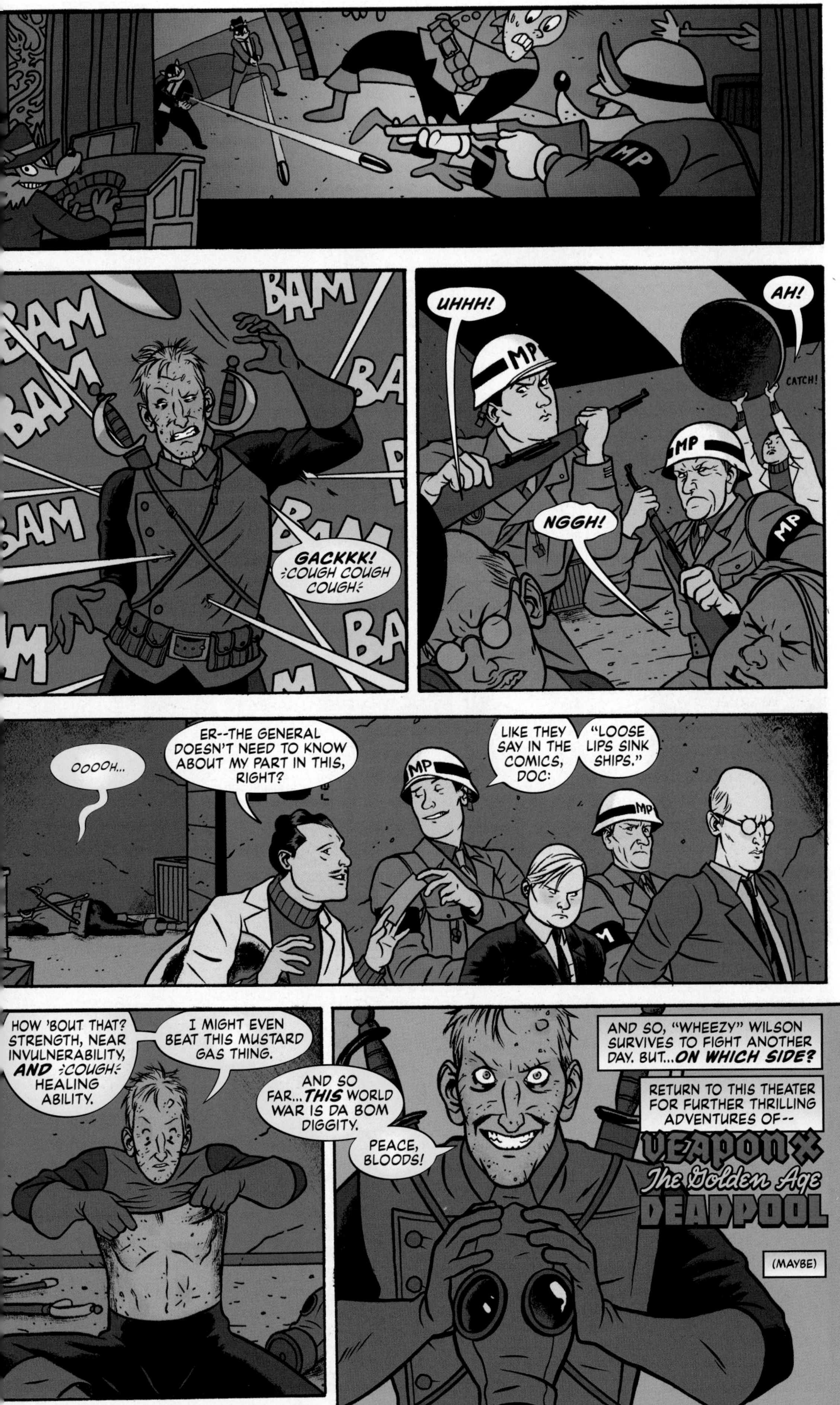

BAM
BAM
BAM
BAM
BAM
GACKKK! COUGH COUGH COUGH
BAM
UHHH!
AH!
CATCH!
NGGH!
OOOOH...
ER--THE GENERAL DOESN'T NEED TO KNOW ABOUT MY PART IN THIS, RIGHT?
LIKE THEY SAY IN THE COMICS, DOC:
"LOOSE LIPS SINK SHIPS."
HOW 'BOUT THAT? STRENGTH, NEAR INVULNERABILITY, AND COUGH HEALING ABILITY.
I MIGHT EVEN BEAT THIS MUSTARD GAS THING.
AND SO FAR...THIS WORLD WAR IS DA BOM DIGGITY.
PEACE, BLOODS!
AND SO, "WHEEZY" WILSON SURVIVES TO FIGHT ANOTHER DAY. BUT...ON WHICH SIDE?
RETURN TO THIS THEATER FOR FURTHER THRILLING ADVENTURES OF--
WEAPON X
The Golden Age
DEADPOOL
(MAYBE)

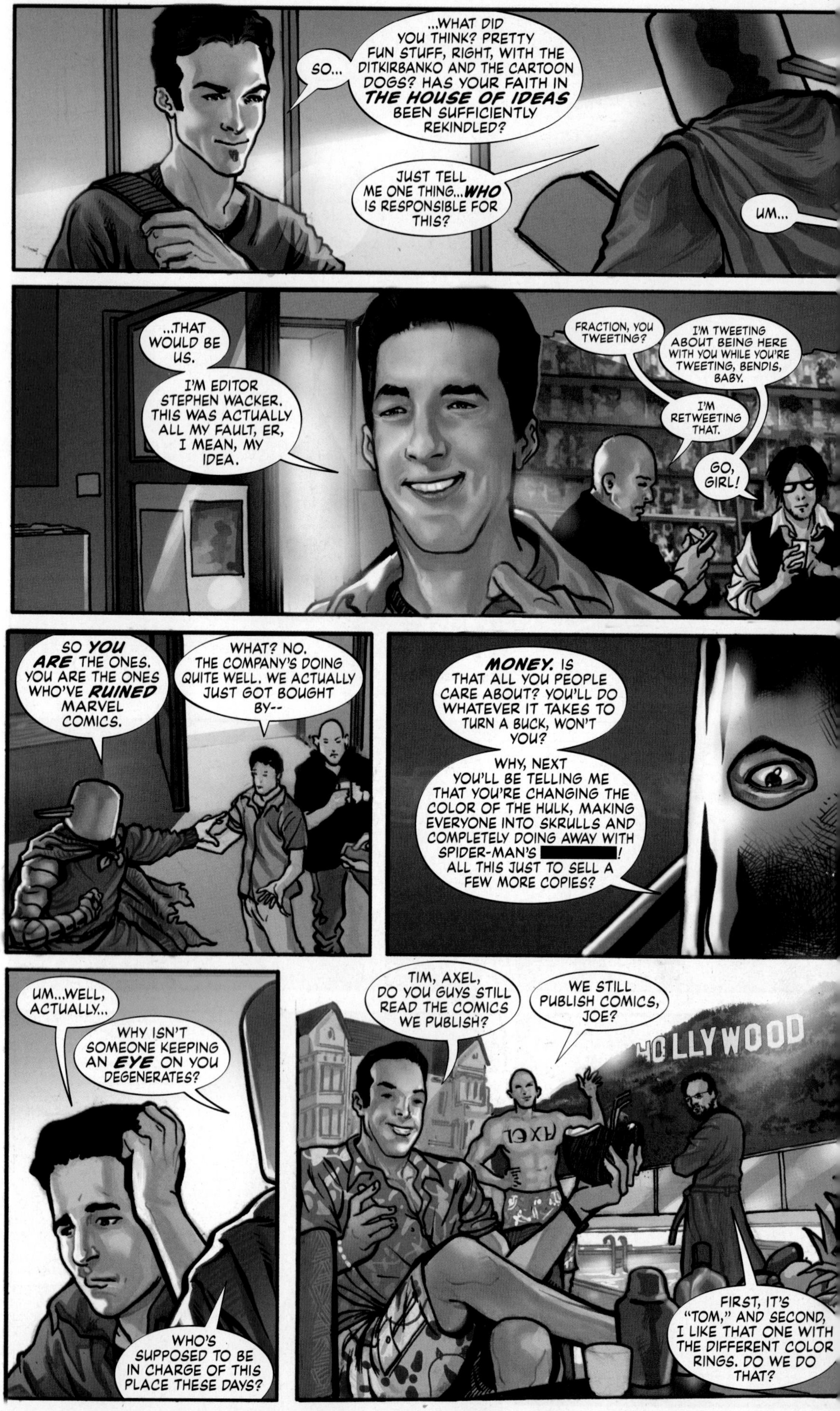
SO...
...WHAT DID YOU THINK? PRETTY FUN STUFF, RIGHT, WITH THE DITKIRBANKO AND THE CARTOON DOGS? HAS YOUR FAITH IN THE HOUSE OF IDEAS BEEN SUFFICIENTLY REKINDLED?
JUST TELL ME ONE THING...WHO IS RESPONSIBLE FOR THIS?
UM...
...THAT WOULD BE US.
I'M EDITOR STEPHEN WACKER. THIS WAS ACTUALLY ALL MY FAULT, ER, I MEAN, MY IDEA.
FRACTION, YOU TWEETING?
I'M TWEETING ABOUT BEING HERE WITH YOU WHILE YOU'RE TWEETING, BENDIS, BABY.
I'M RETWEETING THAT.
GO, GIRL!
SO YOU ARE THE ONES. YOU ARE THE ONES WHO'VE RUINED MARVEL COMICS.
WHAT? NO. THE COMPANY'S DOING QUITE WELL. WE ACTUALLY JUST GOT BOUGHT BY--
MONEY. IS THAT ALL YOU PEOPLE CARE ABOUT? YOU'LL DO WHATEVER IT TAKES TO TURN A BUCK, WON'T YOU?
WHY, NEXT YOU'LL BE TELLING ME THAT YOU'RE CHANGING THE COLOR OF THE HULK, MAKING EVERYONE INTO SKRULLS AND COMPLETELY DOING AWAY WITH SPIDER-MAN'S [redacted]! ALL THIS JUST TO SELL A FEW MORE COPIES?
UM...WELL, ACTUALLY...
WHY ISN'T SOMEONE KEEPING AN EYE ON YOU DEGENERATES?
WHO'S SUPPOSED TO BE IN CHARGE OF THIS PLACE THESE DAYS?
TIM, AXEL, DO YOU GUYS STILL READ THE COMICS WE PUBLISH?
WE STILL PUBLISH COMICS, JOE?
HOLLYWOOD
FIRST, IT'S "TOM," AND SECOND, I LIKE THAT ONE WITH THE DIFFERENT COLOR RINGS. DO WE DO THAT?

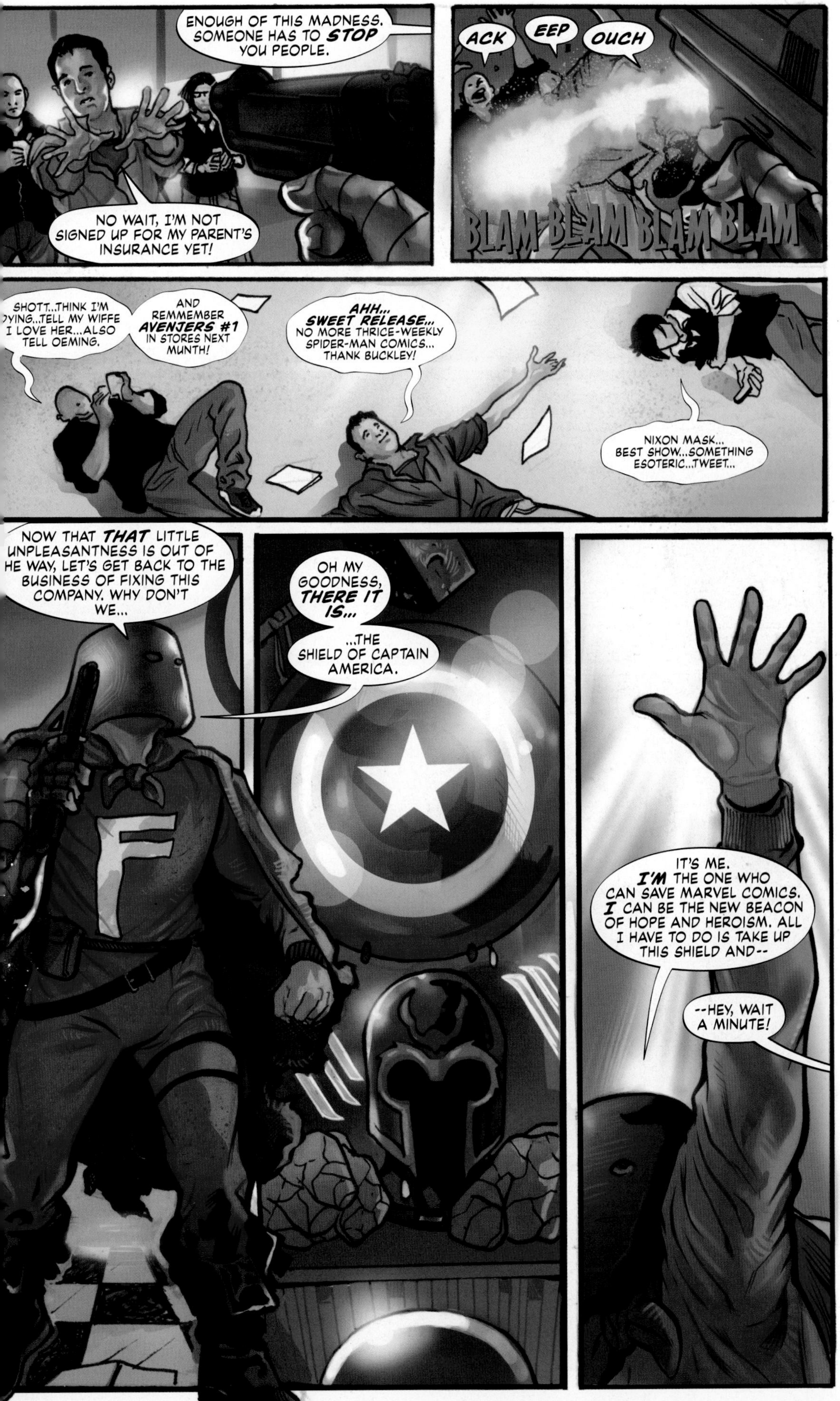
ENOUGH OF THIS MADNESS. SOMEONE HAS TO STOP YOU PEOPLE.
NO WAIT, I'M NOT SIGNED UP FOR MY PARENT'S INSURANCE YET!
ACK
EEP
OUCH
BLAM BLAM BLAM BLAM
SHOTT...THINK I'M DYING...TELL MY WIFFE I LOVE HER...ALSO TELL OEMING.
AND REMMEMBER AVENJERS #1 IN STORES NEXT MUNTH!
AHH... SWEET RELEASE... NO MORE THRICE-WEEKLY SPIDER-MAN COMICS... THANK BUCKLEY!
NIXON MASK... BEST SHOW...SOMETHING ESOTERIC...TWEET...
NOW THAT THAT LITTLE UNPLEASANTNESS IS OUT OF HE WAY, LET'S GET BACK TO THE BUSINESS OF FIXING THIS COMPANY. WHY DON'T WE...
OH MY GOODNESS, THERE IT IS...
...THE SHIELD OF CAPTAIN AMERICA.
IT'S ME. I'M THE ONE WHO CAN SAVE MARVEL COMICS. I CAN BE THE NEW BEACON OF HOPE AND HEROISM. ALL I HAVE TO DO IS TAKE UP THIS SHIELD AND--
--HEY, WAIT A MINUTE!
F

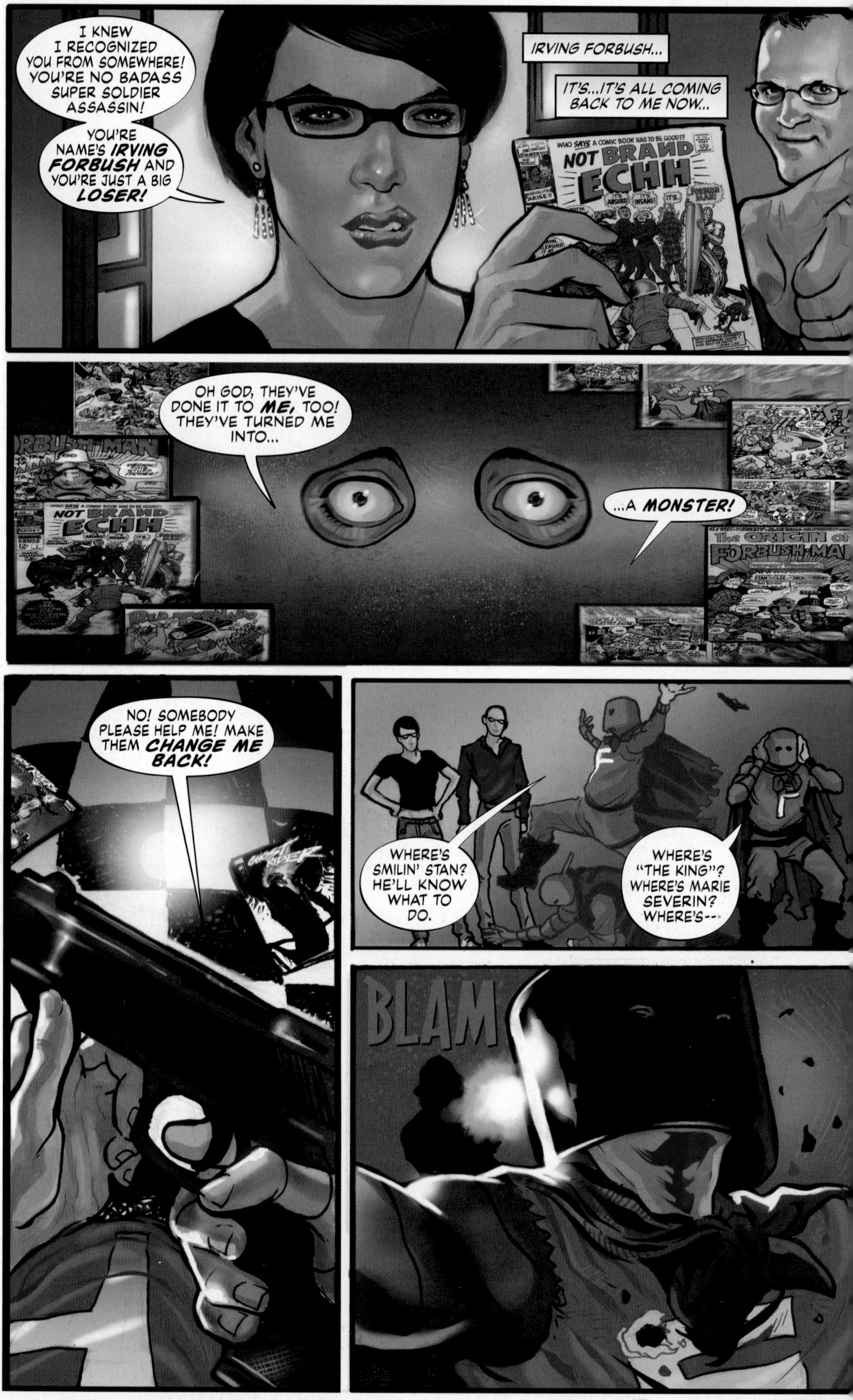
I KNEW I RECOGNIZED YOU FROM SOMEWHERE! YOU'RE NO BADASS SUPER SOLDIER ASSASSIN!
YOU'RE NAME'S IRVING FORBUSH AND YOU'RE JUST A BIG LOSER!
IRVING FORBUSH...
IT'S...IT'S ALL COMING BACK TO ME NOW...
WHO SAYS A COMIC BOOK HAS TO BE GOOD?!
NOT BRAND ECHH
OH GOD, THEY'VE DONE IT TO ME, TOO! THEY'VE TURNED ME INTO...
...A MONSTER!
NO! SOMEBODY PLEASE HELP ME! MAKE THEM CHANGE ME BACK!
WHERE'S SMILIN' STAN? HE'LL KNOW WHAT TO DO.
WHERE'S "THE KING"? WHERE'S MARIE SEVERIN? WHERE'S--
BLAM

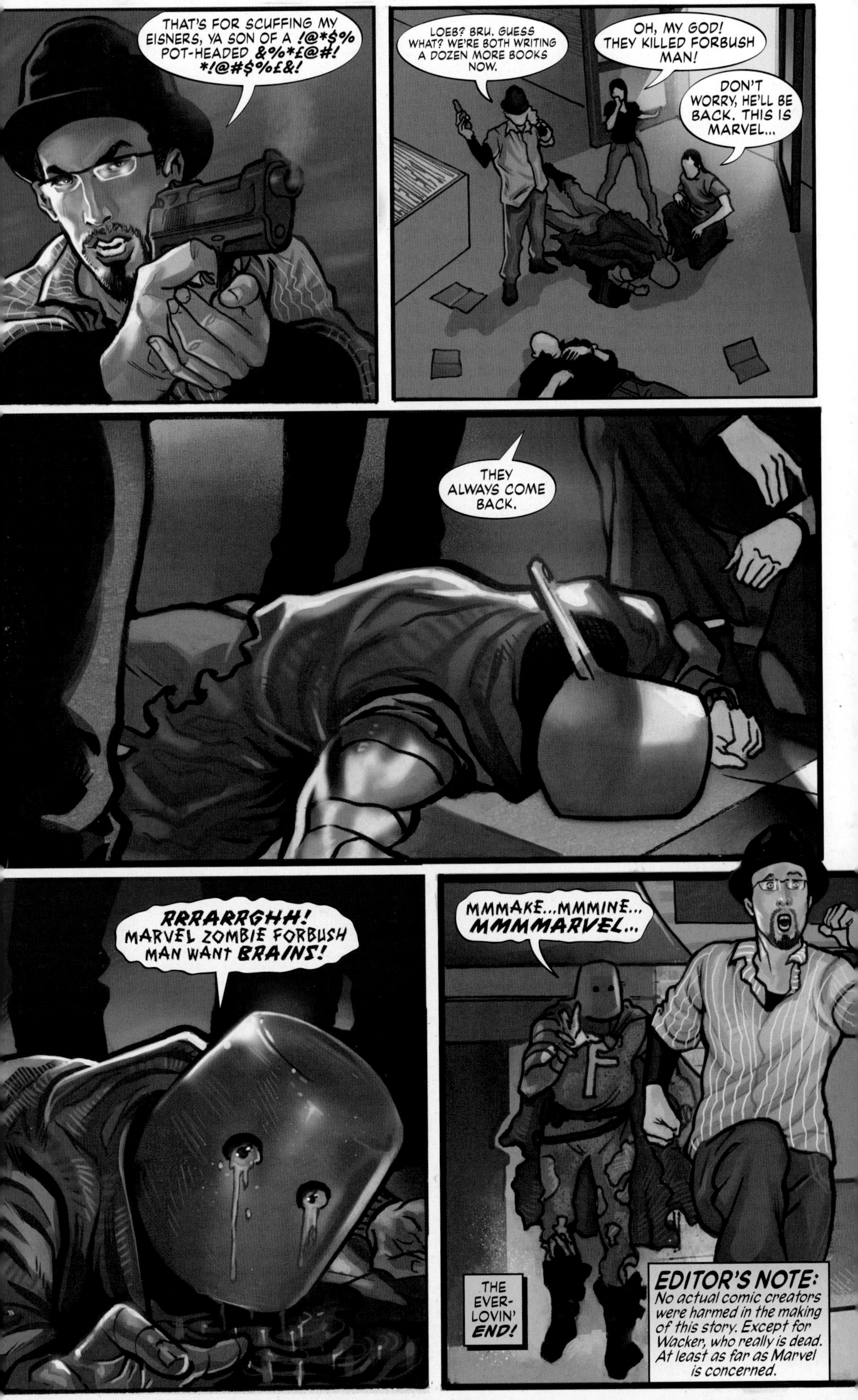
THAT'S FOR SCUFFING MY EISNERS, YA SON OF A !@*$% POT-HEADED &%*£@#! *!@#$%£&!
LOEB? BRU. GUESS WHAT? WE'RE BOTH WRITING A DOZEN MORE BOOKS NOW.
OH, MY GOD! THEY KILLED FORBUSH MAN!
DON'T WORRY, HE'LL BE BACK. THIS IS MARVEL...
THEY ALWAYS COME BACK.
RRRARRGHH! MARVEL ZOMBIE FORBUSH MAN WANT BRAINS!
MMMAKE...MMMINE... MMMMARVEL...
THE EVER-LOVIN' END!
EDITOR'S NOTE: No actual comic creators were harmed in the making of this story. Except for Wacker, who really is dead. At least as far as Marvel is concerned.

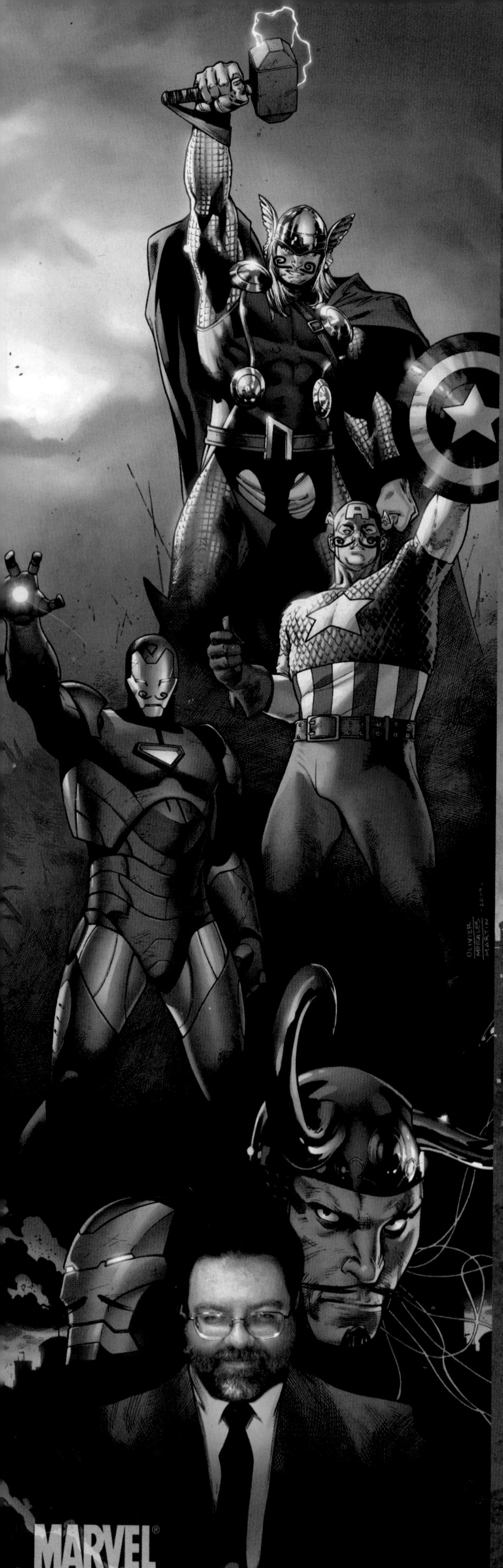

SLEEGE CHECKLIST

DEKREMBER
☐ SLEEGE: BEFOREMATH #1
☐ SLEEGE PROLOGUE: GROUP OF CLASSIC CHARACTERS SITTING AROUND TABLE DISCUSSING PLOT #1
☐ GULF COAST AVENGERS: THE INTIATIVE #86
☐ ORIGINS OF SELLING CLIP ART OF PREVIOUS MARVEL EVENTS #3

CRANUARY
☐ SLEEGE #1
☐ SLEEGE #1: Director's Cut
☐ SLEEGE #1 (variant cover)
☐ SLEEGE #1 (other variant cover)
☐ SLEEGE #1 (variant of other variant cover)
☐ SLEEGE #1 (black and white version of variant cover)
☐ SLEEGE #1 (color variant of black and white version of variant cover)
☐ LIGHT WOLVERINE #86
☐ NUDE AVENGERS #61
☐ SLEEGE: TENUOUSLY CONNECTED NEWSPAPER STORY #1
☐ SLEEGE #1 (Deadpool variant)

FEBRUBRAKERARY
☐ SLEEGE #2
☐ SLEEGE #2 (with variant interiors)
☐ DORK AVENGERS #43
☐ SLEEGE #1: Director's of the Director's Cut
☐ THE MIGHTY SNORE #
☐ SLEEGE OMNIBUS HARDCOVER
☐ BLUNDERDOLTS #87

MARTS
☐ SLEEGE #4
☐ SLEEGE OMNIBUS DIG
☐ PEOPLE COMPLAINING ABOUT GIRL COMICS #4 - SLEEGE STRIKES!
☐ DARK SLEEGE: THE AGENDA OBJECTIVE GAMB

APERIL
☐ *Sorry no Sleege comics April. Try Red Hulk!*
☐ SLEEGE #1, 2, AND 4: TH STORY SO FAR!
☐ SLEEGE: PRELUDE TO T AFTERMATH #Wha-?

MAY
☐ SLEEGE #3 (FINALLY!)
☐ (NAME CLASSIFIED) #7
☐ SLEEGE: FUNERAL FOR CHARACTER COMING BACK SOON #1
☐ SLEEGE PROLOGUE TO EPILOGUE #2
☐ SLEEGE: HEROES ARGUI WHILE PEOPLE DIE #5
☐ SLEEGE: EVERYTHING IS LIGHT AND HAPPY #1

INSERT GENERIC TAGLINE HERE!!

MARVEL

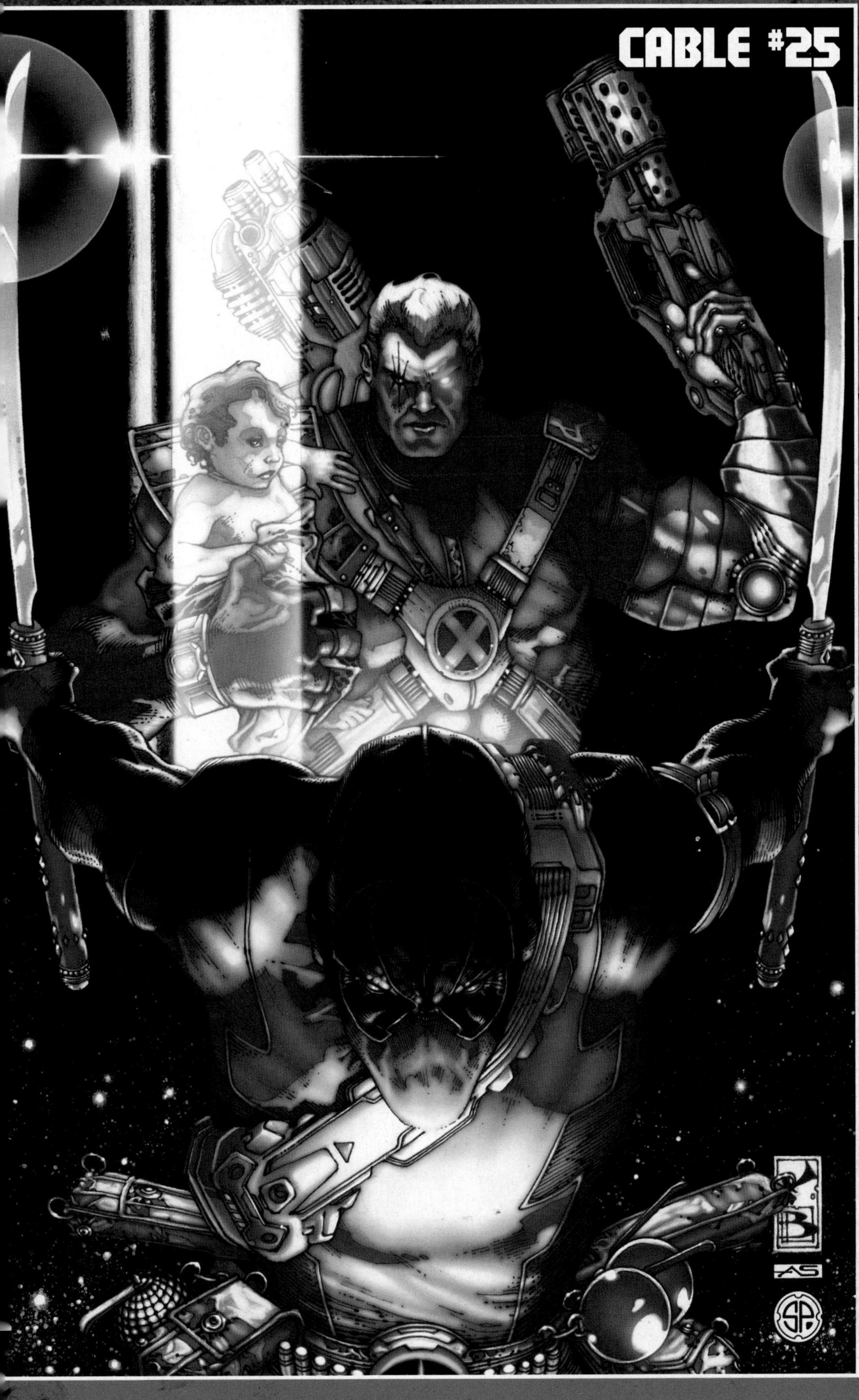
CABLE #25

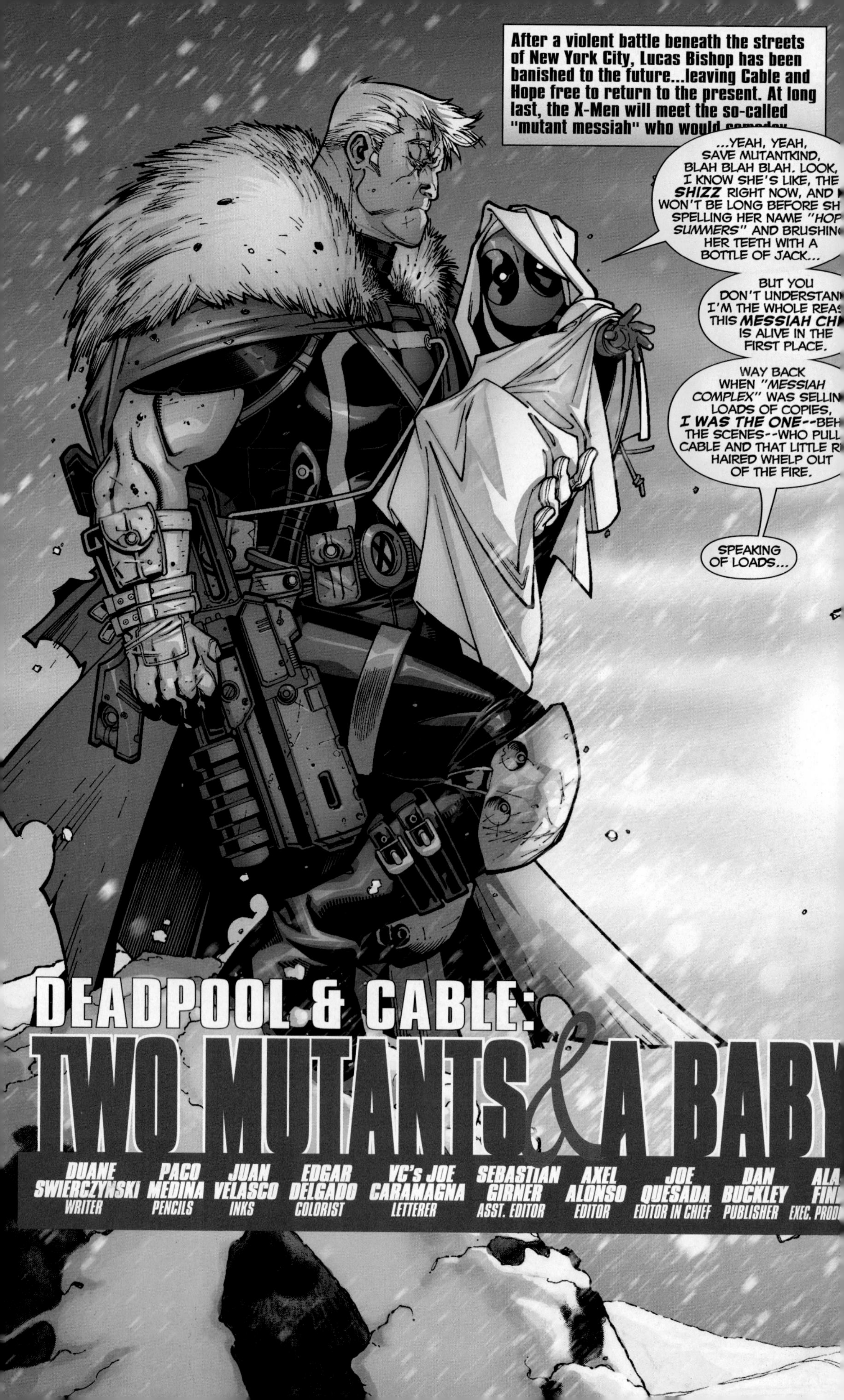
After a violent battle beneath the streets of New York City, Lucas Bishop has been banished to the future...leaving Cable and Hope free to return to the present. At long last, the X-Men will meet the so-called "mutant messiah" who would
...YEAH, YEAH, SAVE MUTANTKIND, BLAH BLAH BLAH. LOOK, I KNOW SHE'S LIKE, THE SHIZZ RIGHT NOW, AND WON'T BE LONG BEFORE SH SPELLING HER NAME "HOP SUMMERS" AND BRUSHIN HER TEETH WITH A BOTTLE OF JACK...
BUT YOU DON'T UNDERSTAN I'M THE WHOLE REAS THIS MESSIAH CH IS ALIVE IN THE FIRST PLACE.
WAY BACK WHEN "MESSIAH COMPLEX" WAS SELLIN LOADS OF COPIES, I WAS THE ONE--BEH THE SCENES--WHO PULL CABLE AND THAT LITTLE R HAIRED WHELP OUT OF THE FIRE.
SPEAKING OF LOADS...
DEADPOOL & CABLE:
TWO MUTANTS & A BABY
DUANE SWIERCZYNSKI WRITER
PACO MEDINA PENCILS
JUAN VELASCO INKS
EDGAR DELGADO COLORIST
VC's JOE CARAMAGNA LETTERER
SEBASTIAN GIRNER ASST. EDITOR
AXEL ALONSO EDITOR
JOE QUESADA EDITOR IN CHIEF
DAN BUCKLEY PUBLISHER
ALA FIN EXEC. PROD

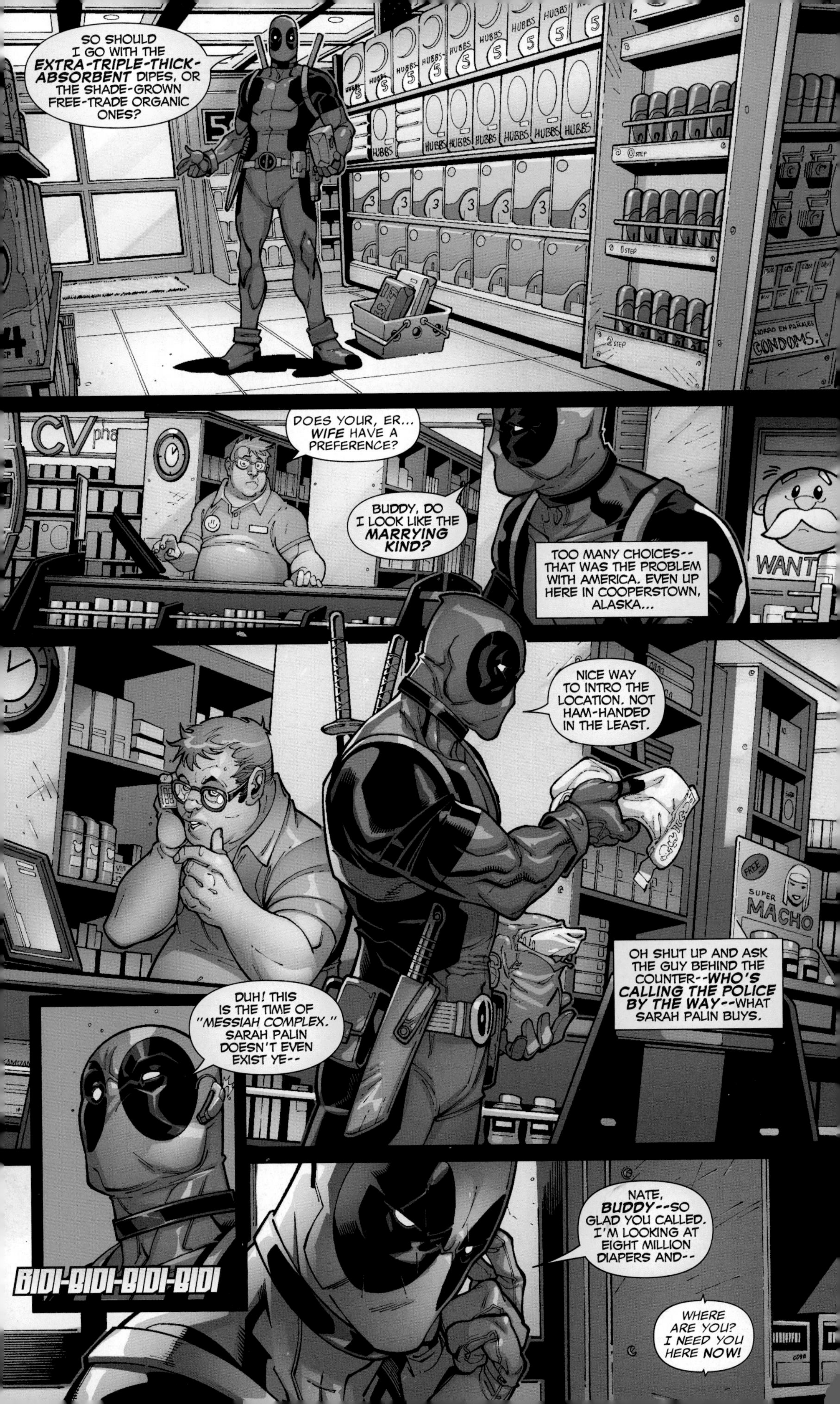

SO SHOULD I GO WITH THE EXTRA-TRIPLE-THICK-ABSORBENT DIPES, OR THE SHADE-GROWN FREE-TRADE ORGANIC ONES?
HUBBS
CONDOMS.
DOES YOUR, ER... WIFE HAVE A PREFERENCE?
BUDDY, DO I LOOK LIKE THE MARRYING KIND?
TOO MANY CHOICES--THAT WAS THE PROBLEM WITH AMERICA. EVEN UP HERE IN COOPERSTOWN, ALASKA...
WANT
NICE WAY TO INTRO THE LOCATION. NOT HAM-HANDED IN THE LEAST.
SUPER MACHO
OH SHUT UP AND ASK THE GUY BEHIND THE COUNTER--WHO'S CALLING THE POLICE BY THE WAY--WHAT SARAH PALIN BUYS.
DUH! THIS IS THE TIME OF "MESSIAH COMPLEX." SARAH PALIN DOESN'T EVEN EXIST YE--
BIDI-BIDI-BIDI-BIDI
NATE, BUDDY--SO GLAD YOU CALLED. I'M LOOKING AT EIGHT MILLION DIAPERS AND--
WHERE ARE YOU? I NEED YOU HERE NOW!

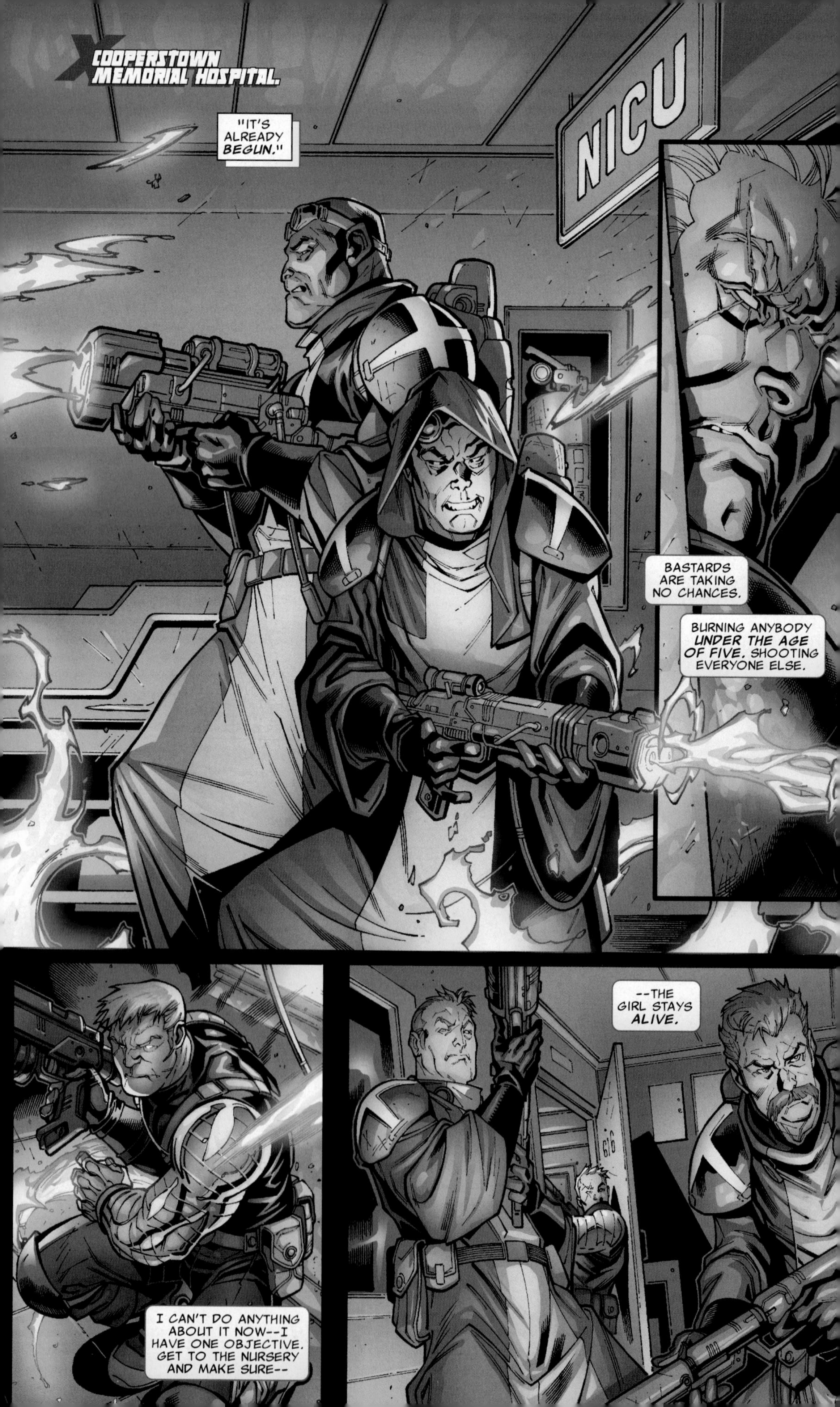
COOPERSTOWN MEMORIAL HOSPITAL.
"IT'S ALREADY BEGUN."
NICU
BASTARDS ARE TAKING NO CHANCES.
BURNING ANYBODY UNDER THE AGE OF FIVE. SHOOTING EVERYONE ELSE.
I CAN'T DO ANYTHING ABOUT IT NOW--I HAVE ONE OBJECTIVE. GET TO THE NURSERY AND MAKE SURE--
--THE GIRL STAYS ALIVE.

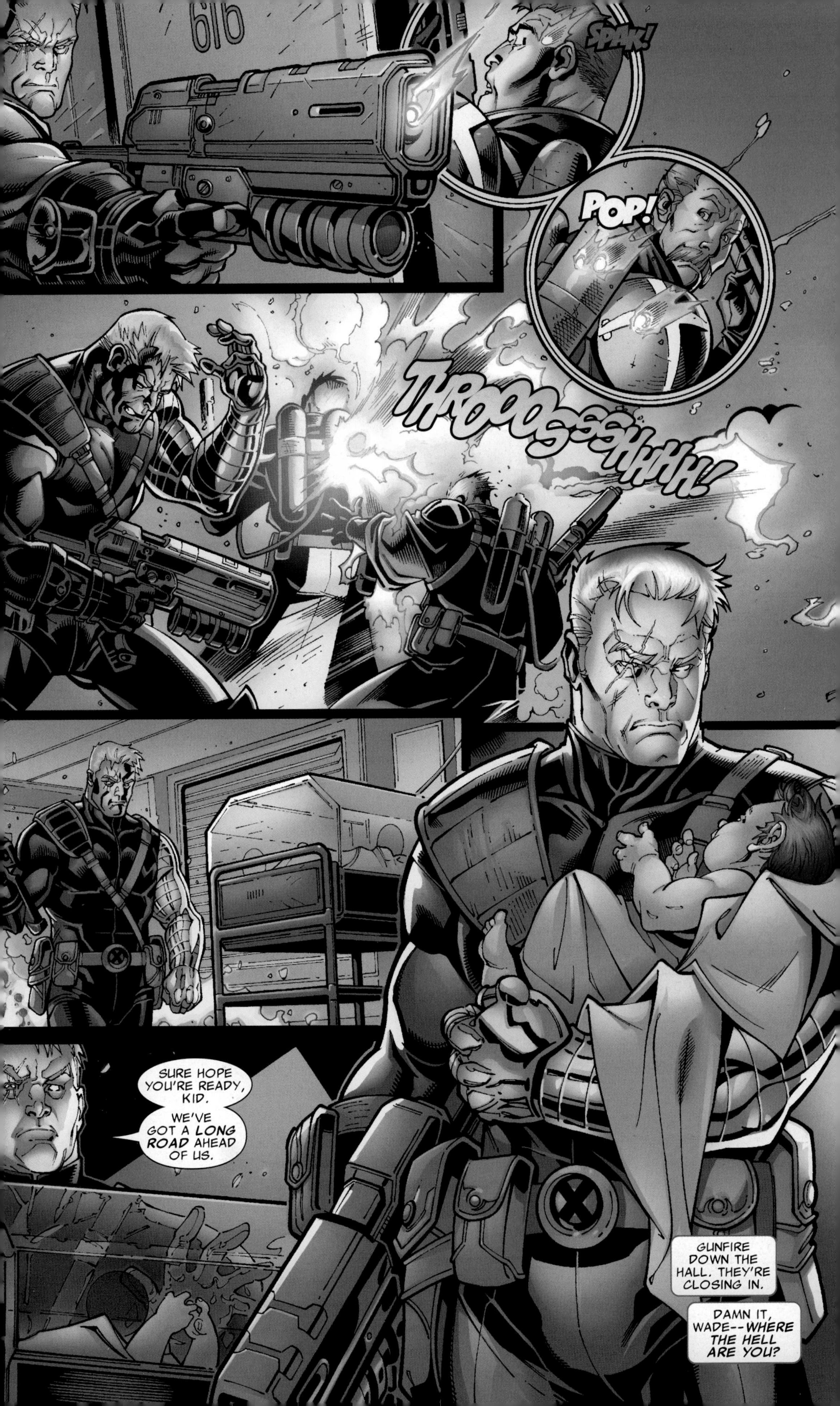

616
SPAK!
POP!
THROOOSSHHHH!
SURE HOPE YOU'RE READY, KID.
WE'VE GOT A LONG ROAD AHEAD OF US.
GUNFIRE DOWN THE HALL. THEY'RE CLOSING IN.
DAMN IT, WADE--WHERE THE HELL ARE YOU?

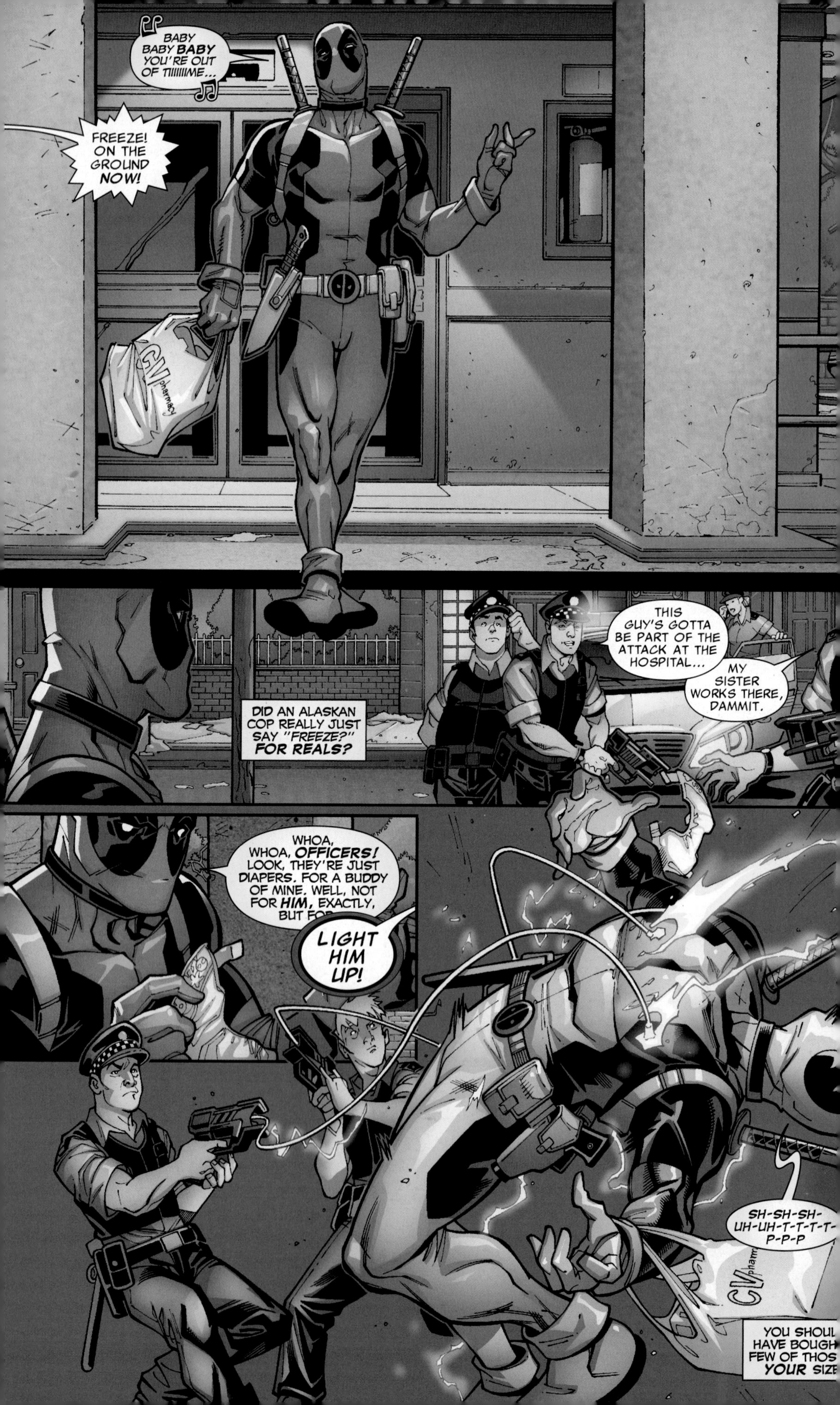

BABY BABY BABY YOU'RE OUT OF TIIIIIIME...
FREEZE! ON THE GROUND NOW!
DID AN ALASKAN COP REALLY JUST SAY "FREEZE?" FOR REALS?
THIS GUY'S GOTTA BE PART OF THE ATTACK AT THE HOSPITAL...
MY SISTER WORKS THERE, DAMMIT.
WHOA, WHOA, OFFICERS! LOOK, THEY'RE JUST DIAPERS. FOR A BUDDY OF MINE. WELL, NOT FOR HIM, EXACTLY, BUT FOR
LIGHT HIM UP!
SH-SH-SH-UH-UH-T-T-T-T-P-P-P
YOU SHOUL HAVE BOUGH FEW OF THOS YOUR SIZE

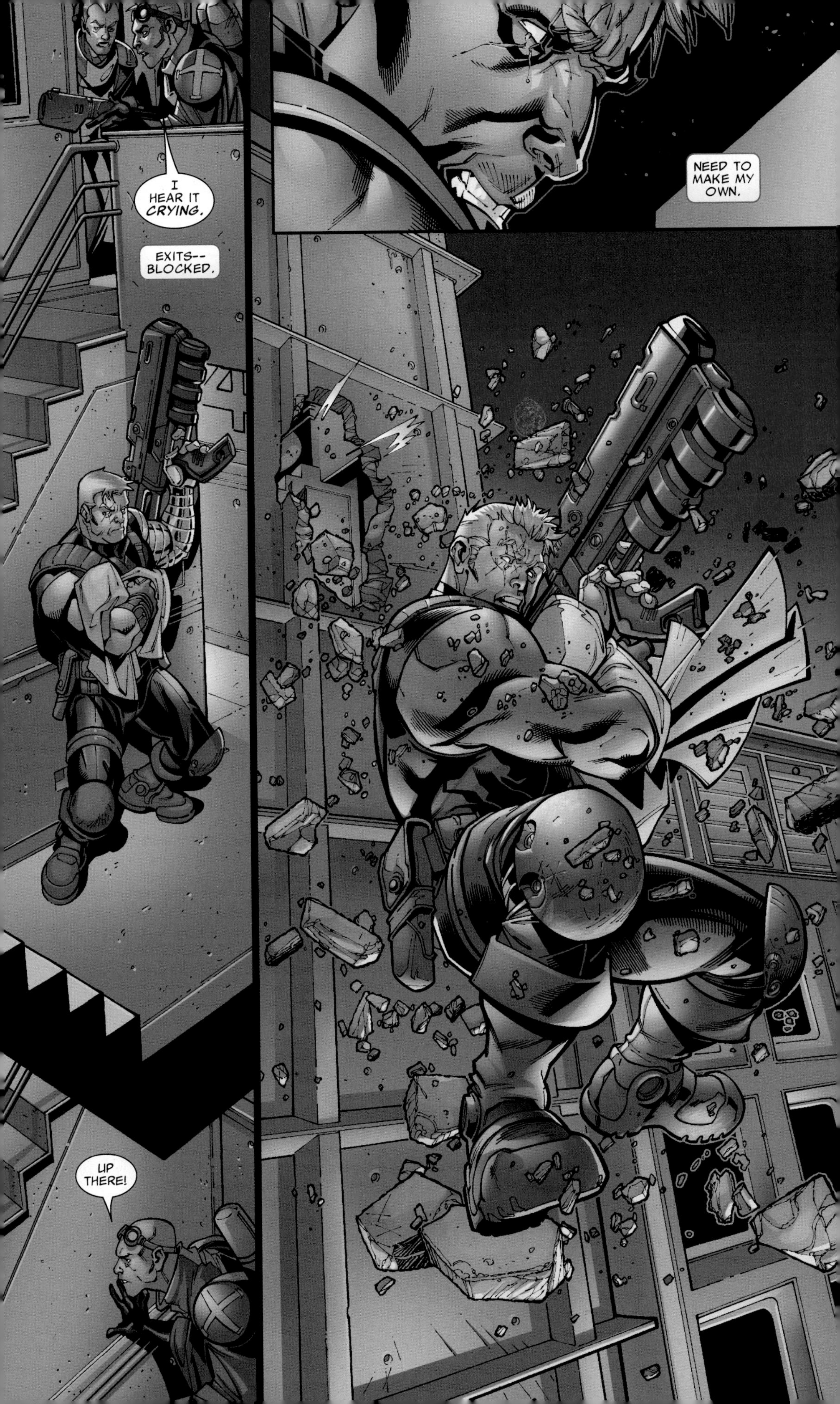

I HEAR IT CRYING.
EXITS-- BLOCKED.
NEED TO MAKE MY OWN.
UP THERE!

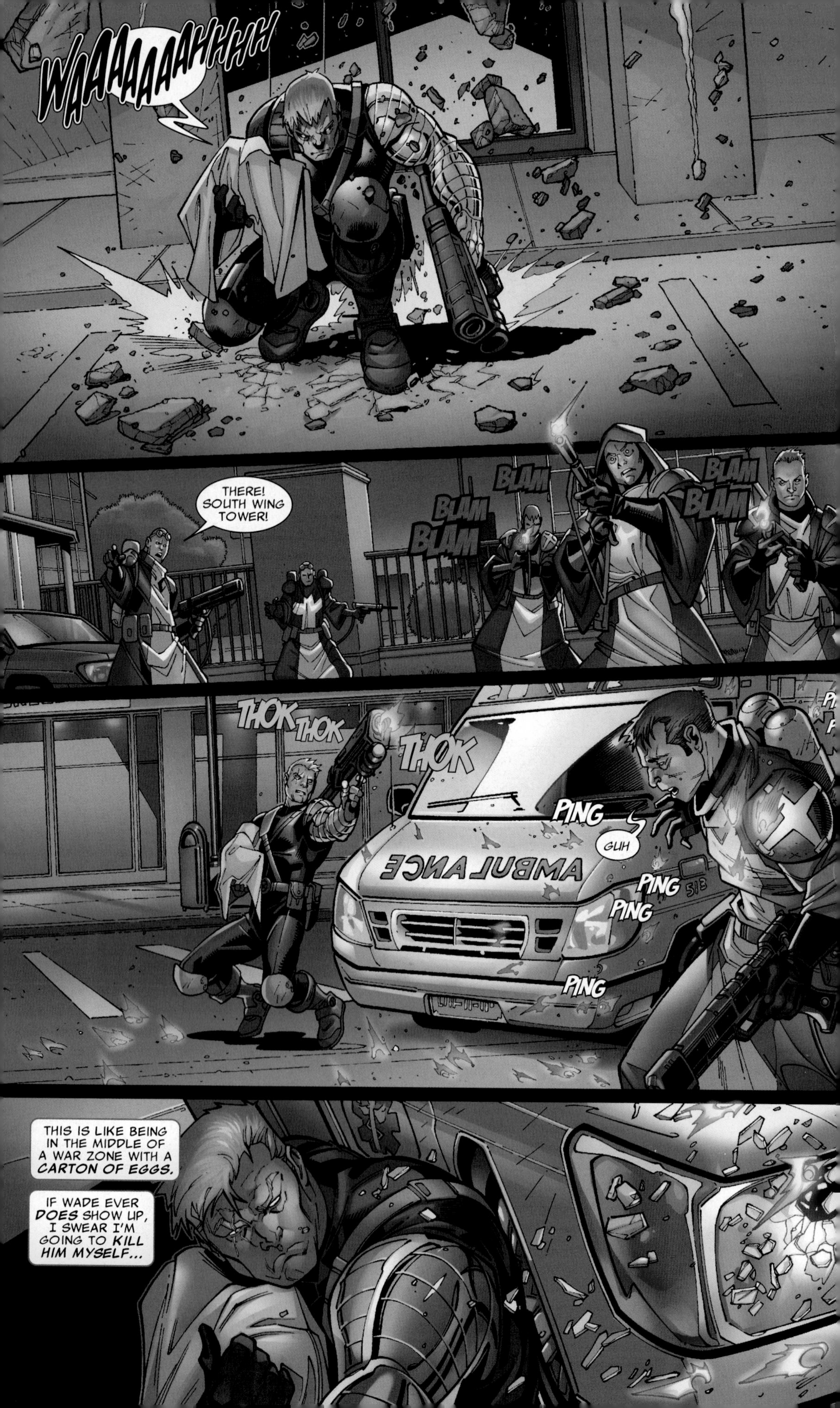
WAAAAAAAHHHH
THERE! SOUTH WING TOWER!
BLAM
BLAM
BLAM
BLAM
BLAM
THOK THOK
THOK
PING
GUH
AMBULANCE
PING
PING
PING
THIS IS LIKE BEING IN THE MIDDLE OF A WAR ZONE WITH A CARTON OF EGGS.
IF WADE EVER DOES SHOW UP, I SWEAR I'M GOING TO KILL HIM MYSELF...

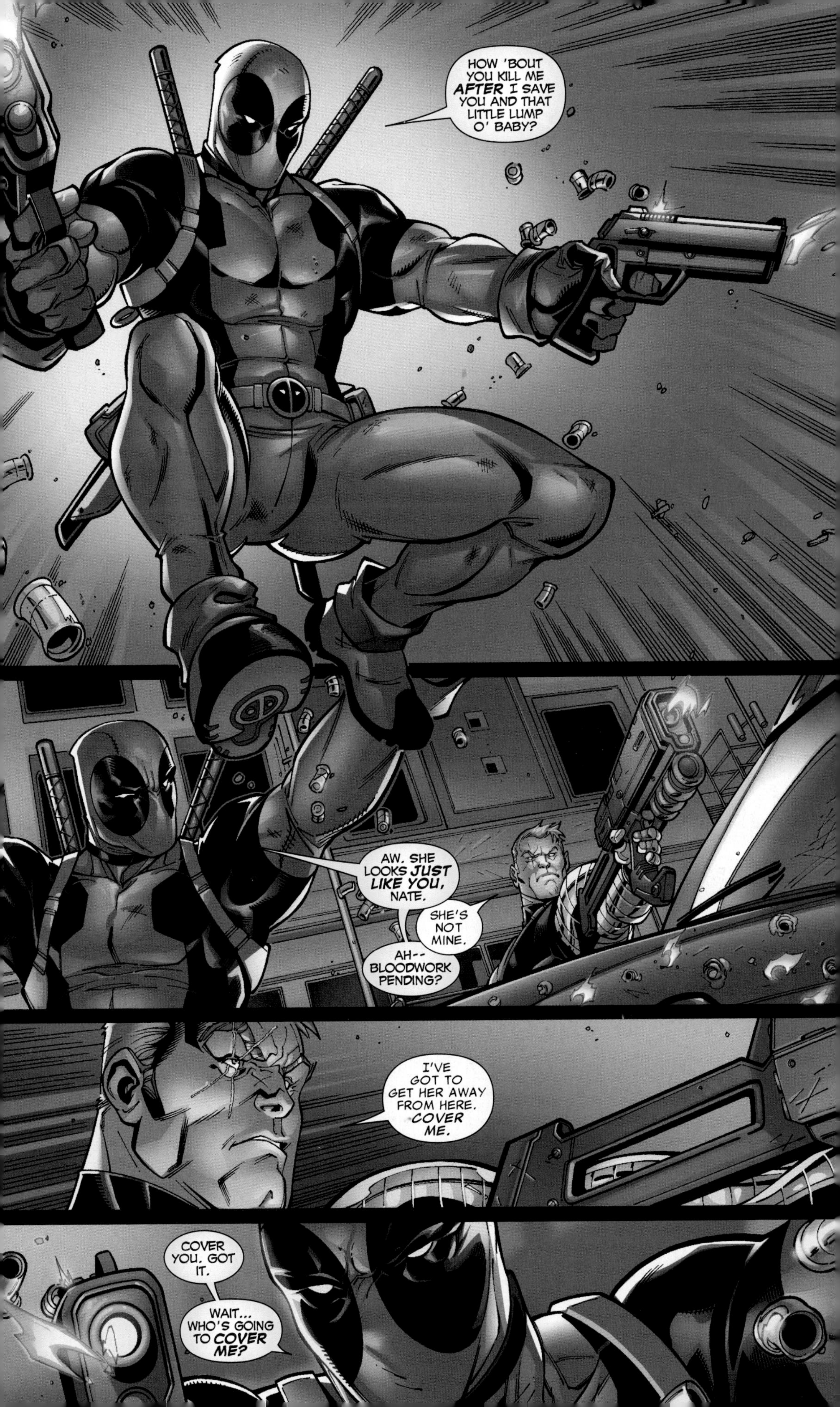

HOW 'BOUT YOU KILL ME AFTER I SAVE YOU AND THAT LITTLE LUMP O' BABY?
AW. SHE LOOKS JUST LIKE YOU, NATE.
SHE'S NOT MINE.
AH--BLOODWORK PENDING?
I'VE GOT TO GET HER AWAY FROM HERE. COVER ME.
COVER YOU, GOT IT.
WAIT... WHO'S GOING TO COVER ME?

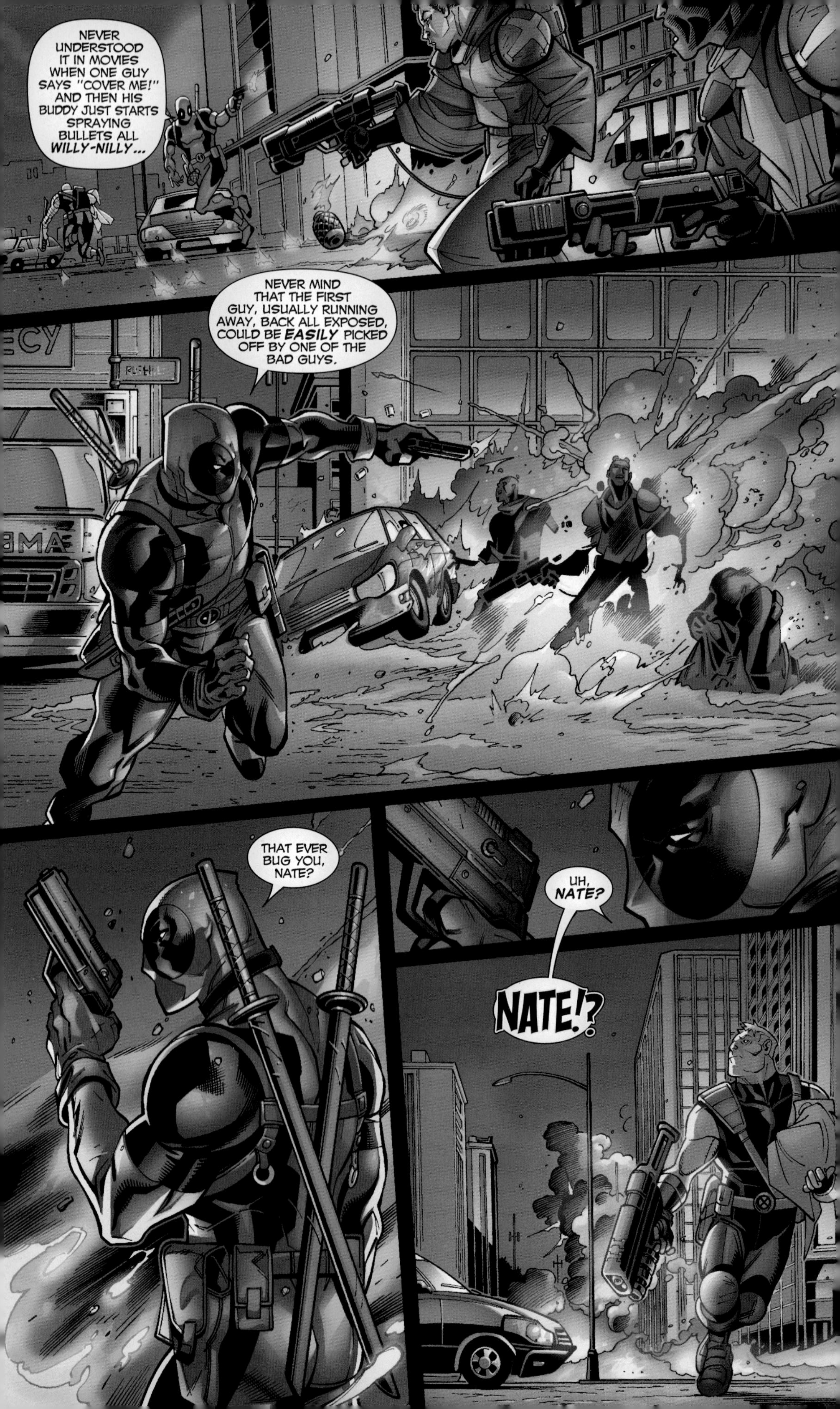
NEVER UNDERSTOOD IT IN MOVIES WHEN ONE GUY SAYS "COVER ME!" AND THEN HIS BUDDY JUST STARTS SPRAYING BULLETS ALL WILLY-NILLY...
NEVER MIND THAT THE FIRST GUY, USUALLY RUNNING AWAY, BACK ALL EXPOSED, COULD BE EASILY PICKED OFF BY ONE OF THE BAD GUYS.
THAT EVER BUG YOU, NATE?
UH, NATE?
NATE!?

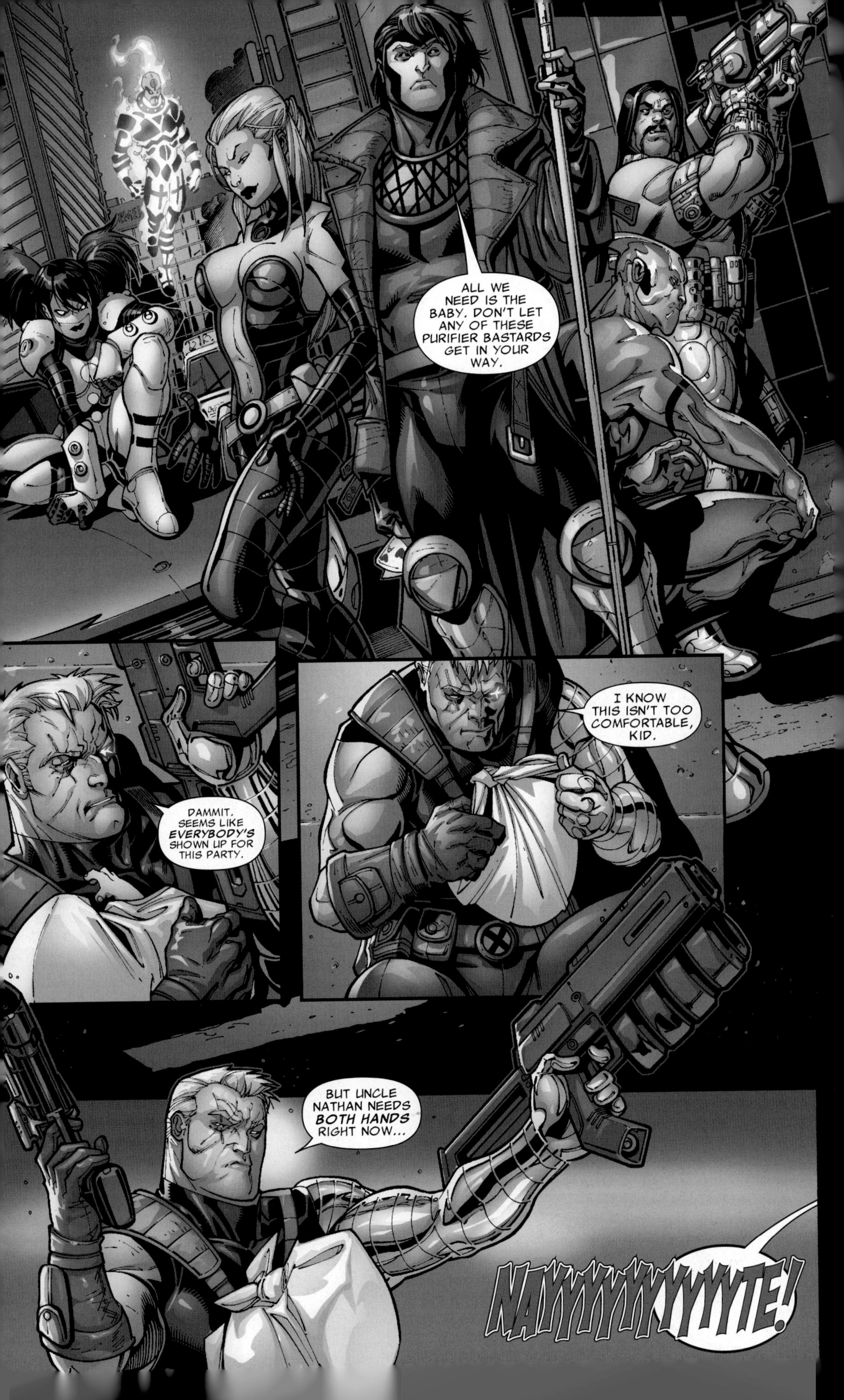
ALL WE NEED IS THE BABY. DON'T LET ANY OF THESE PURIFIER BASTARDS GET IN YOUR WAY.
DAMMIT. SEEMS LIKE EVERYBODY'S SHOWN UP FOR THIS PARTY.
I KNOW THIS ISN'T TOO COMFORTABLE, KID.
BUT UNCLE NATHAN NEEDS BOTH HANDS RIGHT NOW...
NAYYYYYYYYYYTE!

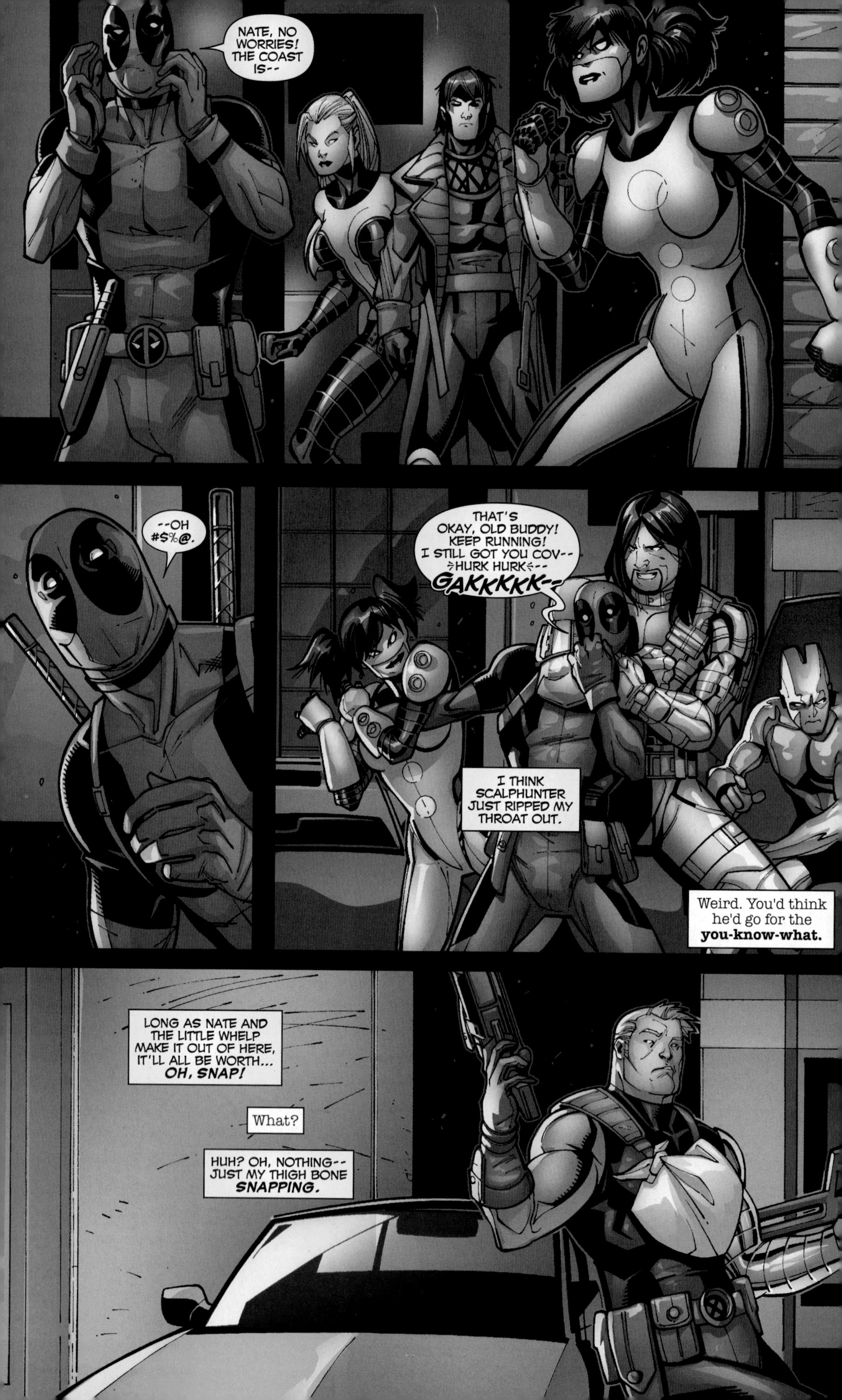
NATE, NO WORRIES! THE COAST IS--
--OH #$%@.
THAT'S OKAY, OLD BUDDY! KEEP RUNNING! I STILL GOT YOU COV-- ≠HURK HURK≠-- GAKKKKK--
I THINK SCALPHUNTER JUST RIPPED MY THROAT OUT.
Weird. You'd think he'd go for the **you-know-what.**
LONG AS NATE AND THE LITTLE WHELP MAKE IT OUT OF HERE, IT'LL ALL BE WORTH... **OH, SNAP!**
What?
HUH? OH, NOTHING-- JUST MY THIGH BONE **SNAPPING.**

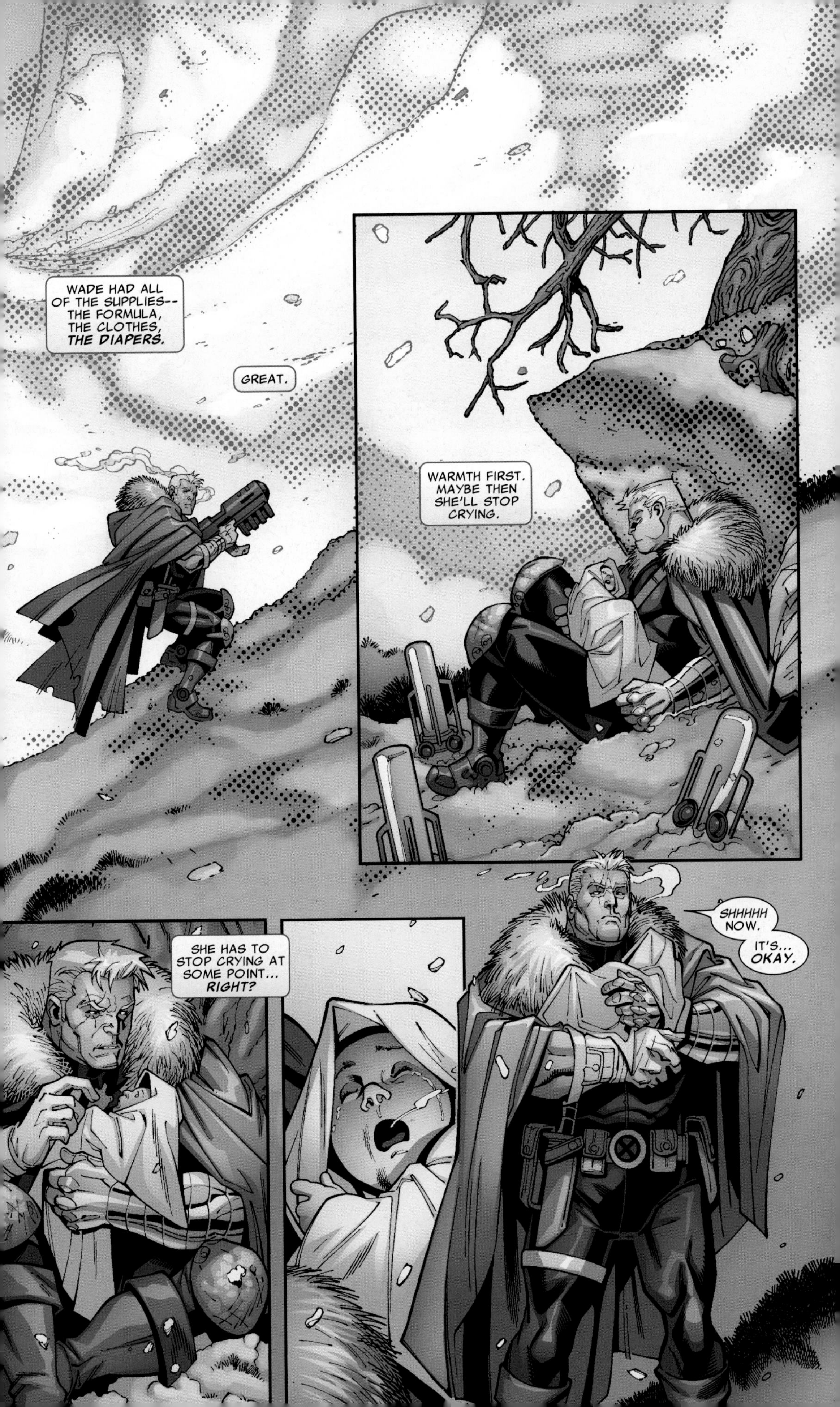
WADE HAD ALL OF THE SUPPLIES-- THE FORMULA, THE CLOTHES, *THE DIAPERS.*
GREAT.
WARMTH FIRST. MAYBE THEN SHE'LL STOP CRYING.
SHE HAS TO STOP CRYING AT SOME POINT... *RIGHT?*
SHHHHH NOW.
IT'S... *OKAY.*

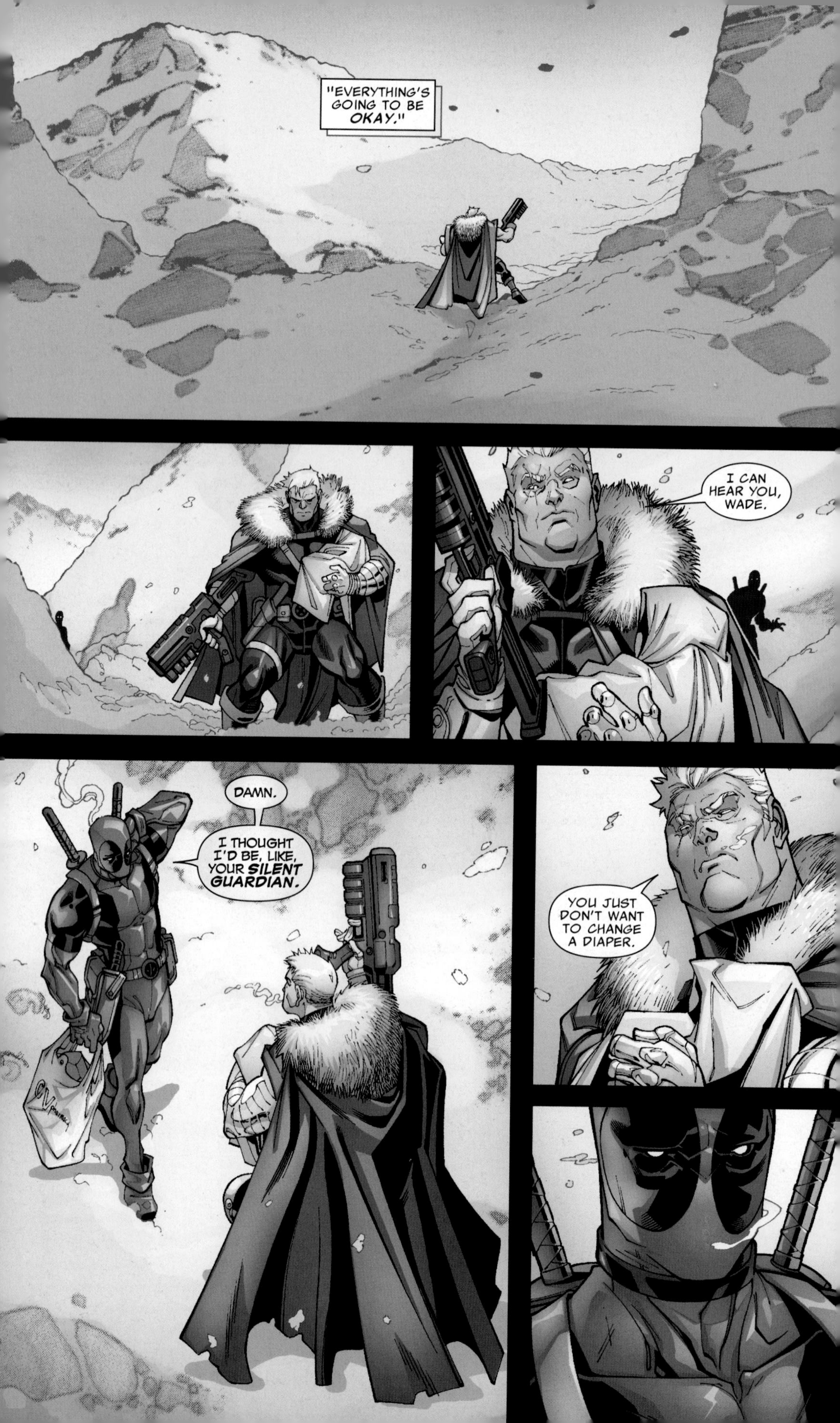
"EVERYTHING'S GOING TO BE OKAY."
I CAN HEAR YOU, WADE.
DAMN.
I THOUGHT I'D BE, LIKE, YOUR SILENT GUARDIAN.
YOU JUST DON'T WANT TO CHANGE A DIAPER.

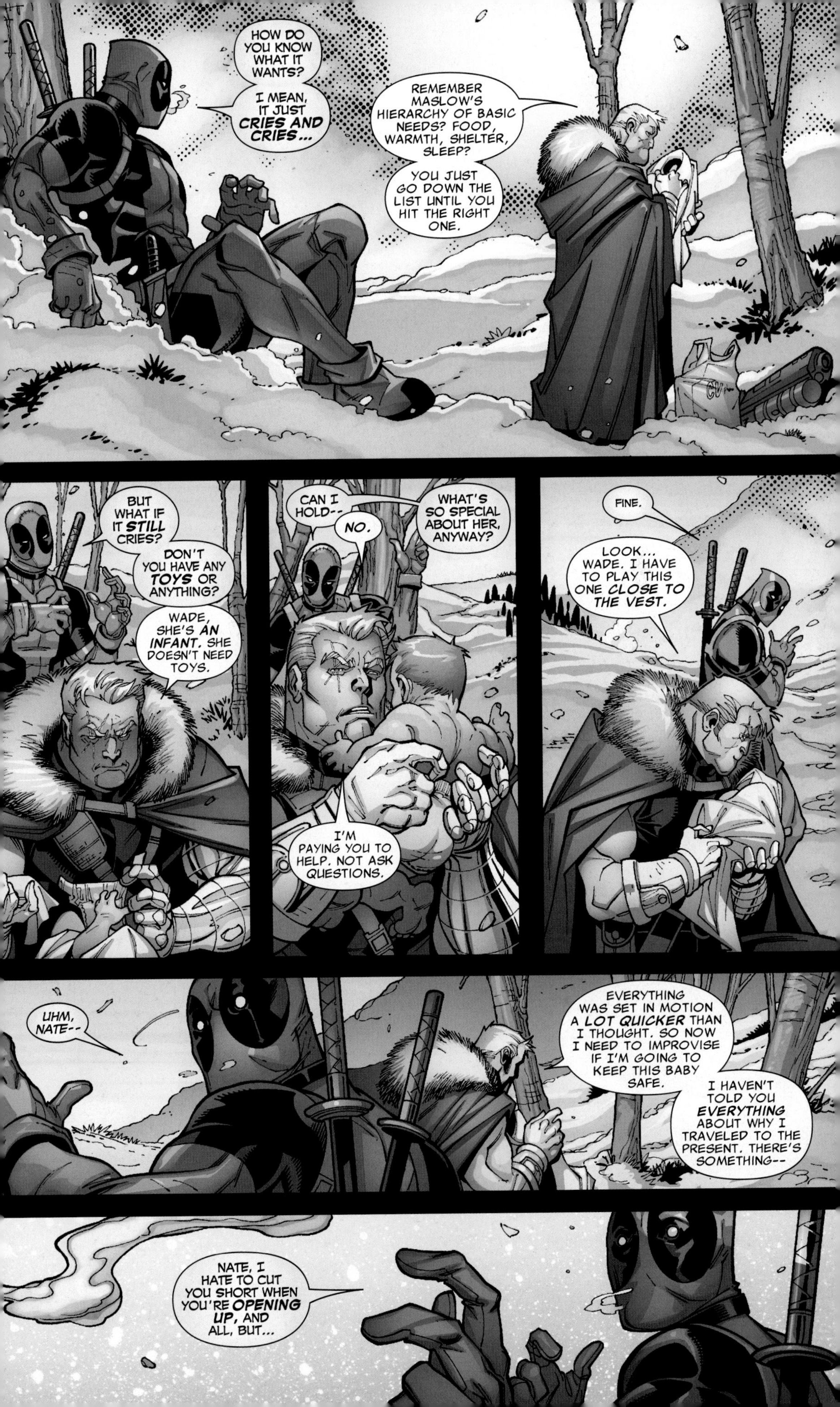

HOW DO YOU KNOW WHAT IT WANTS?
I MEAN, IT JUST CRIES AND CRIES...
REMEMBER MASLOW'S HIERARCHY OF BASIC NEEDS? FOOD, WARMTH, SHELTER, SLEEP?
YOU JUST GO DOWN THE LIST UNTIL YOU HIT THE RIGHT ONE.
BUT WHAT IF IT STILL CRIES?
DON'T YOU HAVE ANY TOYS OR ANYTHING?
WADE, SHE'S AN INFANT. SHE DOESN'T NEED TOYS.
CAN I HOLD--
NO.
WHAT'S SO SPECIAL ABOUT HER, ANYWAY?
I'M PAYING YOU TO HELP. NOT ASK QUESTIONS.
FINE.
LOOK... WADE. I HAVE TO PLAY THIS ONE CLOSE TO THE VEST.
UHM, NATE--
EVERYTHING WAS SET IN MOTION A LOT QUICKER THAN I THOUGHT. SO NOW I NEED TO IMPROVISE IF I'M GOING TO KEEP THIS BABY SAFE.
I HAVEN'T TOLD YOU EVERYTHING ABOUT WHY I TRAVELED TO THE PRESENT. THERE'S SOMETHING--
NATE, I HATE TO CUT YOU SHORT WHEN YOU'RE OPENING UP, AND ALL, BUT...

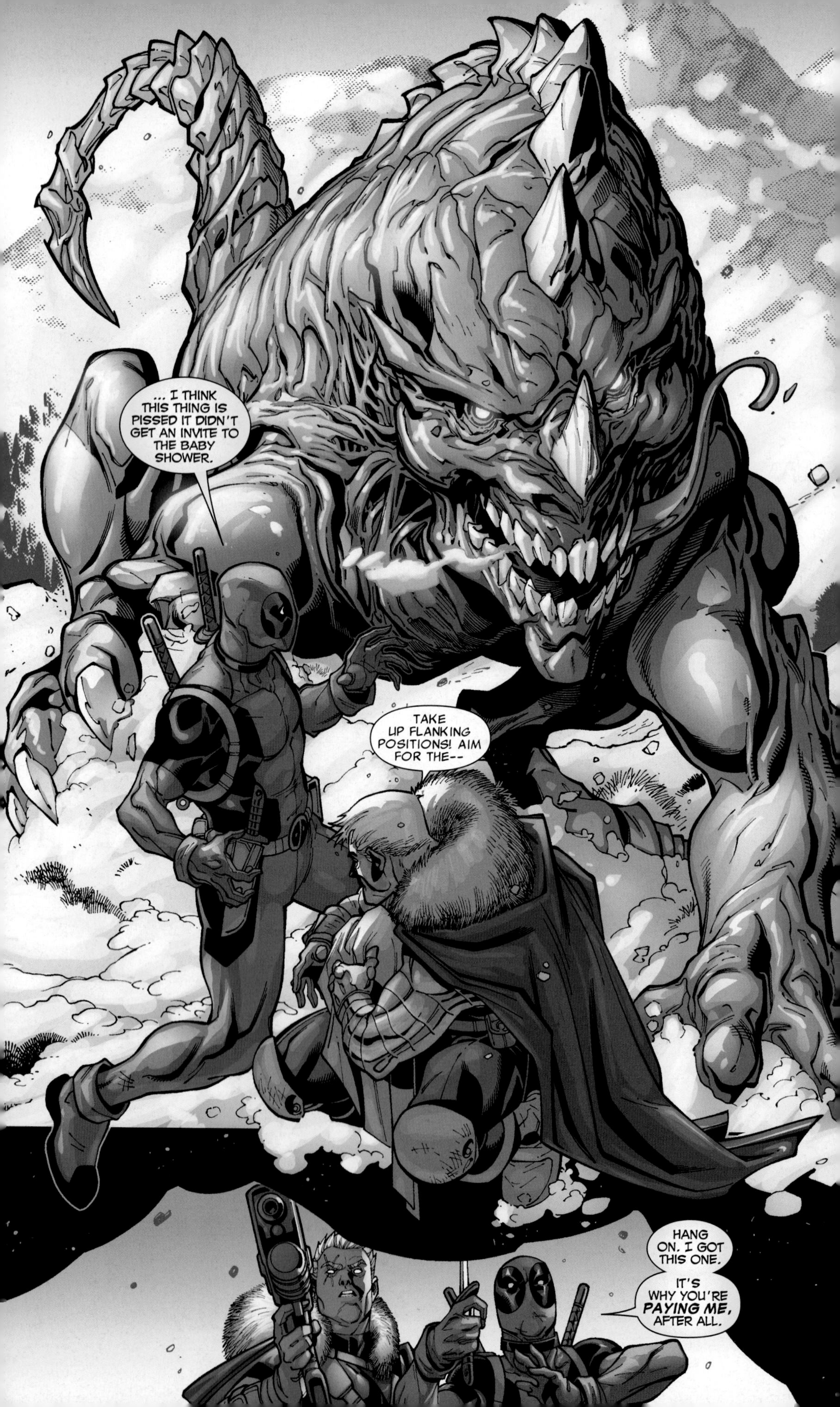
... I THINK THIS THING IS PISSED IT DIDN'T GET AN INVITE TO THE BABY SHOWER.
TAKE UP FLANKING POSITIONS! AIM FOR THE--
HANG ON. I GOT THIS ONE.
IT'S WHY YOU'RE PAYING ME, AFTER ALL.

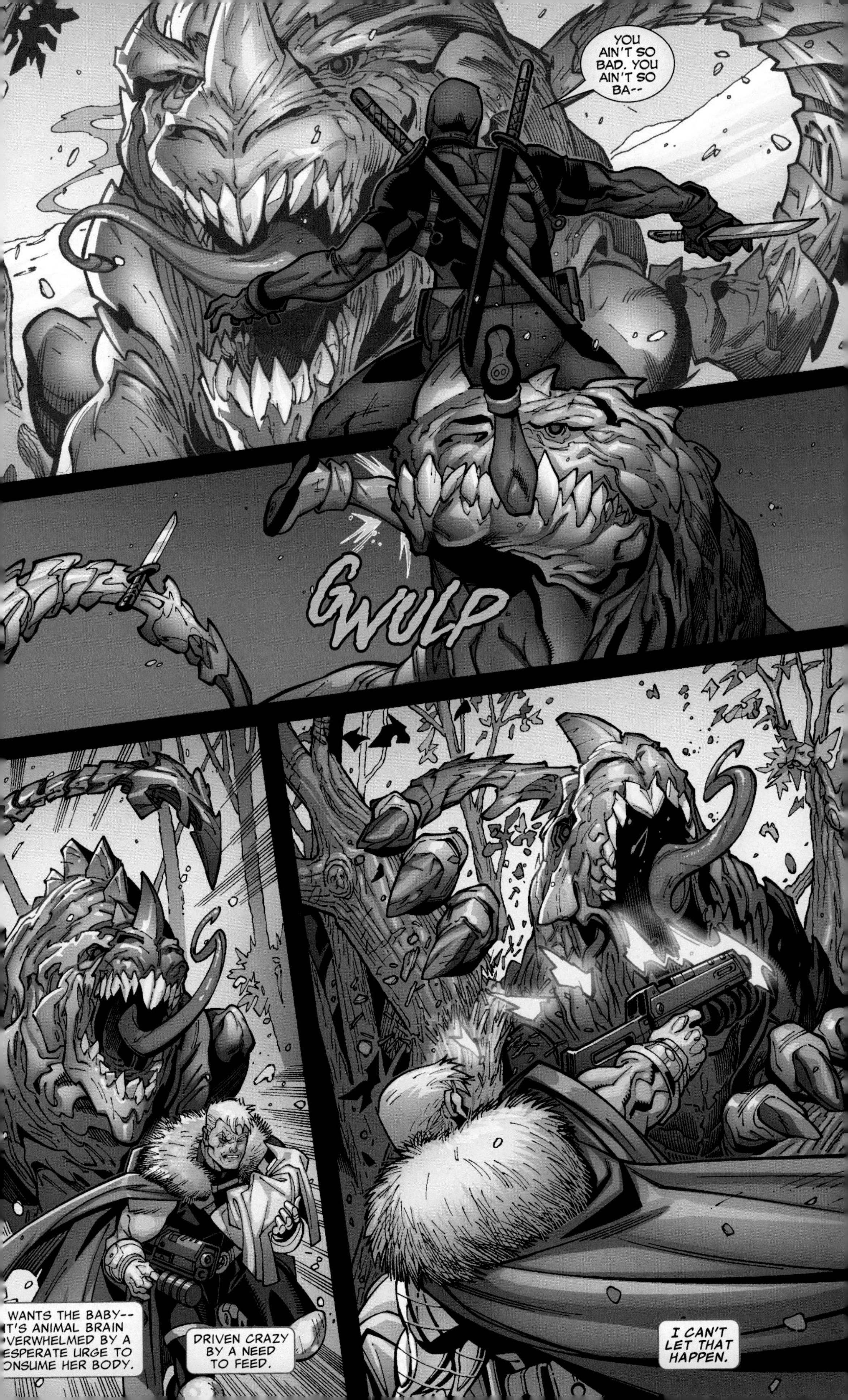
YOU AIN'T SO BAD. YOU AIN'T SO BA--
GWULP
WANTS THE BABY-- 'T'S ANIMAL BRAIN VERWHELMED BY A ESPERATE URGE TO ONSUME HER BODY.
DRIVEN CRAZY BY A NEED TO FEED.
I CAN'T LET THAT HAPPEN.

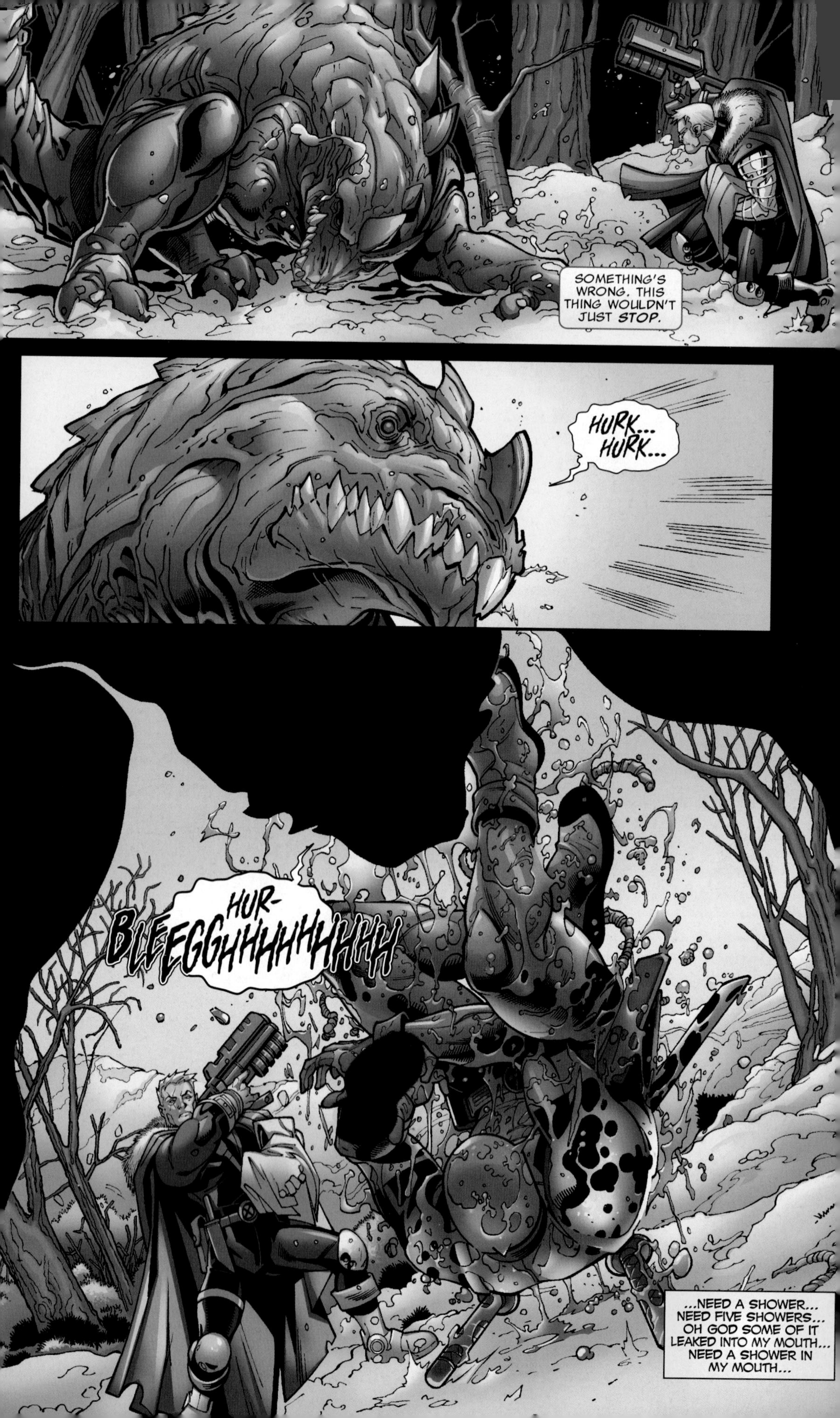

SOMETHING'S WRONG. THIS THING WOULDN'T JUST STOP.
HURK... HURK...
HUR-BLEEGGHHHHHHHH
...NEED A SHOWER... NEED FIVE SHOWERS... OH GOD SOME OF IT LEAKED INTO MY MOUTH... NEED A SHOWER IN MY MOUTH...

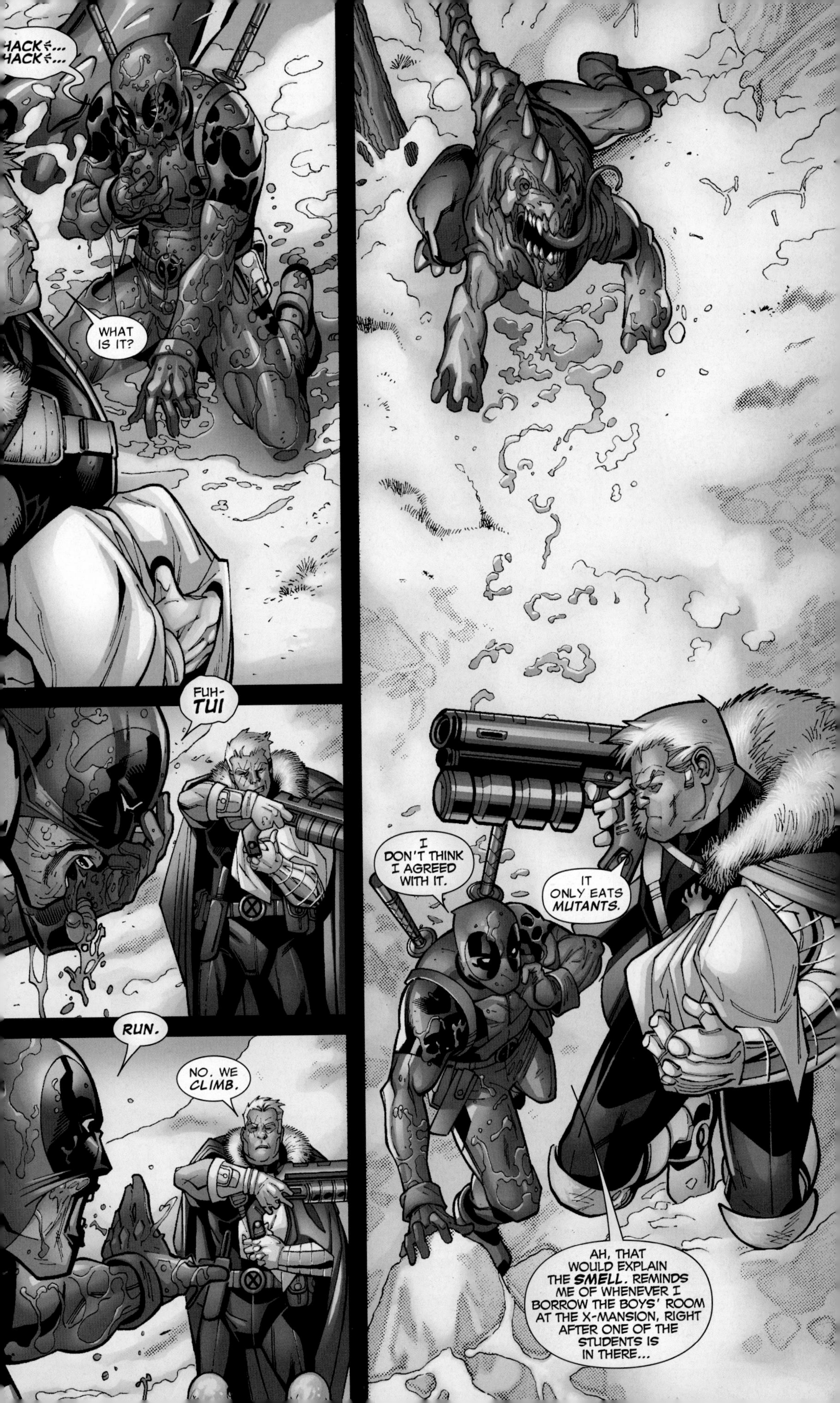
HACK...
HACK...
WHAT IS IT?
FUH-TUI
RUN.
NO. WE CLIMB.
IT ONLY EATS MUTANTS.
I DON'T THINK I AGREED WITH IT.
AH, THAT WOULD EXPLAIN THE SMELL. REMINDS ME OF WHENEVER I BORROW THE BOYS' ROOM AT THE X-MANSION, RIGHT AFTER ONE OF THE STUDENTS IS IN THERE...

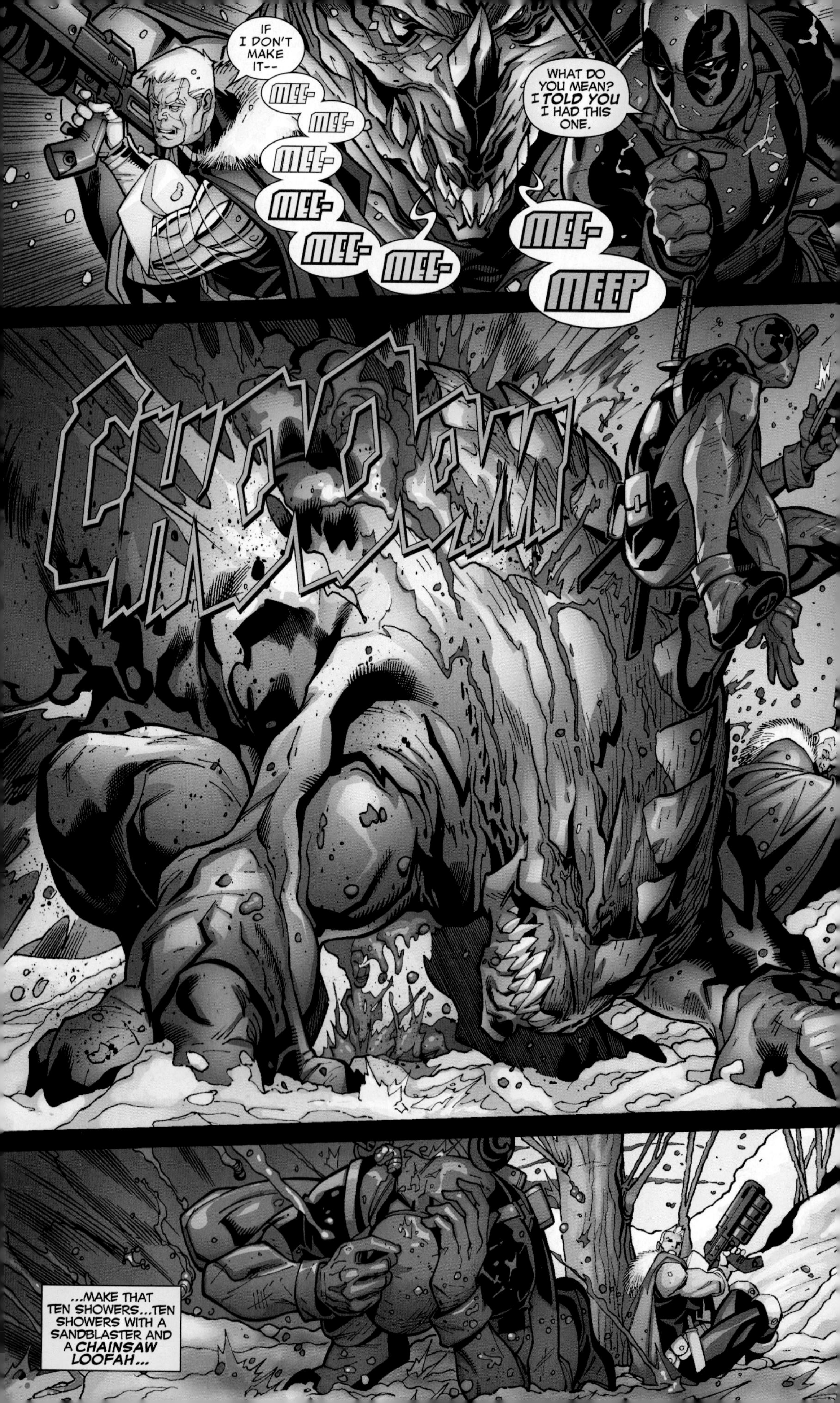

IF I DON'T MAKE IT--
MEE-
MEE-
MEE-
MEE-
MEE-
MEE-
WHAT DO YOU MEAN? I *TOLD YOU* I HAD THIS ONE.
MEE-
MEEP
...MAKE THAT TEN SHOWERS...TEN SHOWERS WITH A SANDBLASTER AND A *CHAINSAW LOOFAH*...

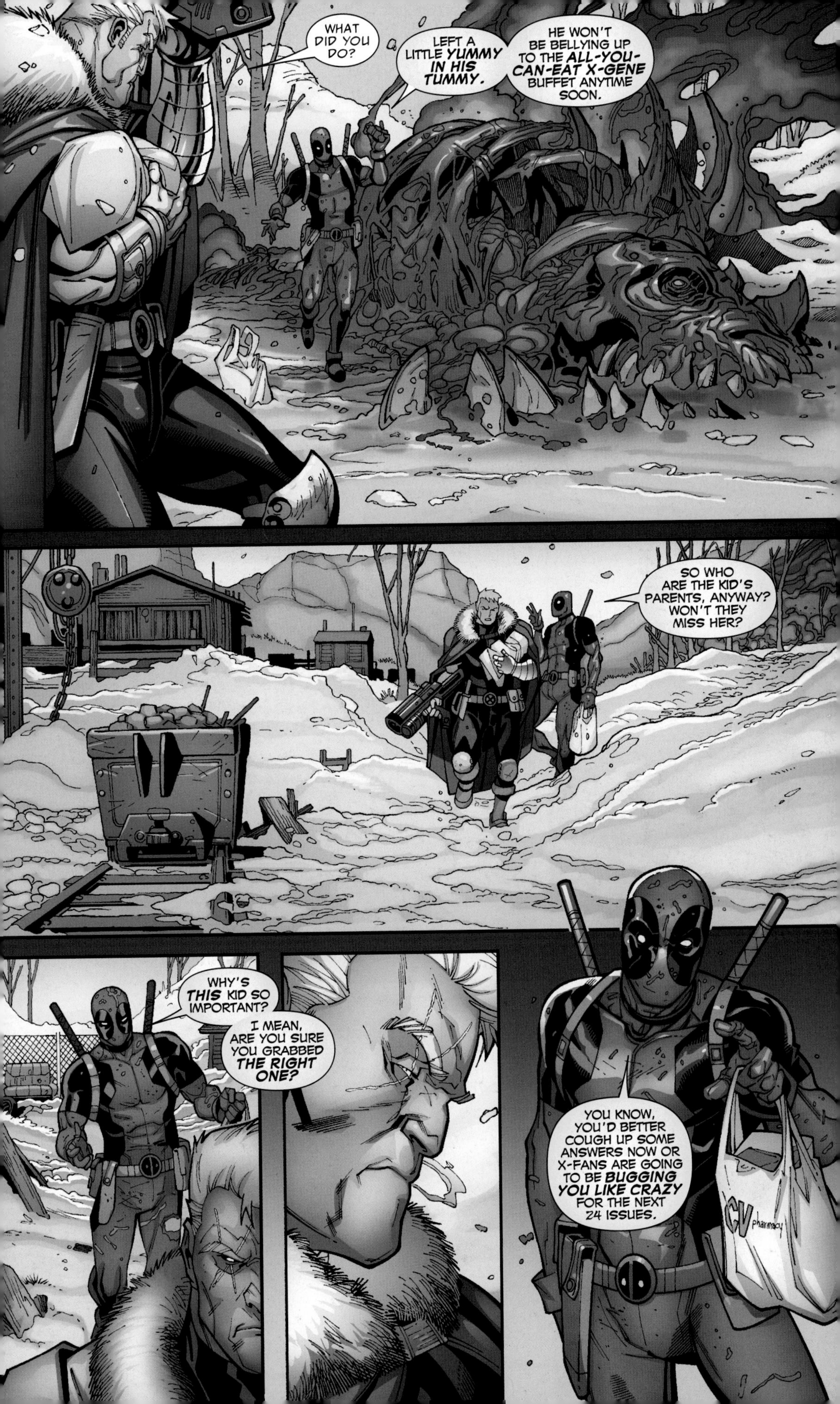
WHAT DID YOU DO?
LEFT A LITTLE YUMMY IN HIS TUMMY.
HE WON'T BE BELLYING UP TO THE ALL-YOU-CAN-EAT X-GENE BUFFET ANYTIME SOON.
SO WHO ARE THE KID'S PARENTS, ANYWAY? WON'T THEY MISS HER?
WHY'S THIS KID SO IMPORTANT?
I MEAN, ARE YOU SURE YOU GRABBED THE RIGHT ONE?
YOU KNOW, YOU'D BETTER COUGH UP SOME ANSWERS NOW OR X-FANS ARE GOING TO BE BUGGING YOU LIKE CRAZY FOR THE NEXT 24 ISSUES.
CV pharmacy

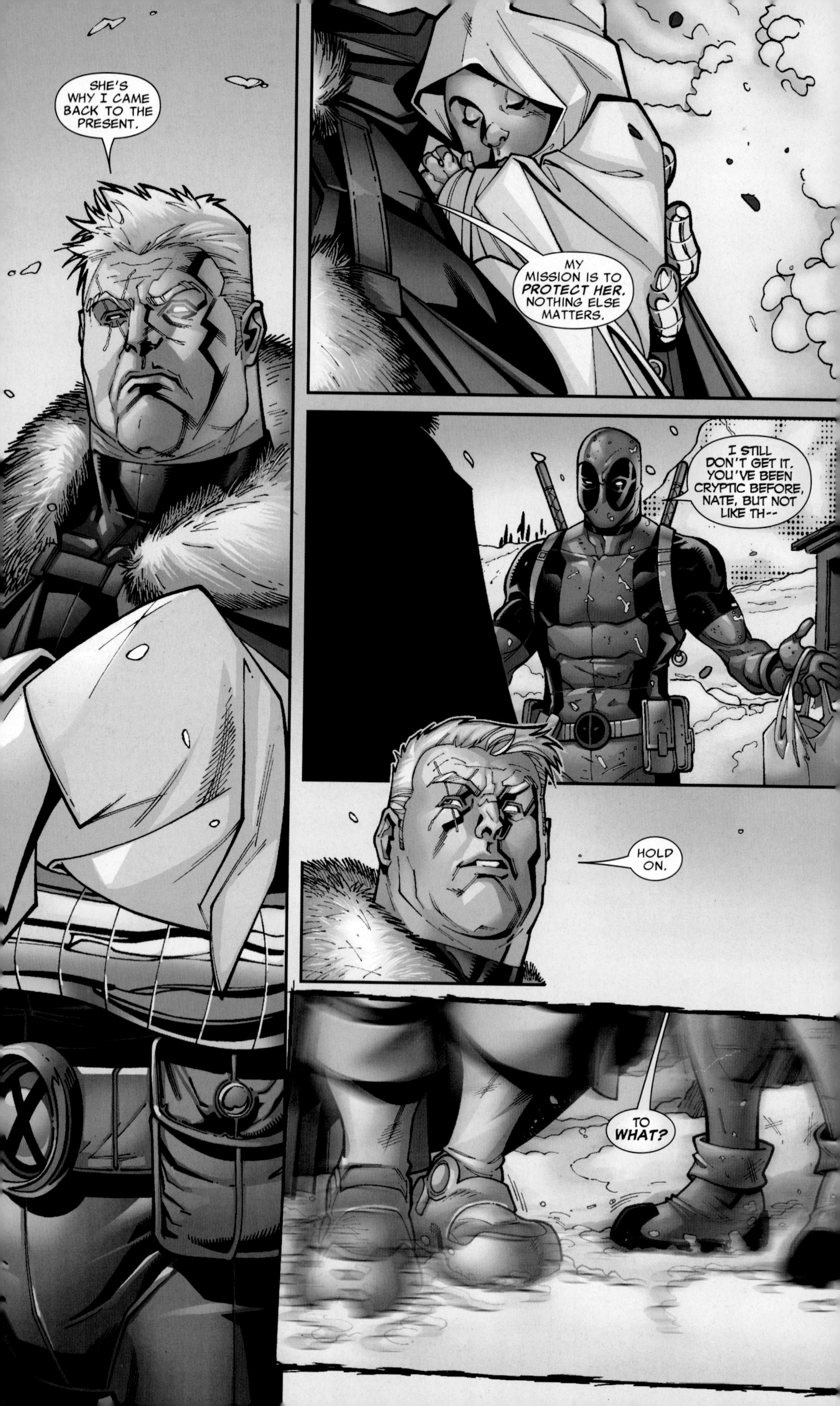
SHE'S WHY I CAME BACK TO THE PRESENT.
MY MISSION IS TO PROTECT HER. NOTHING ELSE MATTERS.
I STILL DON'T GET IT. YOU'VE BEEN CRYPTIC BEFORE, NATE, BUT NOT LIKE TH--
HOLD ON.
TO WHAT?

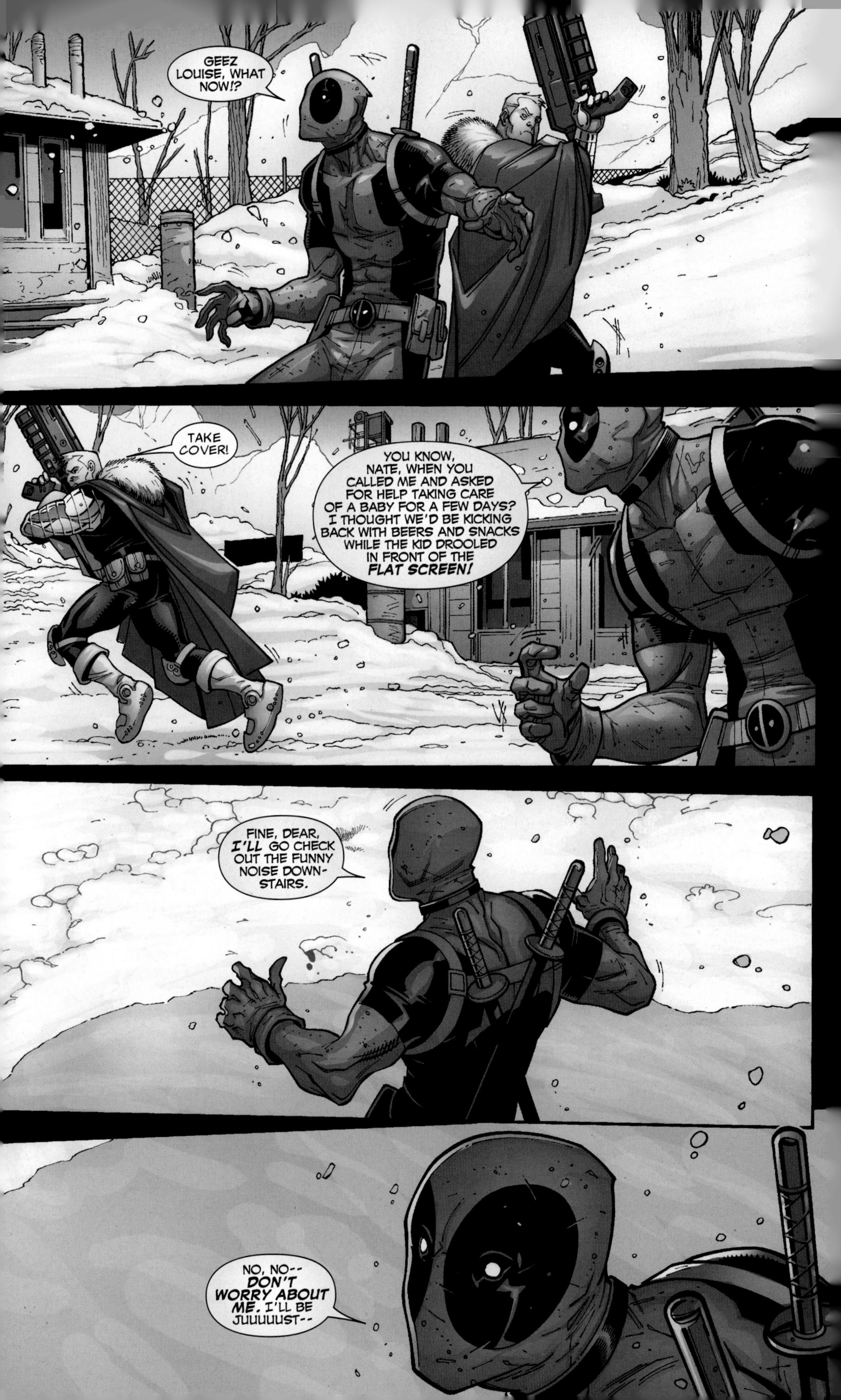
GEEZ LOUISE, WHAT NOW!?
TAKE COVER!
YOU KNOW, NATE, WHEN YOU CALLED ME AND ASKED FOR HELP TAKING CARE OF A BABY FOR A FEW DAYS? I THOUGHT WE'D BE KICKING BACK WITH BEERS AND SNACKS WHILE THE KID DROOLED IN FRONT OF THE FLAT SCREEN!
FINE, DEAR, I'LL GO CHECK OUT THE FUNNY NOISE DOWN-STAIRS.
NO, NO-- DON'T WORRY ABOUT ME. I'LL BE JUUUUUST--

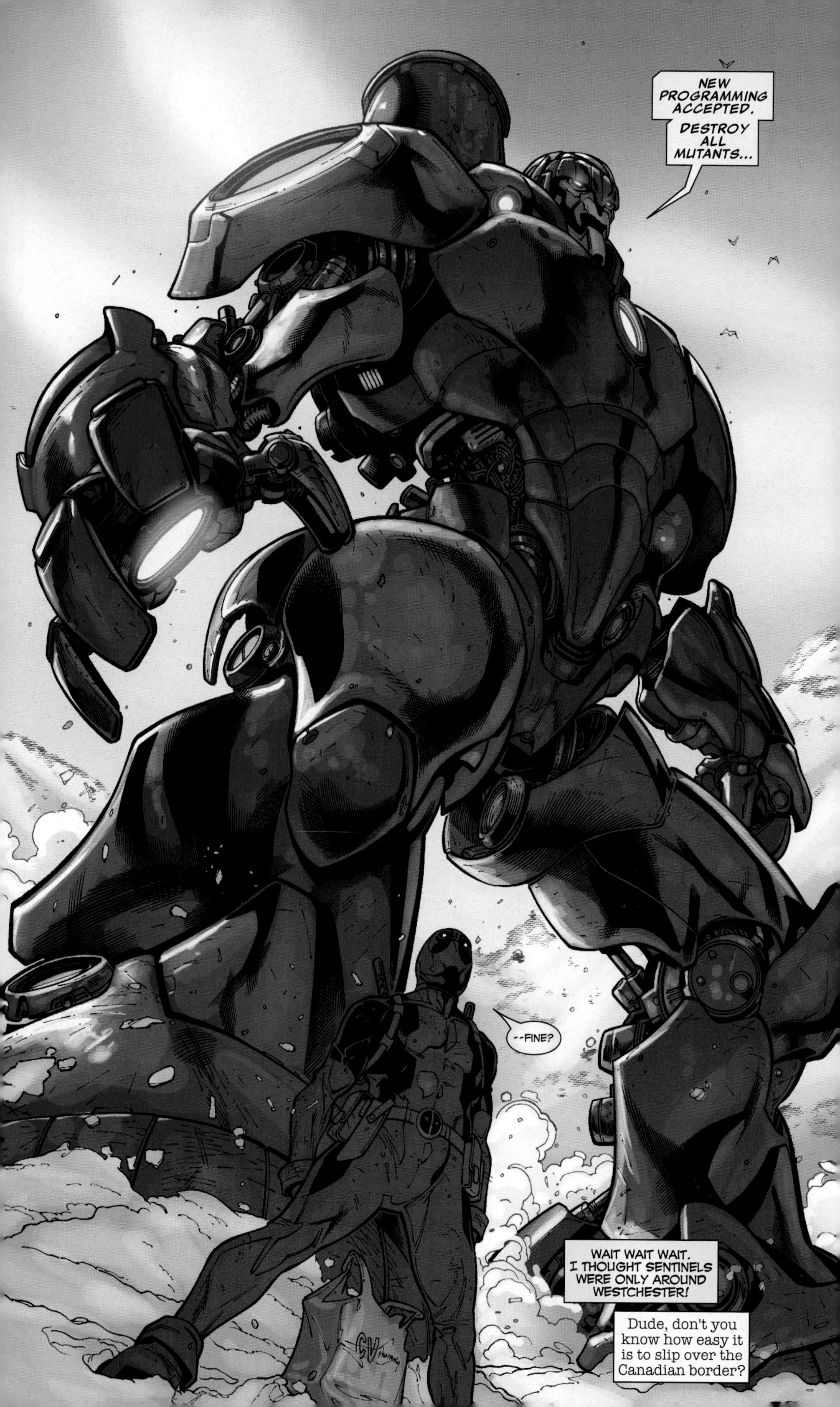

NEW PROGRAMMING ACCEPTED. DESTROY ALL MUTANTS...
--FINE?
WAIT WAIT WAIT. I THOUGHT SENTINELS WERE ONLY AROUND WESTCHESTER!
Dude, don't you know how easy it is to slip over the Canadian border?

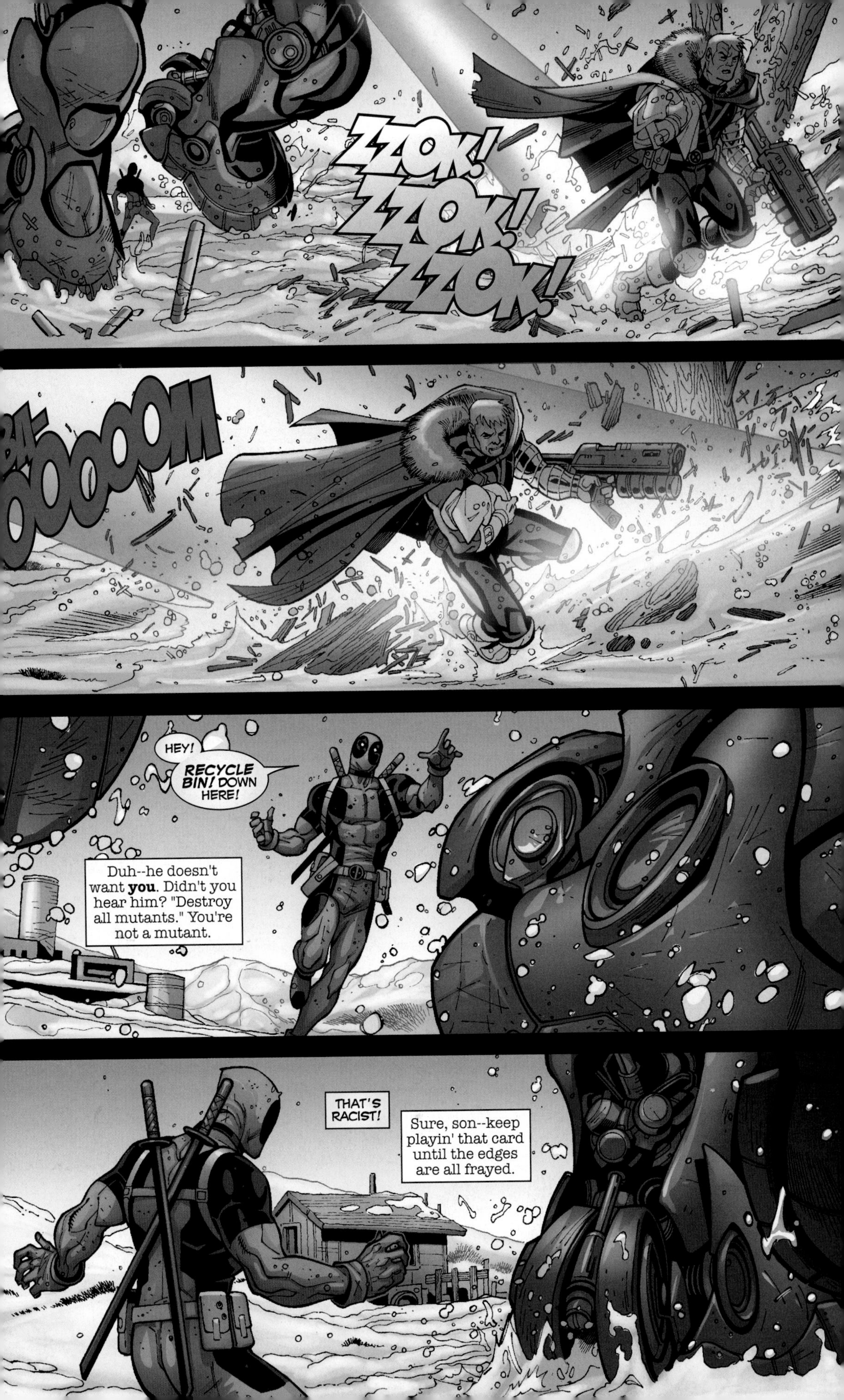
ZZOK! ZZOK! ZZOK!
BA-OOOOOOM
HEY!
RECYCLE BIN! DOWN HERE!
Duh--he doesn't want **you**. Didn't you hear him? "Destroy all mutants." You're not a mutant.
THAT'S RACIST!
Sure, son--keep playin' that card until the edges are all frayed.

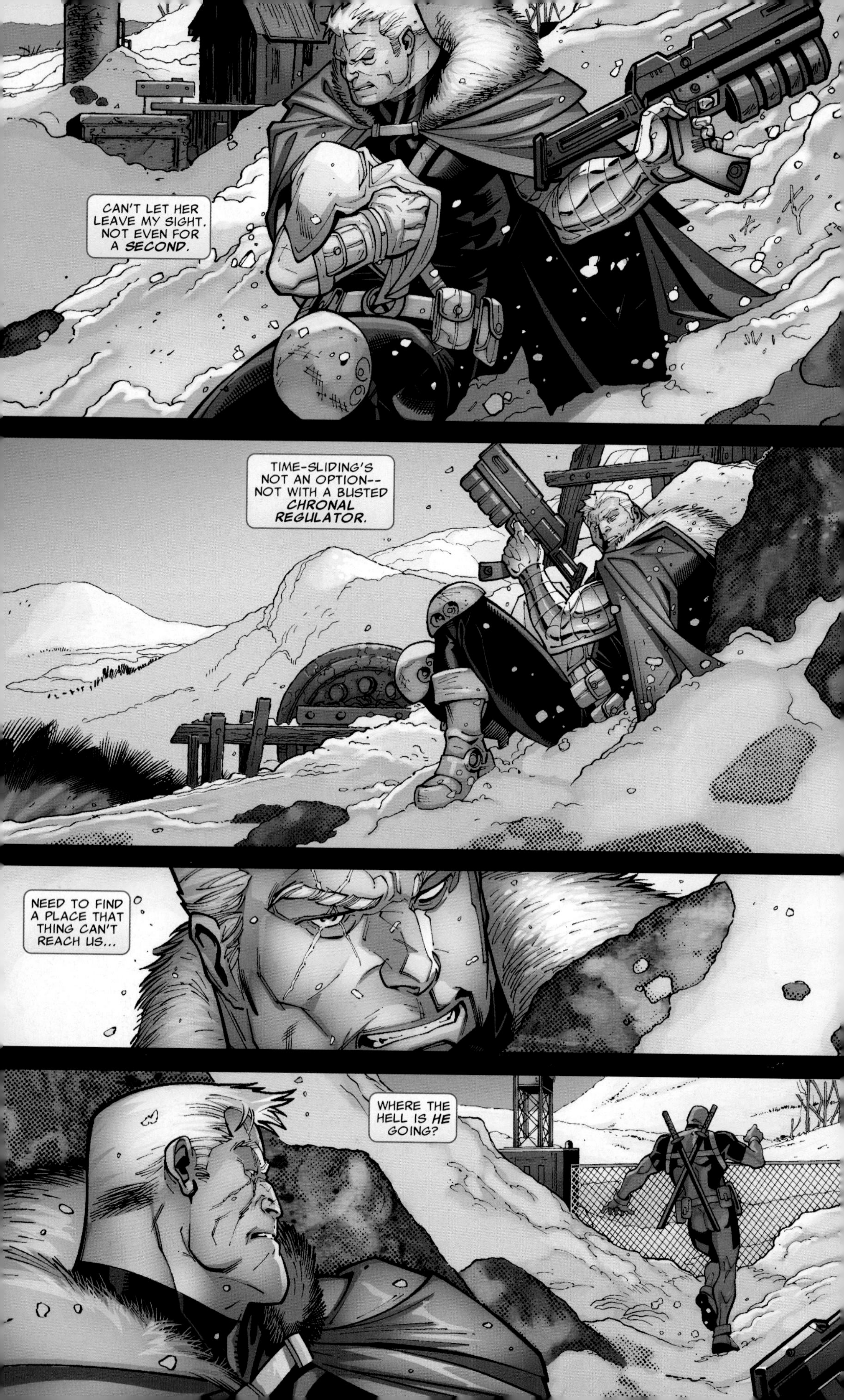
CAN'T LET HER LEAVE MY SIGHT. NOT EVEN FOR A SECOND.
TIME-SLIDING'S NOT AN OPTION-- NOT WITH A BUSTED CHRONAL REGULATOR.
NEED TO FIND A PLACE THAT THING CAN'T REACH US...
WHERE THE HELL IS HE GOING?

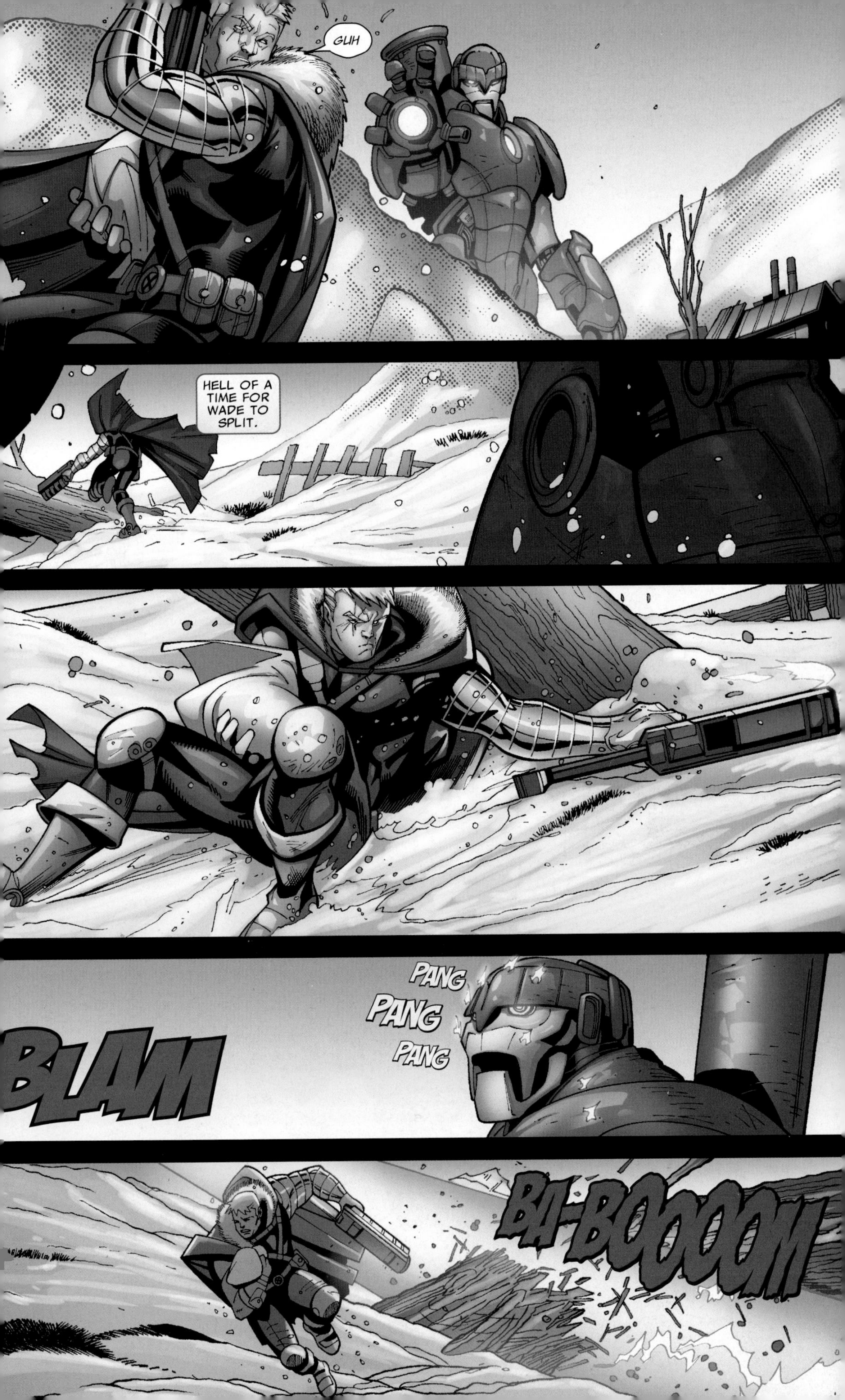
GUH
HELL OF A TIME FOR WADE TO SPLIT.
PANG
PANG
PANG
BLAM
BA-BOOOOOM

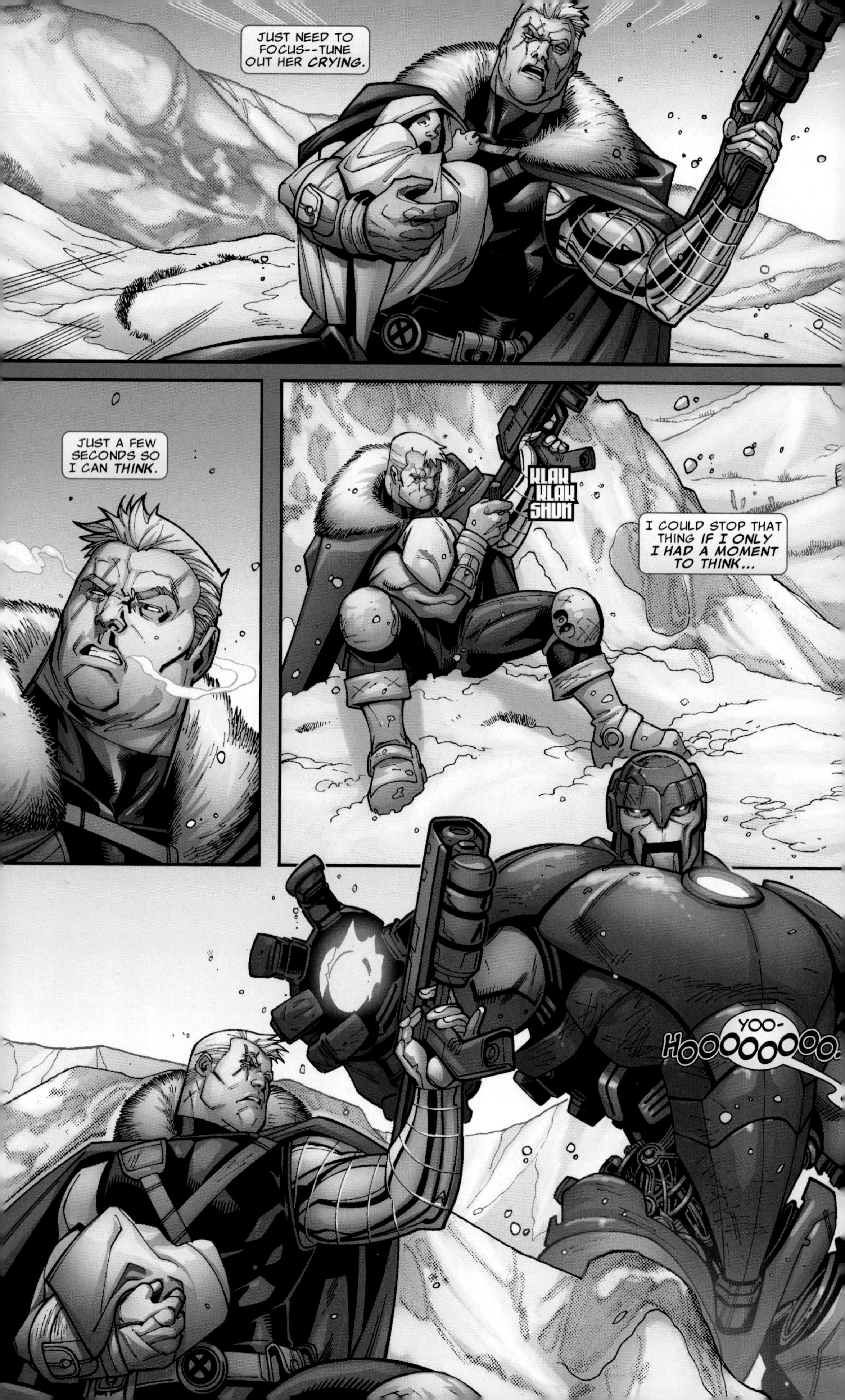
JUST NEED TO FOCUS--TUNE OUT HER CRYING.
JUST A FEW SECONDS SO I CAN THINK.
KLAK KLAK SHUK
I COULD STOP THAT THING IF I ONLY I HAD A MOMENT TO THINK...
YOO-HOOOOOOOO.

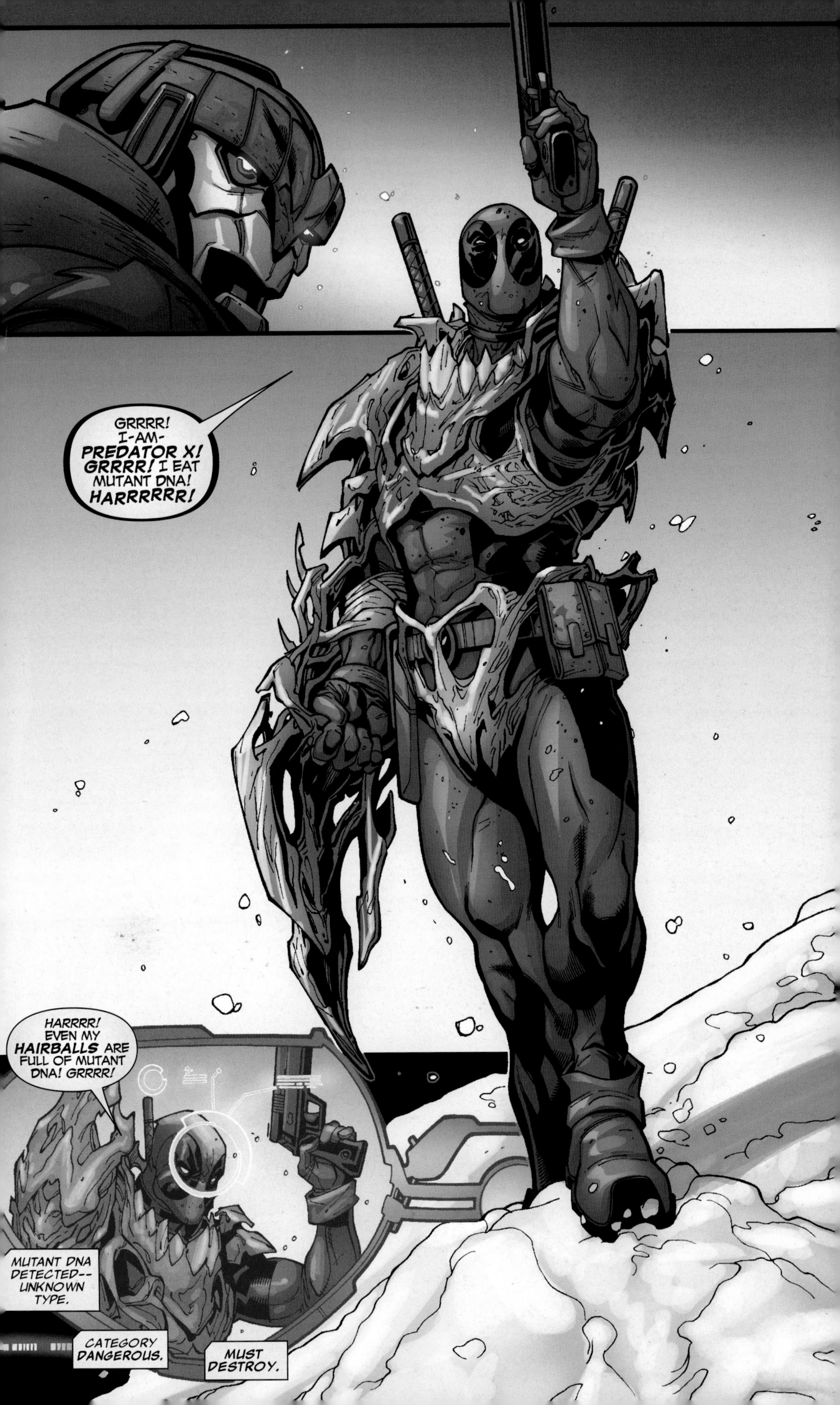
GRRRR! I-AM- PREDATOR X! GRRRR! I EAT MUTANT DNA! HARRRRRR!
HARRRR! EVEN MY HAIRBALLS ARE FULL OF MUTANT DNA! GRRRR!
MUTANT DNA DETECTED-- UNKNOWN TYPE.
CATEGORY DANGEROUS.
MUST DESTROY.

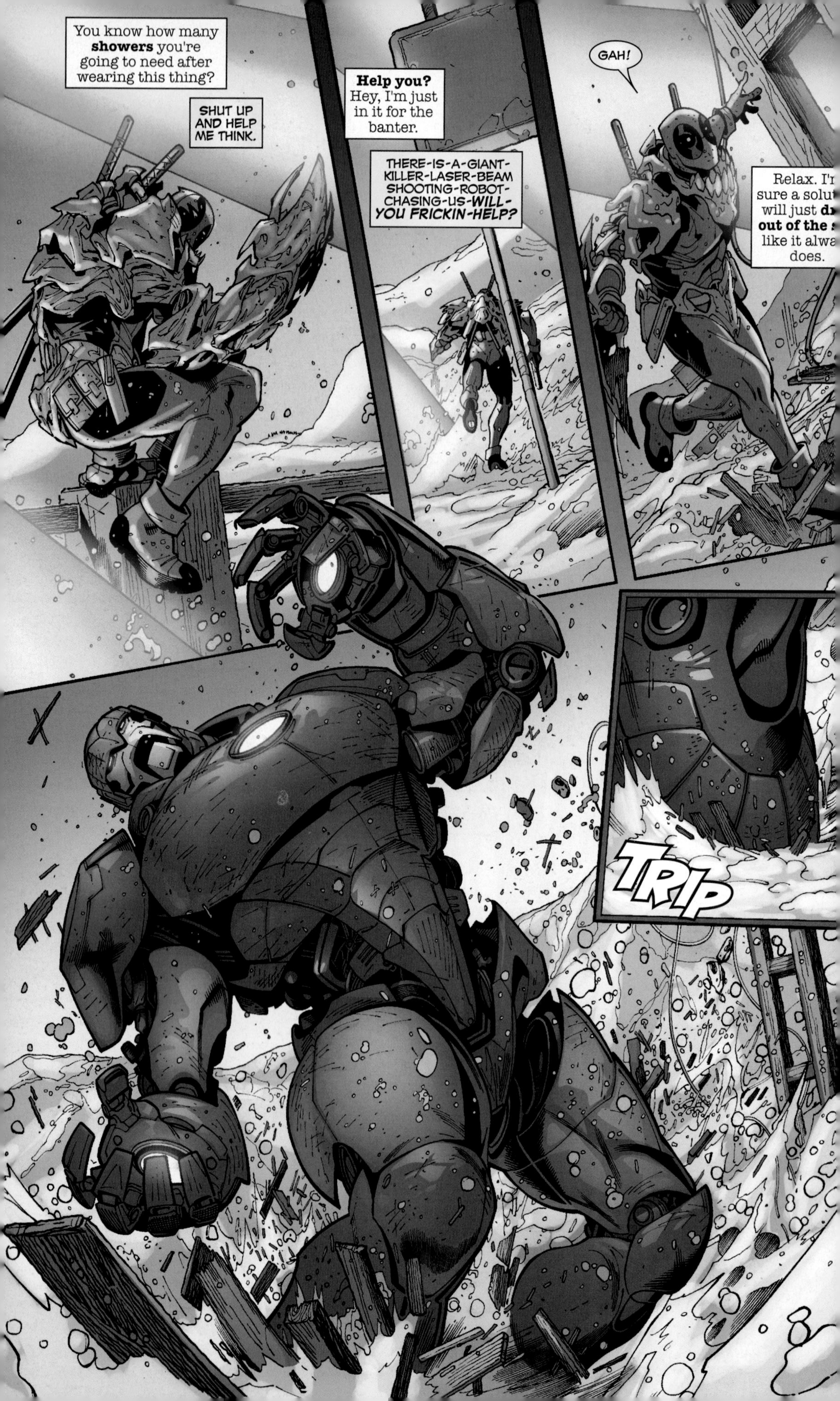

You know how many **showers** you're going to need after wearing this thing?
SHUT UP AND HELP ME THINK.
Help you? Hey, I'm just in it for the banter.
THERE-IS-A-GIANT-KILLER-LASER-BEAM SHOOTING-ROBOT-CHASING-US-*WILL-YOU FRICKIN-HELP?*
GAH!
TRIP

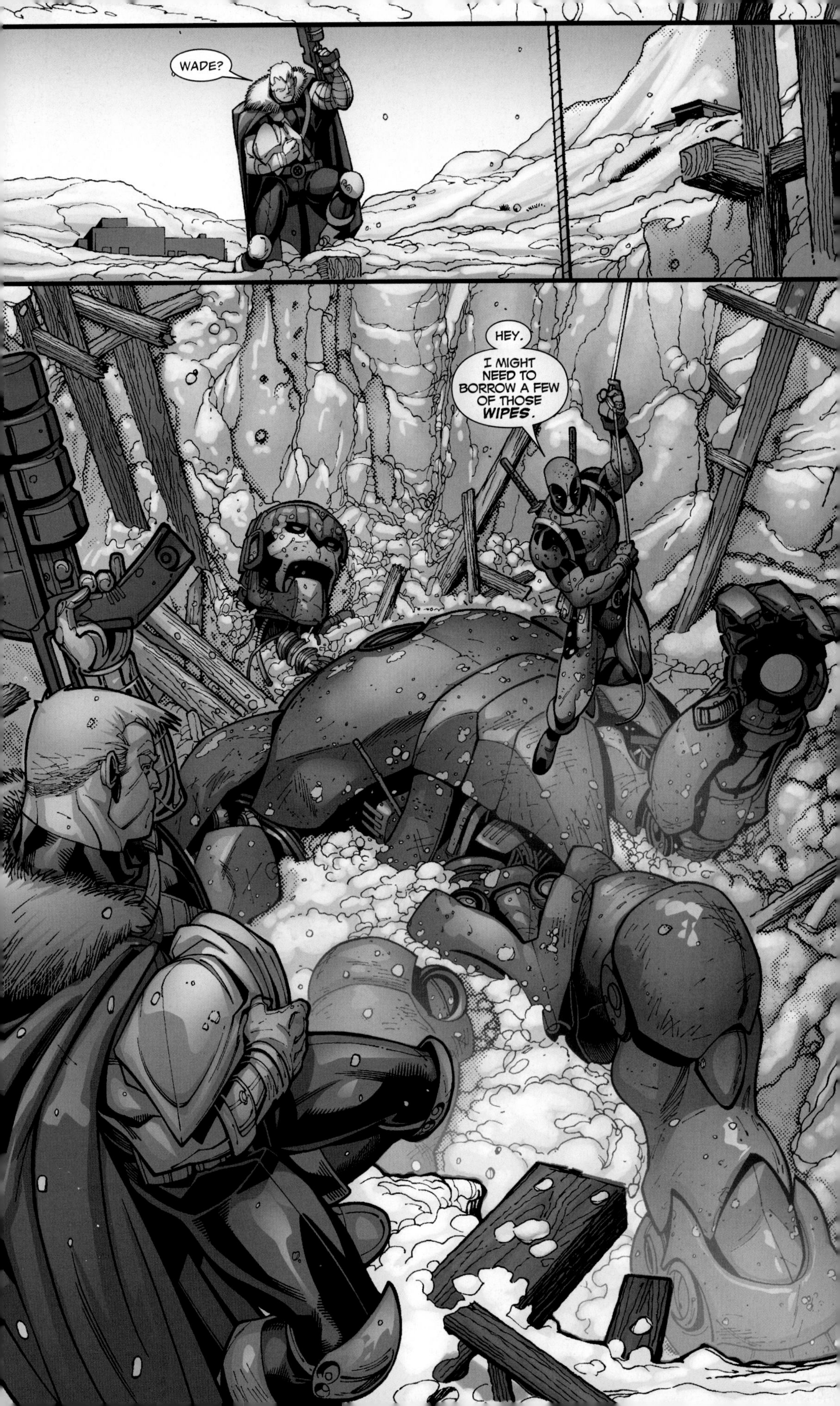
WADE?
HEY.
I MIGHT NEED TO BORROW A FEW OF THOSE WIPES.

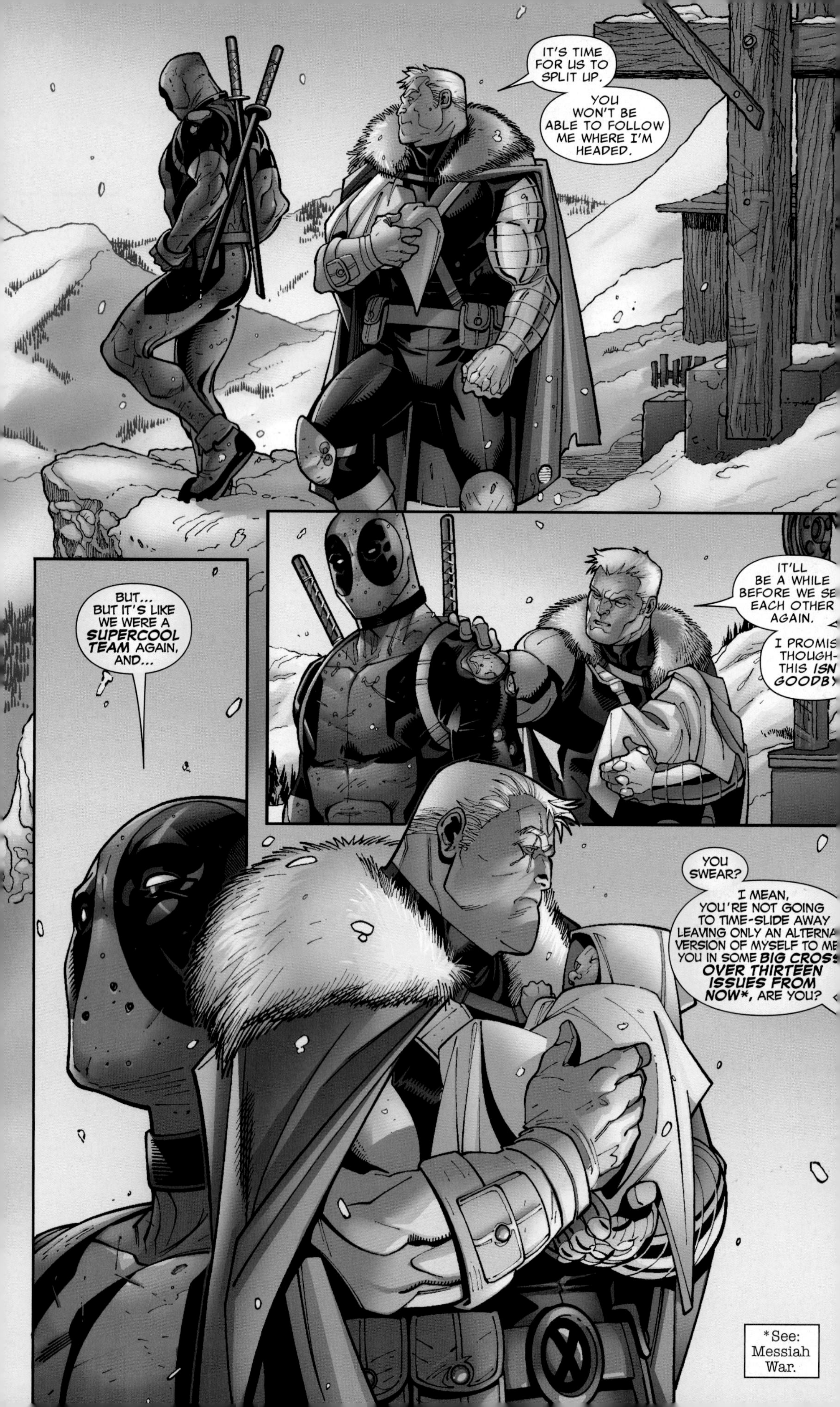

IT'S TIME FOR US TO SPLIT UP.
YOU WON'T BE ABLE TO FOLLOW ME WHERE I'M HEADED.
BUT... BUT IT'S LIKE WE WERE A **SUPERCOOL TEAM** AGAIN, AND...
IT'LL BE A WHILE BEFORE WE SE EACH OTHER AGAIN.
I PROMIS THOUGH- THIS *ISN GOODBY*
YOU SWEAR?
I MEAN, YOU'RE NOT GOING TO TIME-SLIDE AWAY LEAVING ONLY AN ALTERNA VERSION OF MYSELF TO ME YOU IN SOME **BIG CROSS OVER THIRTEEN ISSUES FROM NOW***, ARE YOU?
*See: Messiah War.

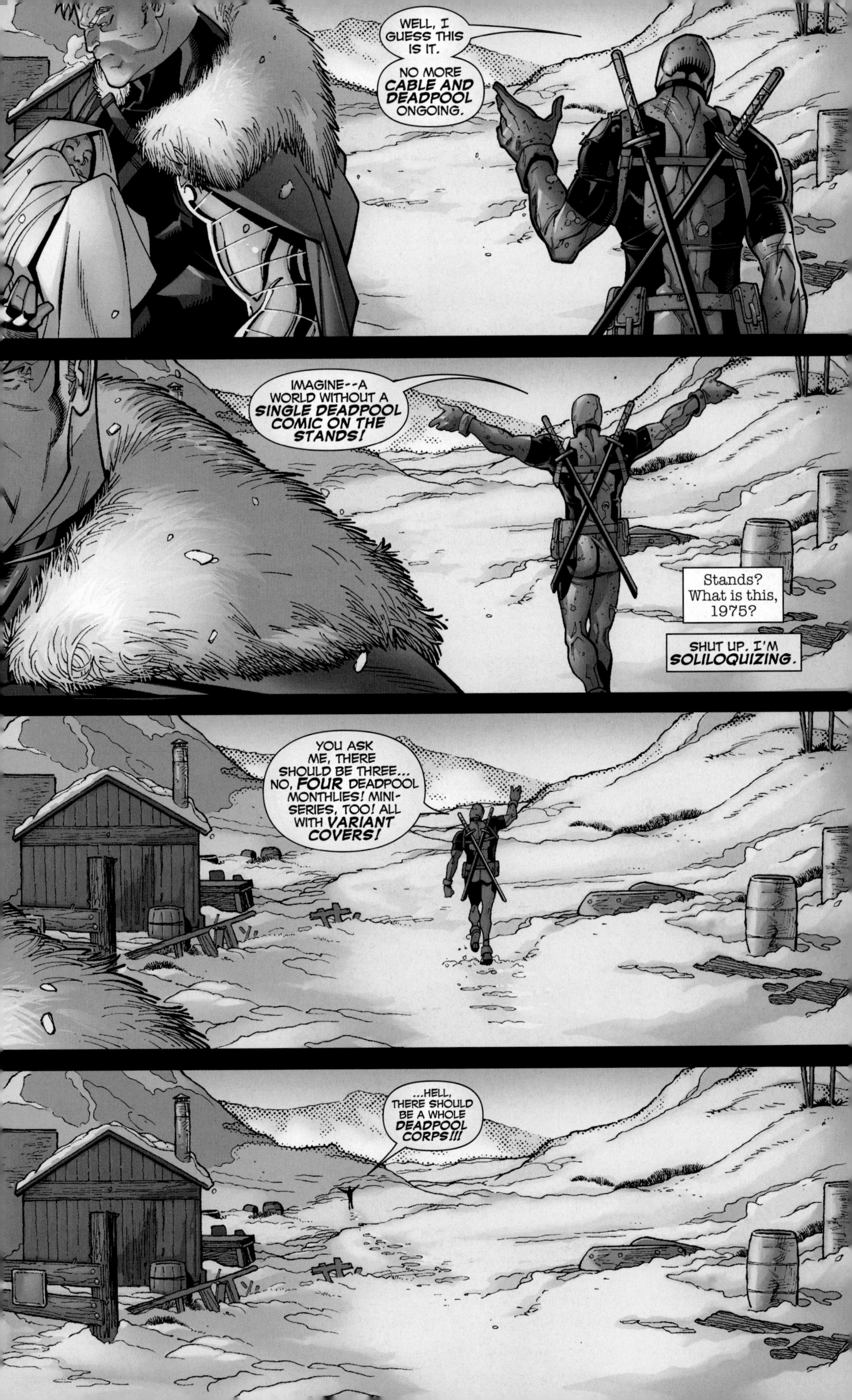
WELL, I GUESS THIS IS IT.
NO MORE CABLE AND DEADPOOL ONGOING.
IMAGINE--A WORLD WITHOUT A SINGLE DEADPOOL COMIC ON THE STANDS!
Stands? What is this, 1975?
SHUT UP. I'M SOLILOQUIZING.
YOU ASK ME, THERE SHOULD BE THREE... NO, FOUR DEADPOOL MONTHLIES! MINI-SERIES, TOO! ALL WITH VARIANT COVERS!
...HELL, THERE SHOULD BE A WHOLE DEADPOOL CORPS!!!

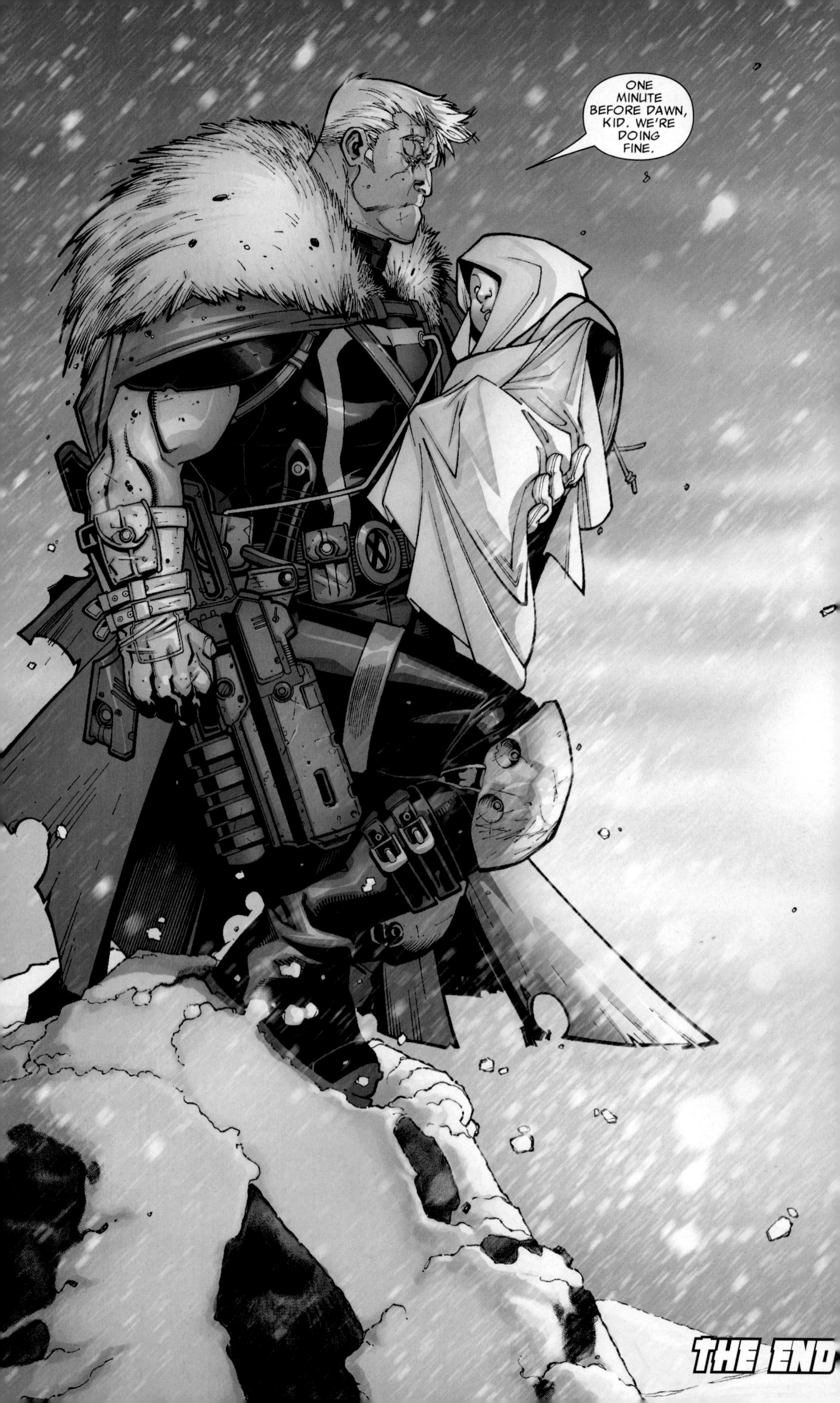
ONE MINUTE BEFORE DAWN, KID. WE'RE DOING FINE.
THE END

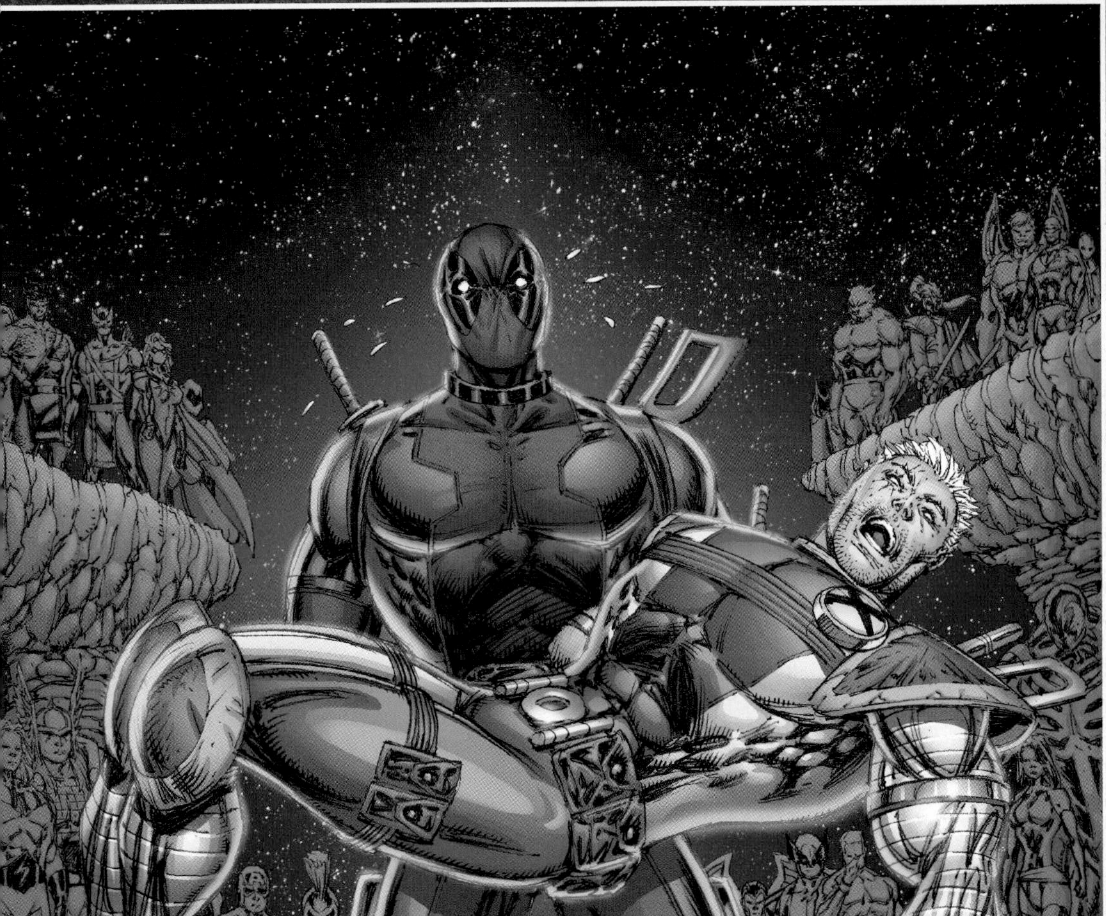
AFTER PEREZ
YACKEY

CABLE #25 (2008) VARIANT
BY ROB LIEFELD & MATT YACKEY

DEADPOOL & CABLE #26

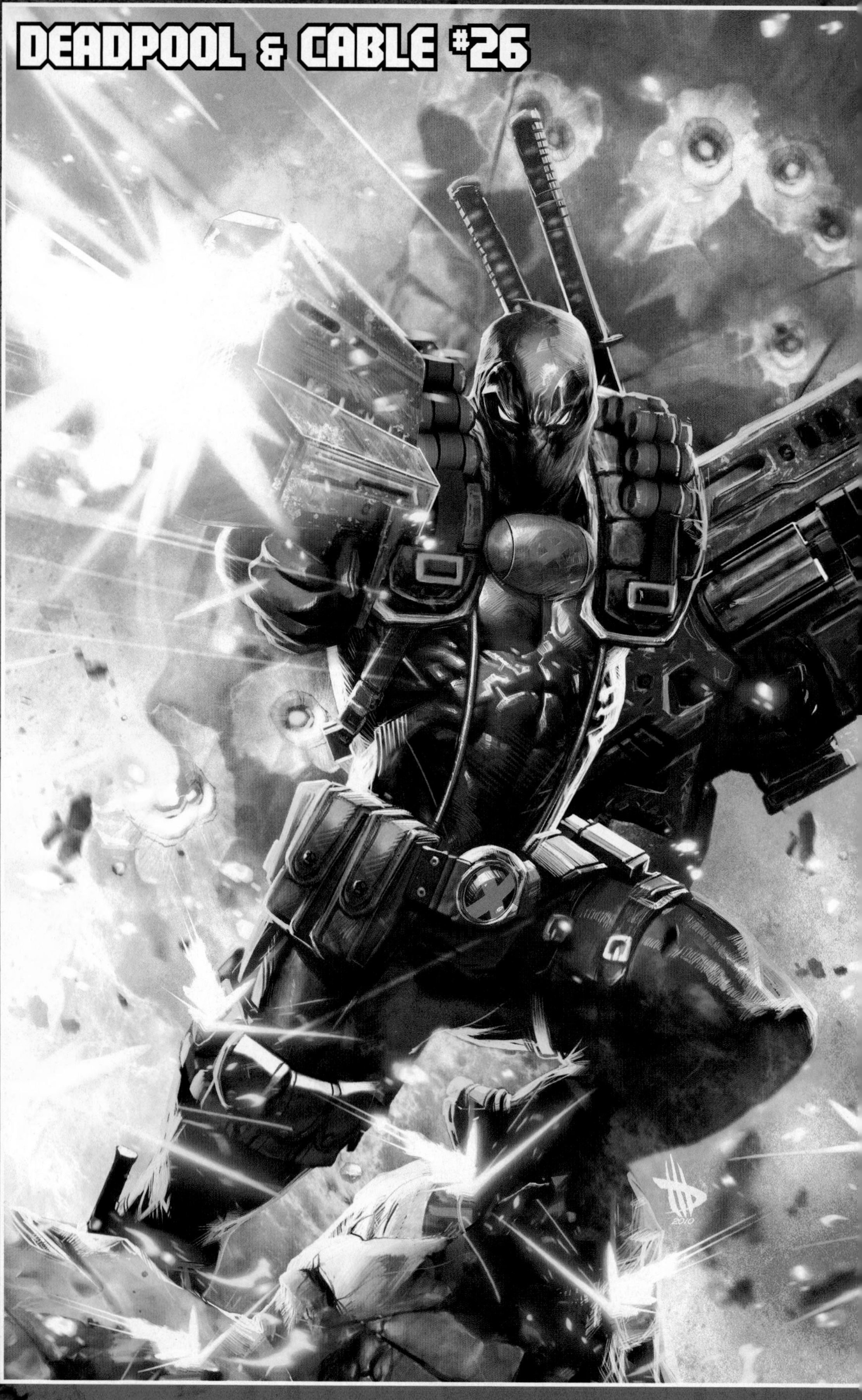

WRITER
DUANE SWIERCZYNSKI

ART
LEANDRO FERNANDEZ

COLORS
STEVE BUCCELLATO

LETTERS
JEFF ECKLEBERRY

COVER
DAVE WILKINS

PRODUCTION
IRENE Y. LEE

ASST EDITOR
SEBASTIAN GIRNER

EDITOR
AXEL ALONSO

EDITOR IN CHIEF
JOE QUESADA

PUBLISHER
DAN BUCKLEY

EXEC. PRODUCER
ALAN FINE

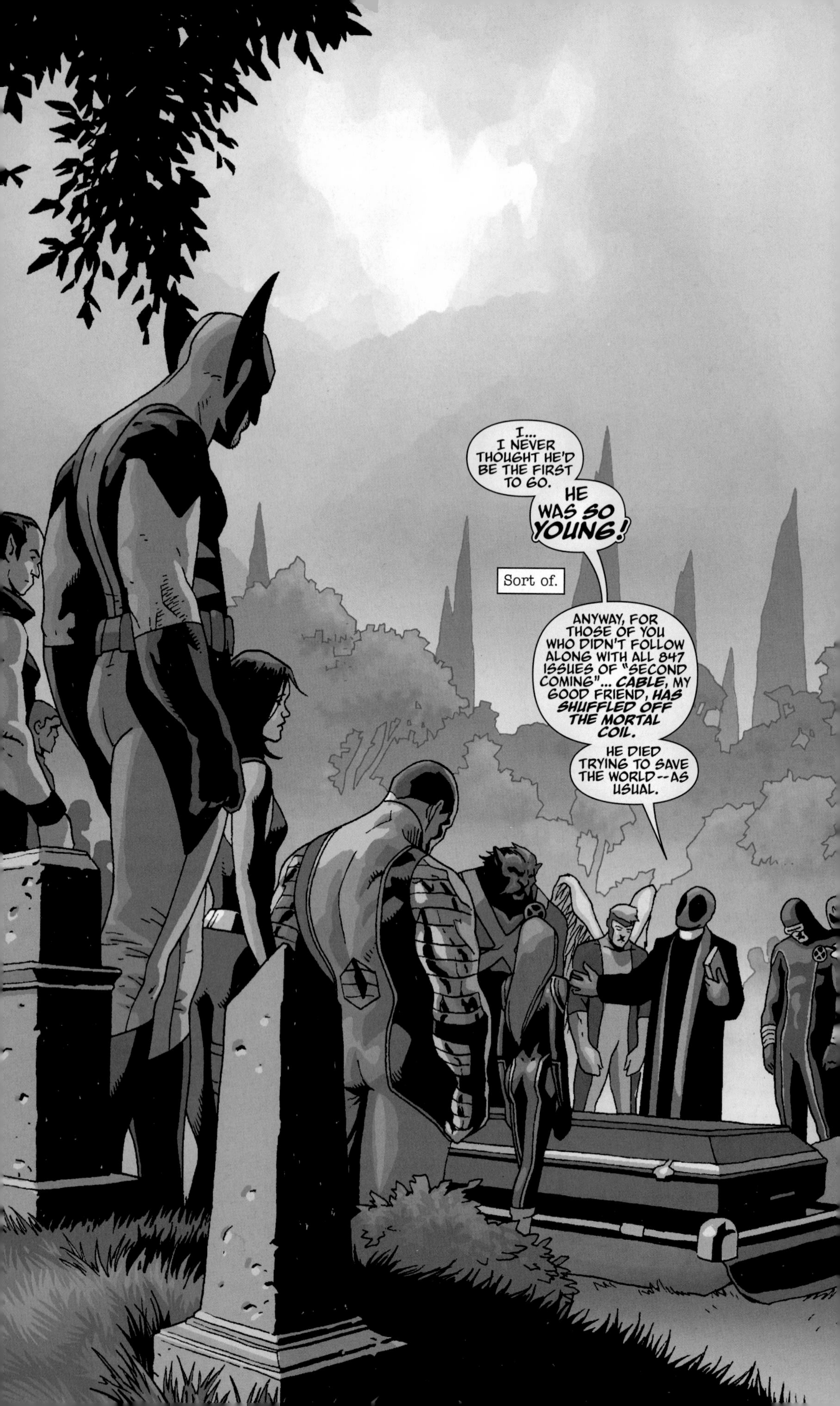
I... I NEVER THOUGHT HE'D BE THE FIRST TO GO.
HE WAS SO YOUNG!
Sort of.
ANYWAY, FOR THOSE OF YOU WHO DIDN'T FOLLOW ALONG WITH ALL 847 ISSUES OF "SECOND COMING"... CABLE, MY GOOD FRIEND, HAS SHUFFLED OFF THE MORTAL COIL.
HE DIED TRYING TO SAVE THE WORLD--AS USUAL.

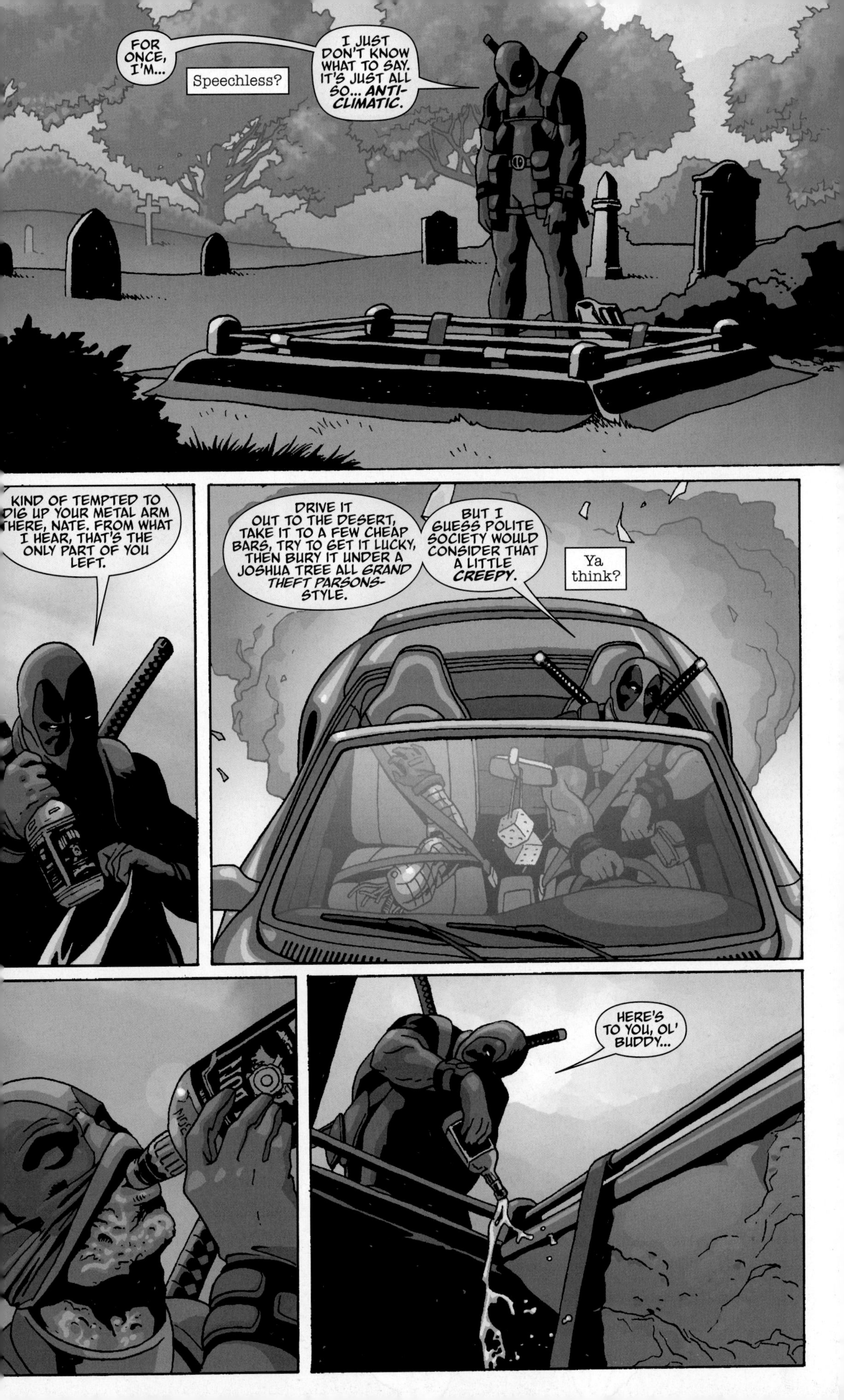
FOR ONCE, I'M...
Speechless?
I JUST DON'T KNOW WHAT TO SAY. IT'S JUST ALL SO... ANTI-CLIMATIC.
KIND OF TEMPTED TO DIG UP YOUR METAL ARM THERE, NATE. FROM WHAT I HEAR, THAT'S THE ONLY PART OF YOU LEFT.
DRIVE IT OUT TO THE DESERT, TAKE IT TO A FEW CHEAP BARS, TRY TO GET IT LUCKY, THEN BURY IT UNDER A JOSHUA TREE ALL GRAND THEFT PARSONS-STYLE.
BUT I GUESS POLITE SOCIETY WOULD CONSIDER THAT A LITTLE CREEPY.
Ya think?
HERE'S TO YOU, OL' BUDDY...

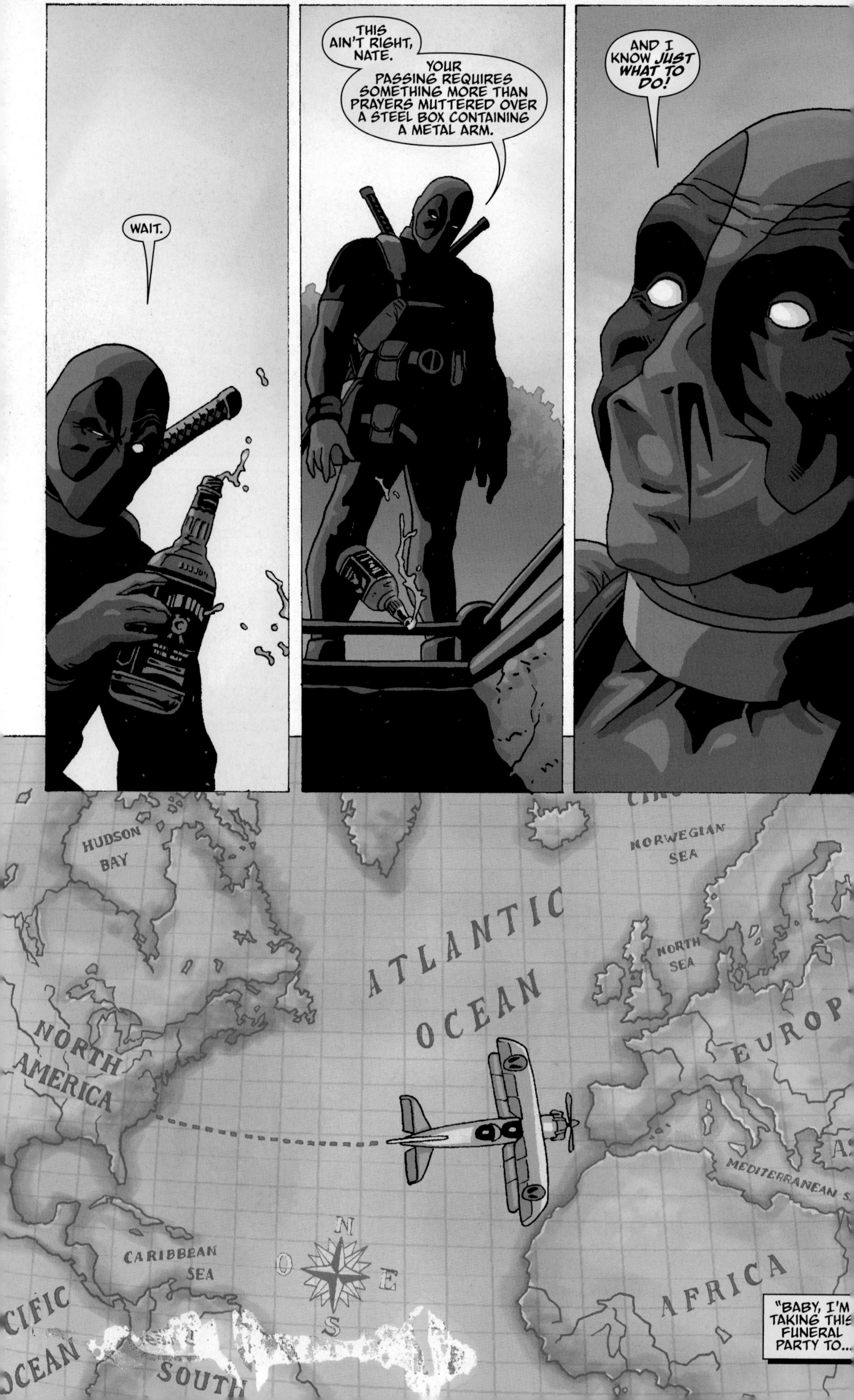

WAIT.
THIS AIN'T RIGHT, NATE.
YOUR PASSING REQUIRES SOMETHING MORE THAN PRAYERS MUTTERED OVER A STEEL BOX CONTAINING A METAL ARM.
AND I KNOW JUST WHAT TO DO!
HUDSON BAY
NORWEGIAN SEA
NORTH SEA
ATLANTIC OCEAN
NORTH AMERICA
EUROP
MEDITERRANEAN S
CARIBBEAN SEA
N
O
E
S
AFRICA
CIFIC OCEAN
SOUTH
"BABY, I'M TAKING THIS FUNERAL PARTY TO...

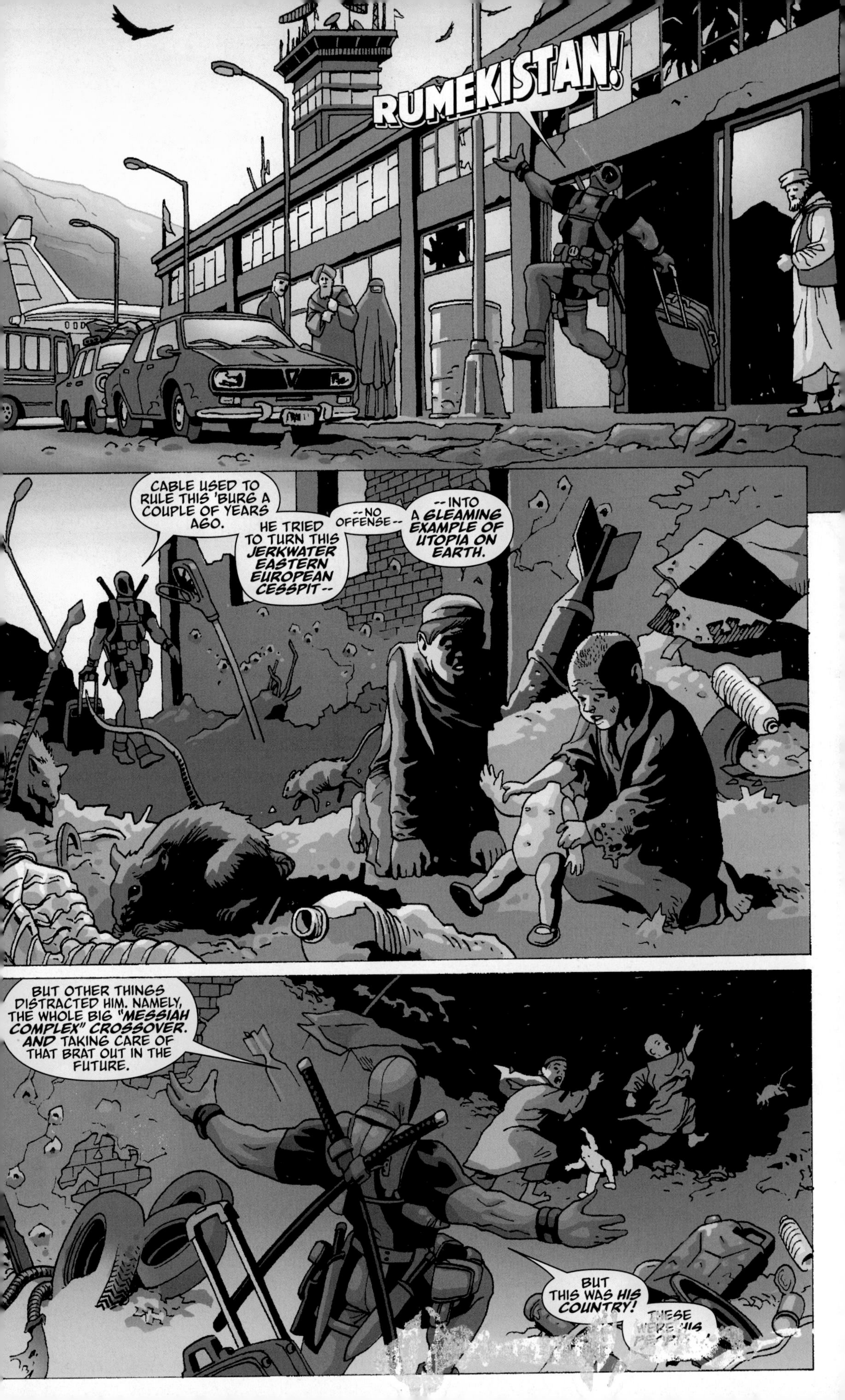
RUMEKISTAN!
CABLE USED TO RULE THIS 'BURG A COUPLE OF YEARS AGO.
HE TRIED TO TURN THIS *JERKWATER EASTERN EUROPEAN CESSPIT* --
--NO OFFENSE--
--INTO A *GLEAMING EXAMPLE OF UTOPIA ON EARTH.*
BUT OTHER THINGS DISTRACTED HIM. NAMELY, THE WHOLE BIG *"MESSIAH COMPLEX" CROSSOVER. AND* TAKING CARE OF THAT BRAT OUT IN THE FUTURE.
BUT THIS WAS *HIS COUNTRY!*
THESE WERE HIS

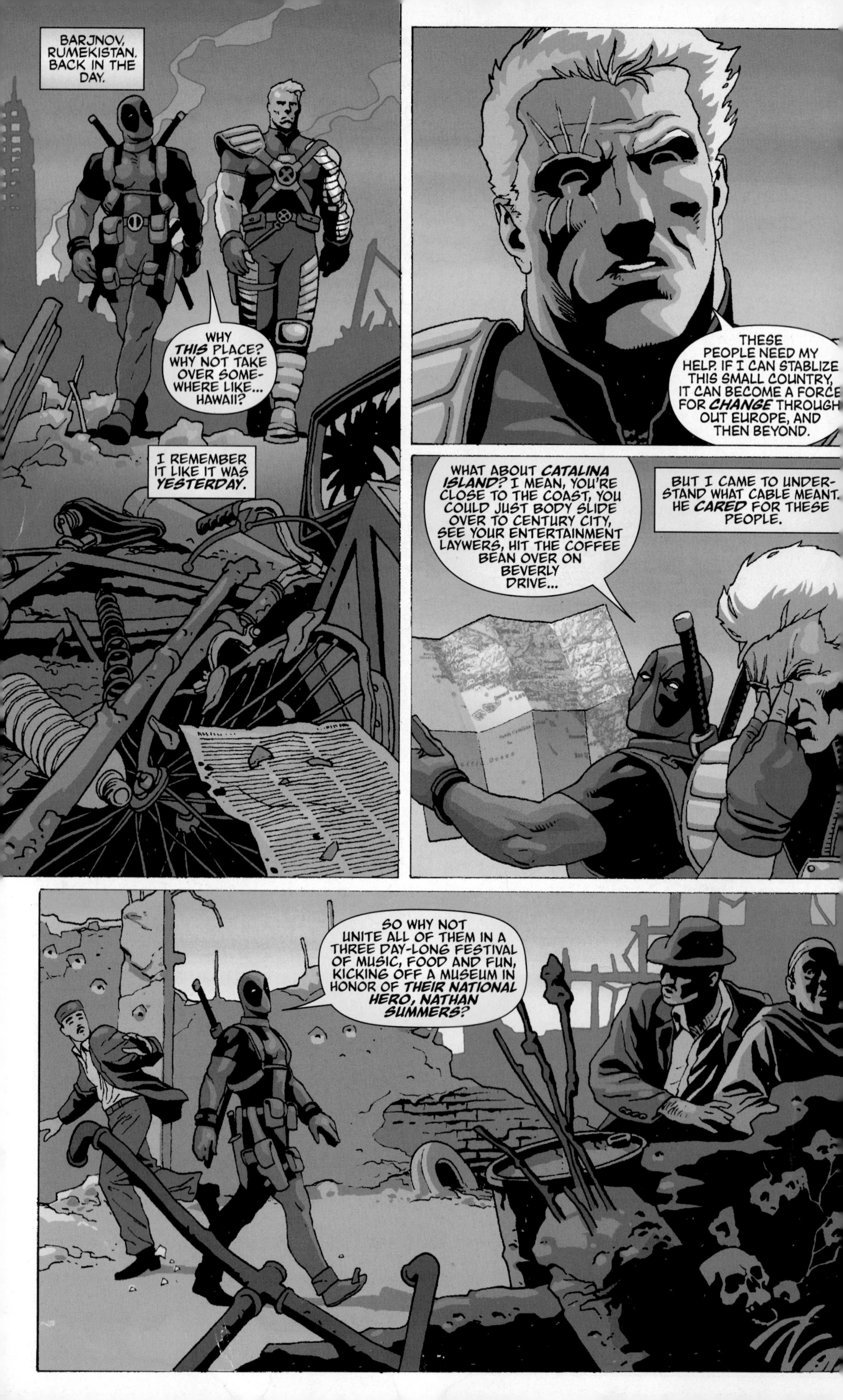
BARJNOV, RUMEKISTAN. BACK IN THE DAY.
WHY THIS PLACE? WHY NOT TAKE OVER SOME-WHERE LIKE... HAWAII?
I REMEMBER IT LIKE IT WAS YESTERDAY.
THESE PEOPLE NEED MY HELP. IF I CAN STABLIZE THIS SMALL COUNTRY, IT CAN BECOME A FORCE FOR CHANGE THROUGH-OUT EUROPE, AND THEN BEYOND.
WHAT ABOUT CATALINA ISLAND? I MEAN, YOU'RE CLOSE TO THE COAST, YOU COULD JUST BODY SLIDE OVER TO CENTURY CITY, SEE YOUR ENTERTAINMENT LAYWERS, HIT THE COFFEE BEAN OVER ON BEVERLY DRIVE...
BUT I CAME TO UNDER-STAND WHAT CABLE MEANT. HE CARED FOR THESE PEOPLE.
SO WHY NOT UNITE ALL OF THEM IN A THREE DAY-LONG FESTIVAL OF MUSIC, FOOD AND FUN, KICKING OFF A MUSEUM IN HONOR OF THEIR NATIONAL HERO, NATHAN SUMMERS?

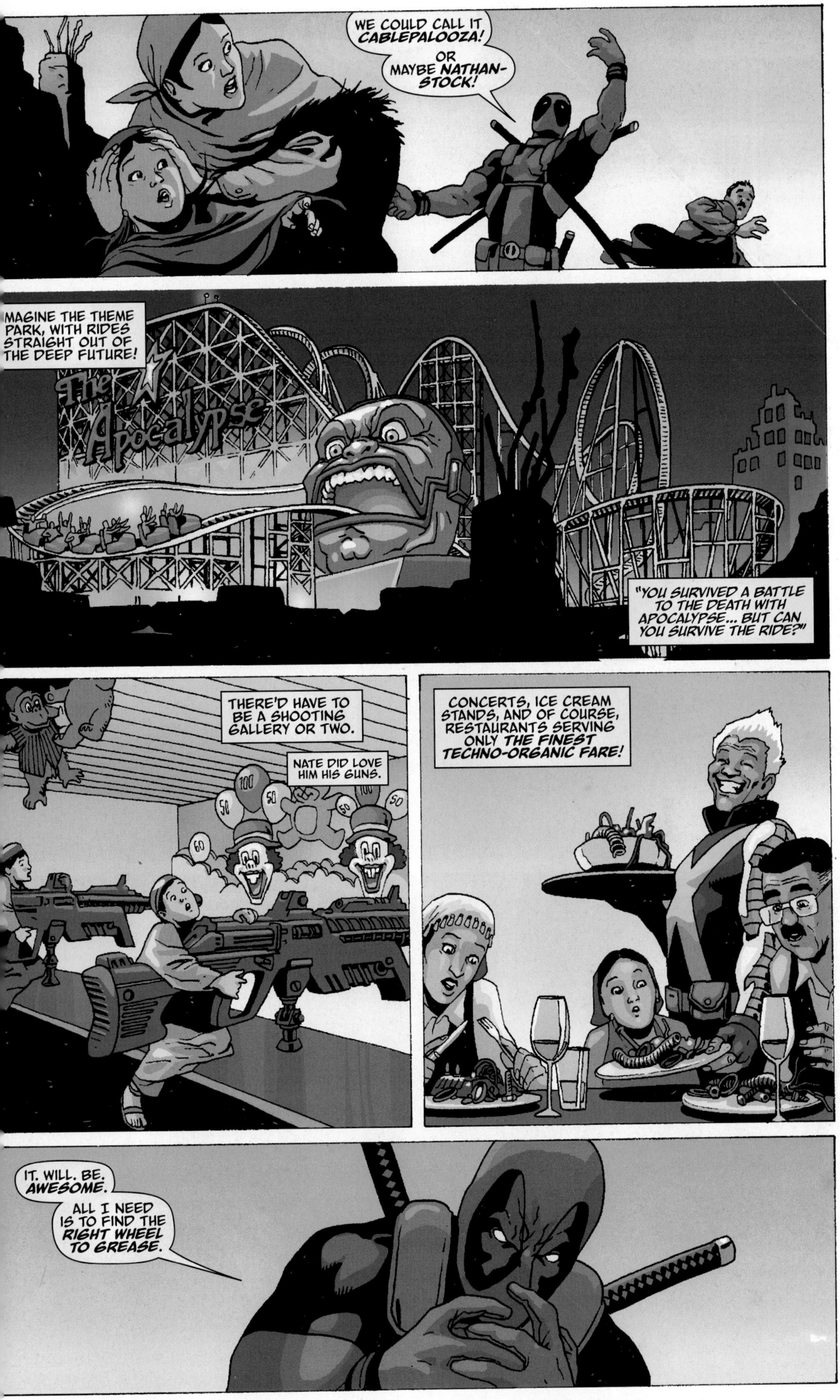
WE COULD CALL IT CABLEPALOOZA!
OR MAYBE NATHAN-STOCK!
MAGINE THE THEME PARK, WITH RIDES STRAIGHT OUT OF THE DEEP FUTURE!
The Apocalypse
"YOU SURVIVED A BATTLE TO THE DEATH WITH APOCALYPSE... BUT CAN YOU SURVIVE THE RIDE?"
THERE'D HAVE TO BE A SHOOTING GALLERY OR TWO.
NATE DID LOVE HIM HIS GUNS.
100
50
50
100
50
50
60
CONCERTS, ICE CREAM STANDS, AND OF COURSE, RESTAURANTS SERVING ONLY THE FINEST TECHNO-ORGANIC FARE!
IT. WILL. BE. AWESOME.
ALL I NEED IS TO FIND THE RIGHT WHEEL TO GREASE.

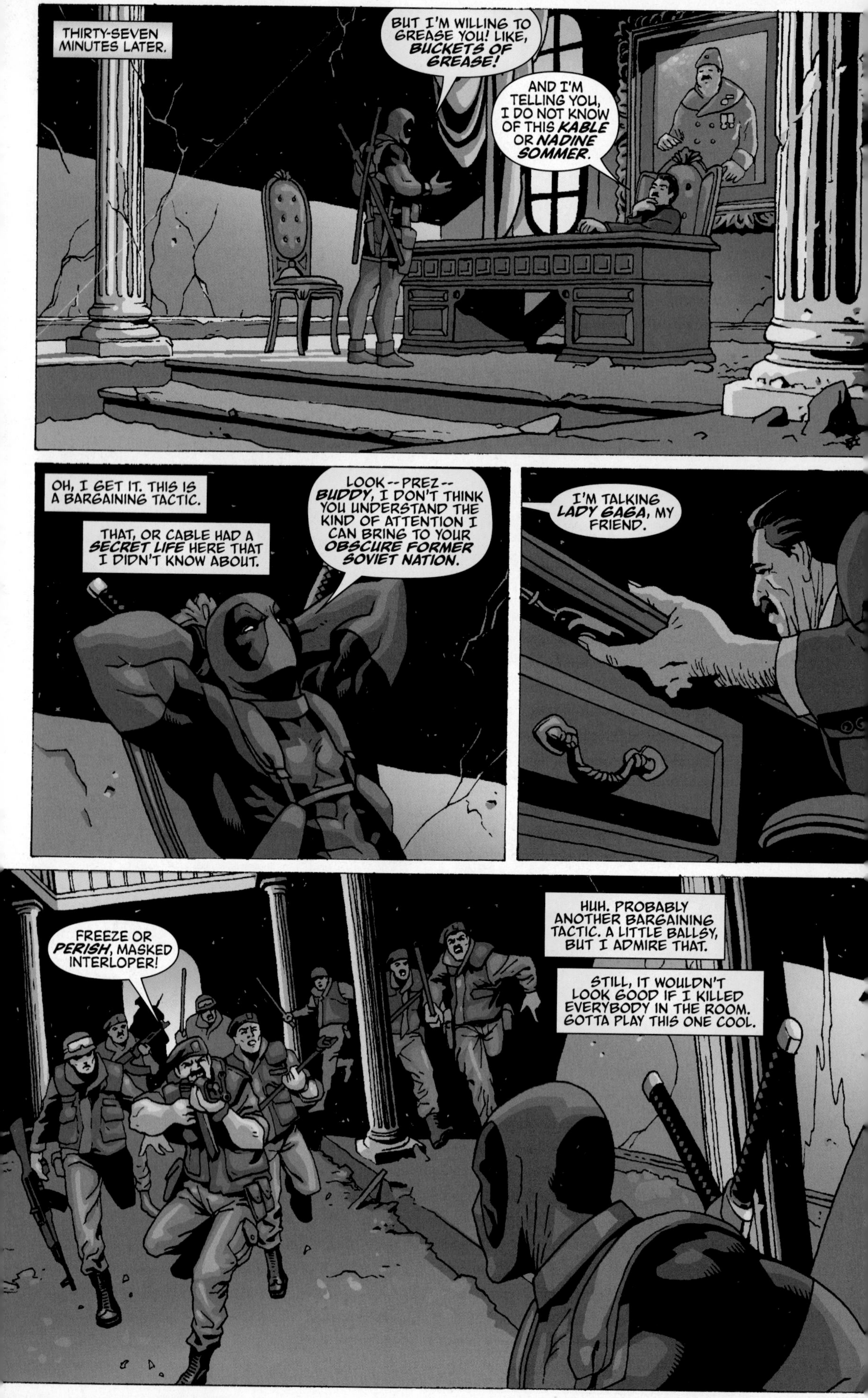
THIRTY-SEVEN MINUTES LATER.
BUT I'M WILLING TO GREASE YOU! LIKE, BUCKETS OF GREASE!
AND I'M TELLING YOU, I DO NOT KNOW OF THIS KABLE OR NADINE SOMMER.
OH, I GET IT. THIS IS A BARGAINING TACTIC.
THAT, OR CABLE HAD A SECRET LIFE HERE THAT I DIDN'T KNOW ABOUT.
LOOK--PREZ--BUDDY, I DON'T THINK YOU UNDERSTAND THE KIND OF ATTENTION I CAN BRING TO YOUR OBSCURE FORMER SOVIET NATION.
I'M TALKING LADY GAGA, MY FRIEND.
FREEZE OR PERISH, MASKED INTERLOPER!
HUH. PROBABLY ANOTHER BARGAINING TACTIC. A LITTLE BALLSY, BUT I ADMIRE THAT.
STILL, IT WOULDN'T LOOK GOOD IF I KILLED EVERYBODY IN THE ROOM. GOTTA PLAY THIS ONE COOL.

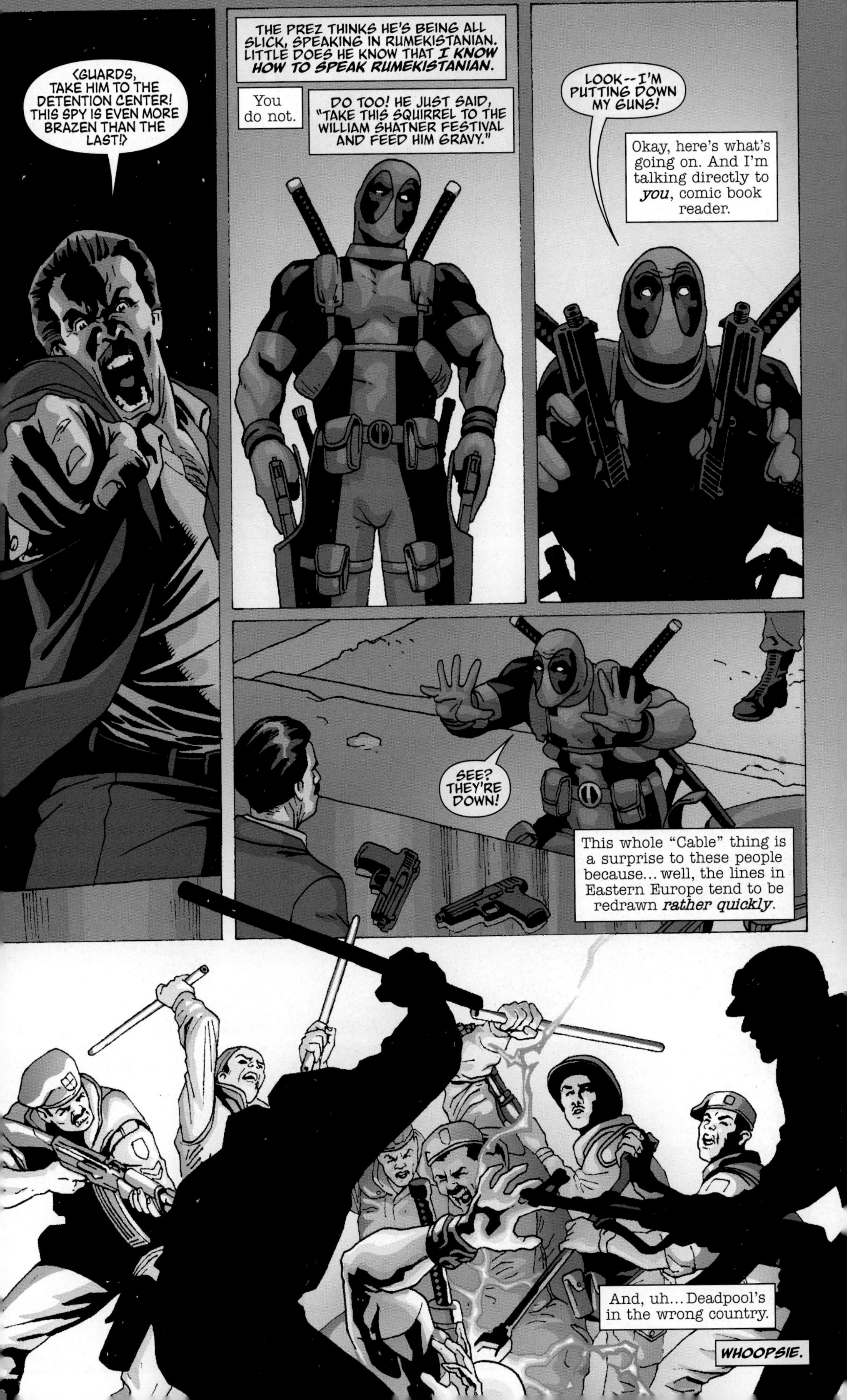
<GUARDS, TAKE HIM TO THE DETENTION CENTER! THIS SPY IS EVEN MORE BRAZEN THAN THE LAST!>
THE PREZ THINKS HE'S BEING ALL SLICK, SPEAKING IN RUMEKISTANIAN. LITTLE DOES HE KNOW THAT *I KNOW HOW TO SPEAK RUMEKISTANIAN.*
You do not.
DO TOO! HE JUST SAID, "TAKE THIS SQUIRREL TO THE WILLIAM SHATNER FESTIVAL AND FEED HIM GRAVY."
LOOK--I'M PUTTING DOWN MY GUNS!
Okay, here's what's going on. And I'm talking directly to ***you***, comic book reader.
SEE? THEY'RE DOWN!
This whole "Cable" thing is a surprise to these people because... well, the lines in Eastern Europe tend to be redrawn ***rather quickly***.
And, uh... Deadpool's in the wrong country.
WHOOPSIE.

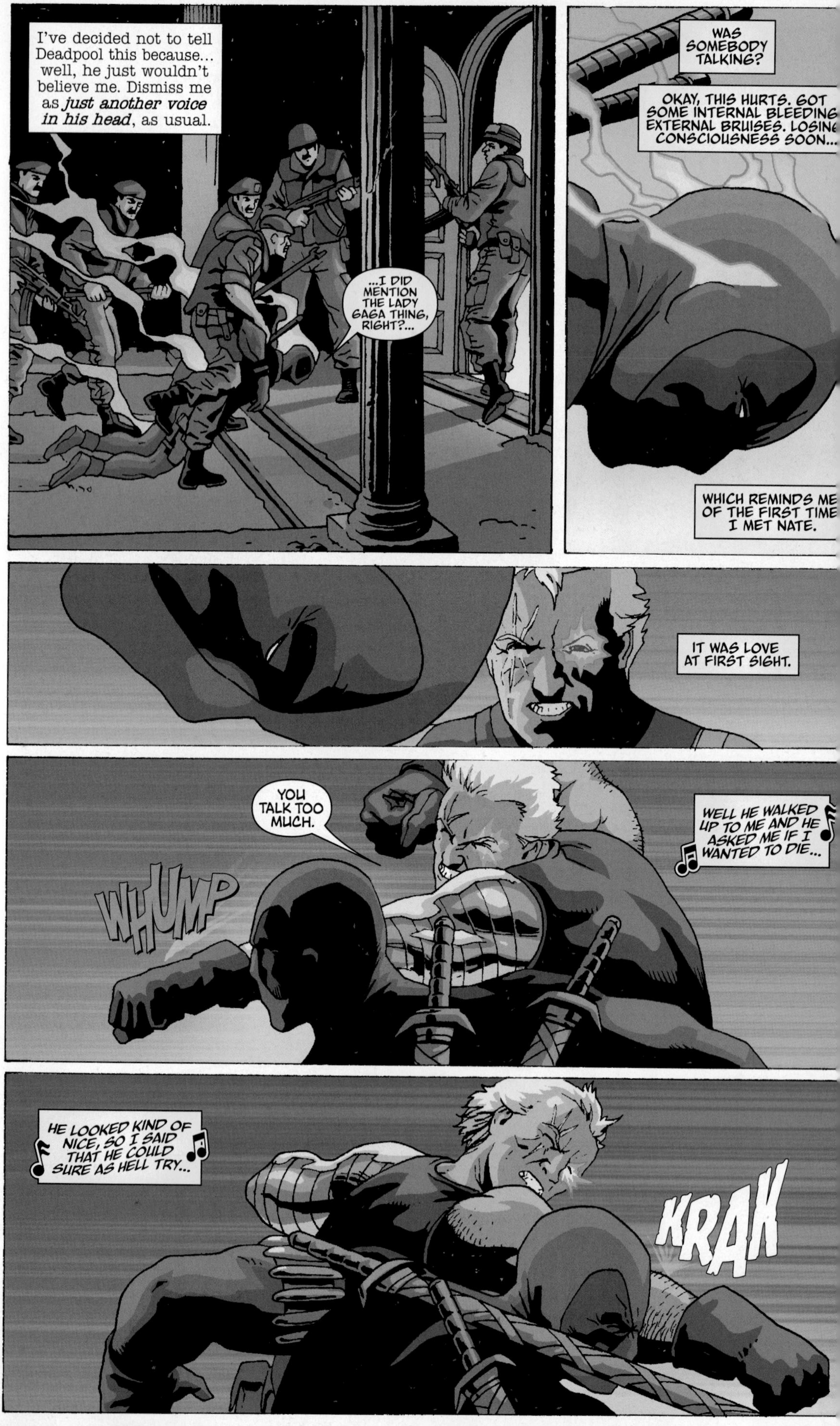
I've decided not to tell Deadpool this because... well, he just wouldn't believe me. Dismiss me as *just another voice in his head*, as usual.
...I DID MENTION THE LADY GAGA THING, RIGHT?...
WAS SOMEBODY TALKING?
OKAY, THIS HURTS. GOT SOME INTERNAL BLEEDING, EXTERNAL BRUISES. LOSING CONSCIOUSNESS SOON...
WHICH REMINDS ME OF THE FIRST TIME I MET NATE.
IT WAS LOVE AT FIRST SIGHT.
YOU TALK TOO MUCH.
WELL HE WALKED UP TO ME AND HE ASKED ME IF I WANTED TO DIE...
WHUMP
HE LOOKED KIND OF NICE, SO I SAID THAT HE COULD SURE AS HELL TRY...
KRAK

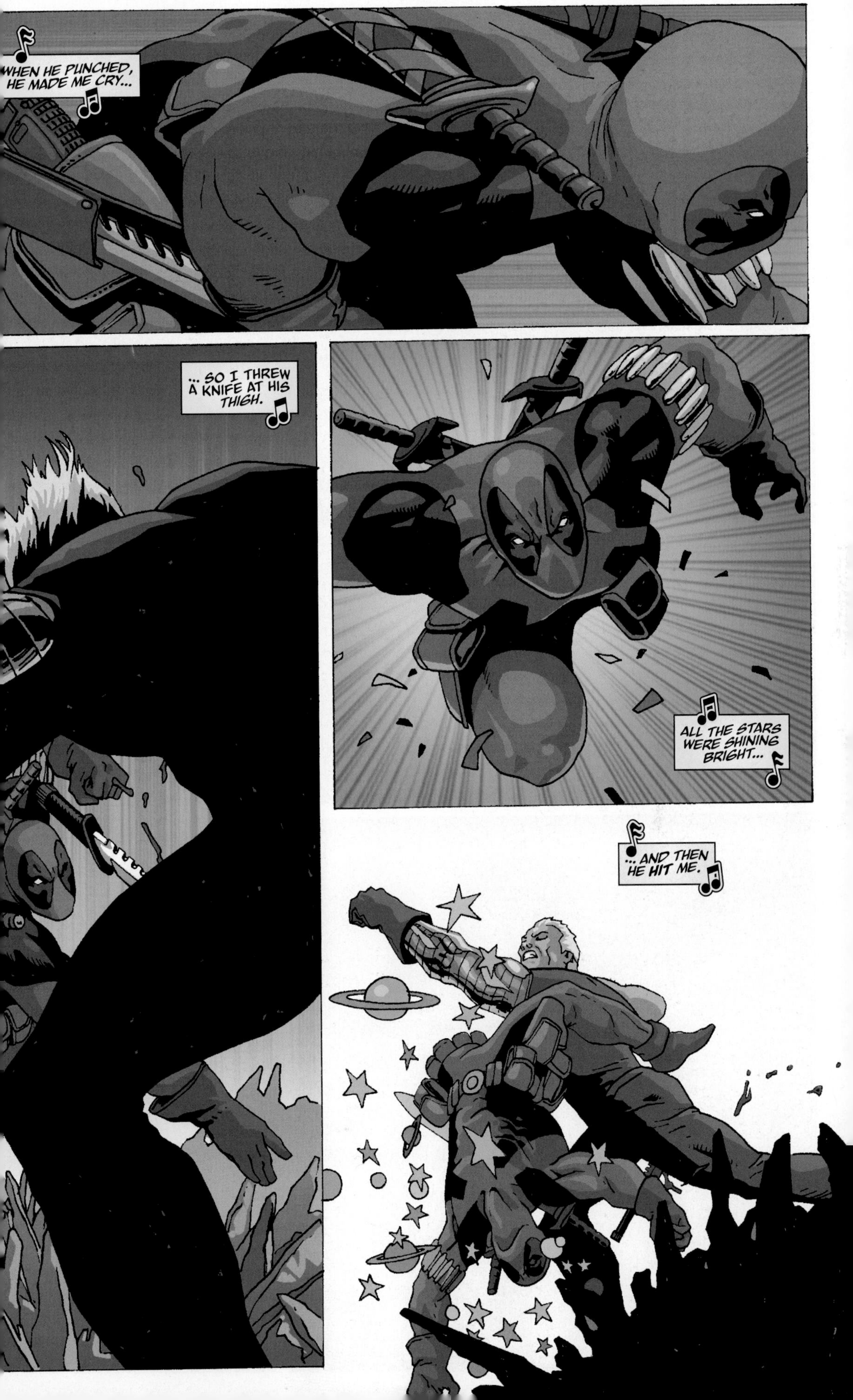
WHEN HE PUNCHED, HE MADE ME CRY...
... SO I THREW A KNIFE AT HIS THIGH.
ALL THE STARS WERE SHINING BRIGHT...
... AND THEN HE HIT ME.

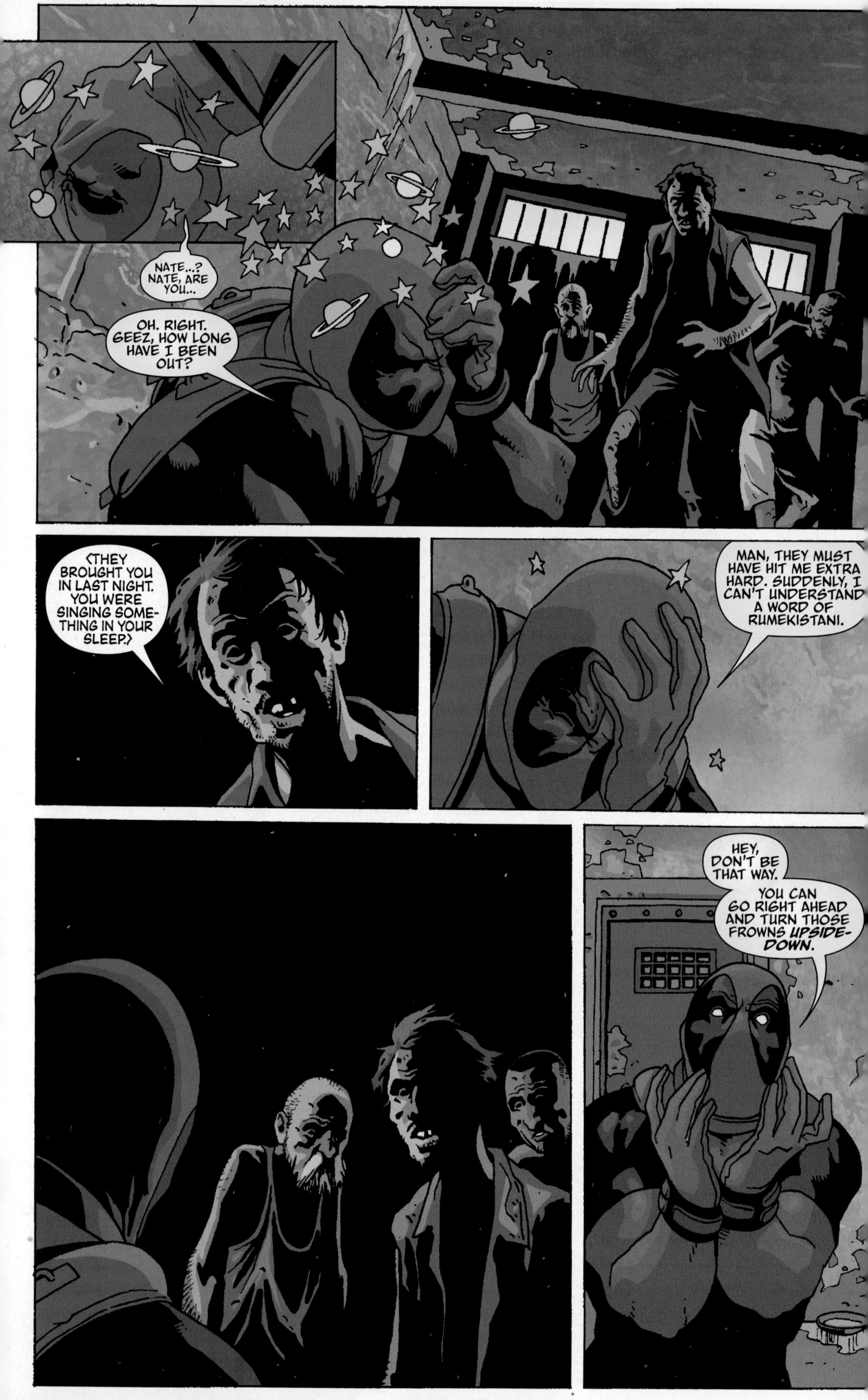
NATE...? NATE, ARE YOU...
OH. RIGHT. GEEZ, HOW LONG HAVE I BEEN OUT?
<THEY BROUGHT YOU IN LAST NIGHT. YOU WERE SINGING SOMETHING IN YOUR SLEEP.>
MAN, THEY MUST HAVE HIT ME EXTRA HARD. SUDDENLY, I CAN'T UNDERSTAND A WORD OF RUMEKISTANI.
HEY, DON'T BE THAT WAY.
YOU CAN GO RIGHT AHEAD AND TURN THOSE FROWNS *UPSIDE-DOWN.*

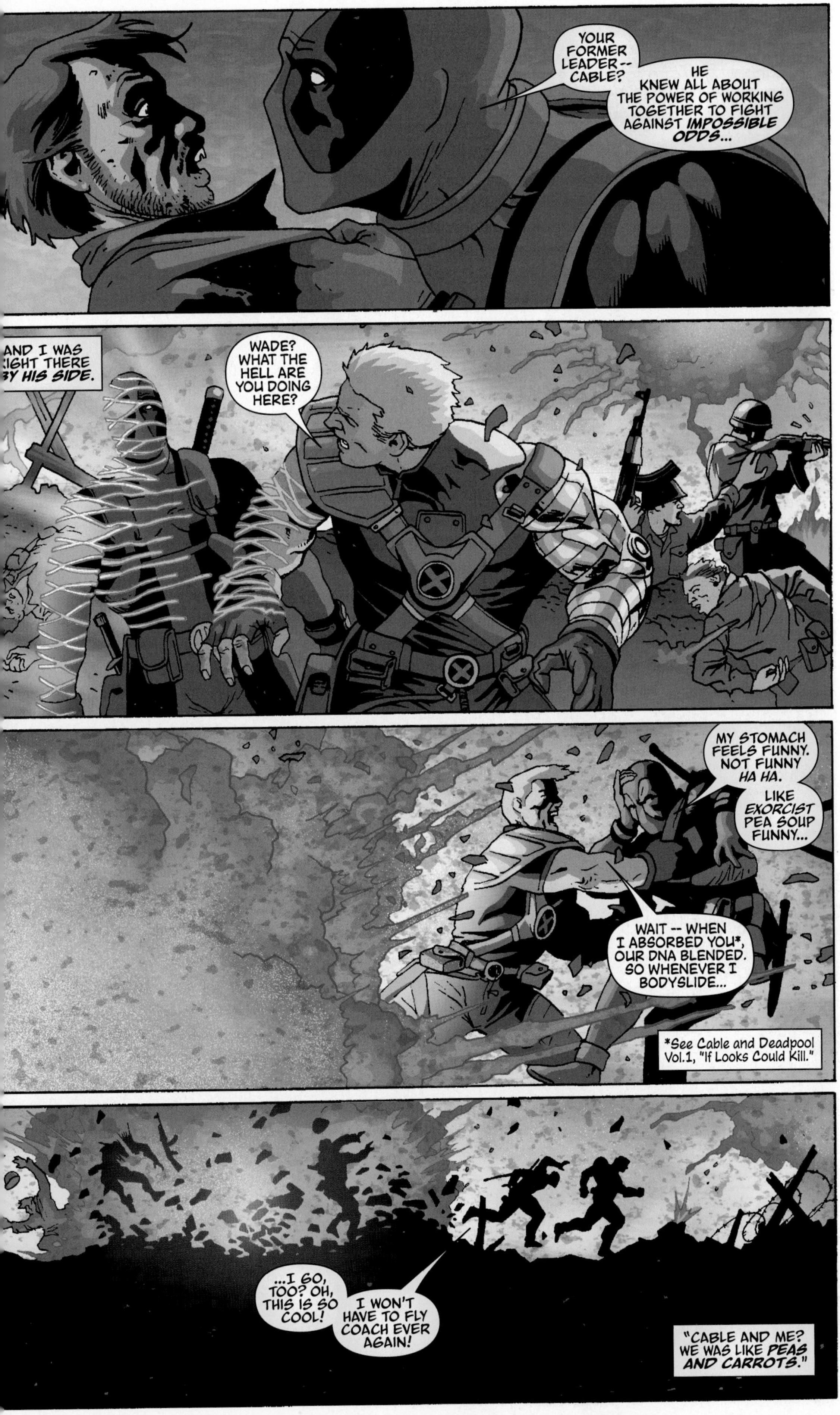
YOUR FORMER LEADER-- CABLE?
HE KNEW ALL ABOUT THE POWER OF WORKING TOGETHER TO FIGHT AGAINST IMPOSSIBLE ODDS...
AND I WAS RIGHT THERE BY HIS SIDE.
WADE? WHAT THE HELL ARE YOU DOING HERE?
MY STOMACH FEELS FUNNY. NOT FUNNY HA HA.
LIKE EXORCIST PEA SOUP FUNNY...
WAIT -- WHEN I ABSORBED YOU*, OUR DNA BLENDED. SO WHENEVER I BODYSLIDE...
*See Cable and Deadpool Vol.1, "If Looks Could Kill."
...I GO, TOO? OH, THIS IS SO COOL!
I WON'T HAVE TO FLY COACH EVER AGAIN!
"CABLE AND ME? WE WAS LIKE PEAS AND CARROTS."

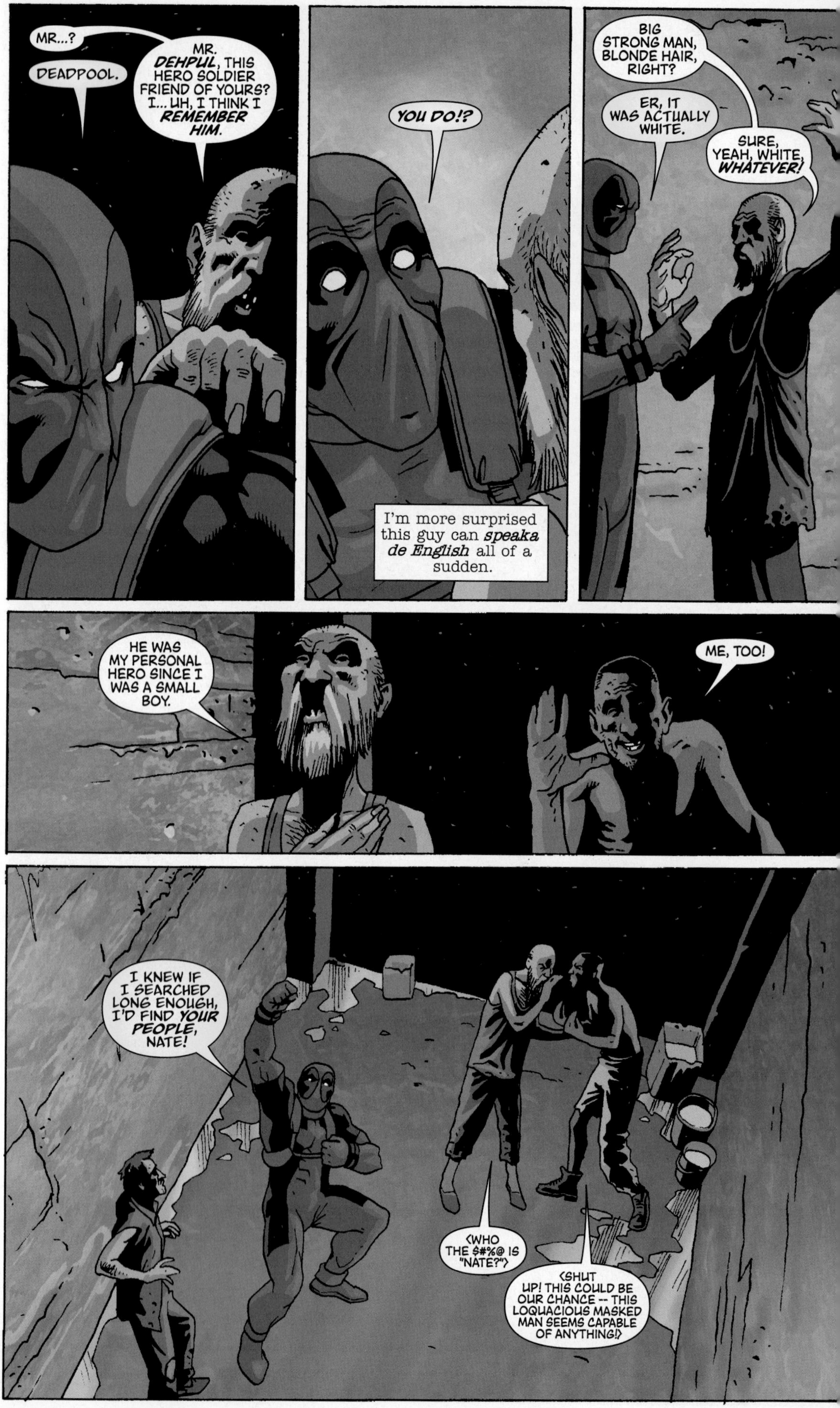
MR...?
DEADPOOL.
MR. DEHPUL, THIS HERO SOLDIER FRIEND OF YOURS? I... UH, I THINK I REMEMBER HIM.
YOU DO!?
I'm more surprised this guy can speaka de English all of a sudden.
BIG STRONG MAN, BLONDE HAIR, RIGHT?
ER, IT WAS ACTUALLY WHITE.
SURE, YEAH, WHITE, WHATEVER!
HE WAS MY PERSONAL HERO SINCE I WAS A SMALL BOY.
ME, TOO!
I KNEW IF I SEARCHED LONG ENOUGH, I'D FIND YOUR PEOPLE, NATE!
<WHO THE $#%@ IS "NATE?">
<SHUT UP! THIS COULD BE OUR CHANCE -- THIS LOQUACIOUS MASKED MAN SEEMS CAPABLE OF ANYTHING!>

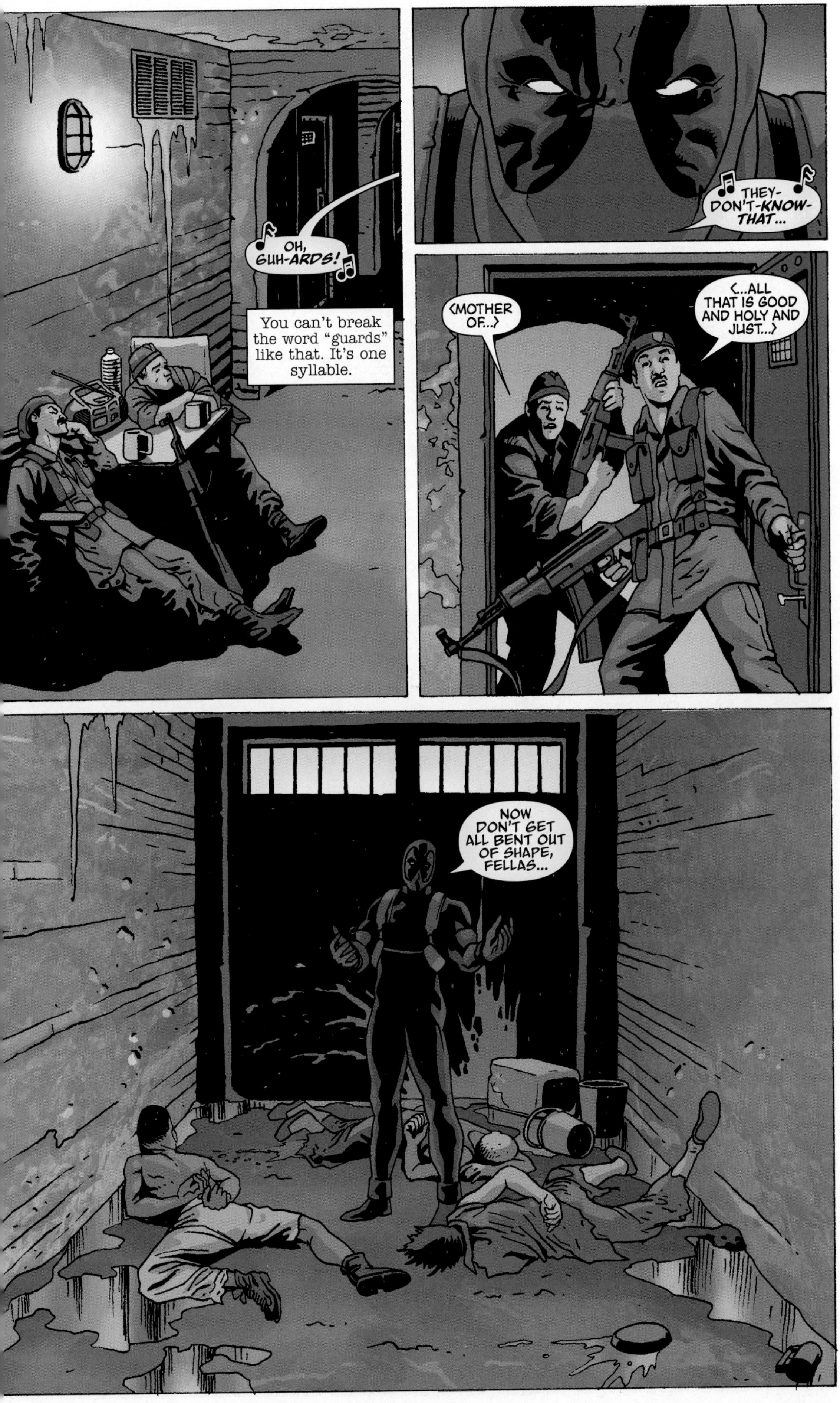
OH, GUH-ARDS!
You can't break the word "guards" like that. It's one syllable.
THEY-DON'T-KNOW-THAT...
<MOTHER OF...>
<...ALL THAT IS GOOD AND HOLY AND JUST...>
NOW DON'T GET ALL BENT OUT OF SHAPE, FELLAS...

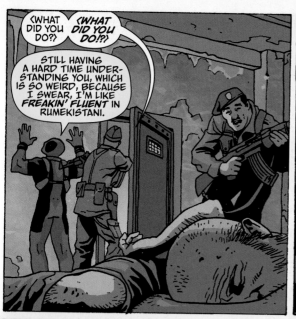

〈WHAT DID YOU DO?〉 〈WHAT *DID YOU DO!?*〉

STILL HAVING A HARD TIME UNDER-STANDING YOU, WHICH IS SO WEIRD, BECAUSE I SWEAR, I'M LIKE *FREAKIN' FLUENT* IN RUMEKISTANI.

FOR INSTANCE, I'M INTIMATELY FAMILIAR WITH THE WORD --

〈SUCKA!〉

VIVA LA RUMEKISTAN!

〈MR. DEHPUL, YOU MUST COME WITH US. THERE IS AN INVASION SET FOR DAWN. YOUR SKILLS WOULD BE INVALUABLE TO OUR CAUSE!〉

YEAH... UH...

You still have no idea what he's saying, do you?

DO, TOO...

LOOK, I WOULDN'T MIND PARTYING WITH YOU GUYS, BUT I HAVE A *MEMORIAL CONCERT* TO PLAN.

AND THAT LADY GAGA WENCH HASN'T BEEN RETURNING MY TEXTS.

MAYBE I SHOULD TRY THE CONVENTION AND VISITORS BUREAU...

WAAAHH

HUH -- WHAT'S THAT?

OH, POOCHYKINS... NO MORE CRY CRY NOW! NO MORE CRY CRY!

YEAH, THAT'S A GOOD WOOBSIE FLOOBSIE NANNY NANNY POO POO FACE...

SCREWSIE YOUSIE, INTERNAL NARRATION MAN.

Hey -- you're finally speaking fluent Rumekistani!

"YOU DON'T UNDERSTAND. THIS BRINGS ME RIGHT BACK TO THE TIME POOR NATE REVERTED TO INFANTHOOD, AND I HAD TO RAISE HIM -- ALL BY MY LONESOME.

"IT WAS THE CLOSEST WE'D EVER BEEN.

"OH, HOW I MISS THOSE DAYS.

"SO VERY BADLY."

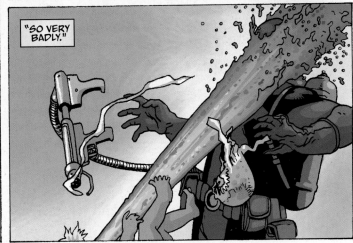

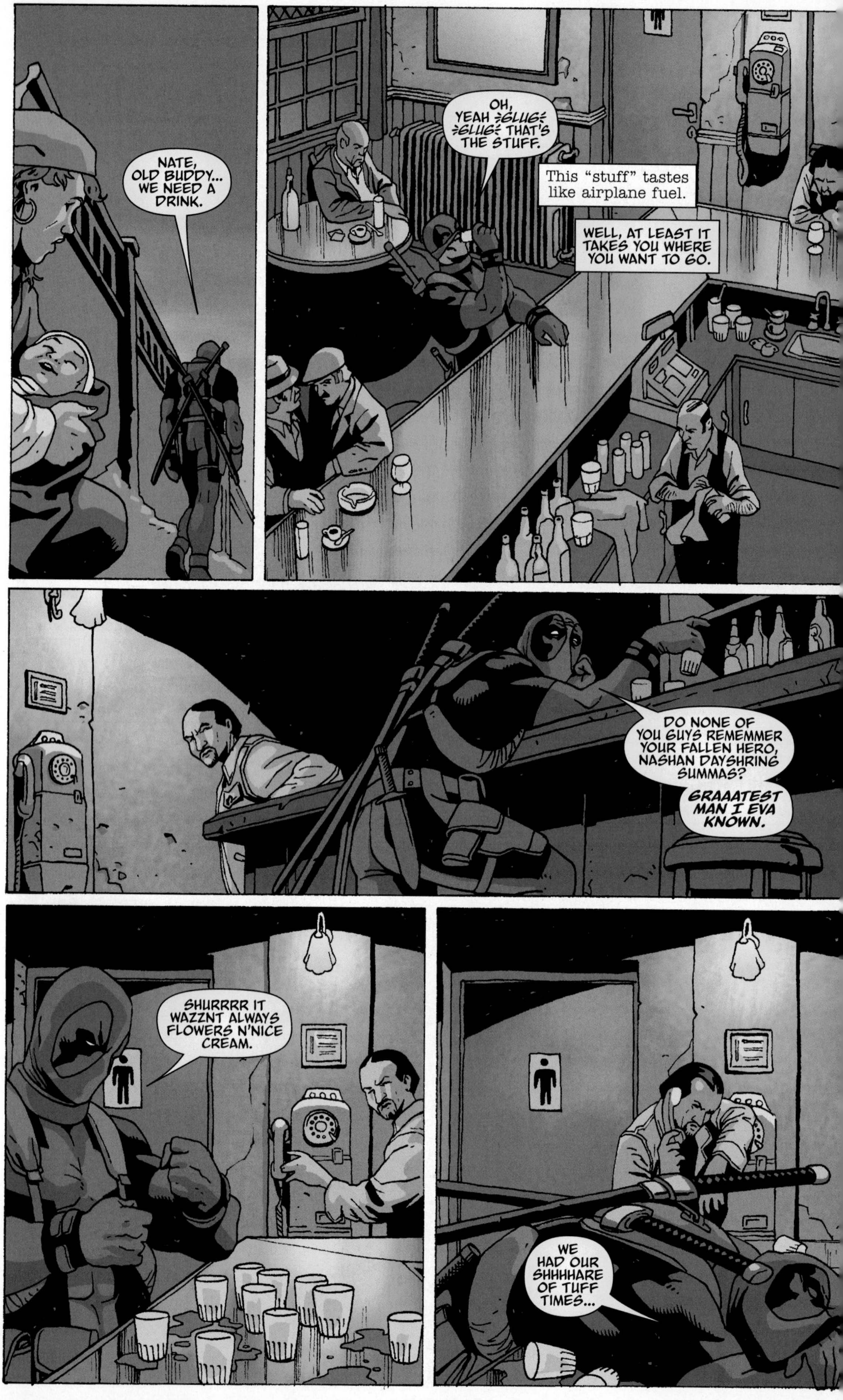
NATE, OLD BUDDY... WE NEED A DRINK.
OH, YEAH *GLUG* *GLUG* THAT'S THE STUFF.
This "stuff" tastes like airplane fuel.
WELL, AT LEAST IT TAKES YOU WHERE YOU WANT TO GO.
DO NONE OF YOU GUYS REMEMMER YOUR FALLEN HERO, NASHAN DAYSHRING SUMMAS?
GRAAATEST MAN I EVA KNOWN.
SHURRRR IT WAZZNT ALWAYS FLOWERS N'NICE CREAM.
WE HAD OUR SHHHHARE OF TUFF TIMES...

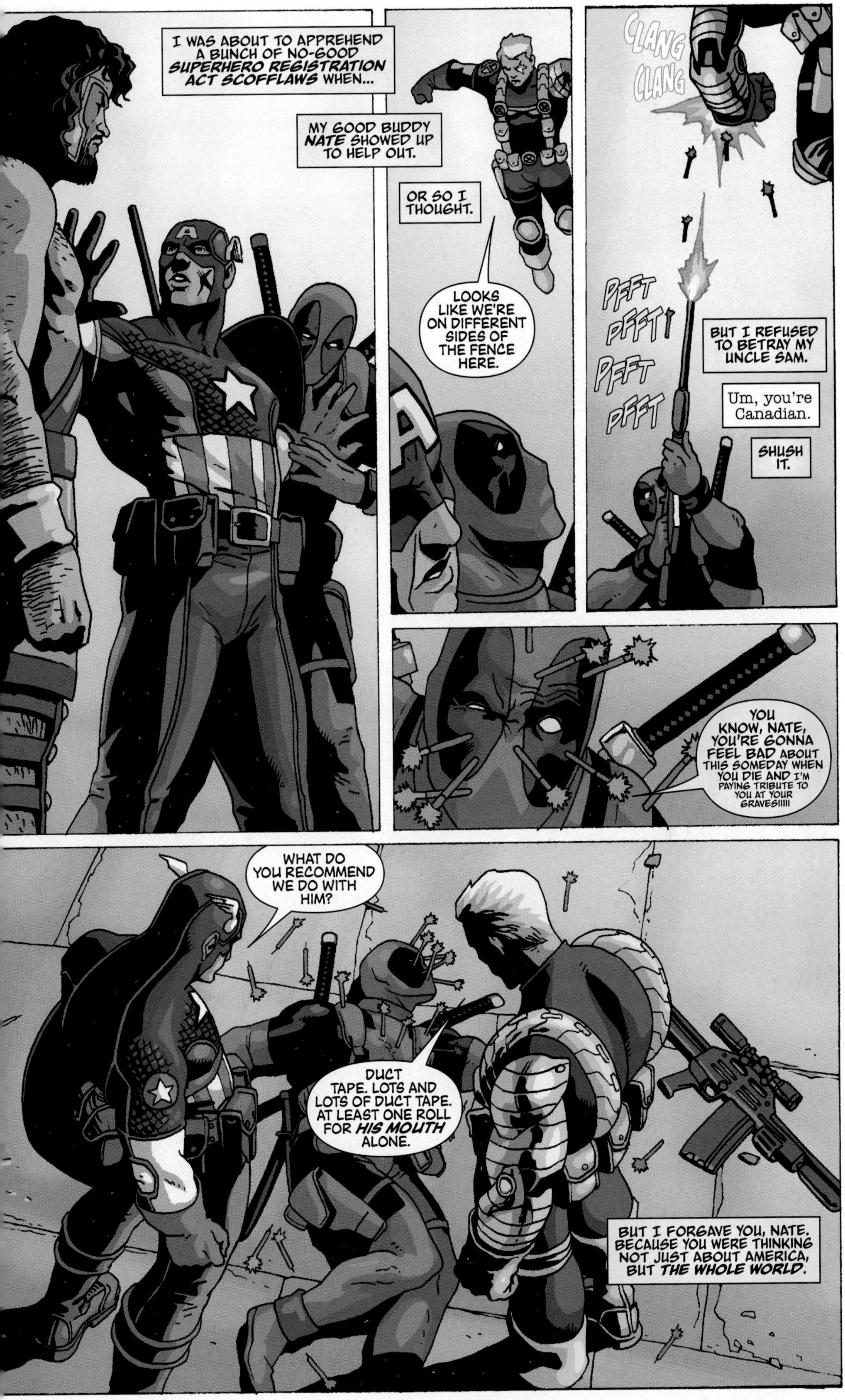
I WAS ABOUT TO APPREHEND A BUNCH OF NO-GOOD SUPERHERO REGISTRATION ACT SCOFFLAWS WHEN...
MY GOOD BUDDY NATE SHOWED UP TO HELP OUT.
OR SO I THOUGHT.
LOOKS LIKE WE'RE ON DIFFERENT SIDES OF THE FENCE HERE.
CLANG
CLANG
PFFT
PFFT
PFFT
PFFT
BUT I REFUSED TO BETRAY MY UNCLE SAM.
Um, you're Canadian.
SHUSH IT.
YOU KNOW, NATE, YOU'RE GONNA FEEL BAD ABOUT THIS SOMEDAY WHEN YOU DIE AND I'M PAYING TRIBUTE TO YOU AT YOUR GRAVES!!!!!
WHAT DO YOU RECOMMEND WE DO WITH HIM?
DUCT TAPE. LOTS AND LOTS OF DUCT TAPE. AT LEAST ONE ROLL FOR HIS MOUTH ALONE.
BUT I FORGAVE YOU, NATE. BECAUSE YOU WERE THINKING NOT JUST ABOUT AMERICA, BUT THE WHOLE WORLD.

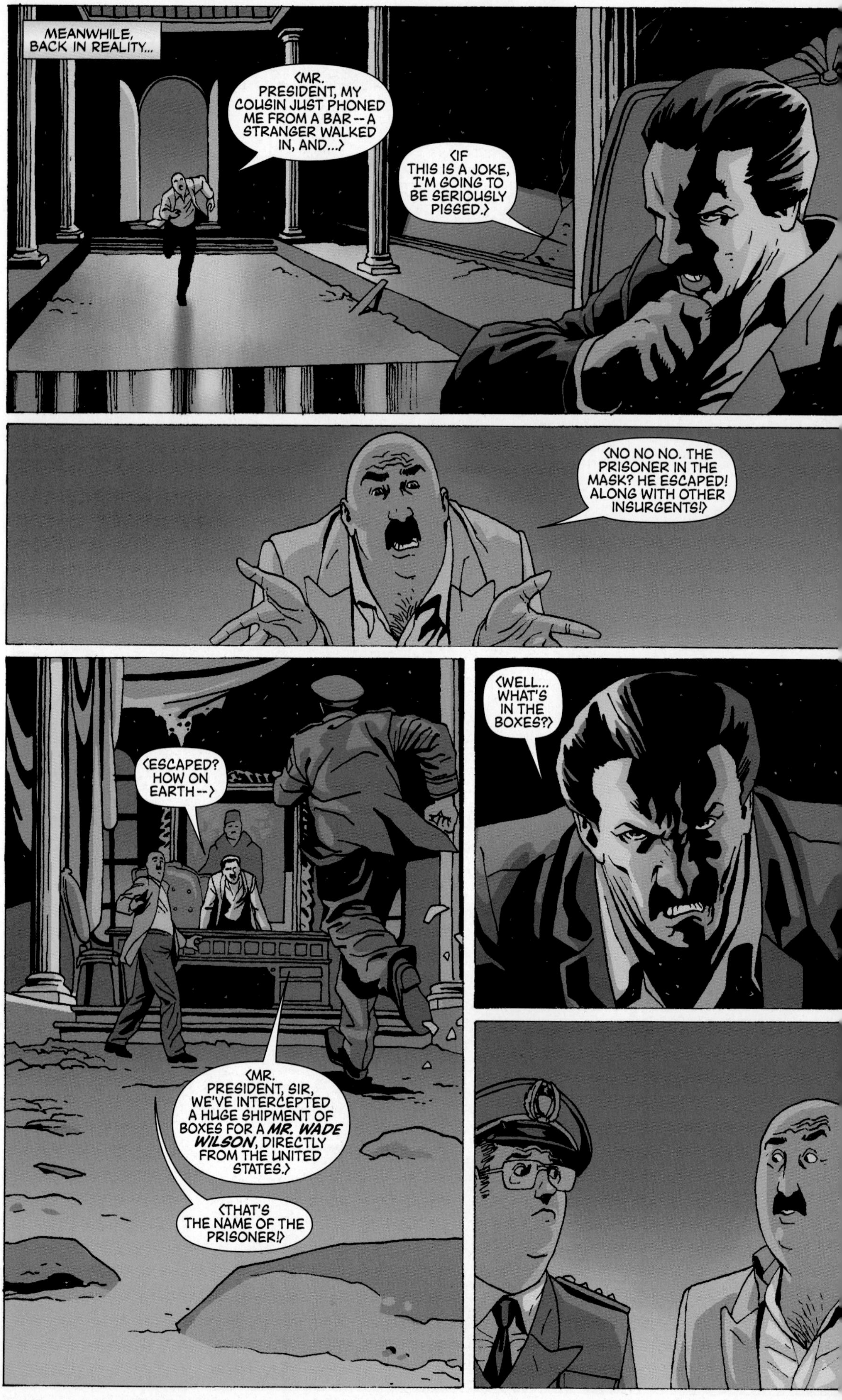
MEANWHILE, BACK IN REALITY...
<MR. PRESIDENT, MY COUSIN JUST PHONED ME FROM A BAR -- A STRANGER WALKED IN, AND...>
<IF THIS IS A JOKE, I'M GOING TO BE SERIOUSLY PISSED.>
<NO NO NO. THE PRISONER IN THE MASK? HE ESCAPED! ALONG WITH OTHER INSURGENTS!>
<ESCAPED? HOW ON EARTH -->
<MR. PRESIDENT, SIR, WE'VE INTERCEPTED A HUGE SHIPMENT OF BOXES FOR A MR. WADE WILSON, DIRECTLY FROM THE UNITED STATES.>
<THAT'S THE NAME OF THE PRISONER!>
<WELL... WHAT'S IN THE BOXES?>

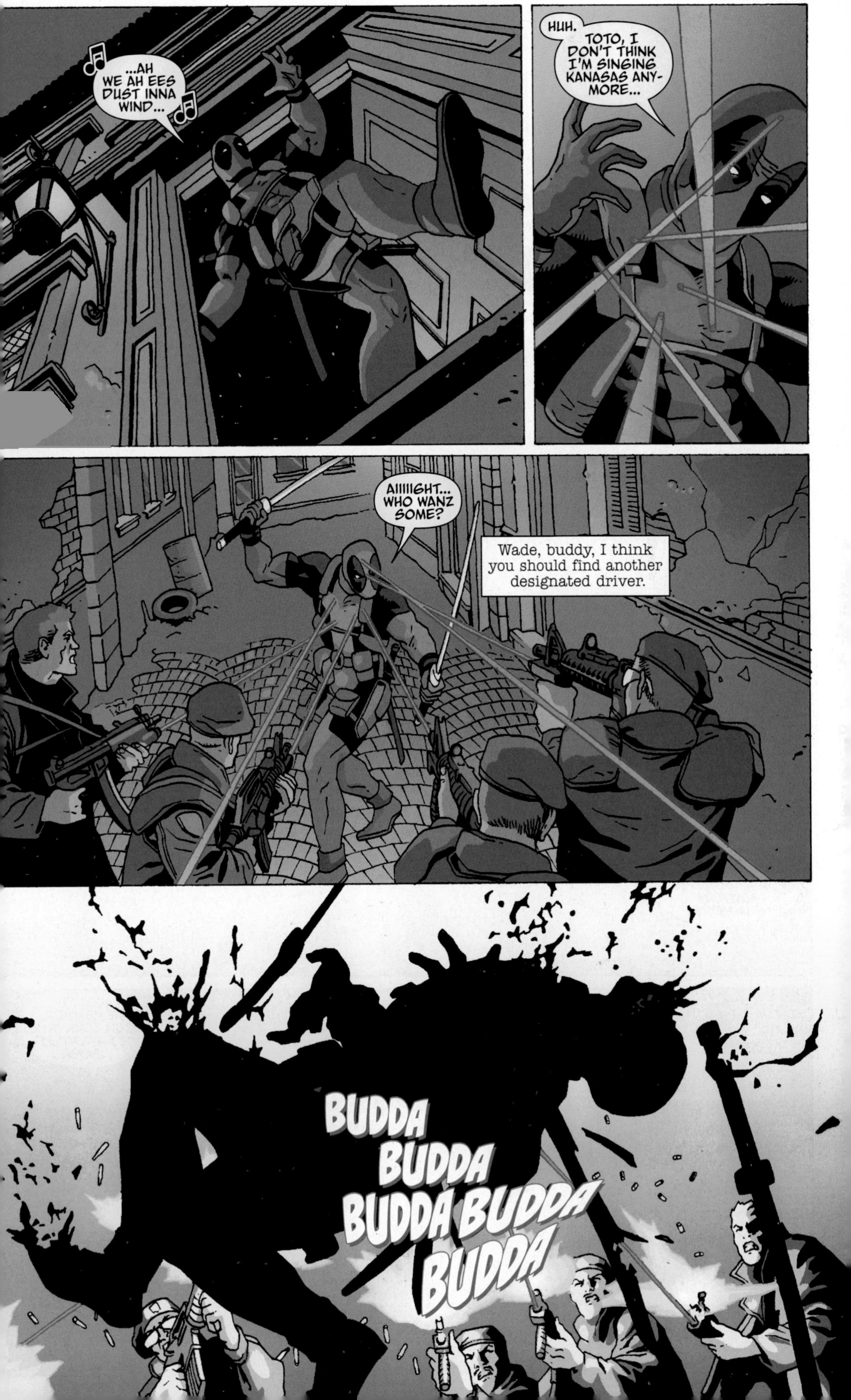
...AH WE AH EES DUST INNA WIND...
HUH.
TOTO, I DON'T THINK I'M SINGING KANASAS ANY-MORE...
AIIIIIGHT... WHO WANZ SOME?
Wade, buddy, I think you should find another designated driver.
BUDDA BUDDA BUDDA BUDDA BUDDA

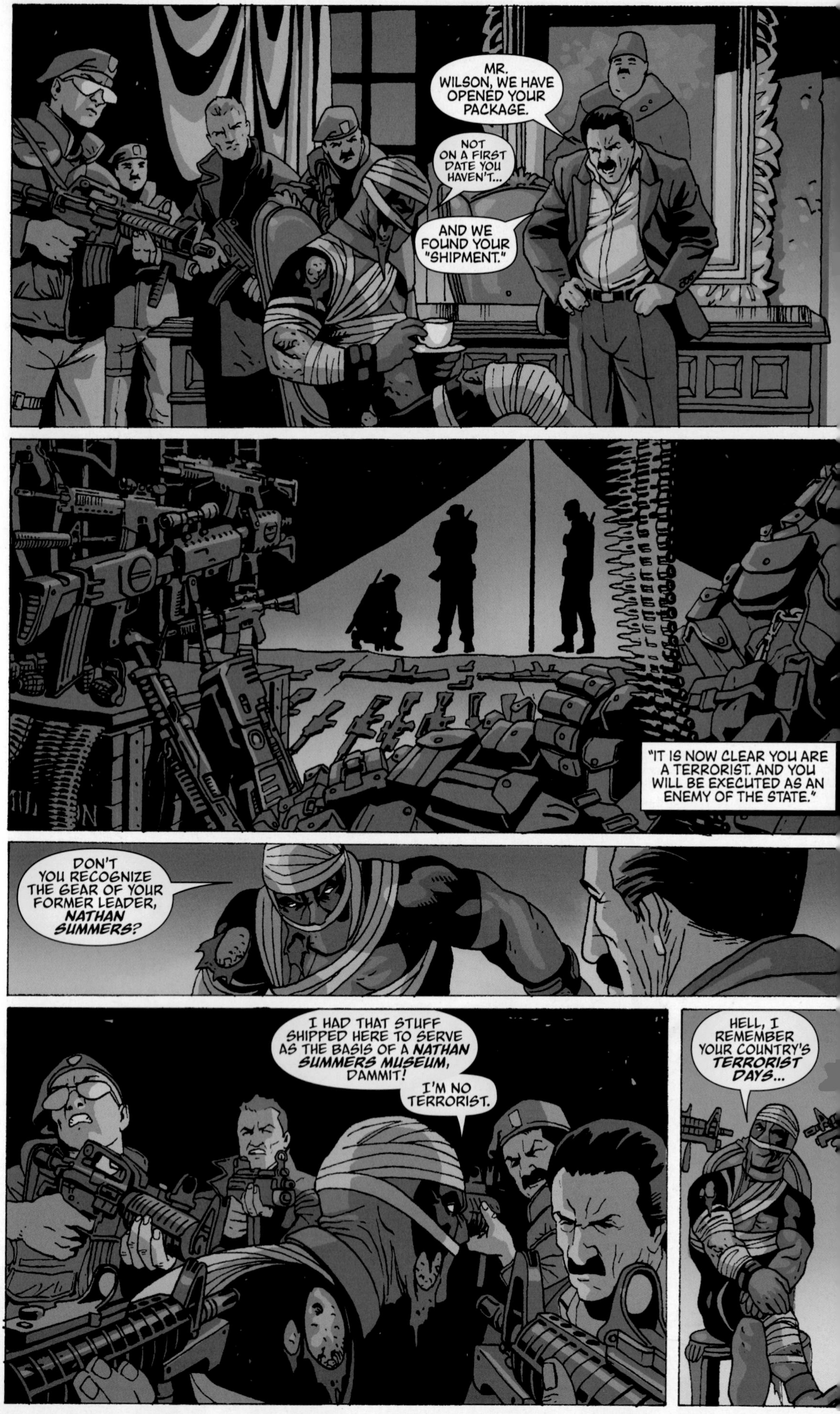

MR. WILSON, WE HAVE OPENED YOUR PACKAGE.
NOT ON A FIRST DATE YOU HAVEN'T...
AND WE FOUND YOUR "SHIPMENT."
"IT IS NOW CLEAR YOU ARE A TERRORIST. AND YOU WILL BE EXECUTED AS AN ENEMY OF THE STATE."
DON'T YOU RECOGNIZE THE GEAR OF YOUR FORMER LEADER, NATHAN SUMMERS?
I HAD THAT STUFF SHIPPED HERE TO SERVE AS THE BASIS OF A NATHAN SUMMERS MUSEUM, DAMMIT!
I'M NO TERRORIST.
HELL, I REMEMBER YOUR COUNTRY'S TERRORIST DAYS...

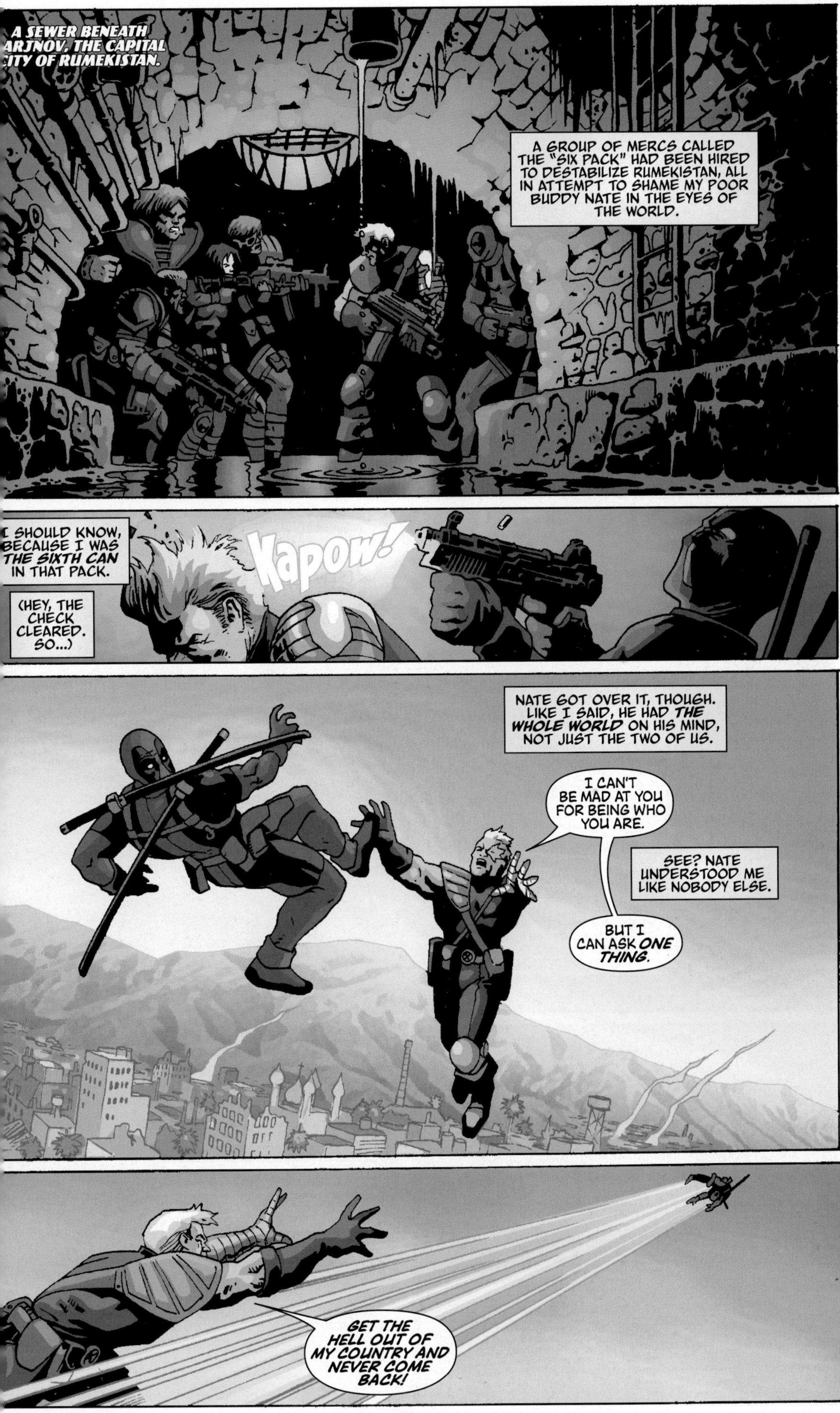
A SEWER BENEATH
ARJNOV, THE CAPITAL
ITY OF RUMEKISTAN.
A GROUP OF MERCS CALLED THE "SIX PACK" HAD BEEN HIRED TO DESTABILIZE RUMEKISTAN, ALL IN ATTEMPT TO SHAME MY POOR BUDDY NATE IN THE EYES OF THE WORLD.
I SHOULD KNOW, BECAUSE I WAS THE SIXTH CAN IN THAT PACK.
(HEY, THE CHECK CLEARED. SO...)
KAPOW!
NATE GOT OVER IT, THOUGH. LIKE I SAID, HE HAD THE WHOLE WORLD ON HIS MIND, NOT JUST THE TWO OF US.
I CAN'T BE MAD AT YOU FOR BEING WHO YOU ARE.
SEE? NATE UNDERSTOOD ME LIKE NOBODY ELSE.
BUT I CAN ASK ONE THING.
GET THE HELL OUT OF MY COUNTRY AND NEVER COME BACK!

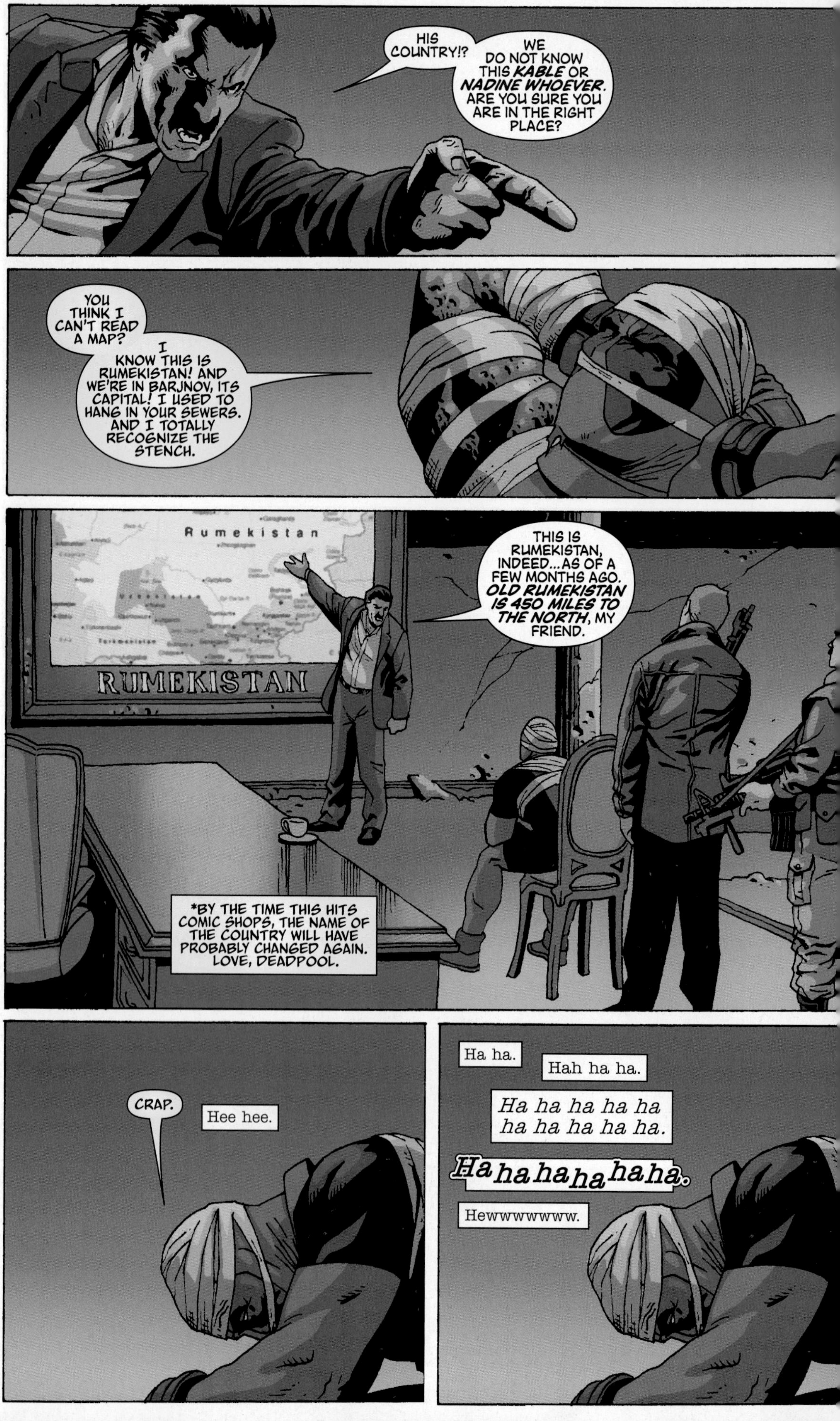

HIS COUNTRY!?
WE DO NOT KNOW THIS *KABLE* OR ***NADINE WHOEVER***. ARE YOU SURE YOU ARE IN THE RIGHT PLACE?
YOU THINK I CAN'T READ A MAP?
I KNOW THIS IS RUMEKISTAN! AND WE'RE IN BARJNOV, ITS CAPITAL! I USED TO HANG IN YOUR SEWERS. AND I TOTALLY RECOGNIZE THE STENCH.
Rumekistan
RUMEKISTAN
THIS IS RUMEKISTAN, INDEED...AS OF A FEW MONTHS AGO. ***OLD RUMEKISTAN IS 450 MILES TO THE NORTH***, MY FRIEND.
*BY THE TIME THIS HITS COMIC SHOPS, THE NAME OF THE COUNTRY WILL HAVE PROBABLY CHANGED AGAIN. LOVE, DEADPOOL.
CRAP.
Hee hee.
Ha ha.
Hah ha ha.
Ha ha ha ha ha ha ha ha ha ha.
Hahahahahaha.
Hewwwwwwww.

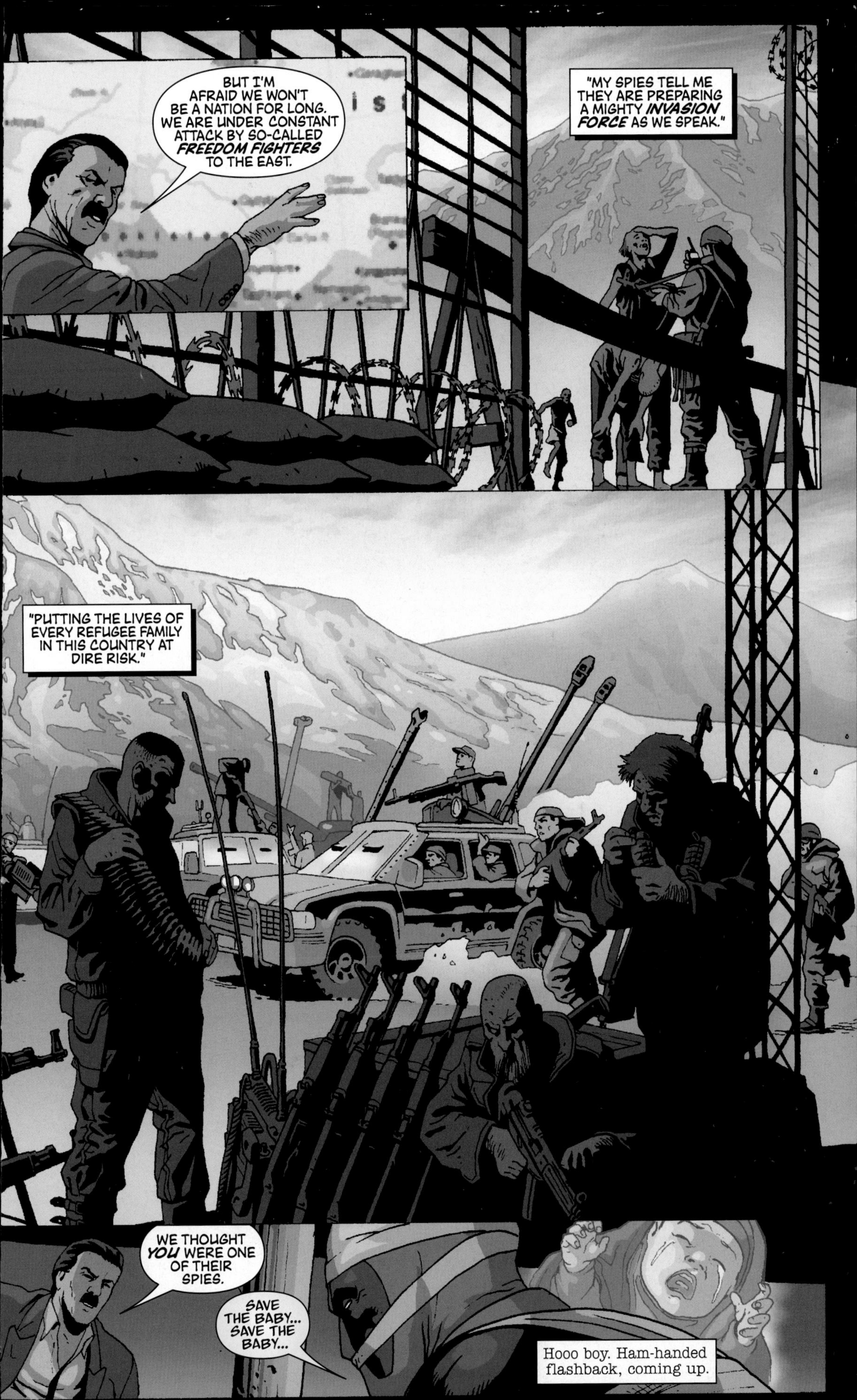
BUT I'M AFRAID WE WON'T BE A NATION FOR LONG. WE ARE UNDER CONSTANT ATTACK BY SO-CALLED FREEDOM FIGHTERS TO THE EAST.
"MY SPIES TELL ME THEY ARE PREPARING A MIGHTY INVASION FORCE AS WE SPEAK."
"PUTTING THE LIVES OF EVERY REFUGEE FAMILY IN THIS COUNTRY AT DIRE RISK."
WE THOUGHT YOU WERE ONE OF THEIR SPIES.
SAVE THE BABY... SAVE THE BABY...
Hooo boy. Ham-handed flashback, coming up.

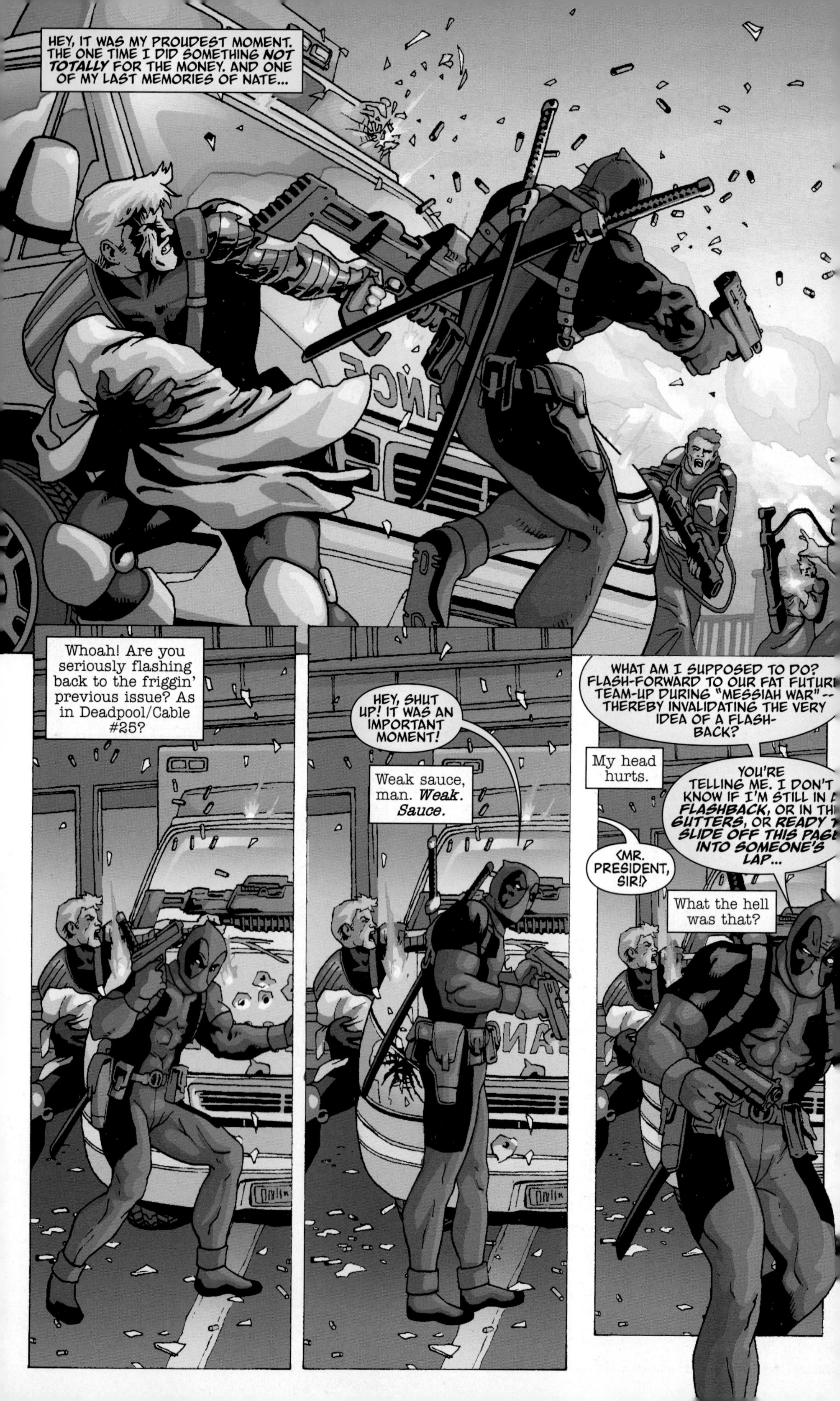

HEY, IT WAS MY PROUDEST MOMENT. THE ONE TIME I DID SOMETHING *NOT TOTALLY* FOR THE MONEY. AND ONE OF MY LAST MEMORIES OF NATE...
Whoah! Are you seriously flashing back to the friggin' previous issue? As in Deadpool/Cable #25?
HEY, SHUT UP! IT WAS AN IMPORTANT MOMENT!
Weak sauce, man. *Weak. Sauce.*
WHAT AM I SUPPOSED TO DO? FLASH-FORWARD TO OUR FAT FUTUR TEAM-UP DURING "MESSIAH WAR" -- THEREBY INVALIDATING THE VERY IDEA OF A FLASH-BACK?
My head hurts.
YOU'RE TELLING ME. I DON'T KNOW IF I'M STILL IN A *FLASHBACK*, OR IN TH *GUTTERS*, OR *READY* T *SLIDE OFF THIS PAG INTO SOMEONE'S LAP...*
<MR. PRESIDENT, SIR!>
What the hell was that?

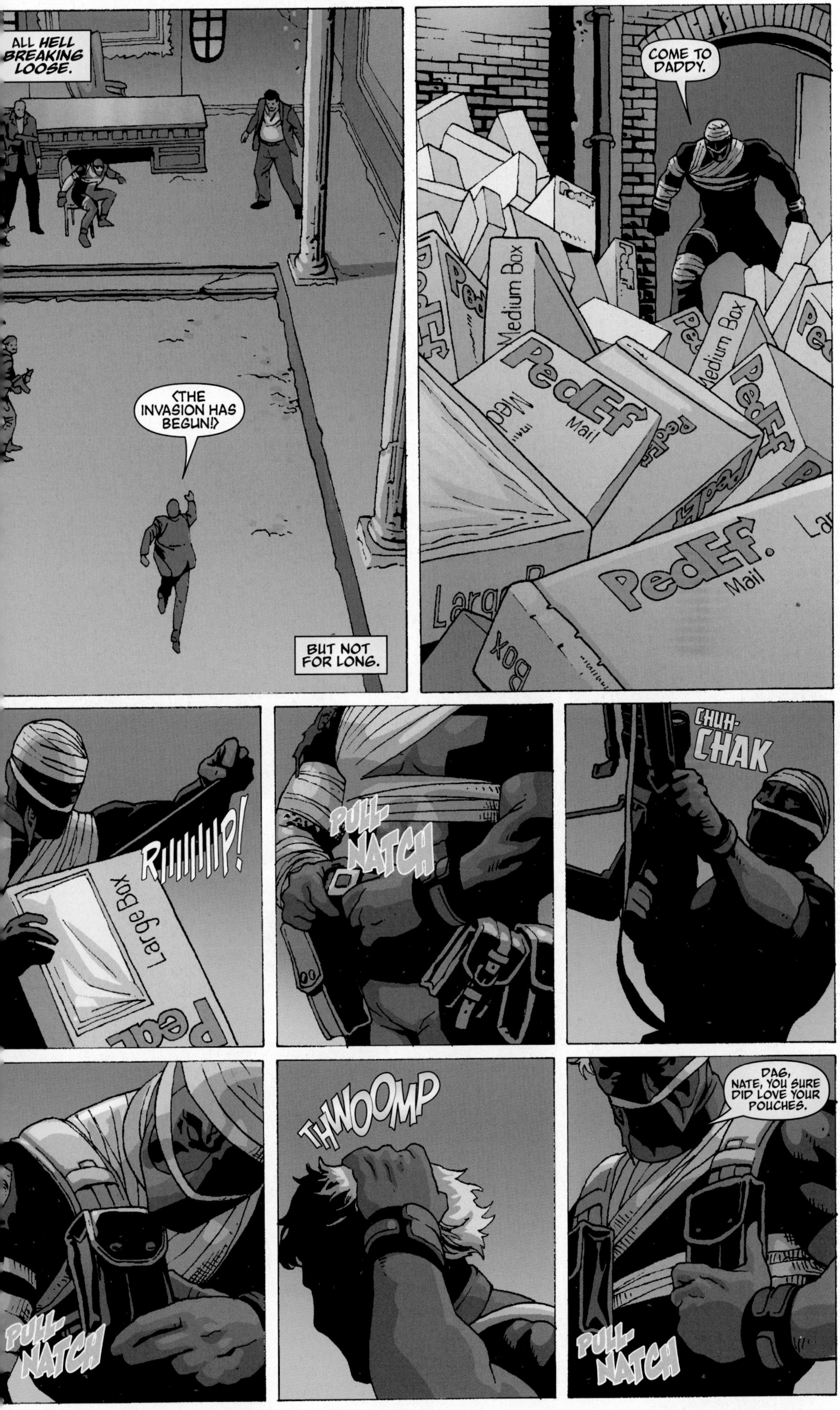
ALL HELL BREAKING LOOSE.
<THE INVASION HAS BEGUN!>
BUT NOT FOR LONG.
COME TO DADDY.
PedEf Mail
Medium Box
Large Box
RIIIIIIIP!
PULL-NATCH
CHUH-CHAK
PULL-NATCH
THWOOMP
DAG, NATE, YOU SURE DID LOVE YOUR POUCHES.
PULL-NATCH

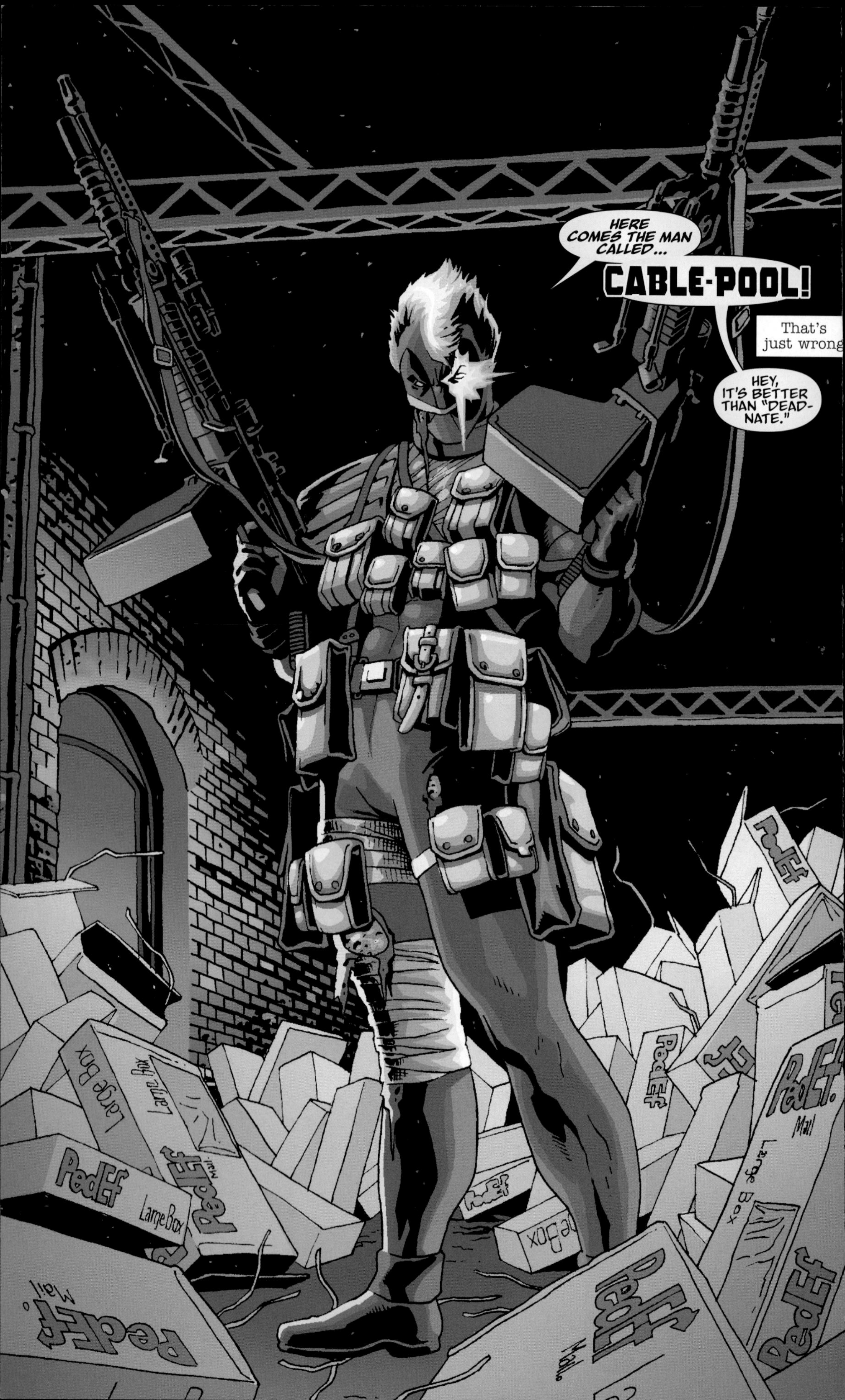
HERE COMES THE MAN CALLED...
CABLE-POOL!
That's just wrong
HEY, IT'S BETTER THAN "DEAD-NATE."

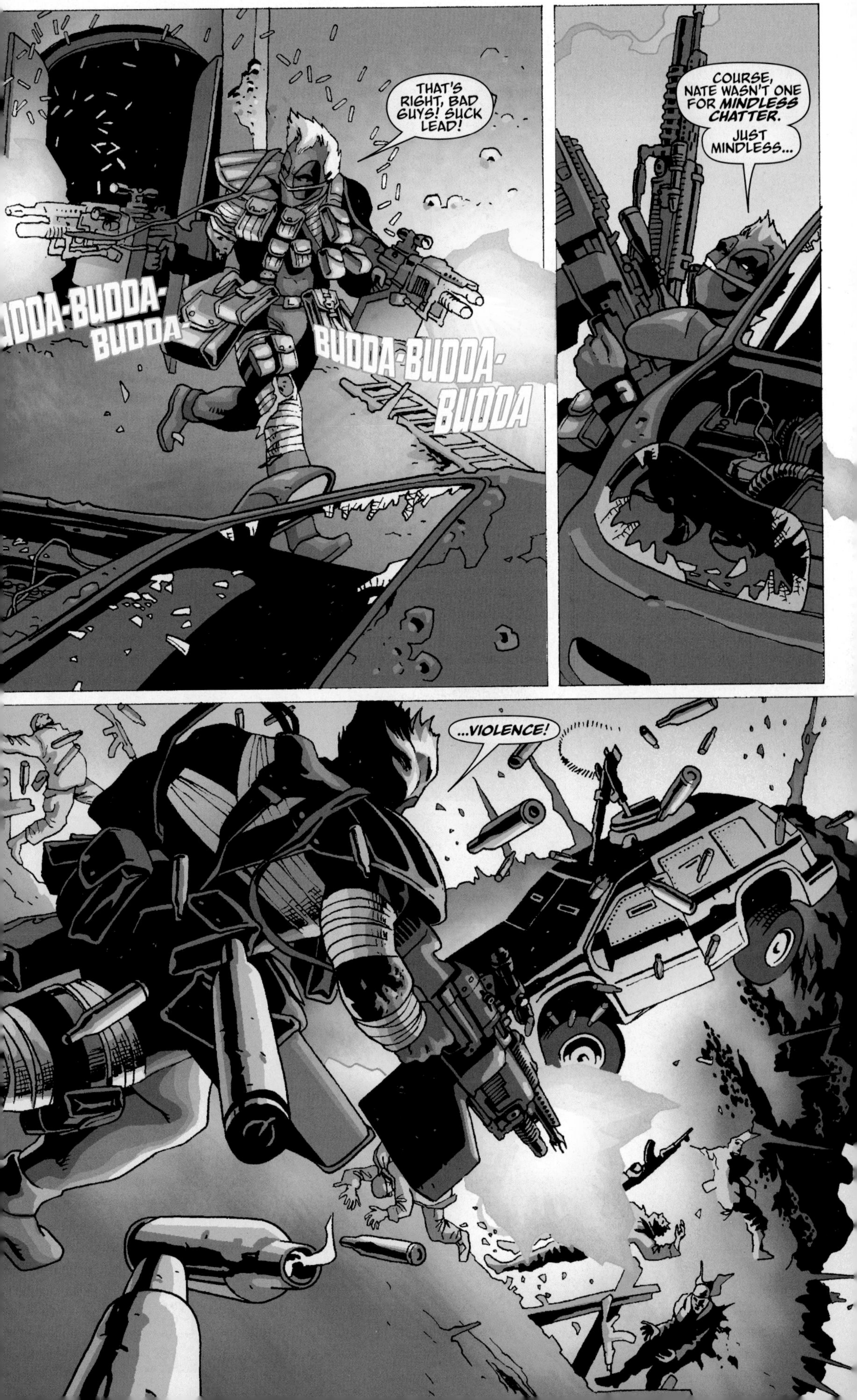
THAT'S RIGHT, BAD GUYS! SUCK LEAD!
UDDA-BUDDA-BUDDA-
BUDDA-BUDDA-BUDDA
COURSE, NATE WASN'T ONE FOR MINDLESS CHATTER.
JUST MINDLESS...
...VIOLENCE!

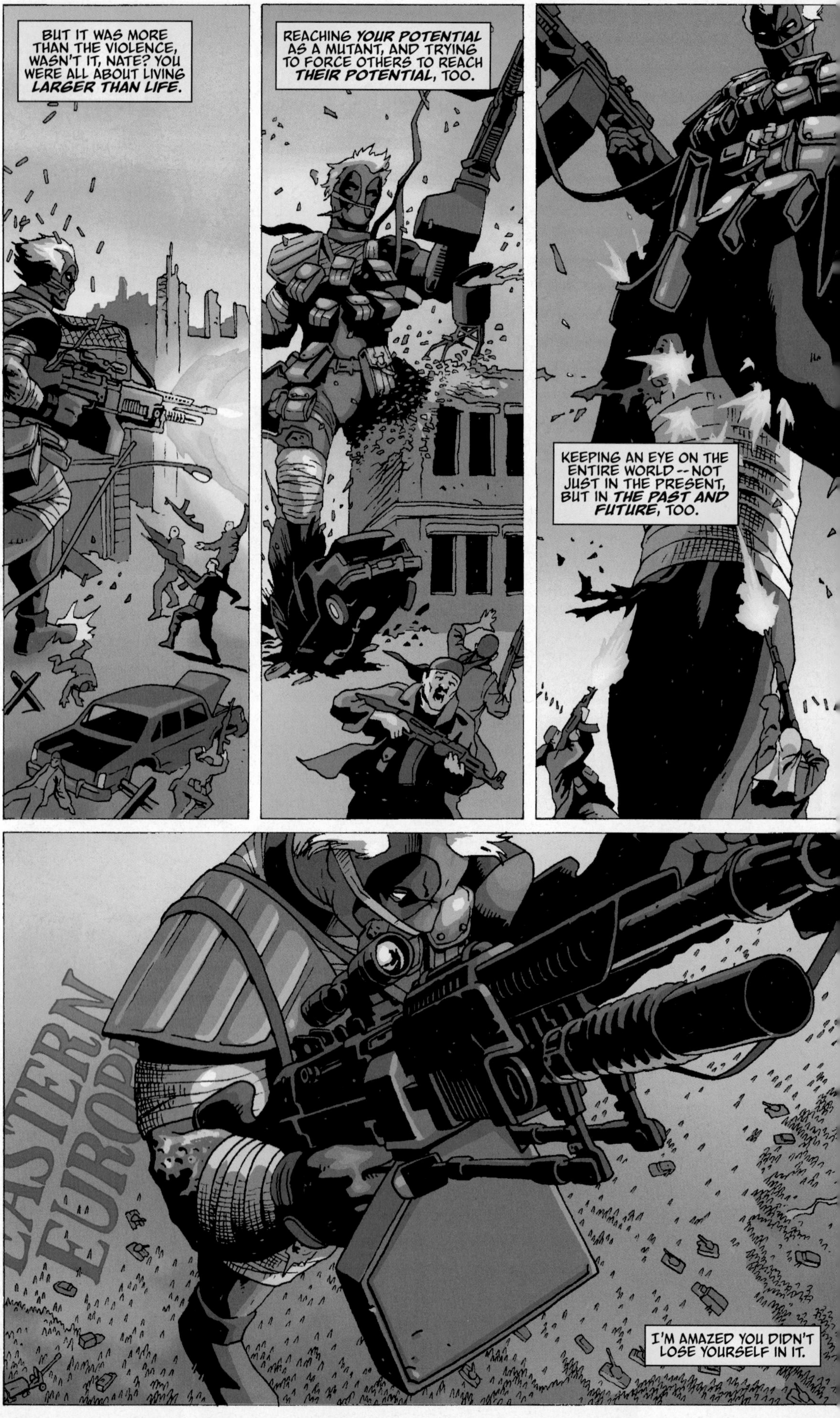
BUT IT WAS MORE THAN THE VIOLENCE, WASN'T IT, NATE? YOU WERE ALL ABOUT LIVING *LARGER THAN LIFE*.
REACHING *YOUR POTENTIAL* AS A MUTANT, AND TRYING TO FORCE OTHERS TO REACH *THEIR POTENTIAL*, TOO.
KEEPING AN EYE ON THE ENTIRE WORLD -- NOT JUST IN THE PRESENT, BUT IN *THE PAST AND FUTURE*, TOO.
I'M AMAZED YOU DIDN'T LOSE YOURSELF IN IT.

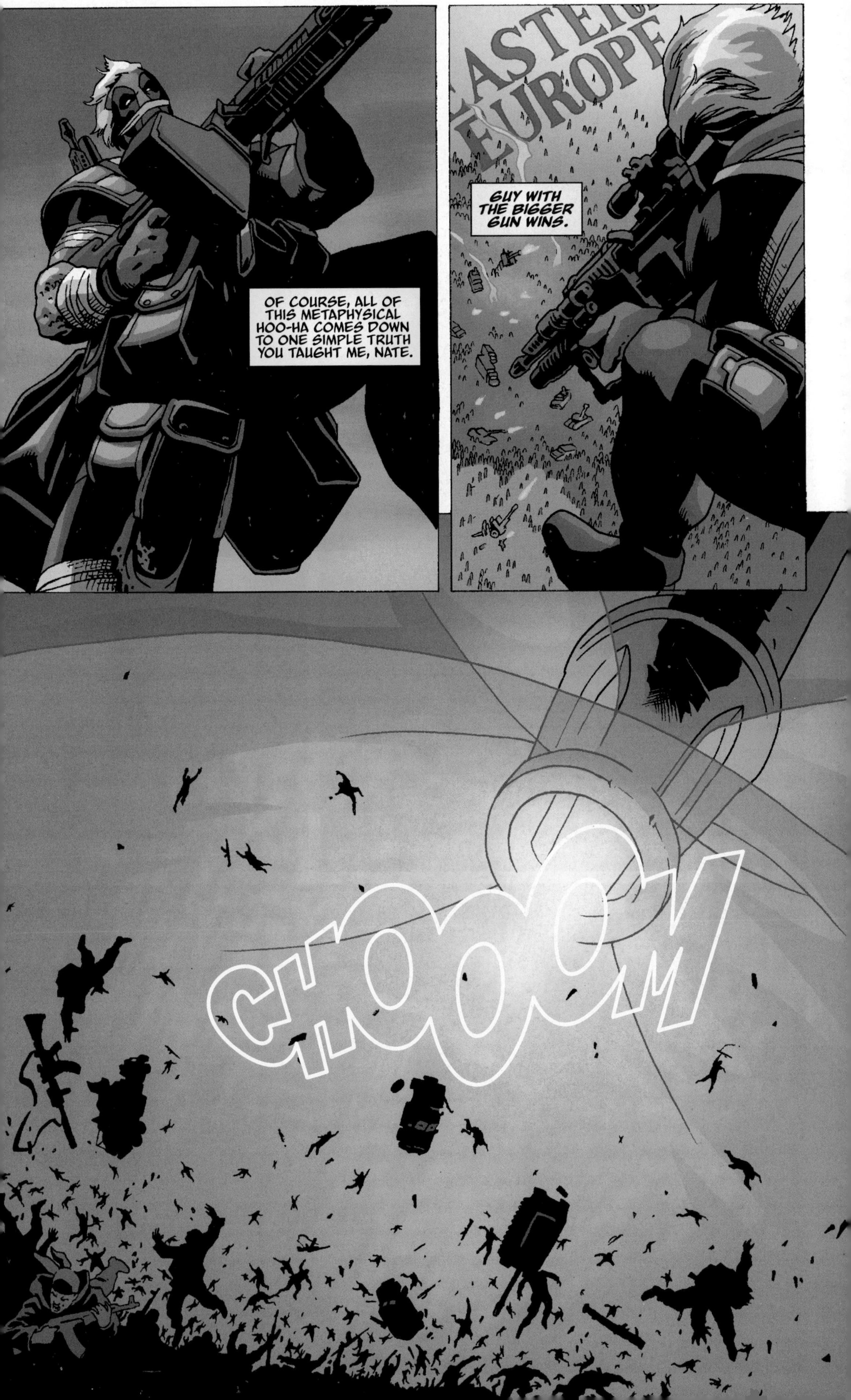
OF COURSE, ALL OF THIS METAPHYSICAL HOO-HA COMES DOWN TO ONE SIMPLE TRUTH YOU TAUGHT ME, NATE.
EASTERN EUROPE
GUY WITH THE BIGGER GUN WINS.
CHOOOOM

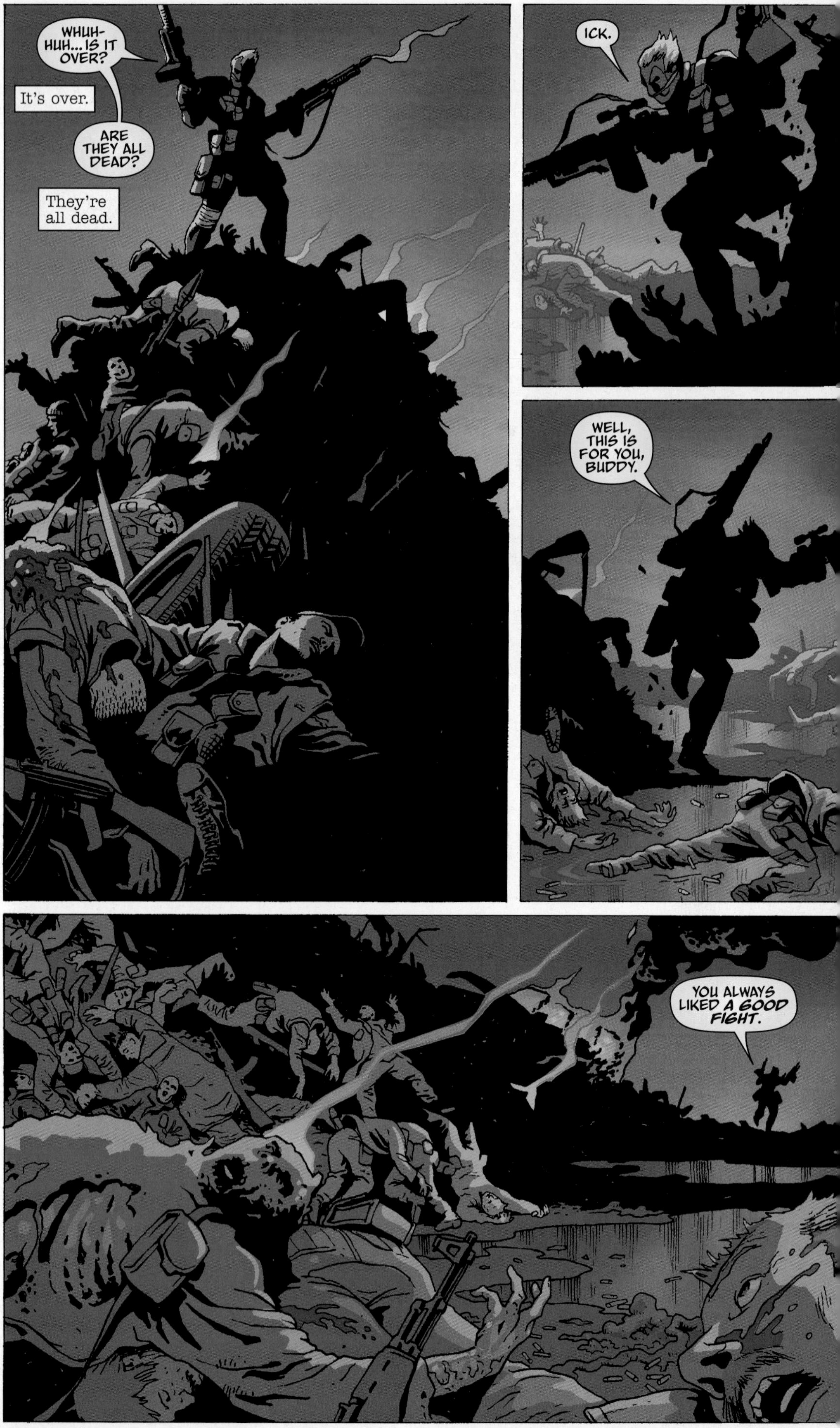
WHUH-HUH... IS IT OVER?
It's over.
ARE THEY ALL DEAD?
They're all dead.
ICK.
WELL, THIS IS FOR YOU, BUDDY.
YOU ALWAYS LIKED A GOOD FIGHT.

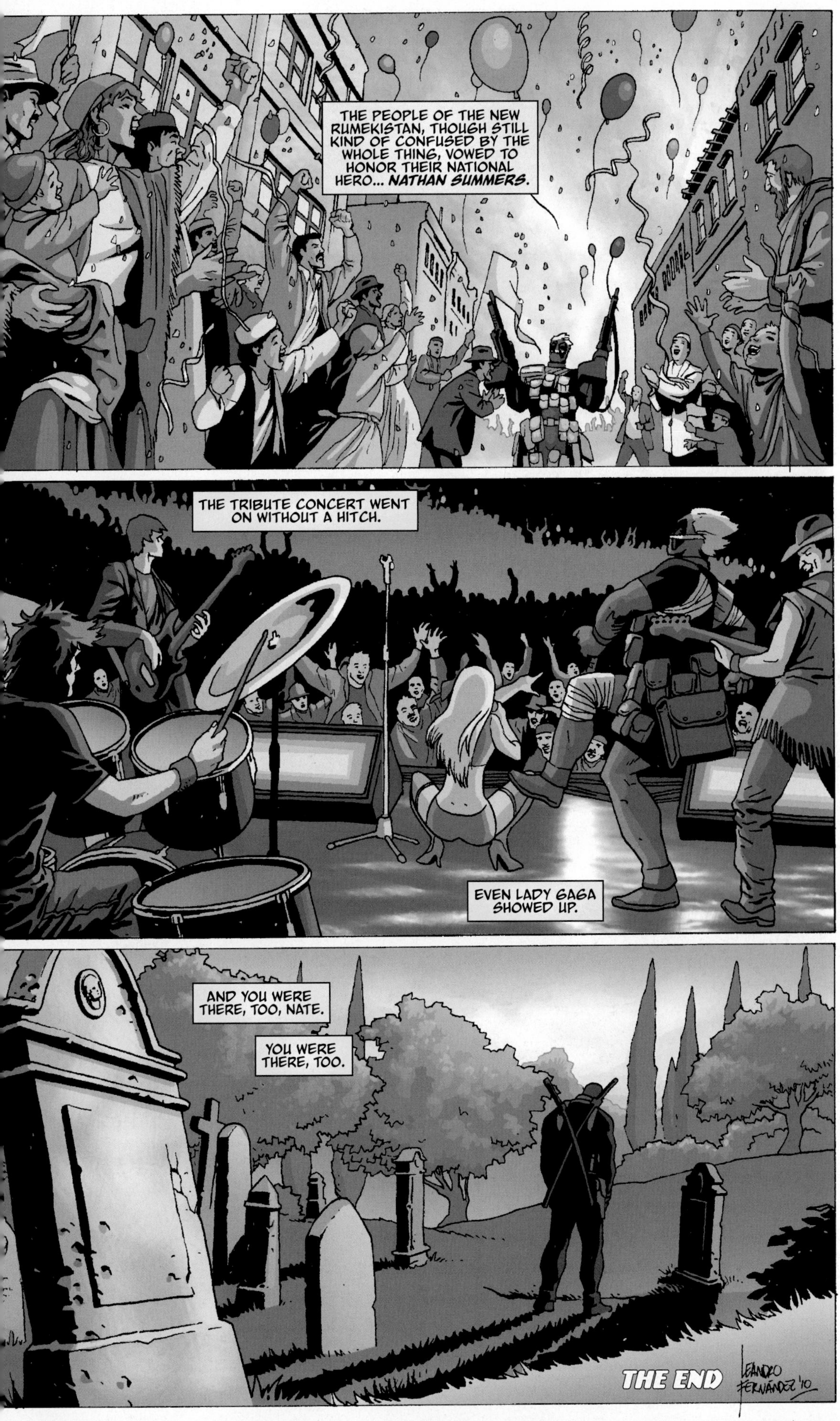
THE PEOPLE OF THE NEW RUMEKISTAN, THOUGH STILL KIND OF CONFUSED BY THE WHOLE THING, VOWED TO HONOR THEIR NATIONAL HERO... NATHAN SUMMERS.
THE TRIBUTE CONCERT WENT ON WITHOUT A HITCH.
EVEN LADY GAGA SHOWED UP.
AND YOU WERE THERE, TOO, NATE.
YOU WERE THERE, TOO.
THE END

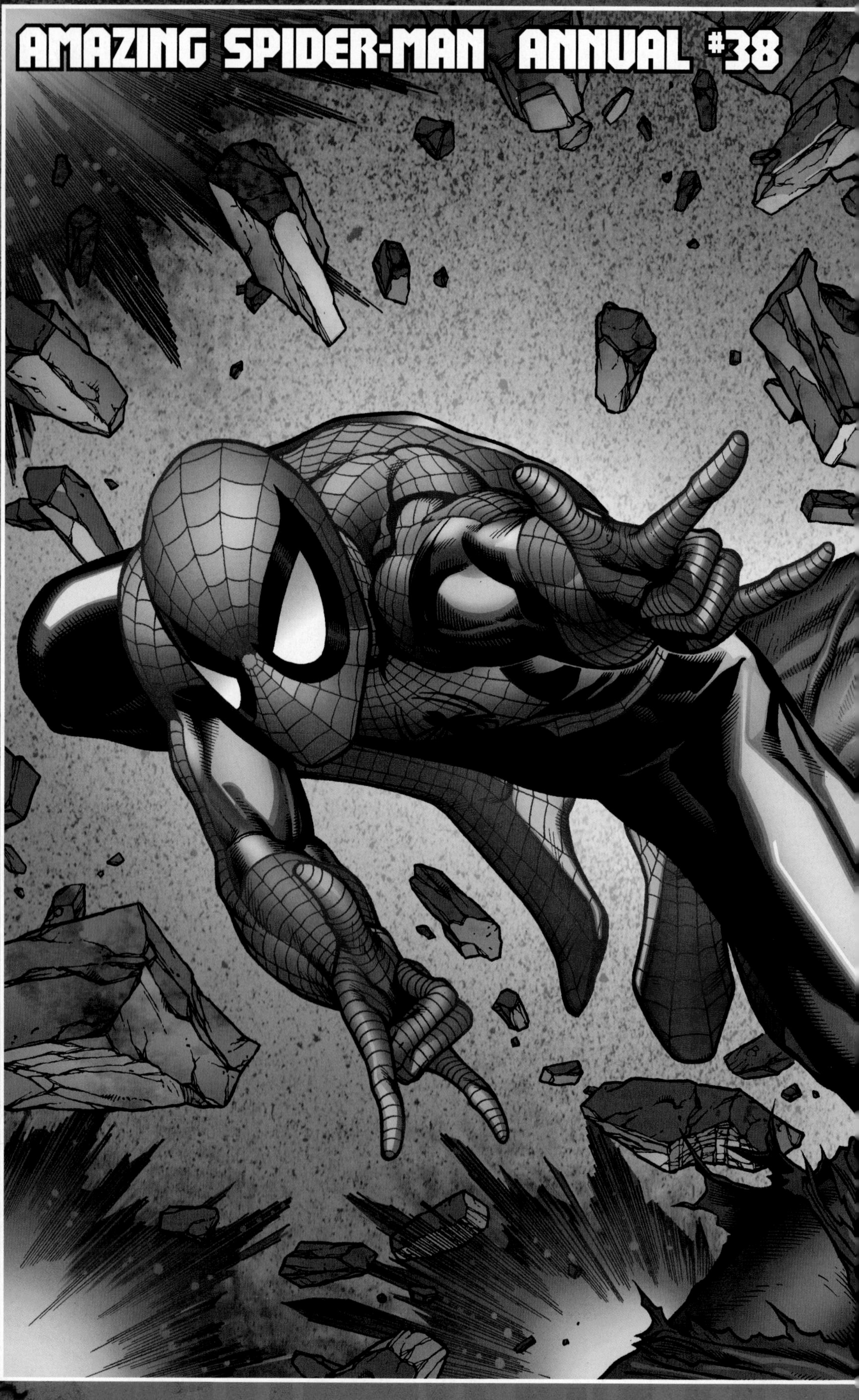
AMAZING SPIDER-MAN ANNUAL #38

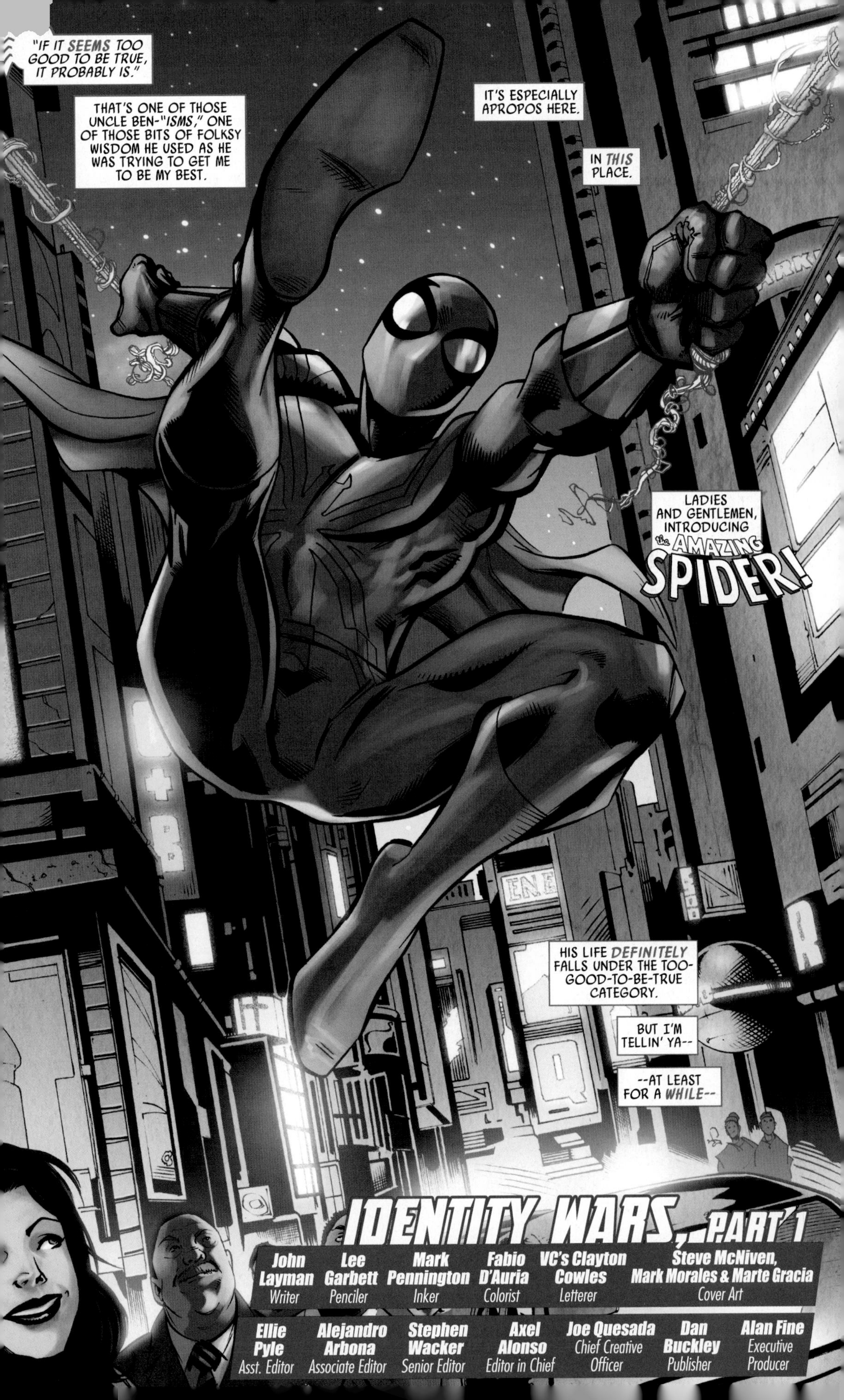

"IF IT SEEMS TOO GOOD TO BE TRUE, IT PROBABLY IS."
THAT'S ONE OF THOSE UNCLE BEN-"ISMS," ONE OF THOSE BITS OF FOLKSY WISDOM HE USED AS HE WAS TRYING TO GET ME TO BE MY BEST.
IT'S ESPECIALLY APROPOS HERE.
IN THIS PLACE.
LADIES AND GENTLEMEN, INTRODUCING the AMAZING SPIDER!
HIS LIFE DEFINITELY FALLS UNDER THE TOO-GOOD-TO-BE-TRUE CATEGORY.
BUT I'M TELLIN' YA--
--AT LEAST FOR A WHILE--
IDENTITY WARS, PART 1
John Layman Writer
Lee Garbett Penciler
Mark Pennington Inker
Fabio D'Auria Colorist
VC's Clayton Cowles Letterer
Steve McNiven, Mark Morales & Marte Gracia Cover Art
Ellie Pyle Asst. Editor
Alejandro Arbona Associate Editor
Stephen Wacker Senior Editor
Axel Alonso Editor in Chief
Joe Quesada Chief Creative Officer
Dan Buckley Publisher
Alan Fine Executive Producer

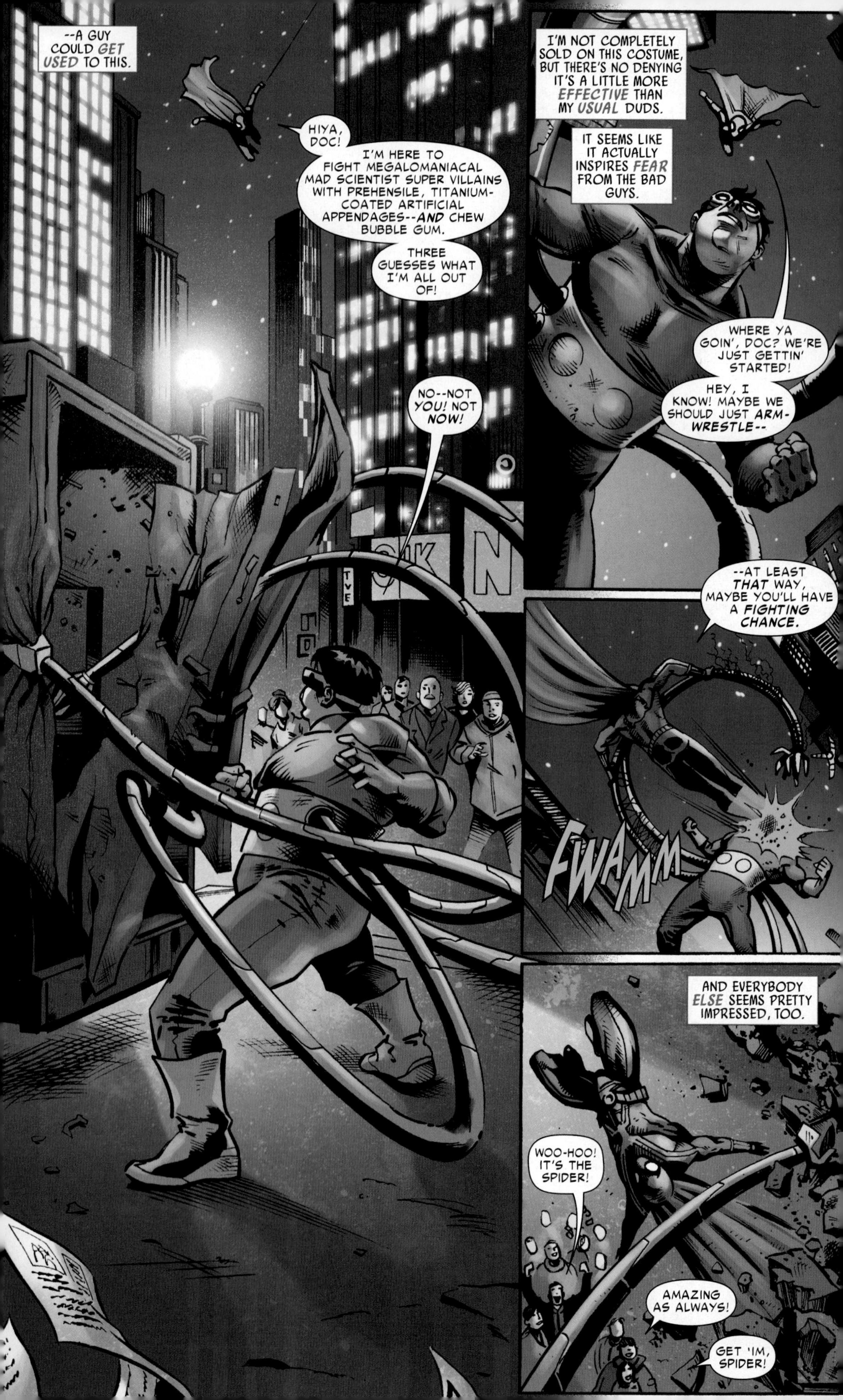

--A GUY COULD GET USED TO THIS.
HIYA, DOC!
I'M HERE TO FIGHT MEGALOMANIACAL MAD SCIENTIST SUPER VILLAINS WITH PREHENSILE, TITANIUM-COATED ARTIFICIAL APPENDAGES--AND CHEW BUBBLE GUM.
THREE GUESSES WHAT I'M ALL OUT OF!
NO--NOT YOU! NOT NOW!
I'M NOT COMPLETELY SOLD ON THIS COSTUME, BUT THERE'S NO DENYING IT'S A LITTLE MORE EFFECTIVE THAN MY USUAL DUDS.
IT SEEMS LIKE IT ACTUALLY INSPIRES FEAR FROM THE BAD GUYS.
WHERE YA GOIN', DOC? WE'RE JUST GETTIN' STARTED!
HEY, I KNOW! MAYBE WE SHOULD JUST ARM-WRESTLE--
--AT LEAST THAT WAY, MAYBE YOU'LL HAVE A FIGHTING CHANCE.
FWAMM
AND EVERYBODY ELSE SEEMS PRETTY IMPRESSED, TOO.
WOO-HOO! IT'S THE SPIDER!
AMAZING AS ALWAYS!
GET 'IM, SPIDER!

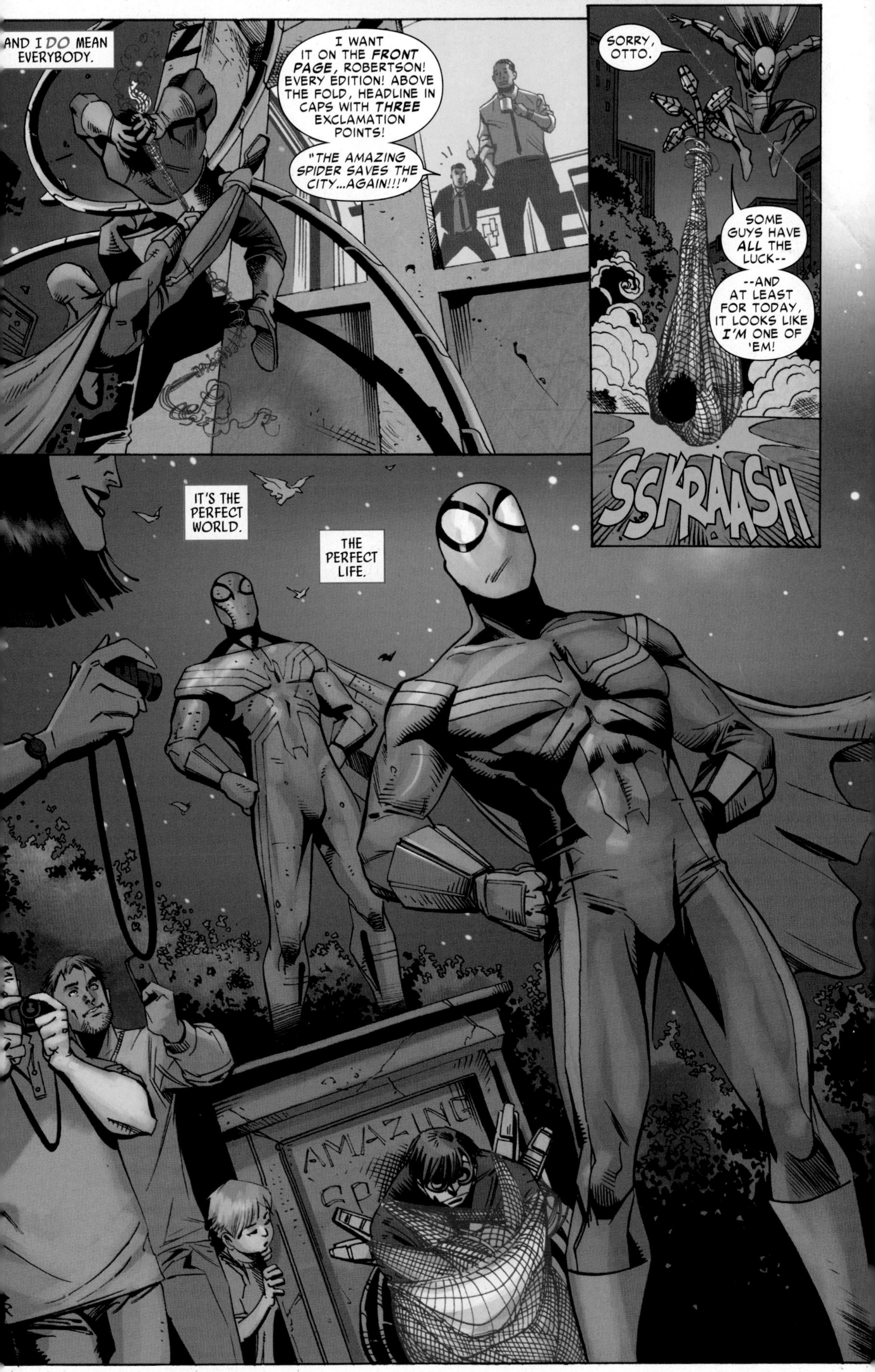
AND I DO MEAN EVERYBODY.
I WANT IT ON THE FRONT PAGE, ROBERTSON! EVERY EDITION! ABOVE THE FOLD, HEADLINE IN CAPS WITH THREE EXCLAMATION POINTS!
"THE AMAZING SPIDER SAVES THE CITY...AGAIN!!!"
SORRY, OTTO.
SOME GUYS HAVE ALL THE LUCK--
--AND AT LEAST FOR TODAY, IT LOOKS LIKE I'M ONE OF 'EM!
SSKRAASH
IT'S THE PERFECT WORLD.
THE PERFECT LIFE.
AMAZING

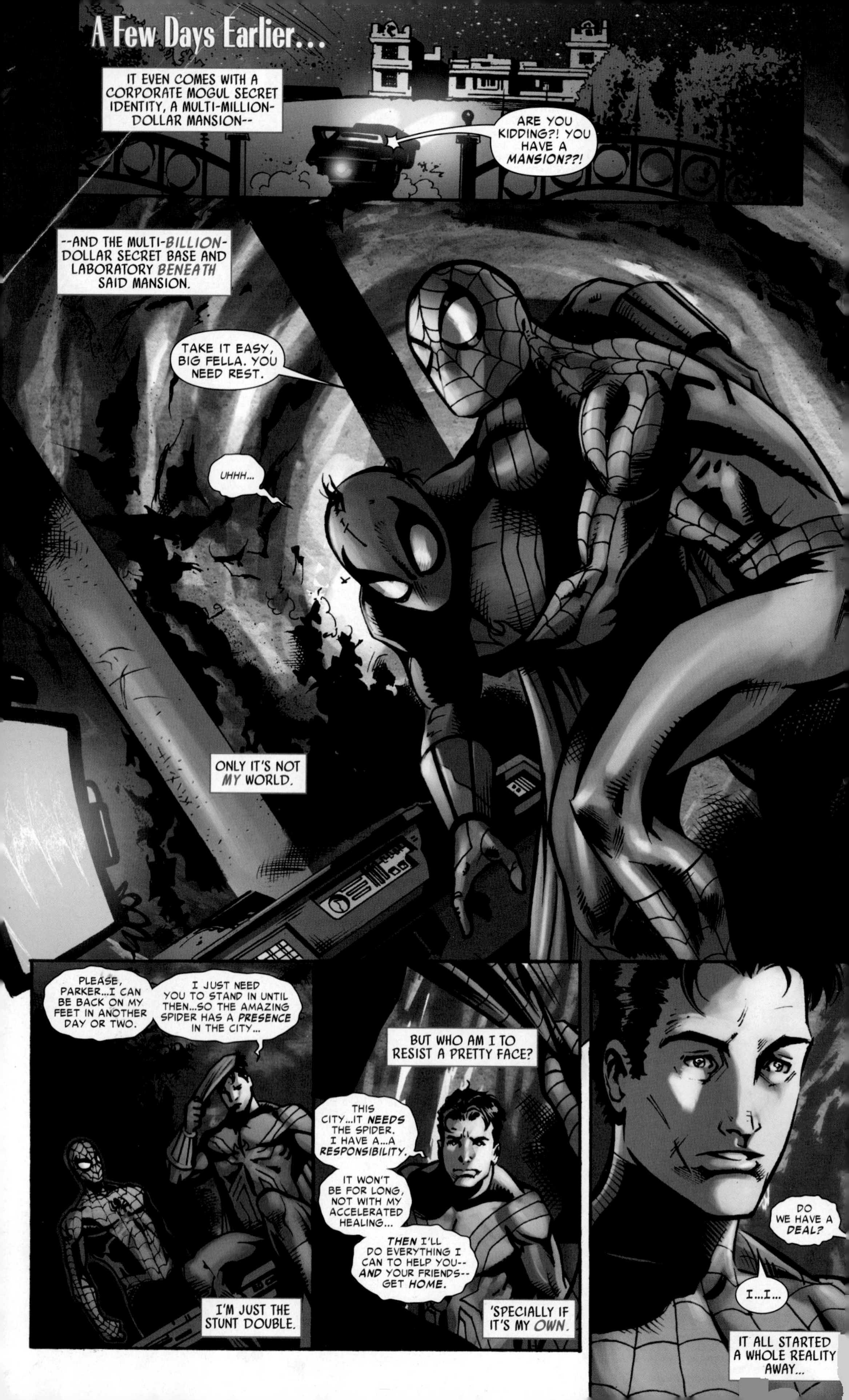
A Few Days Earlier...
IT EVEN COMES WITH A CORPORATE MOGUL SECRET IDENTITY, A MULTI-MILLION-DOLLAR MANSION--
ARE YOU KIDDING?! YOU HAVE A MANSION??!
--AND THE MULTI-BILLION-DOLLAR SECRET BASE AND LABORATORY BENEATH SAID MANSION.
TAKE IT EASY, BIG FELLA. YOU NEED REST.
UHHH...
ONLY IT'S NOT MY WORLD.
PLEASE, PARKER...I CAN BE BACK ON MY FEET IN ANOTHER DAY OR TWO.
I JUST NEED YOU TO STAND IN UNTIL THEN...SO THE AMAZING SPIDER HAS A PRESENCE IN THE CITY...
I'M JUST THE STUNT DOUBLE.
BUT WHO AM I TO RESIST A PRETTY FACE?
THIS CITY...IT NEEDS THE SPIDER. I HAVE A...A RESPONSIBILITY.
IT WON'T BE FOR LONG, NOT WITH MY ACCELERATED HEALING...
THEN I'LL DO EVERYTHING I CAN TO HELP YOU--AND YOUR FRIENDS--GET HOME.
'SPECIALLY IF IT'S MY OWN.
DO WE HAVE A DEAL?
I...I...
IT ALL STARTED A WHOLE REALITY AWAY...

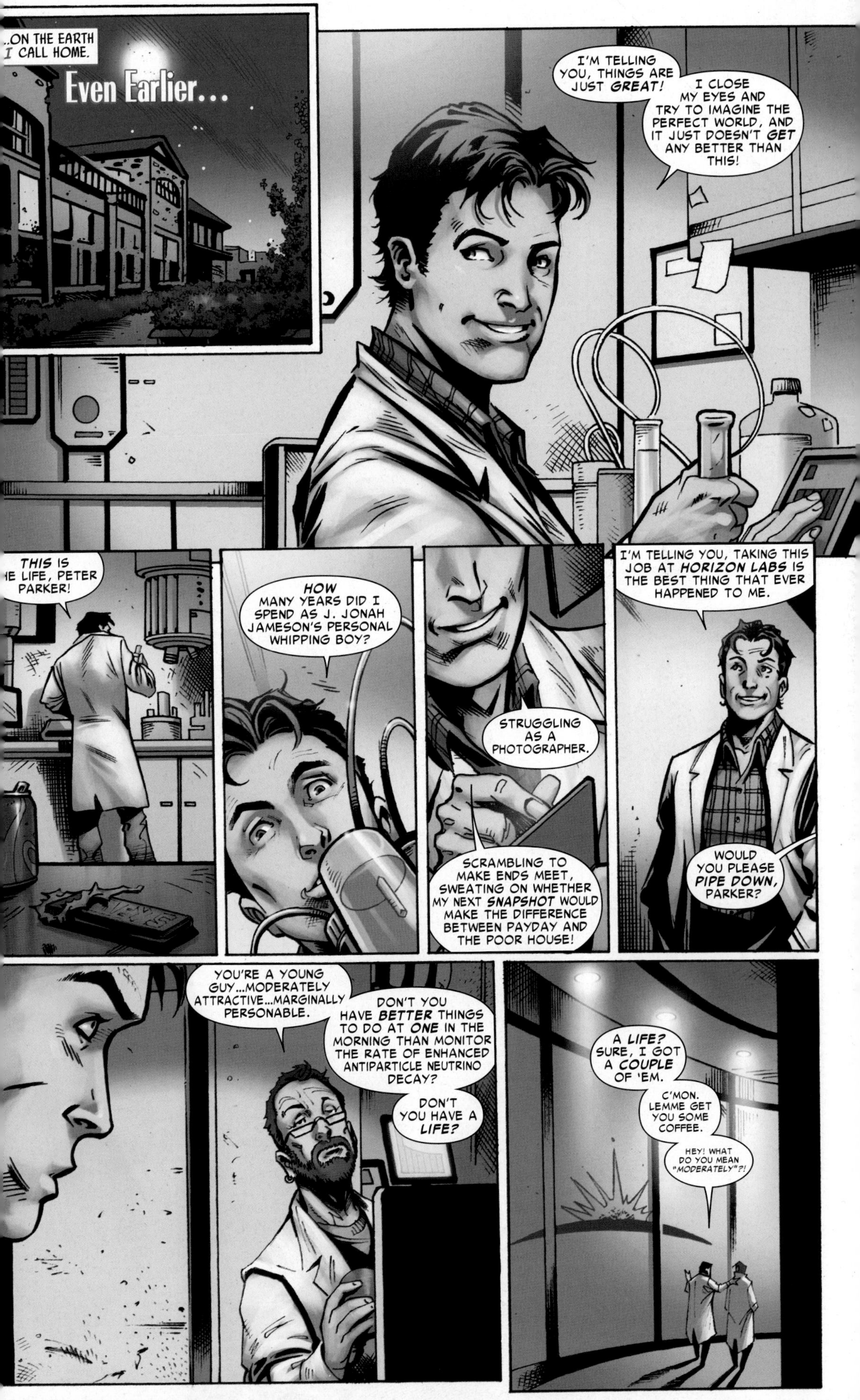

..ON THE EARTH I CALL HOME.
Even Earlier...
I'M TELLING YOU, THINGS ARE JUST GREAT!
I CLOSE MY EYES AND TRY TO IMAGINE THE PERFECT WORLD, AND IT JUST DOESN'T GET ANY BETTER THAN THIS!
THIS IS HE LIFE, PETER PARKER!
HOW MANY YEARS DID I SPEND AS J. JONAH JAMESON'S PERSONAL WHIPPING BOY?
STRUGGLING AS A PHOTOGRAPHER.
SCRAMBLING TO MAKE ENDS MEET, SWEATING ON WHETHER MY NEXT SNAPSHOT WOULD MAKE THE DIFFERENCE BETWEEN PAYDAY AND THE POOR HOUSE!
I'M TELLING YOU, TAKING THIS JOB AT HORIZON LABS IS THE BEST THING THAT EVER HAPPENED TO ME.
WOULD YOU PLEASE PIPE DOWN, PARKER?
YOU'RE A YOUNG GUY...MODERATELY ATTRACTIVE...MARGINALLY PERSONABLE.
DON'T YOU HAVE BETTER THINGS TO DO AT ONE IN THE MORNING THAN MONITOR THE RATE OF ENHANCED ANTIPARTICLE NEUTRINO DECAY?
DON'T YOU HAVE A LIFE?
A LIFE? SURE, I GOT A COUPLE OF 'EM.
C'MON. LEMME GET YOU SOME COFFEE.
HEY! WHAT DO YOU MEAN "MODERATELY"?!

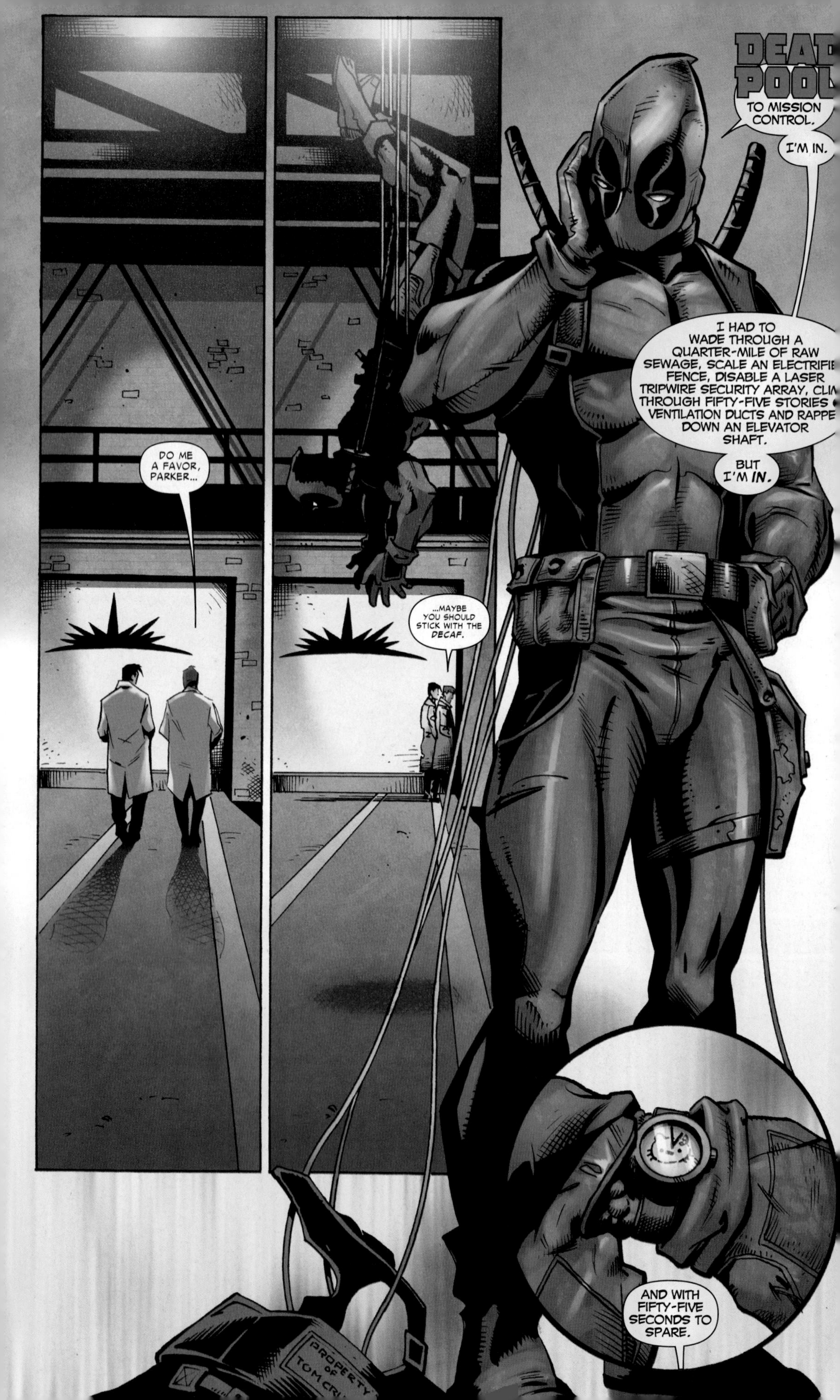
DEADPOOL
DO ME A FAVOR, PARKER...
...MAYBE YOU SHOULD STICK WITH THE DECAF.
TO MISSION CONTROL.
I'M IN.
I HAD TO WADE THROUGH A QUARTER-MILE OF RAW SEWAGE, SCALE AN ELECTRIFIE FENCE, DISABLE A LASER TRIPWIRE SECURITY ARRAY, CLI THROUGH FIFTY-FIVE STORIES VENTILATION DUCTS AND RAPPE DOWN AN ELEVATOR SHAFT.
BUT I'M IN.
AND WITH FIFTY-FIVE SECONDS TO SPARE.
PROPERTY OF TOM CRU

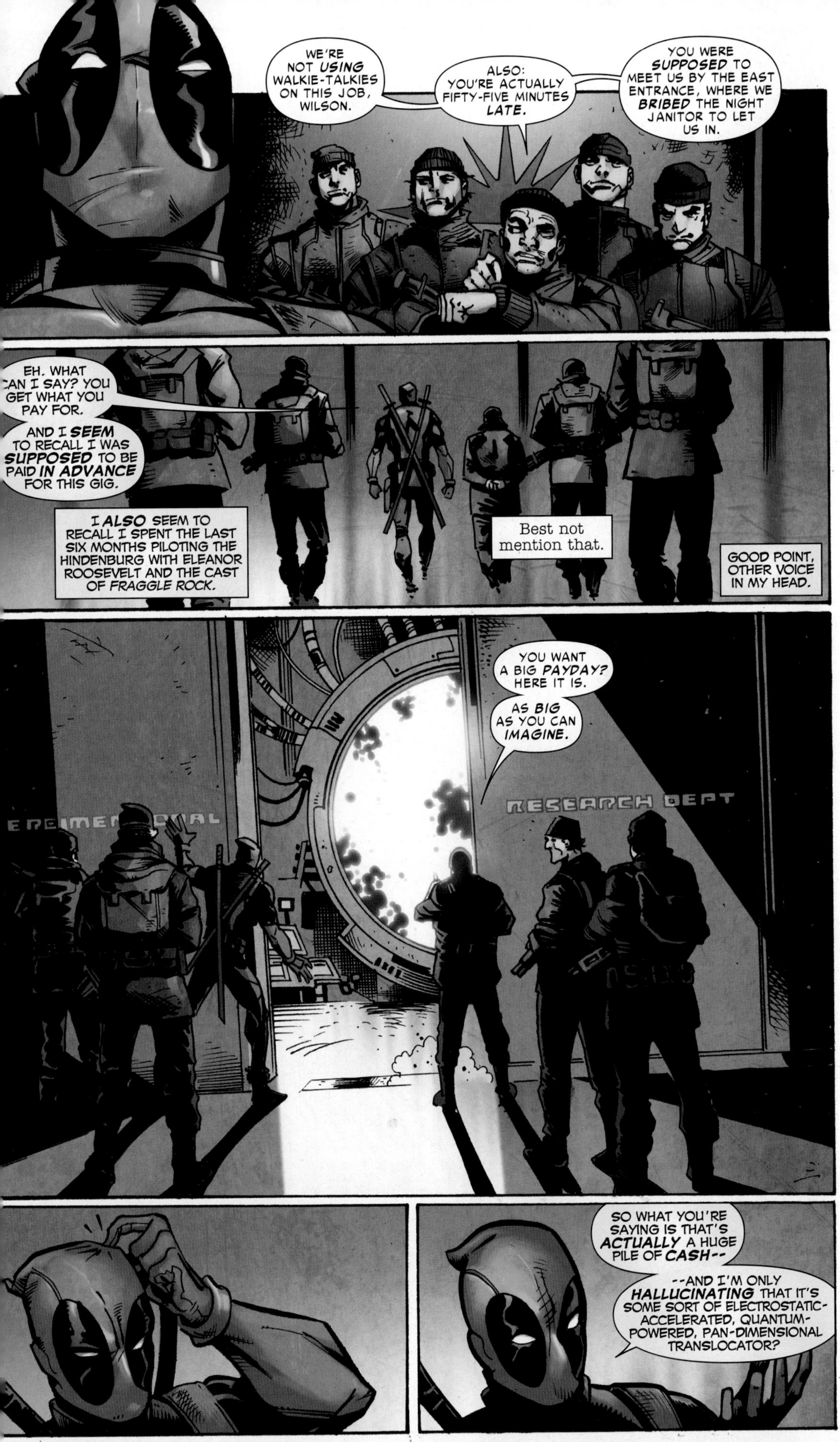
WE'RE NOT *USING* WALKIE-TALKIES ON THIS JOB, WILSON.
ALSO: YOU'RE ACTUALLY FIFTY-FIVE MINUTES *LATE.*
YOU WERE *SUPPOSED* TO MEET US BY THE EAST ENTRANCE, WHERE WE *BRIBED* THE NIGHT JANITOR TO LET US IN.
EH. WHAT AN I SAY? YOU GET WHAT YOU PAY FOR.
AND I *SEEM* TO RECALL I WAS *SUPPOSED* TO BE PAID *IN ADVANCE* FOR THIS GIG.
I *ALSO* SEEM TO RECALL I SPENT THE LAST SIX MONTHS PILOTING THE HINDENBURG WITH ELEANOR ROOSEVELT AND THE CAST OF *FRAGGLE ROCK.*
Best not mention that.
GOOD POINT, OTHER VOICE IN MY HEAD.
YOU WANT A BIG *PAYDAY?* HERE IT IS.
AS *BIG* AS YOU CAN *IMAGINE.*
RESEARCH DEPT
SO WHAT YOU'RE SAYING IS THAT'S *ACTUALLY* A HUGE PILE OF *CASH--*
--AND I'M ONLY *HALLUCINATING* THAT IT'S SOME SORT OF ELECTROSTATIC-ACCELERATED, QUANTUM-POWERED, PAN-DIMENSIONAL TRANSLOCATOR?

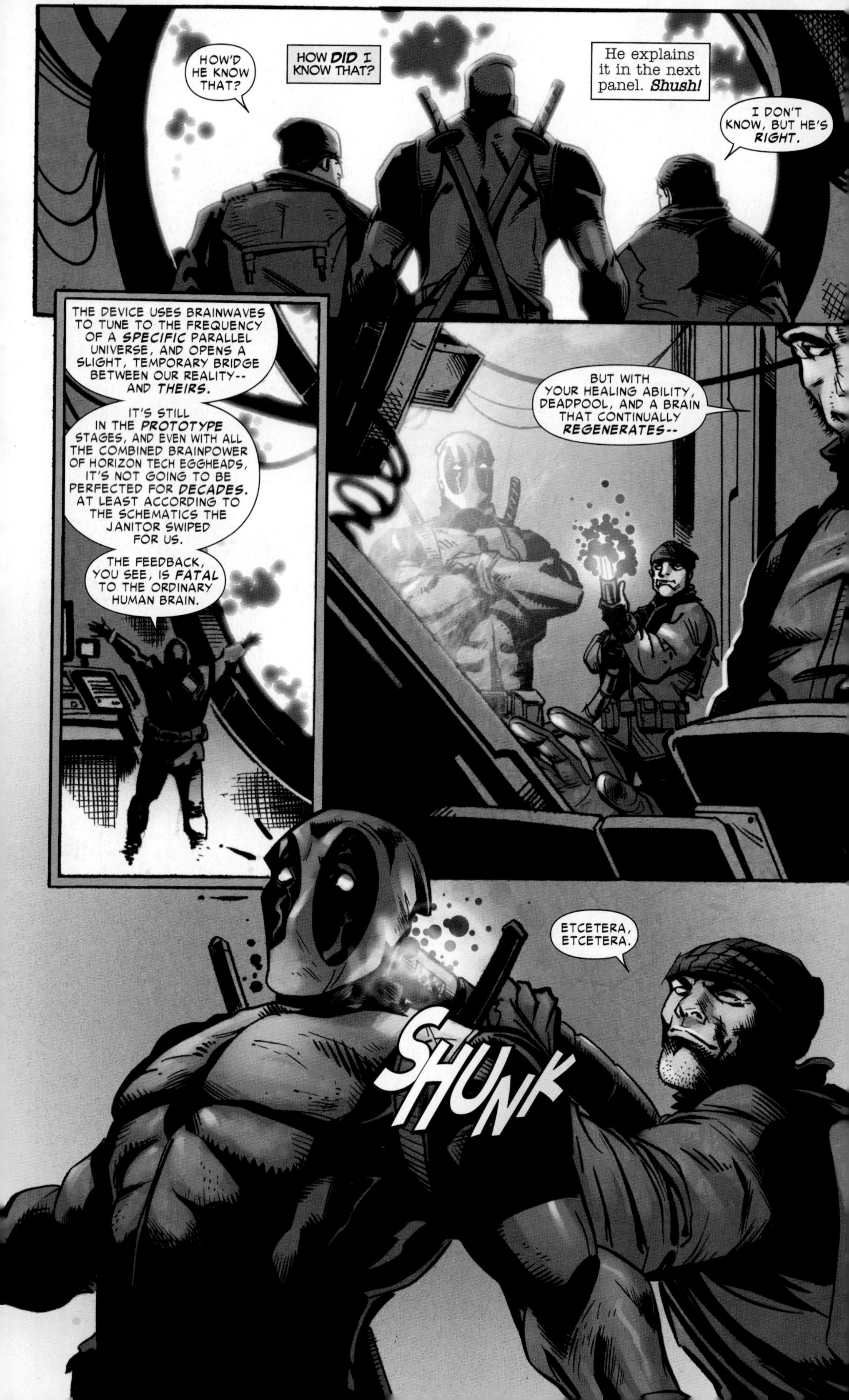

HOW'D HE KNOW THAT?
HOW DID I KNOW THAT?
He explains it in the next panel. Shush!
I DON'T KNOW, BUT HE'S RIGHT.
THE DEVICE USES BRAINWAVES TO TUNE TO THE FREQUENCY OF A SPECIFIC PARALLEL UNIVERSE, AND OPENS A SLIGHT, TEMPORARY BRIDGE BETWEEN OUR REALITY-- AND THEIRS.
IT'S STILL IN THE PROTOTYPE STAGES, AND EVEN WITH ALL THE COMBINED BRAINPOWER OF HORIZON TECH EGGHEADS, IT'S NOT GOING TO BE PERFECTED FOR DECADES. AT LEAST ACCORDING TO THE SCHEMATICS THE JANITOR SWIPED FOR US.
THE FEEDBACK, YOU SEE, IS FATAL TO THE ORDINARY HUMAN BRAIN.
BUT WITH YOUR HEALING ABILITY, DEADPOOL, AND A BRAIN THAT CONTINUALLY REGENERATES--
ETCETERA, ETCETERA.
SHUNK

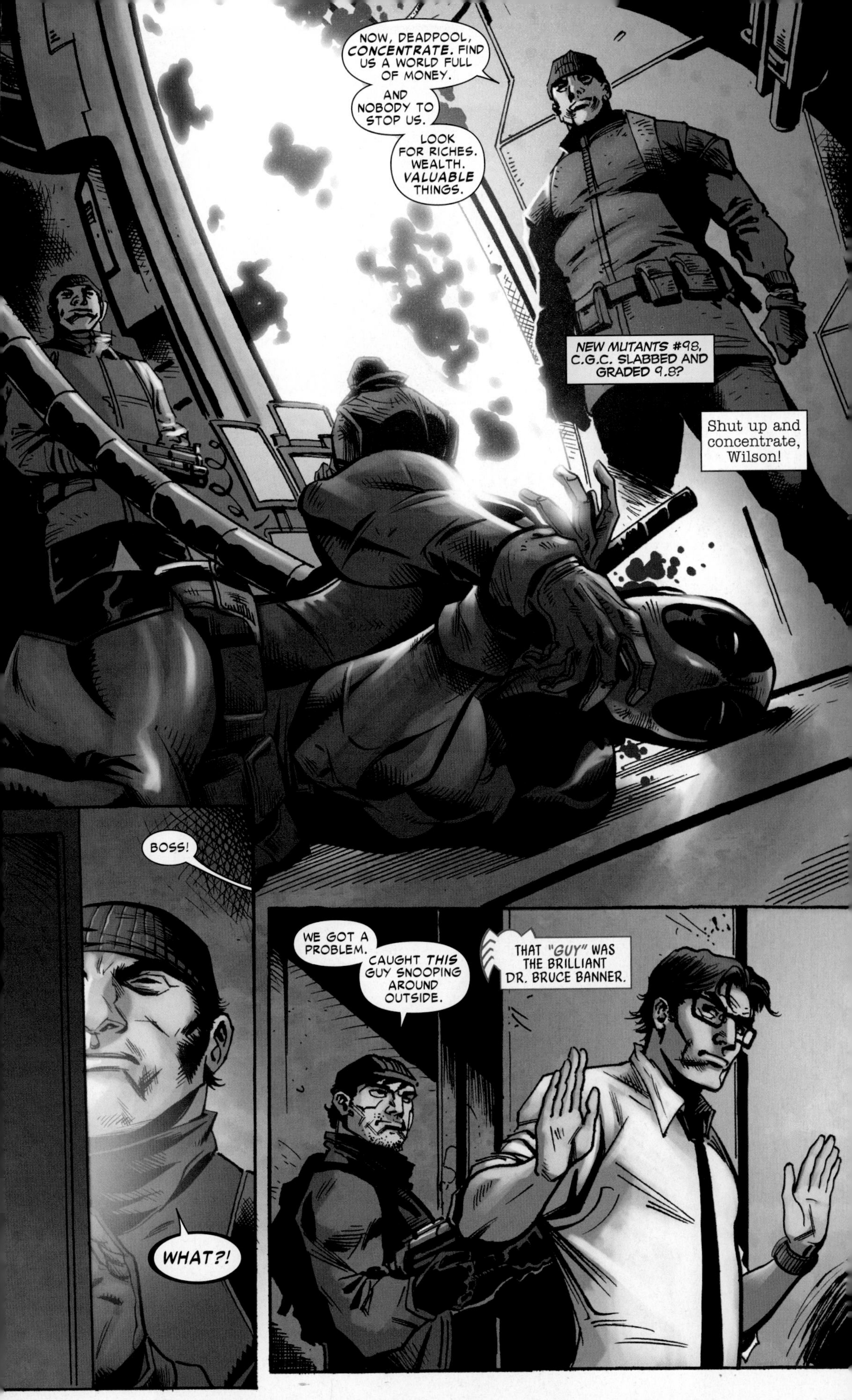

NOW, DEADPOOL, CONCENTRATE. FIND US A WORLD FULL OF MONEY.
AND NOBODY TO STOP US.
LOOK FOR RICHES. WEALTH. VALUABLE THINGS.
NEW MUTANTS #98, C.G.C. SLABBED AND GRADED 9.8?
Shut up and concentrate, Wilson!
BOSS!
WE GOT A PROBLEM.
CAUGHT THIS GUY SNOOPING AROUND OUTSIDE.
THAT "GUY" WAS THE BRILLIANT DR. BRUCE BANNER.
WHAT?!

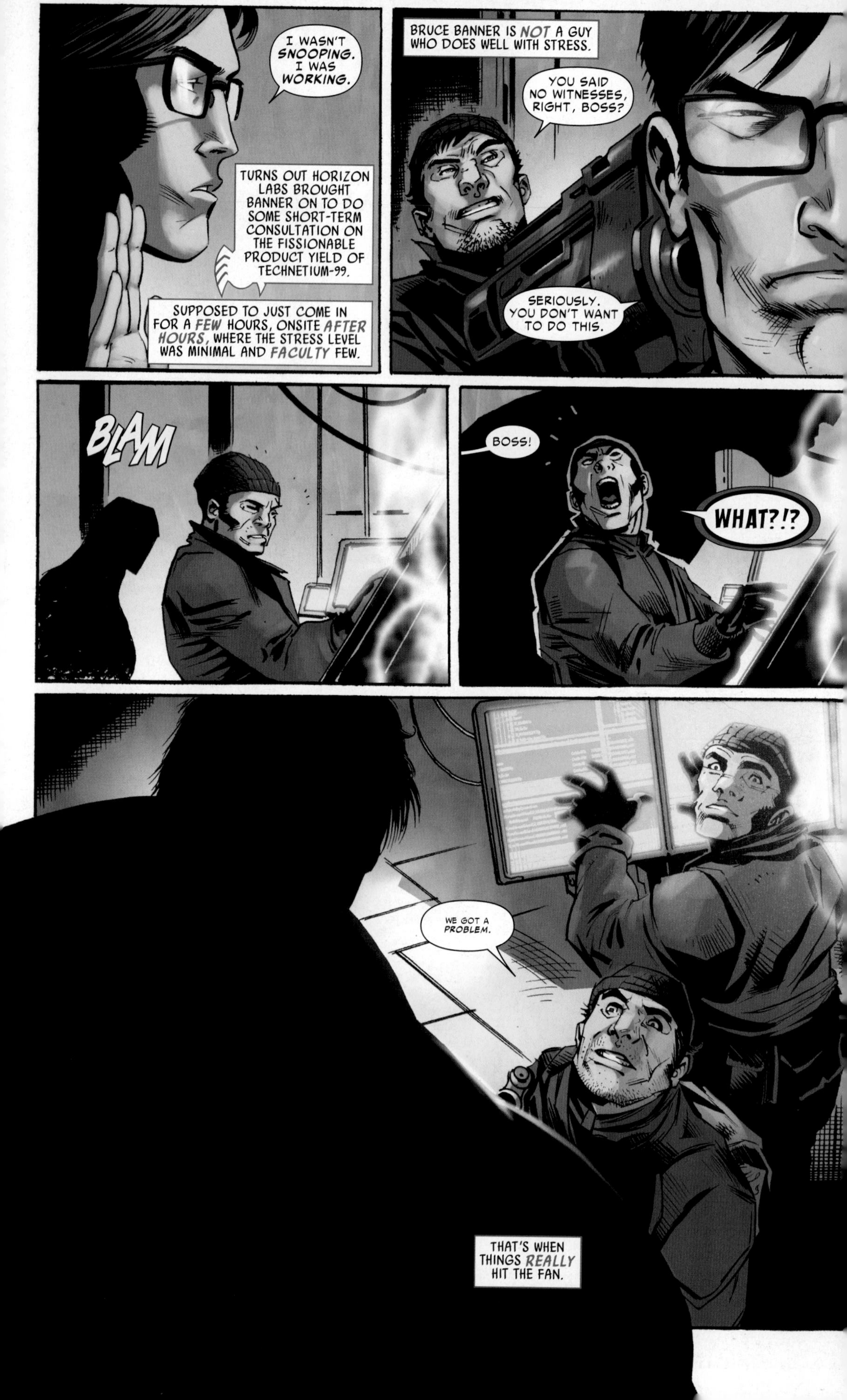
I WASN'T SNOOPING. I WAS WORKING.
TURNS OUT HORIZON LABS BROUGHT BANNER ON TO DO SOME SHORT-TERM CONSULTATION ON THE FISSIONABLE PRODUCT YIELD OF TECHNETIUM-99.
SUPPOSED TO JUST COME IN FOR A FEW HOURS, ONSITE AFTER HOURS, WHERE THE STRESS LEVEL WAS MINIMAL AND FACULTY FEW.
BRUCE BANNER IS NOT A GUY WHO DOES WELL WITH STRESS.
YOU SAID NO WITNESSES, RIGHT, BOSS?
SERIOUSLY. YOU DON'T WANT TO DO THIS.
BLAM
BOSS!
WHAT?!?
WE GOT A PROBLEM.
THAT'S WHEN THINGS REALLY HIT THE FAN.

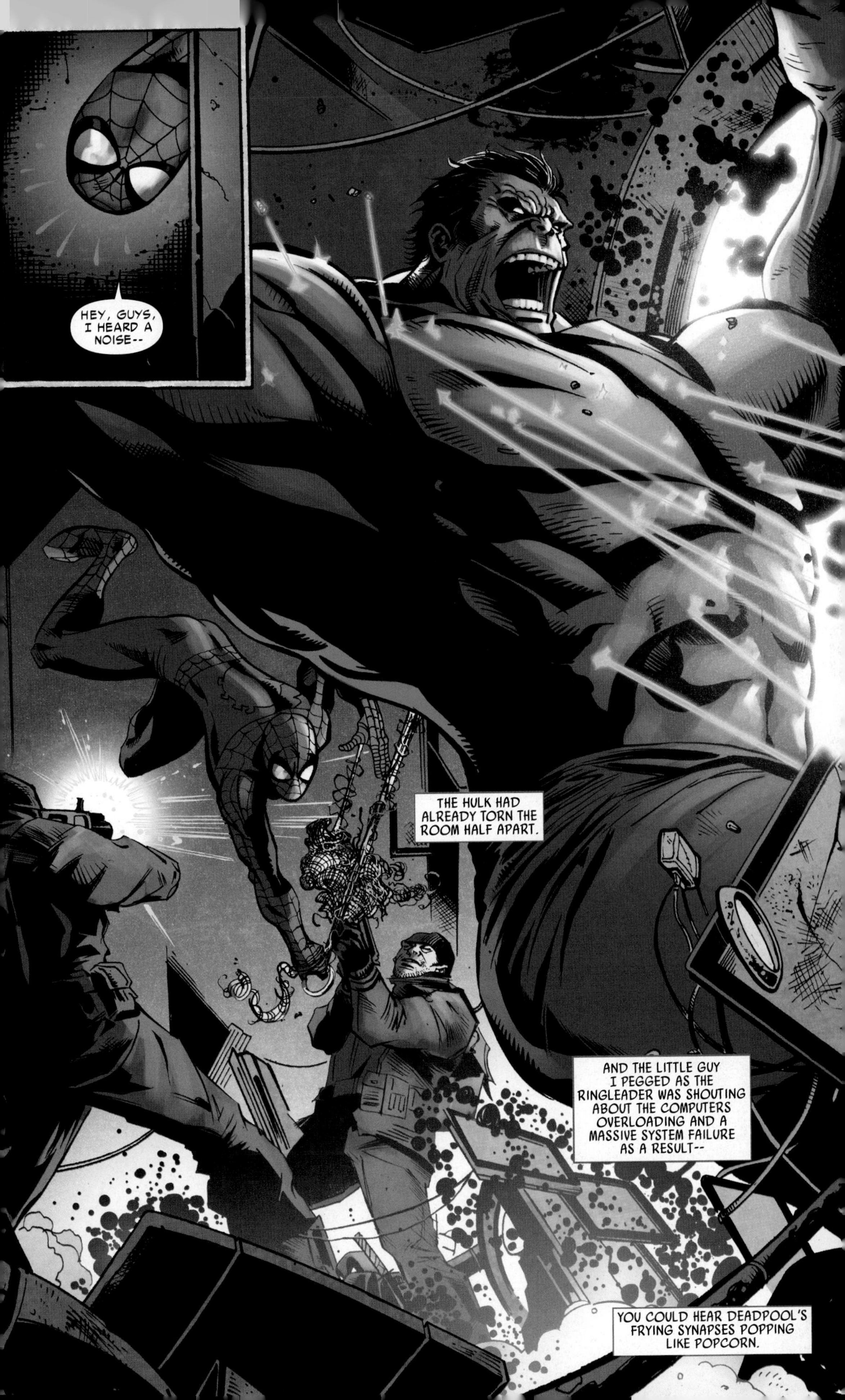
HEY, GUYS, I HEARD A NOISE--
THE HULK HAD ALREADY TORN THE ROOM HALF APART.
AND THE LITTLE GUY I PEGGED AS THE RINGLEADER WAS SHOUTING ABOUT THE COMPUTERS OVERLOADING AND A MASSIVE SYSTEM FAILURE AS A RESULT--
YOU COULD HEAR DEADPOOL'S FRYING SYNAPSES POPPING LIKE POPCORN.

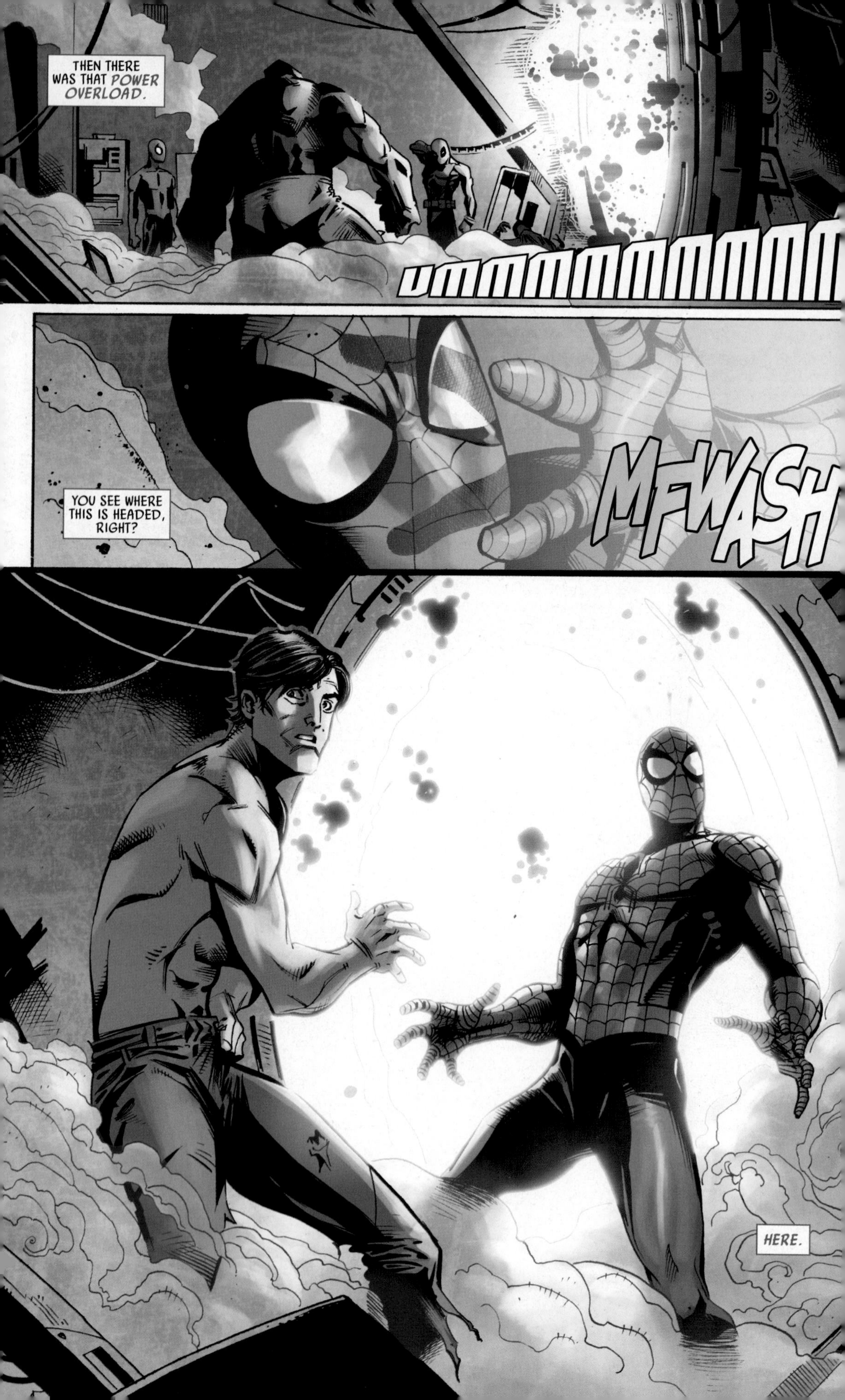
THEN THERE WAS THAT POWER OVERLOAD.
UMMMMMMMMMMM
YOU SEE WHERE THIS IS HEADED, RIGHT?
MFWASH
HERE.

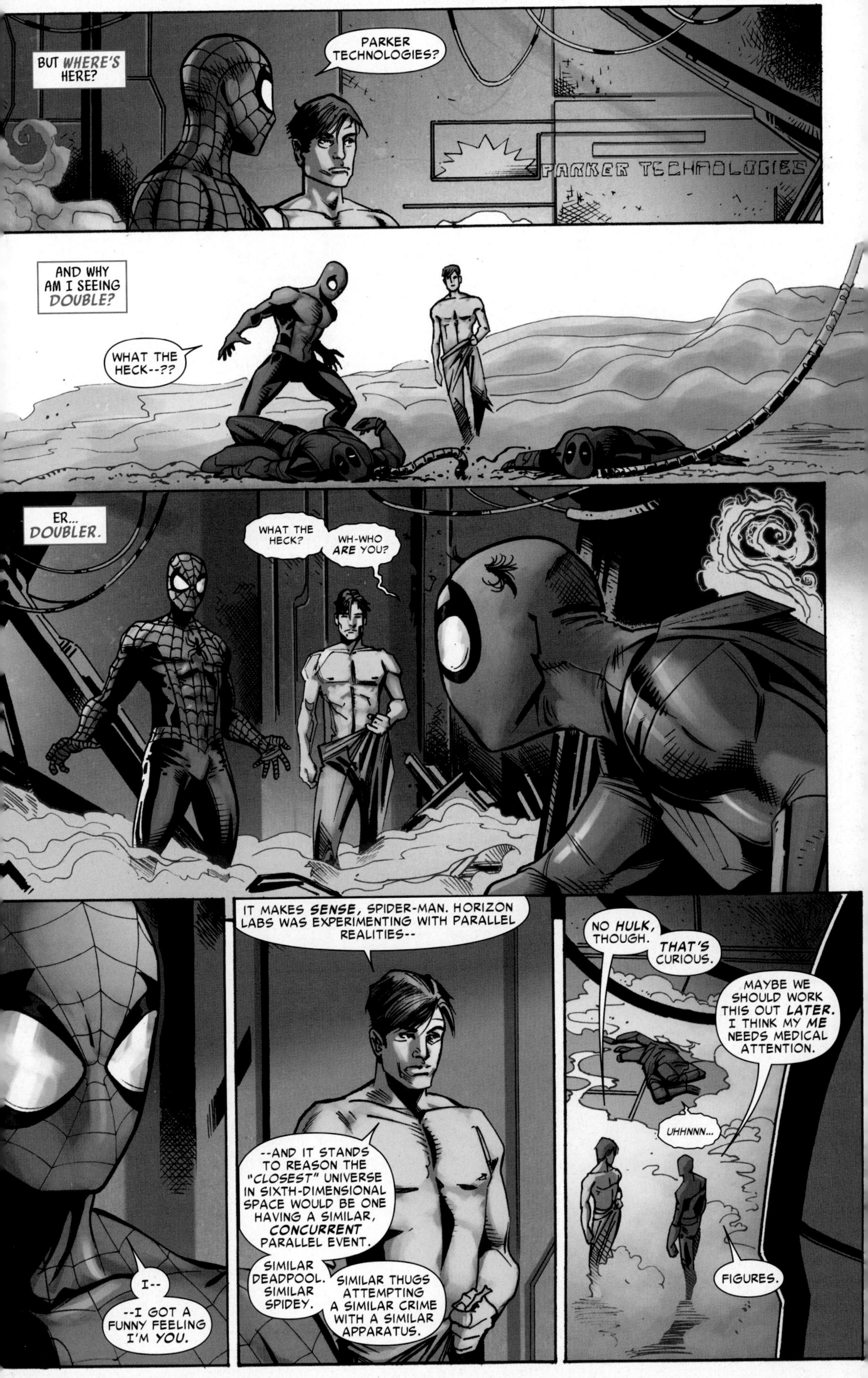
BUT WHERE'S HERE?
PARKER TECHNOLOGIES?
PARKER TECHNOLOGIES
AND WHY AM I SEEING DOUBLE?
WHAT THE HECK--??
ER... DOUBLER.
WHAT THE HECK?
WH-WHO ARE YOU?
IT MAKES SENSE, SPIDER-MAN. HORIZON LABS WAS EXPERIMENTING WITH PARALLEL REALITIES--
--AND IT STANDS TO REASON THE "CLOSEST" UNIVERSE IN SIXTH-DIMENSIONAL SPACE WOULD BE ONE HAVING A SIMILAR, CONCURRENT PARALLEL EVENT.
SIMILAR DEADPOOL. SIMILAR SPIDEY.
SIMILAR THUGS ATTEMPTING A SIMILAR CRIME WITH A SIMILAR APPARATUS.
I--
--I GOT A FUNNY FEELING I'M YOU.
NO HULK, THOUGH.
THAT'S CURIOUS.
MAYBE WE SHOULD WORK THIS OUT LATER. I THINK MY ME NEEDS MEDICAL ATTENTION.
UHHNNN...
FIGURES.

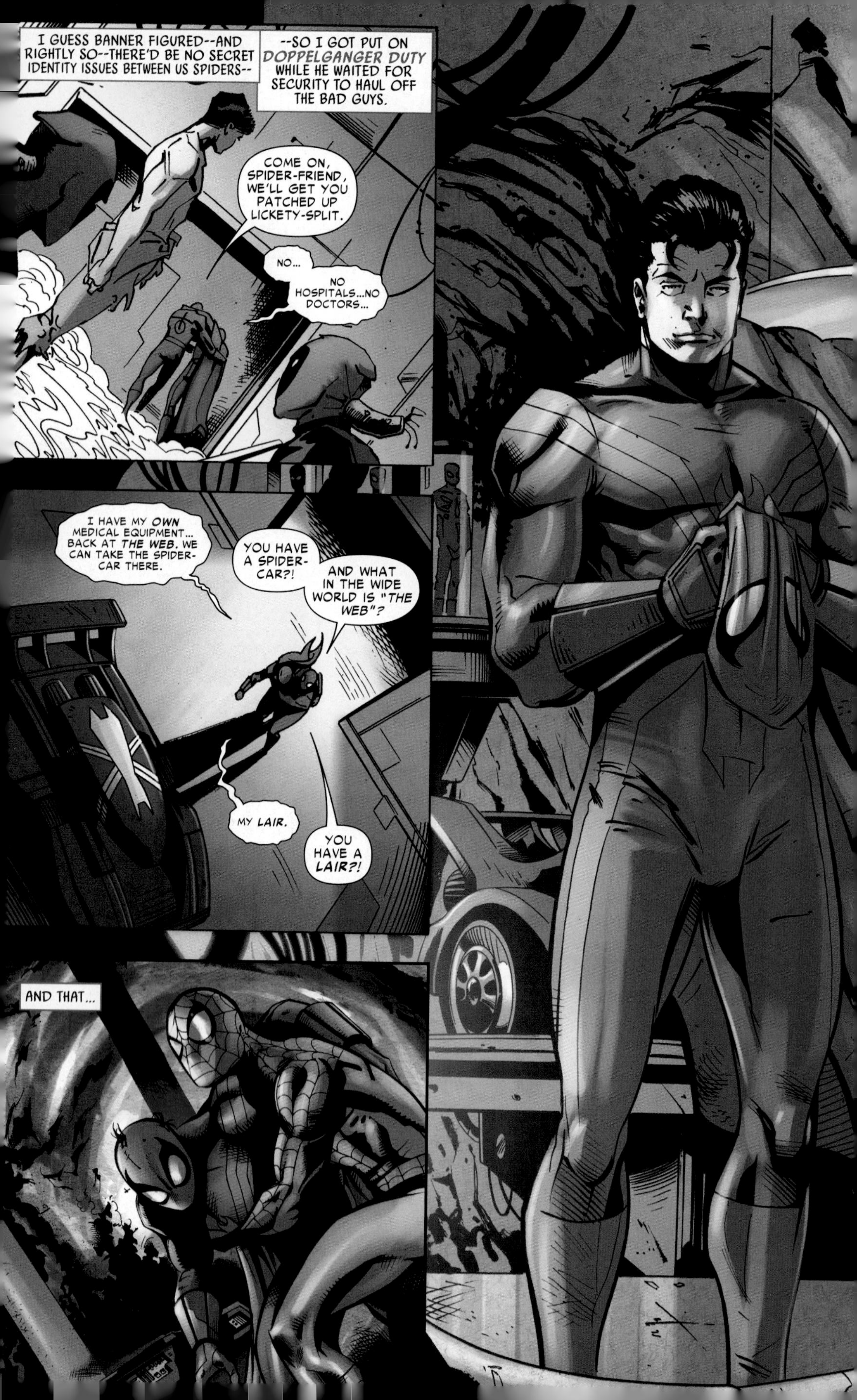
I GUESS BANNER FIGURED--AND RIGHTLY SO--THERE'D BE NO SECRET IDENTITY ISSUES BETWEEN US SPIDERS--
--SO I GOT PUT ON DOPPELGANGER DUTY WHILE HE WAITED FOR SECURITY TO HAUL OFF THE BAD GUYS.
COME ON, SPIDER-FRIEND, WE'LL GET YOU PATCHED UP LICKETY-SPLIT.
NO...
NO HOSPITALS...NO DOCTORS...
I HAVE MY OWN MEDICAL EQUIPMENT... BACK AT THE WEB. WE CAN TAKE THE SPIDER-CAR THERE.
YOU HAVE A SPIDER-CAR?!
AND WHAT IN THE WIDE WORLD IS "THE WEB"?
MY LAIR.
YOU HAVE A LAIR?!
AND THAT...

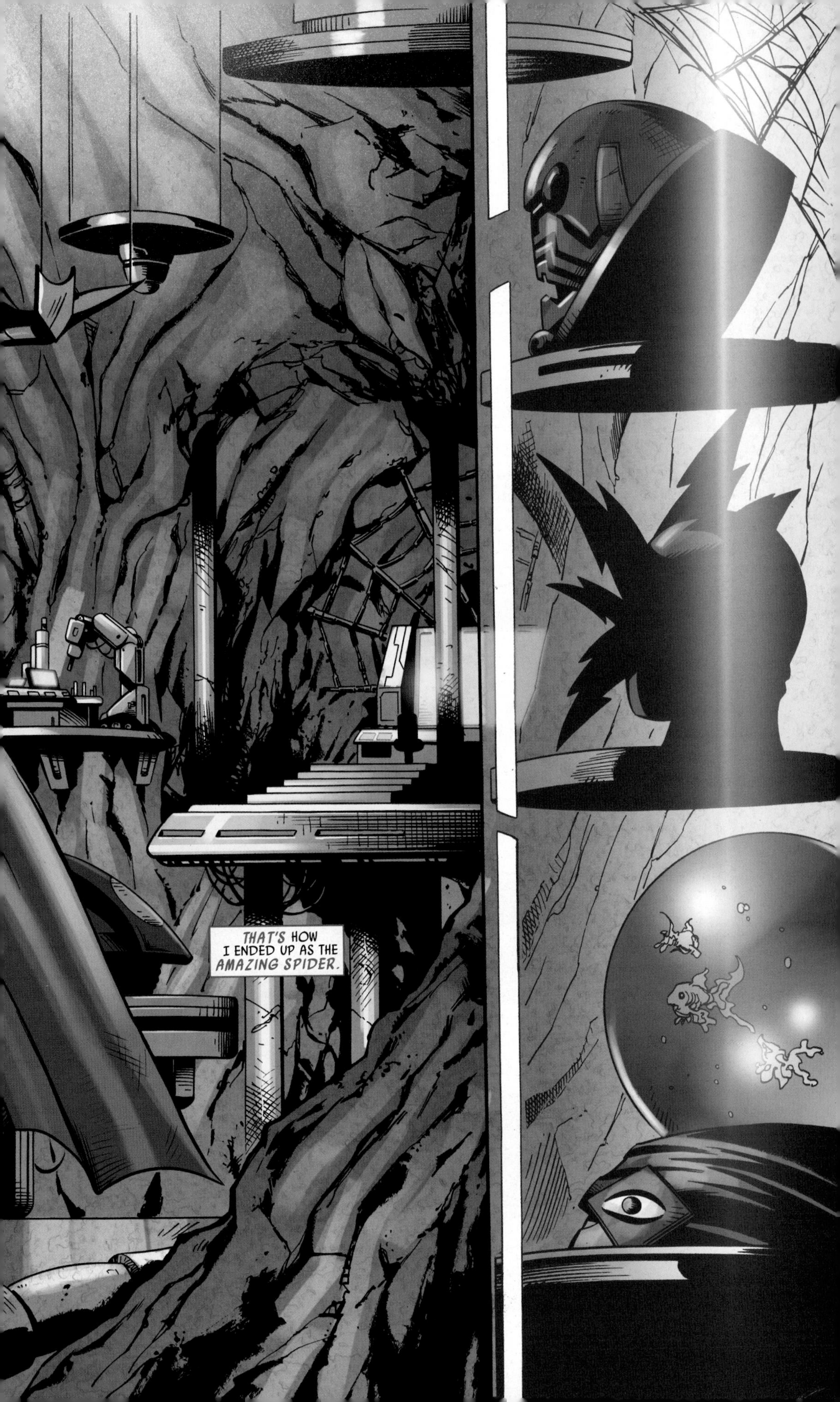
THAT'S HOW I ENDED UP AS THE AMAZING SPIDER.

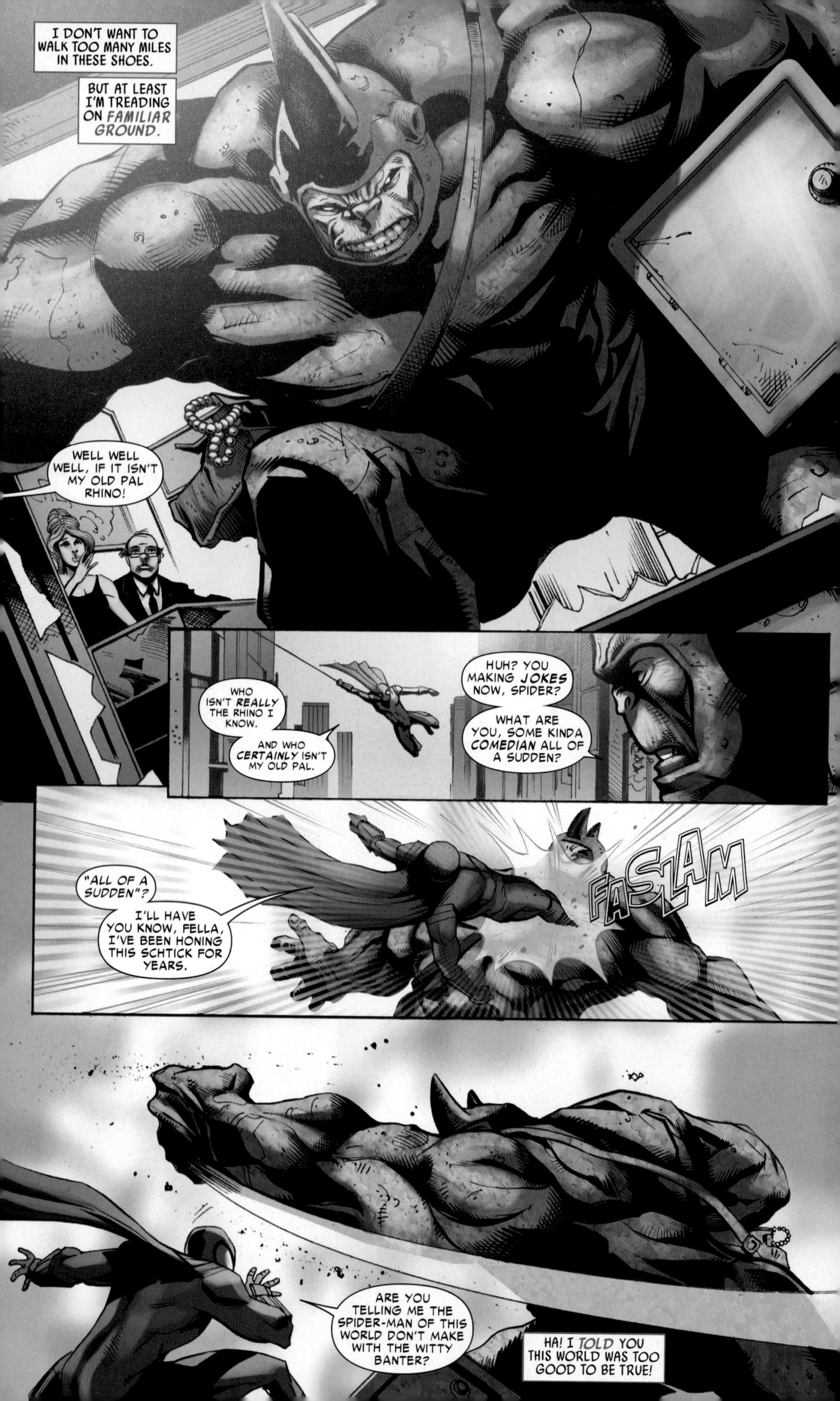

I DON'T WANT TO WALK TOO MANY MILES IN THESE SHOES.
BUT AT LEAST I'M TREADING ON FAMILIAR GROUND.
WELL WELL WELL, IF IT ISN'T MY OLD PAL RHINO!
WHO ISN'T REALLY THE RHINO I KNOW.
AND WHO CERTAINLY ISN'T MY OLD PAL.
HUH? YOU MAKING JOKES NOW, SPIDER?
WHAT ARE YOU, SOME KINDA COMEDIAN ALL OF A SUDDEN?
"ALL OF A SUDDEN"?
I'LL HAVE YOU KNOW, FELLA, I'VE BEEN HONING THIS SCHTICK FOR YEARS.
FASLAM
ARE YOU TELLING ME THE SPIDER-MAN OF THIS WORLD DON'T MAKE WITH THE WITTY BANTER?
HA! I TOLD YOU THIS WORLD WAS TOO GOOD TO BE TRUE!

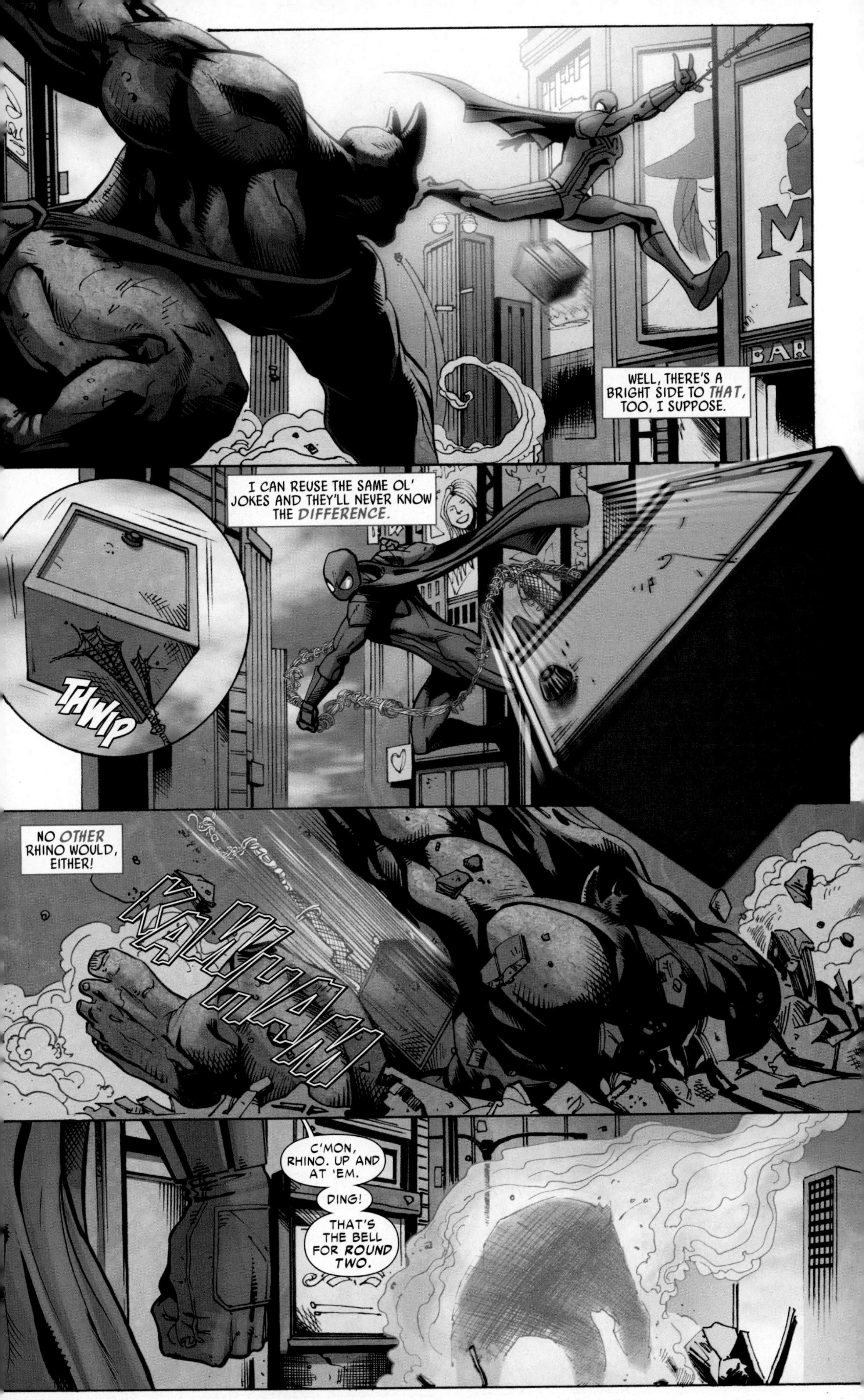
WELL, THERE'S A BRIGHT SIDE TO THAT, TOO, I SUPPOSE.
I CAN REUSE THE SAME OL' JOKES AND THEY'LL NEVER KNOW THE DIFFERENCE.
THWIP
NO OTHER RHINO WOULD, EITHER!
KA-WHAM
C'MON, RHINO. UP AND AT 'EM.
DING!
THAT'S THE BELL FOR ROUND TWO.

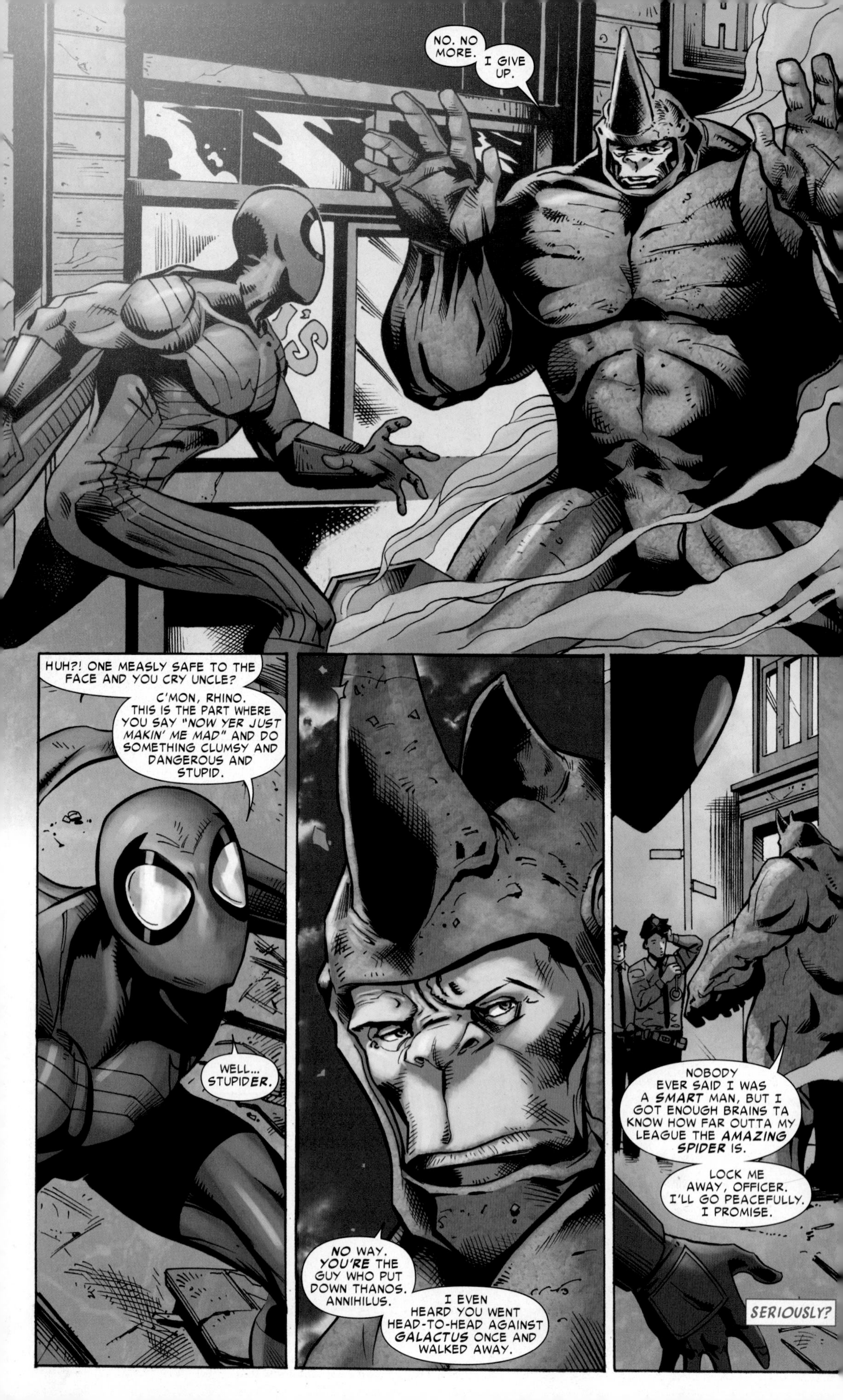
NO. NO MORE.
I GIVE UP.
HUH?! ONE MEASLY SAFE TO THE FACE AND YOU CRY UNCLE?
C'MON, RHINO. THIS IS THE PART WHERE YOU SAY "NOW YER JUST MAKIN' ME MAD" AND DO SOMETHING CLUMSY AND DANGEROUS AND STUPID.
WELL... STUPIDER.
NO WAY. YOU'RE THE GUY WHO PUT DOWN THANOS. ANNIHILUS.
I EVEN HEARD YOU WENT HEAD-TO-HEAD AGAINST GALACTUS ONCE AND WALKED AWAY.
NOBODY EVER SAID I WAS A SMART MAN, BUT I GOT ENOUGH BRAINS TA KNOW HOW FAR OUTTA MY LEAGUE THE AMAZING SPIDER IS.
LOCK ME AWAY, OFFICER. I'LL GO PEACEFULLY. I PROMISE.
SERIOUSLY?

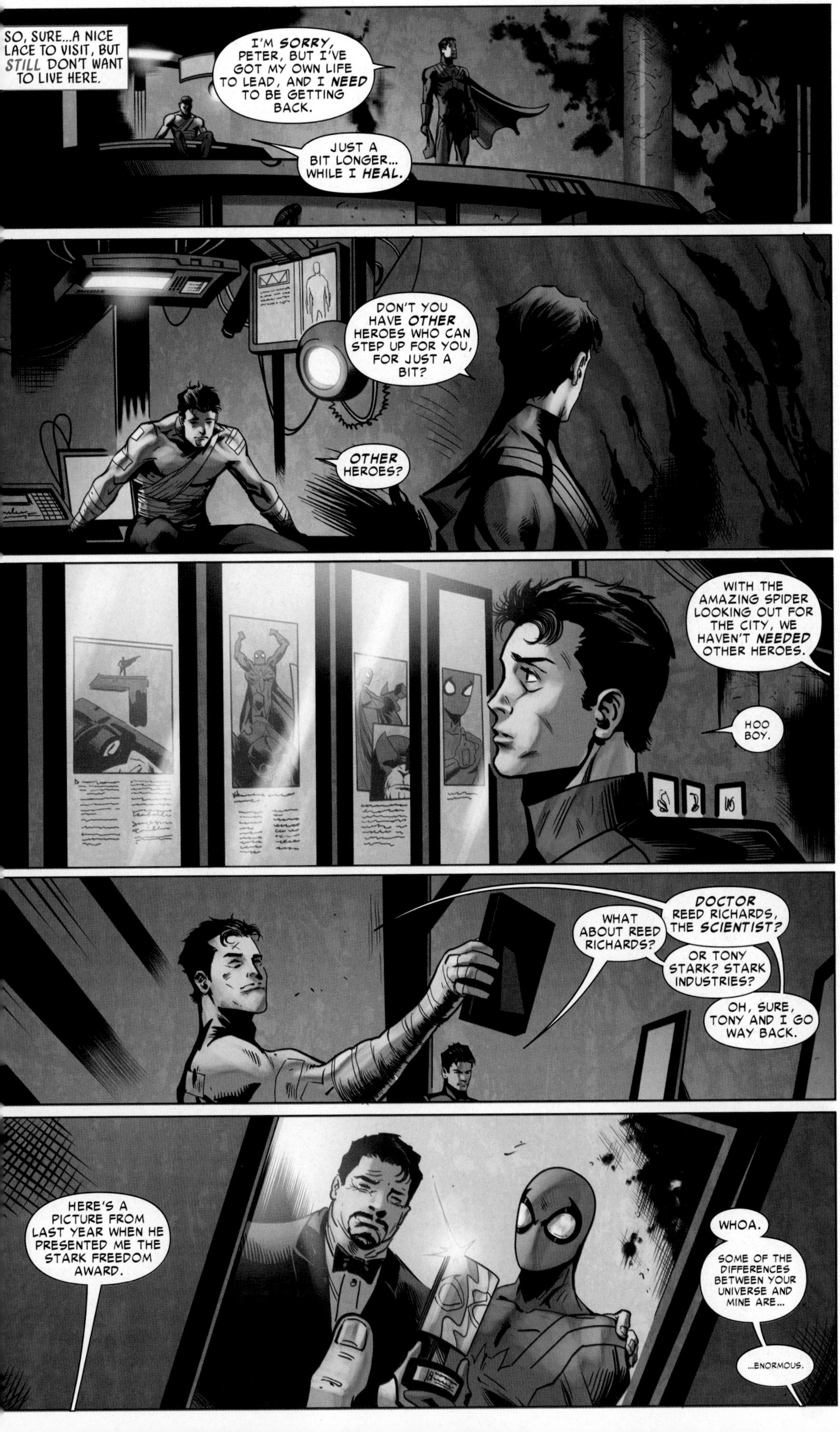

SO, SURE...A NICE LACE TO VISIT, BUT STILL DON'T WANT TO LIVE HERE.
I'M SORRY, PETER, BUT I'VE GOT MY OWN LIFE TO LEAD, AND I NEED TO BE GETTING BACK.
JUST A BIT LONGER... WHILE I HEAL.
DON'T YOU HAVE OTHER HEROES WHO CAN STEP UP FOR YOU, FOR JUST A BIT?
OTHER HEROES?
WITH THE AMAZING SPIDER LOOKING OUT FOR THE CITY, WE HAVEN'T NEEDED OTHER HEROES.
HOO BOY.
WHAT ABOUT REED RICHARDS?
DOCTOR REED RICHARDS, THE SCIENTIST?
OR TONY STARK? STARK INDUSTRIES?
OH, SURE, TONY AND I GO WAY BACK.
HERE'S A PICTURE FROM LAST YEAR WHEN HE PRESENTED ME THE STARK FREEDOM AWARD.
WHOA.
SOME OF THE DIFFERENCES BETWEEN YOUR UNIVERSE AND MINE ARE...
...ENORMOUS.

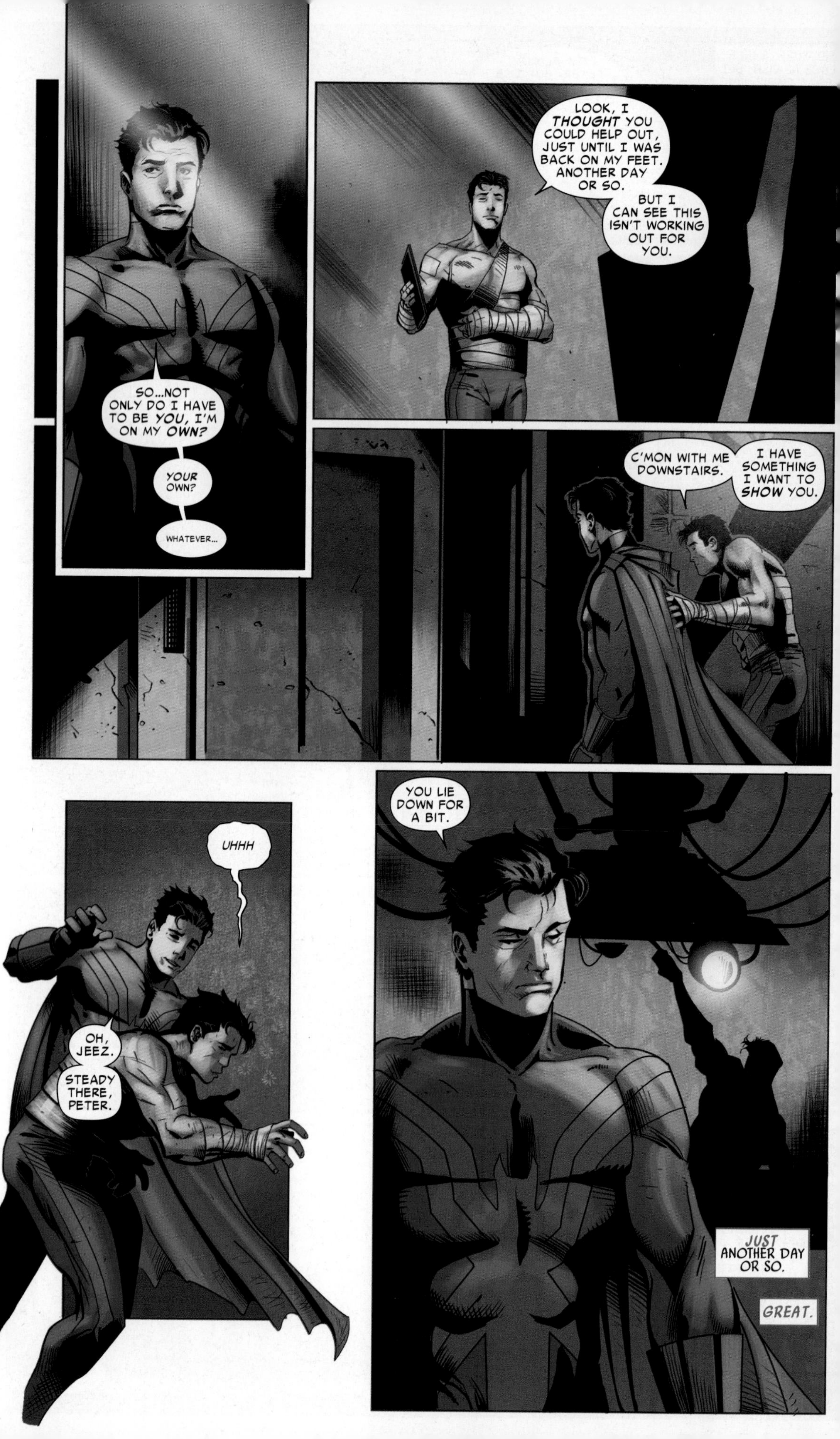
SO...NOT ONLY DO I HAVE TO BE YOU, I'M ON MY OWN?
YOUR OWN?
WHATEVER...
LOOK, I THOUGHT YOU COULD HELP OUT, JUST UNTIL I WAS BACK ON MY FEET. ANOTHER DAY OR SO.
BUT I CAN SEE THIS ISN'T WORKING OUT FOR YOU.
C'MON WITH ME DOWNSTAIRS.
I HAVE SOMETHING I WANT TO SHOW YOU.
UHHH
OH, JEEZ.
STEADY THERE, PETER.
YOU LIE DOWN FOR A BIT.
JUST ANOTHER DAY OR SO.
GREAT.

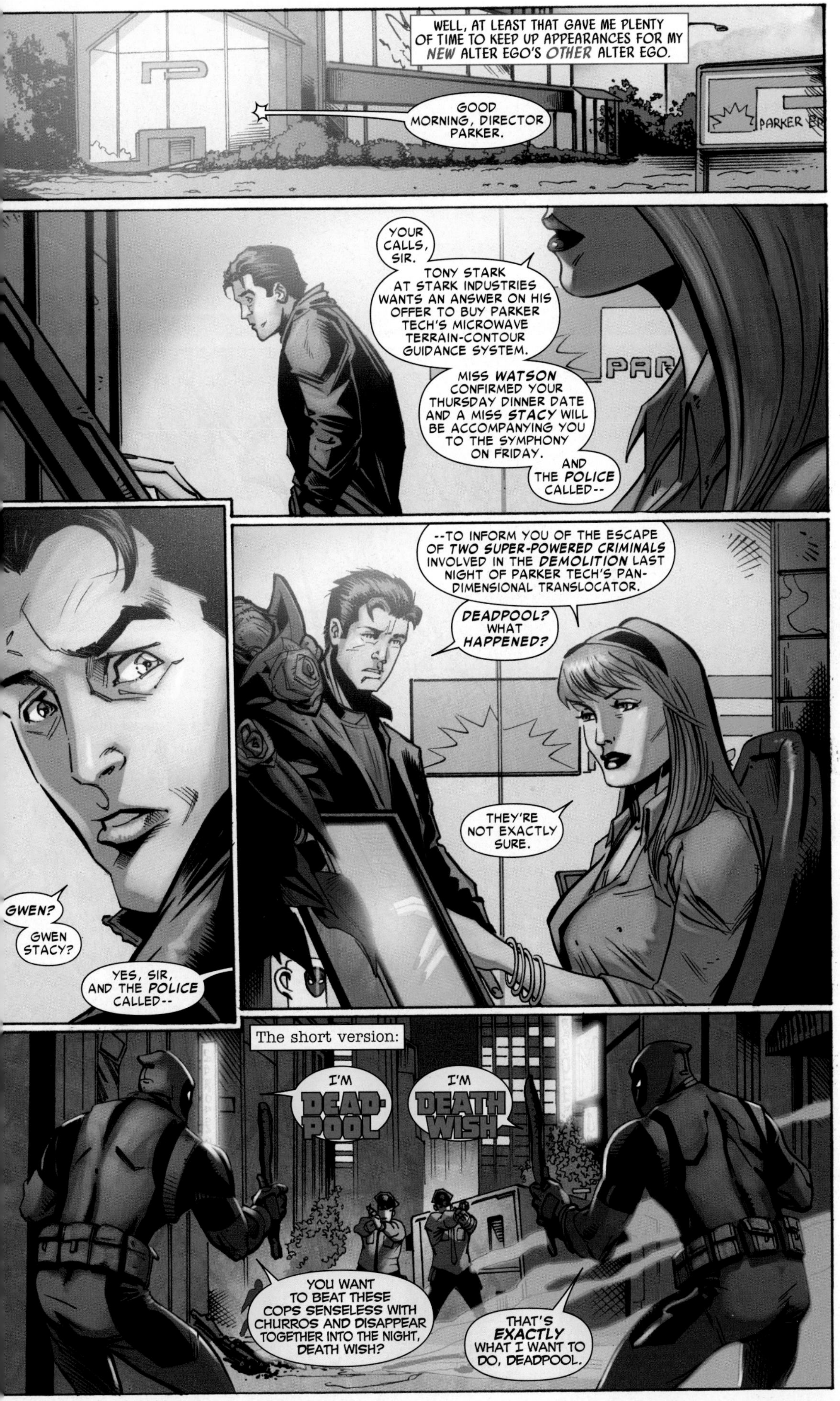

WELL, AT LEAST THAT GAVE ME PLENTY OF TIME TO KEEP UP APPEARANCES FOR MY NEW ALTER EGO'S OTHER ALTER EGO.
GOOD MORNING, DIRECTOR PARKER.
PARKER
YOUR CALLS, SIR.
TONY STARK AT STARK INDUSTRIES WANTS AN ANSWER ON HIS OFFER TO BUY PARKER TECH'S MICROWAVE TERRAIN-CONTOUR GUIDANCE SYSTEM.
MISS WATSON CONFIRMED YOUR THURSDAY DINNER DATE AND A MISS STACY WILL BE ACCOMPANYING YOU TO THE SYMPHONY ON FRIDAY.
AND THE POLICE CALLED--
GWEN?
GWEN STACY?
YES, SIR, AND THE POLICE CALLED--
--TO INFORM YOU OF THE ESCAPE OF TWO SUPER-POWERED CRIMINALS INVOLVED IN THE DEMOLITION LAST NIGHT OF PARKER TECH'S PAN-DIMENSIONAL TRANSLOCATOR.
DEADPOOL? WHAT HAPPENED?
THEY'RE NOT EXACTLY SURE.
The short version:
I'M DEAD-POOL
I'M DEATH WISH
YOU WANT TO BEAT THESE COPS SENSELESS WITH CHURROS AND DISAPPEAR TOGETHER INTO THE NIGHT, DEATH WISH?
THAT'S EXACTLY WHAT I WANT TO DO, DEADPOOL.

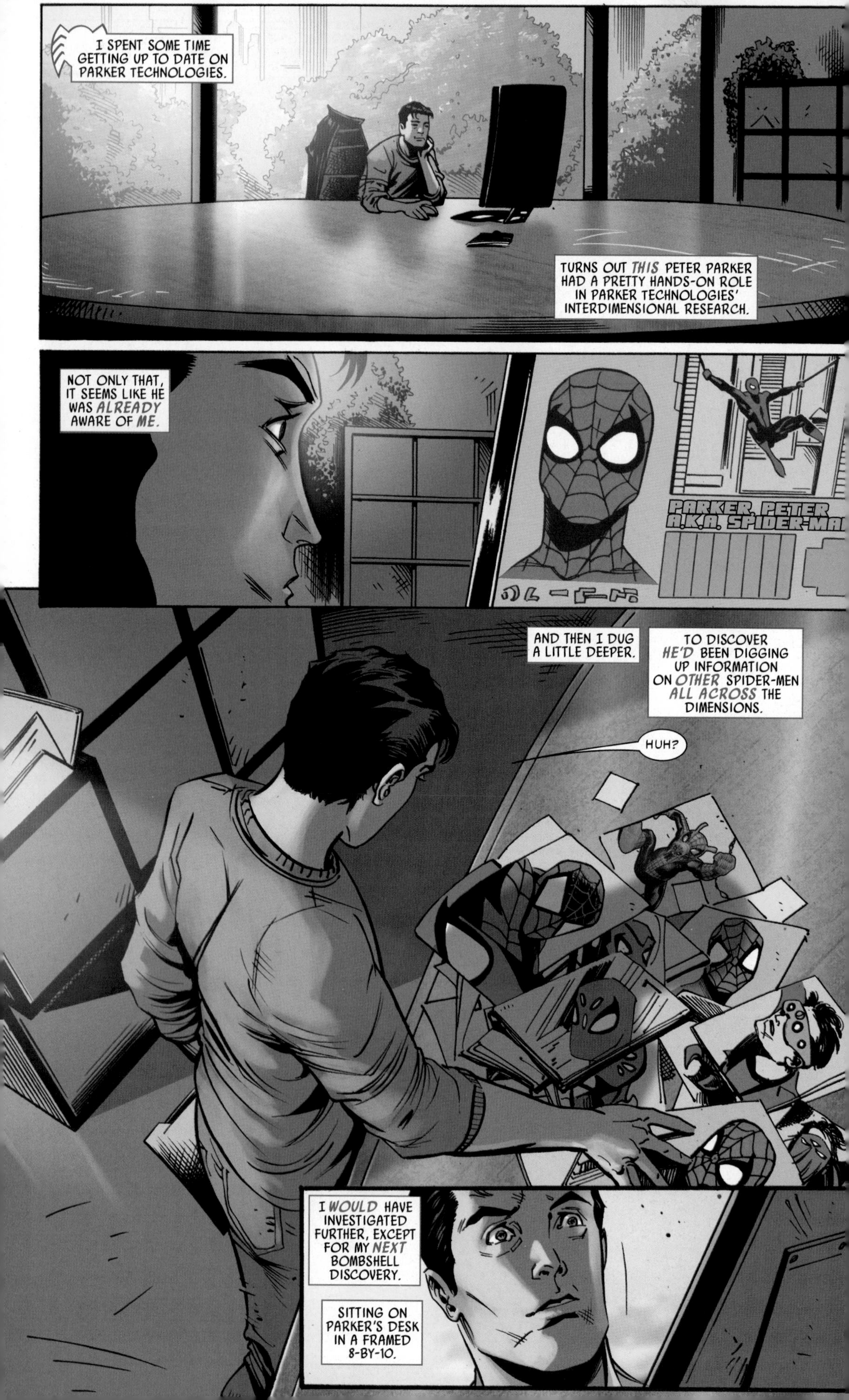

I SPENT SOME TIME GETTING UP TO DATE ON PARKER TECHNOLOGIES.
TURNS OUT THIS PETER PARKER HAD A PRETTY HANDS-ON ROLE IN PARKER TECHNOLOGIES' INTERDIMENSIONAL RESEARCH.
NOT ONLY THAT, IT SEEMS LIKE HE WAS ALREADY AWARE OF ME.
PARKER, PETER
AND THEN I DUG A LITTLE DEEPER.
TO DISCOVER HE'D BEEN DIGGING UP INFORMATION ON OTHER SPIDER-MEN ALL ACROSS THE DIMENSIONS.
HUH?
I WOULD HAVE INVESTIGATED FURTHER, EXCEPT FOR MY NEXT BOMBSHELL DISCOVERY.
SITTING ON PARKER'S DESK IN A FRAMED 8-BY-10.

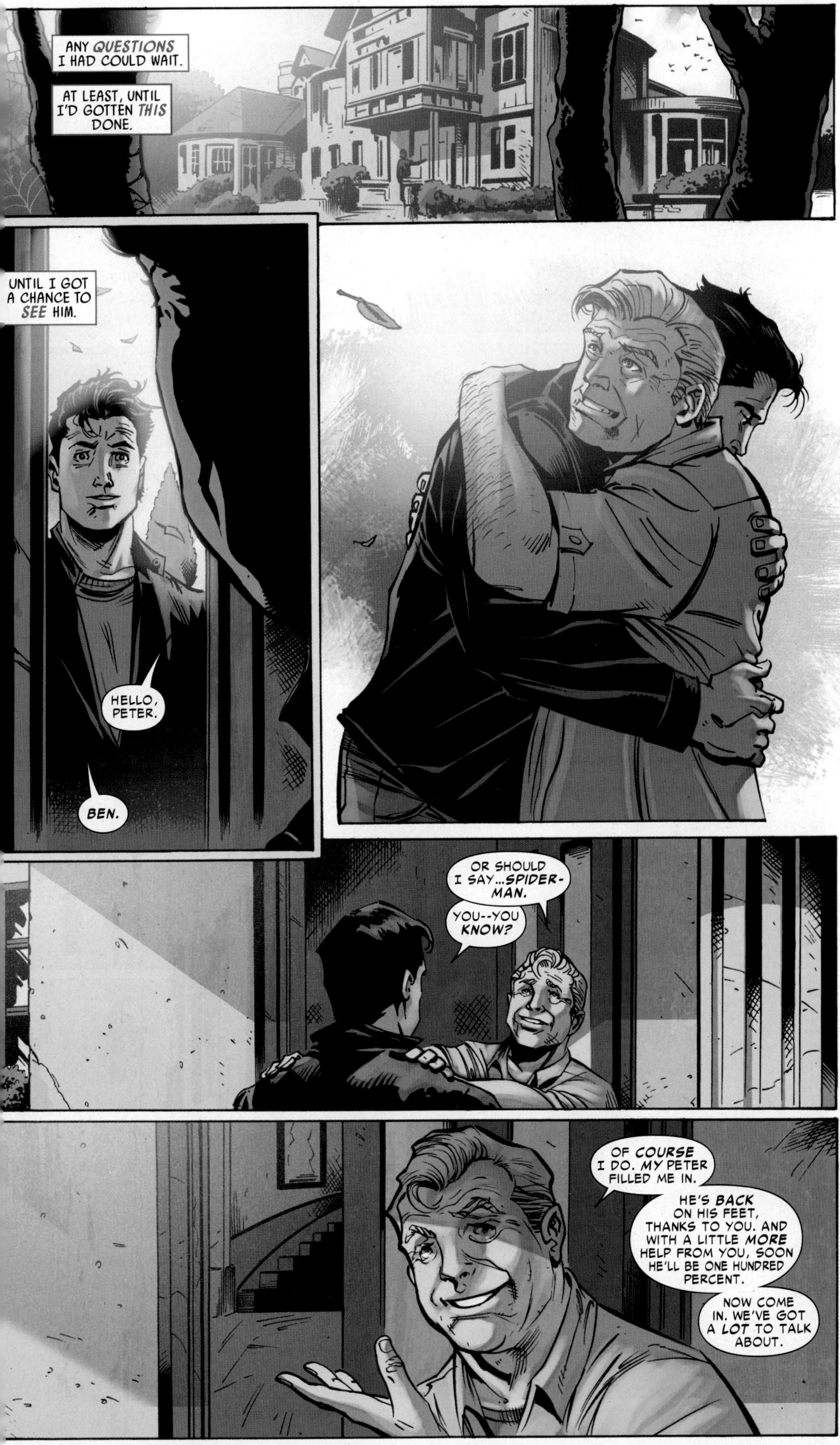
ANY QUESTIONS I HAD COULD WAIT.
AT LEAST, UNTIL I'D GOTTEN THIS DONE.
UNTIL I GOT A CHANCE TO SEE HIM.
HELLO, PETER.
BEN.
OR SHOULD I SAY...SPIDER-MAN.
YOU--YOU KNOW?
OF COURSE I DO. MY PETER FILLED ME IN.
HE'S BACK ON HIS FEET, THANKS TO YOU. AND WITH A LITTLE MORE HELP FROM YOU, SOON HE'LL BE ONE HUNDRED PERCENT.
NOW COME IN. WE'VE GOT A LOT TO TALK ABOUT.

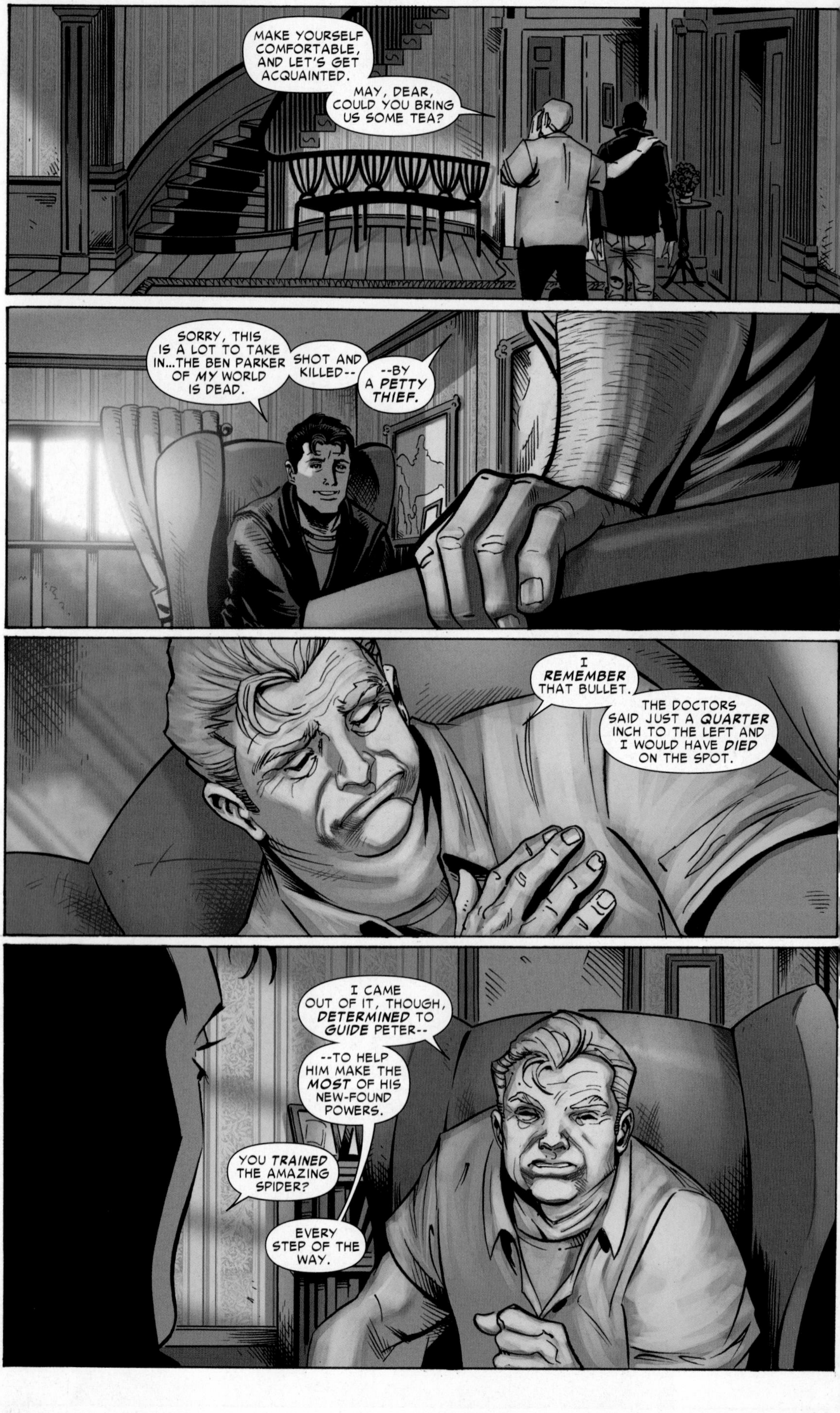
MAKE YOURSELF COMFORTABLE, AND LET'S GET ACQUAINTED.
MAY, DEAR, COULD YOU BRING US SOME TEA?
SORRY, THIS IS A LOT TO TAKE IN...THE BEN PARKER OF MY WORLD IS DEAD.
SHOT AND KILLED--
--BY A PETTY THIEF.
I REMEMBER THAT BULLET.
THE DOCTORS SAID JUST A QUARTER INCH TO THE LEFT AND I WOULD HAVE DIED ON THE SPOT.
I CAME OUT OF IT, THOUGH, DETERMINED TO GUIDE PETER--
--TO HELP HIM MAKE THE MOST OF HIS NEW-FOUND POWERS.
YOU TRAINED THE AMAZING SPIDER?
EVERY STEP OF THE WAY.

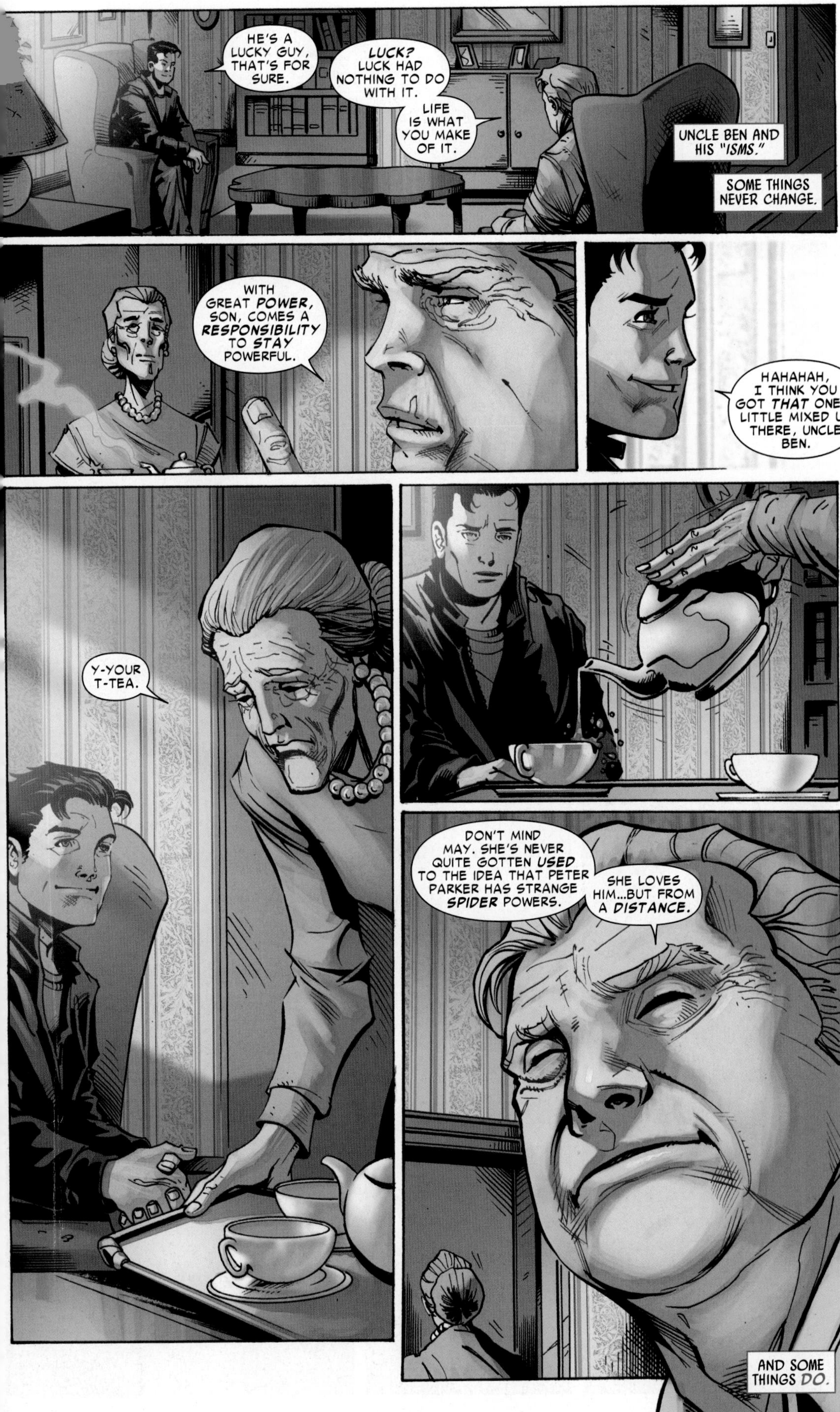
HE'S A LUCKY GUY, THAT'S FOR SURE.
LUCK? LUCK HAD NOTHING TO DO WITH IT.
LIFE IS WHAT YOU MAKE OF IT.
UNCLE BEN AND HIS "ISMS."
SOME THINGS NEVER CHANGE.
WITH GREAT POWER, SON, COMES A RESPONSIBILITY TO STAY POWERFUL.
HAHAHAH, I THINK YOU GOT THAT ONE A LITTLE MIXED UP THERE, UNCLE BEN.
Y-YOUR T-TEA.
DON'T MIND MAY. SHE'S NEVER QUITE GOTTEN USED TO THE IDEA THAT PETER PARKER HAS STRANGE SPIDER POWERS.
SHE LOVES HIM...BUT FROM A DISTANCE.
AND SOME THINGS DO.

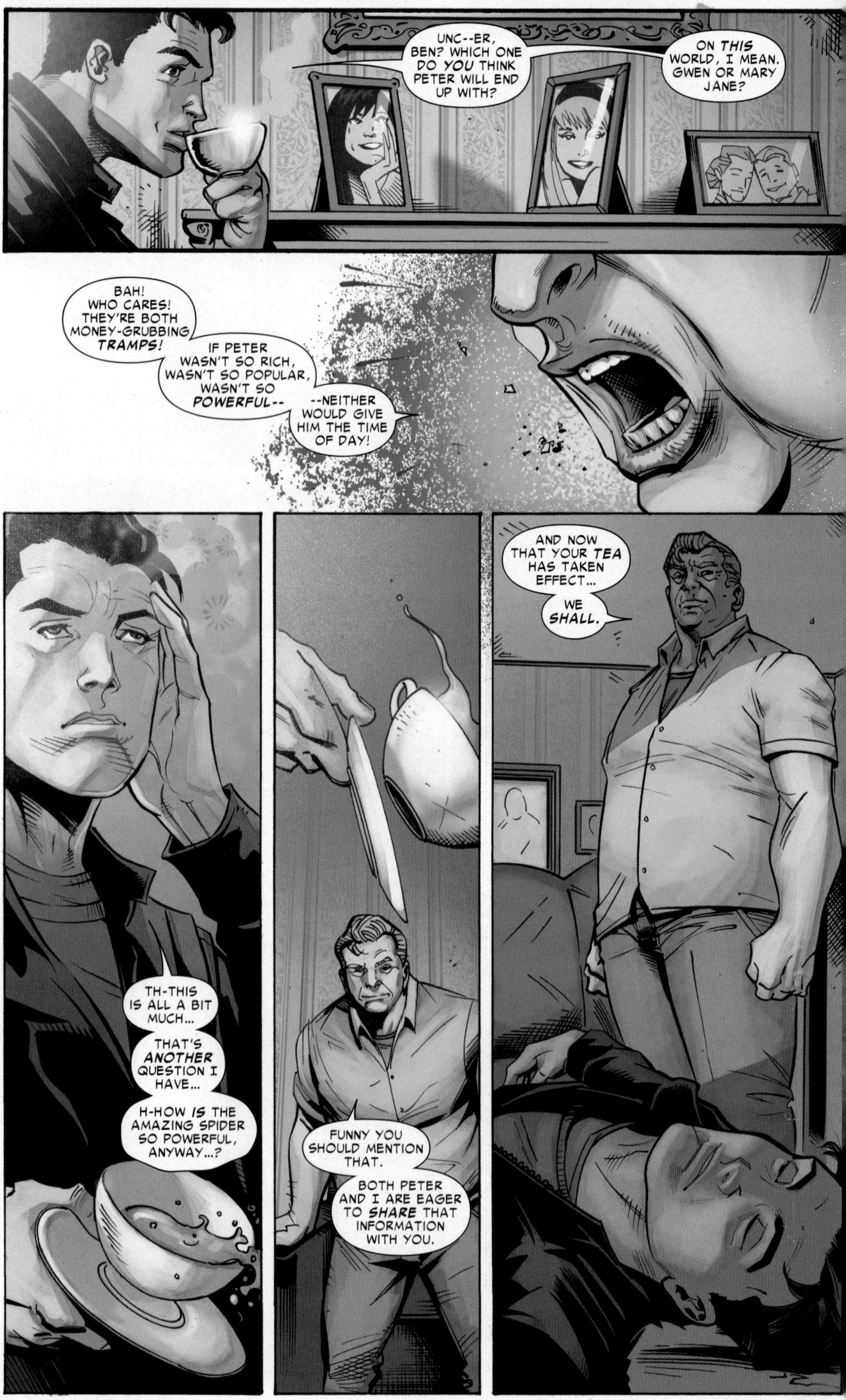
UNC--ER, BEN? WHICH ONE DO YOU THINK PETER WILL END UP WITH?
ON THIS WORLD, I MEAN. GWEN OR MARY JANE?
BAH! WHO CARES! THEY'RE BOTH MONEY-GRUBBING TRAMPS!
IF PETER WASN'T SO RICH, WASN'T SO POPULAR, WASN'T SO POWERFUL--
--NEITHER WOULD GIVE HIM THE TIME OF DAY!
TH-THIS IS ALL A BIT MUCH...
THAT'S ANOTHER QUESTION I HAVE...
H-HOW IS THE AMAZING SPIDER SO POWERFUL, ANYWAY...?
FUNNY YOU SHOULD MENTION THAT.
BOTH PETER AND I ARE EAGER TO SHARE THAT INFORMATION WITH YOU.
AND NOW THAT YOUR TEA HAS TAKEN EFFECT...
WE SHALL.

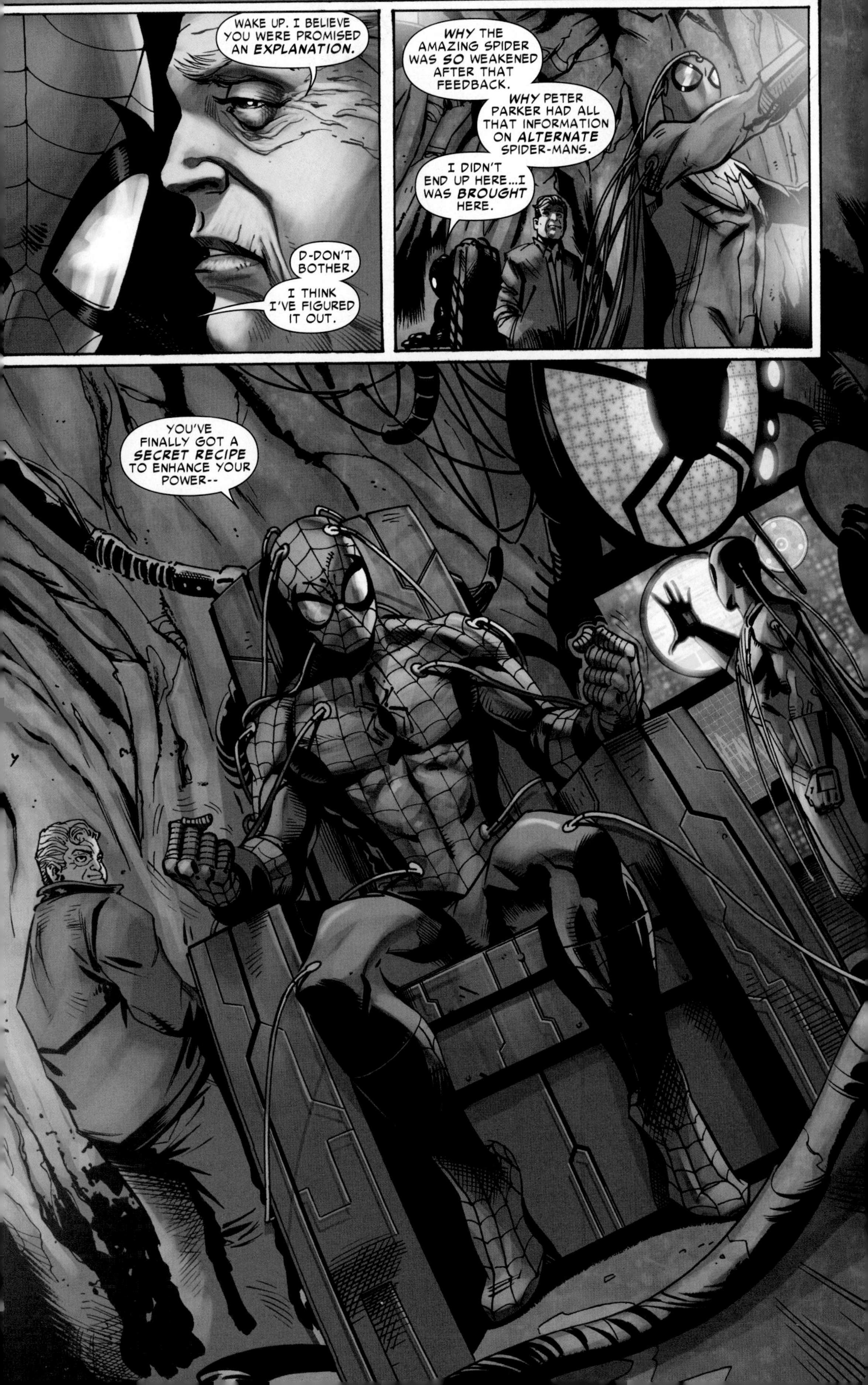
WAKE UP. I BELIEVE YOU WERE PROMISED AN EXPLANATION.
D-DON'T BOTHER.
I THINK I'VE FIGURED IT OUT.
WHY THE AMAZING SPIDER WAS SO WEAKENED AFTER THAT FEEDBACK.
WHY PETER PARKER HAD ALL THAT INFORMATION ON ALTERNATE SPIDER-MANS.
I DIDN'T END UP HERE...I WAS BROUGHT HERE.
YOU'VE FINALLY GOT A SECRET RECIPE TO ENHANCE YOUR POWER--

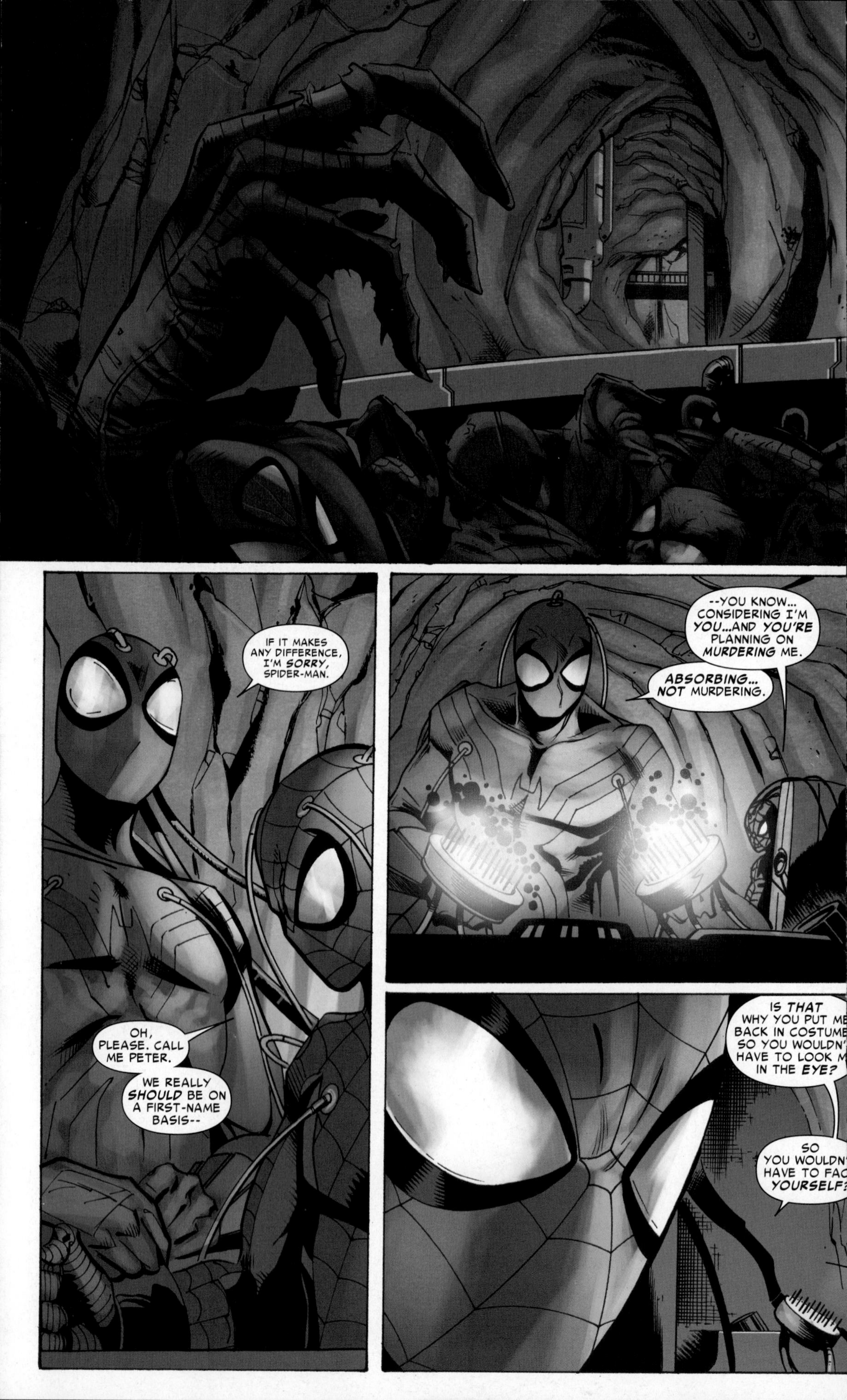
IF IT MAKES ANY DIFFERENCE, I'M SORRY, SPIDER-MAN.
--YOU KNOW... CONSIDERING I'M YOU...AND YOU'RE PLANNING ON MURDERING ME.
ABSORBING... NOT MURDERING.
OH, PLEASE. CALL ME PETER.
WE REALLY SHOULD BE ON A FIRST-NAME BASIS--
IS THAT WHY YOU PUT ME BACK IN COSTUME SO YOU WOULDN' HAVE TO LOOK M IN THE EYE?
SO YOU WOULDN HAVE TO FAC YOURSELF?

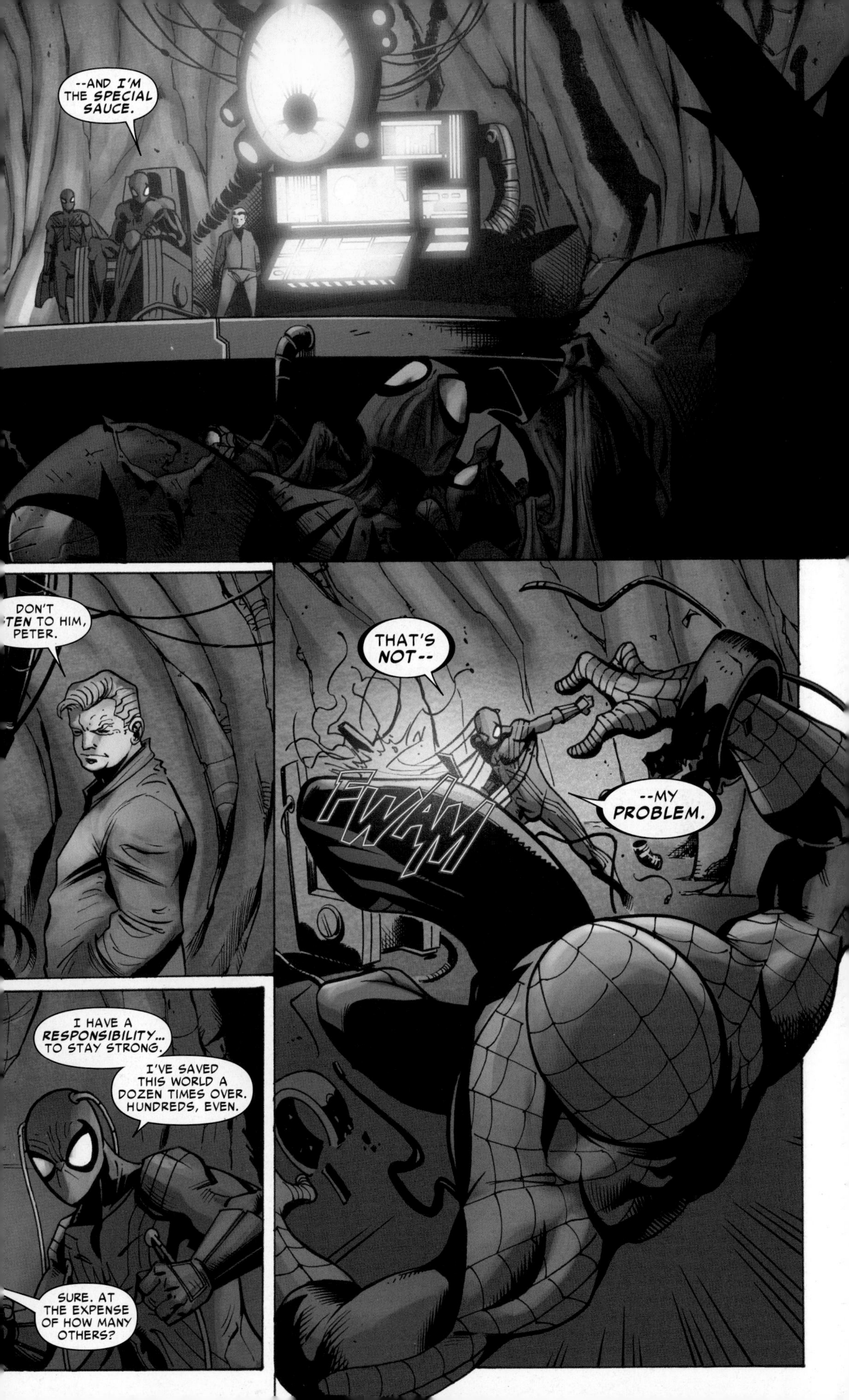
--AND I'M THE SPECIAL SAUCE.
DON'T TEN TO HIM, PETER.
I HAVE A RESPONSIBILITY... TO STAY STRONG.
I'VE SAVED THIS WORLD A DOZEN TIMES OVER. HUNDREDS, EVEN.
SURE. AT THE EXPENSE OF HOW MANY OTHERS?
THAT'S NOT--
FWAM
--MY PROBLEM.

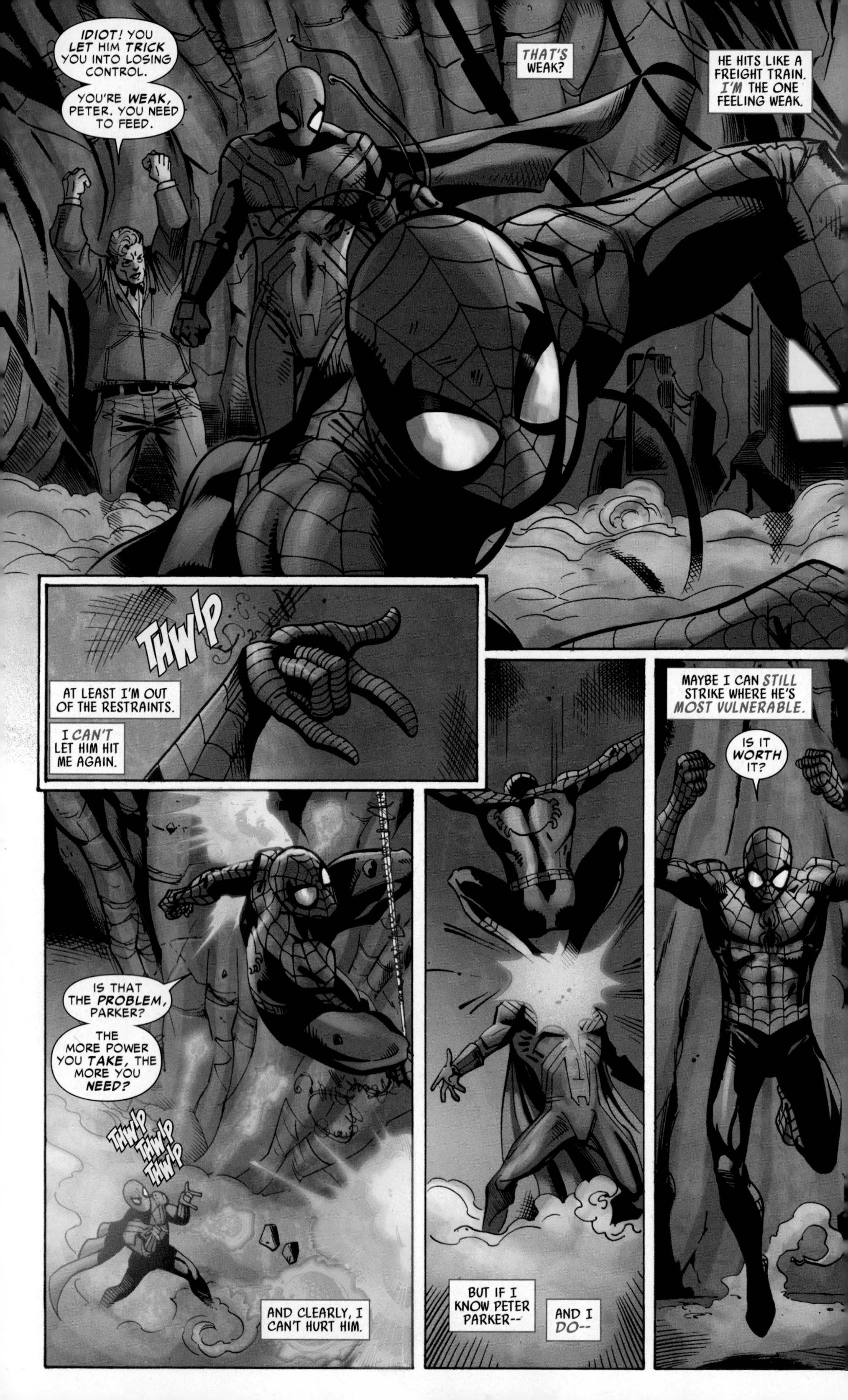
IDIOT! YOU LET HIM TRICK YOU INTO LOSING CONTROL.
YOU'RE WEAK, PETER. YOU NEED TO FEED.
THAT'S WEAK?
HE HITS LIKE A FREIGHT TRAIN. I'M THE ONE FEELING WEAK.
THWIP
AT LEAST I'M OUT OF THE RESTRAINTS.
I CAN'T LET HIM HIT ME AGAIN.
IS THAT THE PROBLEM, PARKER?
THE MORE POWER YOU TAKE, THE MORE YOU NEED?
THWIP THWIP THWIP
AND CLEARLY, I CAN'T HURT HIM.
BUT IF I KNOW PETER PARKER--
AND I DO--
MAYBE I CAN STILL STRIKE WHERE HE'S MOST VULNERABLE.
IS IT WORTH IT?

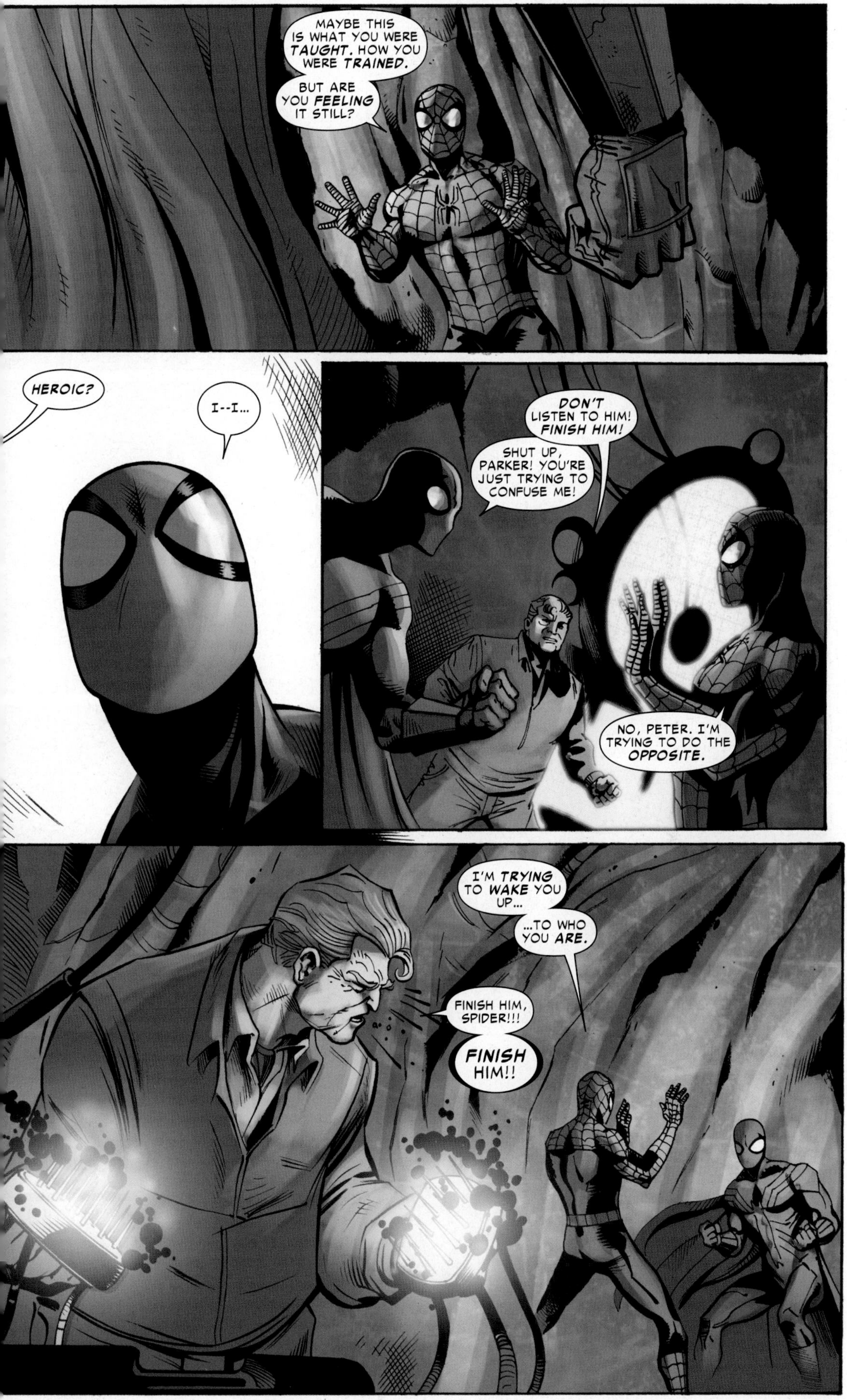

MAYBE THIS IS WHAT YOU WERE TAUGHT. HOW YOU WERE TRAINED.
BUT ARE YOU FEELING IT STILL?
HEROIC?
I--I...
DON'T LISTEN TO HIM! FINISH HIM!
SHUT UP, PARKER! YOU'RE JUST TRYING TO CONFUSE ME!
NO, PETER. I'M TRYING TO DO THE OPPOSITE.
I'M TRYING TO WAKE YOU UP...
...TO WHO YOU ARE.
FINISH HIM, SPIDER!!!
FINISH HIM!!

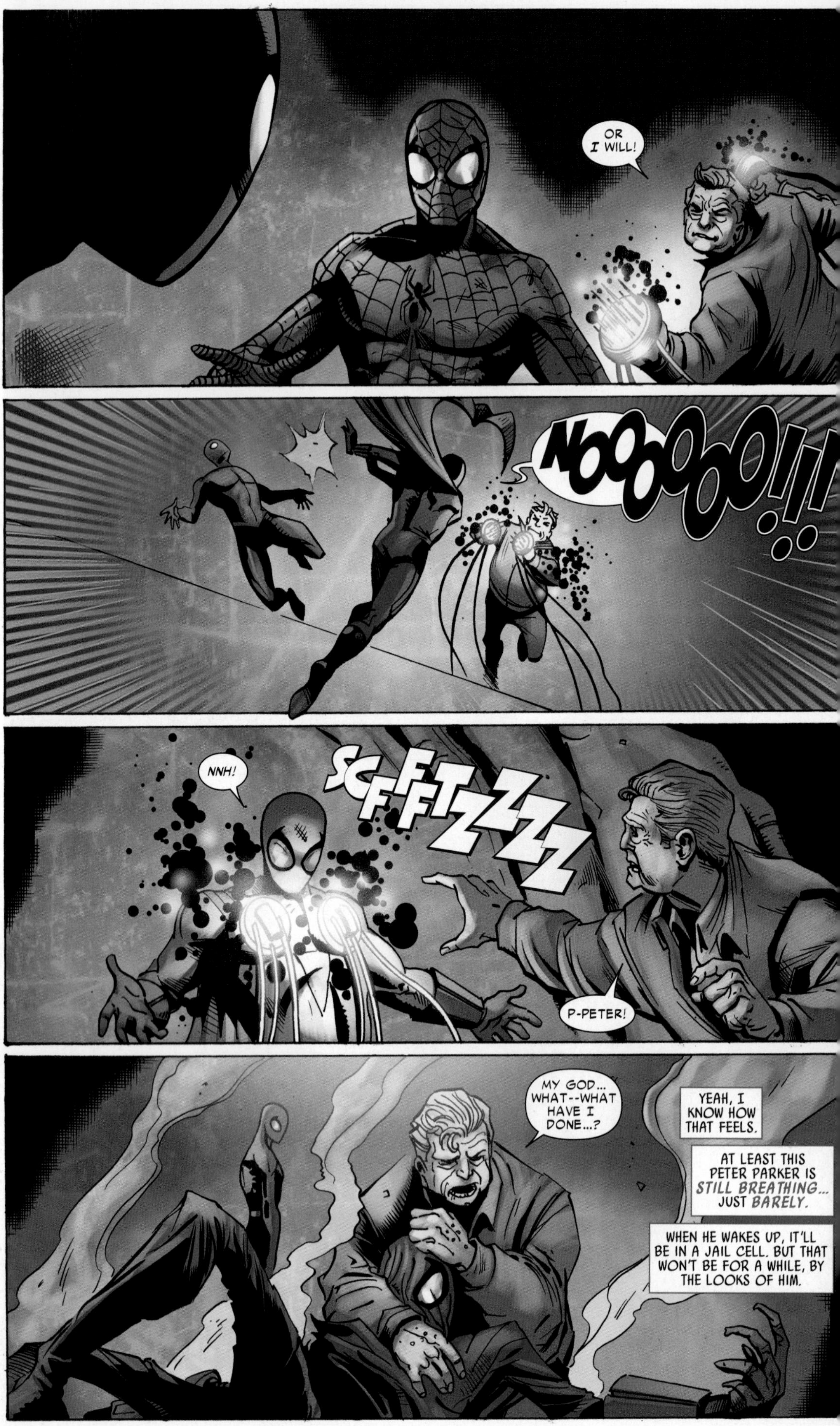
OR I WILL!
NOOOOOOO!!!
NNH!
SCFFFTZZZZ
P-PETER!
MY GOD... WHAT--WHAT HAVE I DONE...?
YEAH, I KNOW HOW THAT FEELS.
AT LEAST THIS PETER PARKER IS STILL BREATHING... JUST BARELY.
WHEN HE WAKES UP, IT'LL BE IN A JAIL CELL. BUT THAT WON'T BE FOR A WHILE, BY THE LOOKS OF HIM.

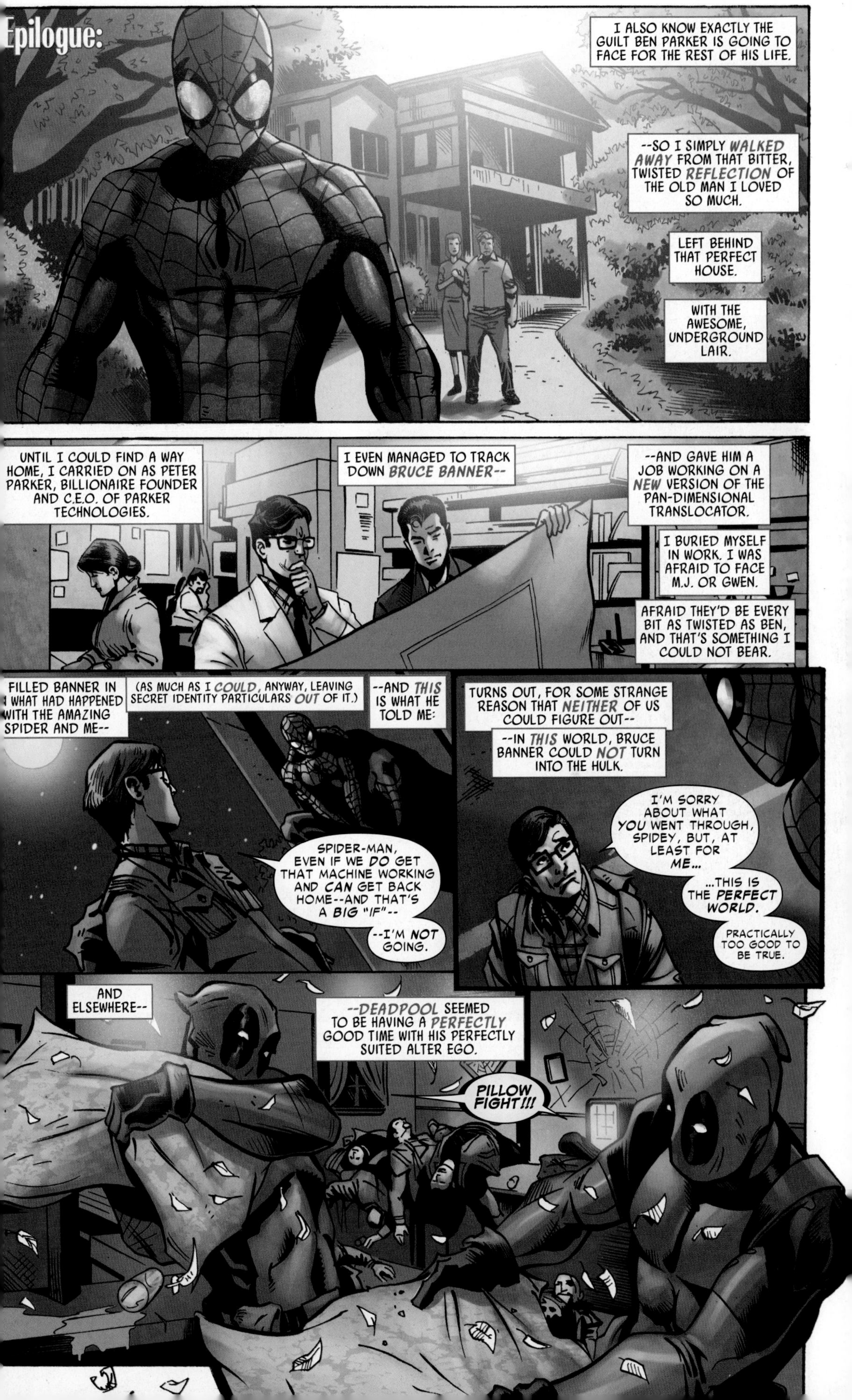
Epilogue:
I ALSO KNOW EXACTLY THE GUILT BEN PARKER IS GOING TO FACE FOR THE REST OF HIS LIFE.
--SO I SIMPLY WALKED AWAY FROM THAT BITTER, TWISTED REFLECTION OF THE OLD MAN I LOVED SO MUCH.
LEFT BEHIND THAT PERFECT HOUSE.
WITH THE AWESOME, UNDERGROUND LAIR.
UNTIL I COULD FIND A WAY HOME, I CARRIED ON AS PETER PARKER, BILLIONAIRE FOUNDER AND C.E.O. OF PARKER TECHNOLOGIES.
I EVEN MANAGED TO TRACK DOWN BRUCE BANNER--
--AND GAVE HIM A JOB WORKING ON A NEW VERSION OF THE PAN-DIMENSIONAL TRANSLOCATOR.
I BURIED MYSELF IN WORK. I WAS AFRAID TO FACE M.J. OR GWEN.
AFRAID THEY'D BE EVERY BIT AS TWISTED AS BEN, AND THAT'S SOMETHING I COULD NOT BEAR.
FILLED BANNER IN WHAT HAD HAPPENED WITH THE AMAZING SPIDER AND ME--
(AS MUCH AS I COULD, ANYWAY, LEAVING SECRET IDENTITY PARTICULARS OUT OF IT.)
--AND THIS IS WHAT HE TOLD ME:
SPIDER-MAN, EVEN IF WE DO GET THAT MACHINE WORKING AND CAN GET BACK HOME--AND THAT'S A BIG "IF"--
--I'M NOT GOING.
TURNS OUT, FOR SOME STRANGE REASON THAT NEITHER OF US COULD FIGURE OUT--
--IN THIS WORLD, BRUCE BANNER COULD NOT TURN INTO THE HULK.
I'M SORRY ABOUT WHAT YOU WENT THROUGH, SPIDEY, BUT, AT LEAST FOR ME...
...THIS IS THE PERFECT WORLD.
PRACTICALLY TOO GOOD TO BE TRUE.
AND ELSEWHERE--
--DEADPOOL SEEMED TO BE HAVING A PERFECTLY GOOD TIME WITH HIS PERFECTLY SUITED ALTER EGO.
PILLOW FIGHT!!!

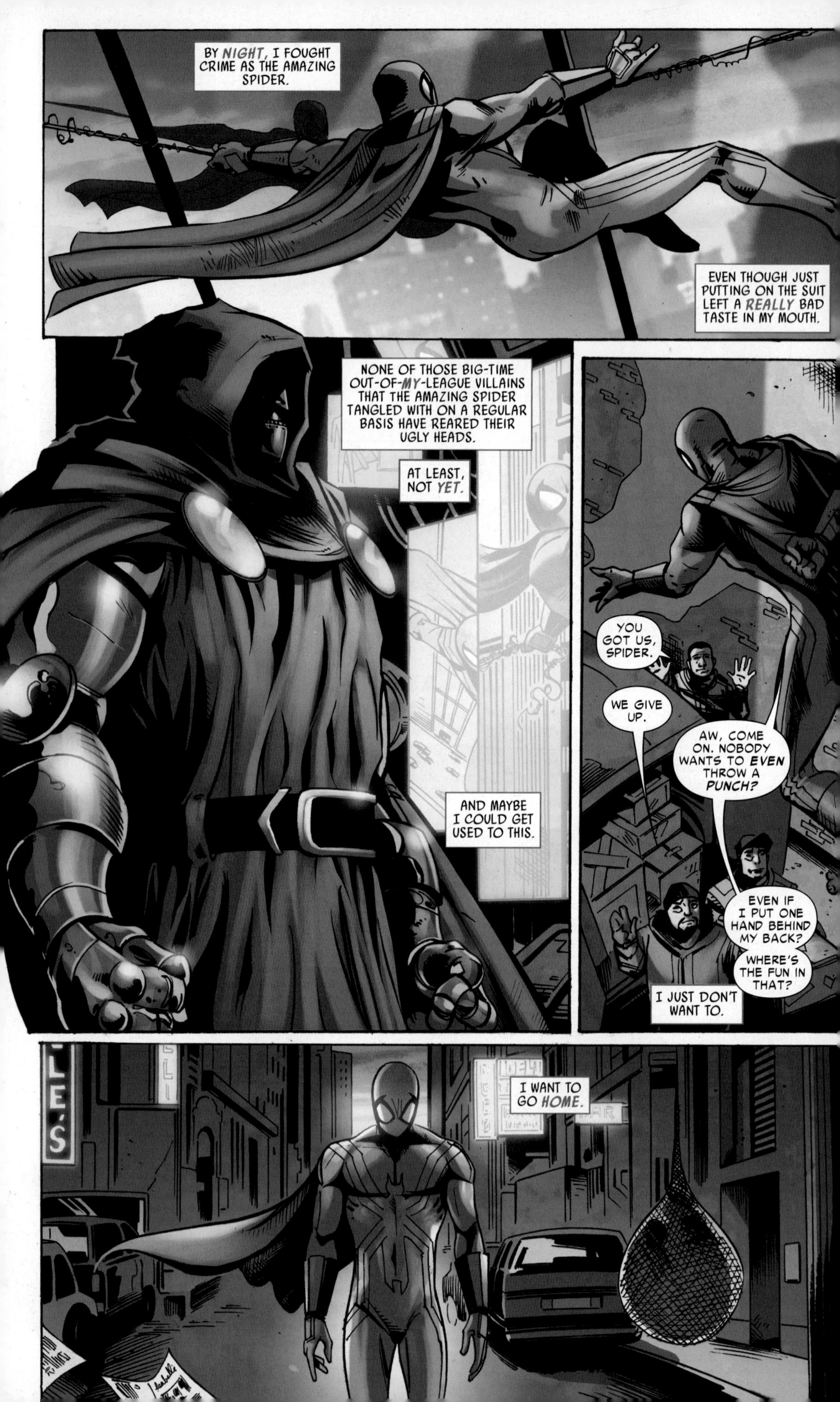
BY NIGHT, I FOUGHT CRIME AS THE AMAZING SPIDER.
EVEN THOUGH JUST PUTTING ON THE SUIT LEFT A REALLY BAD TASTE IN MY MOUTH.
NONE OF THOSE BIG-TIME OUT-OF-MY-LEAGUE VILLAINS THAT THE AMAZING SPIDER TANGLED WITH ON A REGULAR BASIS HAVE REARED THEIR UGLY HEADS.
AT LEAST, NOT YET.
AND MAYBE I COULD GET USED TO THIS.
YOU GOT US, SPIDER.
WE GIVE UP.
AW, COME ON. NOBODY WANTS TO EVEN THROW A PUNCH?
EVEN IF I PUT ONE HAND BEHIND MY BACK?
WHERE'S THE FUN IN THAT?
I JUST DON'T WANT TO.
I WANT TO GO HOME.
LE'S
BAR

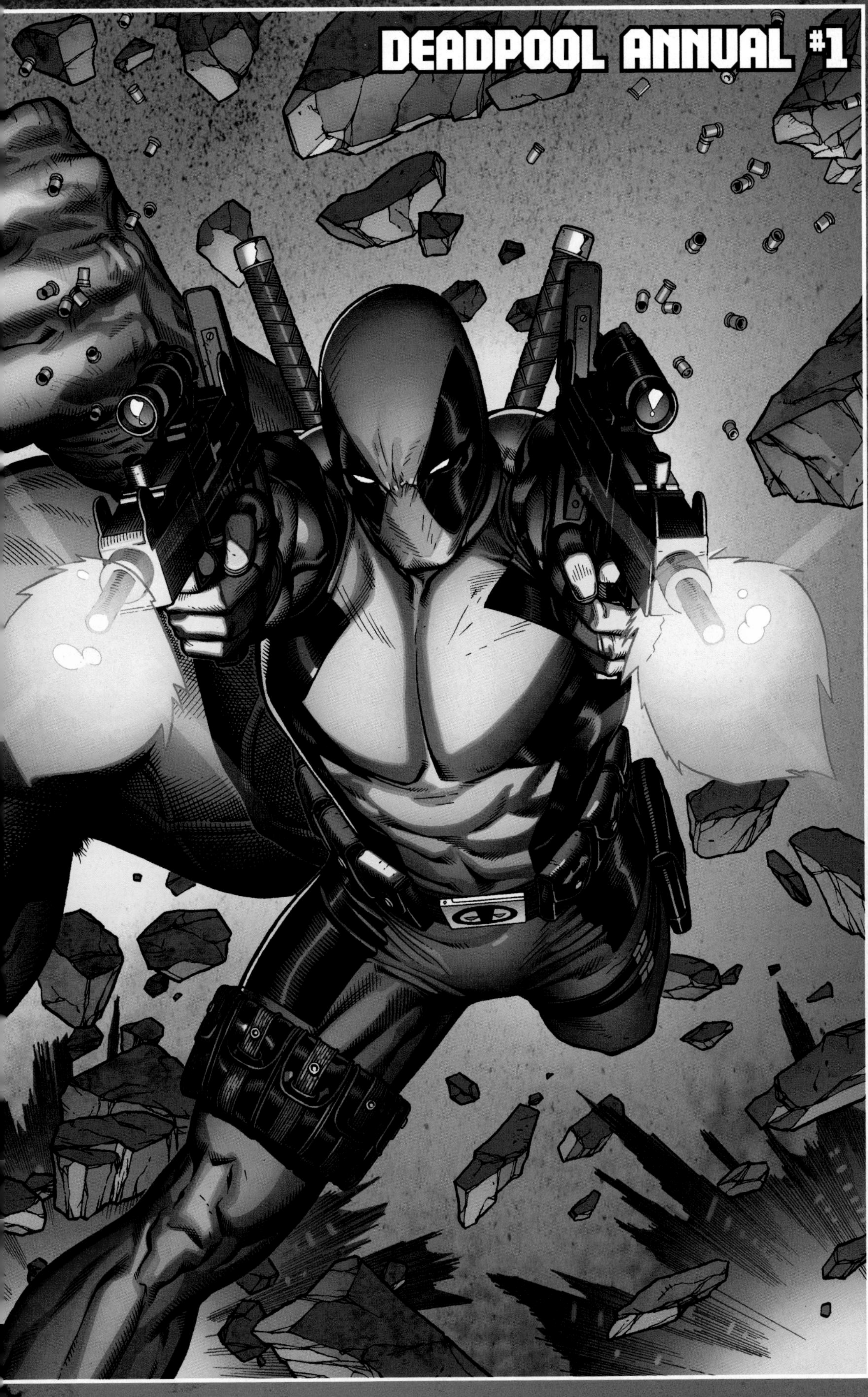
DEADPOOL ANNUAL #1

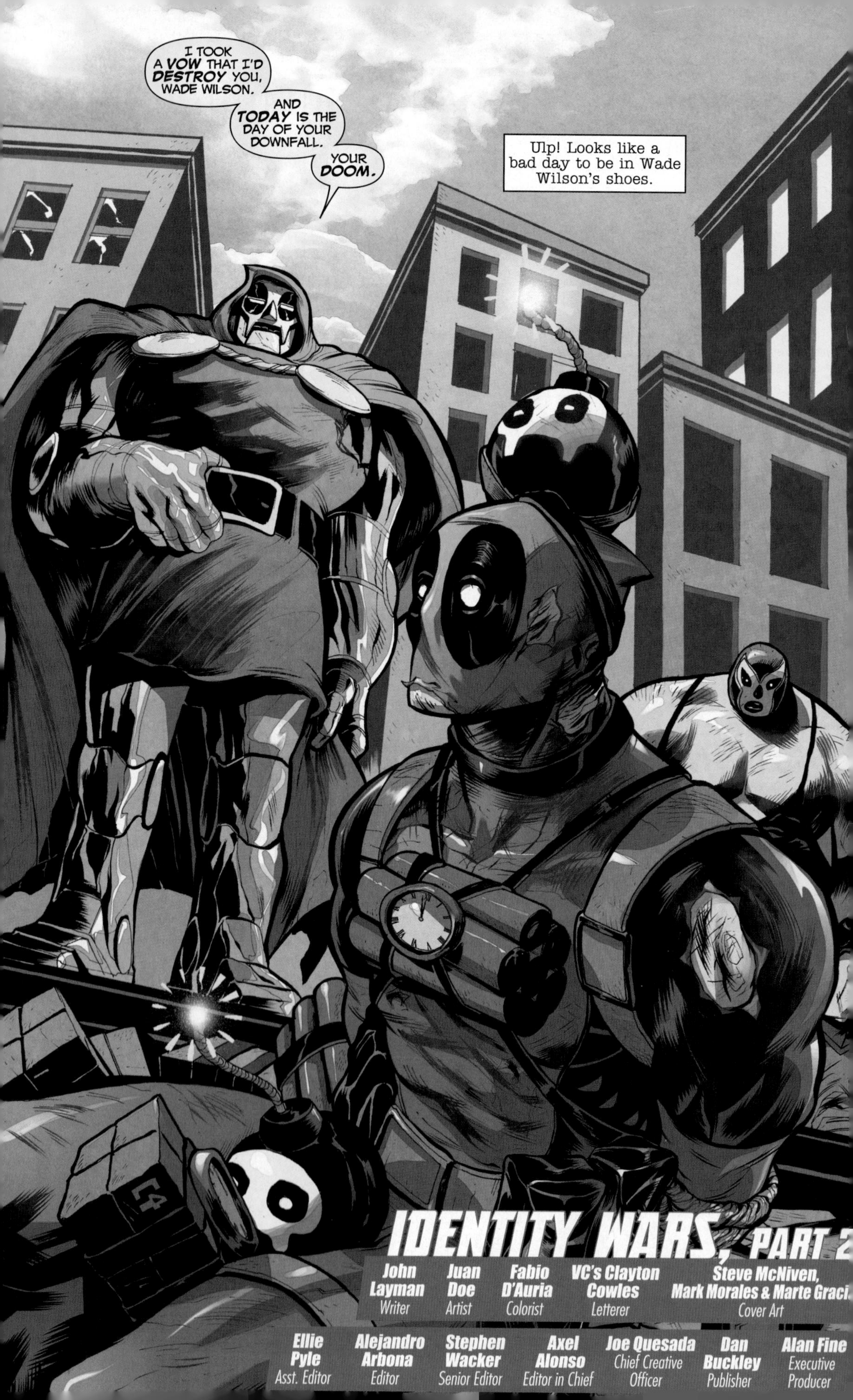

I TOOK A VOW THAT I'D DESTROY YOU, WADE WILSON.
AND TODAY IS THE DAY OF YOUR DOWNFALL.
YOUR DOOM.
Ulp! Looks like a bad day to be in Wade Wilson's shoes.
C4
IDENTITY WARS, PART 2
John Layman Writer
Juan Doe Artist
Fabio D'Auria Colorist
VC's Clayton Cowles Letterer
Steve McNiven, Mark Morales & Marte Graci. Cover Art
Ellie Pyle Asst. Editor
Alejandro Arbona Editor
Stephen Wacker Senior Editor
Axel Alonso Editor in Chief
Joe Quesada Chief Creative Officer
Dan Buckley Publisher
Alan Fine Executive Producer

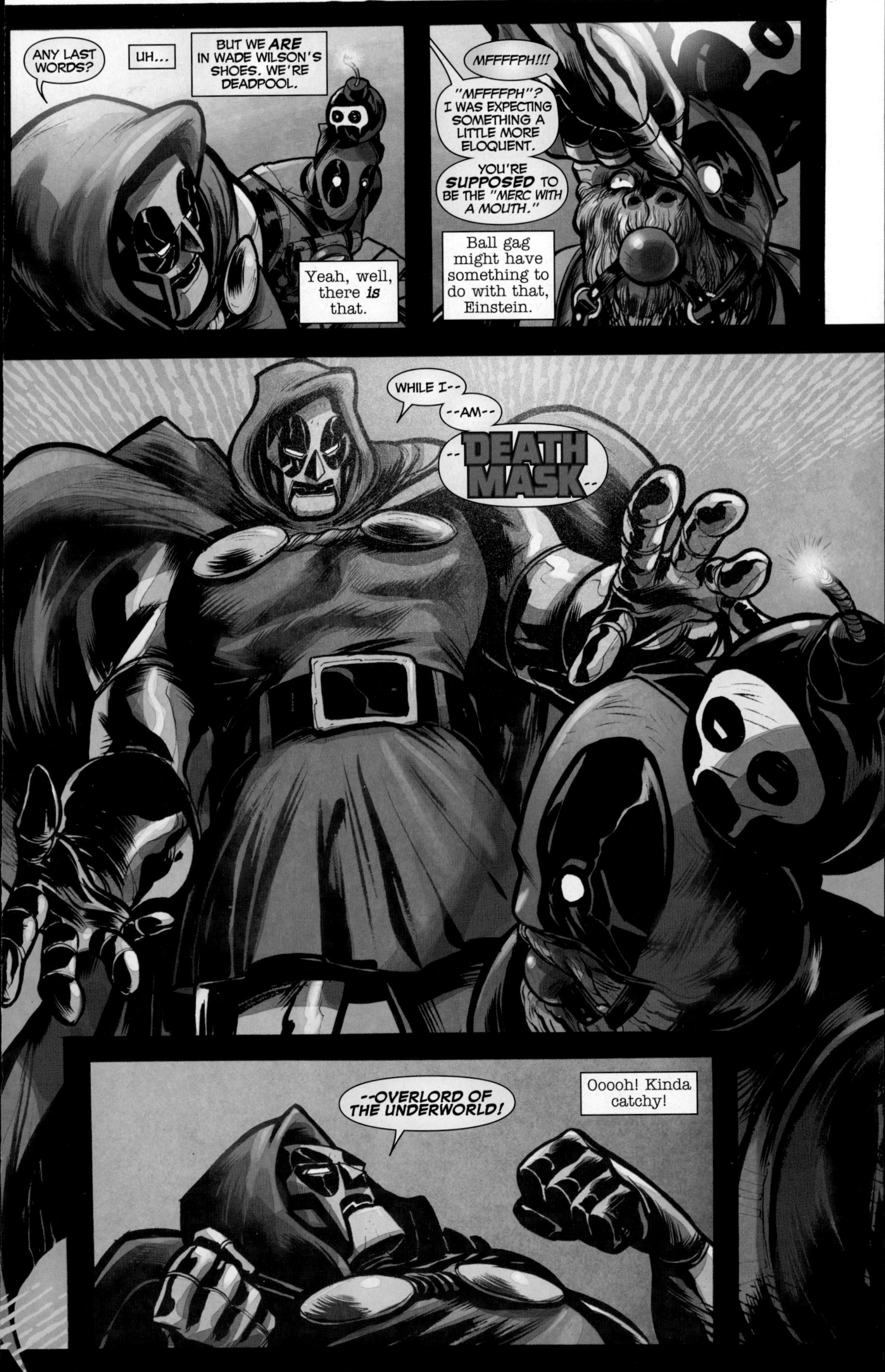
ANY LAST WORDS?
UH...
BUT WE ARE IN WADE WILSON'S SHOES. WE'RE DEADPOOL.
Yeah, well, there is that.
MFFFFPH!!!
"MFFFFPH"? I WAS EXPECTING SOMETHING A LITTLE MORE ELOQUENT.
YOU'RE SUPPOSED TO BE THE "MERC WITH A MOUTH."
Ball gag might have something to do with that, Einstein.
WHILE I--
--AM--
--DEATH MASK--
--OVERLORD OF THE UNDERWORLD!
Ooooh! Kinda catchy!

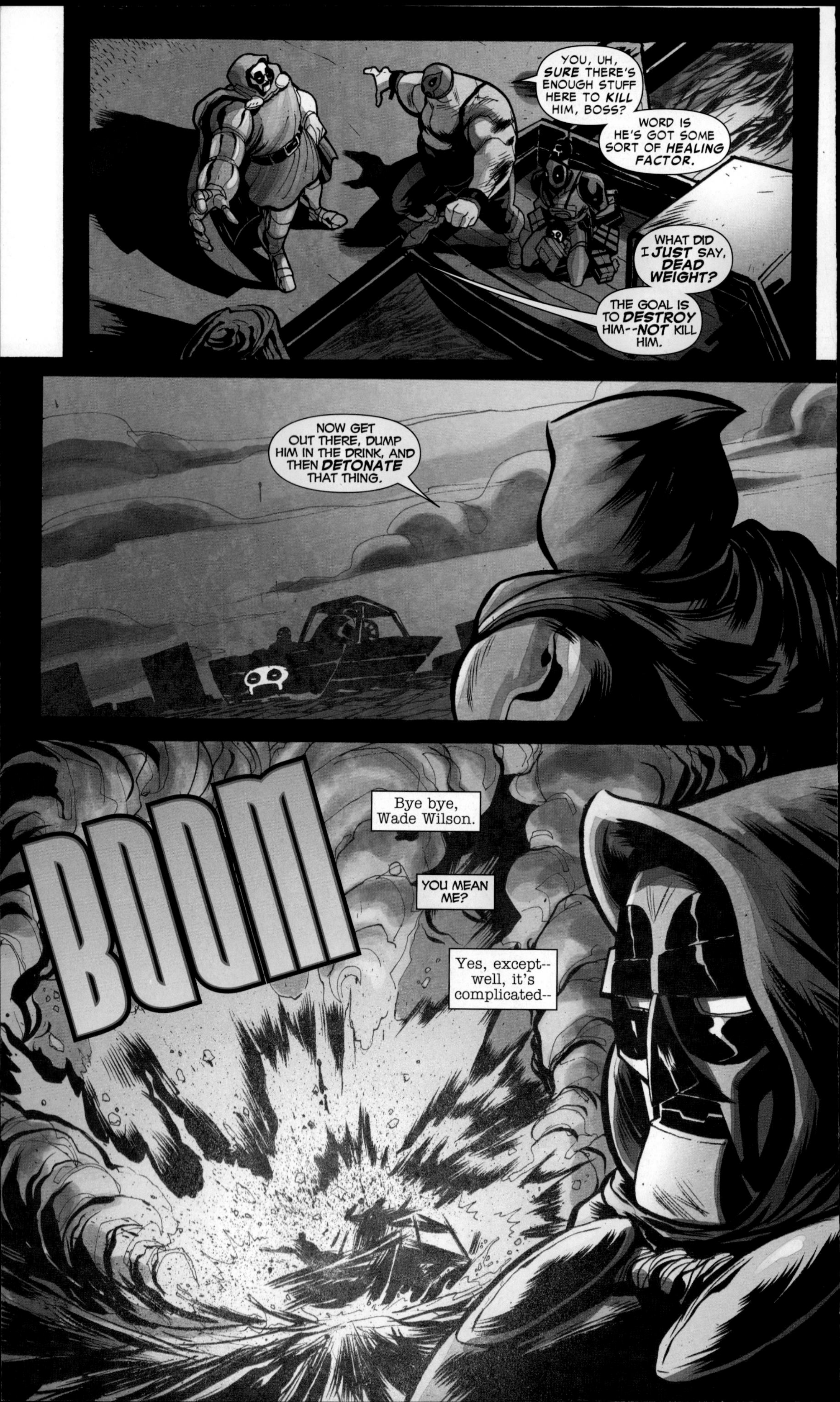
YOU, UH, SURE THERE'S ENOUGH STUFF HERE TO KILL HIM, BOSS?
WORD IS HE'S GOT SOME SORT OF HEALING FACTOR.
WHAT DID I JUST SAY, DEAD WEIGHT?
THE GOAL IS TO DESTROY HIM--NOT KILL HIM.
NOW GET OUT THERE, DUMP HIM IN THE DRINK, AND THEN DETONATE THAT THING.
BOOM
Bye bye, Wade Wilson.
YOU MEAN ME?
Yes, except--well, it's complicated--

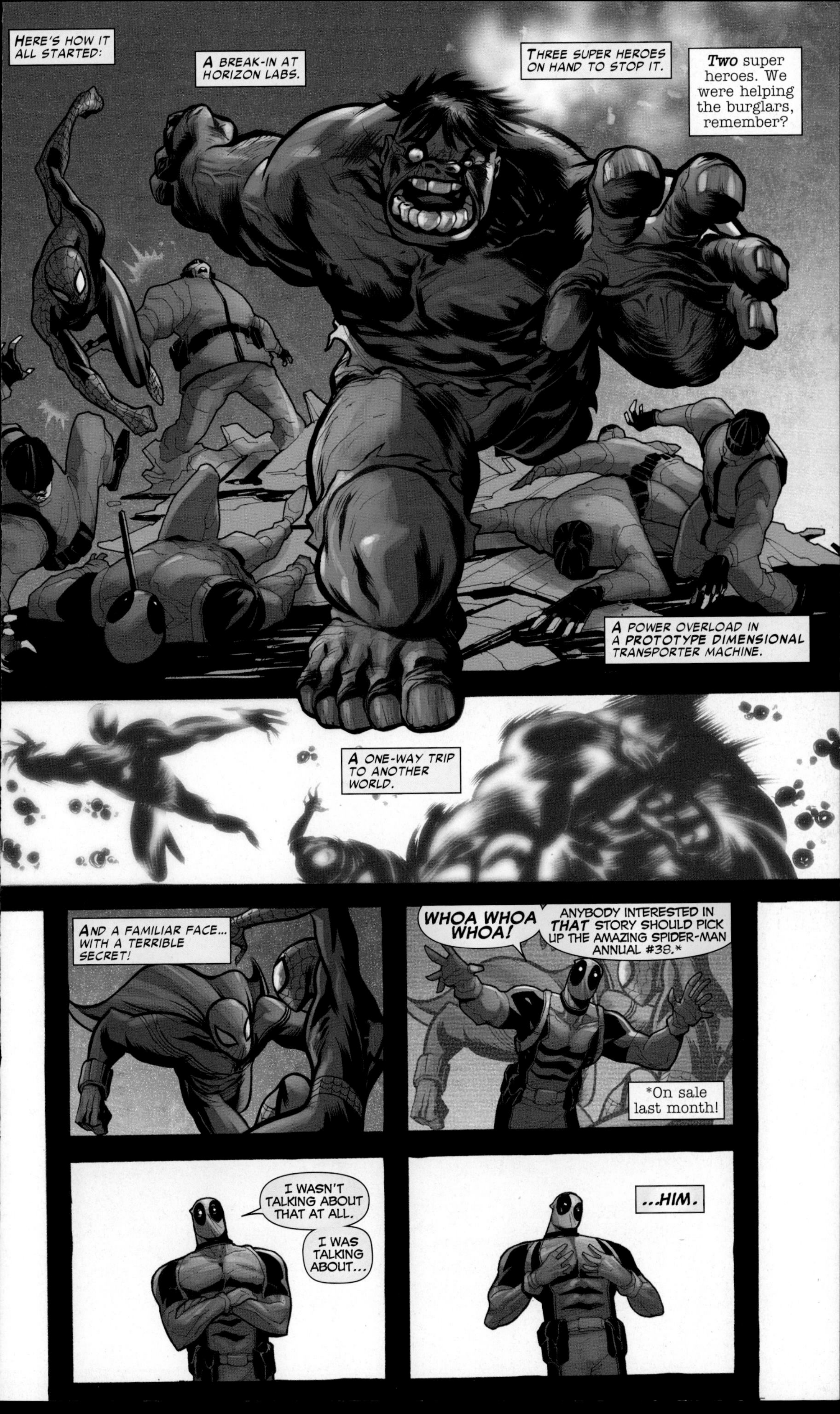
HERE'S HOW IT ALL STARTED:
A BREAK-IN AT HORIZON LABS.
THREE SUPER HEROES ON HAND TO STOP IT.
Two super heroes. We were helping the burglars, remember?
A POWER OVERLOAD IN A PROTOTYPE DIMENSIONAL TRANSPORTER MACHINE.
A ONE-WAY TRIP TO ANOTHER WORLD.
AND A FAMILIAR FACE... WITH A TERRIBLE SECRET!
WHOA WHOA WHOA!
ANYBODY INTERESTED IN THAT STORY SHOULD PICK UP THE AMAZING SPIDER-MAN ANNUAL #38.*
*On sale last month!
I WASN'T TALKING ABOUT THAT AT ALL.
I WAS TALKING ABOUT...
...HIM.

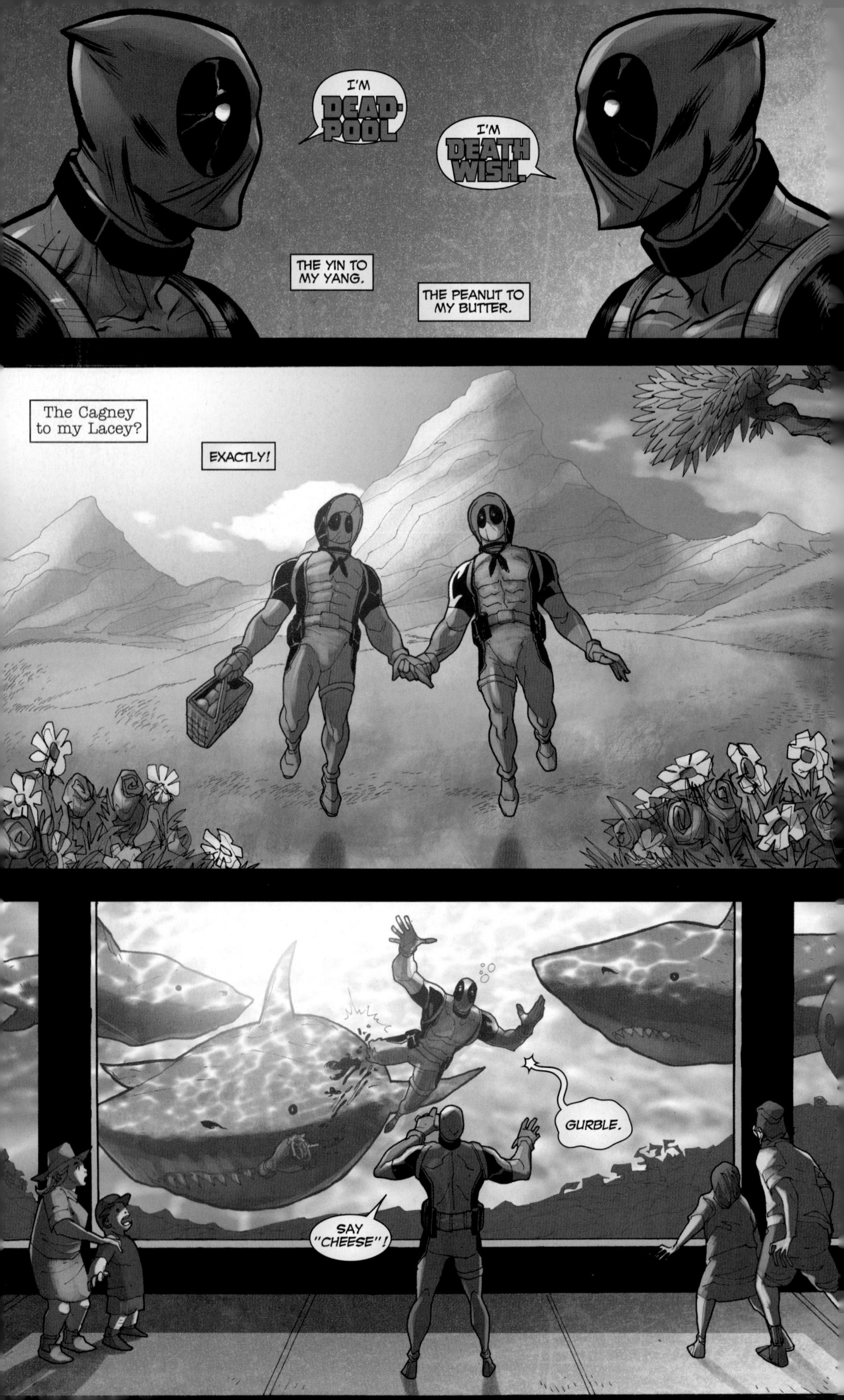
I'M DEAD-POOL
I'M DEATH WISH.
THE YIN TO MY YANG.
THE PEANUT TO MY BUTTER.
The Cagney to my Lacey?
EXACTLY!
GURBLE.
SAY "CHEESE"!

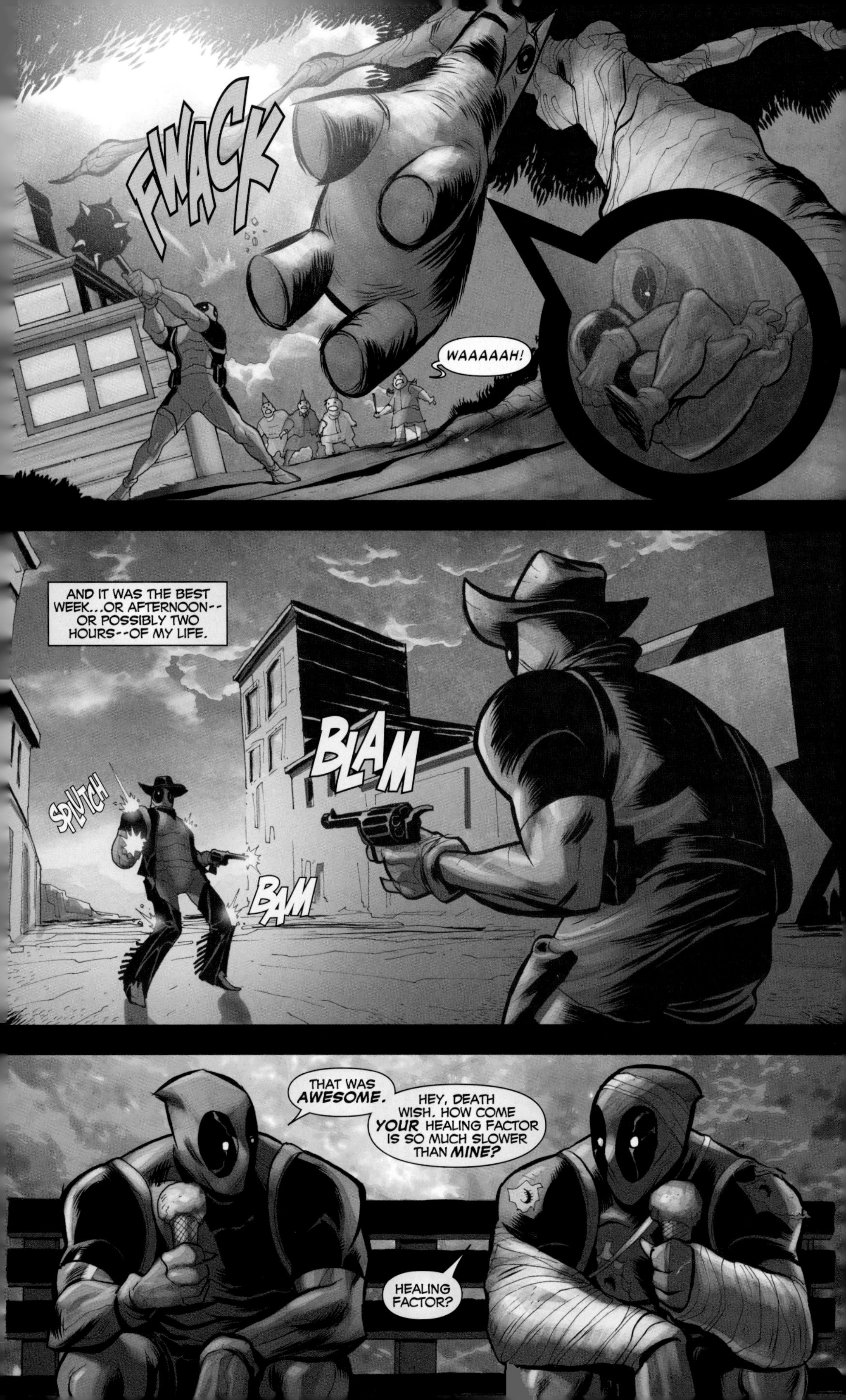
FWACK
WAAAAAH!
AND IT WAS THE BEST WEEK...OR AFTERNOON--OR POSSIBLY TWO HOURS--OF MY LIFE.
BLAM
SPLUTCH
BAM
THAT WAS **AWESOME.**
HEY, DEATH WISH. HOW COME ***YOUR*** HEALING FACTOR IS SO MUCH SLOWER THAN ***MINE?***
HEALING FACTOR?

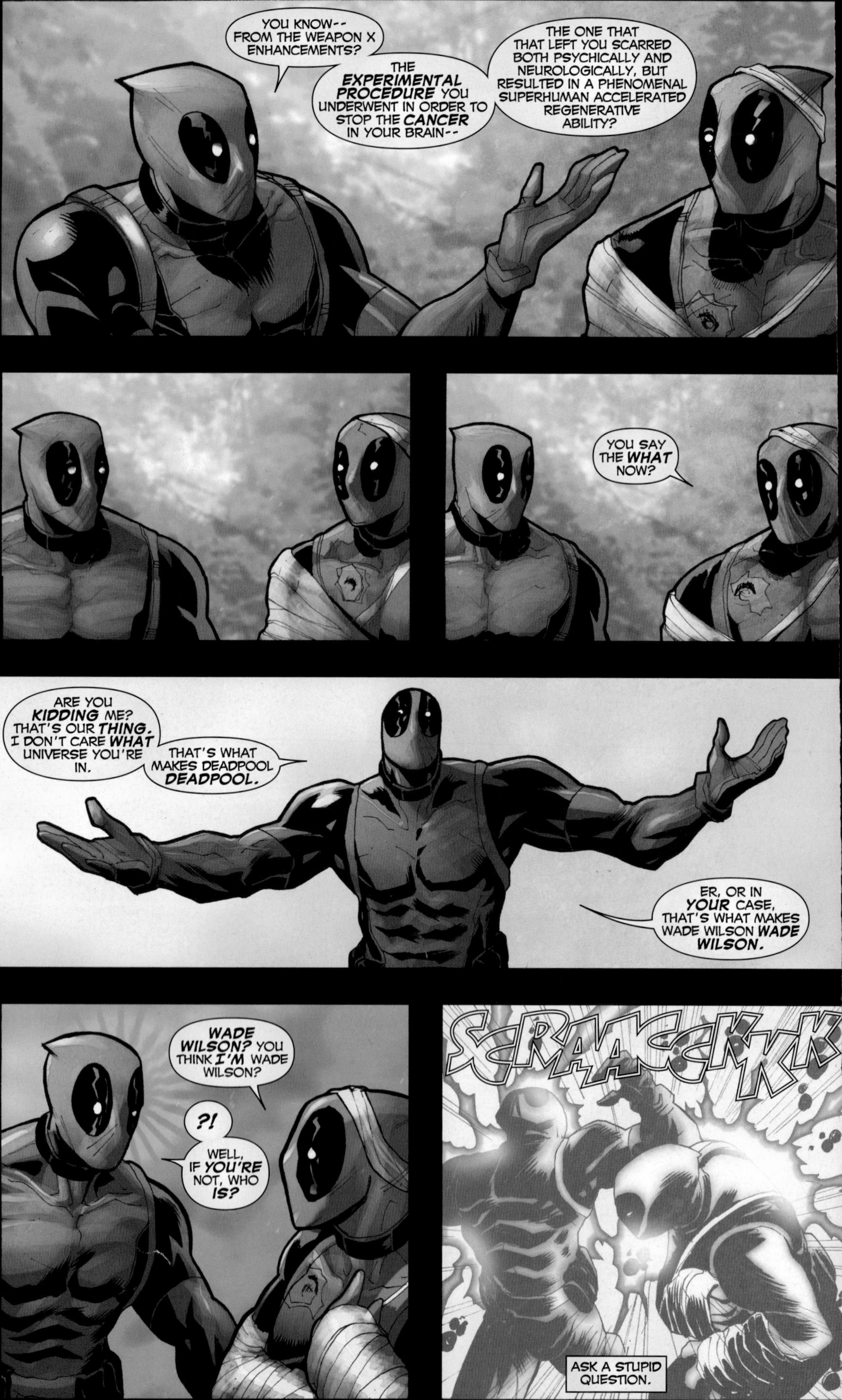

YOU KNOW-- FROM THE WEAPON X ENHANCEMENTS?
THE EXPERIMENTAL PROCEDURE YOU UNDERWENT IN ORDER TO STOP THE CANCER IN YOUR BRAIN--
THE ONE THAT THAT LEFT YOU SCARRED BOTH PSYCHICALLY AND NEUROLOGICALLY, BUT RESULTED IN A PHENOMENAL SUPERHUMAN ACCELERATED REGENERATIVE ABILITY?
YOU SAY THE WHAT NOW?
ARE YOU KIDDING ME? THAT'S OUR THING. I DON'T CARE WHAT UNIVERSE YOU'RE IN.
THAT'S WHAT MAKES DEADPOOL DEADPOOL.
ER, OR IN YOUR CASE, THAT'S WHAT MAKES WADE WILSON WADE WILSON.
WADE WILSON? YOU THINK I'M WADE WILSON?
?!
WELL, IF YOU'RE NOT, WHO IS?
SCRAACKKK
ASK A STUPID QUESTION.

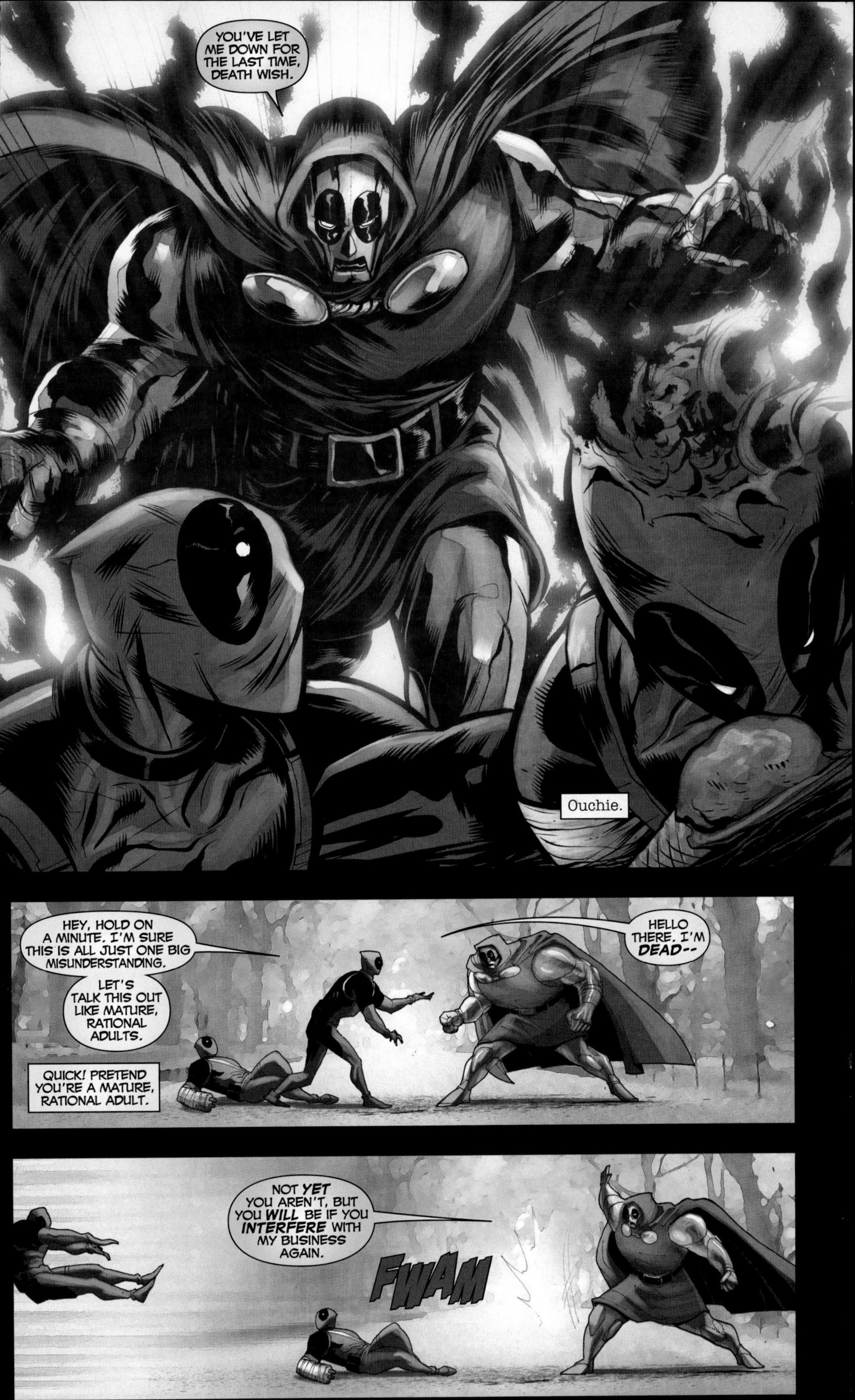
YOU'VE LET ME DOWN FOR THE LAST TIME, DEATH WISH.
Ouchie.
HEY, HOLD ON A MINUTE. I'M SURE THIS IS ALL JUST ONE BIG MISUNDERSTANDING.
LET'S TALK THIS OUT LIKE MATURE, RATIONAL ADULTS.
QUICK! PRETEND YOU'RE A MATURE, RATIONAL ADULT.
HELLO THERE. I'M DEAD--
NOT YET YOU AREN'T, BUT YOU WILL BE IF YOU INTERFERE WITH MY BUSINESS AGAIN.
FWAM

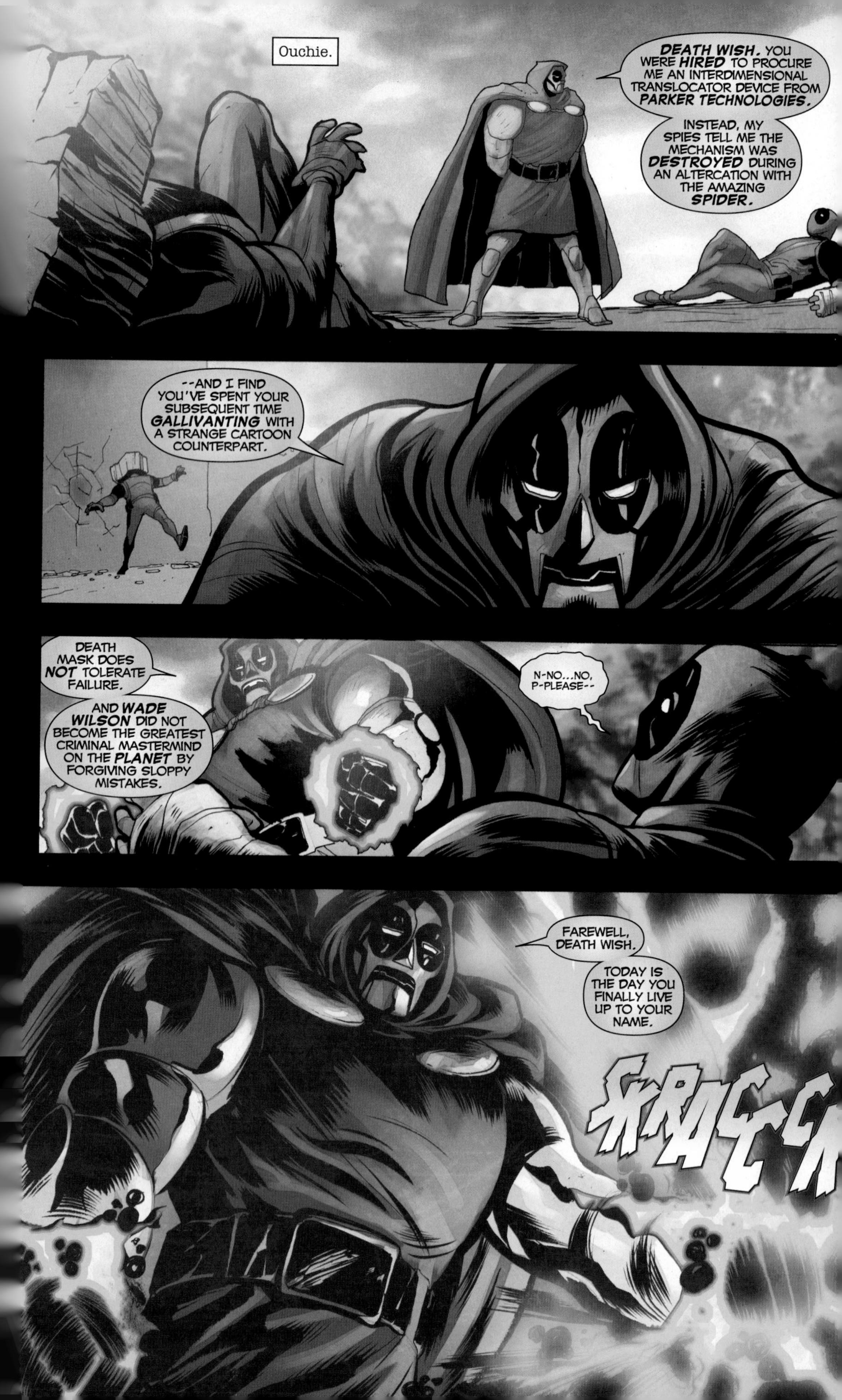
Ouchie.
DEATH WISH. YOU WERE HIRED TO PROCURE ME AN INTERDIMENSIONAL TRANSLOCATOR DEVICE FROM PARKER TECHNOLOGIES.
INSTEAD, MY SPIES TELL ME THE MECHANISM WAS DESTROYED DURING AN ALTERCATION WITH THE AMAZING SPIDER.
--AND I FIND YOU'VE SPENT YOUR SUBSEQUENT TIME GALLIVANTING WITH A STRANGE CARTOON COUNTERPART.
DEATH MASK DOES NOT TOLERATE FAILURE.
AND WADE WILSON DID NOT BECOME THE GREATEST CRIMINAL MASTERMIND ON THE PLANET BY FORGIVING SLOPPY MISTAKES.
N-NO...NO, P-PLEASE--
FAREWELL, DEATH WISH.
TODAY IS THE DAY YOU FINALLY LIVE UP TO YOUR NAME.

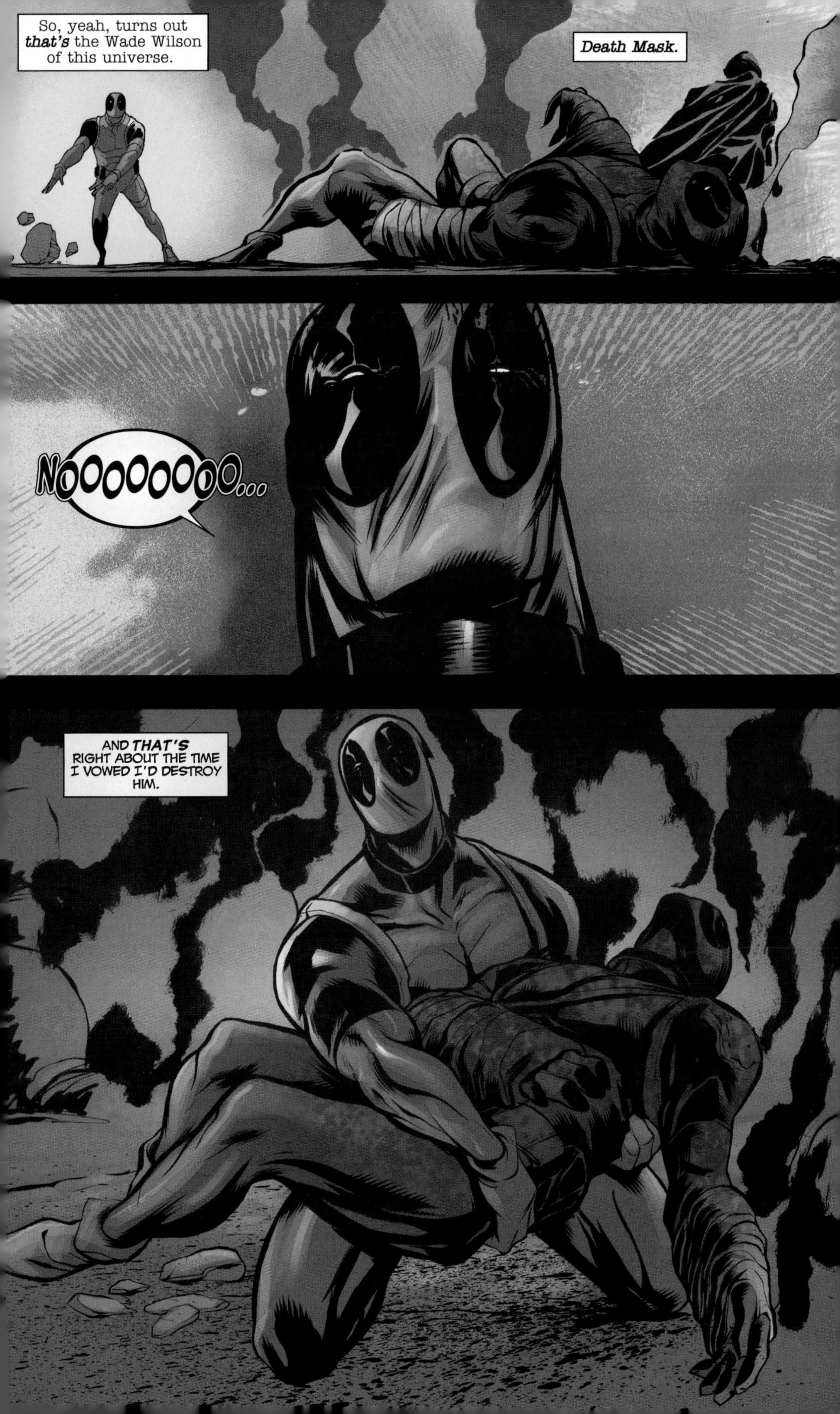

So, yeah, turns out *that's* the Wade Wilson of this universe.
Death Mask.
NOOOOOOOO...
AND *THAT'S* RIGHT ABOUT THE TIME I VOWED I'D DESTROY HIM.

Soon:

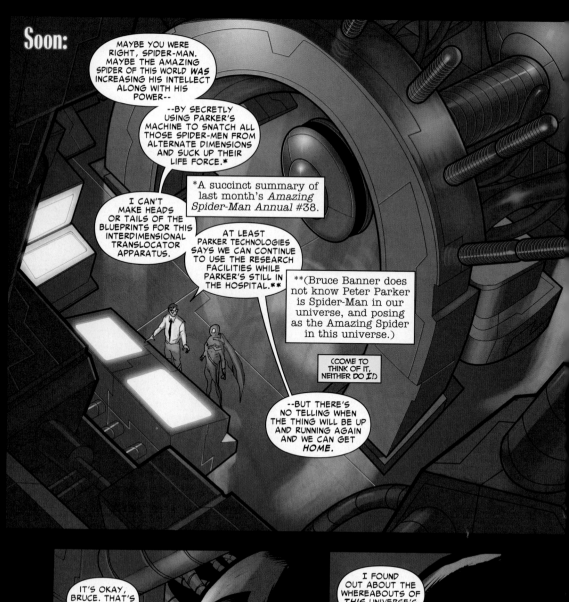

MAYBE YOU WERE RIGHT, SPIDER-MAN. MAYBE THE AMAZING SPIDER OF THIS WORLD *WAS* INCREASING HIS INTELLECT ALONG WITH HIS POWER--

--BY SECRETLY USING PARKER'S MACHINE TO SNATCH ALL THOSE SPIDER-MEN FROM ALTERNATE DIMENSIONS AND SUCK UP THEIR LIFE FORCE.*

*A succinct summary of last month's *Amazing Spider-Man Annual #38.*

I CAN'T MAKE HEADS OR TAILS OF THE BLUEPRINTS FOR THIS INTERDIMENSIONAL TRANSLOCATOR APPARATUS.

AT LEAST PARKER TECHNOLOGIES SAYS WE CAN CONTINUE TO USE THE RESEARCH FACILITIES WHILE PARKER'S STILL IN THE HOSPITAL.**

**(Bruce Banner does not know Peter Parker is Spider-Man in our universe, and posing as the Amazing Spider in this universe.)

(COME TO THINK OF IT, NEITHER DO *I*.)

--BUT THERE'S NO TELLING WHEN THE THING WILL BE UP AND RUNNING AGAIN AND WE CAN GET *HOME*.

IT'S OKAY, BRUCE. THAT'S NOT WHY I'M HERE.

WHILE I'VE BEEN DOUBLING AS THE AMAZING SPIDER, I'VE HAD A CHANCE TO SNOOP AROUND INTO HIS FILES.

I FOUND SOME *OTHER* STUFF-- A *DATABASE* ON ALL THE SUPERHUMANS ON THIS PLANET, FRIENDS *AND* FOES.

I FOUND OUT ABOUT THE WHEREABOUTS OF *THIS* UNIVERSE'S BRUCE BANNER.

AND I FOUND OUT HOW HE WAS ABLE TO BANISH *THE HULK* FROM THIS WORLD.

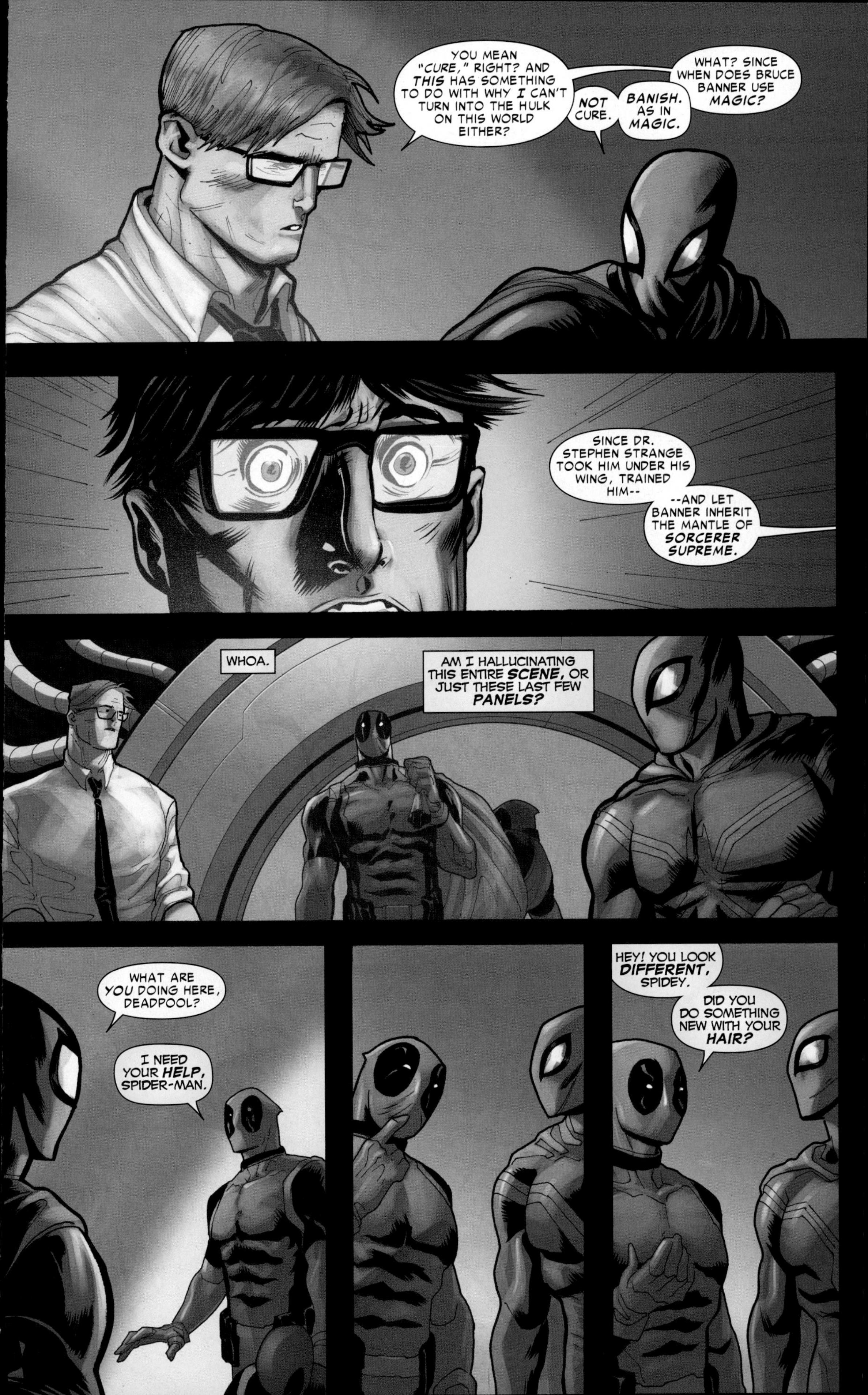
YOU MEAN "CURE," RIGHT? AND THIS HAS SOMETHING TO DO WITH WHY I CAN'T TURN INTO THE HULK ON THIS WORLD EITHER?
NOT CURE.
BANISH. AS IN MAGIC.
WHAT? SINCE WHEN DOES BRUCE BANNER USE MAGIC?
SINCE DR. STEPHEN STRANGE TOOK HIM UNDER HIS WING, TRAINED HIM--
--AND LET BANNER INHERIT THE MANTLE OF SORCERER SUPREME.
WHOA.
AM I HALLUCINATING THIS ENTIRE SCENE, OR JUST THESE LAST FEW PANELS?
WHAT ARE YOU DOING HERE, DEADPOOL?
I NEED YOUR HELP, SPIDER-MAN.
HEY! YOU LOOK DIFFERENT, SPIDEY.
DID YOU DO SOMETHING NEW WITH YOUR HAIR?

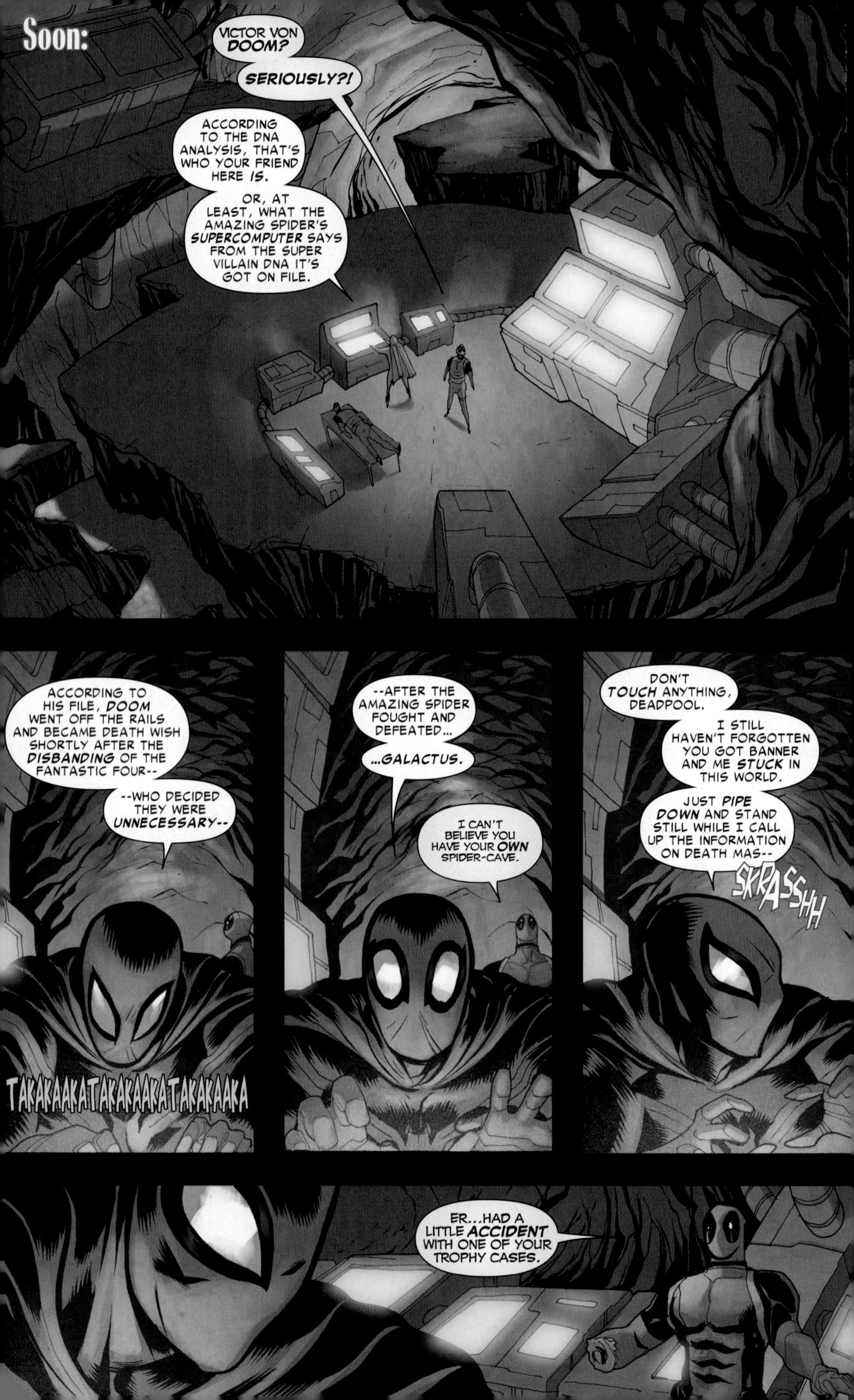
Soon:
VICTOR VON DOOM?
SERIOUSLY?!
ACCORDING TO THE DNA ANALYSIS, THAT'S WHO YOUR FRIEND HERE IS.
OR, AT LEAST, WHAT THE AMAZING SPIDER'S SUPERCOMPUTER SAYS FROM THE SUPER VILLAIN DNA IT'S GOT ON FILE.
ACCORDING TO HIS FILE, DOOM WENT OFF THE RAILS AND BECAME DEATH WISH SHORTLY AFTER THE DISBANDING OF THE FANTASTIC FOUR--
--WHO DECIDED THEY WERE UNNECESSARY--
TAKAKAAKATAKAKAAKATAKAKAAKA
--AFTER THE AMAZING SPIDER FOUGHT AND DEFEATED...
...GALACTUS.
I CAN'T BELIEVE YOU HAVE YOUR OWN SPIDER-CAVE.
DON'T TOUCH ANYTHING, DEADPOOL.
I STILL HAVEN'T FORGOTTEN YOU GOT BANNER AND ME STUCK IN THIS WORLD.
JUST PIPE DOWN AND STAND STILL WHILE I CALL UP THE INFORMATION ON DEATH MAS--
SKRASSHH
ER...HAD A LITTLE ACCIDENT WITH ONE OF YOUR TROPHY CASES.

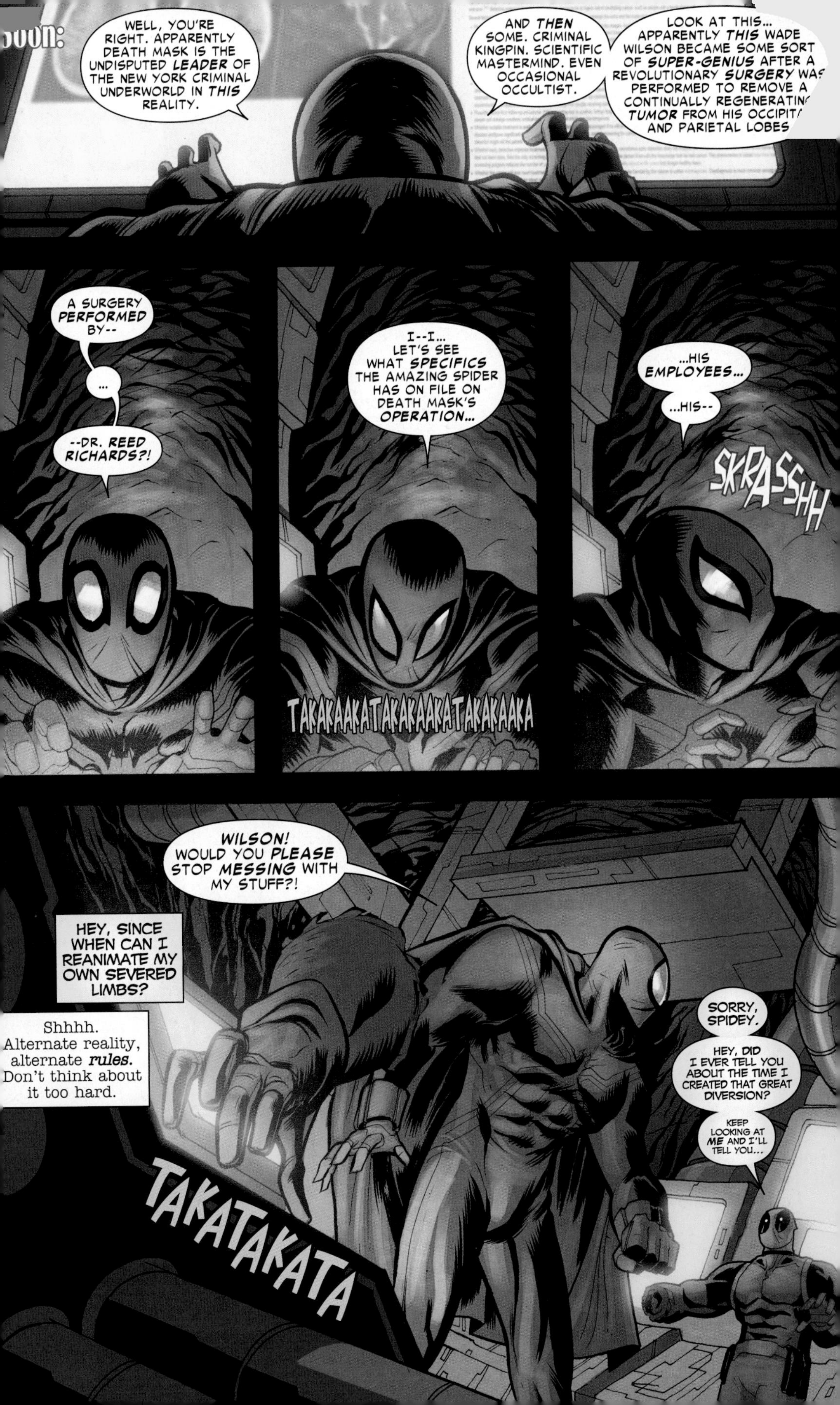

WELL, YOU'RE RIGHT. APPARENTLY DEATH MASK IS THE UNDISPUTED LEADER OF THE NEW YORK CRIMINAL UNDERWORLD IN THIS REALITY.
AND THEN SOME. CRIMINAL KINGPIN. SCIENTIFIC MASTERMIND. EVEN OCCASIONAL OCCULTIST.
LOOK AT THIS... APPARENTLY THIS WADE WILSON BECAME SOME SORT OF SUPER-GENIUS AFTER A REVOLUTIONARY SURGERY WAS PERFORMED TO REMOVE A CONTINUALLY REGENERATING TUMOR FROM HIS OCCIPITAL AND PARIETAL LOBES
A SURGERY PERFORMED BY--
...
--DR. REED RICHARDS?!
I--I... LET'S SEE WHAT SPECIFICS THE AMAZING SPIDER HAS ON FILE ON DEATH MASK'S OPERATION...
TAKAKAAKATAKAKAAKATAKAKAAKA
...HIS EMPLOYEES...
...HIS--
SKRASSHH
WILSON! WOULD YOU PLEASE STOP MESSING WITH MY STUFF?!
HEY, SINCE WHEN CAN I REANIMATE MY OWN SEVERED LIMBS?
Shhhh. Alternate reality, alternate rules. Don't think about it too hard.
SORRY, SPIDEY.
HEY, DID I EVER TELL YOU ABOUT THE TIME I CREATED THAT GREAT DIVERSION?
KEEP LOOKING AT ME AND I'LL TELL YOU...
TAKATAKATA

FILES ON DEATH MASK! ➜

♪

WELL, THAT WASN'T VERY NICE.

TRICKING THE NICE SPIDER-MAN.

...MM. NO RECORDS ON DEATH MASK'S OPERATION.

LOOKS LIKE IT MIGHT HAVE BEEN *ERASED* AT SOME POINT.

POSSIBLY *RECENTLY.*

HUH, GEE.

LYING TO THE NICE SPIDER-MAN.

MANIPULATING THE NICE SPIDER-MAN.

WELL, *YOU* NEED TO LOOK *INTO* THIS, SPIDEY. THIS DEATH MASK GUY IS A DANGEROUS *PSYCHOPATH.*

I'VE *GOOD INFORMATION* THERE'S A *GANG WAR* ABOUT TO START UP--

--AND *WADE WILSON* IS GOING TO CAUSE A LOT *MORE* DEAD BODIES TO PILE UP.

Notice I didn't say *which* Wade Wilson would be doing the killin'?

BWOOM

BAD GUYS WAREHOUSE HEATING SUPPLY CO.
WHO... 618

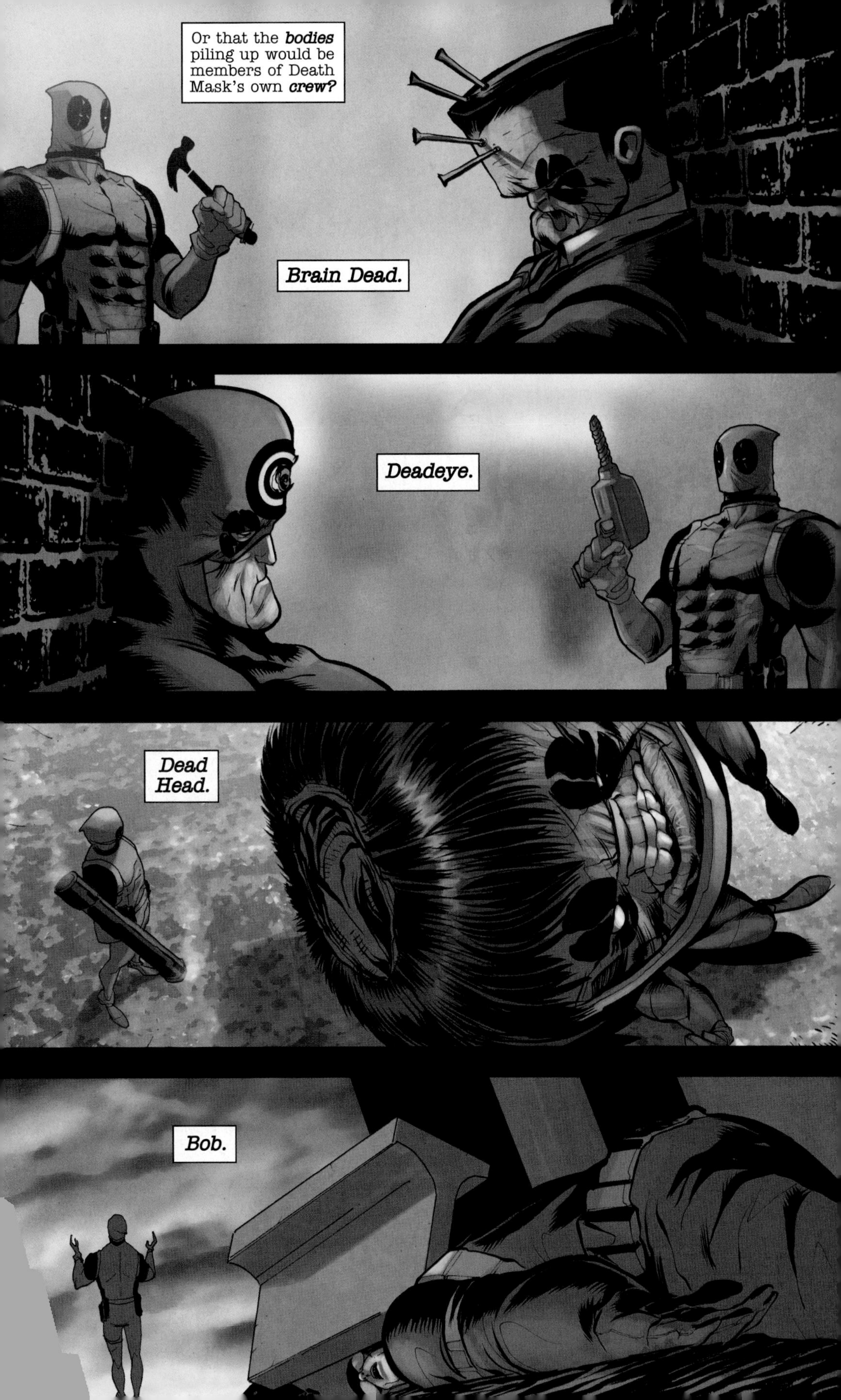
Or that the *bodies* piling up would be members of Death Mask's own *crew?*
Brain Dead.
Deadeye.
Dead Head.
Bob.

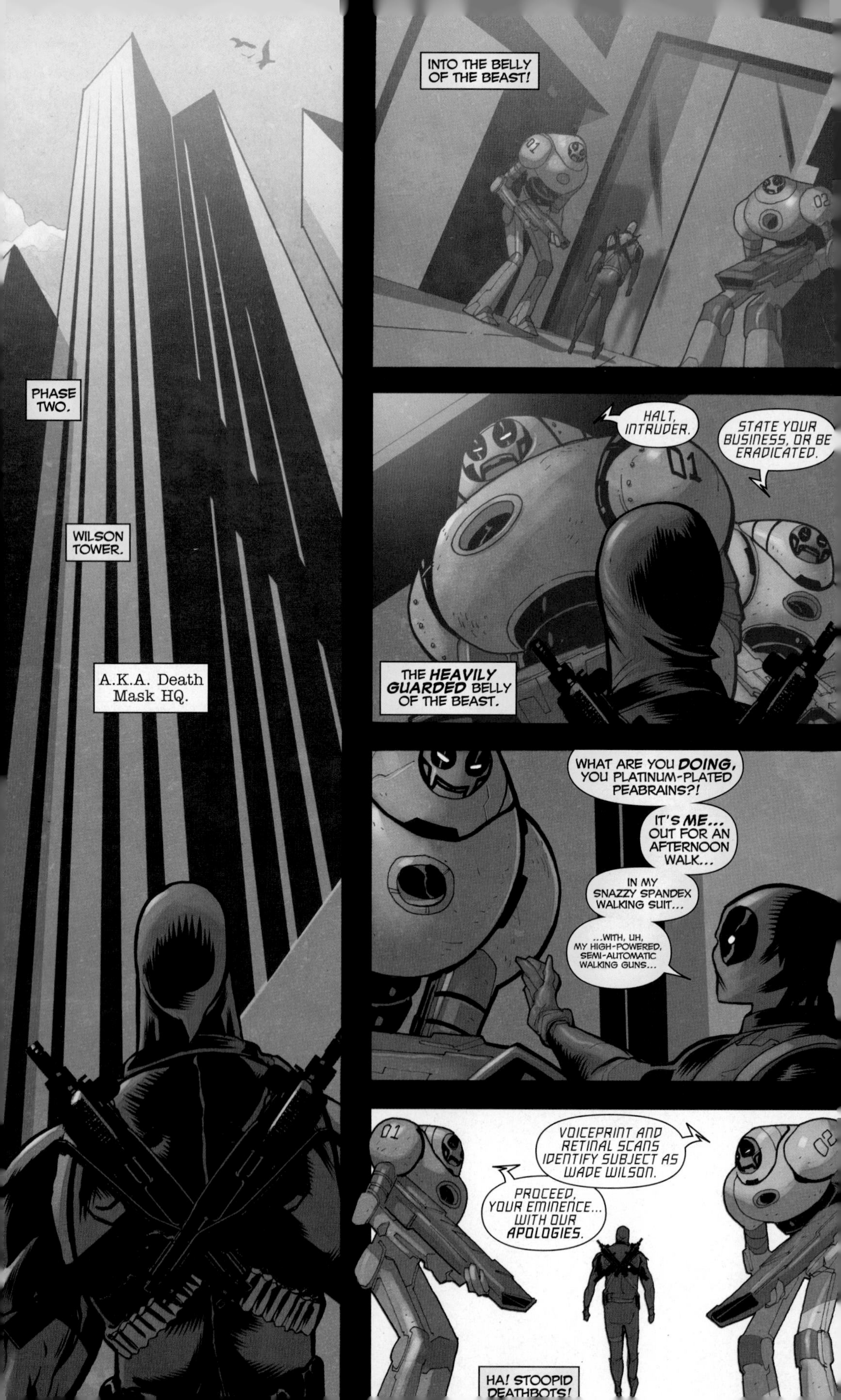

PHASE TWO.
WILSON TOWER.
A.K.A. Death Mask HQ.
INTO THE BELLY OF THE BEAST!
HALT, INTRUDER.
STATE YOUR BUSINESS, OR BE ERADICATED.
THE HEAVILY GUARDED BELLY OF THE BEAST.
WHAT ARE YOU DOING, YOU PLATINUM-PLATED PEABRAINS?!
IT'S ME... OUT FOR AN AFTERNOON WALK...
IN MY SNAZZY SPANDEX WALKING SUIT...
...WITH, UH, MY HIGH-POWERED, SEMI-AUTOMATIC WALKING GUNS...
VOICEPRINT AND RETINAL SCANS IDENTIFY SUBJECT AS WADE WILSON.
PROCEED, YOUR EMINENCE... WITH OUR APOLOGIES.
HA! STOOPID DEATHBOTS!

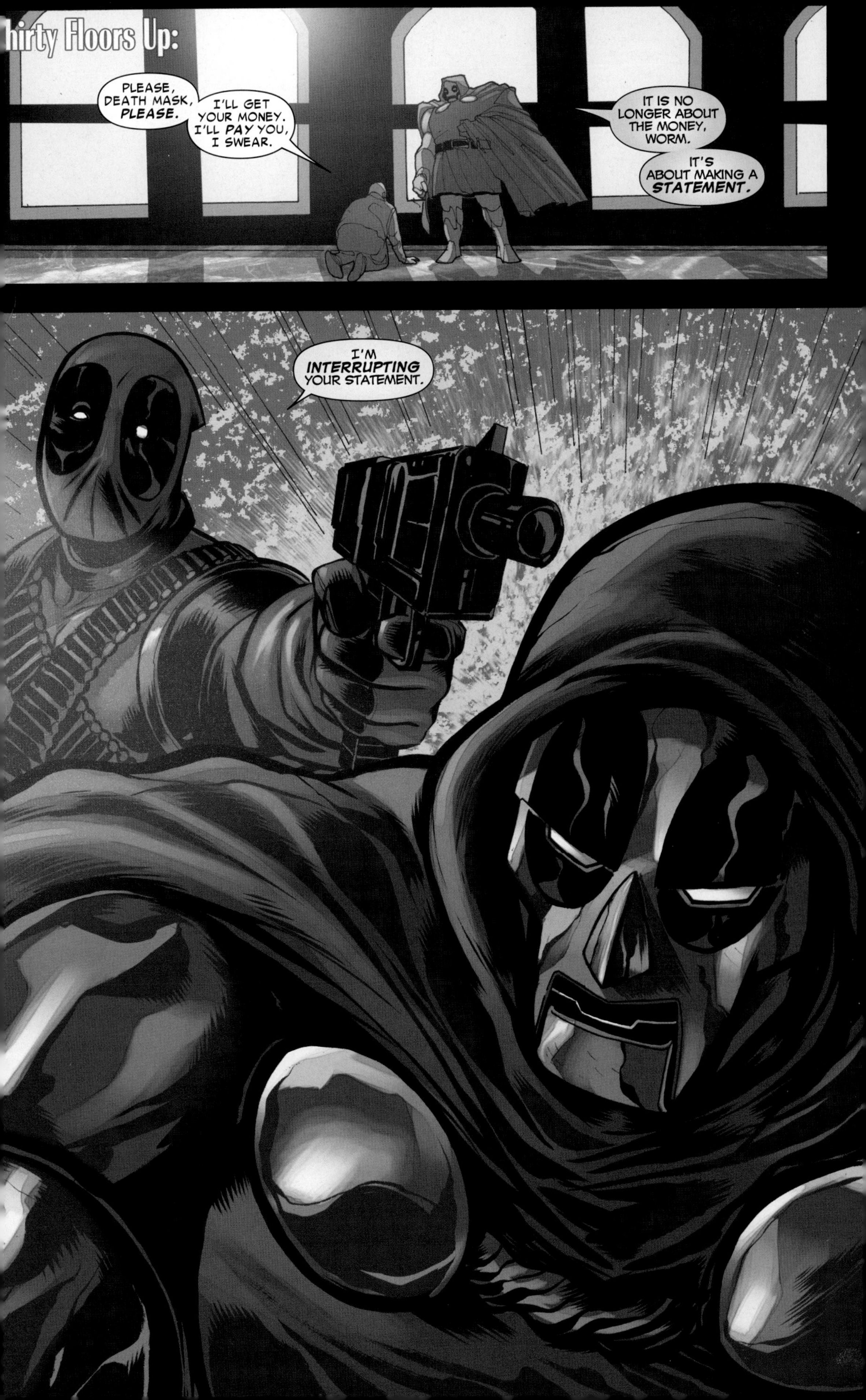
hirty Floors Up:
PLEASE, DEATH MASK, PLEASE.
I'LL GET YOUR MONEY. I'LL PAY YOU, I SWEAR.
IT IS NO LONGER ABOUT THE MONEY, WORM.
IT'S ABOUT MAKING A STATEMENT.
I'M INTERRUPTING YOUR STATEMENT.

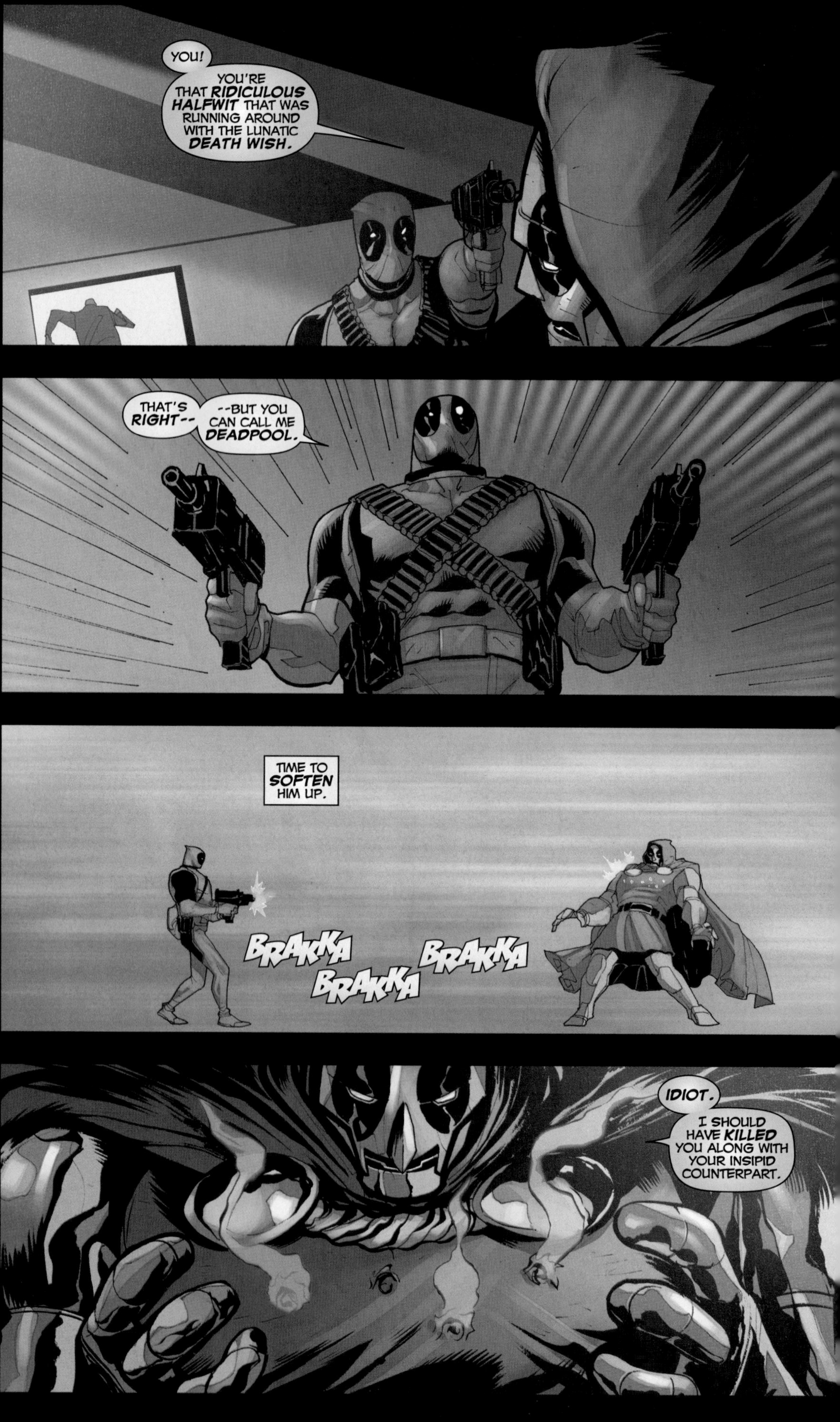

YOU!
YOU'RE THAT RIDICULOUS HALFWIT THAT WAS RUNNING AROUND WITH THE LUNATIC DEATH WISH.
THAT'S RIGHT--
--BUT YOU CAN CALL ME DEADPOOL.
TIME TO SOFTEN HIM UP.
BRAKKA
BRAKKA
BRAKKA
IDIOT.
I SHOULD HAVE KILLED YOU ALONG WITH YOUR INSIPID COUNTERPART.

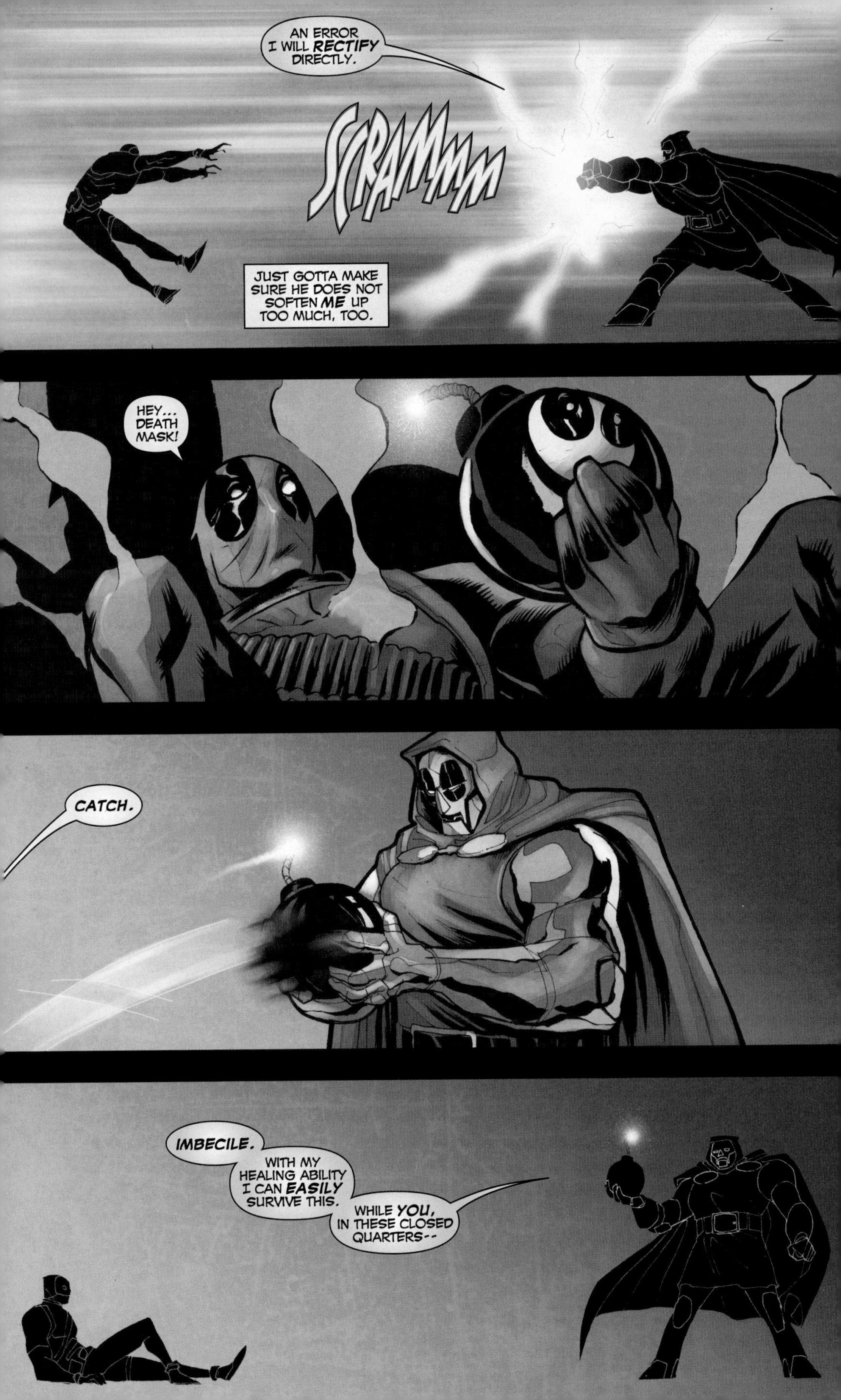
AN ERROR I WILL RECTIFY DIRECTLY.
SCRAMMMM
JUST GOTTA MAKE SURE HE DOES NOT SOFTEN ME UP TOO MUCH, TOO.
HEY... DEATH MASK!
CATCH.
IMBECILE.
WITH MY HEALING ABILITY I CAN EASILY SURVIVE THIS.
WHILE YOU, IN THESE CLOSED QUARTERS--

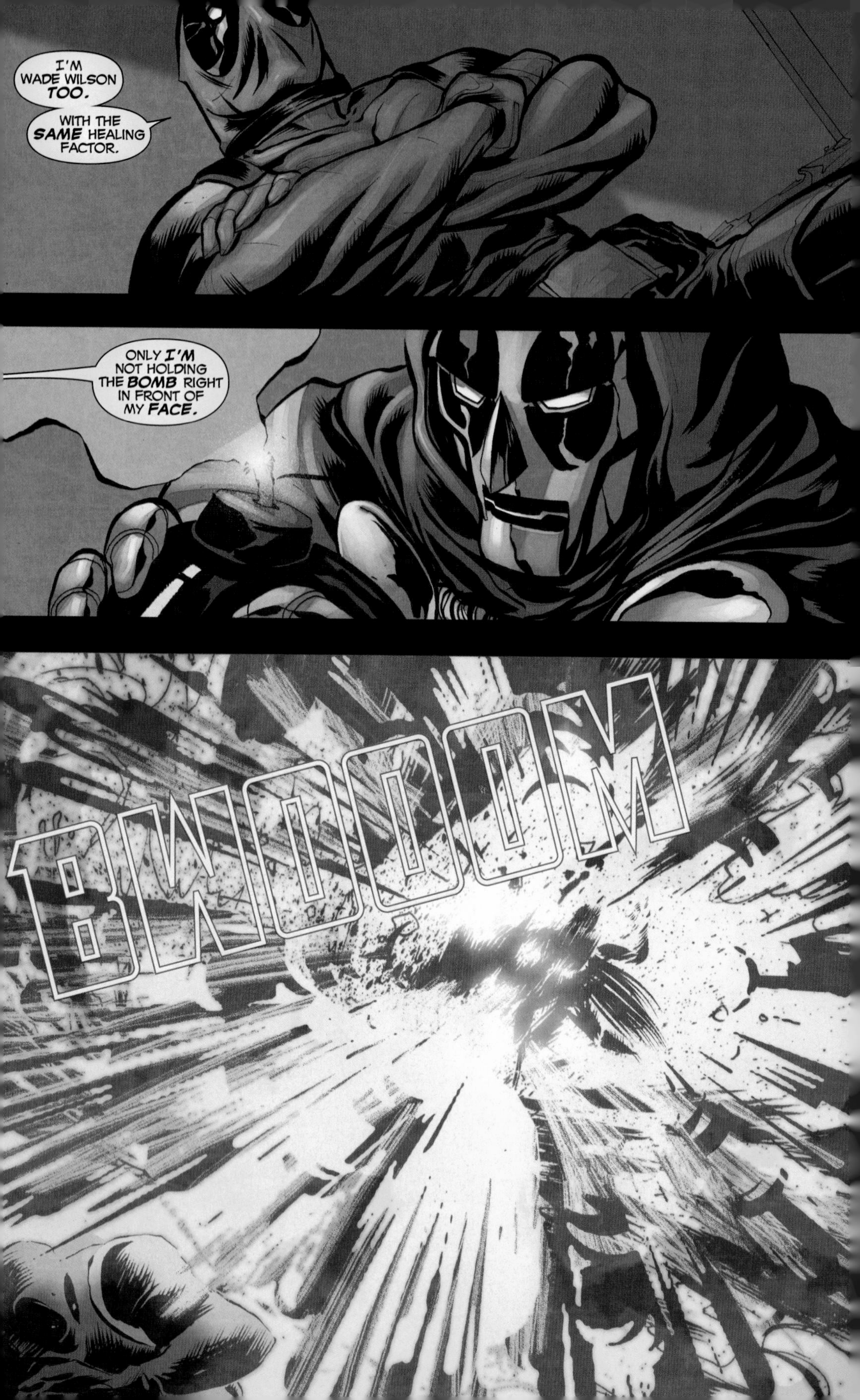
I'M WADE WILSON TOO.
WITH THE SAME HEALING FACTOR.
ONLY I'M NOT HOLDING THE BOMB RIGHT IN FRONT OF MY FACE.
BWOOOM

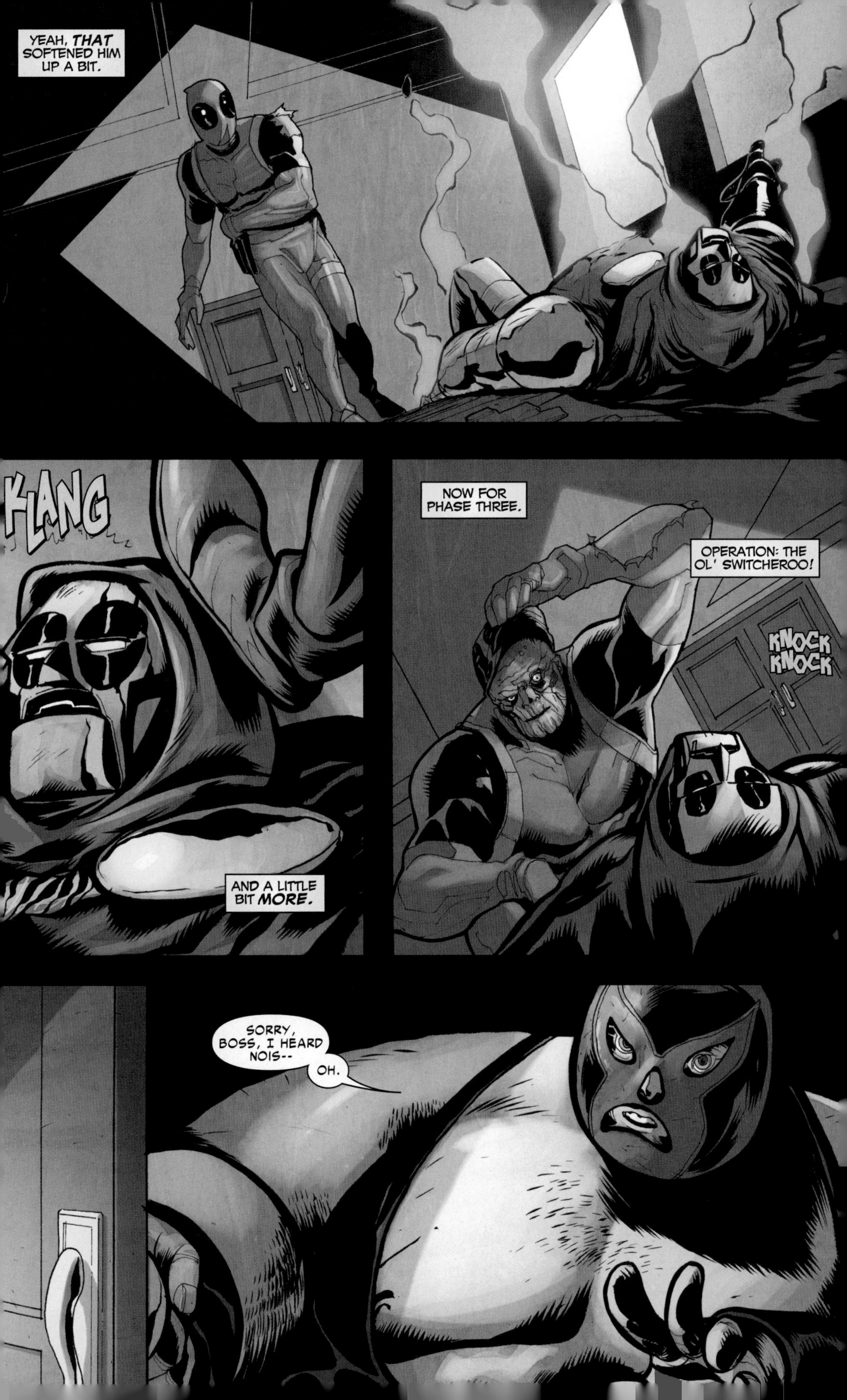
YEAH, *THAT* SOFTENED HIM UP A BIT.
KLANG
AND A LITTLE BIT *MORE.*
NOW FOR PHASE THREE.
OPERATION: THE OL' SWITCHEROO!
KNOCK KNOCK
SORRY, BOSS, I HEARD NOIS--
OH.

AM I INTERRUPTING SOMETHING?

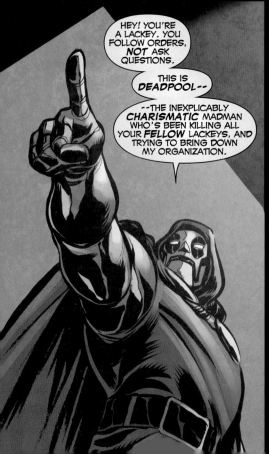

HEY! YOU'RE A LACKEY. YOU FOLLOW ORDERS, *NOT* ASK QUESTIONS.

THIS IS *DEADPOOL*--

--THE INEXPLICABLY *CHARISMATIC* MADMAN WHO'S BEEN KILLING ALL YOUR *FELLOW* LACKEYS, AND TRYING TO BRING DOWN MY ORGANIZATION.

WHAT'S YOUR NAME AGAIN, LACKEY?

WILSON FISK, BOSS...*DEAD WEIGHT.*

HEH...

WELL, HELP ME CARRY HIM DOWNSTAIRS, FISK. WE'RE TAKING HIM TO THE PIER.

OH YEAH? WHY WE DOING THAT, BOSS?

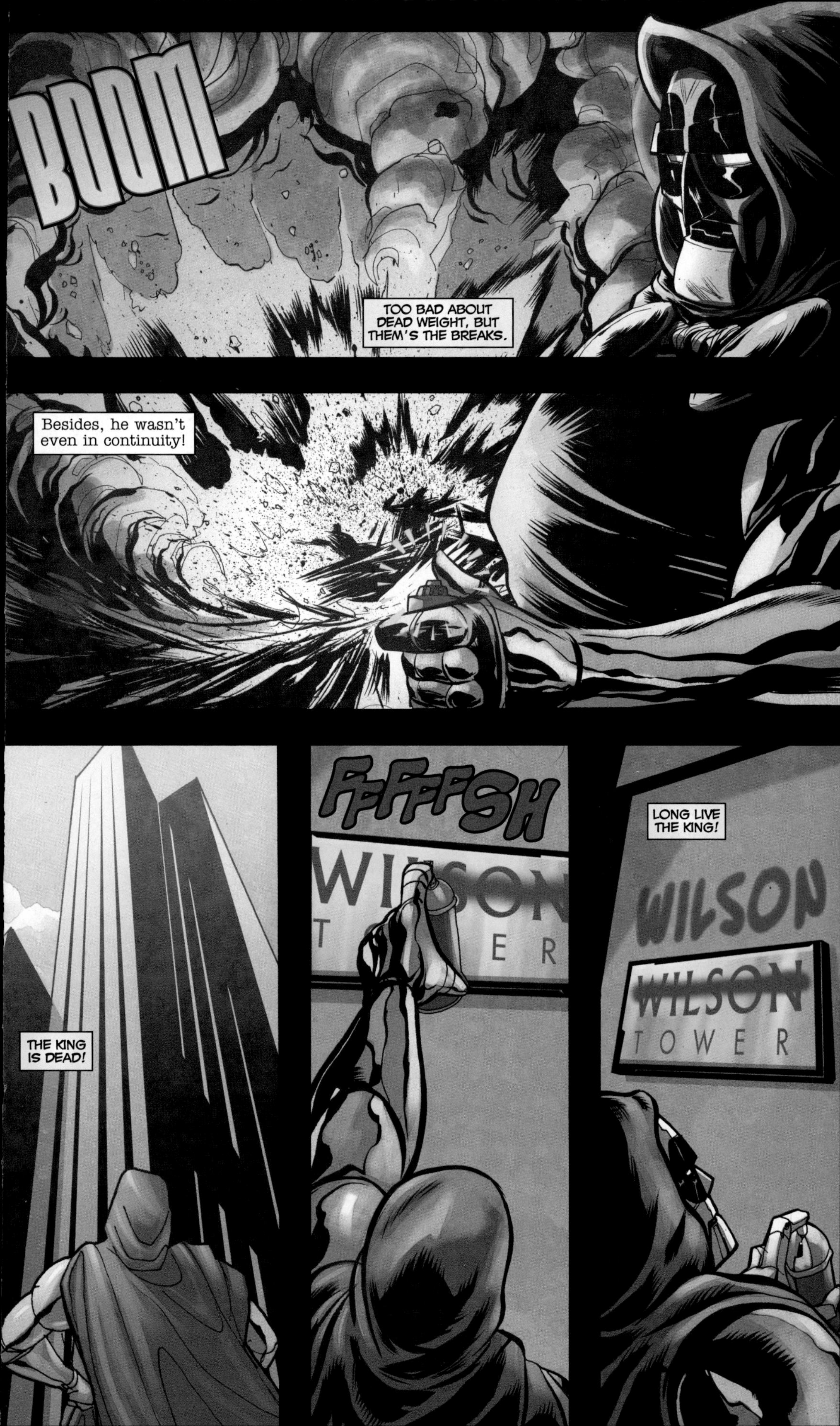
BOOM
TOO BAD ABOUT DEAD WEIGHT, BUT THEM'S THE BREAKS.
Besides, he wasn't even in continuity!
THE KING IS DEAD!
FFFFFSH
WILSON TOWER
LONG LIVE THE KING!
WILSON
WILSON TOWER

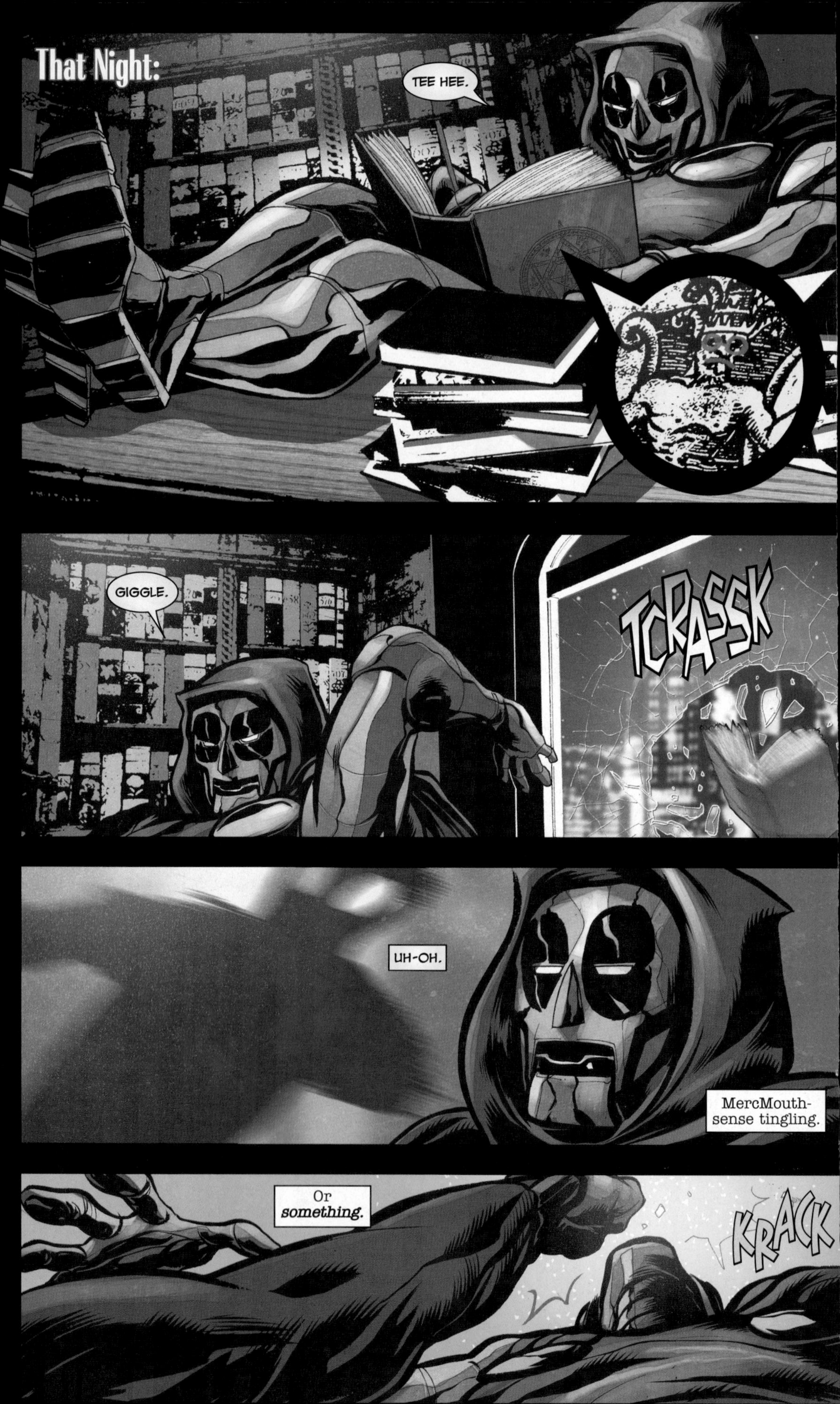

That Night:
TEE HEE.
GIGGLE.
TCRASSK
UH-OH.
MercMouth-
sense tingling.
Or
something.
KRACK

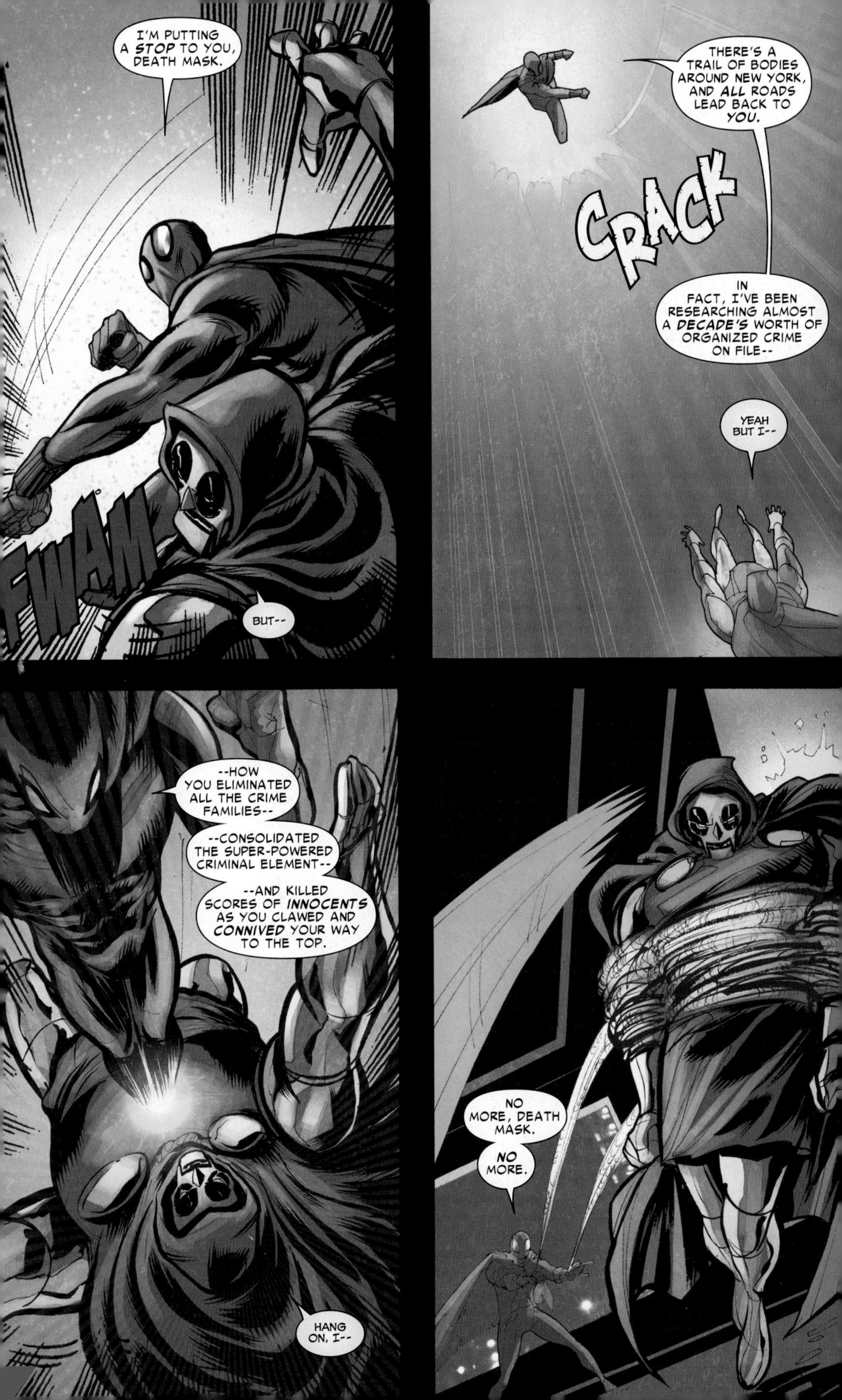
I'M PUTTING A STOP TO YOU, DEATH MASK.
FWAM
BUT--
THERE'S A TRAIL OF BODIES AROUND NEW YORK, AND ALL ROADS LEAD BACK TO YOU.
CRACK
IN FACT, I'VE BEEN RESEARCHING ALMOST A DECADE'S WORTH OF ORGANIZED CRIME ON FILE--
YEAH BUT I--
--HOW YOU ELIMINATED ALL THE CRIME FAMILIES--
--CONSOLIDATED THE SUPER-POWERED CRIMINAL ELEMENT--
--AND KILLED SCORES OF INNOCENTS AS YOU CLAWED AND CONNIVED YOUR WAY TO THE TOP.
HANG ON, I--
NO MORE, DEATH MASK.
NO MORE.

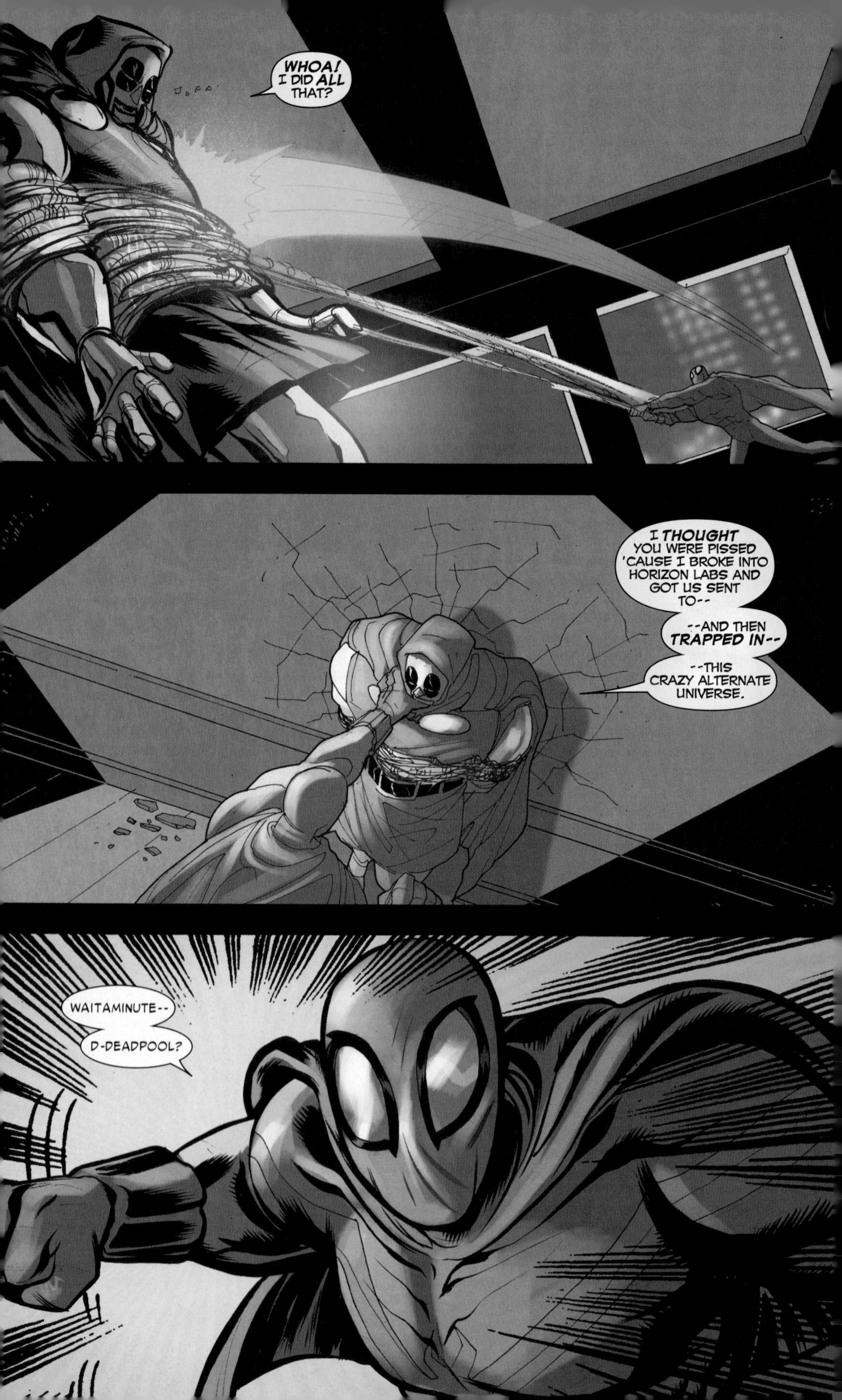
WHOA! I DID ALL THAT?
I THOUGHT YOU WERE PISSED 'CAUSE I BROKE INTO HORIZON LABS AND GOT US SENT TO--
--AND THEN TRAPPED IN--
--THIS CRAZY ALTERNATE UNIVERSE.
WAITAMINUTE--
D-DEADPOOL?

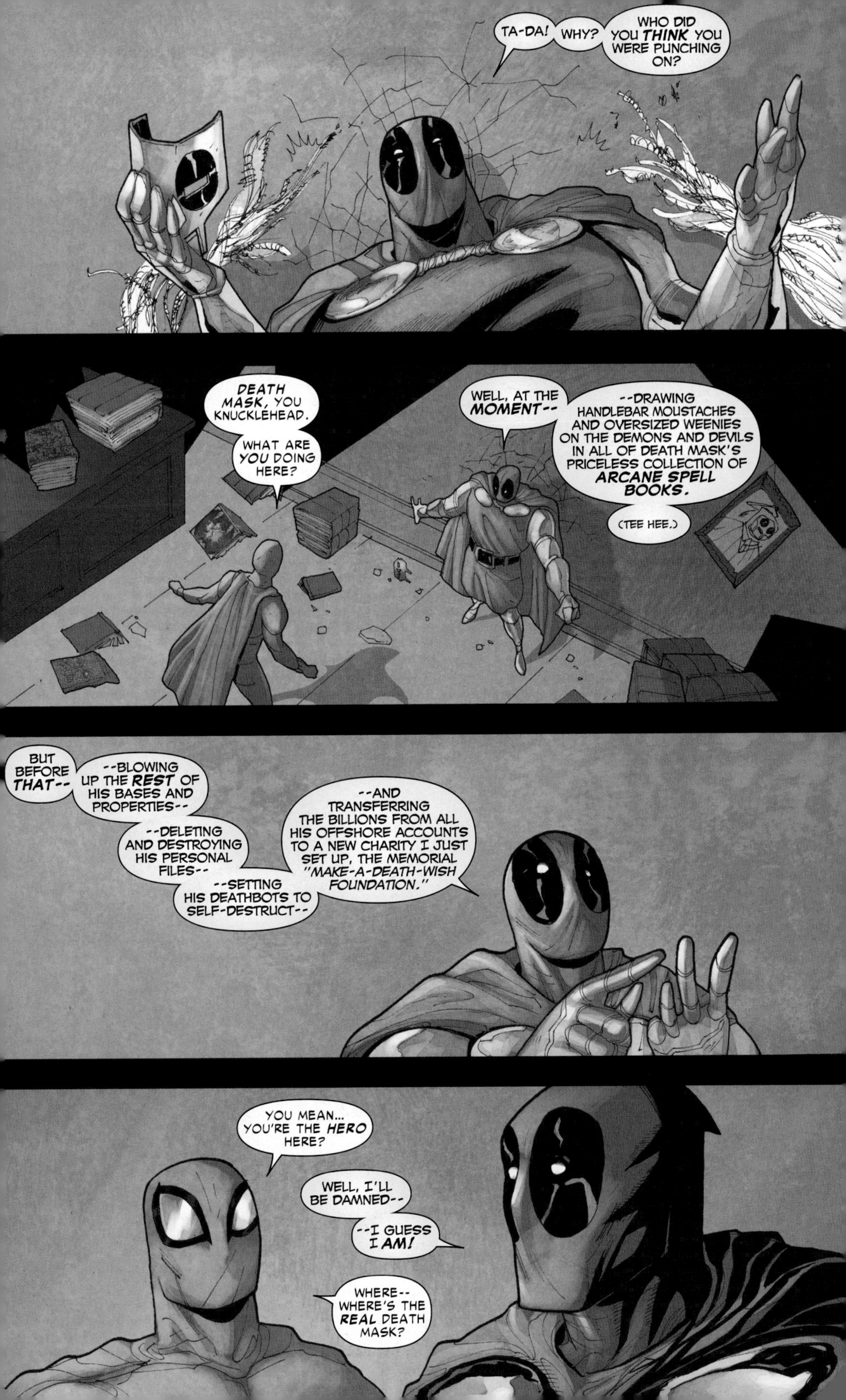
TA-DA!
WHY?
WHO DID YOU THINK YOU WERE PUNCHING ON?
DEATH MASK, YOU KNUCKLEHEAD.
WHAT ARE YOU DOING HERE?
WELL, AT THE MOMENT--
--DRAWING HANDLEBAR MOUSTACHES AND OVERSIZED WEENIES ON THE DEMONS AND DEVILS IN ALL OF DEATH MASK'S PRICELESS COLLECTION OF ARCANE SPELL BOOKS.
(TEE HEE.)
BUT BEFORE THAT--
--BLOWING UP THE REST OF HIS BASES AND PROPERTIES--
--DELETING AND DESTROYING HIS PERSONAL FILES--
--SETTING HIS DEATHBOTS TO SELF-DESTRUCT--
--AND TRANSFERRING THE BILLIONS FROM ALL HIS OFFSHORE ACCOUNTS TO A NEW CHARITY I JUST SET UP, THE MEMORIAL "MAKE-A-DEATH-WISH FOUNDATION."
YOU MEAN... YOU'RE THE HERO HERE?
WELL, I'LL BE DAMNED--
--I GUESS I AM!
WHERE-- WHERE'S THE REAL DEATH MASK?

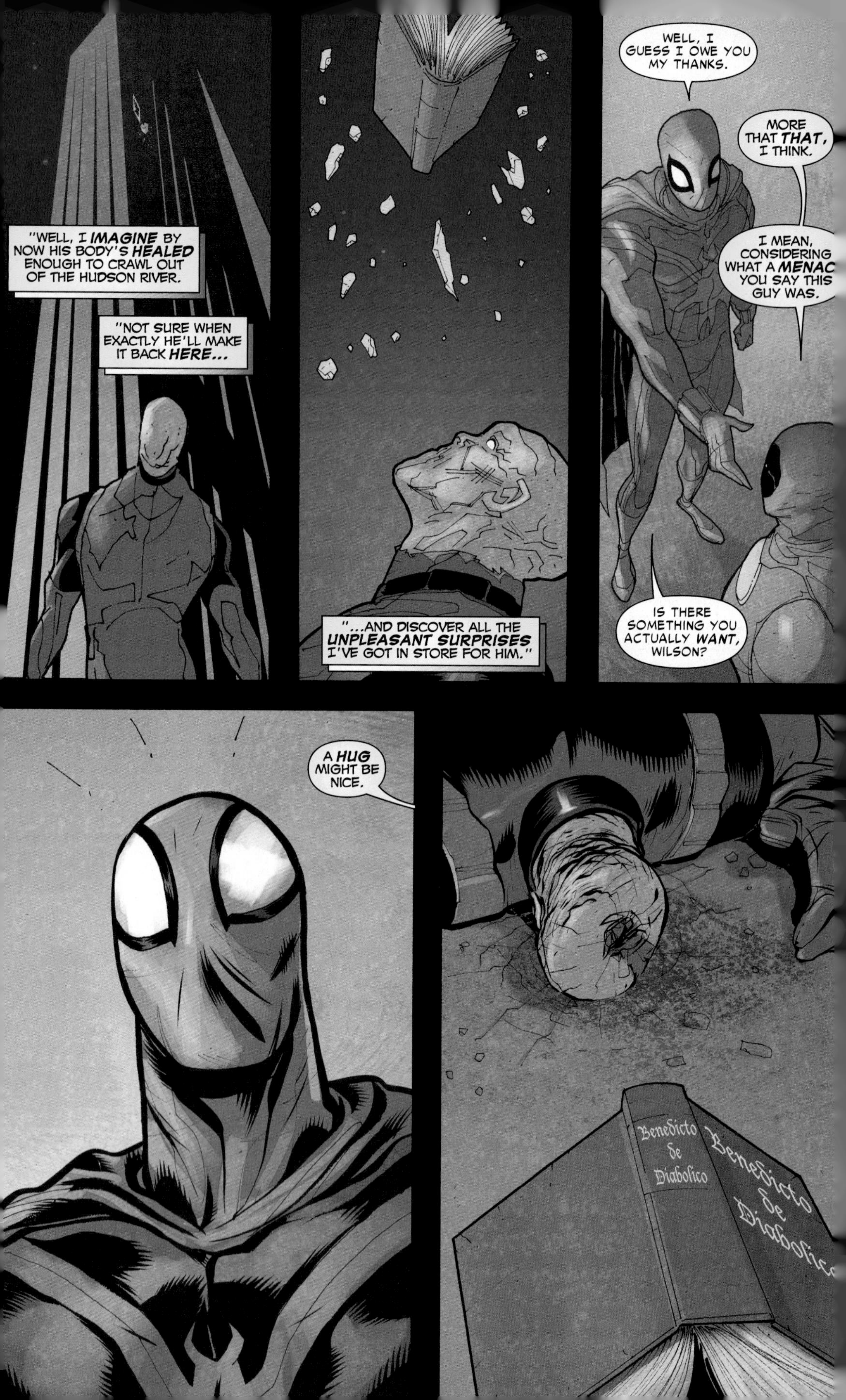
"WELL, I IMAGINE BY NOW HIS BODY'S HEALED ENOUGH TO CRAWL OUT OF THE HUDSON RIVER.
"NOT SURE WHEN EXACTLY HE'LL MAKE IT BACK HERE...
"...AND DISCOVER ALL THE UNPLEASANT SURPRISES I'VE GOT IN STORE FOR HIM."
WELL, I GUESS I OWE YOU MY THANKS.
MORE THAT THAT, I THINK.
I MEAN, CONSIDERING WHAT A MENAC YOU SAY THIS GUY WAS.
IS THERE SOMETHING YOU ACTUALLY WANT, WILSON?
A HUG MIGHT BE NICE.
Benedicto de Diabolico
Benedicto de Diabolica

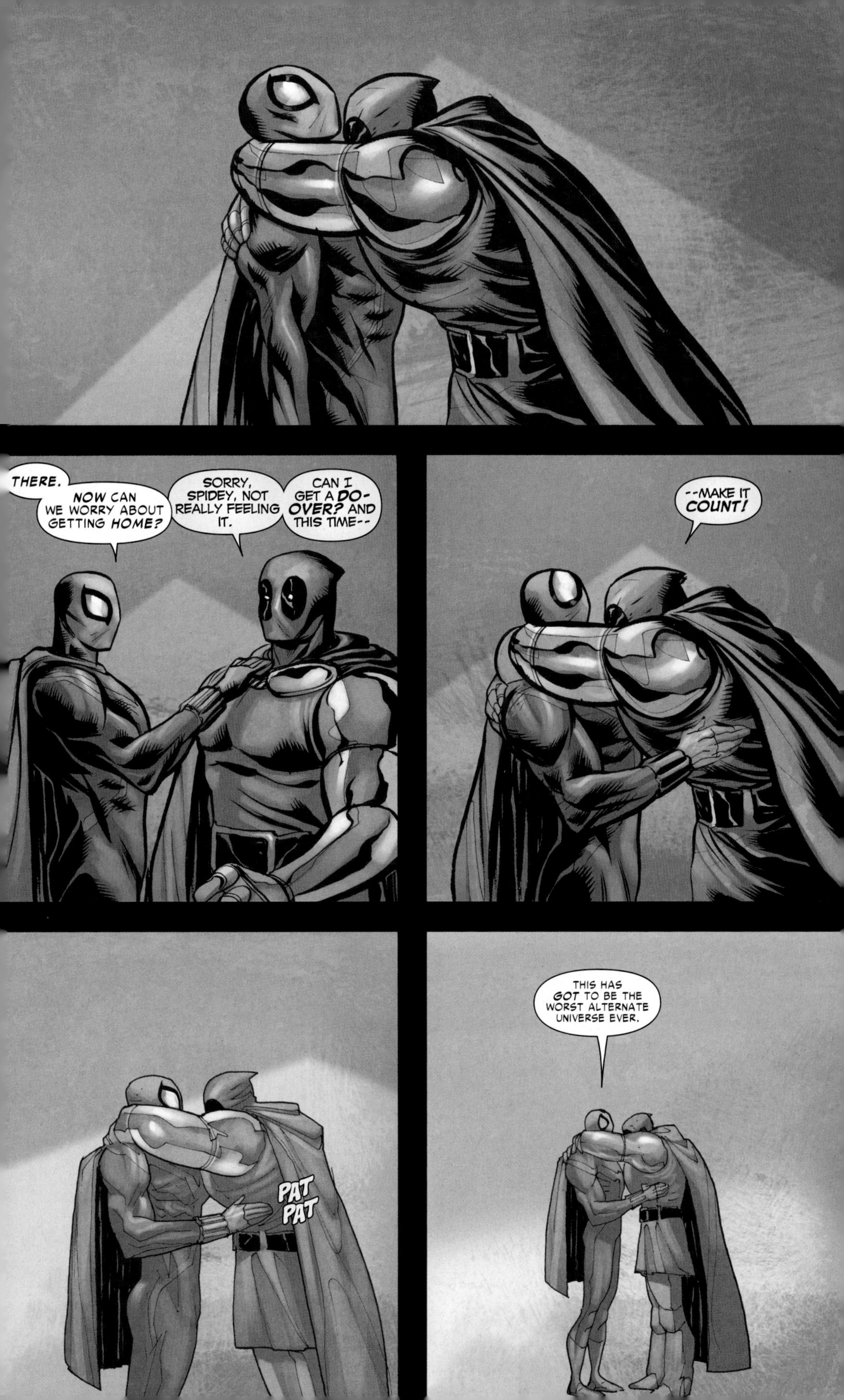
THERE. NOW CAN WE WORRY ABOUT GETTING HOME?
SORRY, SPIDEY, NOT REALLY FEELING IT.
CAN I GET A DO-OVER? AND THIS TIME--
--MAKE IT COUNT!
PAT PAT
THIS HAS GOT TO BE THE WORST ALTERNATE UNIVERSE EVER.

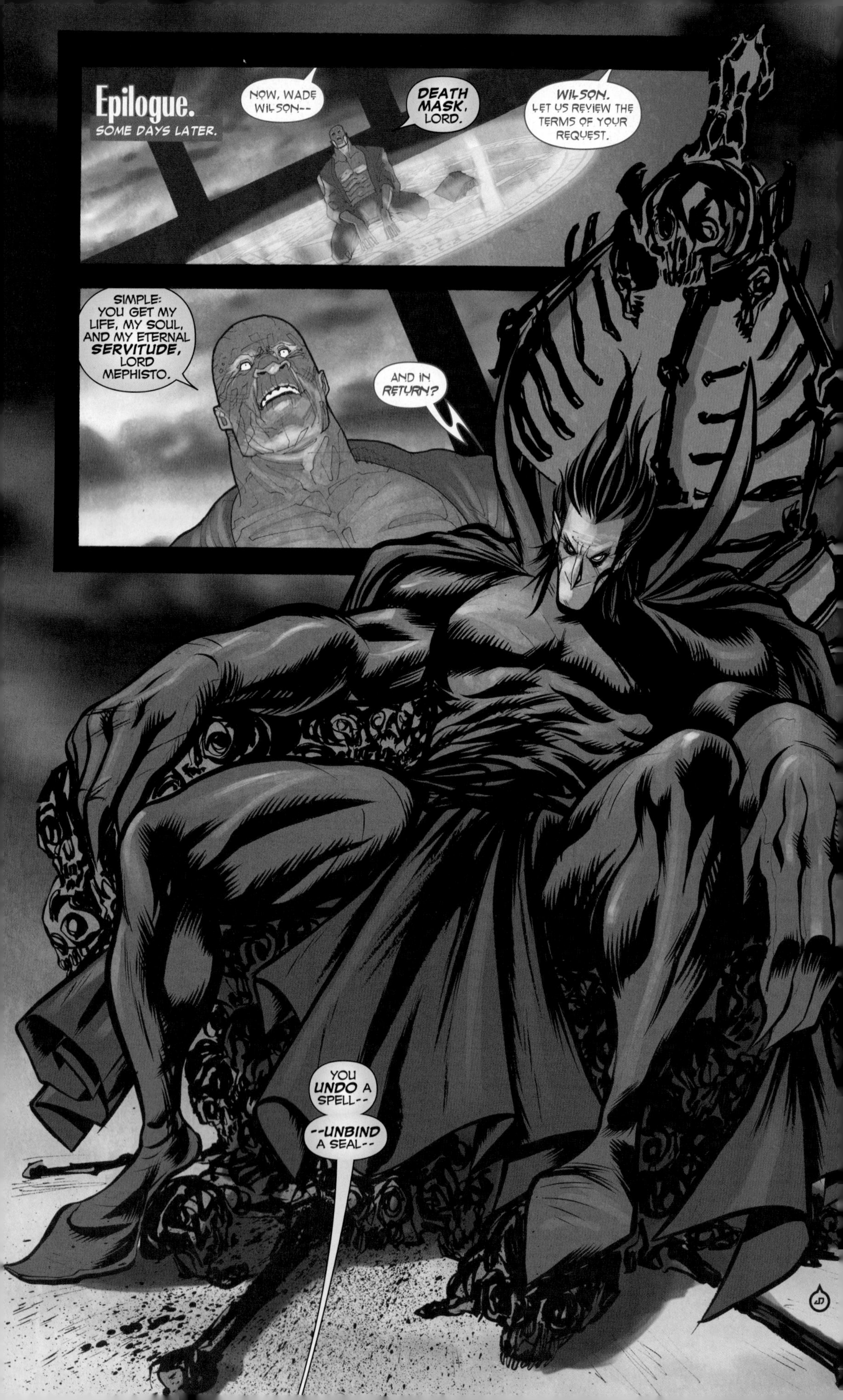
Epilogue.
SOME DAYS LATER.
NOW, WADE WILSON--
DEATH MASK, LORD.
WILSON. LET US REVIEW THE TERMS OF YOUR REQUEST.
SIMPLE: YOU GET MY LIFE, MY SOUL, AND MY ETERNAL SERVITUDE, LORD MEPHISTO.
AND IN RETURN?
YOU UNDO A SPELL--
--UNBIND A SEAL--

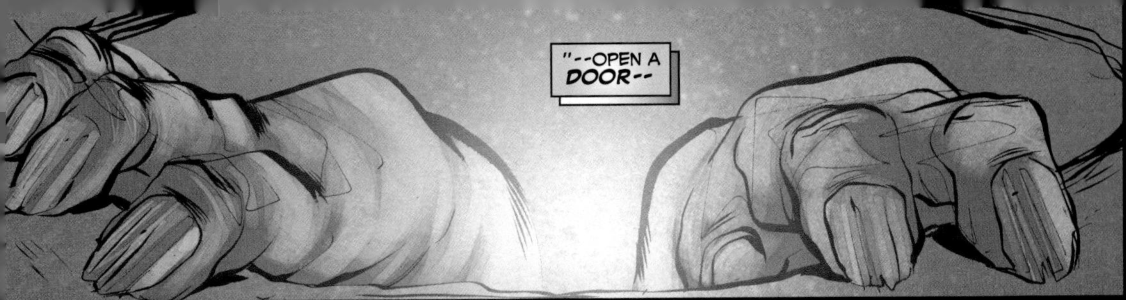
"--OPEN A DOOR--

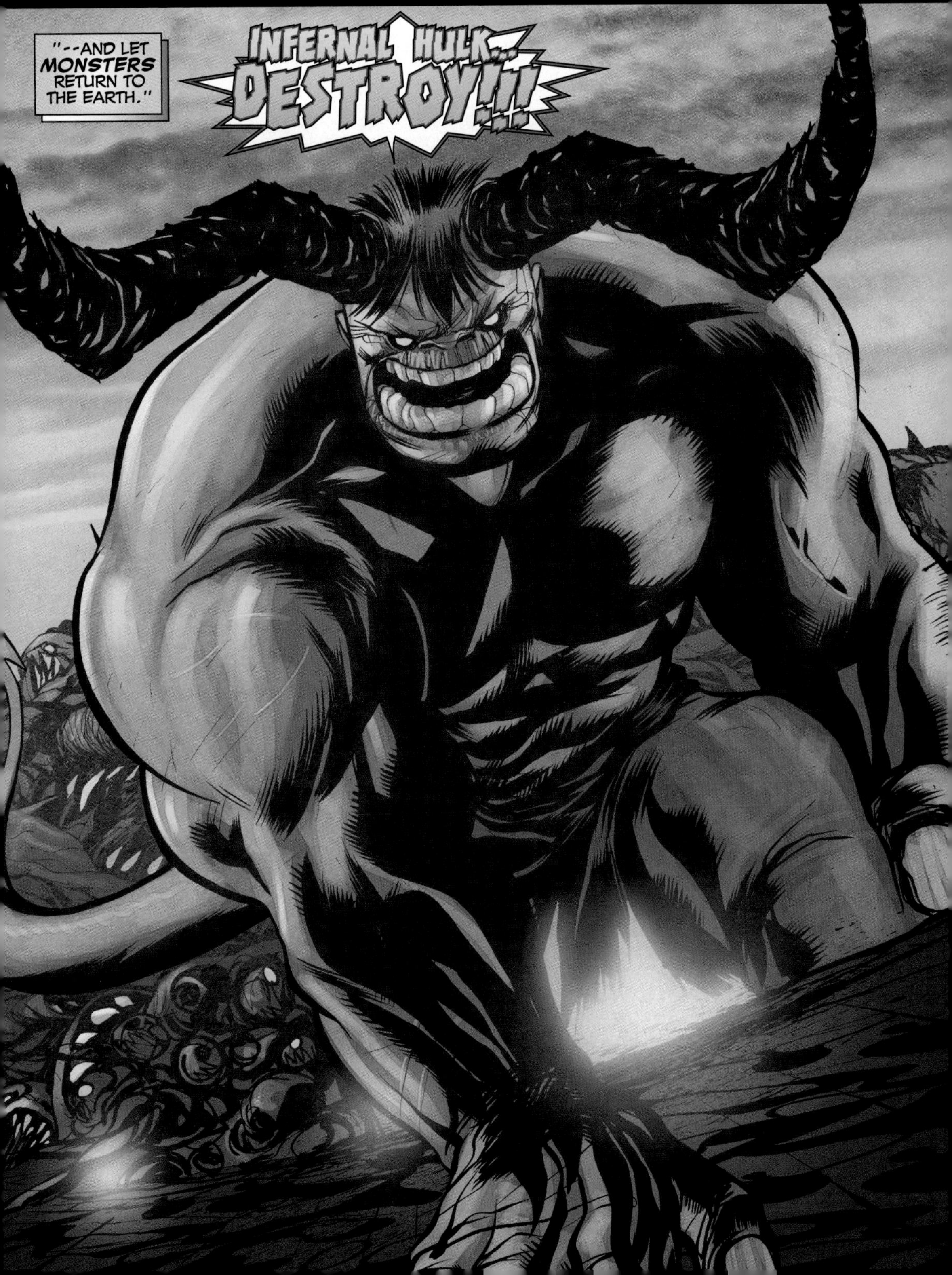
"--AND LET MONSTERS RETURN TO THE EARTH."
INFERNAL HULK... DESTROY!!!

INCREDIBLE HULKS ANNUAL #1

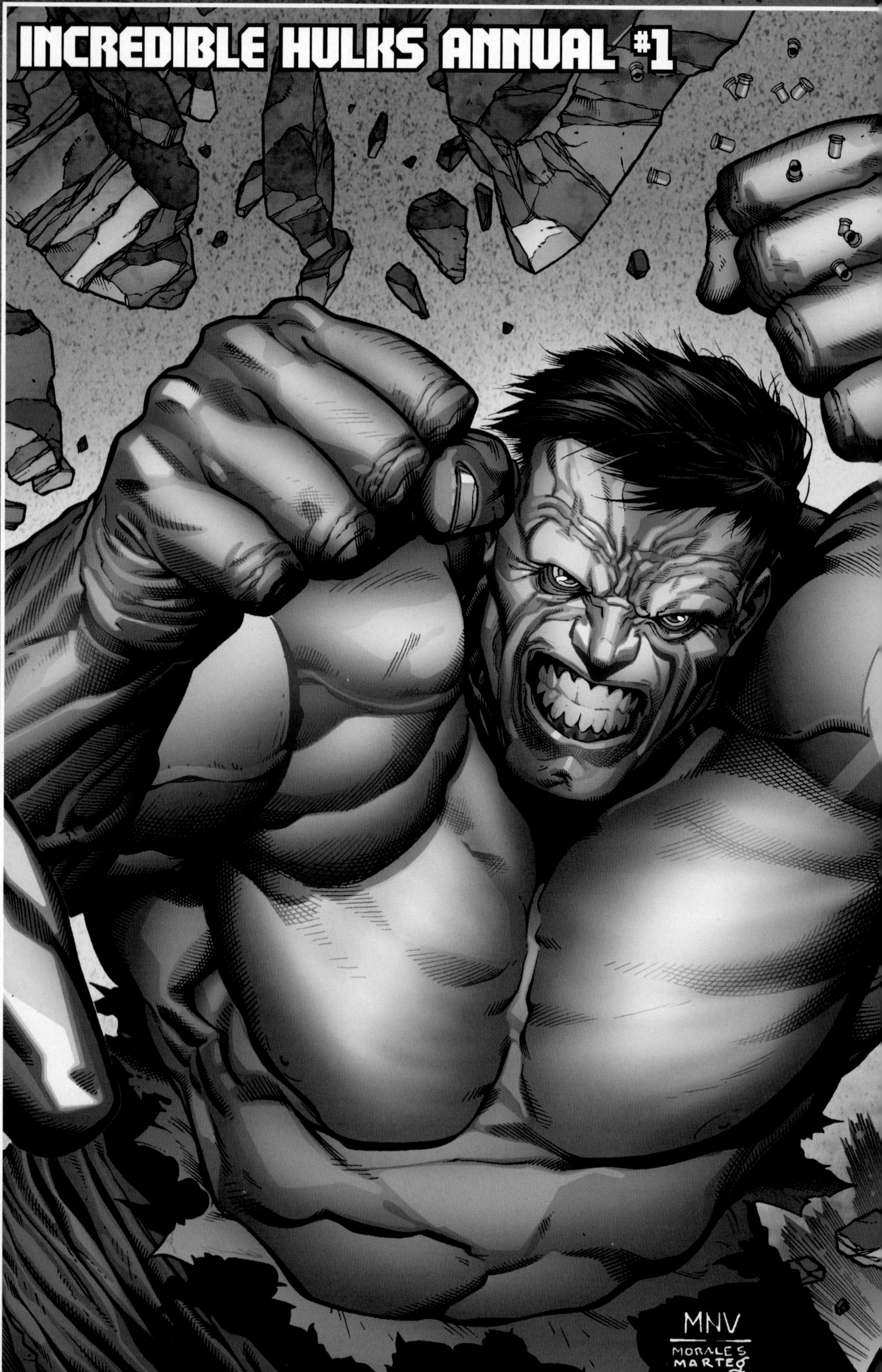
MNV
MORALES
MARTEG

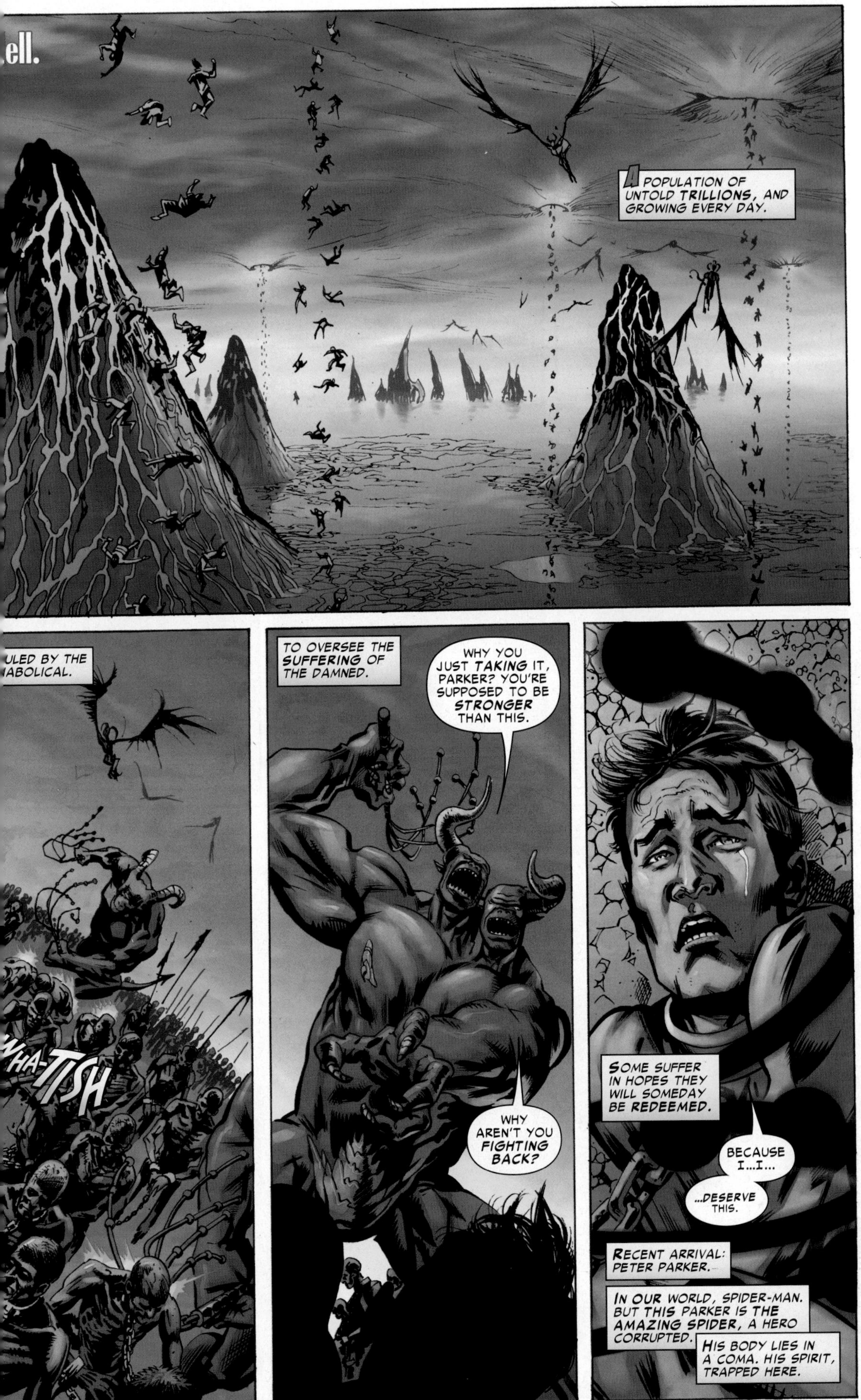
...ell.
A POPULATION OF UNTOLD TRILLIONS, AND GROWING EVERY DAY.
...ULED BY THE ...ABOLICAL.
WHA-TISH
TO OVERSEE THE SUFFERING OF THE DAMNED.
WHY YOU JUST TAKING IT, PARKER? YOU'RE SUPPOSED TO BE STRONGER THAN THIS.
WHY AREN'T YOU FIGHTING BACK?
SOME SUFFER IN HOPES THEY WILL SOMEDAY BE REDEEMED.
BECAUSE I...I...
...DESERVE THIS.
RECENT ARRIVAL: PETER PARKER.
IN OUR WORLD, SPIDER-MAN. BUT THIS PARKER IS THE AMAZING SPIDER, A HERO CORRUPTED.
HIS BODY LIES IN A COMA. HIS SPIRIT, TRAPPED HERE.

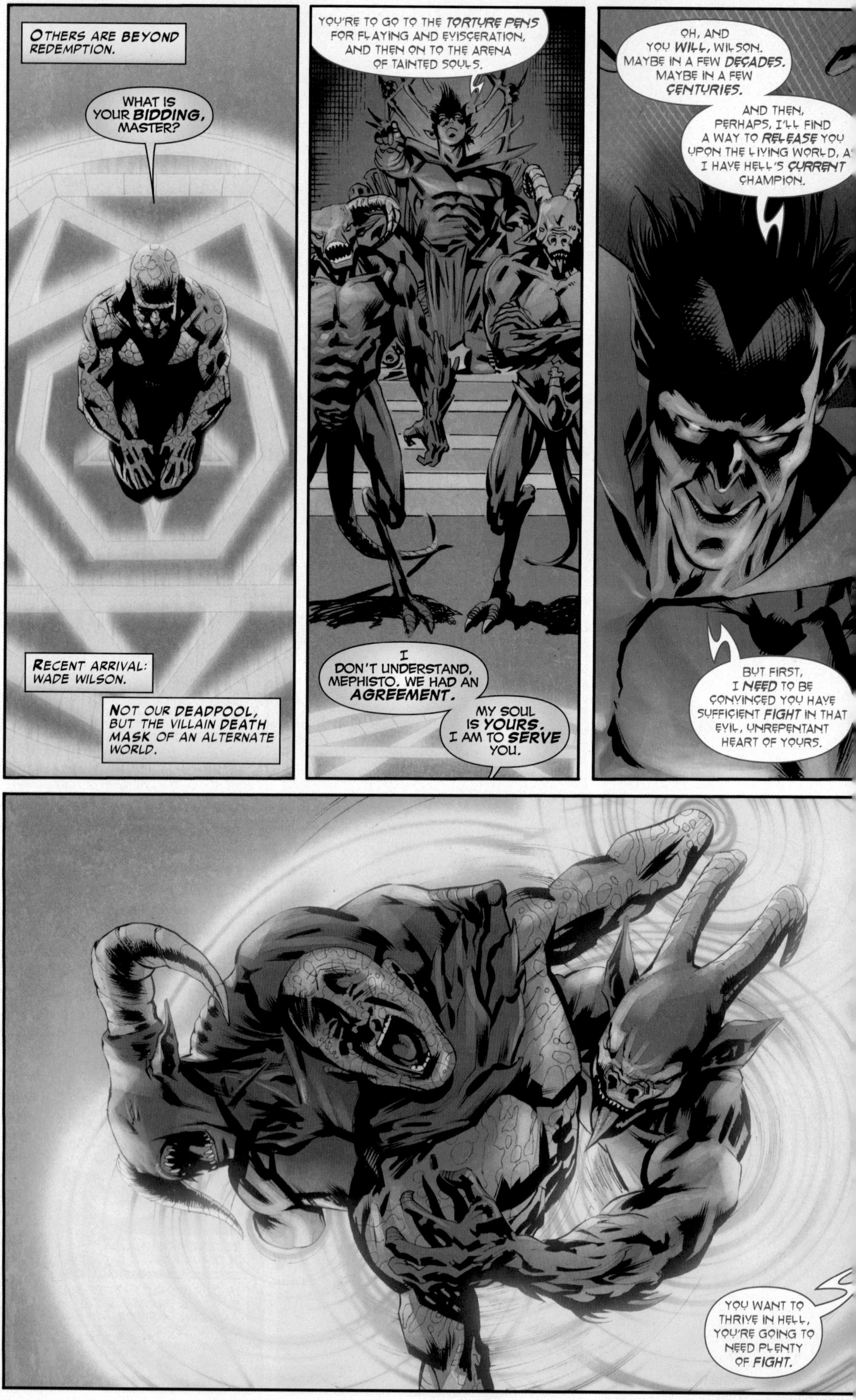
OTHERS ARE BEYOND REDEMPTION.
WHAT IS YOUR BIDDING, MASTER?
RECENT ARRIVAL: WADE WILSON.
NOT OUR DEADPOOL, BUT THE VILLAIN DEATH MASK OF AN ALTERNATE WORLD.
YOU'RE TO GO TO THE TORTURE PENS FOR FLAYING AND EVISCERATION, AND THEN ON TO THE ARENA OF TAINTED SOULS.
I DON'T UNDERSTAND, MEPHISTO. WE HAD AN AGREEMENT.
MY SOUL IS YOURS. I AM TO SERVE YOU.
OH, AND YOU WILL, WILSON. MAYBE IN A FEW DECADES. MAYBE IN A FEW CENTURIES.
AND THEN, PERHAPS, I'LL FIND A WAY TO RELEASE YOU UPON THE LIVING WORLD, A I HAVE HELL'S CURRENT CHAMPION.
BUT FIRST, I NEED TO BE CONVINCED YOU HAVE SUFFICIENT FIGHT IN THAT EVIL, UNREPENTANT HEART OF YOURS.
YOU WANT TO THRIVE IN HELL, YOU'RE GOING TO NEED PLENTY OF FIGHT.

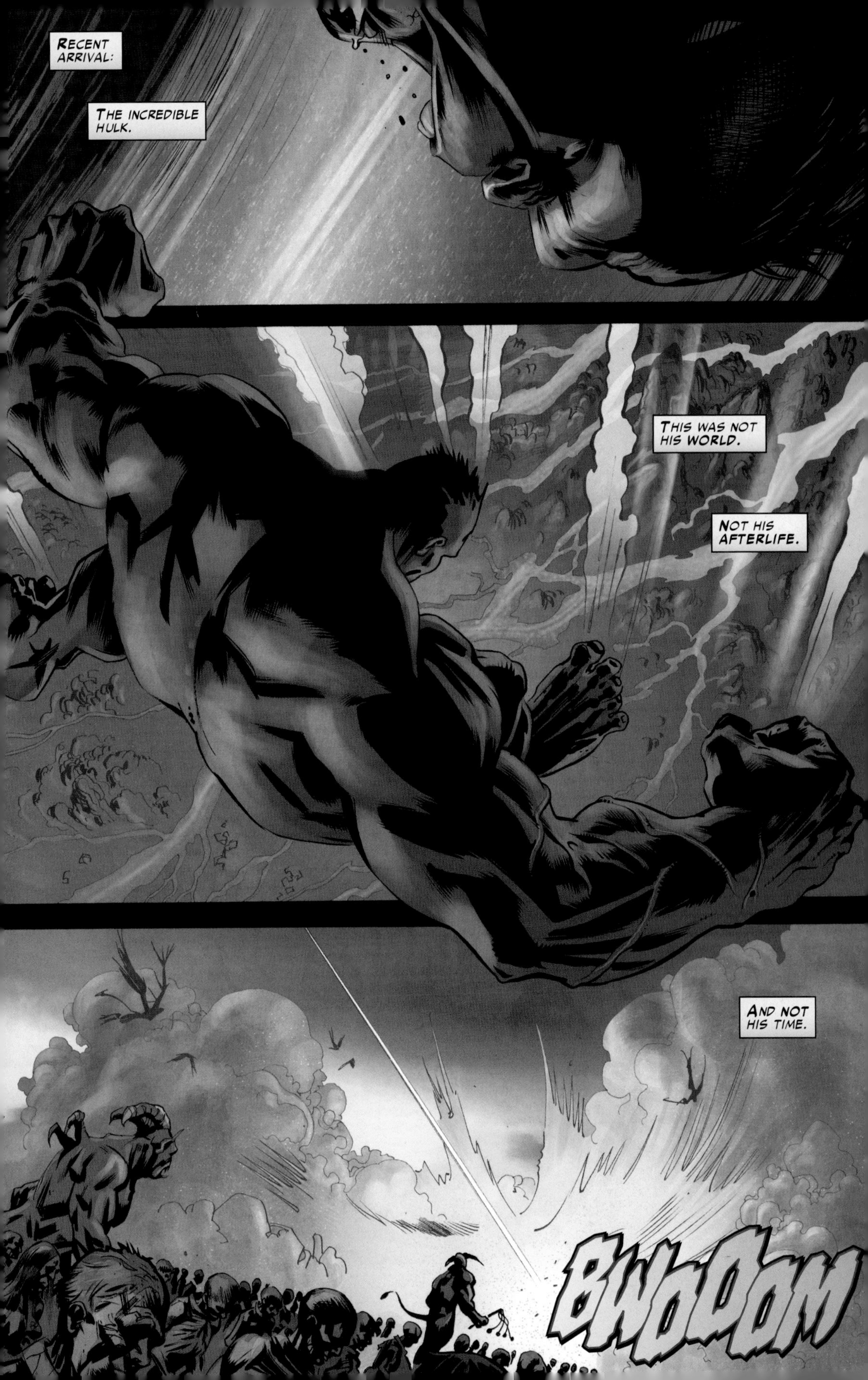
RECENT ARRIVAL:
THE INCREDIBLE HULK.
THIS WAS NOT HIS WORLD.
NOT HIS AFTERLIFE.
AND NOT HIS TIME.
BWOOOM

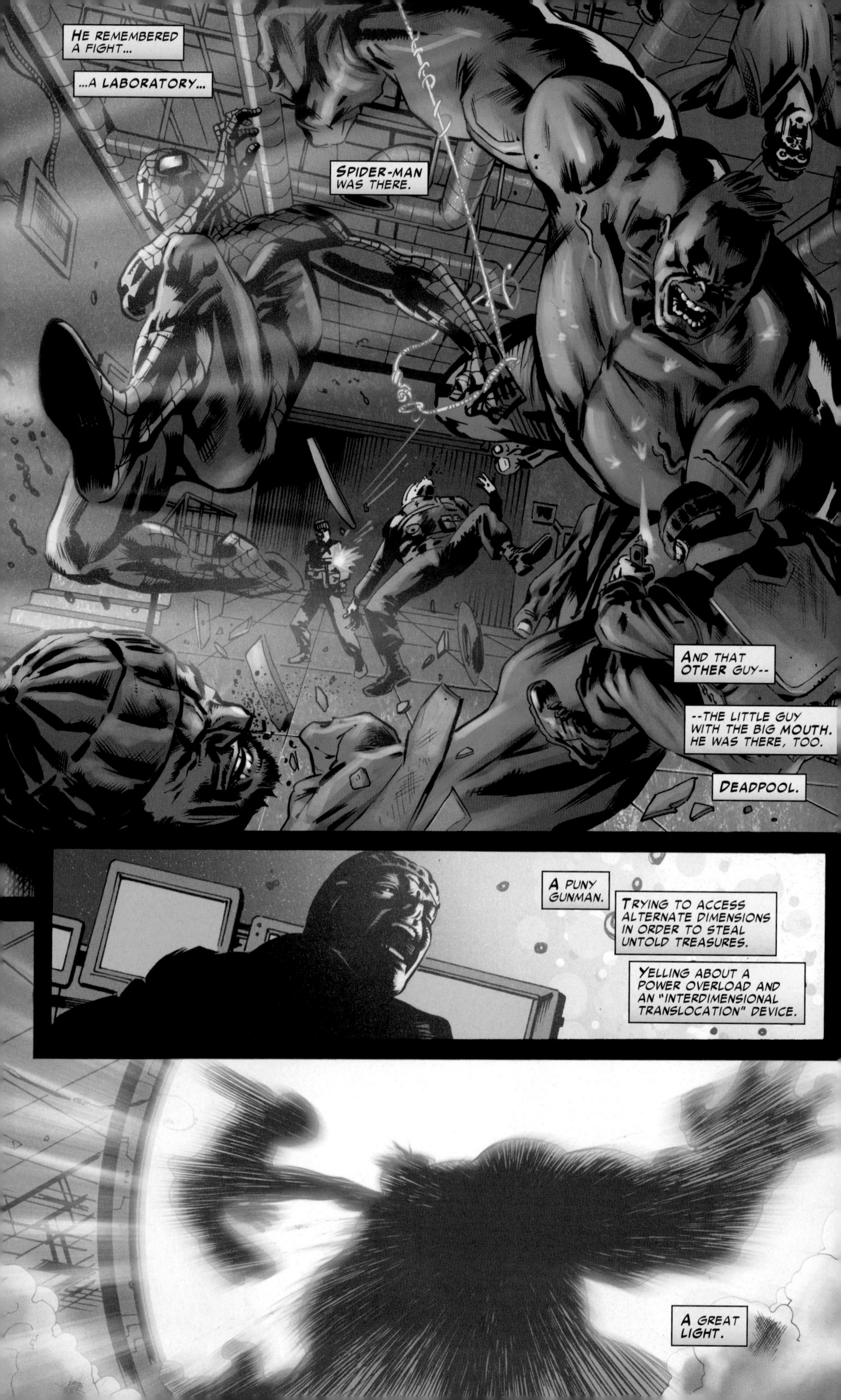

HE REMEMBERED A FIGHT...
...A LABORATORY...
SPIDER-MAN WAS THERE.
AND THAT OTHER GUY--
--THE LITTLE GUY WITH THE BIG MOUTH. HE WAS THERE, TOO.
DEADPOOL.
A PUNY GUNMAN.
TRYING TO ACCESS ALTERNATE DIMENSIONS IN ORDER TO STEAL UNTOLD TREASURES.
YELLING ABOUT A POWER OVERLOAD AND AN "INTERDIMENSIONAL TRANSLOCATION" DEVICE.
A GREAT LIGHT.

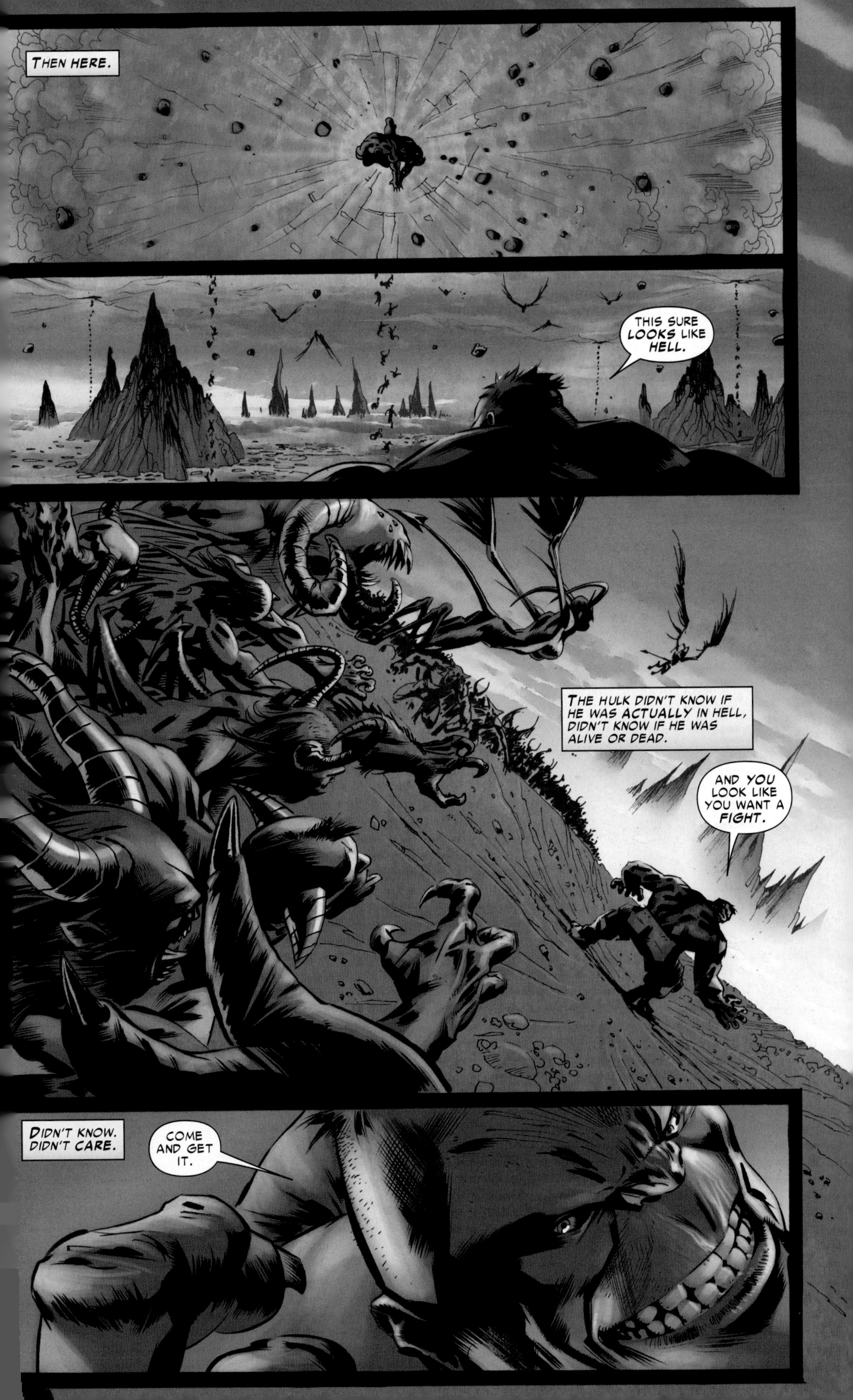
THEN HERE.
THIS SURE LOOKS LIKE HELL.
THE HULK DIDN'T KNOW IF HE WAS ACTUALLY IN HELL, DIDN'T KNOW IF HE WAS ALIVE OR DEAD.
AND YOU LOOK LIKE YOU WANT A FIGHT.
DIDN'T KNOW. DIDN'T CARE.
COME AND GET IT.

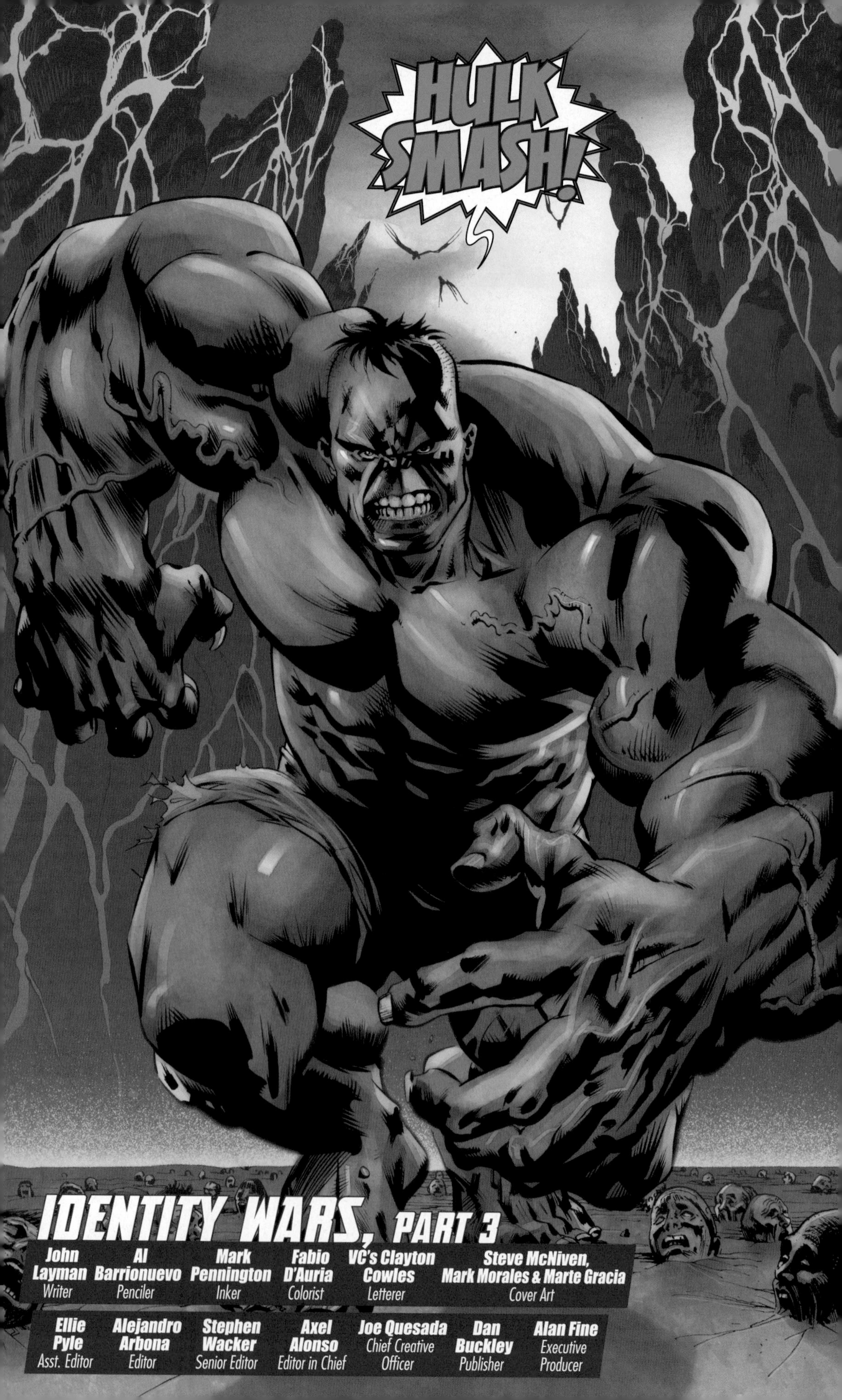
HULK SMASH!
IDENTITY WARS, PART 3
John Layman Writer
Al Barrionuevo Penciler
Mark Pennington Inker
Fabio D'Auria Colorist
VC's Clayton Cowles Letterer
Steve McNiven, Mark Morales & Marte Gracia Cover Art
Ellie Pyle Asst. Editor
Alejandro Arbona Editor
Stephen Wacker Senior Editor
Axel Alonso Editor in Chief
Joe Quesada Chief Creative Officer
Dan Buckley Publisher
Alan Fine Executive Producer

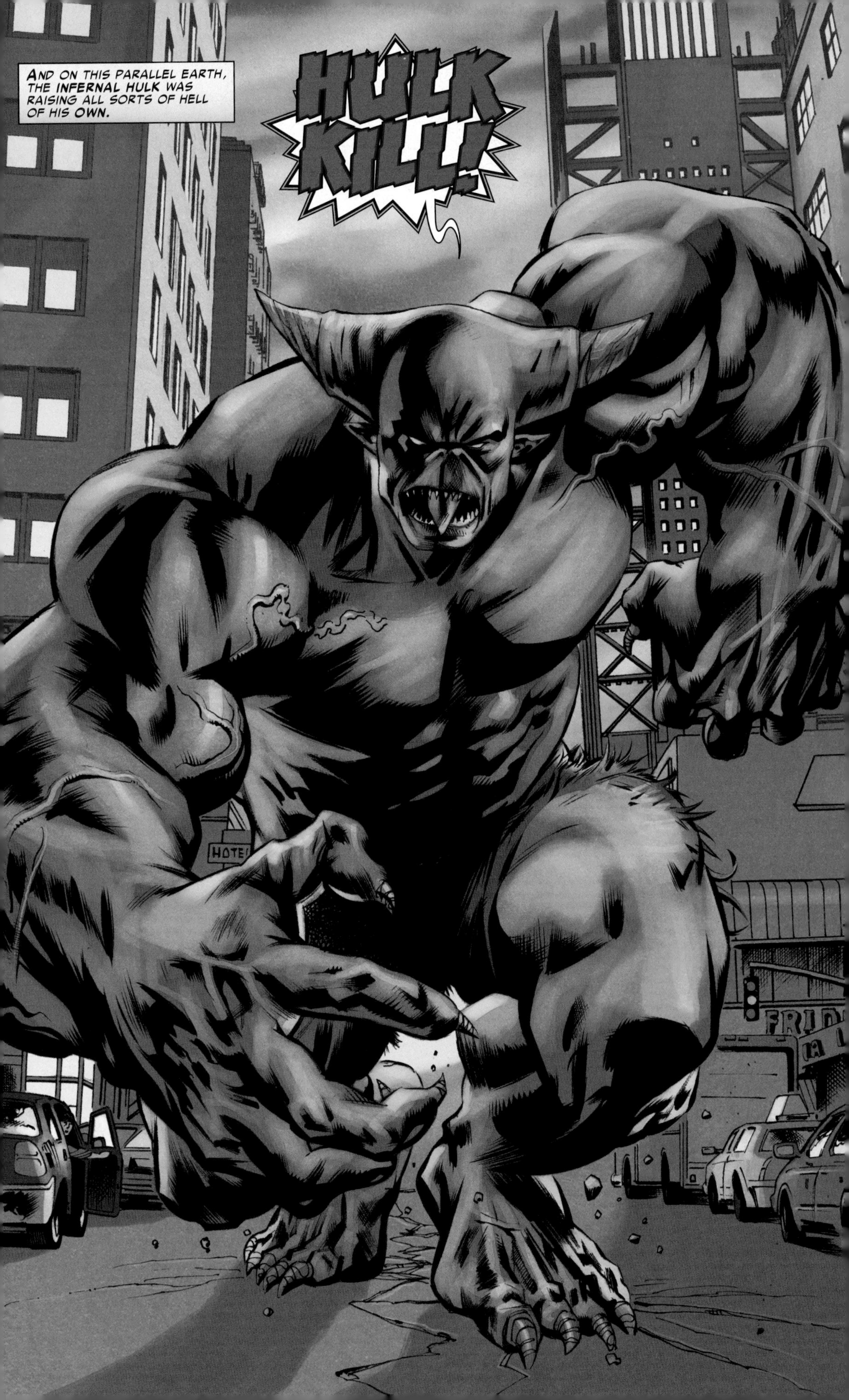
AND ON THIS PARALLEL EARTH, THE INFERNAL HULK WAS RAISING ALL SORTS OF HELL OF HIS OWN.
HULK KILL!
HOTEL

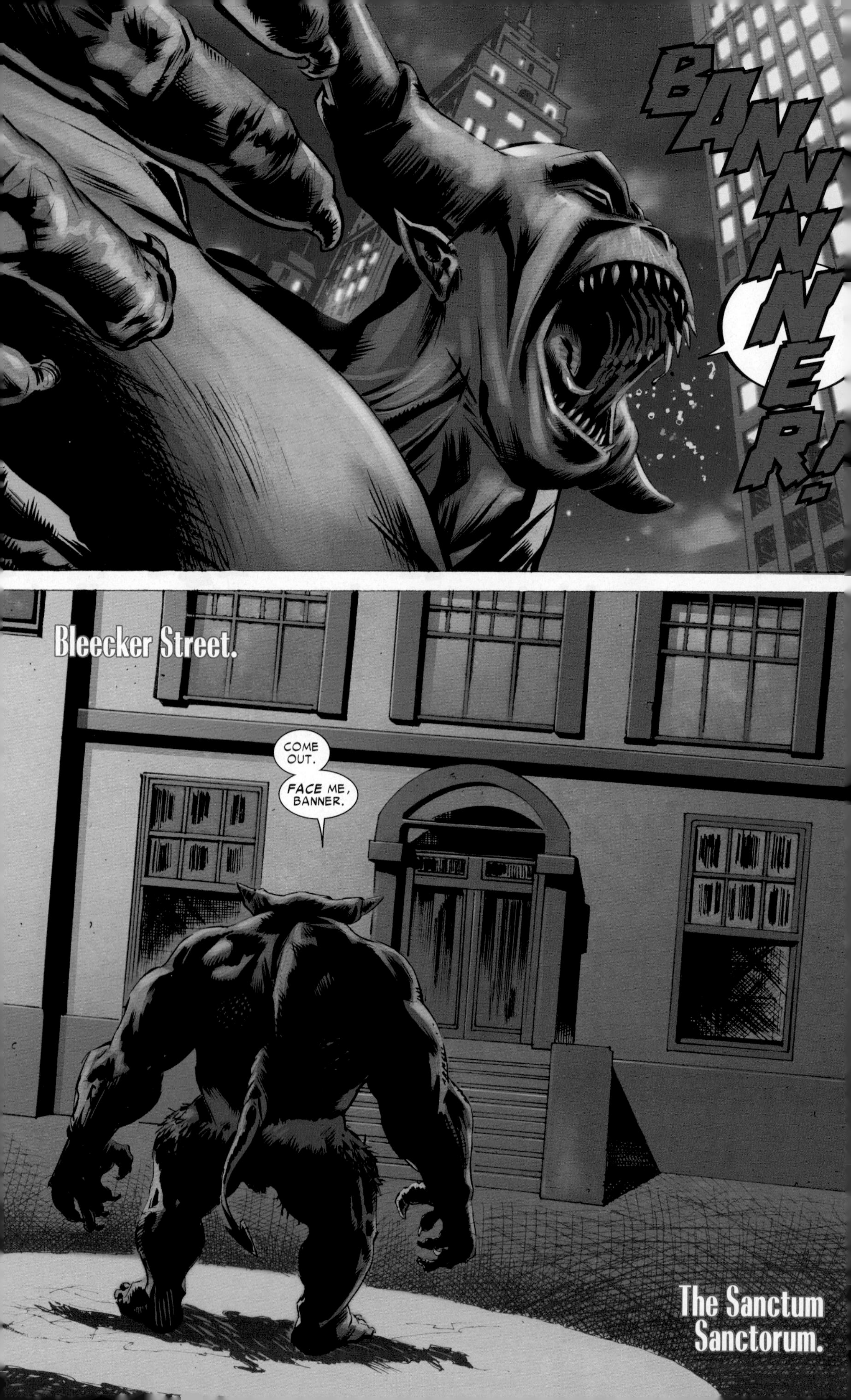
BANNNNER!!
Bleecker Street.
COME OUT.
FACE ME, BANNER.
The Sanctum Sanctorum.

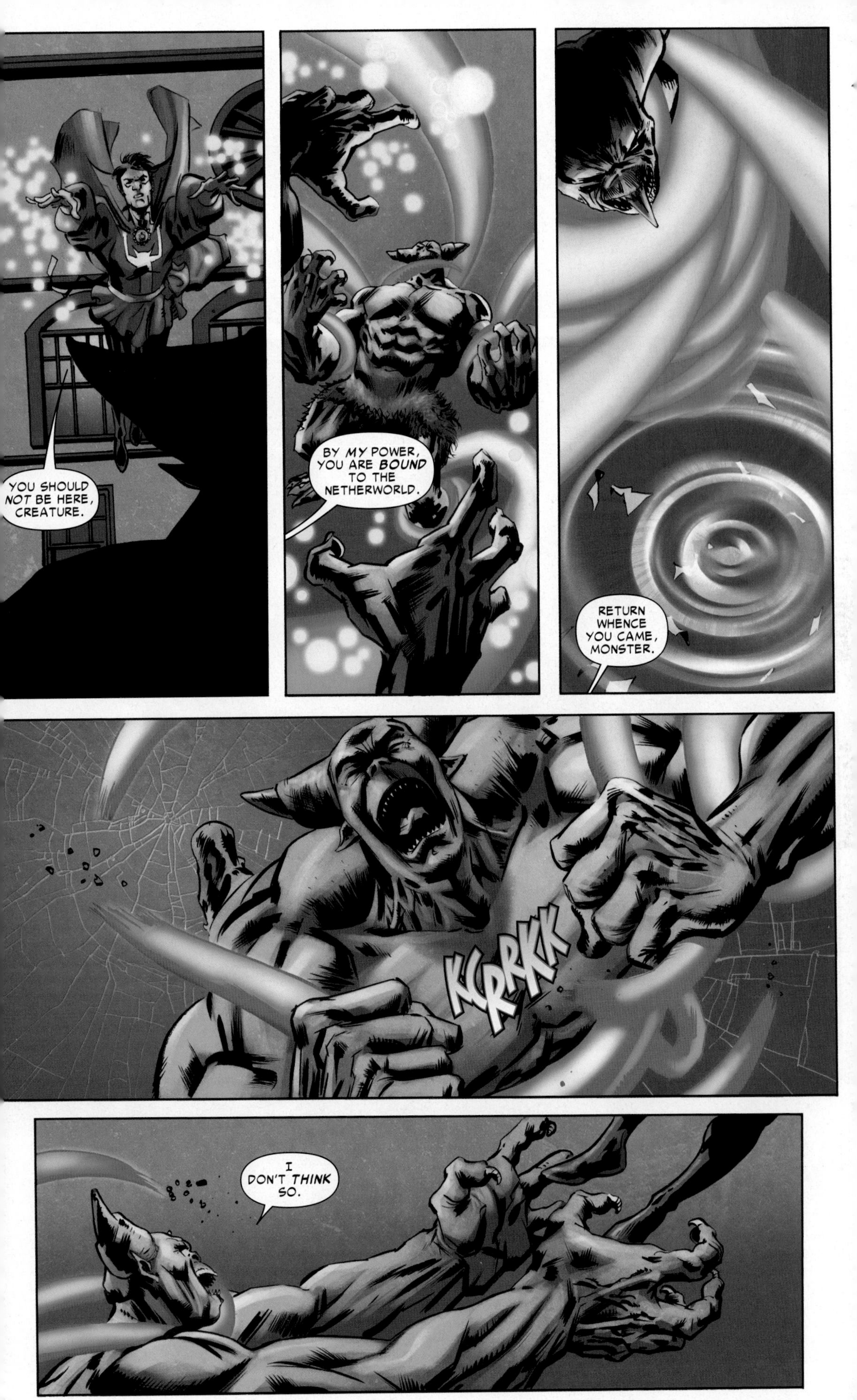
YOU SHOULD NOT BE HERE, CREATURE.
BY MY POWER, YOU ARE BOUND TO THE NETHERWORLD.
RETURN WHENCE YOU CAME, MONSTER.
KCRRKK
I DON'T THINK SO.

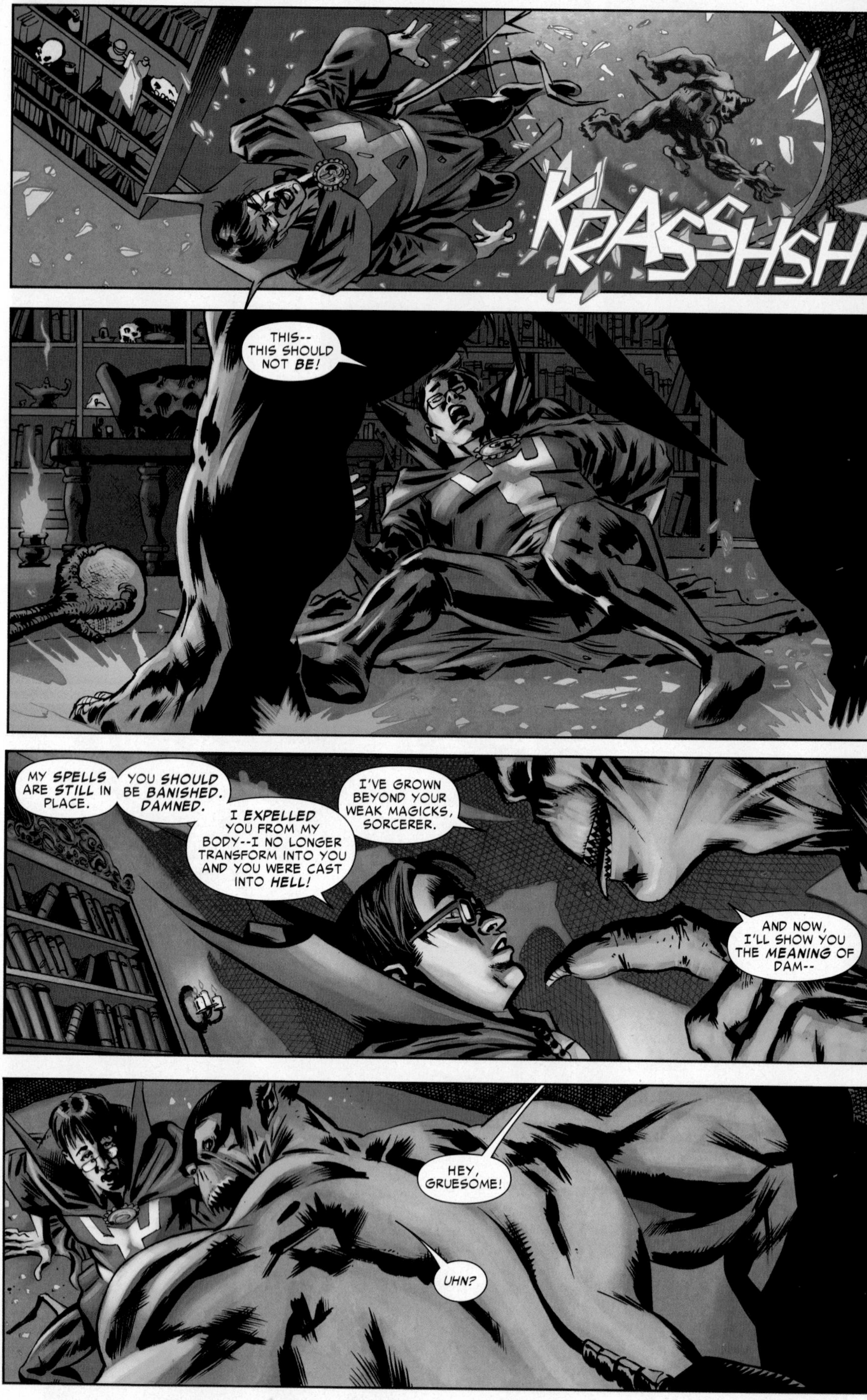
KRASSHSH
THIS-- THIS SHOULD NOT BE!
MY SPELLS ARE STILL IN PLACE.
YOU SHOULD BE BANISHED. DAMNED.
I EXPELLED YOU FROM MY BODY--I NO LONGER TRANSFORM INTO YOU AND YOU WERE CAST INTO HELL!
I'VE GROWN BEYOND YOUR WEAK MAGICKS, SORCERER.
AND NOW, I'LL SHOW YOU THE MEANING OF DAM--
HEY, GRUESOME!
UHN?

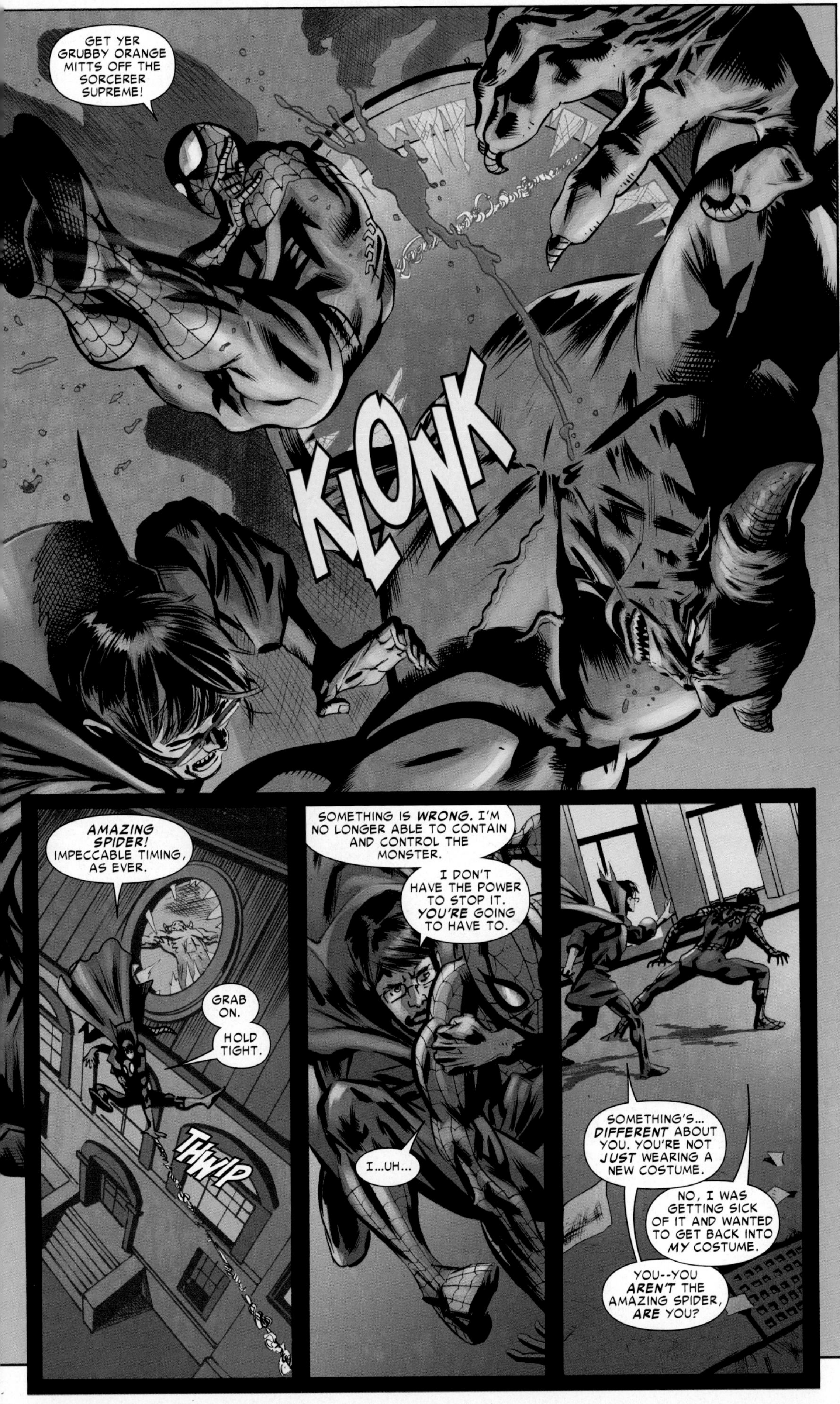
GET YER GRUBBY ORANGE MITTS OFF THE SORCERER SUPREME!
KLONK
AMAZING SPIDER! IMPECCABLE TIMING, AS EVER.
GRAB ON.
HOLD TIGHT.
THWIP
SOMETHING IS WRONG. I'M NO LONGER ABLE TO CONTAIN AND CONTROL THE MONSTER.
I DON'T HAVE THE POWER TO STOP IT. YOU'RE GOING TO HAVE TO.
I...UH...
SOMETHING'S... DIFFERENT ABOUT YOU. YOU'RE NOT JUST WEARING A NEW COSTUME.
NO, I WAS GETTING SICK OF IT AND WANTED TO GET BACK INTO MY COSTUME.
YOU--YOU AREN'T THE AMAZING SPIDER, ARE YOU?

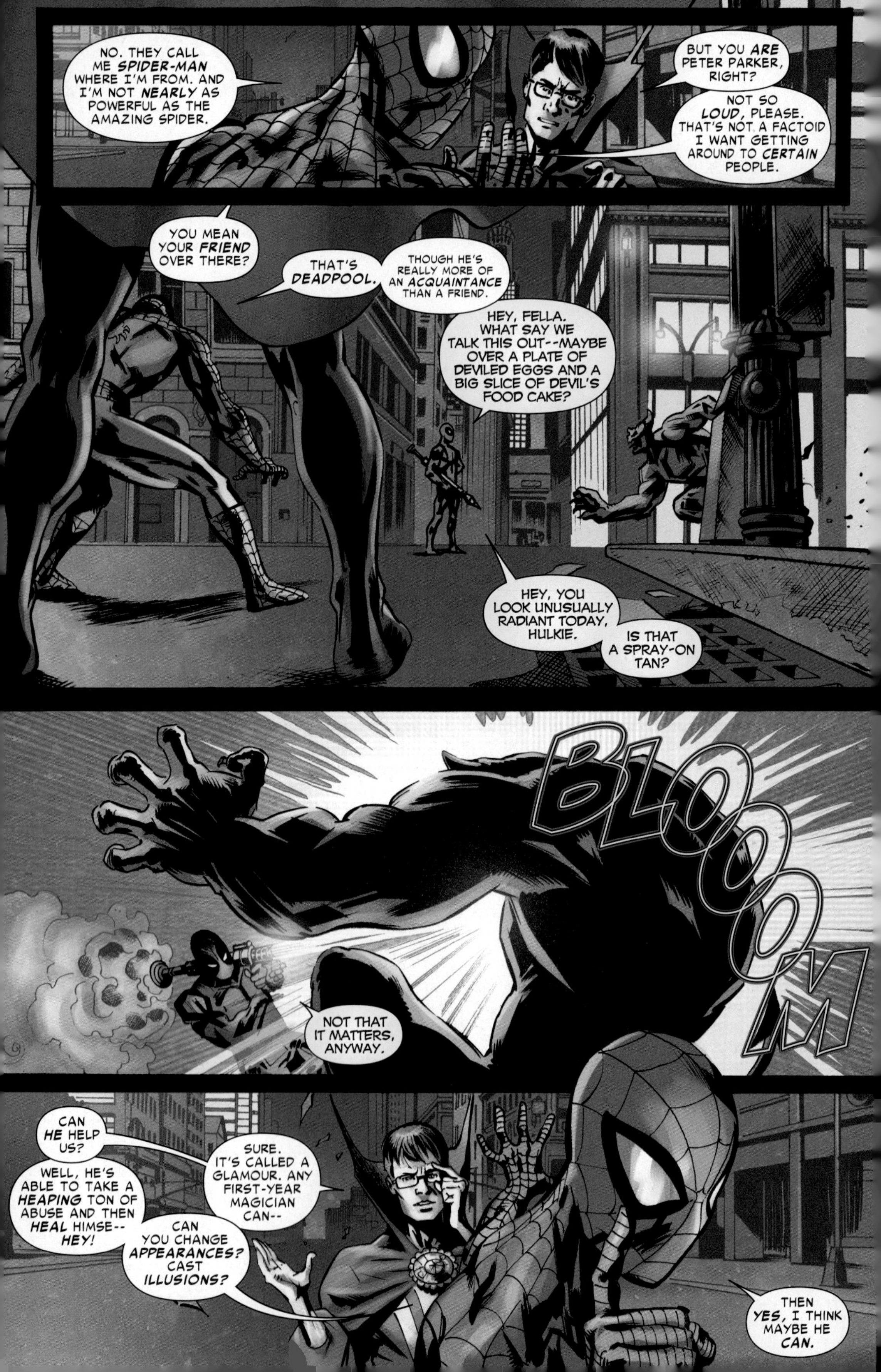
NO. THEY CALL ME SPIDER-MAN WHERE I'M FROM. AND I'M NOT NEARLY AS POWERFUL AS THE AMAZING SPIDER.
BUT YOU ARE PETER PARKER, RIGHT?
NOT SO LOUD, PLEASE. THAT'S NOT A FACTOID I WANT GETTING AROUND TO CERTAIN PEOPLE.
YOU MEAN YOUR FRIEND OVER THERE?
THAT'S DEADPOOL.
THOUGH HE'S REALLY MORE OF AN ACQUAINTANCE THAN A FRIEND.
HEY, FELLA. WHAT SAY WE TALK THIS OUT--MAYBE OVER A PLATE OF DEVILED EGGS AND A BIG SLICE OF DEVIL'S FOOD CAKE?
HEY, YOU LOOK UNUSUALLY RADIANT TODAY, HULKIE.
IS THAT A SPRAY-ON TAN?
BLOOOOOM
NOT THAT IT MATTERS, ANYWAY.
CAN HE HELP US?
WELL, HE'S ABLE TO TAKE A HEAPING TON OF ABUSE AND THEN HEAL HIMSE-- HEY!
SURE. IT'S CALLED A GLAMOUR. ANY FIRST-YEAR MAGICIAN CAN--
CAN YOU CHANGE APPEARANCES? CAST ILLUSIONS?
THEN YES, I THINK MAYBE HE CAN.

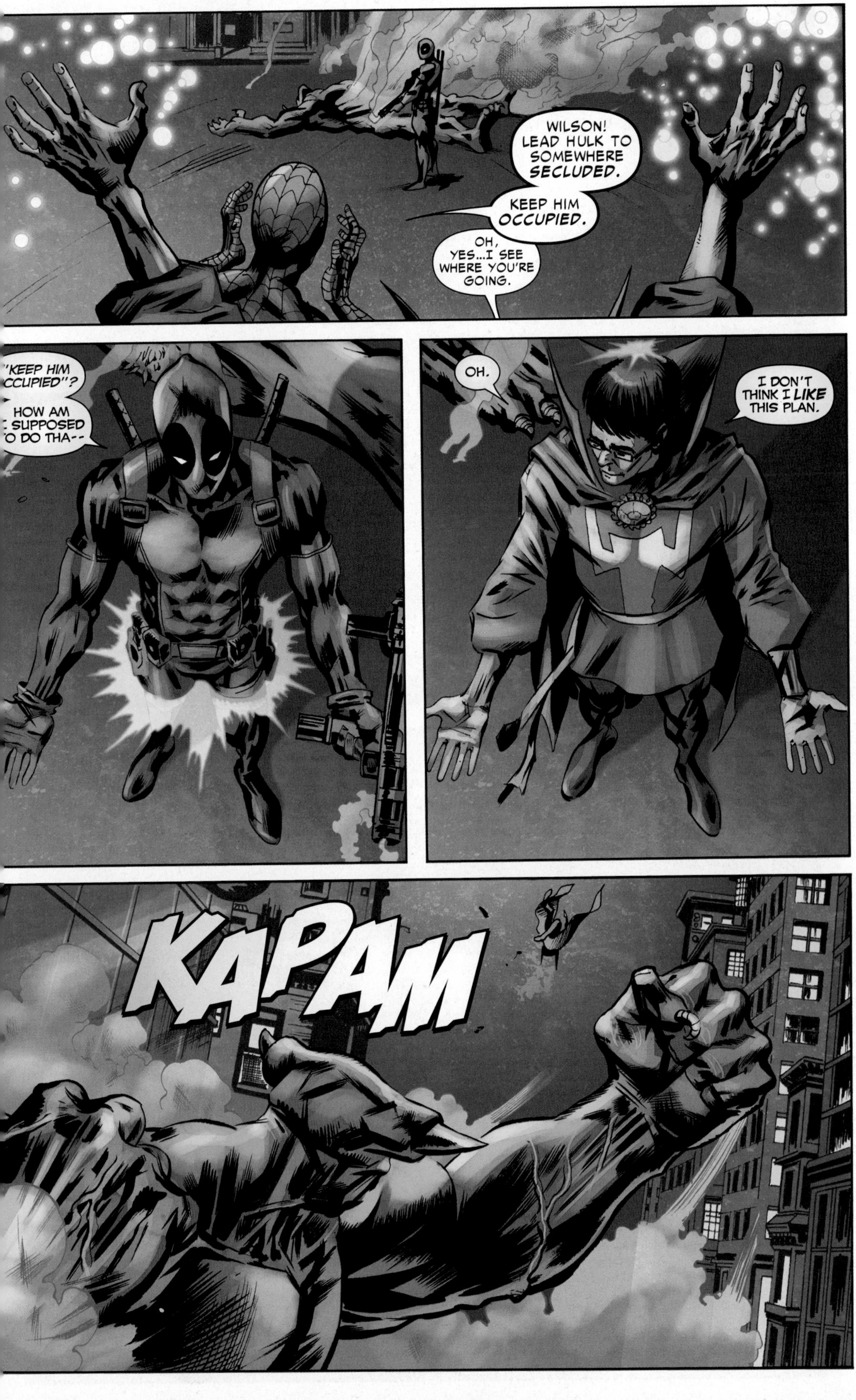
WILSON! LEAD HULK TO SOMEWHERE SECLUDED.
KEEP HIM OCCUPIED.
OH, YES...I SEE WHERE YOU'RE GOING.
"KEEP HIM OCCUPIED"? HOW AM I SUPPOSED TO DO THA--
OH.
I DON'T THINK I LIKE THIS PLAN.
KAPAM

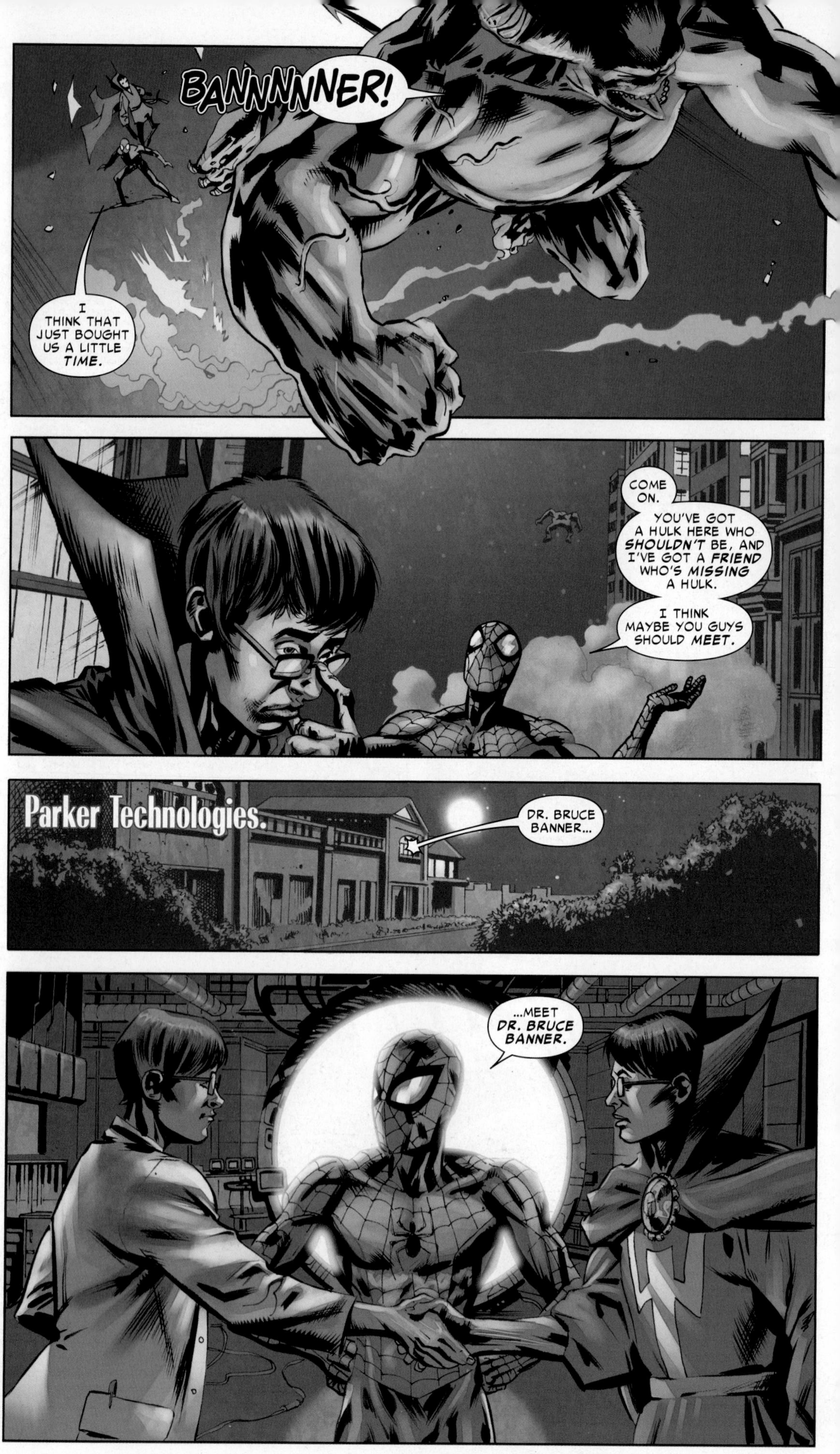
BANNNNNER!
I THINK THAT JUST BOUGHT US A LITTLE *TIME*.
COME ON.
YOU'VE GOT A HULK HERE WHO *SHOULDN'T* BE, AND I'VE GOT A *FRIEND* WHO'S *MISSING* A HULK.
I THINK MAYBE YOU GUYS SHOULD *MEET*.
Parker Technologies.
DR. BRUCE BANNER...
...MEET *DR. BRUCE BANNER*.

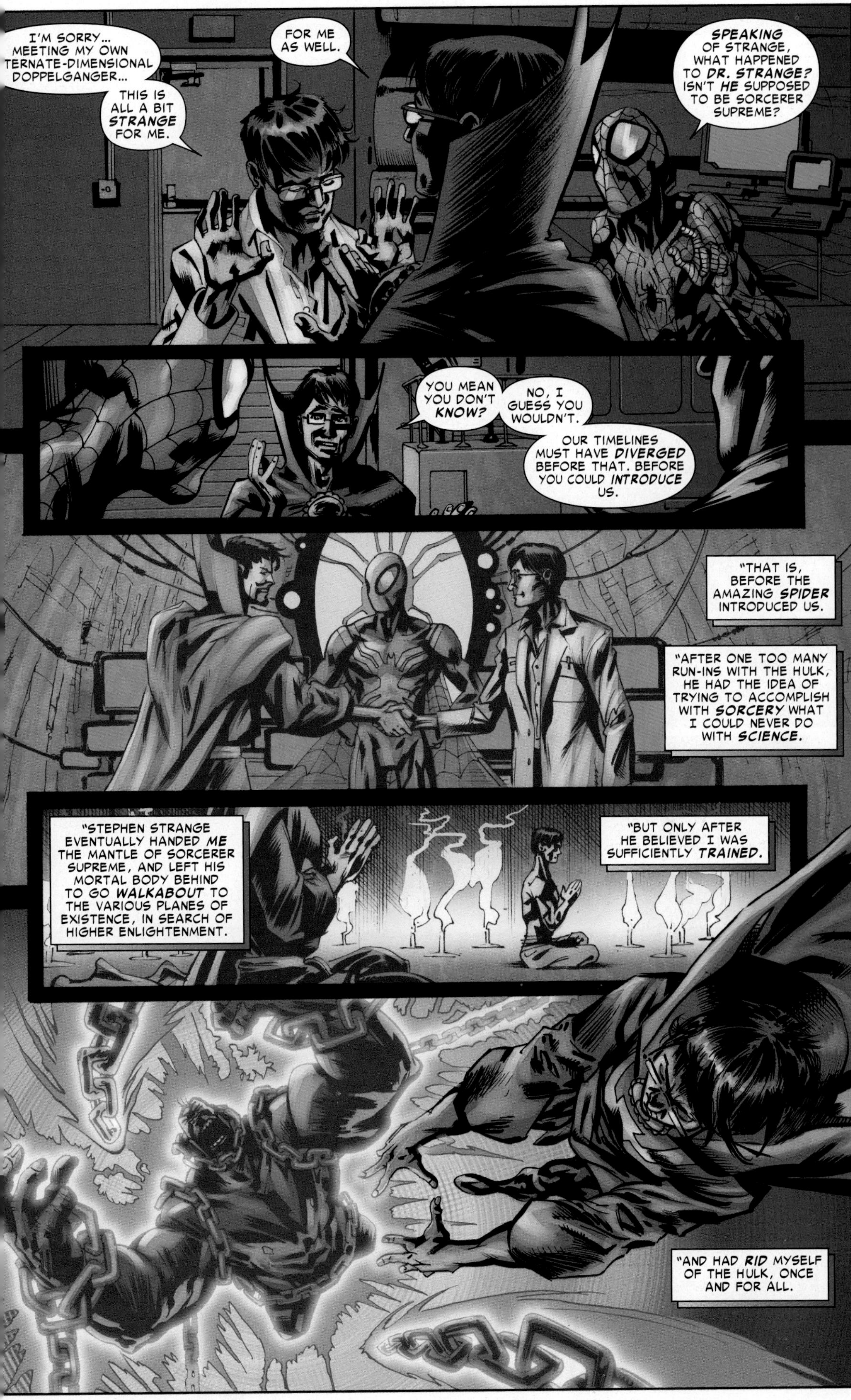
I'M SORRY... MEETING MY OWN TERNATE-DIMENSIONAL DOPPELGANGER...
THIS IS ALL A BIT STRANGE FOR ME.
FOR ME AS WELL.
SPEAKING OF STRANGE, WHAT HAPPENED TO DR. STRANGE? ISN'T HE SUPPOSED TO BE SORCERER SUPREME?
YOU MEAN YOU DON'T KNOW?
NO, I GUESS YOU WOULDN'T.
OUR TIMELINES MUST HAVE DIVERGED BEFORE THAT. BEFORE YOU COULD INTRODUCE US.
"THAT IS, BEFORE THE AMAZING SPIDER INTRODUCED US.
"AFTER ONE TOO MANY RUN-INS WITH THE HULK, HE HAD THE IDEA OF TRYING TO ACCOMPLISH WITH SORCERY WHAT I COULD NEVER DO WITH SCIENCE.
"STEPHEN STRANGE EVENTUALLY HANDED ME THE MANTLE OF SORCERER SUPREME, AND LEFT HIS MORTAL BODY BEHIND TO GO WALKABOUT TO THE VARIOUS PLANES OF EXISTENCE, IN SEARCH OF HIGHER ENLIGHTENMENT.
"BUT ONLY AFTER HE BELIEVED I WAS SUFFICIENTLY TRAINED.
"AND HAD RID MYSELF OF THE HULK, ONCE AND FOR ALL.

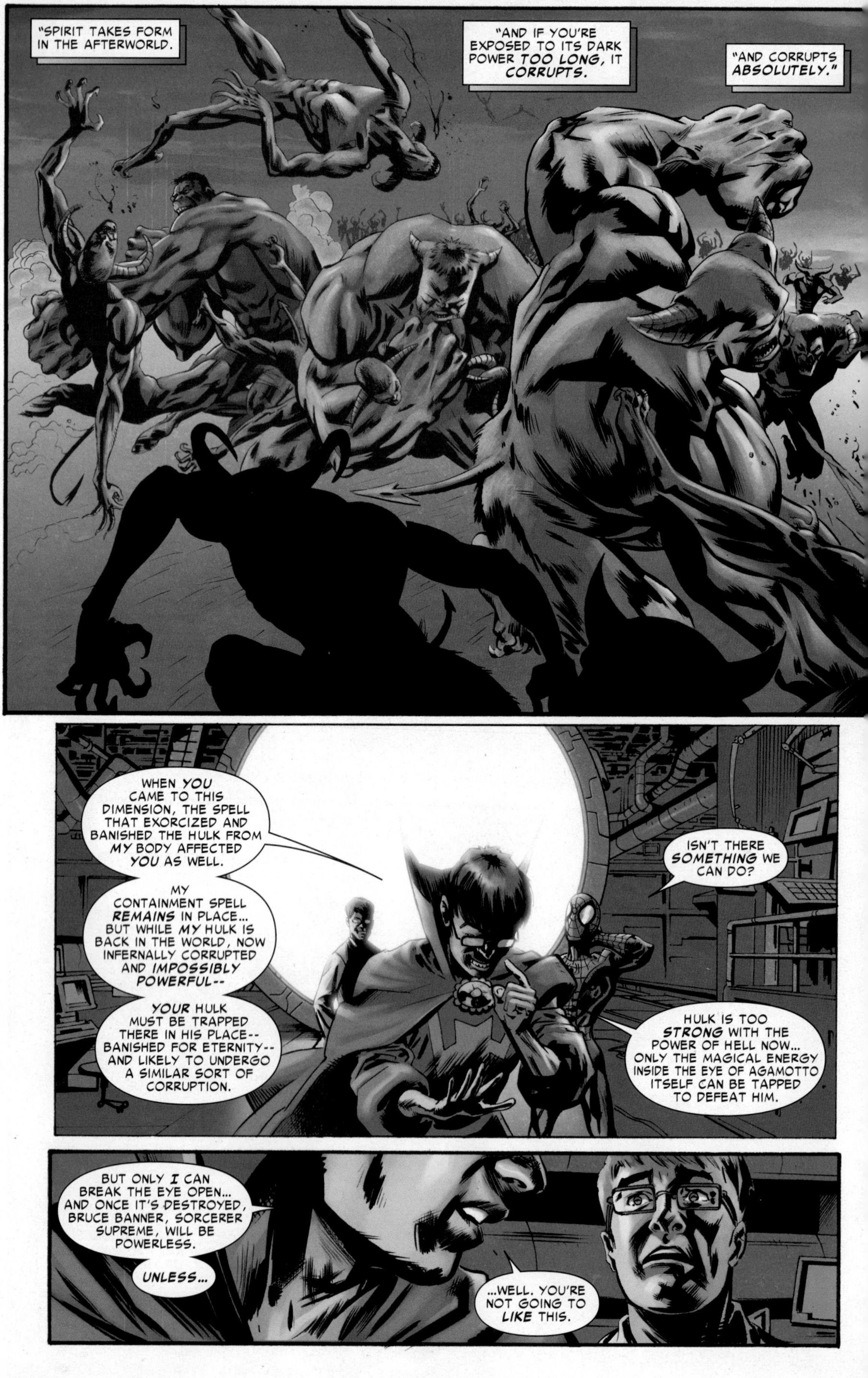
"SPIRIT TAKES FORM IN THE AFTERWORLD.
"AND IF YOU'RE EXPOSED TO ITS DARK POWER TOO LONG, IT CORRUPTS.
"AND CORRUPTS ABSOLUTELY."
WHEN YOU CAME TO THIS DIMENSION, THE SPELL THAT EXORCIZED AND BANISHED THE HULK FROM MY BODY AFFECTED YOU AS WELL.
MY CONTAINMENT SPELL REMAINS IN PLACE... BUT WHILE MY HULK IS BACK IN THE WORLD, NOW INFERNALLY CORRUPTED AND IMPOSSIBLY POWERFUL--
YOUR HULK MUST BE TRAPPED THERE IN HIS PLACE-- BANISHED FOR ETERNITY-- AND LIKELY TO UNDERGO A SIMILAR SORT OF CORRUPTION.
ISN'T THERE SOMETHING WE CAN DO?
HULK IS TOO STRONG WITH THE POWER OF HELL NOW... ONLY THE MAGICAL ENERGY INSIDE THE EYE OF AGAMOTTO ITSELF CAN BE TAPPED TO DEFEAT HIM.
BUT ONLY I CAN BREAK THE EYE OPEN... AND ONCE IT'S DESTROYED, BRUCE BANNER, SORCERER SUPREME, WILL BE POWERLESS.
UNLESS...
...WELL. YOU'RE NOT GOING TO LIKE THIS.

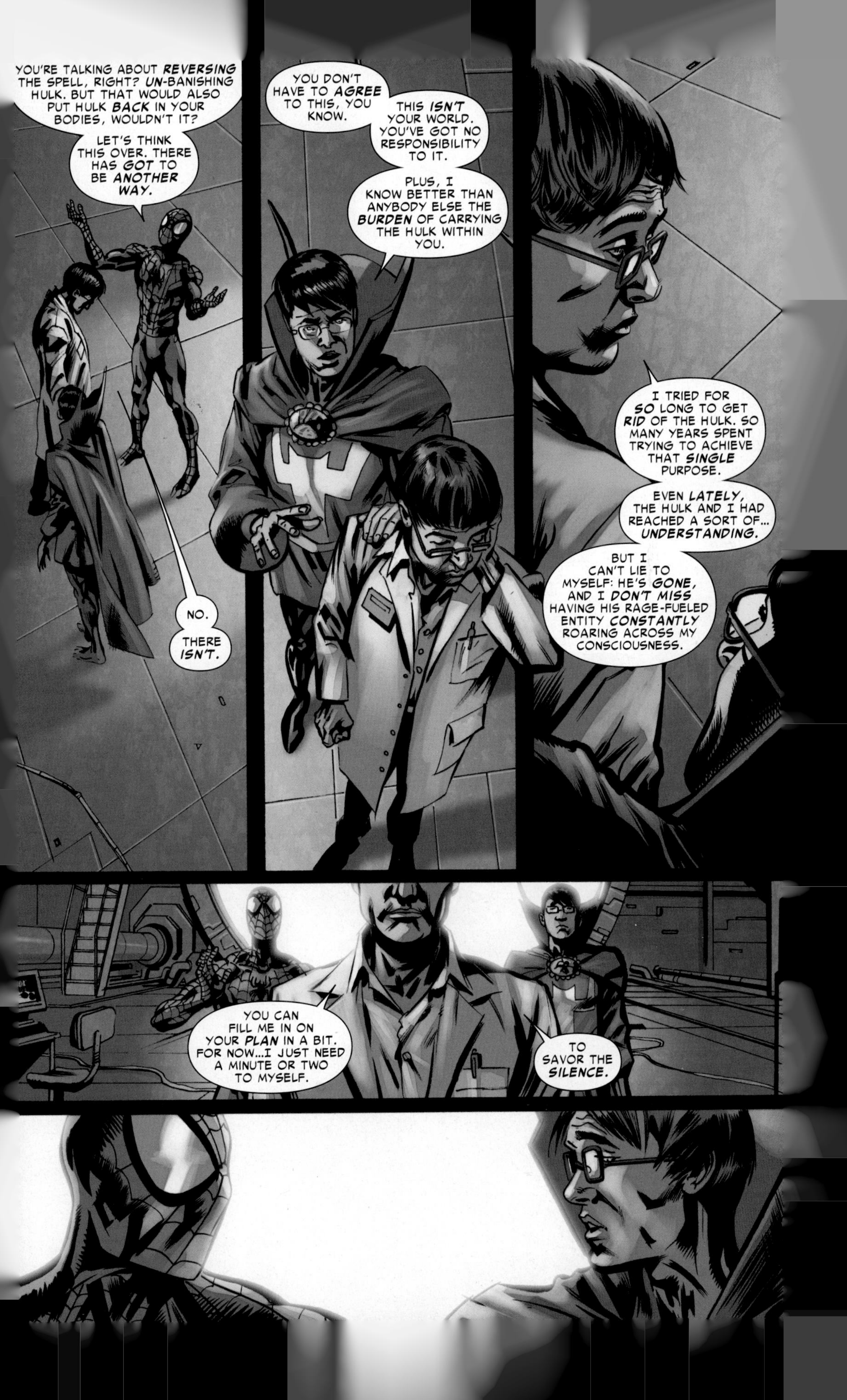
YOU'RE TALKING ABOUT REVERSING THE SPELL, RIGHT? UN-BANISHING HULK. BUT THAT WOULD ALSO PUT HULK BACK IN YOUR BODIES, WOULDN'T IT?
LET'S THINK THIS OVER. THERE HAS GOT TO BE ANOTHER WAY.
NO.
THERE ISN'T.
YOU DON'T HAVE TO AGREE TO THIS, YOU KNOW.
THIS ISN'T YOUR WORLD. YOU'VE GOT NO RESPONSIBILITY TO IT.
PLUS, I KNOW BETTER THAN ANYBODY ELSE THE BURDEN OF CARRYING THE HULK WITHIN YOU.
I TRIED FOR SO LONG TO GET RID OF THE HULK. SO MANY YEARS SPENT TRYING TO ACHIEVE THAT SINGLE PURPOSE.
EVEN LATELY, THE HULK AND I HAD REACHED A SORT OF... UNDERSTANDING.
BUT I CAN'T LIE TO MYSELF: HE'S GONE, AND I DON'T MISS HAVING HIS RAGE-FUELED ENTITY CONSTANTLY ROARING ACROSS MY CONSCIOUSNESS.
YOU CAN FILL ME IN ON YOUR PLAN IN A BIT. FOR NOW...I JUST NEED A MINUTE OR TWO TO MYSELF.
TO SAVOR THE SILENCE.

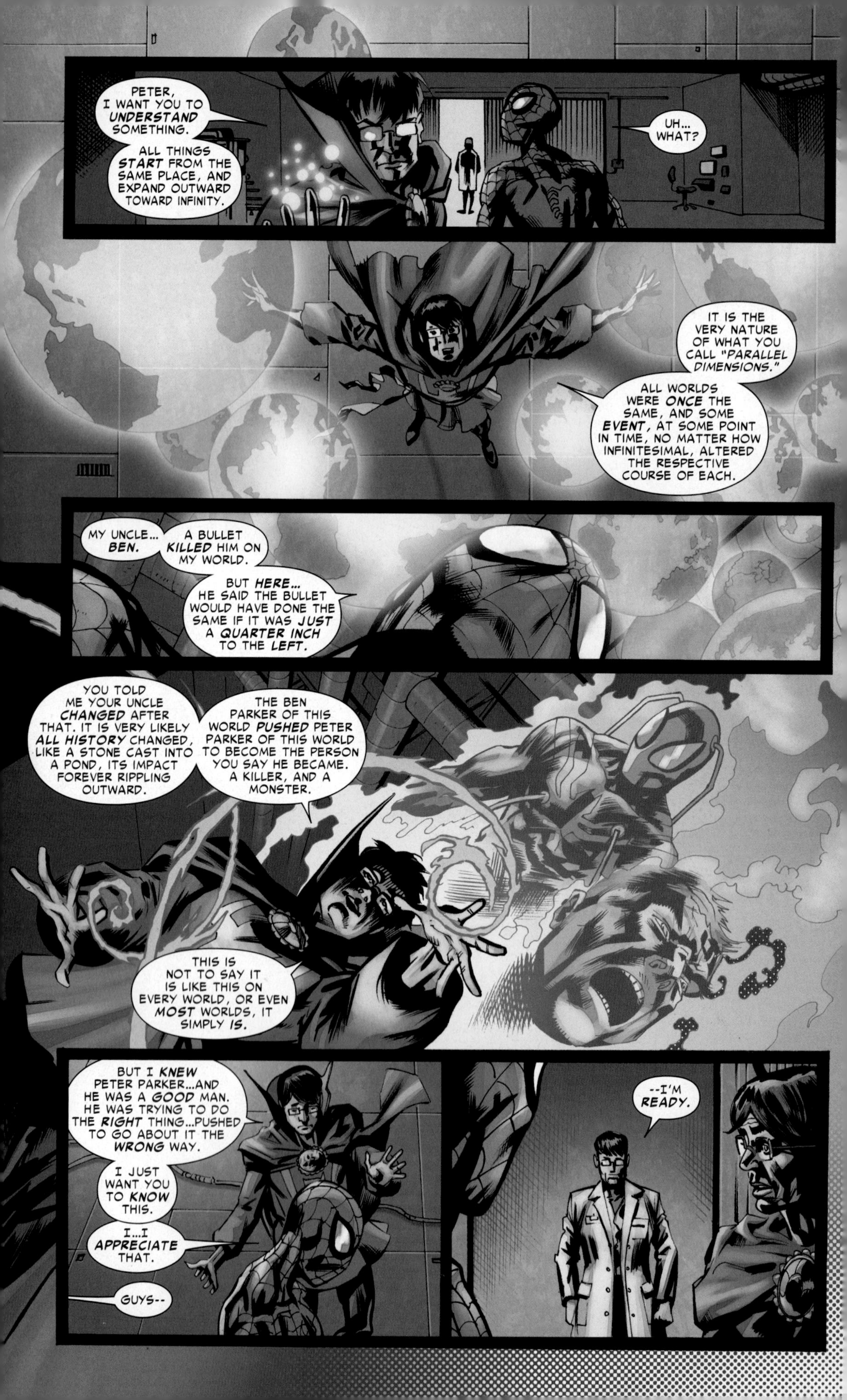
PETER, I WANT YOU TO UNDERSTAND SOMETHING.
ALL THINGS START FROM THE SAME PLACE, AND EXPAND OUTWARD TOWARD INFINITY.
UH... WHAT?
IT IS THE VERY NATURE OF WHAT YOU CALL "PARALLEL DIMENSIONS."
ALL WORLDS WERE ONCE THE SAME, AND SOME EVENT, AT SOME POINT IN TIME, NO MATTER HOW INFINITESIMAL, ALTERED THE RESPECTIVE COURSE OF EACH.
MY UNCLE... BEN.
A BULLET KILLED HIM ON MY WORLD.
BUT HERE... HE SAID THE BULLET WOULD HAVE DONE THE SAME IF IT WAS JUST A QUARTER INCH TO THE LEFT.
YOU TOLD ME YOUR UNCLE CHANGED AFTER THAT. IT IS VERY LIKELY ALL HISTORY CHANGED, LIKE A STONE CAST INTO A POND, ITS IMPACT FOREVER RIPPLING OUTWARD.
THE BEN PARKER OF THIS WORLD PUSHED PETER PARKER OF THIS WORLD TO BECOME THE PERSON YOU SAY HE BECAME. A KILLER, AND A MONSTER.
THIS IS NOT TO SAY IT IS LIKE THIS ON EVERY WORLD, OR EVEN MOST WORLDS, IT SIMPLY IS.
BUT I KNEW PETER PARKER...AND HE WAS A GOOD MAN. HE WAS TRYING TO DO THE RIGHT THING...PUSHED TO GO ABOUT IT THE WRONG WAY.
I JUST WANT YOU TO KNOW THIS.
I...I APPRECIATE THAT.
GUYS--
--I'M READY.

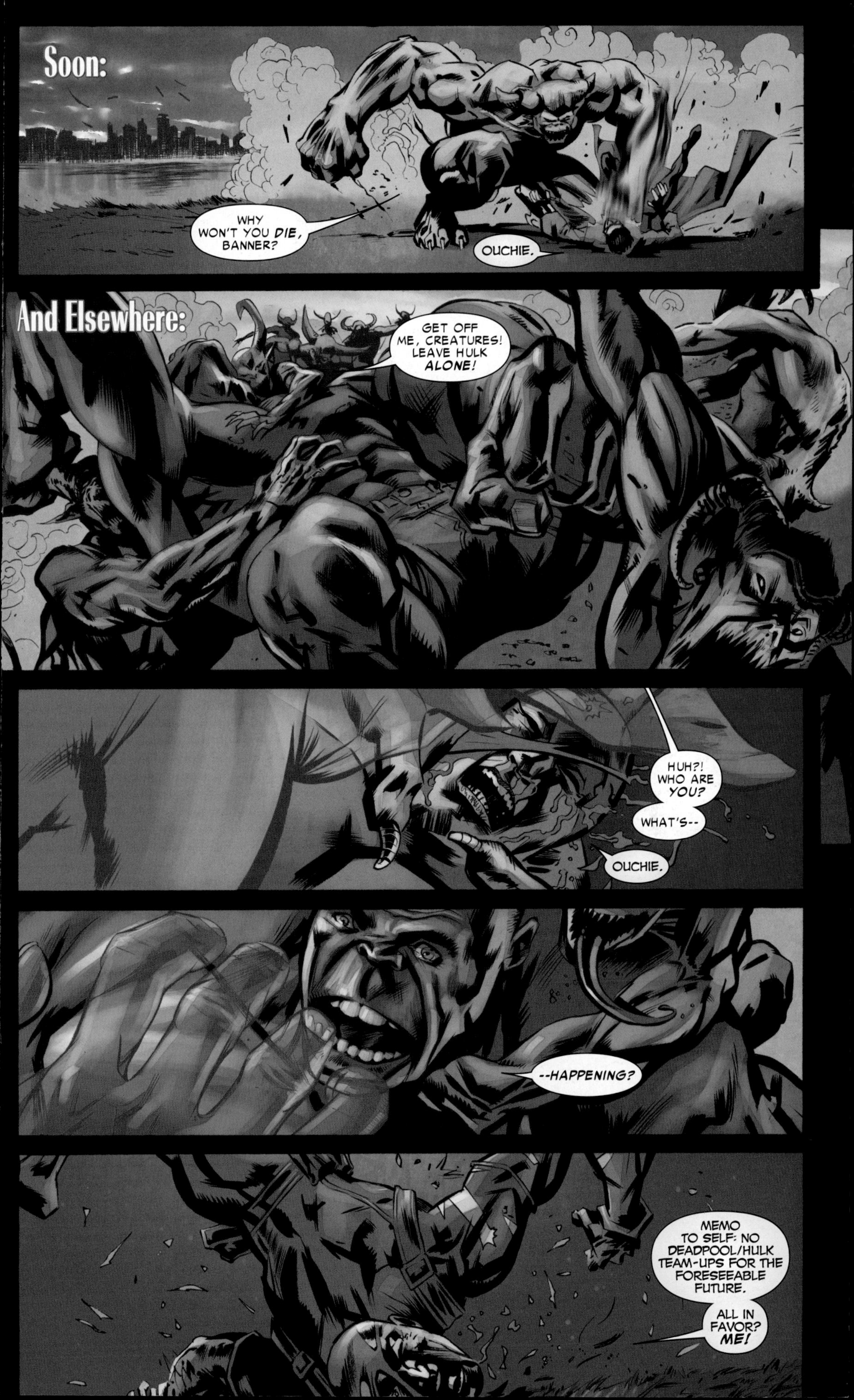
Soon:
WHY WON'T YOU DIE, BANNER?
OUCHIE.
And Elsewhere:
GET OFF ME, CREATURES! LEAVE HULK ALONE!
HUH?! WHO ARE YOU?
WHAT'S--
OUCHIE.
--HAPPENING?
MEMO TO SELF: NO DEADPOOL/HULK TEAM-UPS FOR THE FORESEEABLE FUTURE.
ALL IN FAVOR? ME!

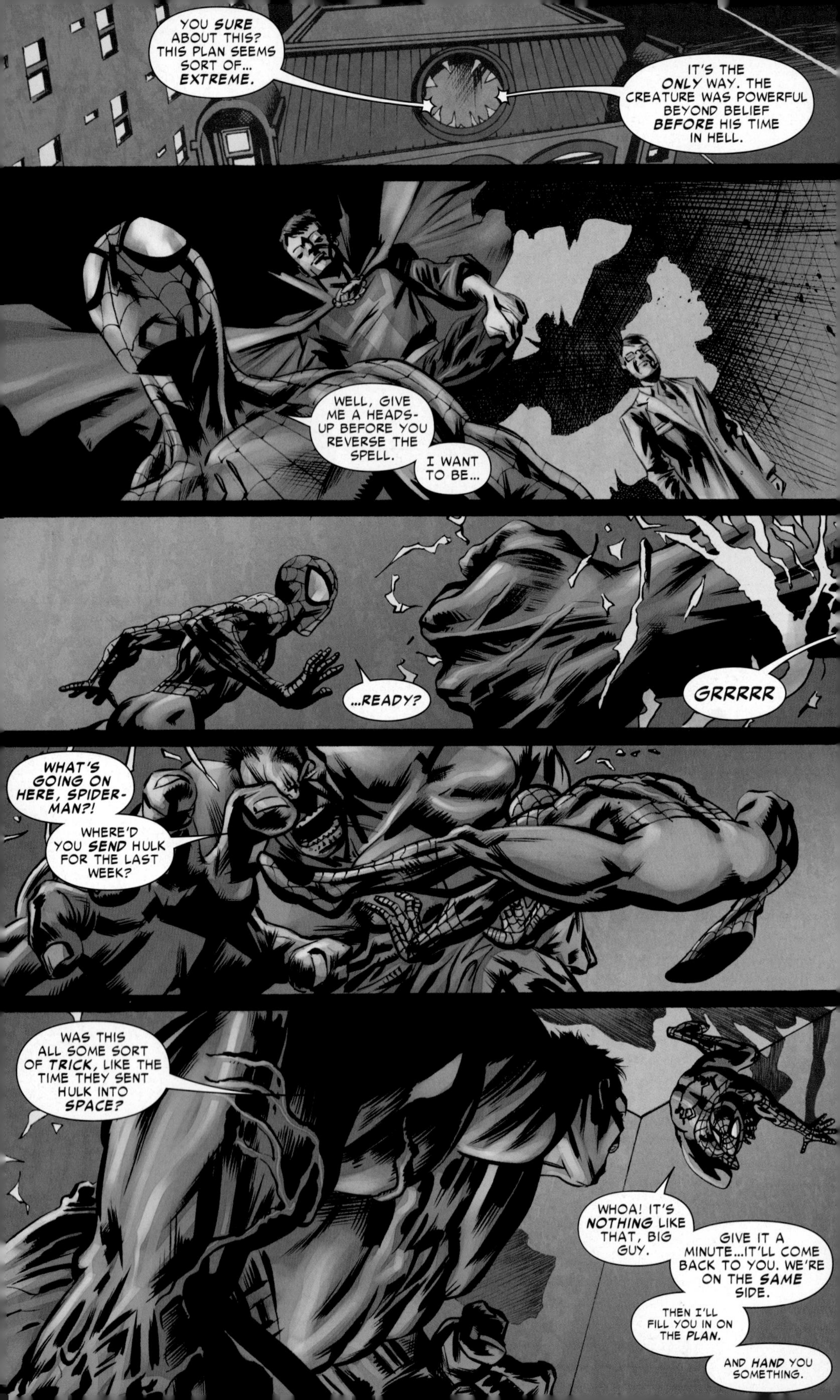
YOU SURE ABOUT THIS? THIS PLAN SEEMS SORT OF... EXTREME.
IT'S THE ONLY WAY. THE CREATURE WAS POWERFUL BEYOND BELIEF BEFORE HIS TIME IN HELL.
WELL, GIVE ME A HEADS-UP BEFORE YOU REVERSE THE SPELL.
I WANT TO BE...
...READY?
GRRRRR
WHAT'S GOING ON HERE, SPIDER-MAN?!
WHERE'D YOU SEND HULK FOR THE LAST WEEK?
WAS THIS ALL SOME SORT OF TRICK, LIKE THE TIME THEY SENT HULK INTO SPACE?
WHOA! IT'S NOTHING LIKE THAT, BIG GUY.
GIVE IT A MINUTE...IT'LL COME BACK TO YOU. WE'RE ON THE SAME SIDE.
THEN I'LL FILL YOU IN ON THE PLAN.
AND HAND YOU SOMETHING.

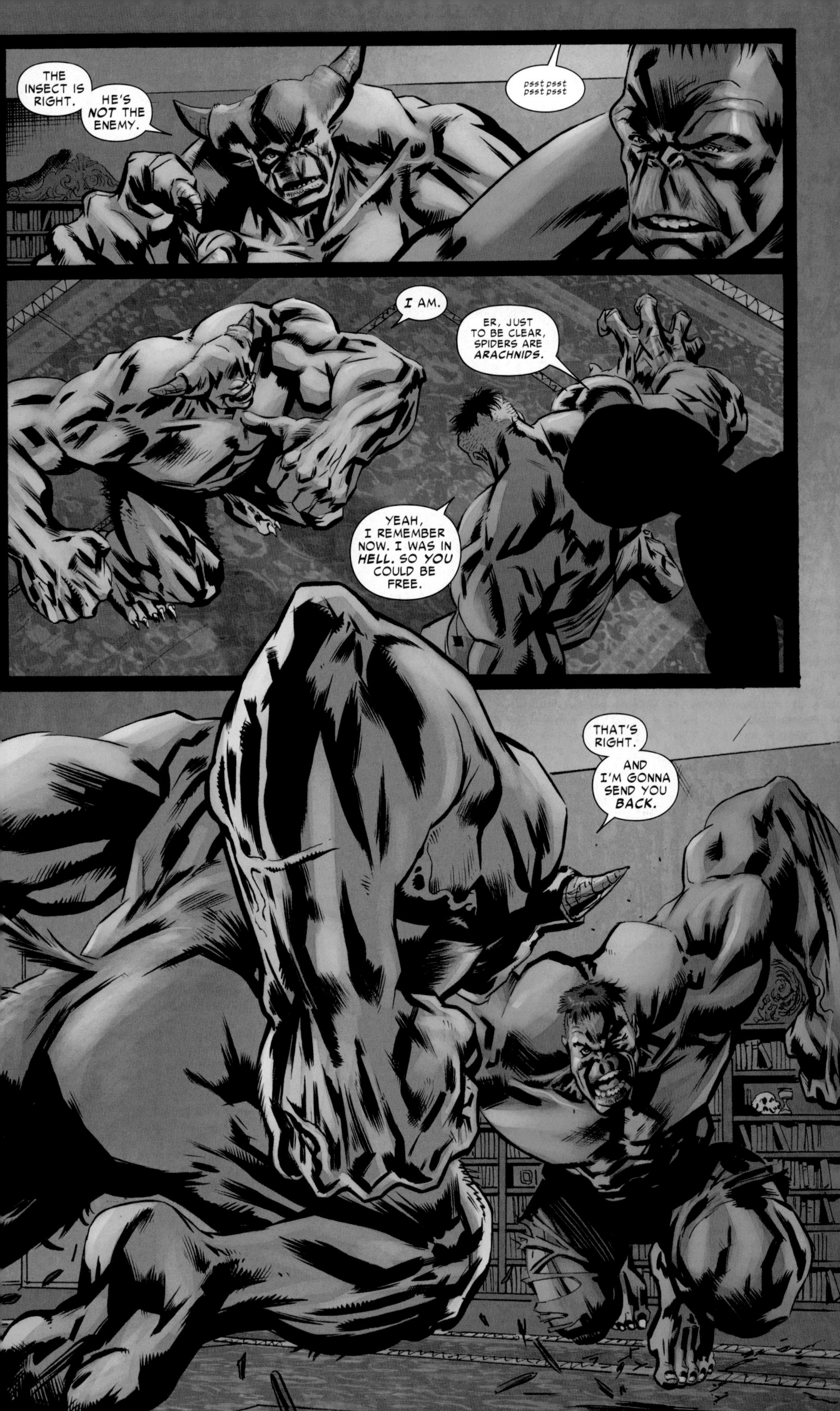
THE INSECT IS RIGHT.
HE'S NOT THE ENEMY.
psst psst psst psst
I AM.
ER, JUST TO BE CLEAR, SPIDERS ARE ARACHNIDS.
YEAH, I REMEMBER NOW. I WAS IN HELL. SO YOU COULD BE FREE.
THAT'S RIGHT.
AND I'M GONNA SEND YOU BACK.

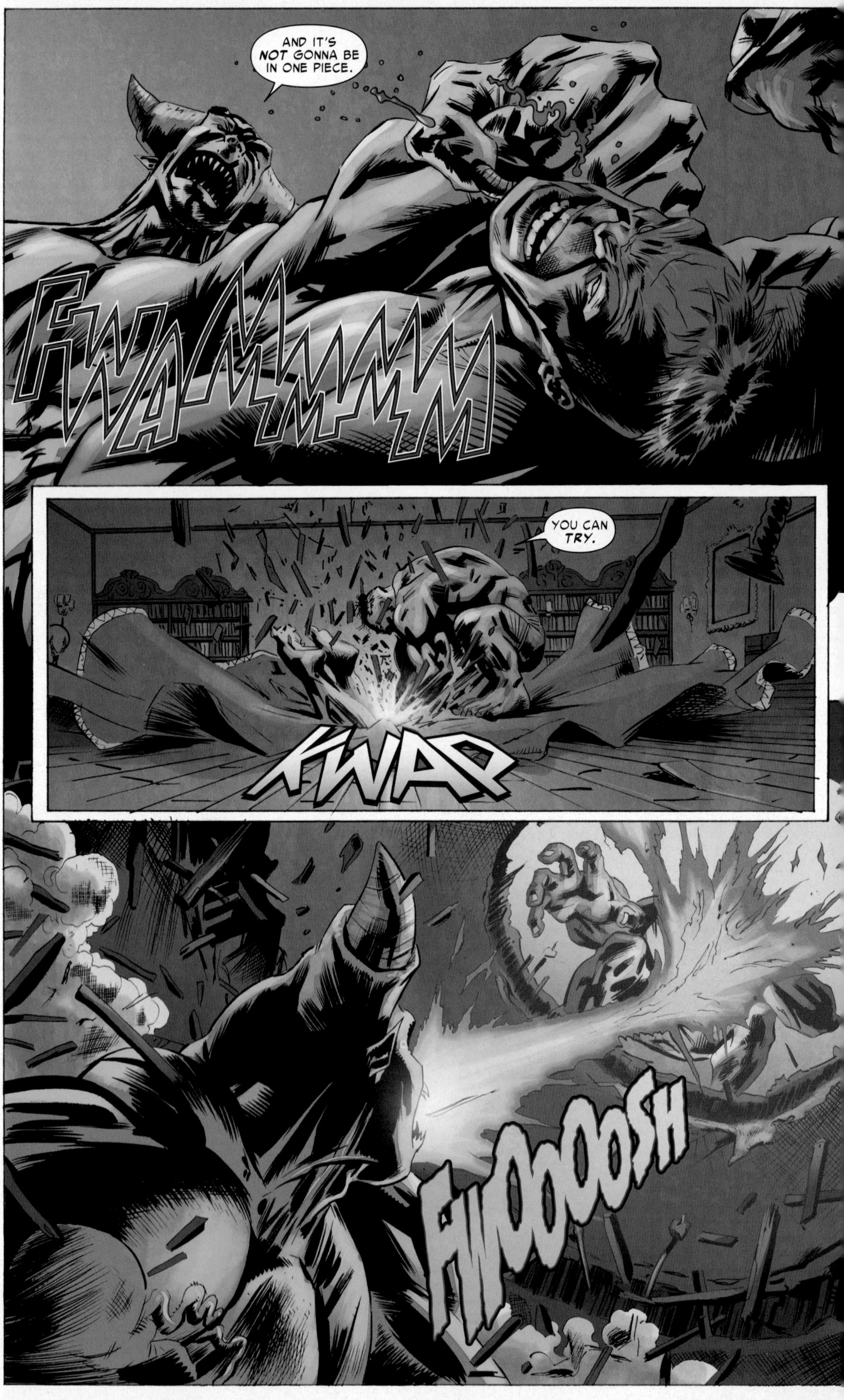
AND IT'S NOT GONNA BE IN ONE PIECE.
FWAMMMM
YOU CAN TRY.
KWAP
FWOOOSH

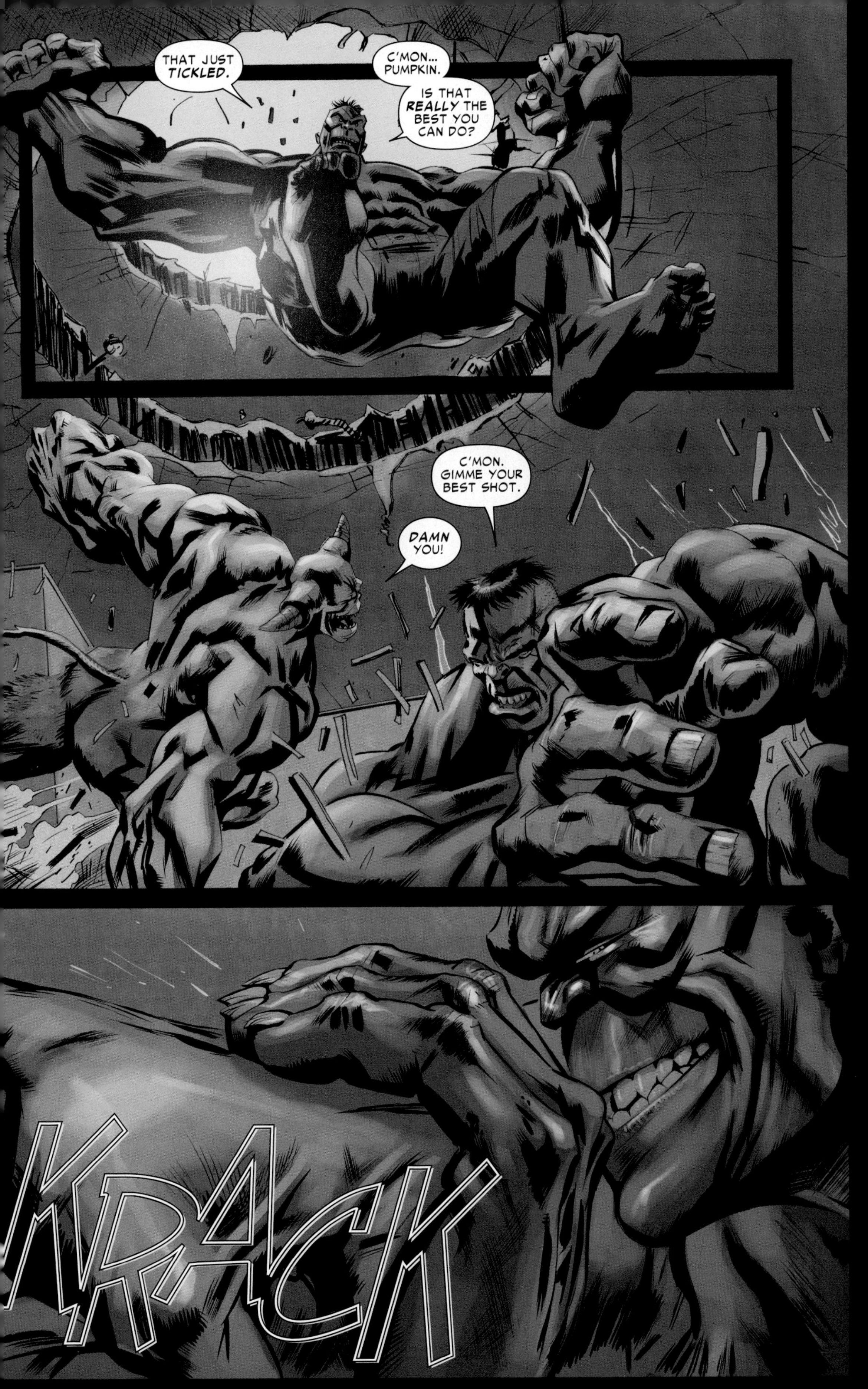
THAT JUST *TICKLED.*
C'MON... PUMPKIN.
IS THAT *REALLY* THE BEST YOU CAN DO?
C'MON. GIMME YOUR BEST SHOT.
DAMN YOU!
KRACK

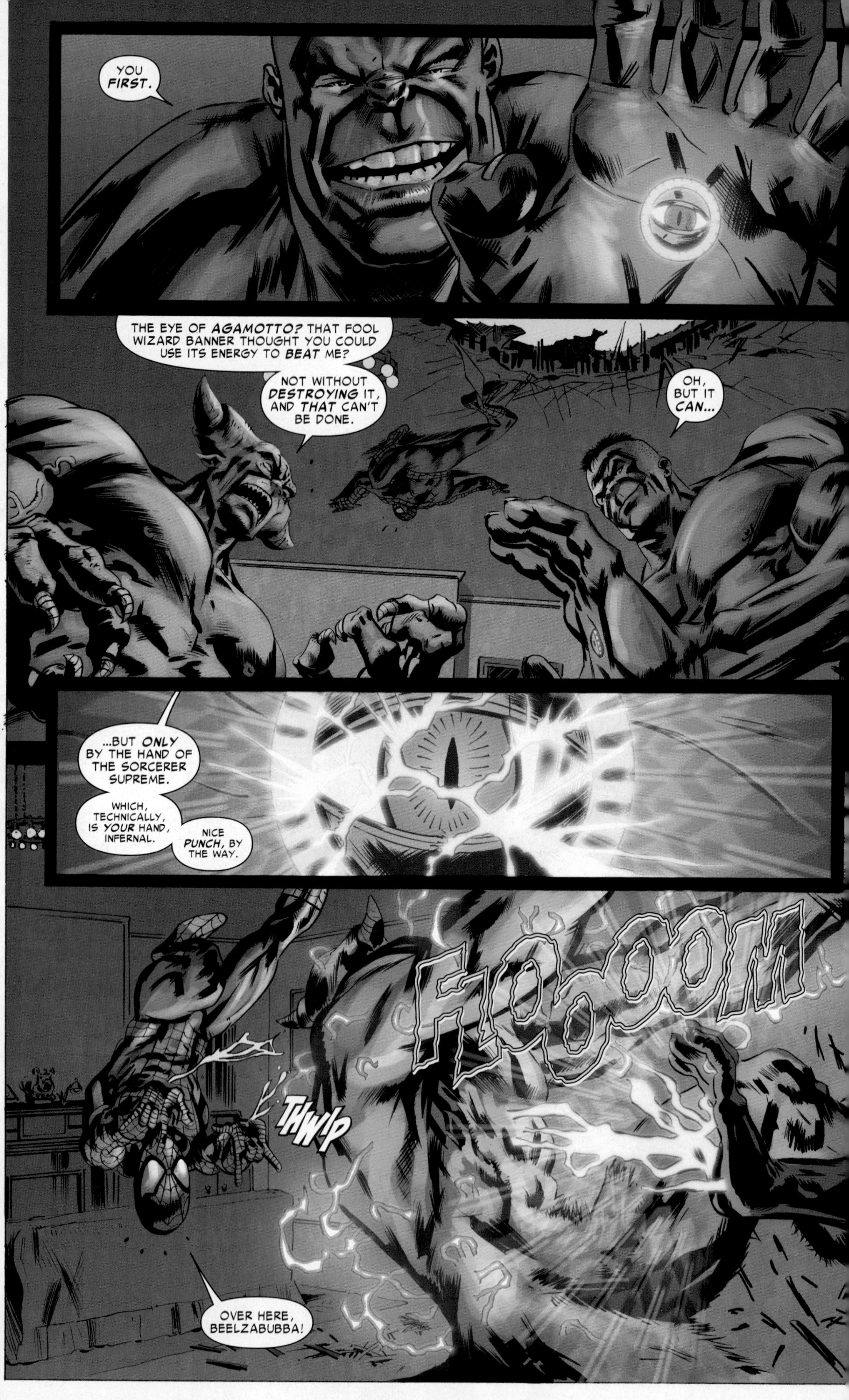

YOU FIRST.
THE EYE OF AGAMOTTO? THAT FOOL WIZARD BANNER THOUGHT YOU COULD USE ITS ENERGY TO BEAT ME?
NOT WITHOUT DESTROYING IT, AND THAT CAN'T BE DONE.
OH, BUT IT CAN...
...BUT ONLY BY THE HAND OF THE SORCERER SUPREME.
WHICH, TECHNICALLY, IS YOUR HAND, INFERNAL.
NICE PUNCH, BY THE WAY.
FZOOOOM
THWIP
OVER HERE, BEELZABUBBA!

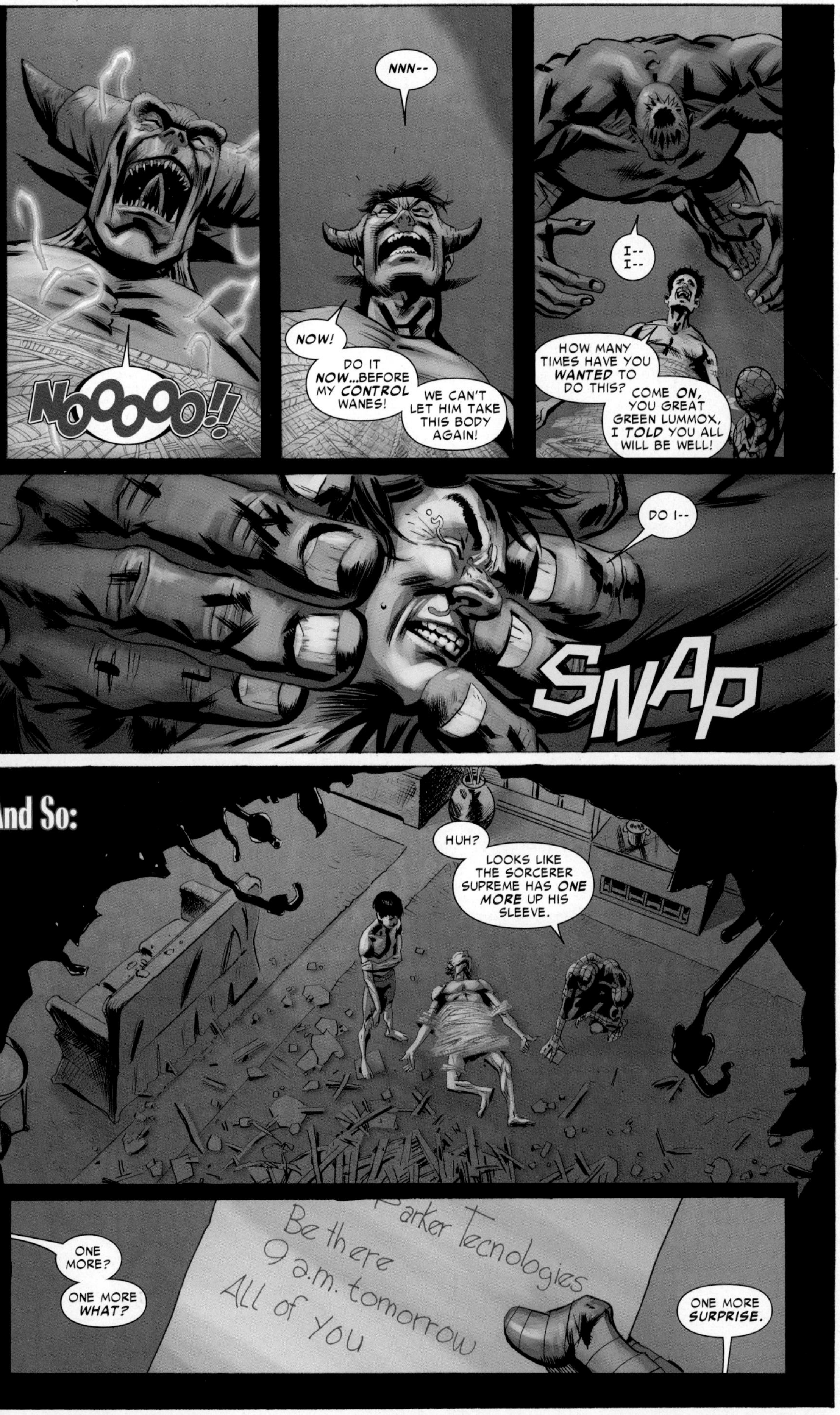
NOOOOO!!
NNN--
NOW!
DO IT NOW...BEFORE MY CONTROL WANES!
WE CAN'T LET HIM TAKE THIS BODY AGAIN!
I-- I--
HOW MANY TIMES HAVE YOU WANTED TO DO THIS?
COME ON, YOU GREAT GREEN LUMMOX, I TOLD YOU ALL WILL BE WELL!
DO I--
SNAP
And So:
HUH?
LOOKS LIKE THE SORCERER SUPREME HAS ONE MORE UP HIS SLEEVE.
ONE MORE?
ONE MORE WHAT?
Parker Tecnologies
Be there
9 a.m. tomorrow
All of You
ONE MORE SURPRISE.

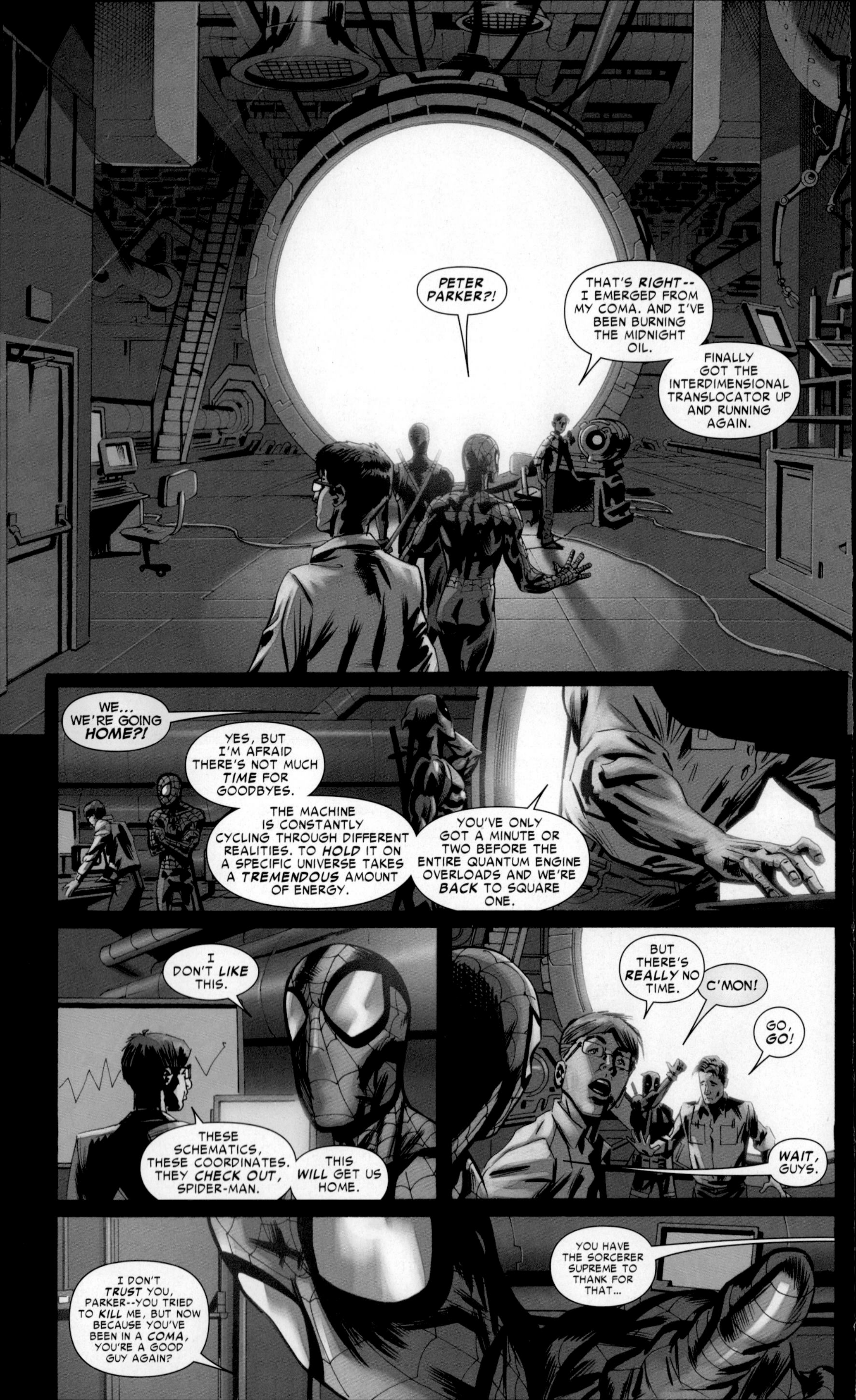
PETER PARKER?!
THAT'S RIGHT-- I EMERGED FROM MY COMA. AND I'VE BEEN BURNING THE MIDNIGHT OIL.
FINALLY GOT THE INTERDIMENSIONAL TRANSLOCATOR UP AND RUNNING AGAIN.
WE... WE'RE GOING HOME?!
YES, BUT I'M AFRAID THERE'S NOT MUCH TIME FOR GOODBYES.
THE MACHINE IS CONSTANTLY CYCLING THROUGH DIFFERENT REALITIES. TO HOLD IT ON A SPECIFIC UNIVERSE TAKES A TREMENDOUS AMOUNT OF ENERGY.
YOU'VE ONLY GOT A MINUTE OR TWO BEFORE THE ENTIRE QUANTUM ENGINE OVERLOADS AND WE'RE BACK TO SQUARE ONE.
I DON'T LIKE THIS.
THESE SCHEMATICS, THESE COORDINATES. THEY CHECK OUT, SPIDER-MAN.
THIS WILL GET US HOME.
BUT THERE'S REALLY NO TIME.
C'MON!
GO, GO!
WAIT, GUYS.
I DON'T TRUST YOU, PARKER--YOU TRIED TO KILL ME, BUT NOW BECAUSE YOU'VE BEEN IN A COMA, YOU'RE A GOOD GUY AGAIN?
YOU HAVE THE SORCERER SUPREME TO THANK FOR THAT...

"...OR HIS *ASTRAL FORM,* ANYWAY.

"BANNER *LEFT* HIS PHYSICAL FORM BEHIND WHEN YOU DEFEATED THE INFERNAL HULK... LIKE HIS PREDECESSOR DR. STRANGE, HE *GRADUATED* TO MOVE ON AND EXPLORE OTHER *PLANES.*

"BUT *FIRST,* HE FREED MY SPIRIT FROM HELL, WHERE I DESERVED TO BE."

HE *INFUSED* ME WITH THE SPIRITS AND *POWER* OF THE REPENTANT DAMNED-- THE SOULS CRYING FOR JUSTICE...AND *REDEMPTION.*

TO GIVE ME A *SECOND CHANCE.*

AND THE HULK?

HIS HULK, I MEAN?

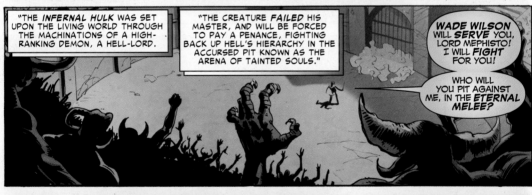

"THE *INFERNAL HULK* WAS SET UPON THE LIVING WORLD THROUGH THE MACHINATIONS OF A HIGH-RANKING DEMON, A HELL-LORD.

"THE CREATURE *FAILED* HIS MASTER, AND WILL BE FORCED TO PAY A PENANCE, FIGHTING BACK UP HELL'S HIERARCHY IN THE ACCURSED PIT KNOWN AS THE ARENA OF TAINTED SOULS."

WADE WILSON WILL *SERVE* YOU, LORD MEPHISTO! I WILL *FIGHT* FOR YOU!

WHO WILL YOU PIT AGAINST ME, IN THE *ETERNAL MELEE?*

THAT WOULD BE ME.

ULP!

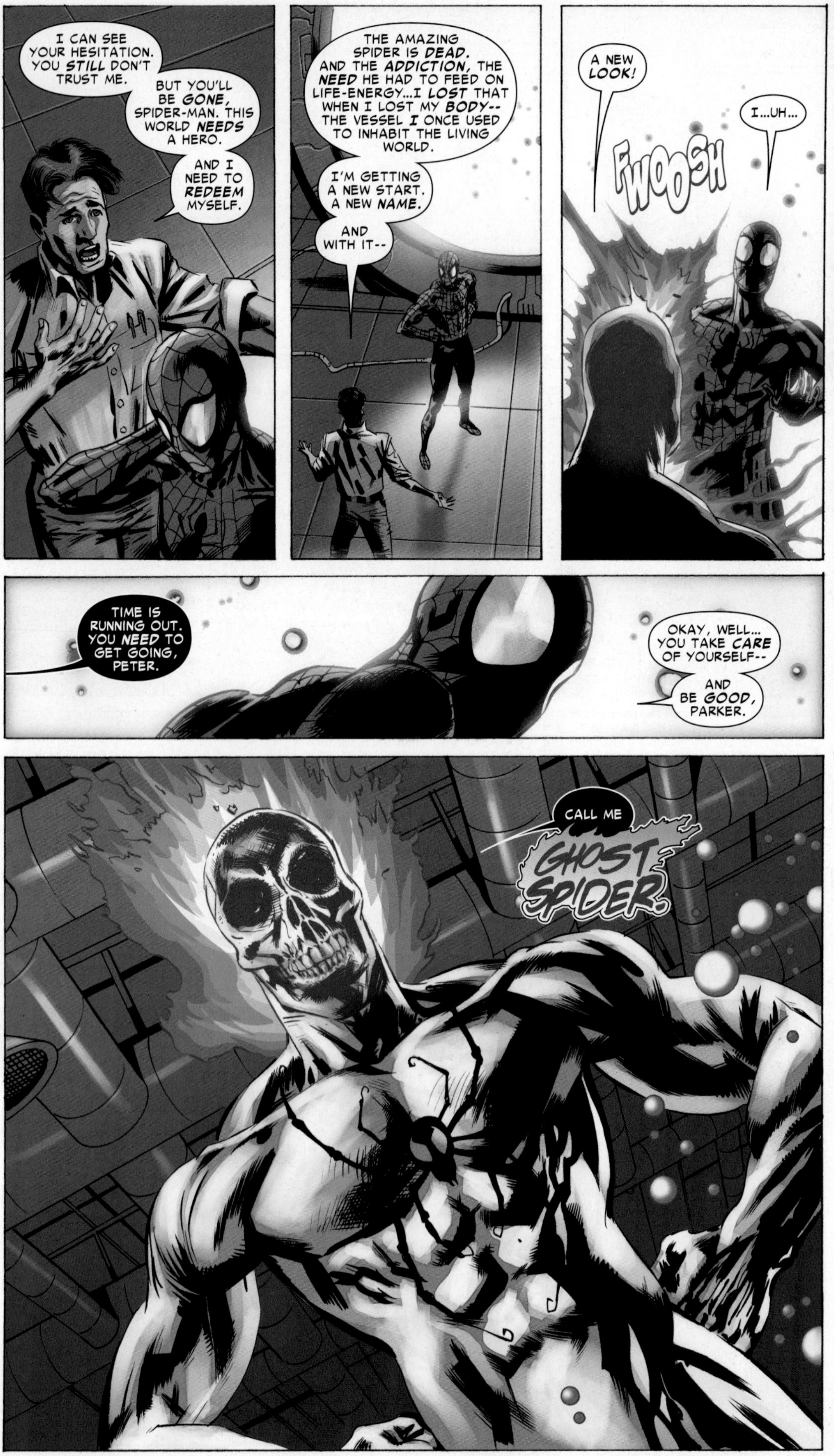
I CAN SEE YOUR HESITATION. YOU STILL DON'T TRUST ME.
BUT YOU'LL BE GONE, SPIDER-MAN. THIS WORLD NEEDS A HERO.
AND I NEED TO REDEEM MYSELF.
THE AMAZING SPIDER IS DEAD. AND THE ADDICTION, THE NEED HE HAD TO FEED ON LIFE-ENERGY...I LOST THAT WHEN I LOST MY BODY-- THE VESSEL I ONCE USED TO INHABIT THE LIVING WORLD.
I'M GETTING A NEW START. A NEW NAME.
AND WITH IT--
A NEW LOOK!
FWOOSH
I...UH...
TIME IS RUNNING OUT. YOU NEED TO GET GOING, PETER.
OKAY, WELL... YOU TAKE CARE OF YOURSELF--
AND BE GOOD, PARKER.
CALL ME
GHOST SPIDER.

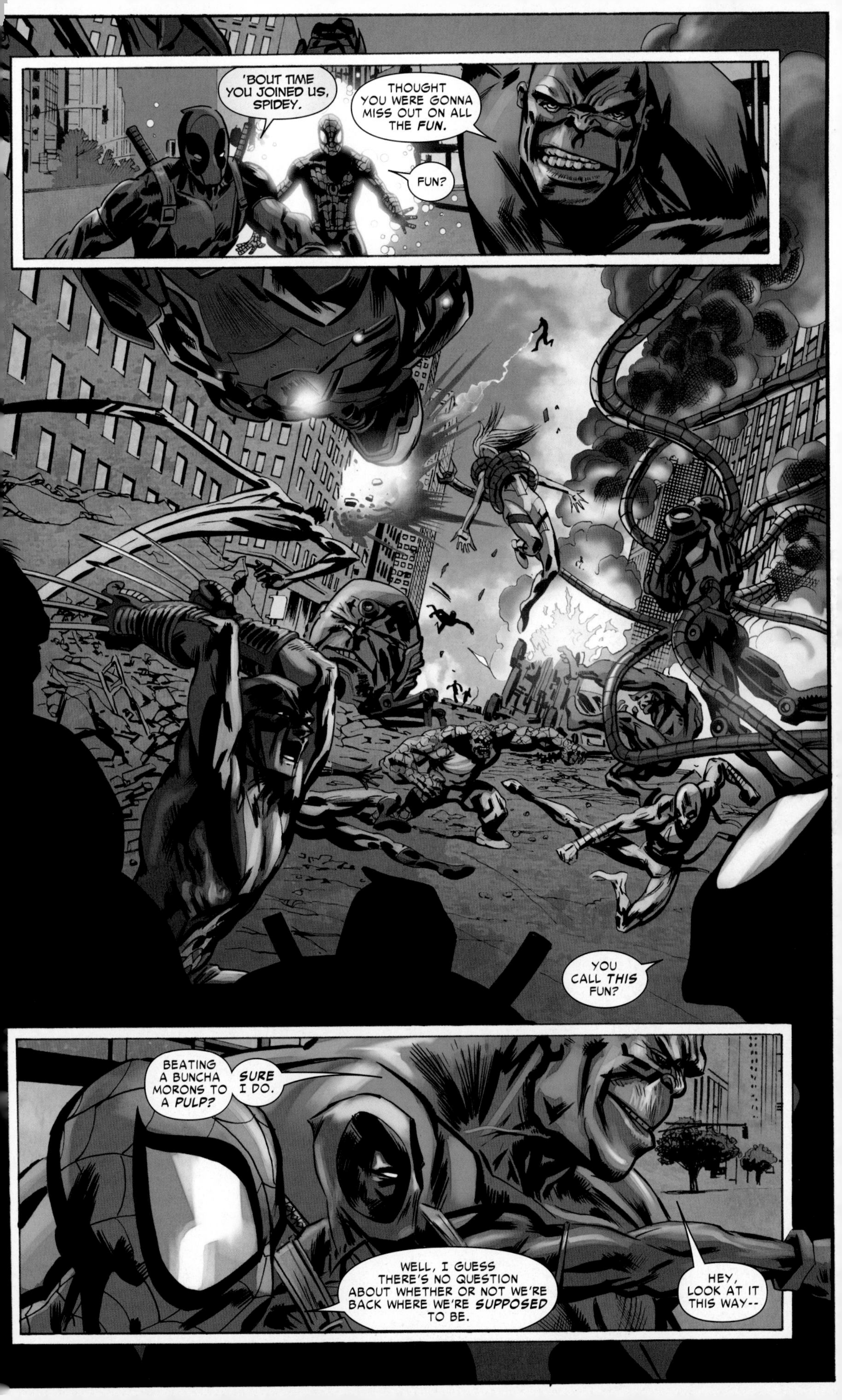
'BOUT TIME YOU JOINED US, SPIDEY.
THOUGHT YOU WERE GONNA MISS OUT ON ALL THE *FUN.*
FUN?
YOU CALL *THIS* FUN?
BEATING A BUNCHA MORONS TO A *PULP?*
SURE I DO.
WELL, I GUESS THERE'S NO QUESTION ABOUT WHETHER OR NOT WE'RE BACK WHERE WE'RE *SUPPOSED* TO BE.
HEY, LOOK AT IT THIS WAY--

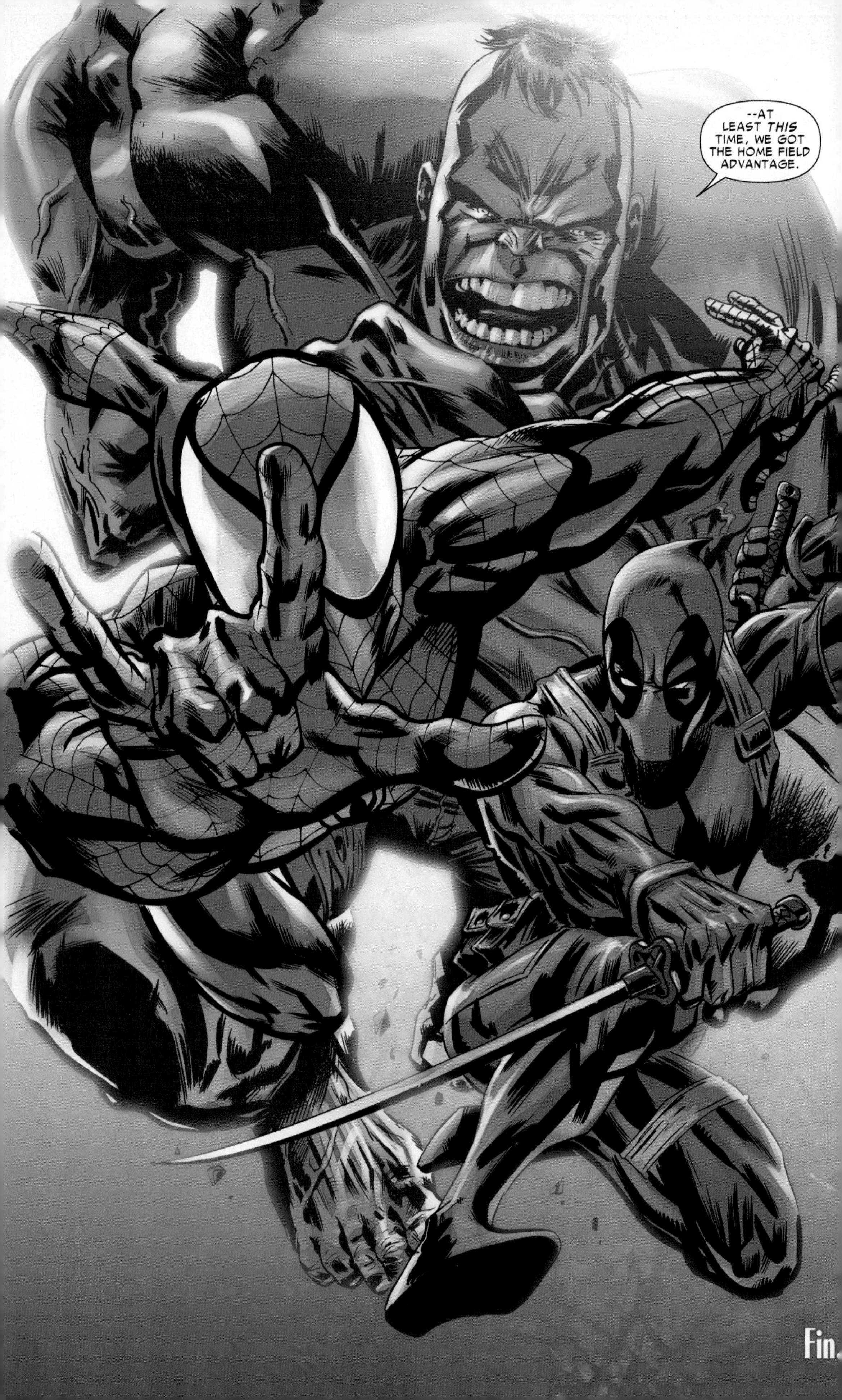
--AT LEAST THIS TIME, WE GOT THE HOME FIELD ADVANTAGE.
Fin.

WOLVERINE/DEADPOOL: THE DECOY

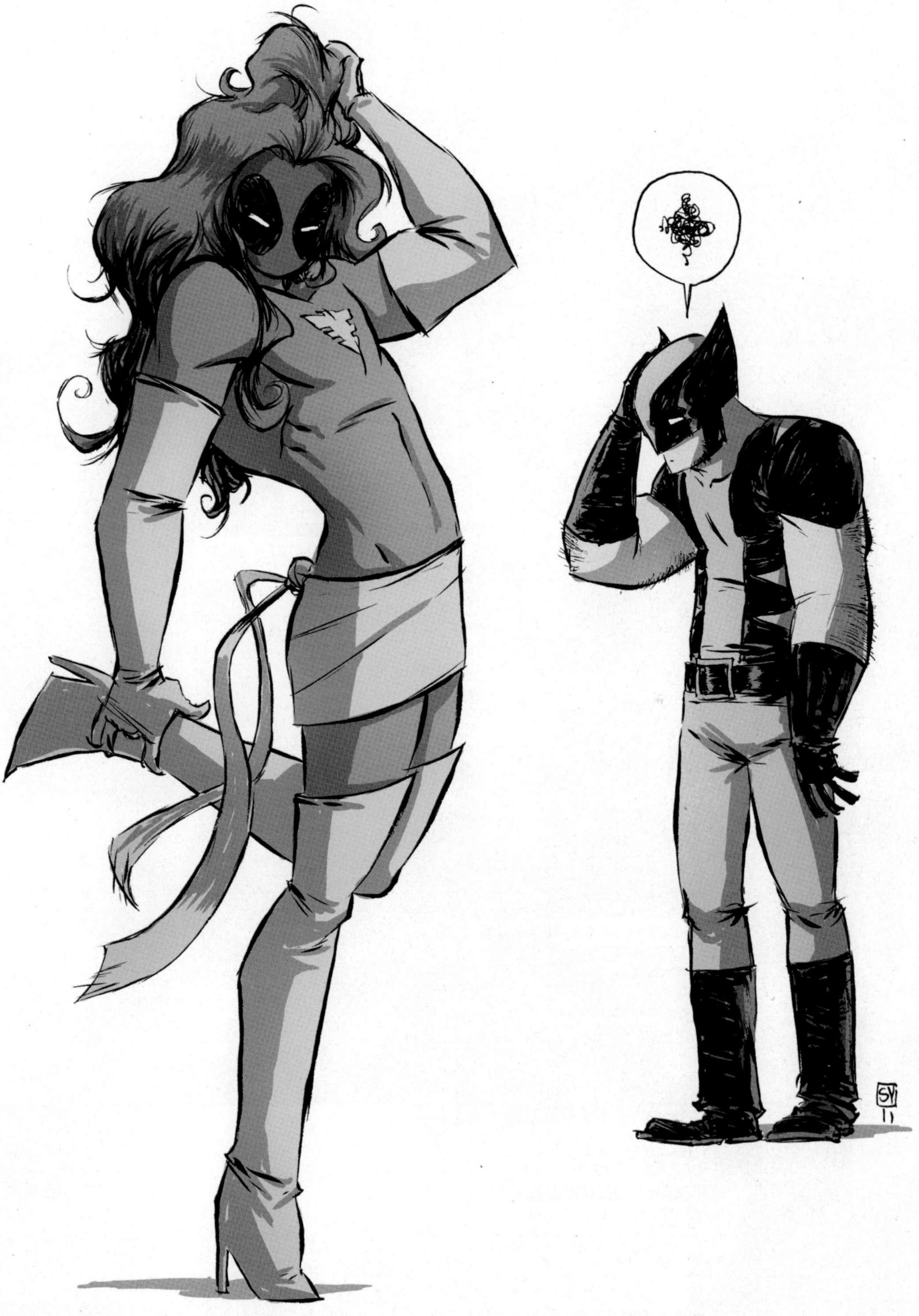

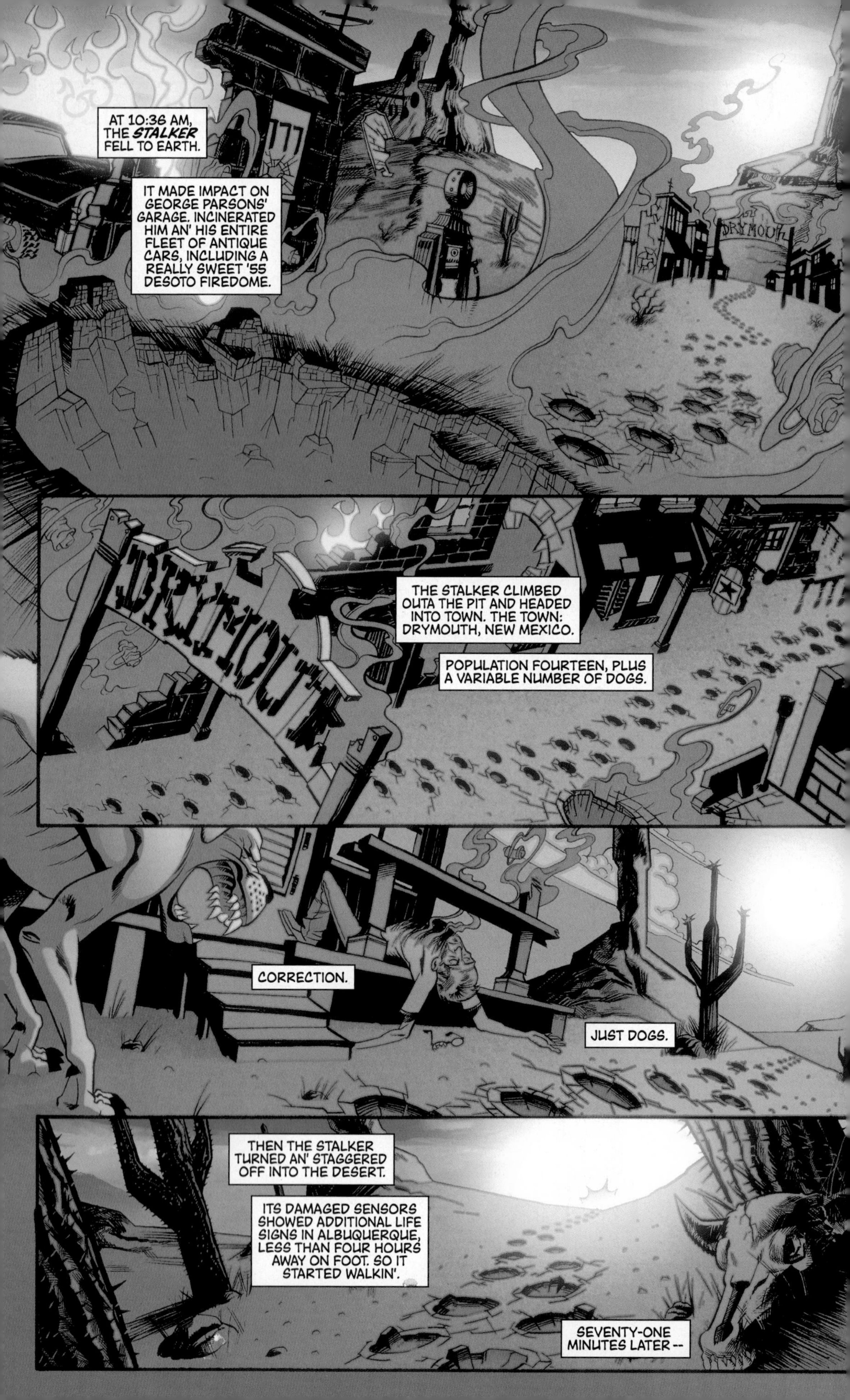
AT 10:36 AM, THE STALKER FELL TO EARTH.
IT MADE IMPACT ON GEORGE PARSONS' GARAGE. INCINERATED HIM AN' HIS ENTIRE FLEET OF ANTIQUE CARS, INCLUDING A REALLY SWEET '55 DESOTO FIREDOME.
DRYMOUTH
THE STALKER CLIMBED OUTA THE PIT AND HEADED INTO TOWN. THE TOWN: DRYMOUTH, NEW MEXICO.
POPULATION FOURTEEN, PLUS A VARIABLE NUMBER OF DOGS.
CORRECTION.
JUST DOGS.
THEN THE STALKER TURNED AN' STAGGERED OFF INTO THE DESERT.
ITS DAMAGED SENSORS SHOWED ADDITIONAL LIFE SIGNS IN ALBUQUERQUE, LESS THAN FOUR HOURS AWAY ON FOOT. SO IT STARTED WALKIN'.
SEVENTY-ONE MINUTES LATER --

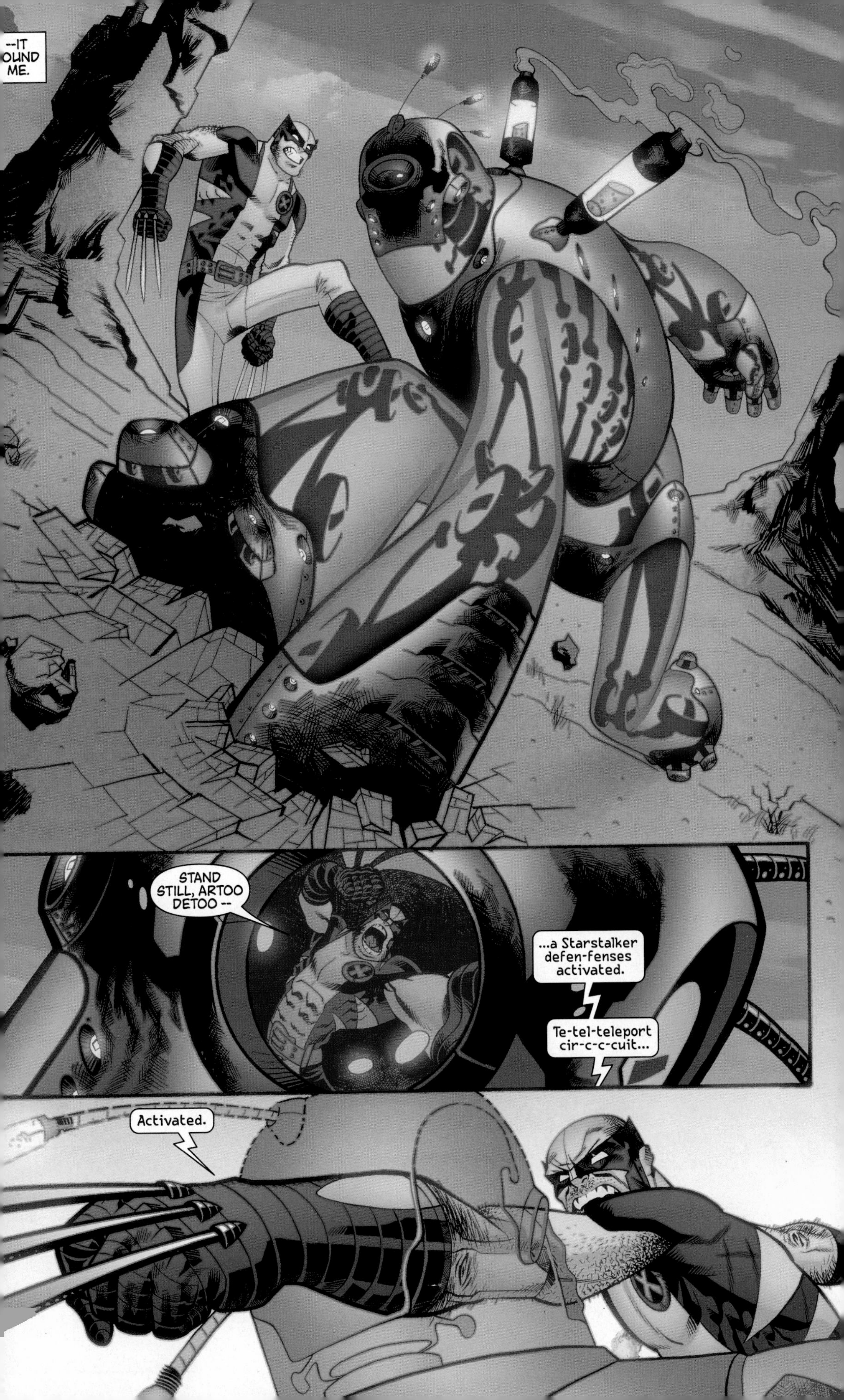
--IT
OUND
ME.
STAND STILL, ARTOO DETOO --
...a Starstalker defen-fenses activated.
Te-tel-teleport cir-c-c-cuit...
Activated.

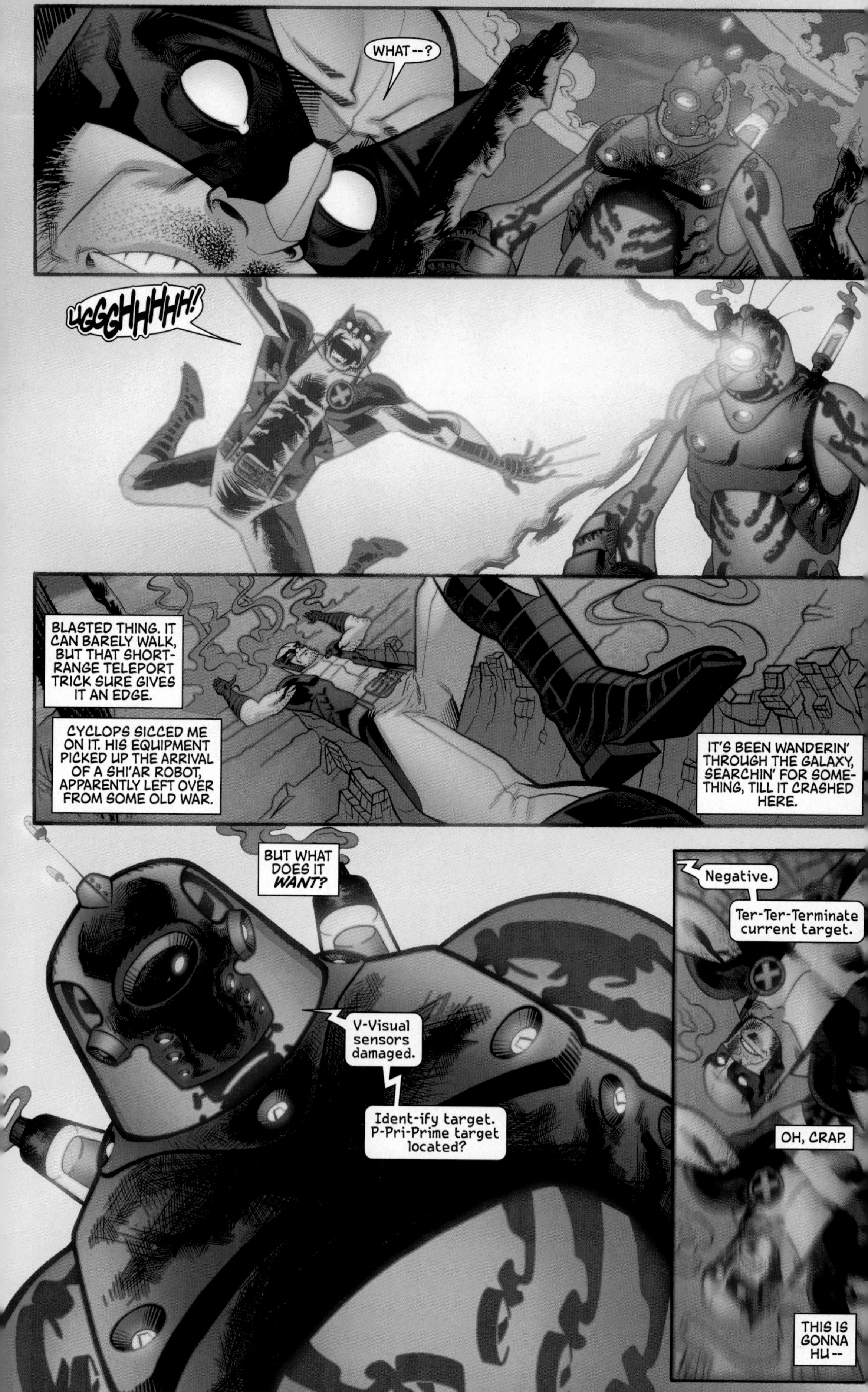
WHAT --?
UGGGHHHHH!
BLASTED THING. IT CAN BARELY WALK, BUT THAT SHORT-RANGE TELEPORT TRICK SURE GIVES IT AN EDGE.
CYCLOPS SICCED ME ON IT. HIS EQUIPMENT PICKED UP THE ARRIVAL OF A SHI'AR ROBOT, APPARENTLY LEFT OVER FROM SOME OLD WAR.
IT'S BEEN WANDERIN' THROUGH THE GALAXY, SEARCHIN' FOR SOME-THING, TILL IT CRASHED HERE.
BUT WHAT DOES IT WANT?
V-Visual sensors damaged.
Ident-ify target. P-Pri-Prime target located?
Negative.
Ter-Ter-Terminate current target.
OH, CRAP.
THIS IS GONNA HU--

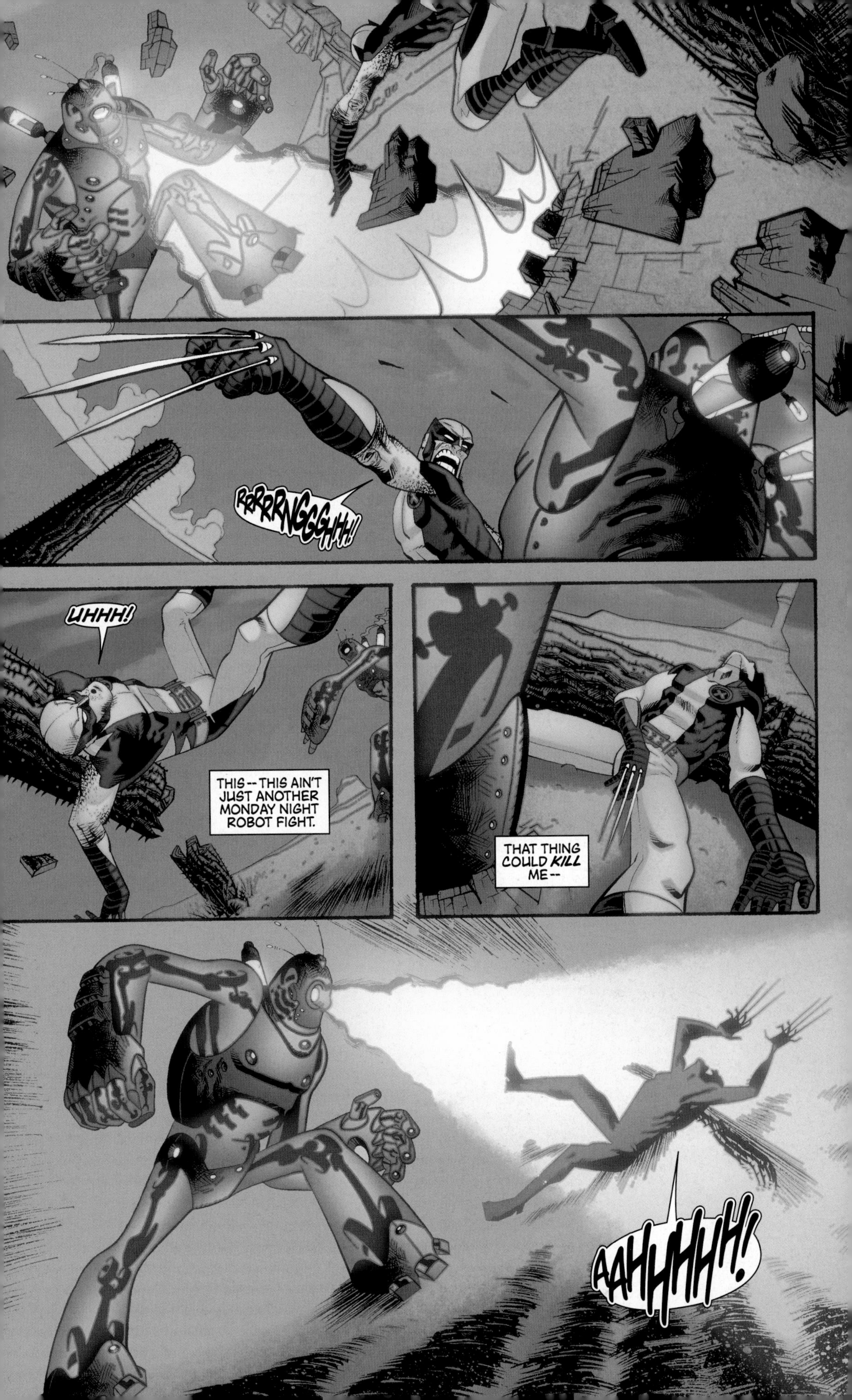
RRRRRNGGGHHH!
UHHH!
THIS -- THIS AIN'T JUST ANOTHER MONDAY NIGHT ROBOT FIGHT.
THAT THING COULD *KILL* ME --
AAHHHHH!

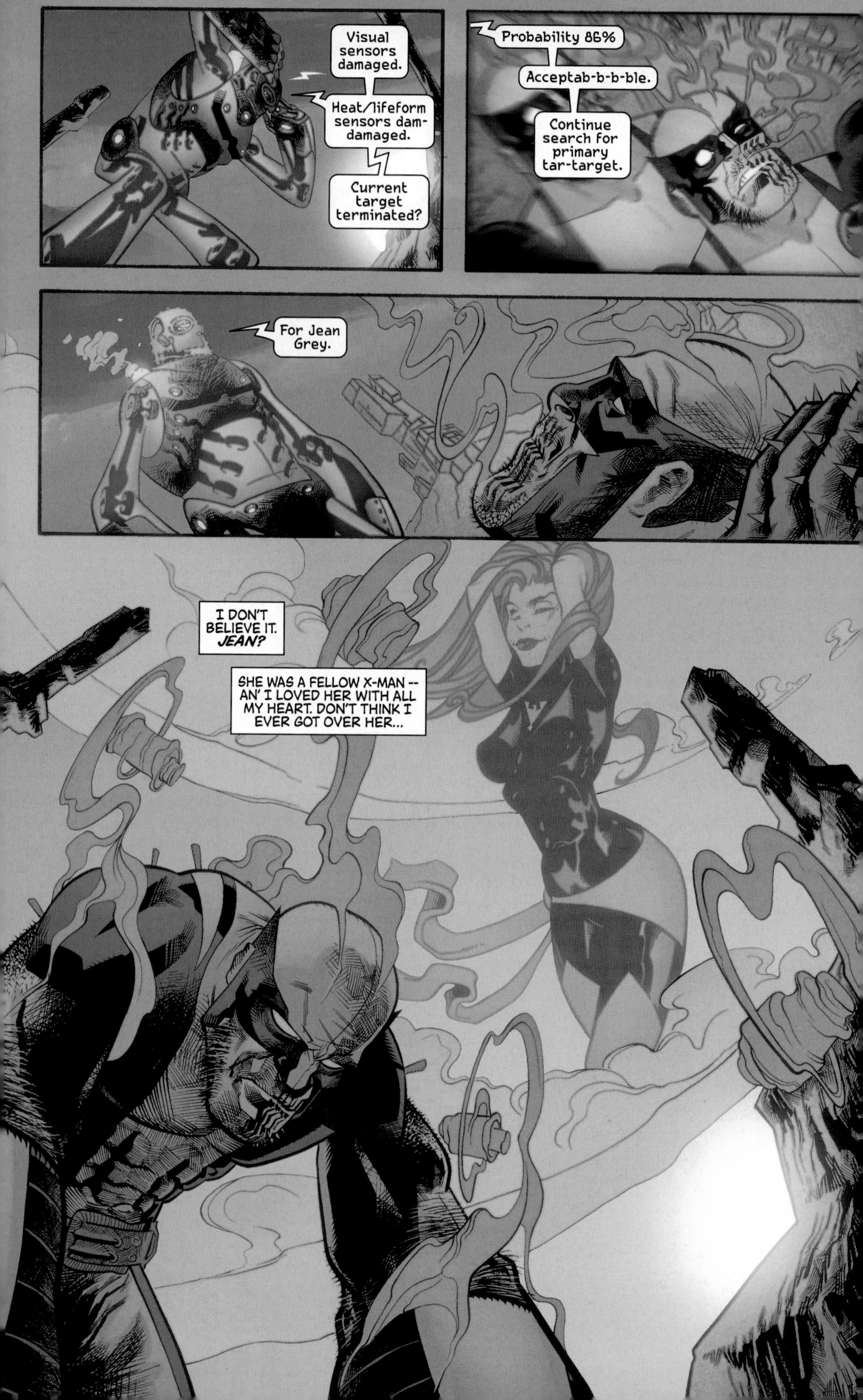
Visual sensors damaged.
Heat/lifeform sensors dam-damaged.
Current target terminated?
Probability 86%
Acceptab-b-b-ble.
Continue search for primary tar-target.
For Jean Grey.
I DON'T BELIEVE IT. JEAN?
SHE WAS A FELLOW X-MAN -- AN' I LOVED HER WITH ALL MY HEART. DON'T THINK I EVER GOT OVER HER...

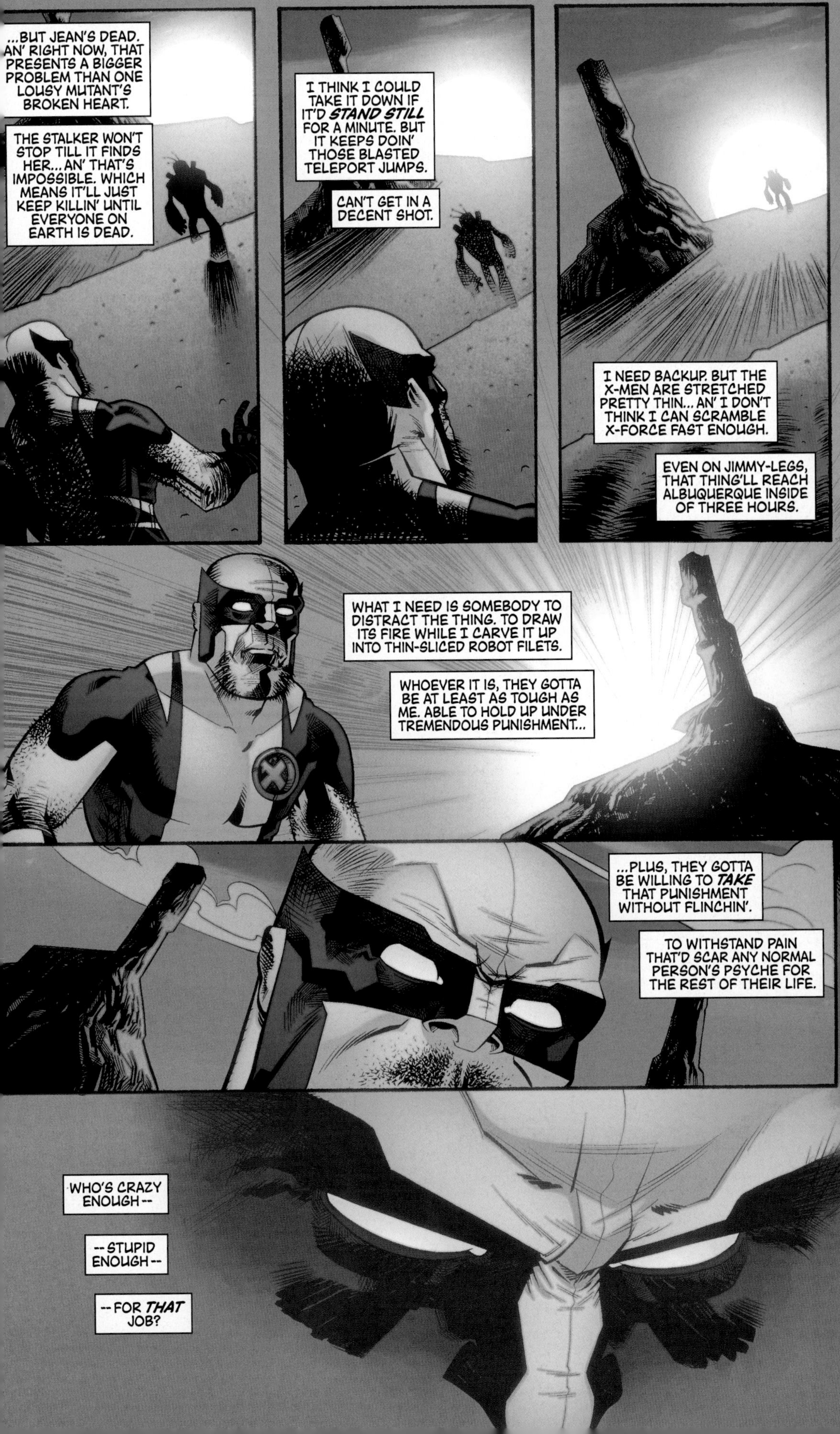
...BUT JEAN'S DEAD. AN' RIGHT NOW, THAT PRESENTS A BIGGER PROBLEM THAN ONE LOUSY MUTANT'S BROKEN HEART.
THE STALKER WON'T STOP TILL IT FINDS HER... AN' THAT'S IMPOSSIBLE. WHICH MEANS IT'LL JUST KEEP KILLIN' UNTIL EVERYONE ON EARTH IS DEAD.
I THINK I COULD TAKE IT DOWN IF IT'D *STAND STILL* FOR A MINUTE. BUT IT KEEPS DOIN' THOSE BLASTED TELEPORT JUMPS.
CAN'T GET IN A DECENT SHOT.
I NEED BACKUP. BUT THE X-MEN ARE STRETCHED PRETTY THIN... AN' I DON'T THINK I CAN SCRAMBLE X-FORCE FAST ENOUGH.
EVEN ON JIMMY-LEGS, THAT THING'LL REACH ALBUQUERQUE INSIDE OF THREE HOURS.
WHAT I NEED IS SOMEBODY TO DISTRACT THE THING. TO DRAW ITS FIRE WHILE I CARVE IT UP INTO THIN-SLICED ROBOT FILETS.
WHOEVER IT IS, THEY GOTTA BE AT LEAST AS TOUGH AS ME. ABLE TO HOLD UP UNDER TREMENDOUS PUNISHMENT...
...PLUS, THEY GOTTA BE WILLING TO *TAKE* THAT PUNISHMENT WITHOUT FLINCHIN'.
TO WITHSTAND PAIN THAT'D SCAR ANY NORMAL PERSON'S PSYCHE FOR THE REST OF THEIR LIFE.
WHO'S CRAZY ENOUGH --
-- STUPID ENOUGH --
-- FOR *THAT* JOB?

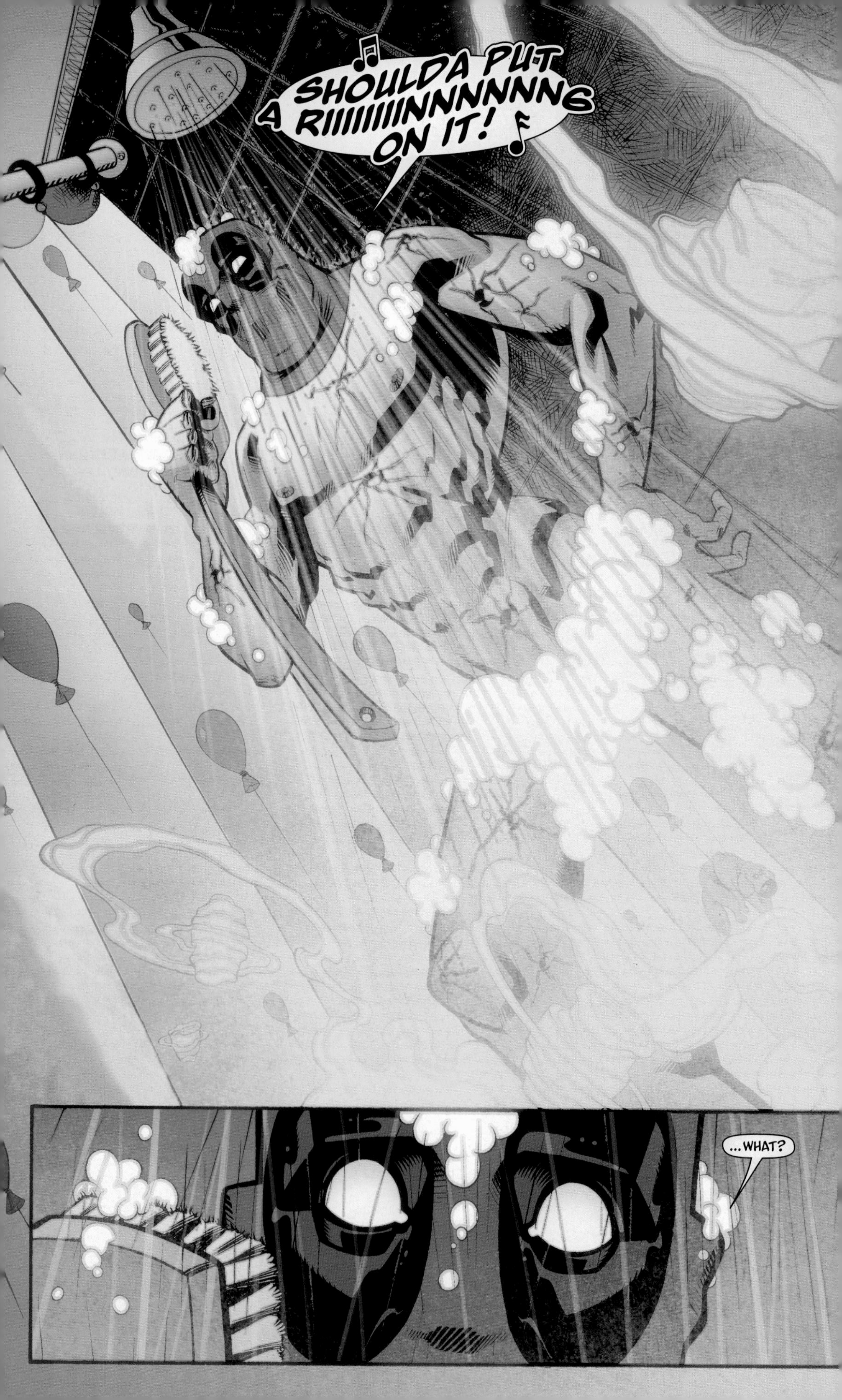
SHOULDA PUT A RIIIIIIIIINNNNNNG ON IT!
...WHAT?

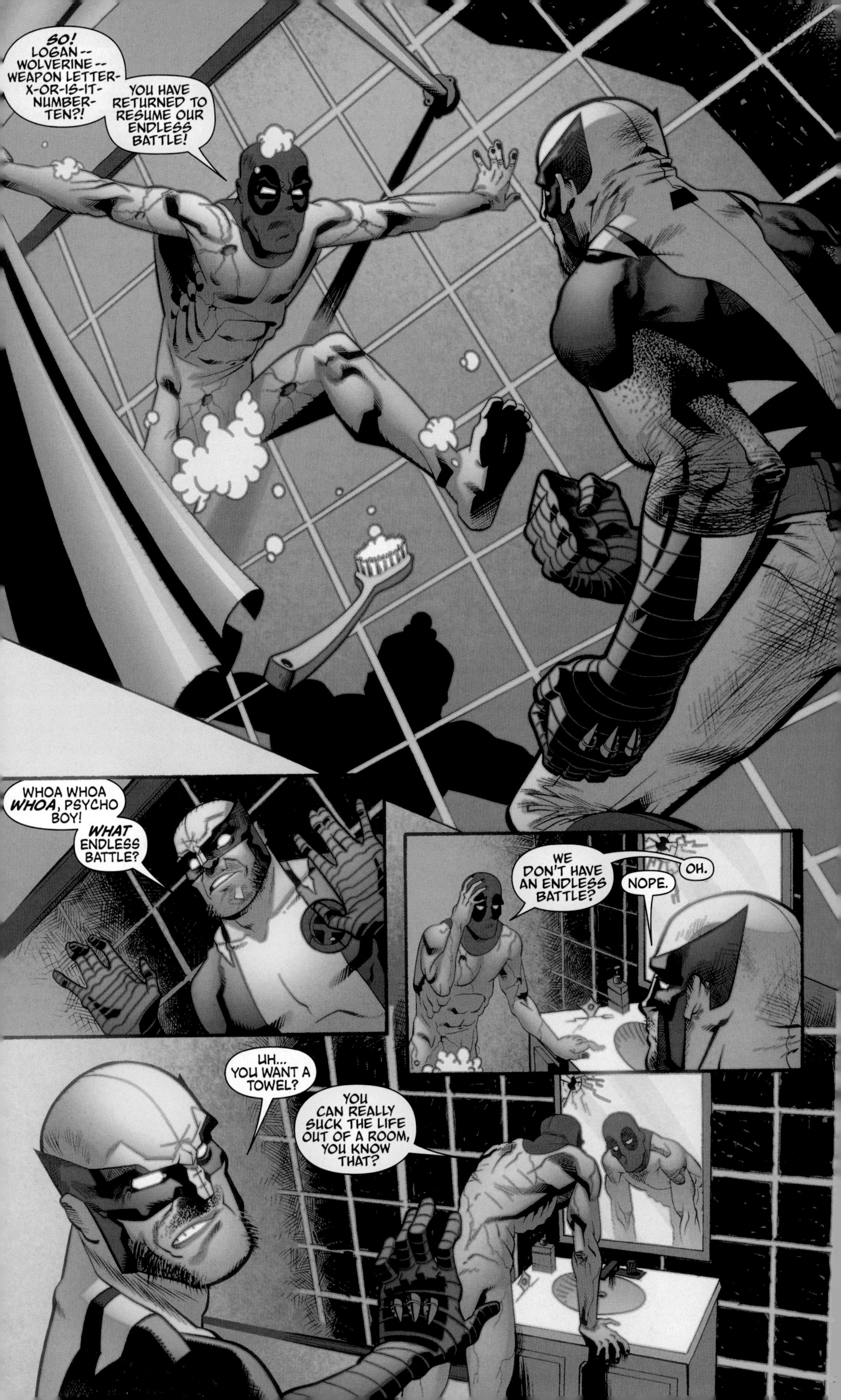

SO! LOGAN -- WOLVERINE -- WEAPON LETTER-X-OR-IS-IT-NUMBER-TEN?!
YOU HAVE RETURNED TO RESUME OUR ENDLESS BATTLE!
WHOA WHOA WHOA, PSYCHO BOY! WHAT ENDLESS BATTLE?
WE DON'T HAVE AN ENDLESS BATTLE?
NOPE.
OH.
UH... YOU WANT A TOWEL?
YOU CAN REALLY SUCK THE LIFE OUT OF A ROOM, YOU KNOW THAT?

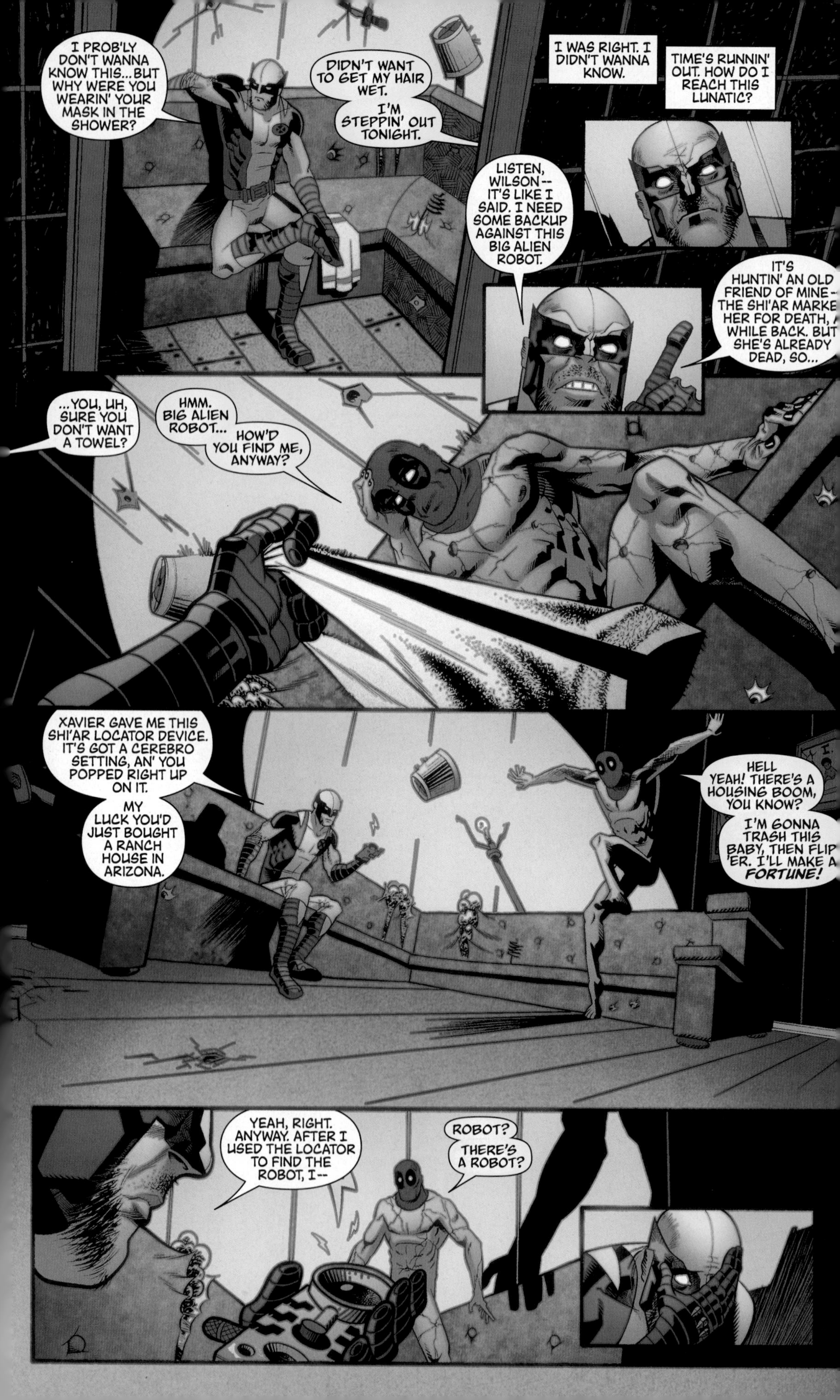
I PROB'LY DON'T WANNA KNOW THIS...BUT WHY WERE YOU WEARIN' YOUR MASK IN THE SHOWER?
DIDN'T WANT TO GET MY HAIR WET.
I'M STEPPIN' OUT TONIGHT.
I WAS RIGHT. I DIDN'T WANNA KNOW.
TIME'S RUNNIN' OUT. HOW DO I REACH THIS LUNATIC?
LISTEN, WILSON-- IT'S LIKE I SAID. I NEED SOME BACKUP AGAINST THIS BIG ALIEN ROBOT.
IT'S HUNTIN' AN OLD FRIEND OF MINE-- THE SHI'AR MARKE HER FOR DEATH, A WHILE BACK. BUT SHE'S ALREADY DEAD, SO...
...YOU, UH, SURE YOU DON'T WANT A TOWEL?
HMM. BIG ALIEN ROBOT...
HOW'D YOU FIND ME, ANYWAY?
XAVIER GAVE ME THIS SHI'AR LOCATOR DEVICE. IT'S GOT A CEREBRO SETTING, AN' YOU POPPED RIGHT UP ON IT.
MY LUCK YOU'D JUST BOUGHT A RANCH HOUSE IN ARIZONA.
HELL YEAH! THERE'S A HOUSING BOOM, YOU KNOW?
I'M GONNA TRASH THIS BABY, THEN FLIP 'ER. I'LL MAKE A FORTUNE!
YEAH, RIGHT. ANYWAY. AFTER I USED THE LOCATOR TO FIND THE ROBOT, I--
ROBOT?
THERE'S A ROBOT?

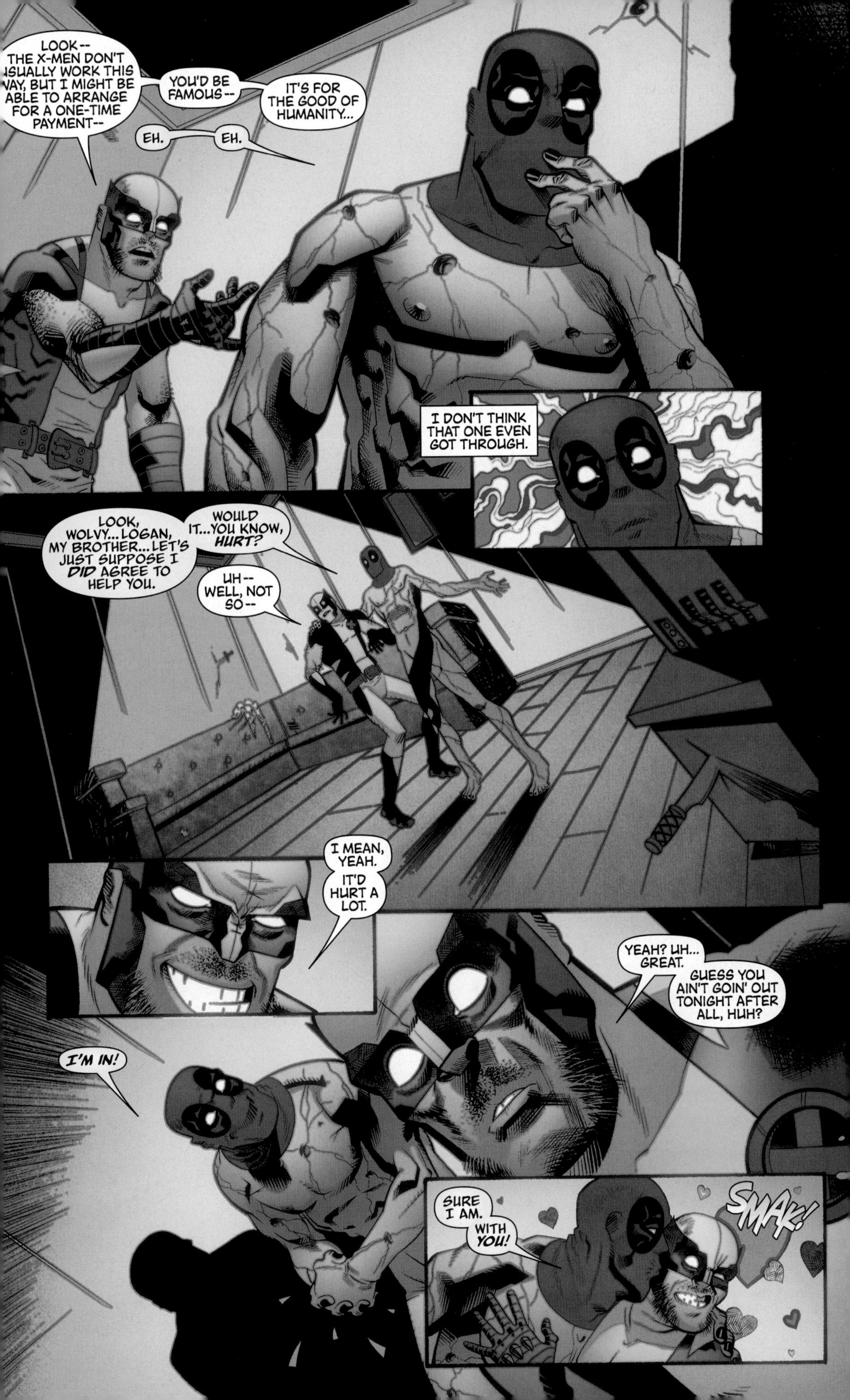
LOOK -- THE X-MEN DON'T USUALLY WORK THIS WAY, BUT I MIGHT BE ABLE TO ARRANGE FOR A ONE-TIME PAYMENT--
EH.
YOU'D BE FAMOUS--
EH.
IT'S FOR THE GOOD OF HUMANITY...
I DON'T THINK THAT ONE EVEN GOT THROUGH.
LOOK, WOLVY...LOGAN, MY BROTHER...LET'S JUST SUPPOSE I DID AGREE TO HELP YOU.
WOULD IT...YOU KNOW, HURT?
UH -- WELL, NOT SO --
I MEAN, YEAH. IT'D HURT A LOT.
I'M IN!
YEAH? UH... GREAT.
GUESS YOU AIN'T GOIN' OUT TONIGHT AFTER ALL, HUH?
SURE I AM.
WITH YOU!
SMAK!

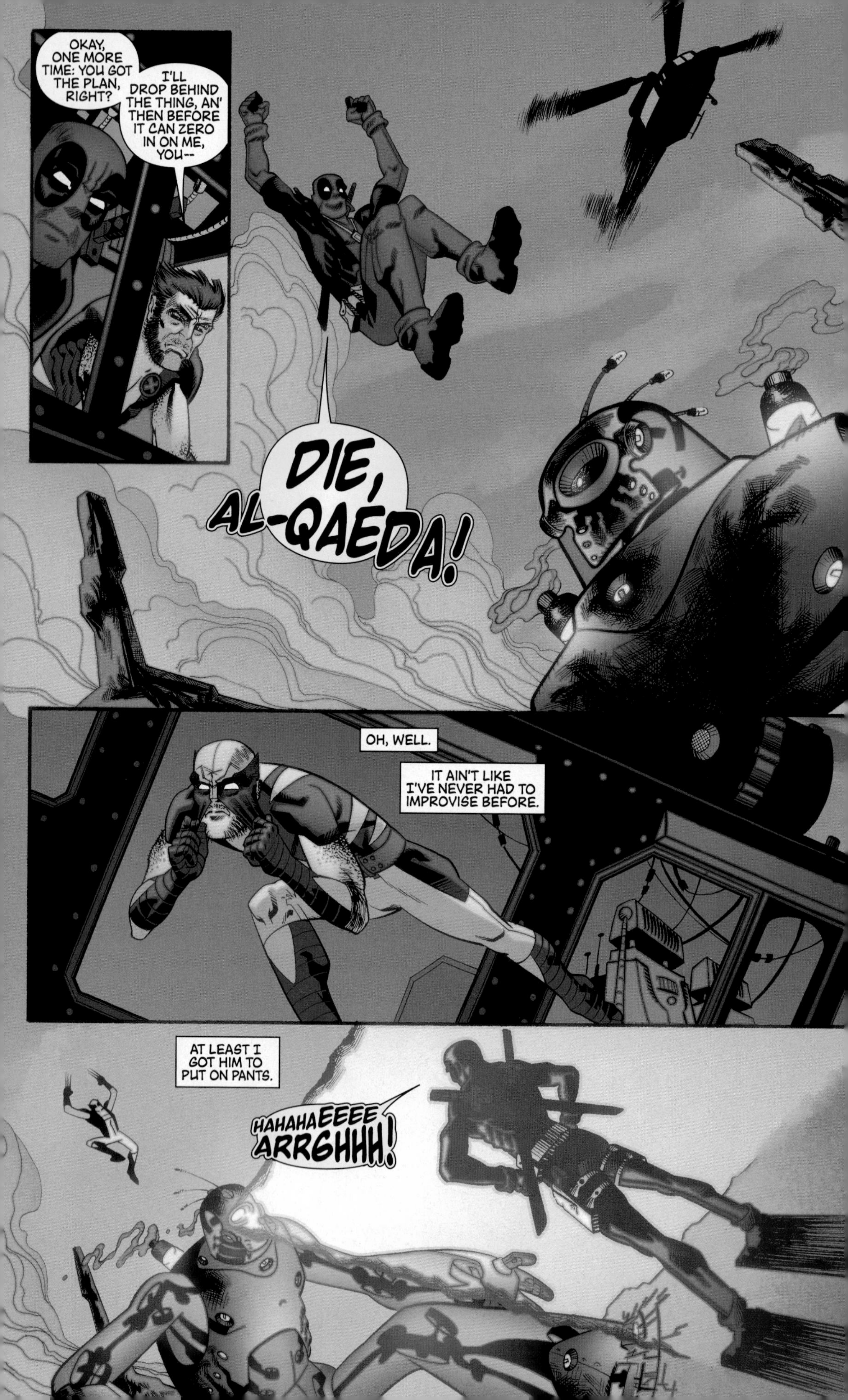
OKAY, ONE MORE TIME: YOU GOT THE PLAN, RIGHT?
I'LL DROP BEHIND THE THING, AN' THEN BEFORE IT CAN ZERO IN ON ME, YOU--
DIE, AL-QAEDA!
OH, WELL.
IT AIN'T LIKE I'VE NEVER HAD TO IMPROVISE BEFORE.
AT LEAST I GOT HIM TO PUT ON PANTS.
HAHAHAEEEE ARRGHHH!

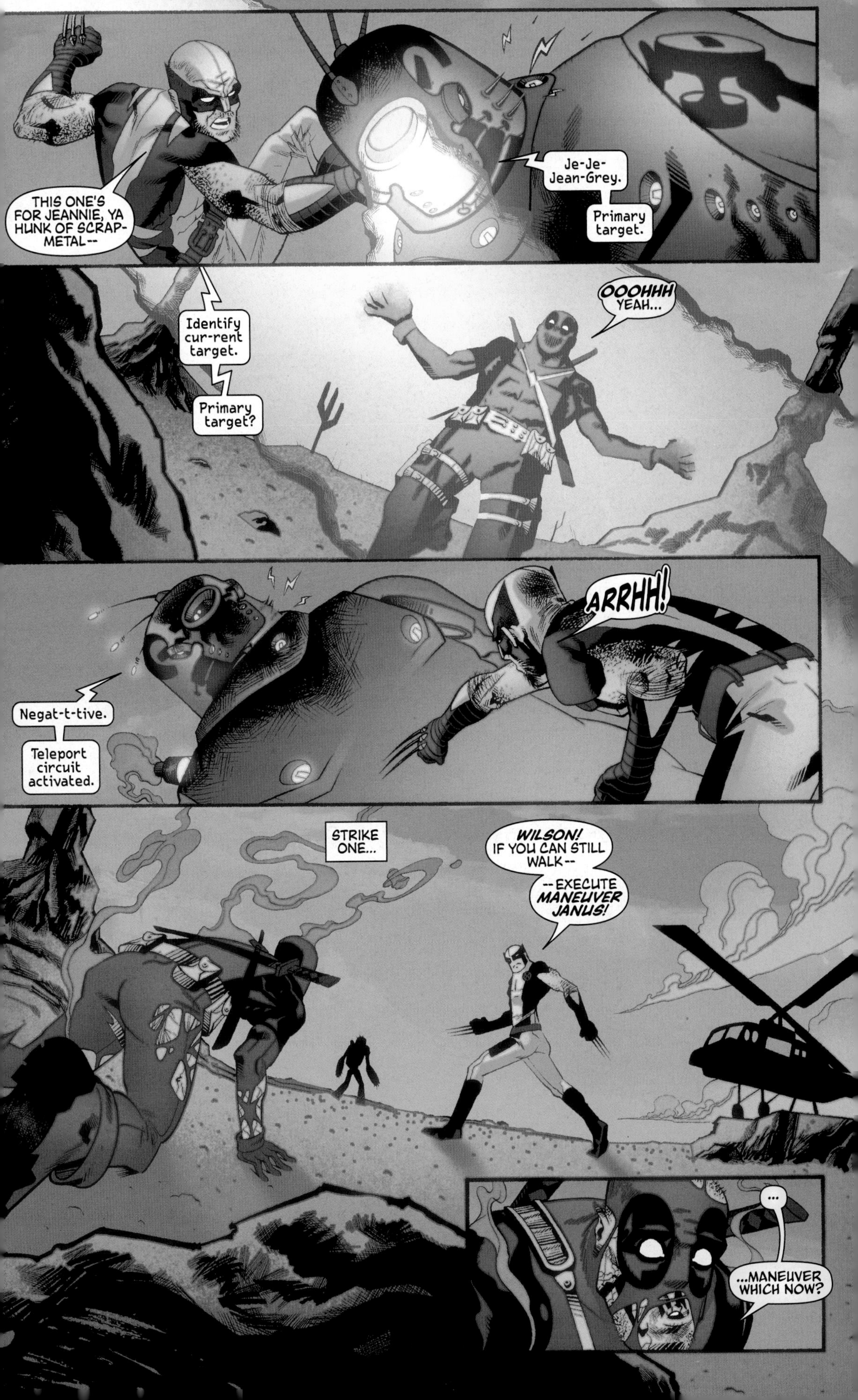
THIS ONE'S FOR JEANNIE, YA HUNK OF SCRAP-METAL--
Je-Je-Jean-Grey.
Primary target.
Identify cur-rent target.
Primary target?
OOOHHH YEAH...
ARRHH!
Negat-t-tive.
Teleport circuit activated.
STRIKE ONE...
WILSON! IF YOU CAN STILL WALK--
--EXECUTE MANEUVER JANUS!
...
...MANEUVER WHICH NOW?

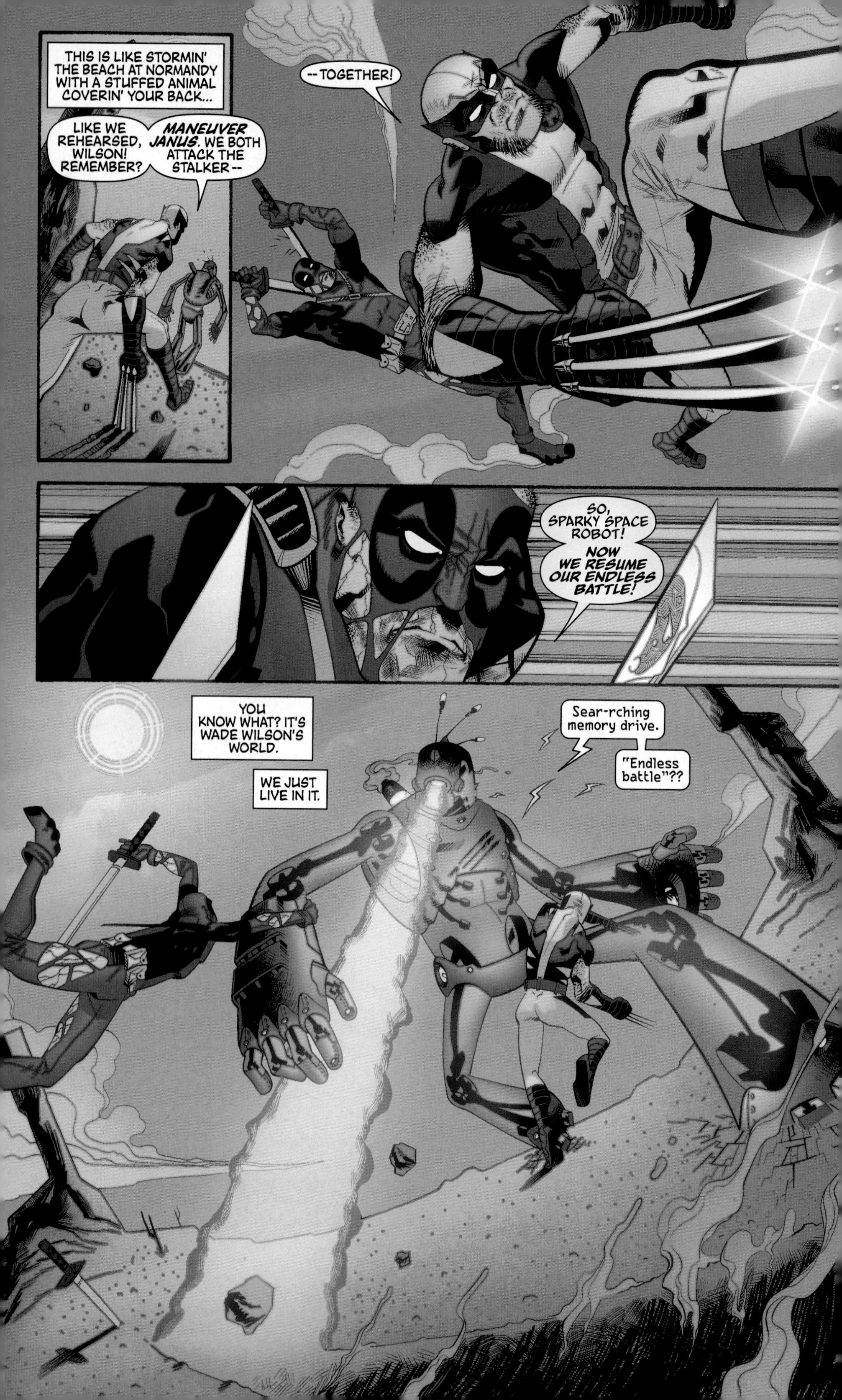

THIS IS LIKE STORMIN' THE BEACH AT NORMANDY WITH A STUFFED ANIMAL COVERIN' YOUR BACK...
LIKE WE REHEARSED, WILSON! REMEMBER?
MANEUVER JANUS. WE BOTH ATTACK THE STALKER --
-- TOGETHER!
SO, SPARKY SPACE ROBOT! NOW WE RESUME OUR ENDLESS BATTLE!
YOU KNOW WHAT? IT'S WADE WILSON'S WORLD.
WE JUST LIVE IN IT.
Sear-rching memory drive.
"Endless battle"??

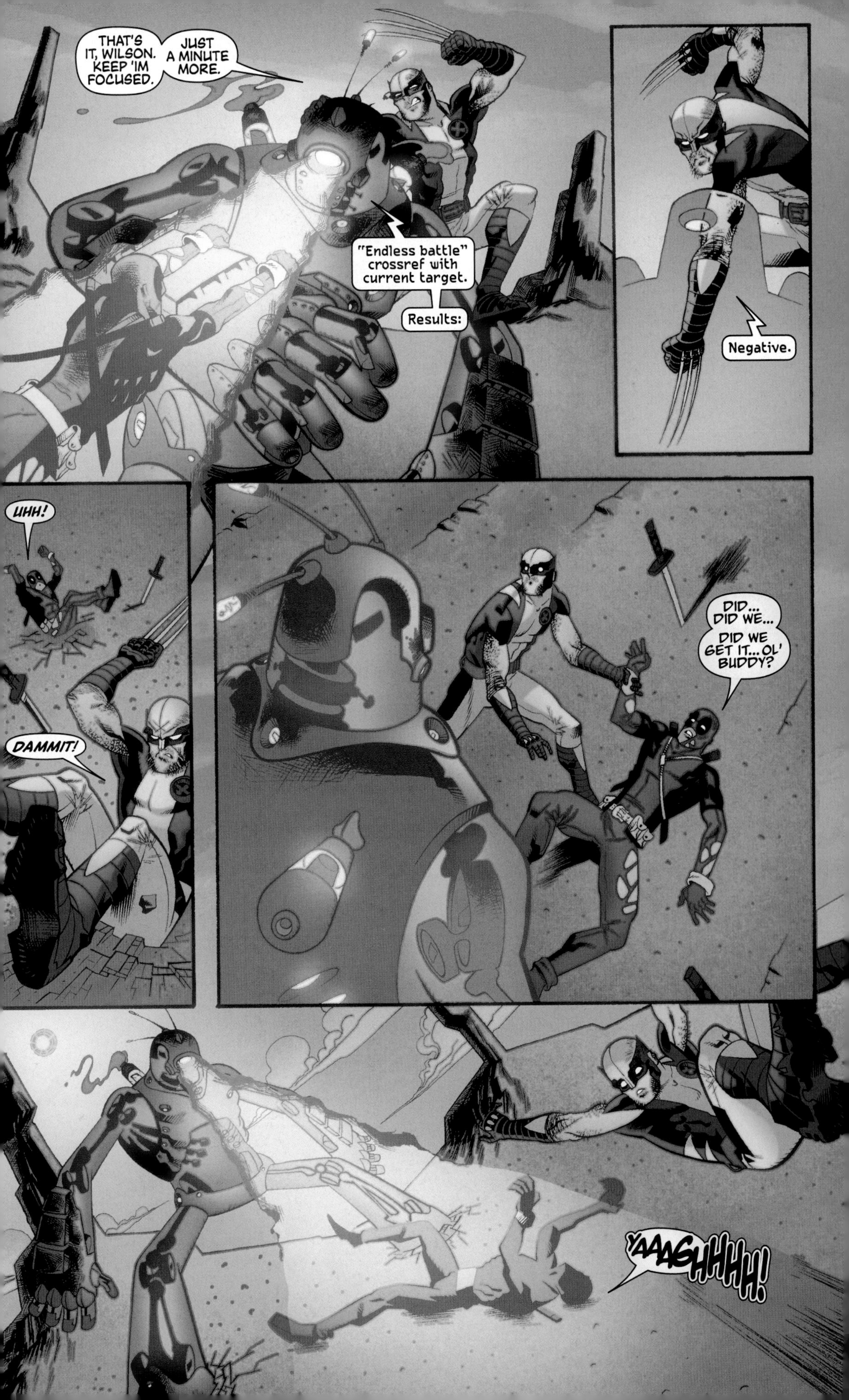

THAT'S IT, WILSON. KEEP 'IM FOCUSED.
JUST A MINUTE MORE.
"Endless battle" crossref with current target.
Results:
Negative.
UHH!
DAMMIT!
DID... DID WE... DID WE GET IT...OL' BUDDY?
YAAAGHHHH!

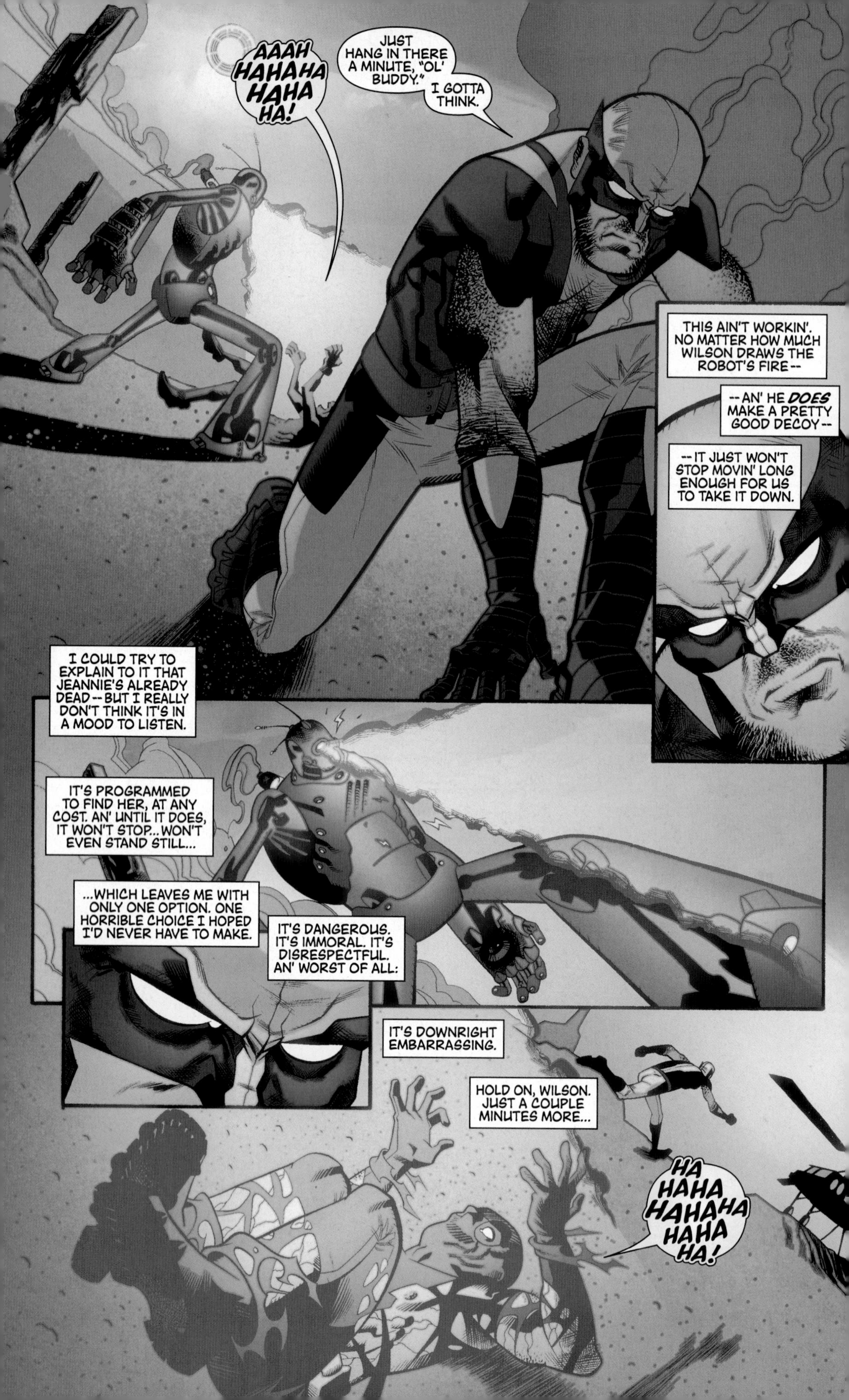
AAAH HAHAHA HAHA HA!
JUST HANG IN THERE A MINUTE, "OL' BUDDY."
I GOTTA THINK.
THIS AIN'T WORKIN'. NO MATTER HOW MUCH WILSON DRAWS THE ROBOT'S FIRE--
--AN' HE DOES MAKE A PRETTY GOOD DECOY--
--IT JUST WON'T STOP MOVIN' LONG ENOUGH FOR US TO TAKE IT DOWN.
I COULD TRY TO EXPLAIN TO IT THAT JEANNIE'S ALREADY DEAD--BUT I REALLY DON'T THINK IT'S IN A MOOD TO LISTEN.
IT'S PROGRAMMED TO FIND HER, AT ANY COST. AN' UNTIL IT DOES, IT WON'T STOP...WON'T EVEN STAND STILL...
...WHICH LEAVES ME WITH ONLY ONE OPTION. ONE HORRIBLE CHOICE I HOPED I'D NEVER HAVE TO MAKE.
IT'S DANGEROUS. IT'S IMMORAL. IT'S DISRESPECTFUL. AN' WORST OF ALL:
IT'S DOWNRIGHT EMBARRASSING.
HOLD ON, WILSON. JUST A COUPLE MINUTES MORE...
HA HAHA HAHAHA HAHA HA!

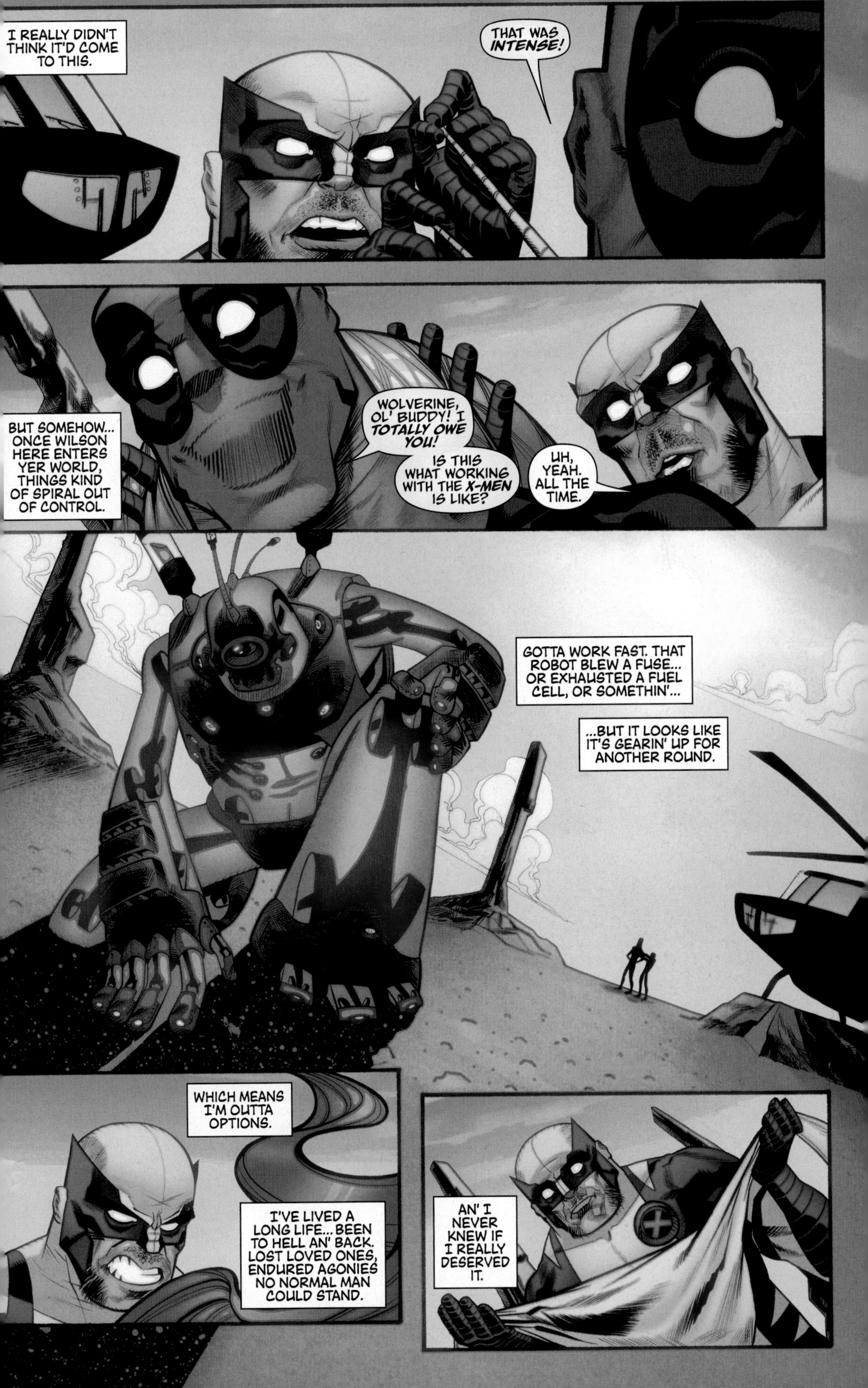
I REALLY DIDN'T THINK IT'D COME TO THIS.
THAT WAS INTENSE!
BUT SOMEHOW... ONCE WILSON HERE ENTERS YER WORLD, THINGS KIND OF SPIRAL OUT OF CONTROL.
WOLVERINE, OL' BUDDY! I TOTALLY OWE YOU!
IS THIS WHAT WORKING WITH THE X-MEN IS LIKE?
UH, YEAH. ALL THE TIME.
GOTTA WORK FAST. THAT ROBOT BLEW A FUSE... OR EXHAUSTED A FUEL CELL, OR SOMETHIN'...
...BUT IT LOOKS LIKE IT'S GEARIN' UP FOR ANOTHER ROUND.
WHICH MEANS I'M OUTTA OPTIONS.
I'VE LIVED A LONG LIFE... BEEN TO HELL AN' BACK. LOST LOVED ONES, ENDURED AGONIES NO NORMAL MAN COULD STAND.
AN' I NEVER KNEW IF I REALLY DESERVED IT.

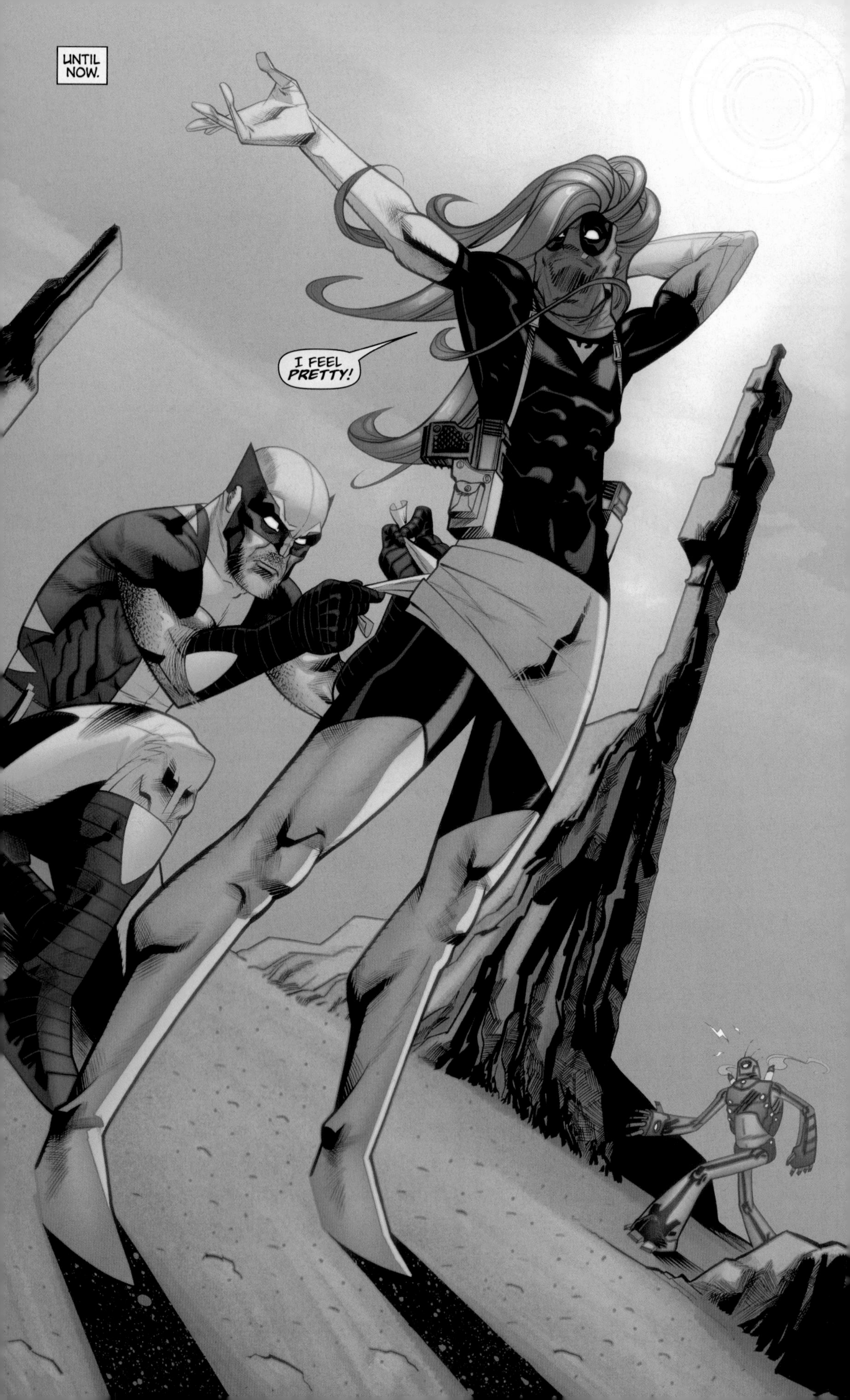
UNTIL NOW.
I FEEL PRETTY!

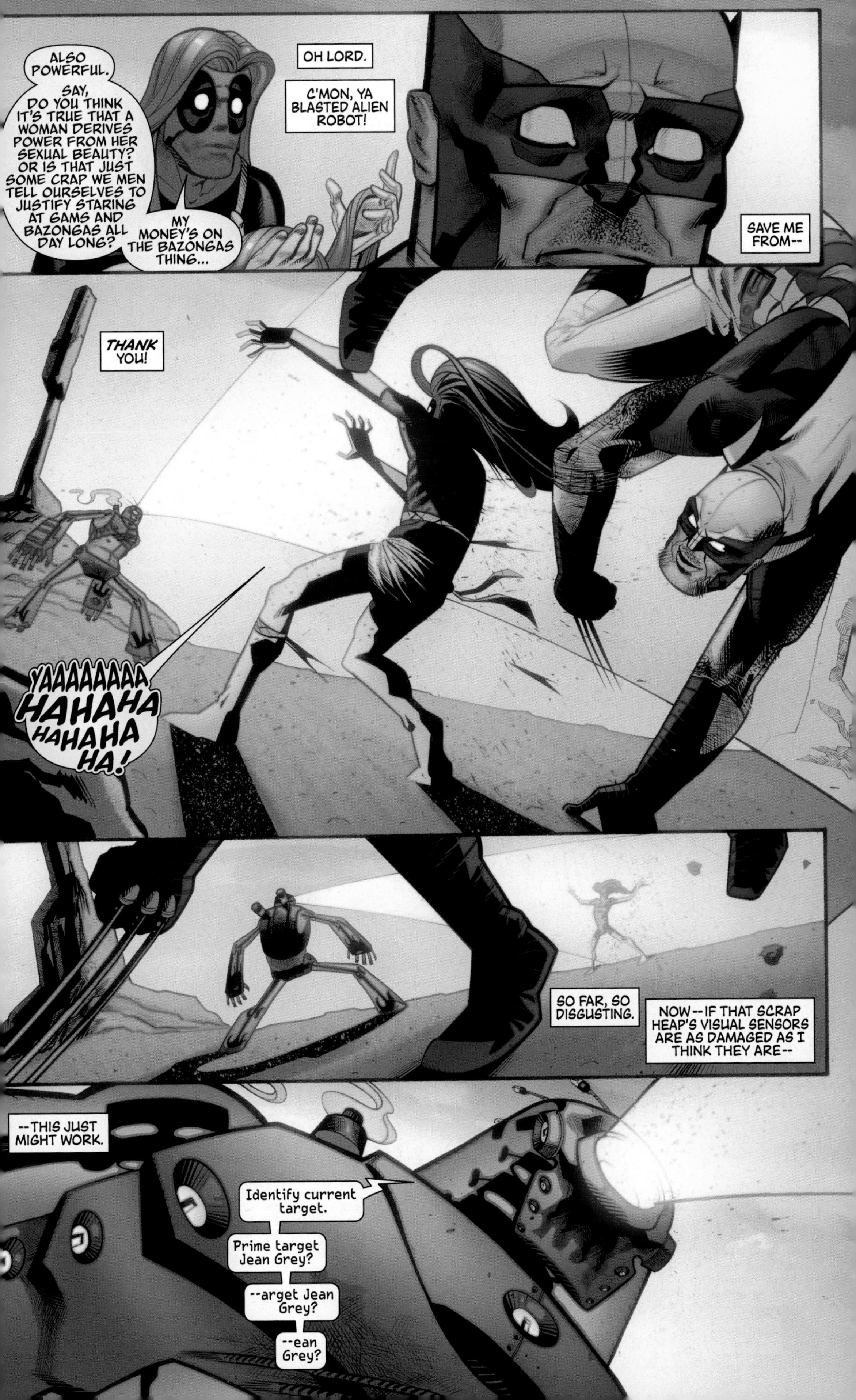
ALSO POWERFUL.
SAY, DO YOU THINK IT'S TRUE THAT A WOMAN DERIVES POWER FROM HER SEXUAL BEAUTY? OR IS THAT JUST SOME CRAP WE MEN TELL OURSELVES TO JUSTIFY STARING AT GAMS AND BAZONGAS ALL DAY LONG?
MY MONEY'S ON THE BAZONGAS THING...
OH LORD.
C'MON, YA BLASTED ALIEN ROBOT!
SAVE ME FROM--
THANK YOU!
YAAAAAAAA HAHAHA HAHAHA HA!
SO FAR, SO DISGUSTING.
NOW--IF THAT SCRAP HEAP'S VISUAL SENSORS ARE AS DAMAGED AS I THINK THEY ARE--
--THIS JUST MIGHT WORK.
Identify current target.
Prime target Jean Grey?
--arget Jean Grey?
--ean Grey?

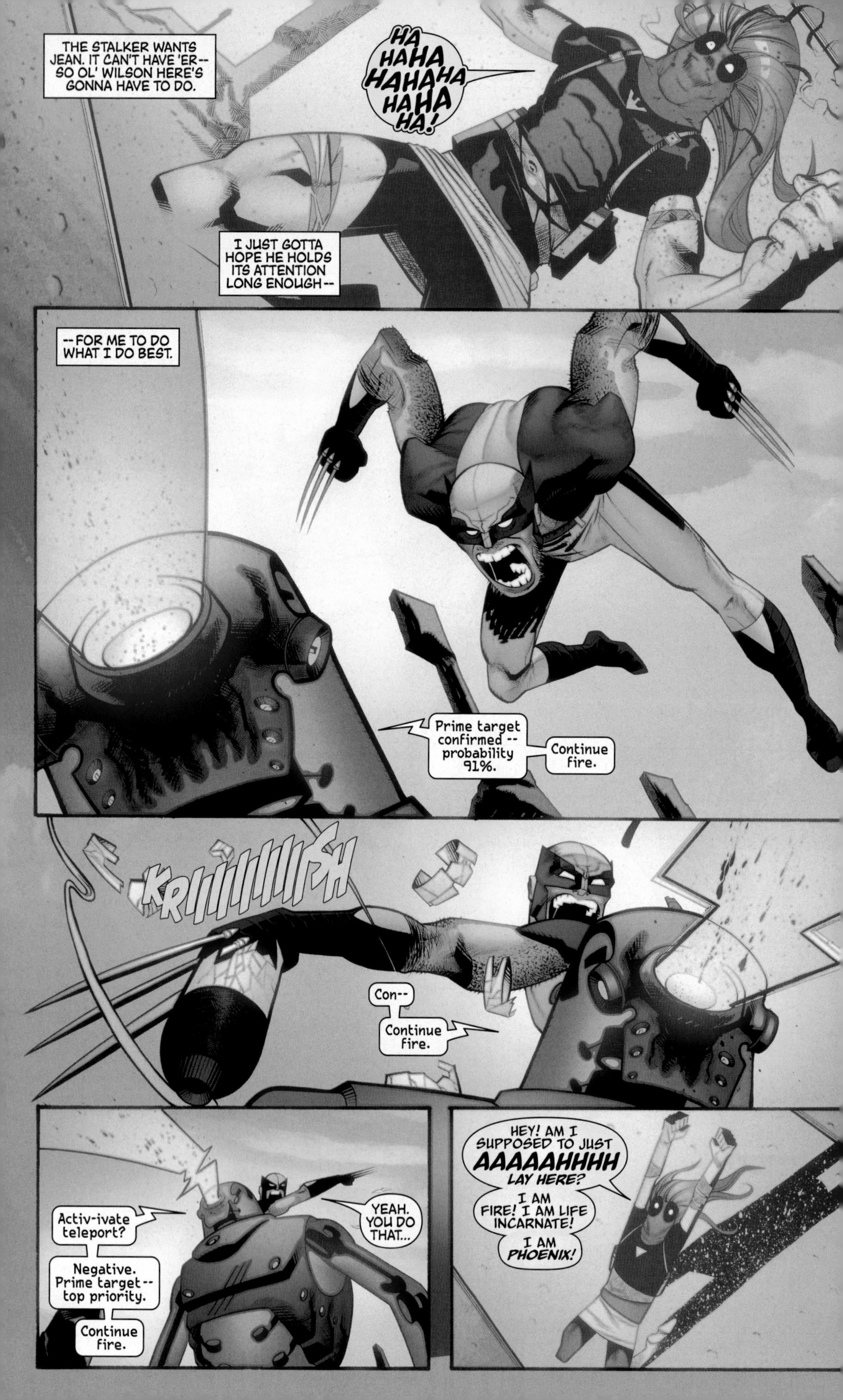
THE STALKER WANTS JEAN. IT CAN'T HAVE 'ER-- SO OL' WILSON HERE'S GONNA HAVE TO DO.
HA HAHA HAHAHA HAHA HA!
I JUST GOTTA HOPE HE HOLDS ITS ATTENTION LONG ENOUGH--
--FOR ME TO DO WHAT I DO BEST.
Prime target confirmed -- probability 91%.
Continue fire.
KRIIIIIIIISH
Con--
Continue fire.
Activ-ivate teleport?
Negative. Prime target -- top priority.
Continue fire.
YEAH. YOU DO THAT...
HEY! AM I SUPPOSED TO JUST AAAAAHHHH LAY HERE?
I AM FIRE! I AM LIFE INCARNATE!
I AM PHOENIX!

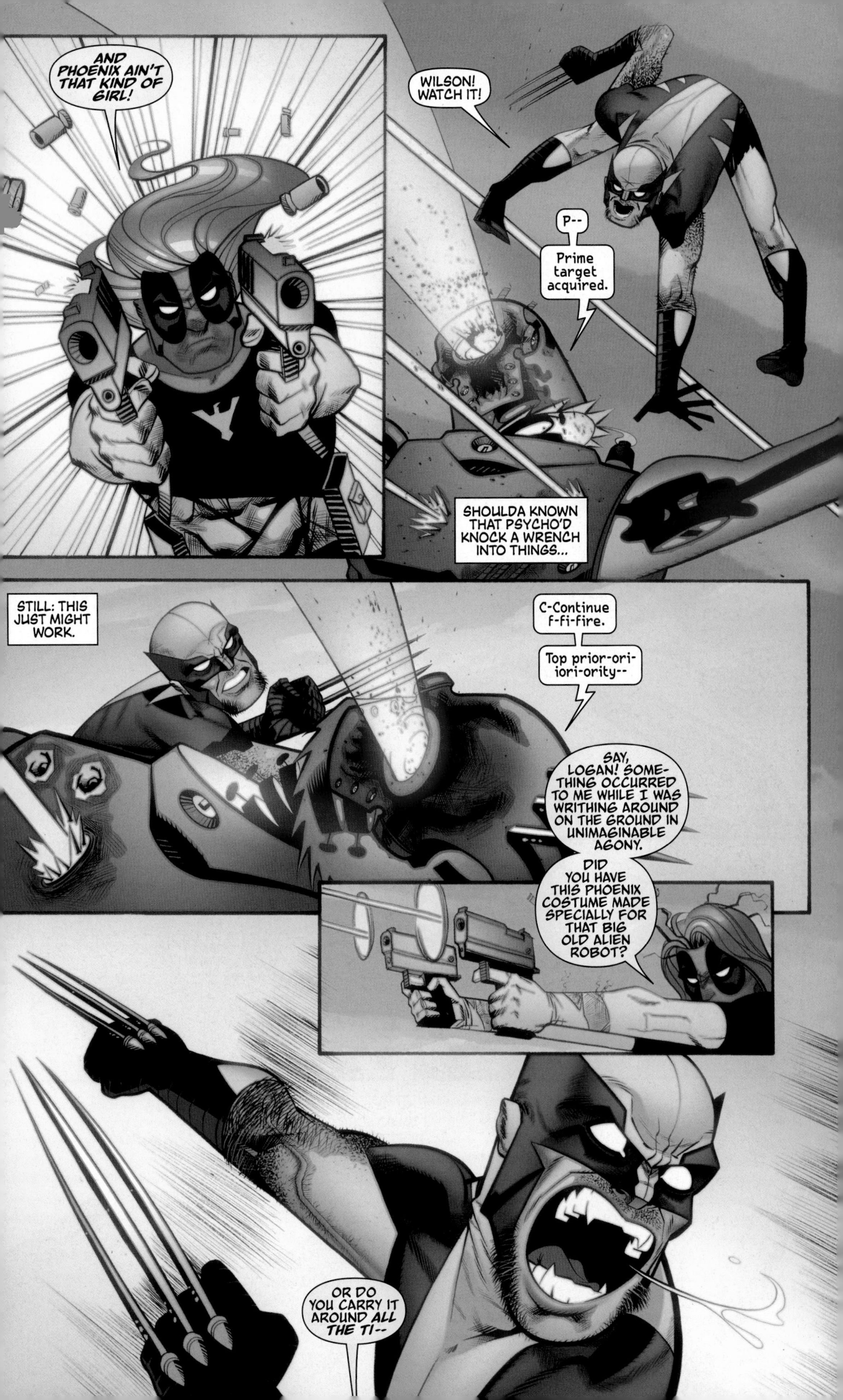
AND PHOENIX AIN'T THAT KIND OF GIRL!
WILSON! WATCH IT!
P--
Prime target acquired.
SHOULDA KNOWN THAT PSYCHO'D KNOCK A WRENCH INTO THINGS...
STILL: THIS JUST MIGHT WORK.
C-Continue f-fi-fire.
Top prior-ori-iori-ority--
SAY, LOGAN! SOME-THING OCCURRED TO ME WHILE I WAS WRITHING AROUND ON THE GROUND IN UNIMAGINABLE AGONY.
DID YOU HAVE THIS PHOENIX COSTUME MADE SPECIALLY FOR THAT BIG OLD ALIEN ROBOT?
OR DO YOU CARRY IT AROUND ALL THE TI--

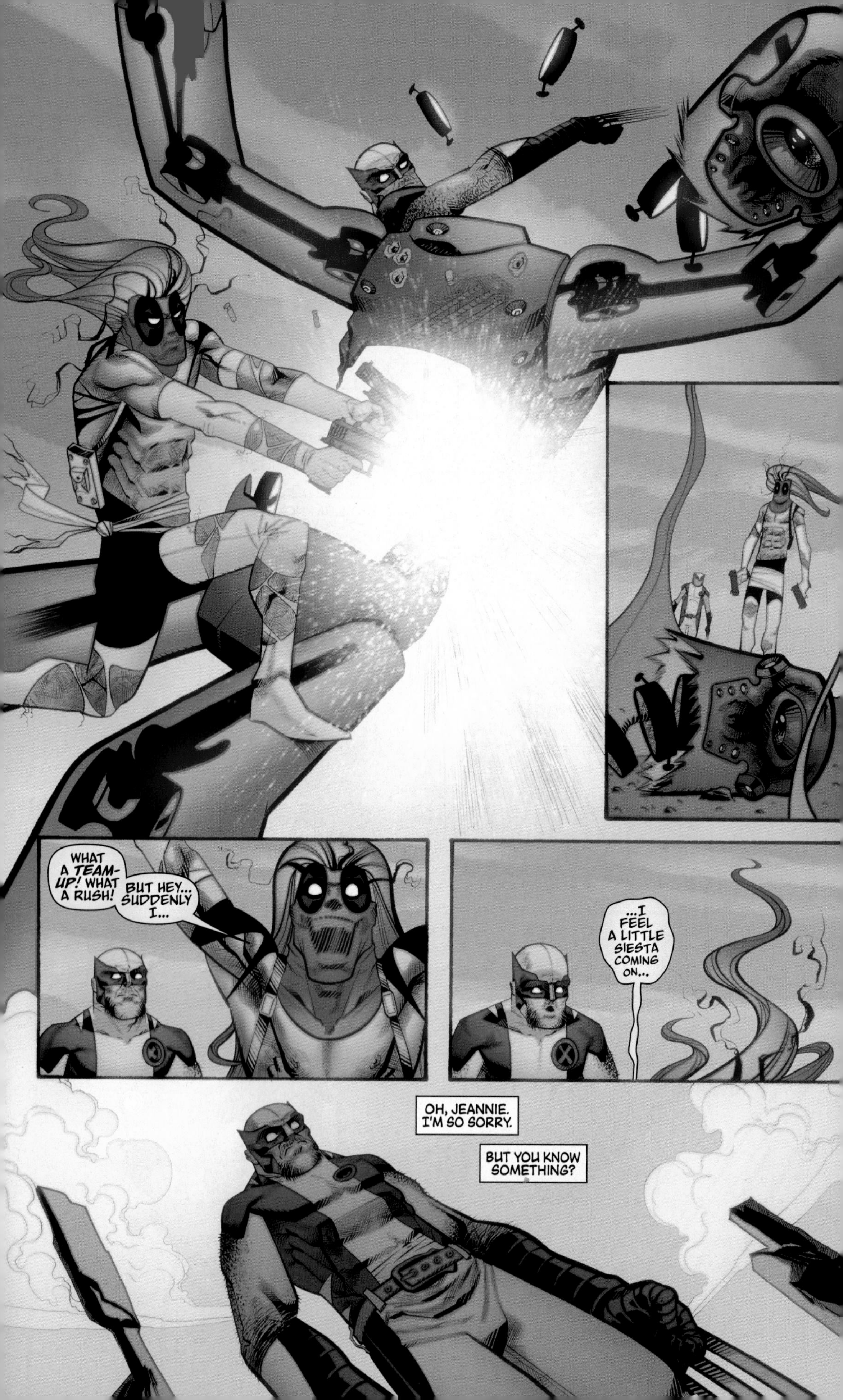
WHAT A *TEAM-UP!* WHAT A RUSH!
BUT HEY... SUDDENLY I...
...I FEEL A LITTLE SIESTA COMING ON...
OH, JEANNIE. I'M SO SORRY.
BUT YOU KNOW SOMETHING?

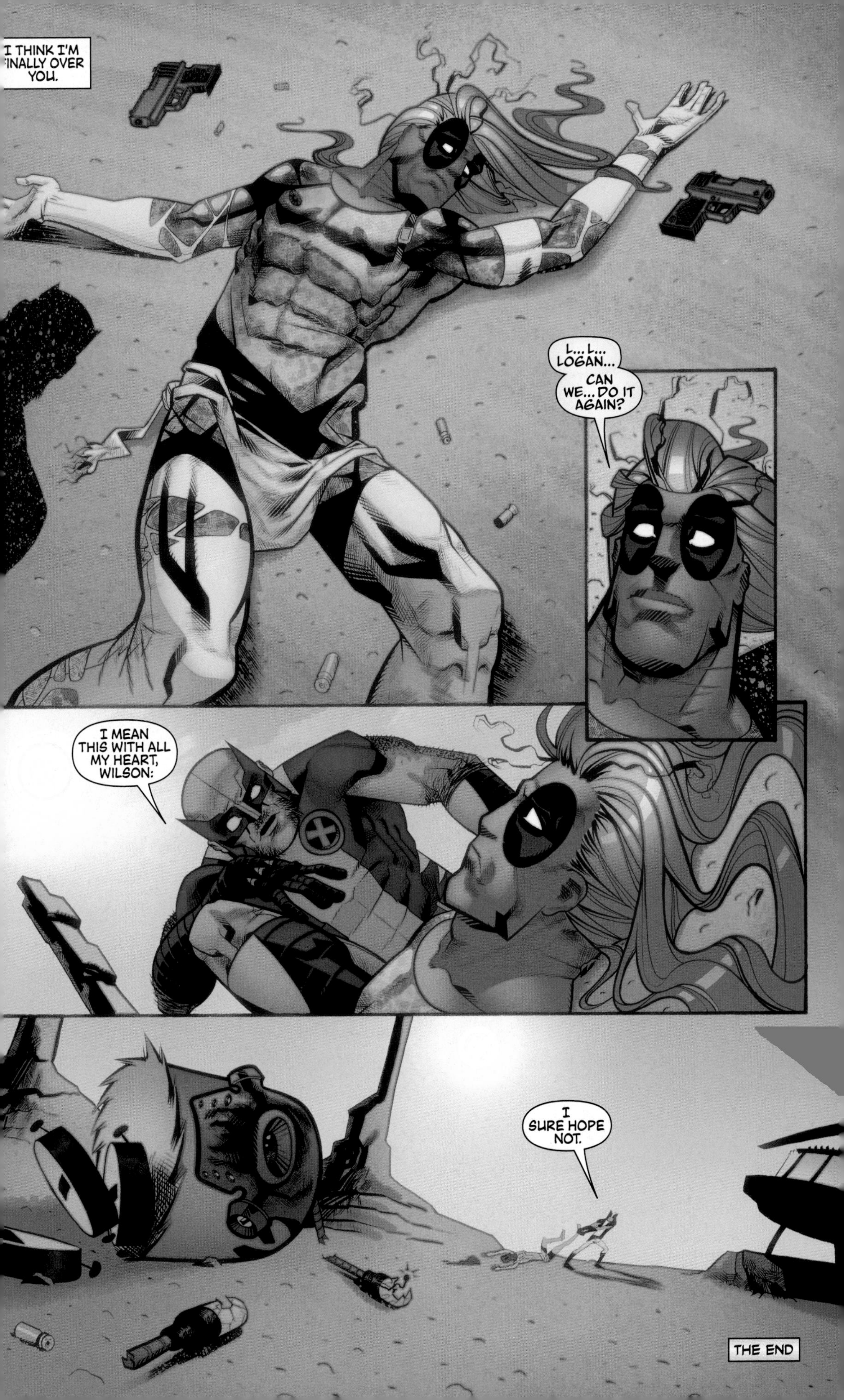
I THINK I'M FINALLY OVER YOU.
L... L... LOGAN... CAN WE... DO IT AGAIN?
I MEAN THIS WITH ALL MY HEART, WILSON:
I SURE HOPE NOT.
THE END

FEAR ITSELF: DEADPOOL #1

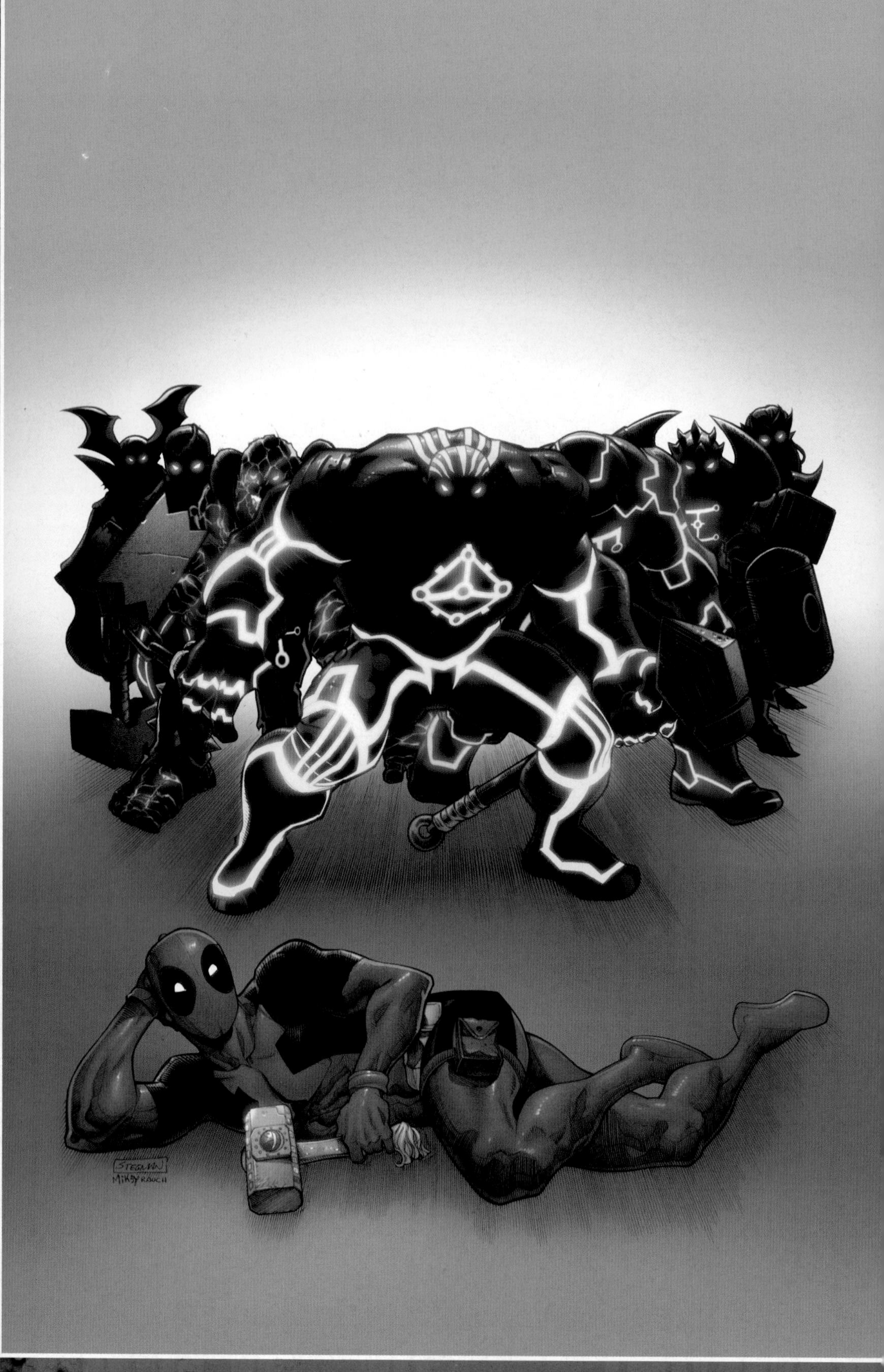

HAMMERS ARE COOL.

EVERYONE LOVES HAMMERS. AND IT SEEMS LIKE ANYBODY WHO'S ***ANYBODY*** HAS THEIR VERY OWN PERSONAL HAMMER NOWADAYS, DOESN'T IT? IT'S ALL THANKS TO THIS BIG BAD GUY CALLED "THE SERPENT". HE CALLED A WHOLE SLEW OF MAGICAL HAMMERS DOWN TO EARTH WITH THE WORDS "IF YE BE TOO LEGIT TO QUIT, THEN YE ***CAN*** TOUCH THIS" ETCHED INTO THE SIDES. OR, SOMETHING LIKE THAT. THOSE DEEMED "THE WORTHY" INCLUDE SIN, THE HULK, THE THING, JUGGERNAUT, ABSORBING MAN, TITANIA, GREY GARGOYLE, AND ATTUMA. WHOA-- HANG ON! WHAT ABOUT OUR BOY, WADE? ISN'T EVERYBODY'S FAVORITE MERC-WITH-A-MOUTH, ***DEADPOOL***, WORTHY OF SOME MAGICAL HAMMA-JAMMA?

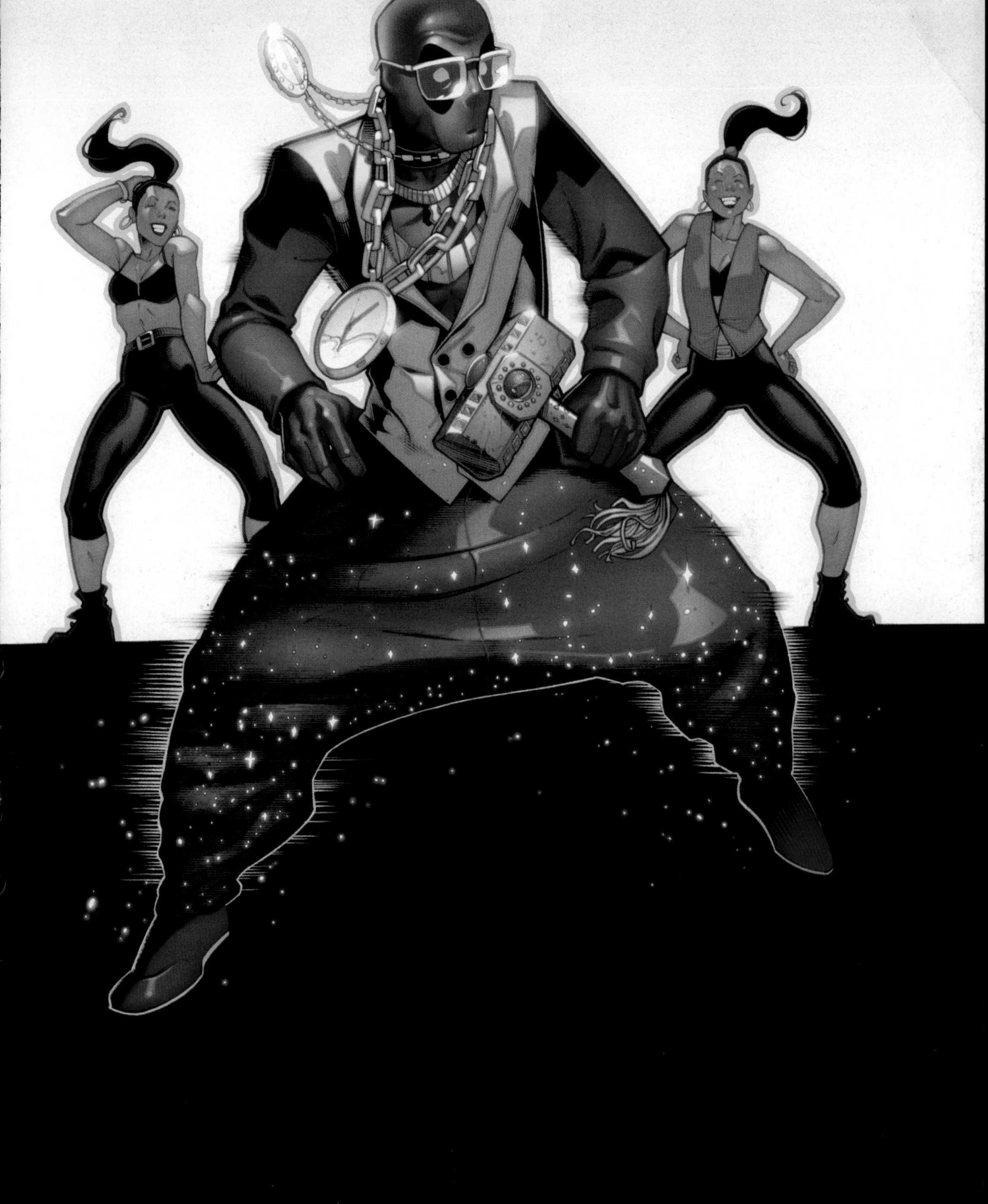

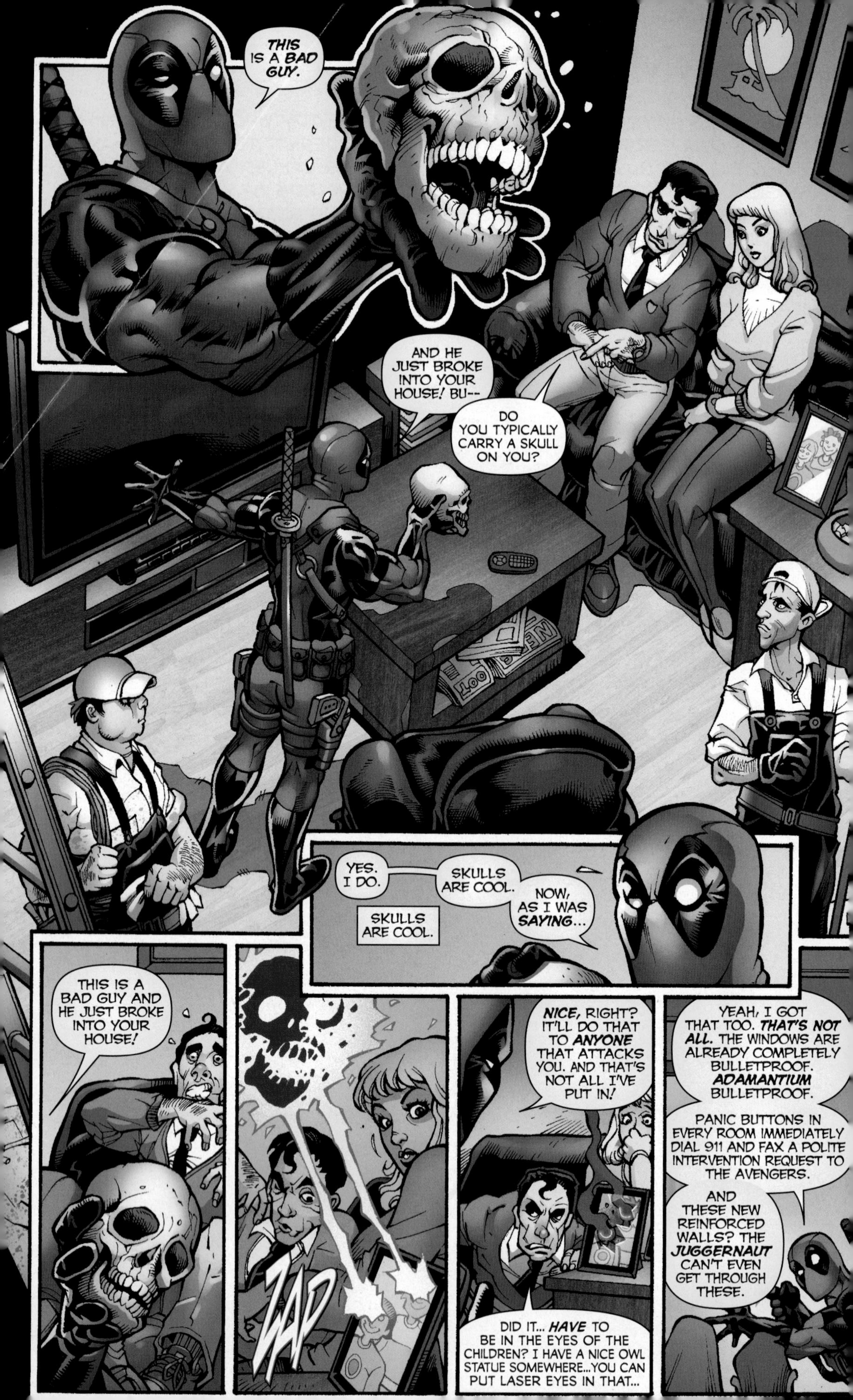

THIS IS A BAD GUY.
AND HE JUST BROKE INTO YOUR HOUSE! BU--
DO YOU TYPICALLY CARRY A SKULL ON YOU?
YES. I DO.
SKULLS ARE COOL.
NOW, AS I WAS SAYING...
SKULLS ARE COOL.
THIS IS A BAD GUY AND HE JUST BROKE INTO YOUR HOUSE!
ZAP
NICE, RIGHT? IT'LL DO THAT TO ANYONE THAT ATTACKS YOU. AND THAT'S NOT ALL I'VE PUT IN!
DID IT... HAVE TO BE IN THE EYES OF THE CHILDREN? I HAVE A NICE OWL STATUE SOMEWHERE...YOU CAN PUT LASER EYES IN THAT...
YEAH, I GOT THAT TOO. THAT'S NOT ALL. THE WINDOWS ARE ALREADY COMPLETELY BULLETPROOF. ADAMANTIUM BULLETPROOF.
PANIC BUTTONS IN EVERY ROOM IMMEDIATELY DIAL 911 AND FAX A POLITE INTERVENTION REQUEST TO THE AVENGERS.
AND THESE NEW REINFORCED WALLS? THE JUGGERNAUT CAN'T EVEN GET THROUGH THESE.

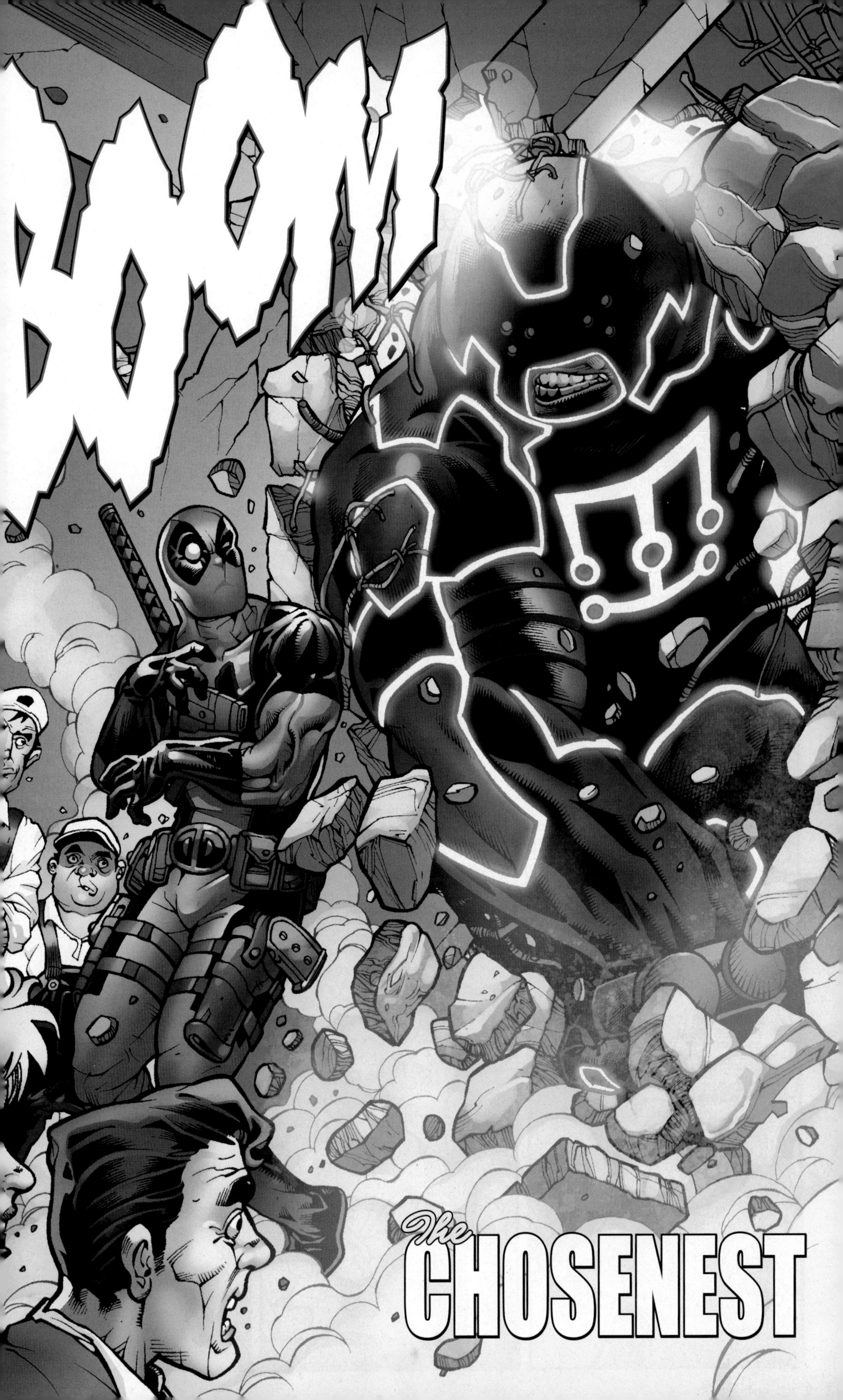
BOOM
The CHOSENEST

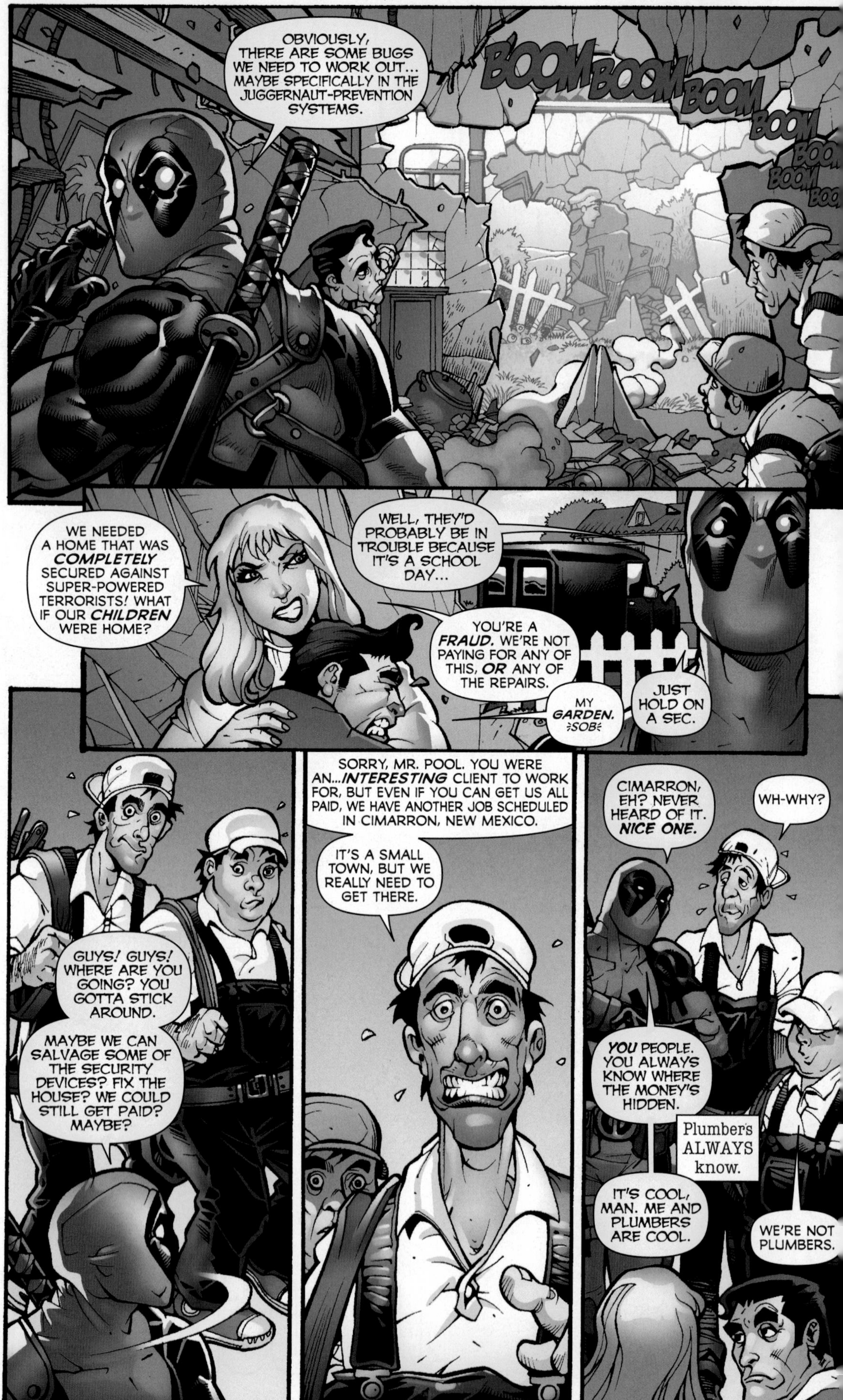
OBVIOUSLY, THERE ARE SOME BUGS WE NEED TO WORK OUT... MAYBE SPECIFICALLY IN THE JUGGERNAUT-PREVENTION SYSTEMS.
BOOM BOOM BOOM BOOM BOOM BOOM BOOM
WE NEEDED A HOME THAT WAS COMPLETELY SECURED AGAINST SUPER-POWERED TERRORISTS! WHAT IF OUR CHILDREN WERE HOME?
WELL, THEY'D PROBABLY BE IN TROUBLE BECAUSE IT'S A SCHOOL DAY...
YOU'RE A FRAUD. WE'RE NOT PAYING FOR ANY OF THIS, OR ANY OF THE REPAIRS.
MY GARDEN. SOB
JUST HOLD ON A SEC.
GUYS! GUYS! WHERE ARE YOU GOING? YOU GOTTA STICK AROUND.
MAYBE WE CAN SALVAGE SOME OF THE SECURITY DEVICES? FIX THE HOUSE? WE COULD STILL GET PAID? MAYBE?
SORRY, MR. POOL. YOU WERE AN...INTERESTING CLIENT TO WORK FOR, BUT EVEN IF YOU CAN GET US ALL PAID, WE HAVE ANOTHER JOB SCHEDULED IN CIMARRON, NEW MEXICO.
IT'S A SMALL TOWN, BUT WE REALLY NEED TO GET THERE.
CIMARRON, EH? NEVER HEARD OF IT. NICE ONE.
WH-WHY?
YOU PEOPLE. YOU ALWAYS KNOW WHERE THE MONEY'S HIDDEN.
Plumbers ALWAYS know.
IT'S COOL, MAN. ME AND PLUMBERS ARE COOL.
WE'RE NOT PLUMBERS.

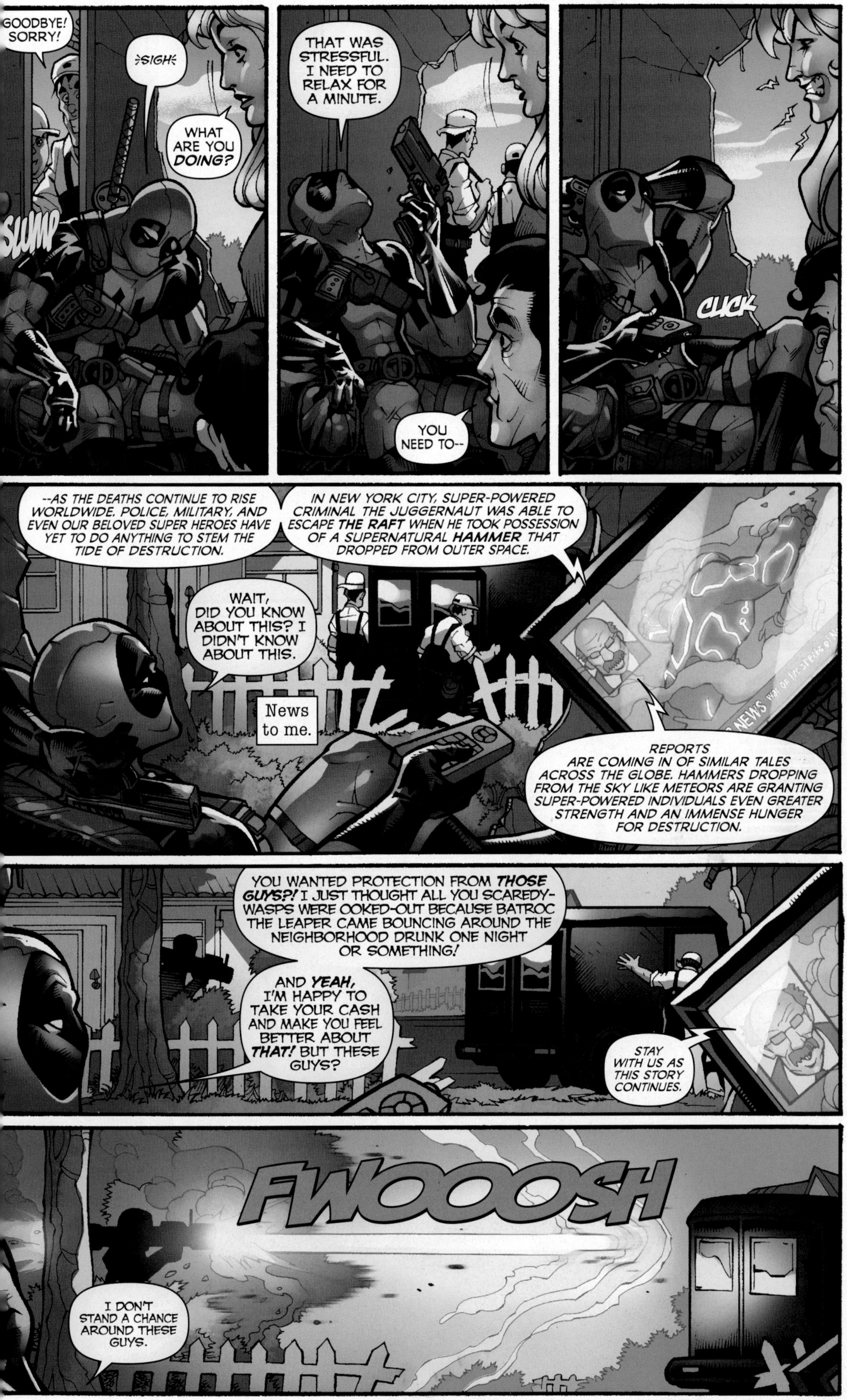
GOODBYE! SORRY!
SIGH
WHAT ARE YOU DOING?
SLUMP
THAT WAS STRESSFUL. I NEED TO RELAX FOR A MINUTE.
YOU NEED TO--
CLICK
--AS THE DEATHS CONTINUE TO RISE WORLDWIDE. POLICE, MILITARY, AND EVEN OUR BELOVED SUPER HEROES HAVE YET TO DO ANYTHING TO STEM THE TIDE OF DESTRUCTION.
IN NEW YORK CITY, SUPER-POWERED CRIMINAL THE JUGGERNAUT WAS ABLE TO ESCAPE THE RAFT WHEN HE TOOK POSSESSION OF A SUPERNATURAL HAMMER THAT DROPPED FROM OUTER SPACE.
WAIT, DID YOU KNOW ABOUT THIS? I DIDN'T KNOW ABOUT THIS.
News to me.
REPORTS ARE COMING IN OF SIMILAR TALES ACROSS THE GLOBE. HAMMERS DROPPING FROM THE SKY LIKE METEORS ARE GRANTING SUPER-POWERED INDIVIDUALS EVEN GREATER STRENGTH AND AN IMMENSE HUNGER FOR DESTRUCTION.
YOU WANTED PROTECTION FROM THOSE GUYS?! I JUST THOUGHT ALL YOU SCAREDY-WASPS WERE OOKED-OUT BECAUSE BATROC THE LEAPER CAME BOUNCING AROUND THE NEIGHBORHOOD DRUNK ONE NIGHT OR SOMETHING!
AND YEAH, I'M HAPPY TO TAKE YOUR CASH AND MAKE YOU FEEL BETTER ABOUT THAT! BUT THESE GUYS?
STAY WITH US AS THIS STORY CONTINUES.
FWOOOSH
I DON'T STAND A CHANCE AROUND THESE GUYS.

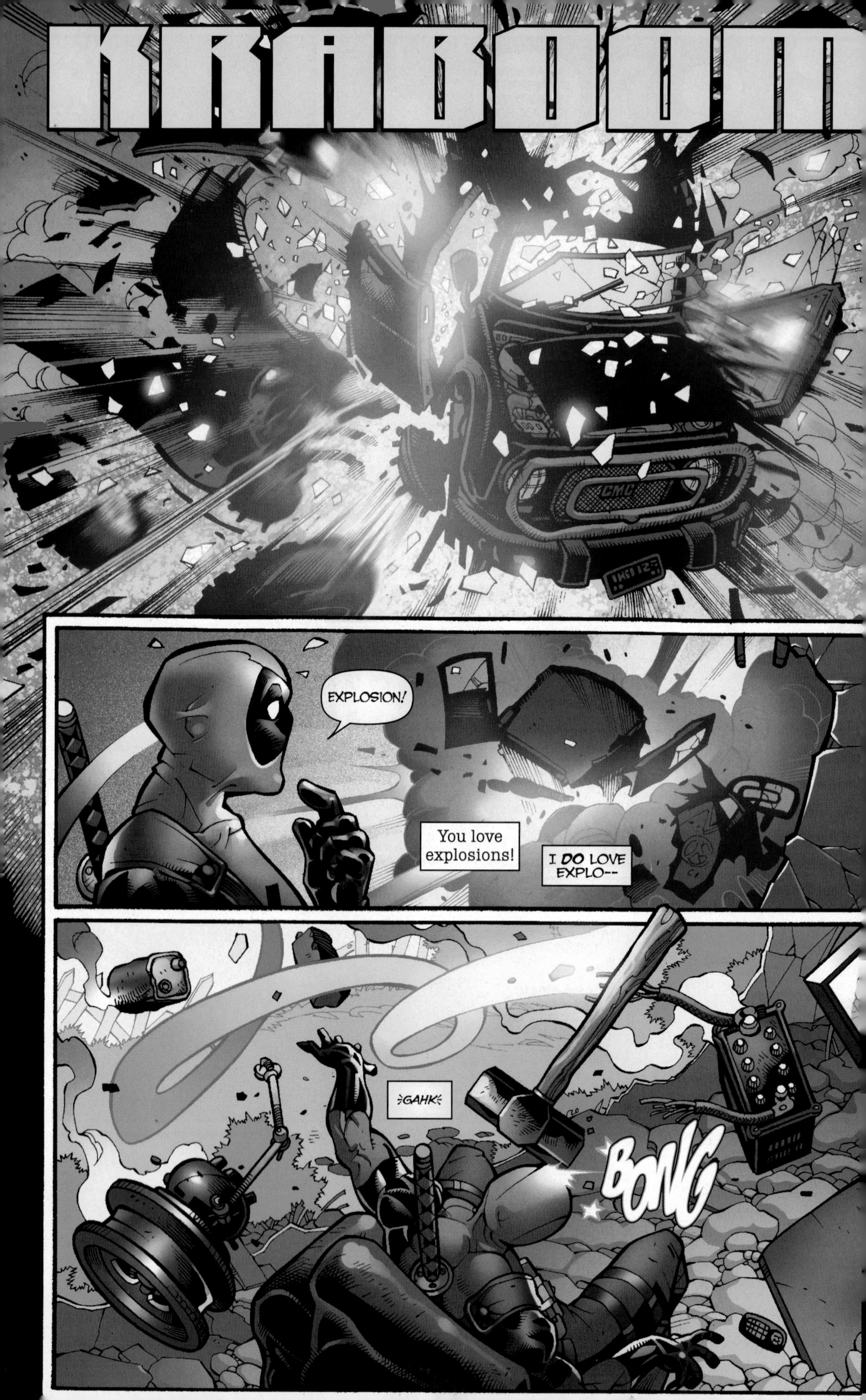
KRABOOM
EXPLOSION!
You love explosions!
I DO LOVE EXPLO--
GAHK
BONG

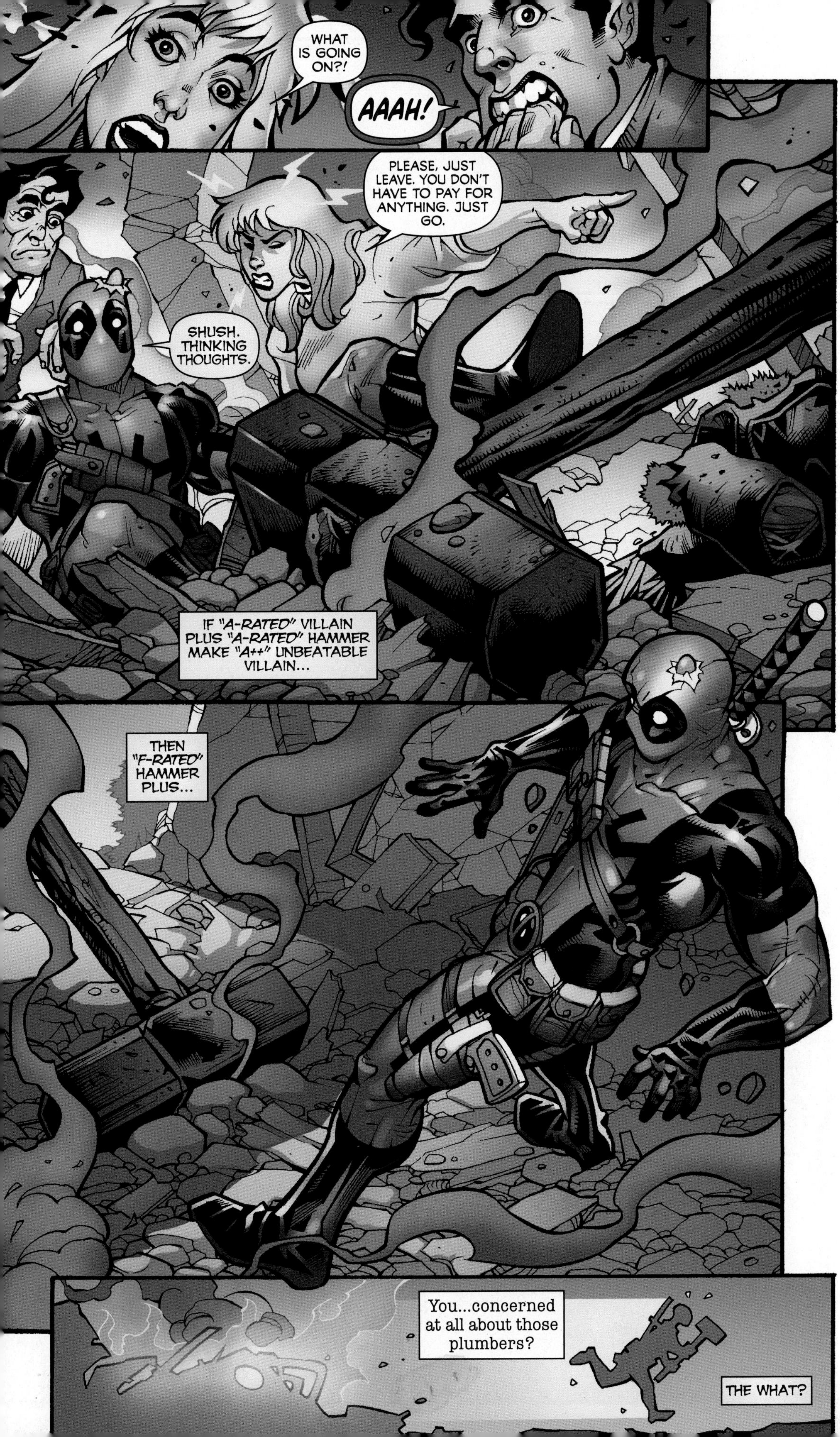
WHAT IS GOING ON?!
AAAH!
PLEASE, JUST LEAVE. YOU DON'T HAVE TO PAY FOR ANYTHING. JUST GO.
SHUSH. THINKING THOUGHTS.
IF "A-RATED" VILLAIN PLUS "A-RATED" HAMMER MAKE "A++" UNBEATABLE VILLAIN...
THEN "F-RATED" HAMMER PLUS...
You...concerned at all about those plumbers?
THE WHAT?

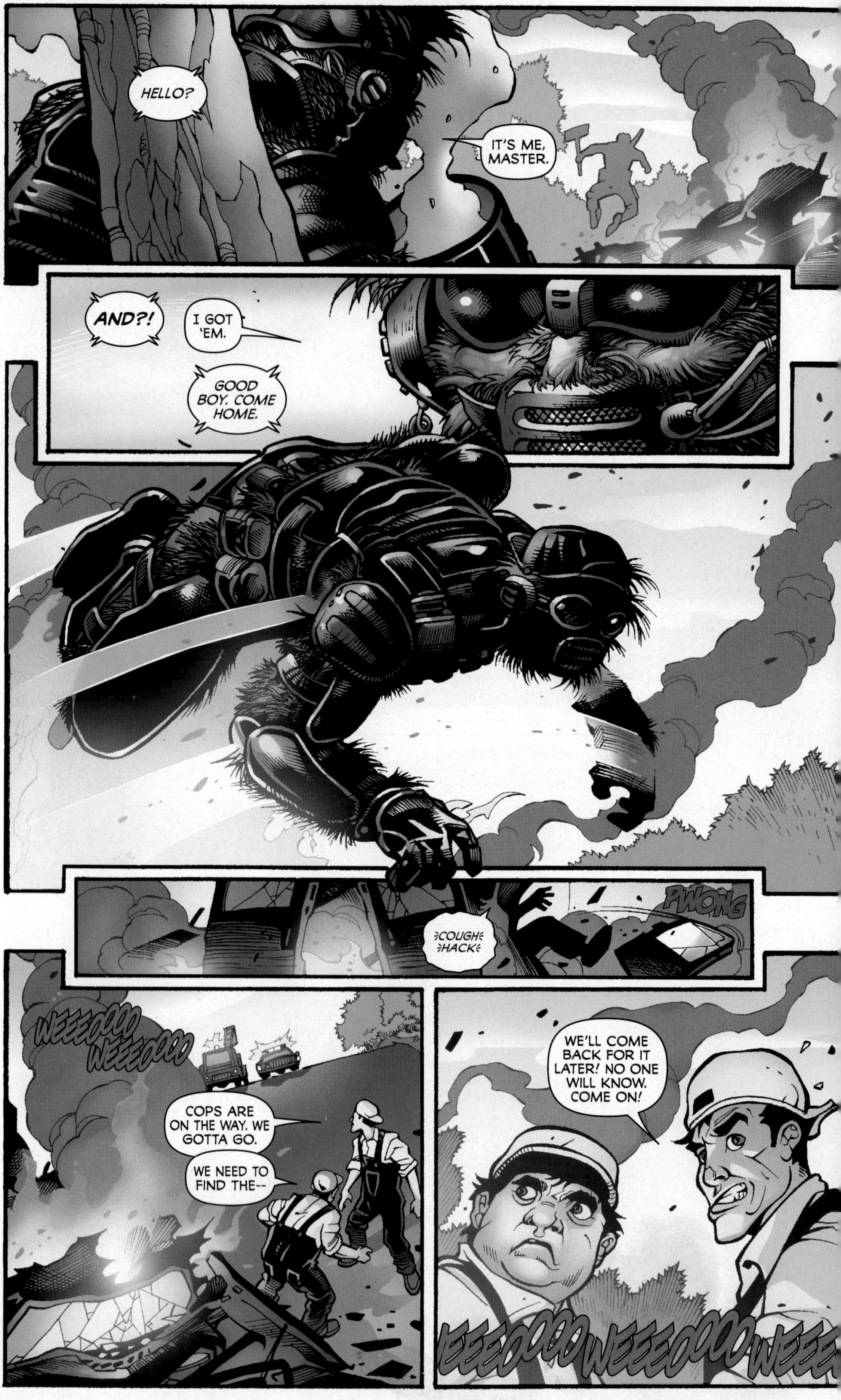
HELLO?
IT'S ME, MASTER.
AND?!
I GOT 'EM.
GOOD BOY. COME HOME.
PWONG
COUGH HACK
WEEEOOOO WEEEOOOO
COPS ARE ON THE WAY. WE GOTTA GO.
WE NEED TO FIND THE--
WE'LL COME BACK FOR IT LATER! NO ONE WILL KNOW. COME ON!
WEEEOOOO WEEEOOOO WEEE

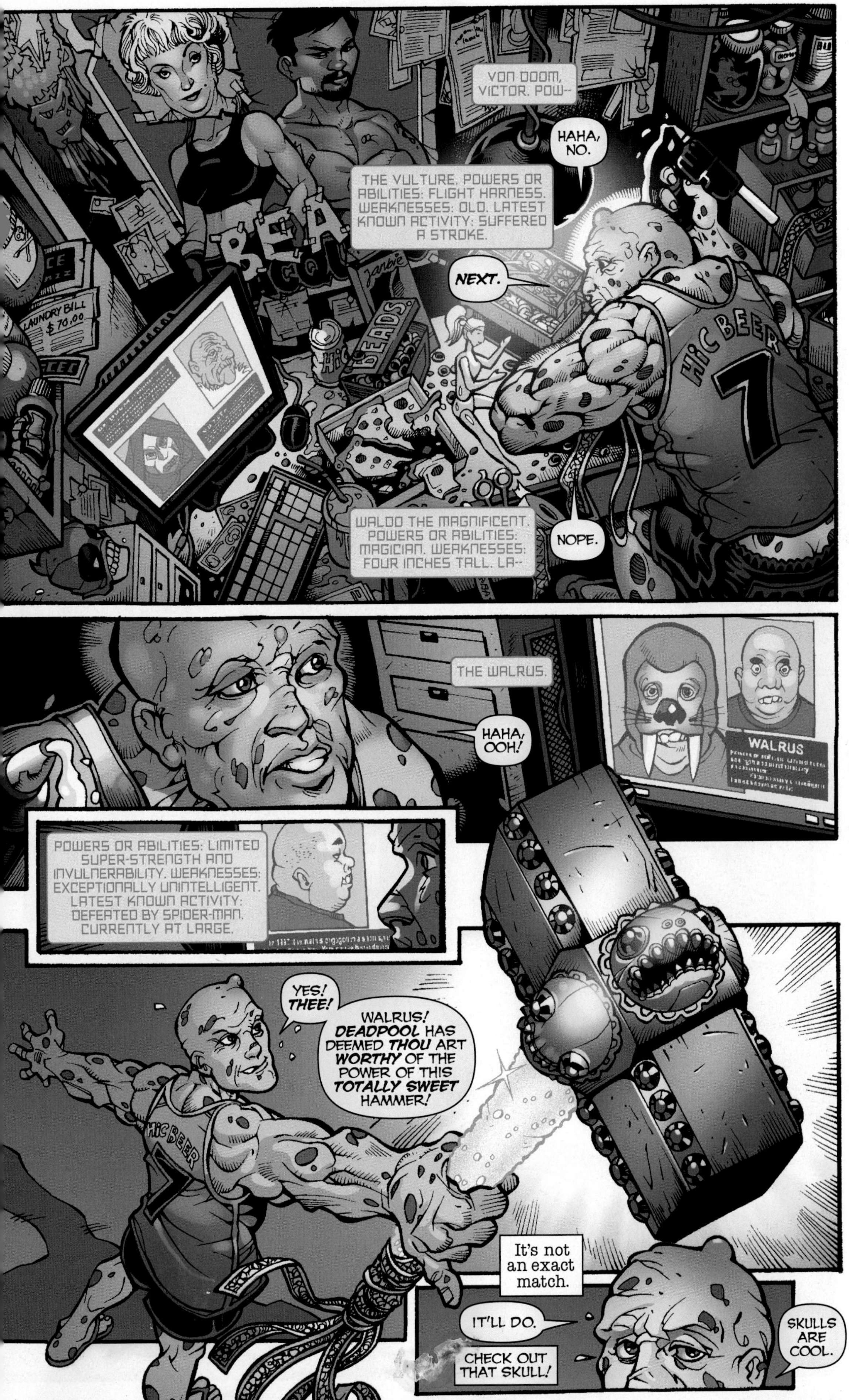
VON DOOM, VICTOR. POW--
HAHA, NO.
THE VULTURE. POWERS OR ABILITIES: FLIGHT HARNESS. WEAKNESSES: OLD. LATEST KNOWN ACTIVITY: SUFFERED A STROKE.
NEXT.
LAUNDRY BILL $70.00
HiC BEER 7
WALDO THE MAGNIFICENT. POWERS OR ABILITIES: MAGICIAN. WEAKNESSES: FOUR INCHES TALL. LA--
NOPE.
THE WALRUS.
HAHA, OOH!
WALRUS
POWERS OR ABILITIES: LIMITED SUPER-STRENGTH AND INVULNERABILITY. WEAKNESSES: EXCEPTIONALLY UNINTELLIGENT. LATEST KNOWN ACTIVITY: DEFEATED BY SPIDER-MAN. CURRENTLY AT LARGE.
YES! THEE!
WALRUS! DEADPOOL HAS DEEMED THOU ART WORTHY OF THE POWER OF THIS TOTALLY SWEET HAMMER!
It's not an exact match.
IT'LL DO.
CHECK OUT THAT SKULL!
SKULLS ARE COOL.

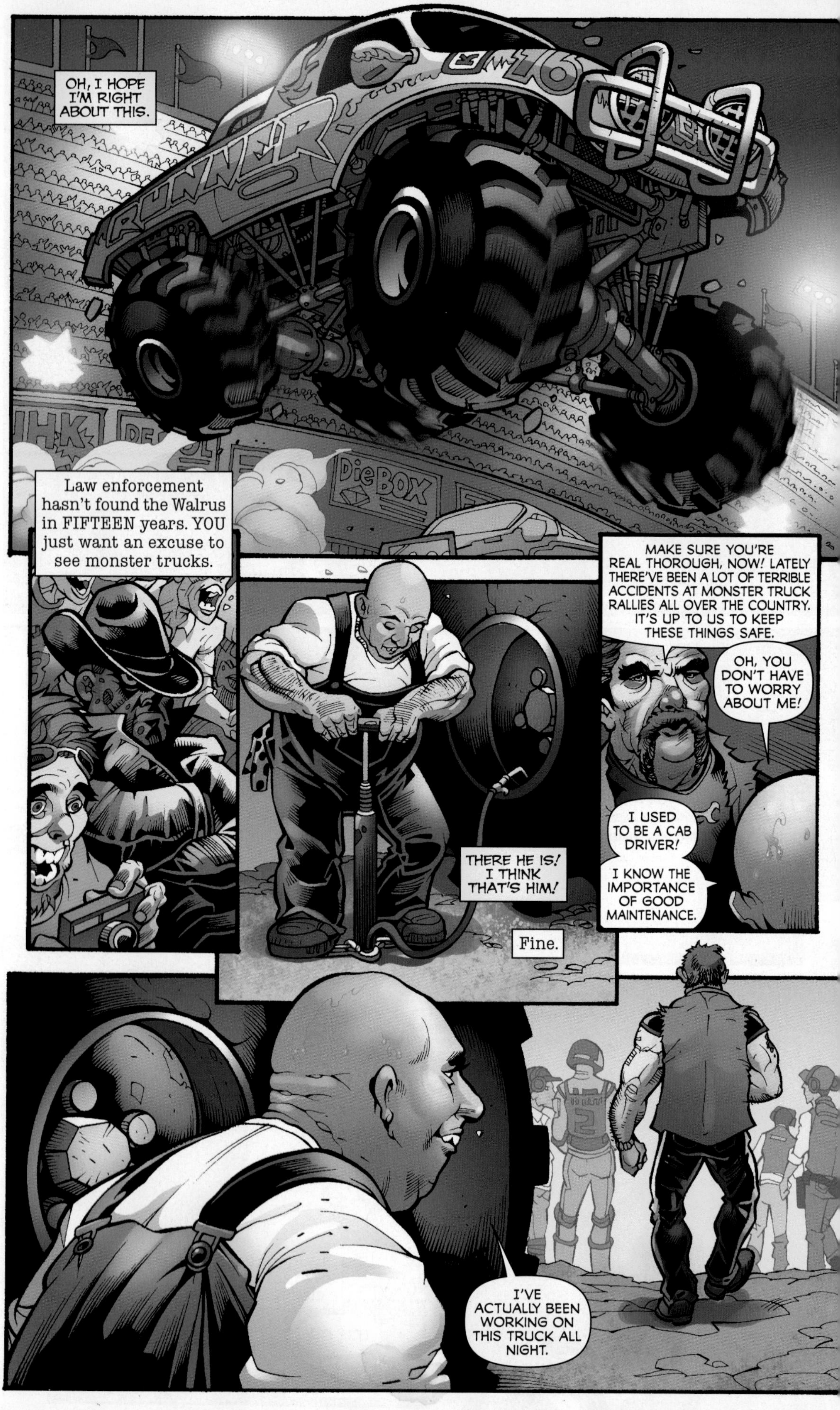
OH, I HOPE I'M RIGHT ABOUT THIS.
RUNNER
16
DieBOX
Law enforcement hasn't found the Walrus in FIFTEEN years. YOU just want an excuse to see monster trucks.
THERE HE IS! I THINK THAT'S HIM!
Fine.
MAKE SURE YOU'RE REAL THOROUGH, NOW! LATELY THERE'VE BEEN A LOT OF TERRIBLE ACCIDENTS AT MONSTER TRUCK RALLIES ALL OVER THE COUNTRY. IT'S UP TO US TO KEEP THESE THINGS SAFE.
OH, YOU DON'T HAVE TO WORRY ABOUT ME!
I USED TO BE A CAB DRIVER!
I KNOW THE IMPORTANCE OF GOOD MAINTENANCE.
I'VE ACTUALLY BEEN WORKING ON THIS TRUCK ALL NIGHT.

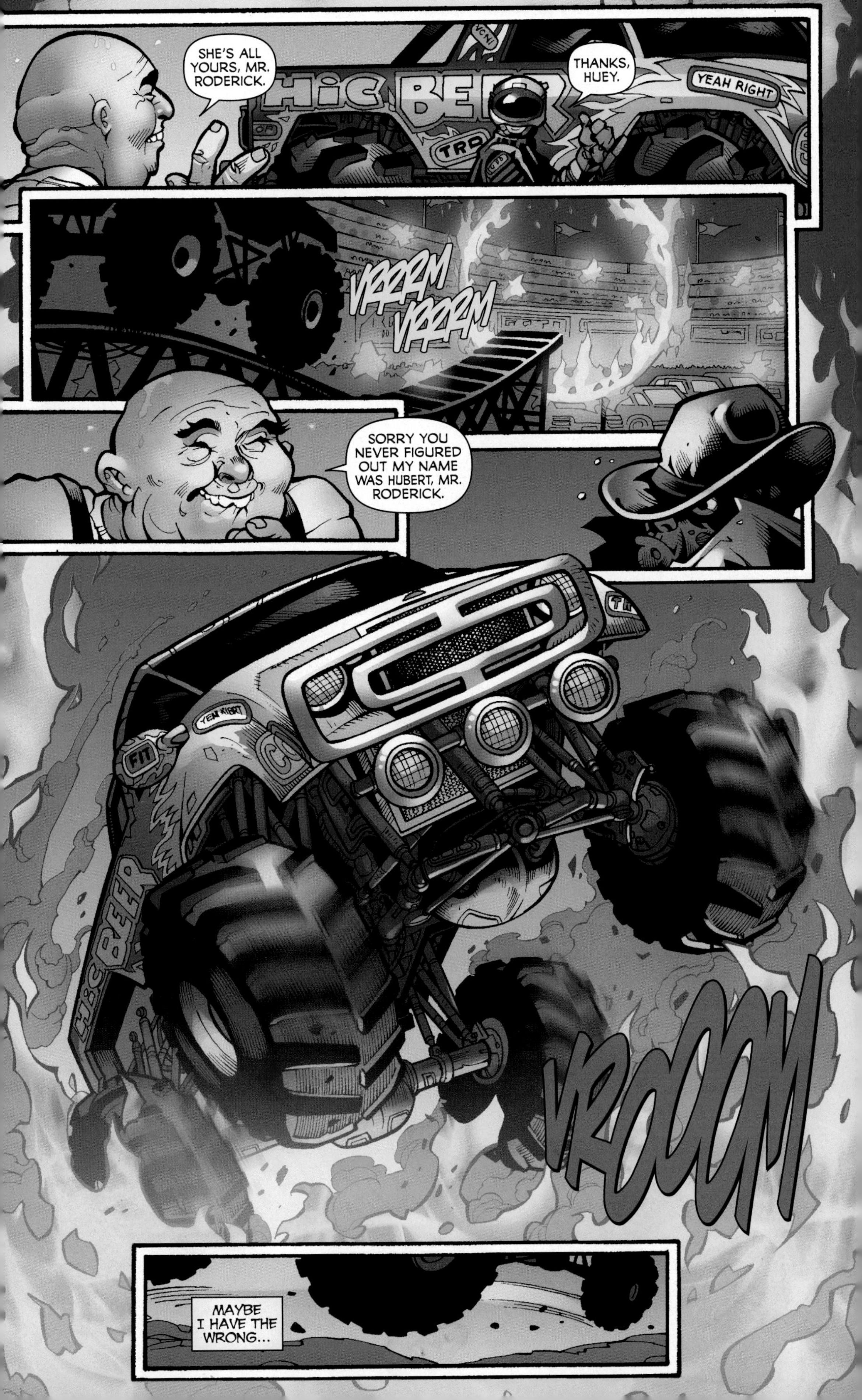
SHE'S ALL YOURS, MR. RODERICK.
THANKS, HUEY.
HiC BEER
YEAH RIGHT
VRRRM VRRRM
SORRY YOU NEVER FIGURED OUT MY NAME WAS HUBERT, MR. RODERICK.
VROOOM
MAYBE I HAVE THE WRONG...

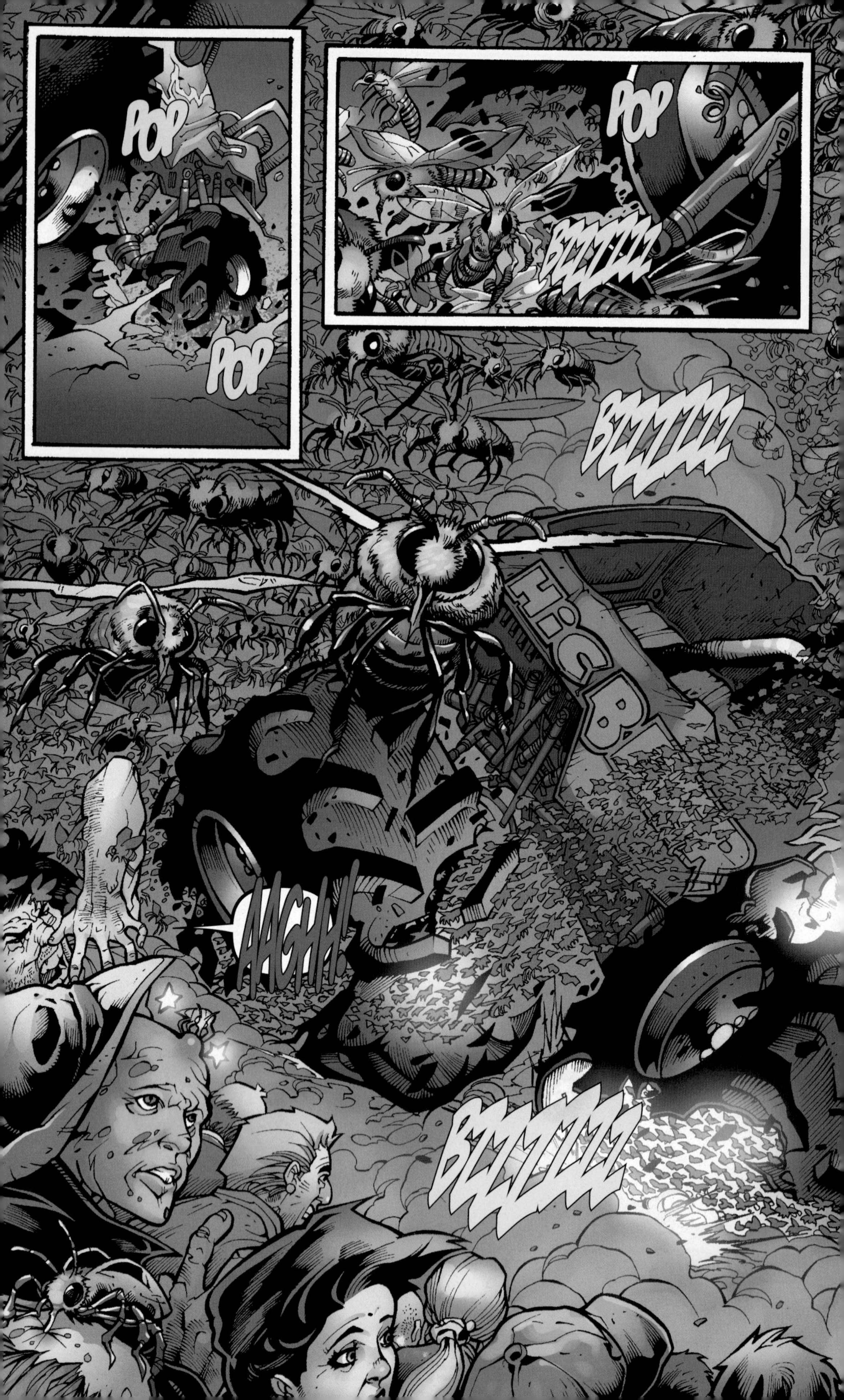
POP
POP
POP
BZZZZZZ
BZZZZZZ
AAGH!
BZZZZZZ

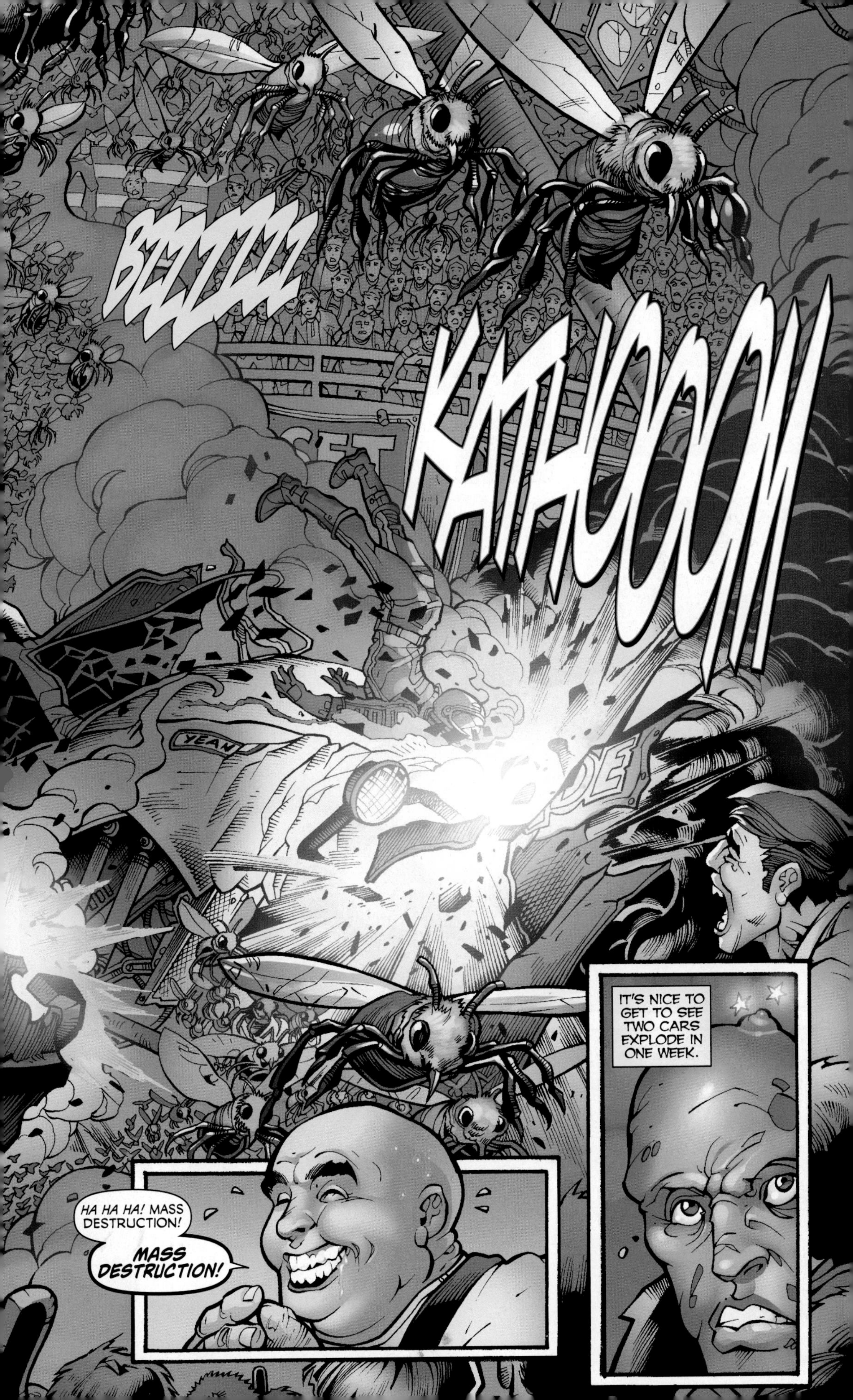
BZZZZZZ
KATHOOOM
IT'S NICE TO GET TO SEE TWO CARS EXPLODE IN ONE WEEK.
HA HA HA! MASS DESTRUCTION!
MASS DESTRUCTION!

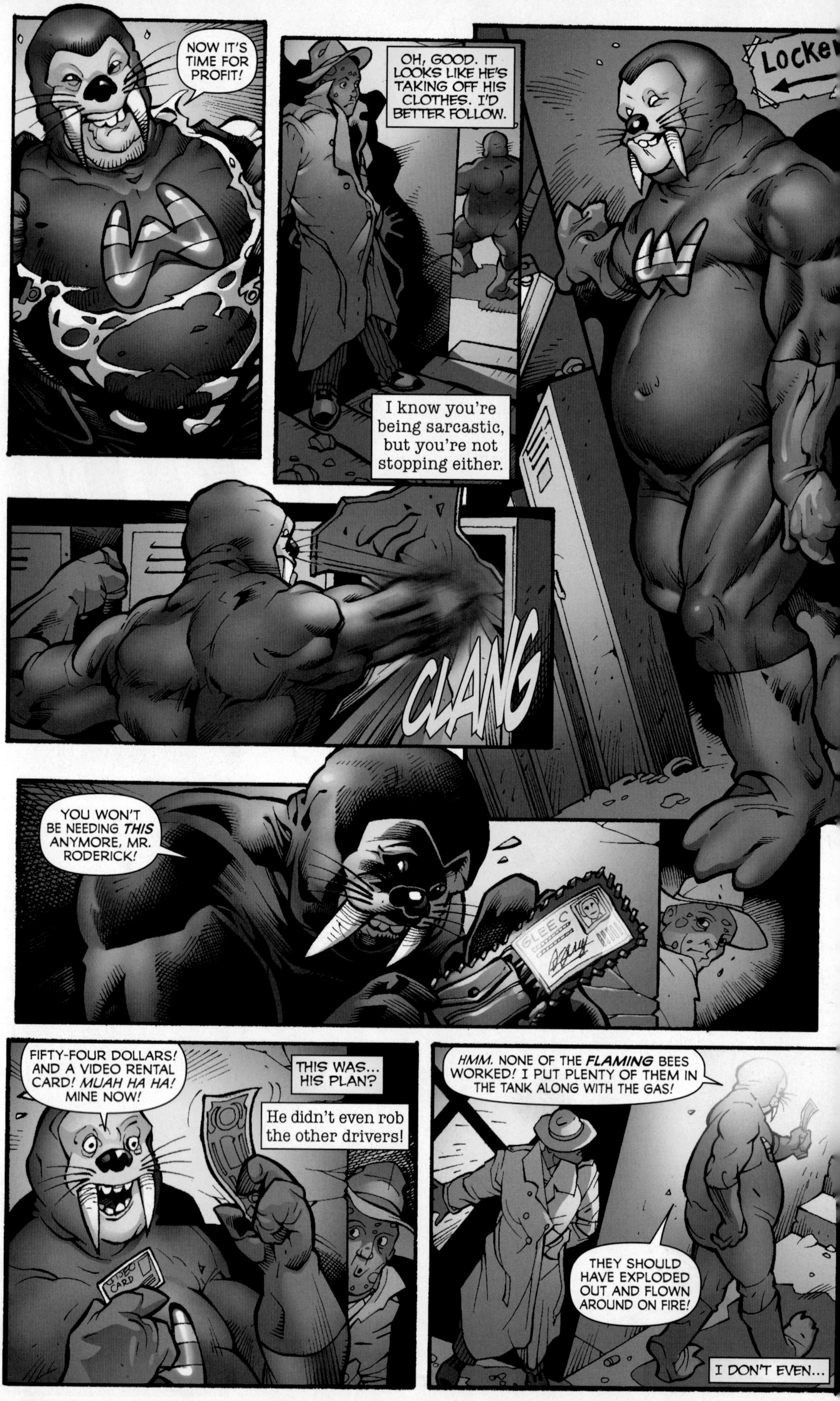
NOW IT'S TIME FOR PROFIT!
OH, GOOD. IT LOOKS LIKE HE'S TAKING OFF HIS CLOTHES. I'D BETTER FOLLOW.
I know you're being sarcastic, but you're not stopping either.
Locker
CLANG
YOU WON'T BE NEEDING THIS ANYMORE, MR. RODERICK!
GLEEC
FIFTY-FOUR DOLLARS! AND A VIDEO RENTAL CARD! MUAH HA HA! MINE NOW!
THIS WAS... HIS PLAN?
He didn't even rob the other drivers!
VIDEO CARD
HMM. NONE OF THE FLAMING BEES WORKED! I PUT PLENTY OF THEM IN THE TANK ALONG WITH THE GAS!
THEY SHOULD HAVE EXPLODED OUT AND FLOWN AROUND ON FIRE!
I DON'T EVEN...

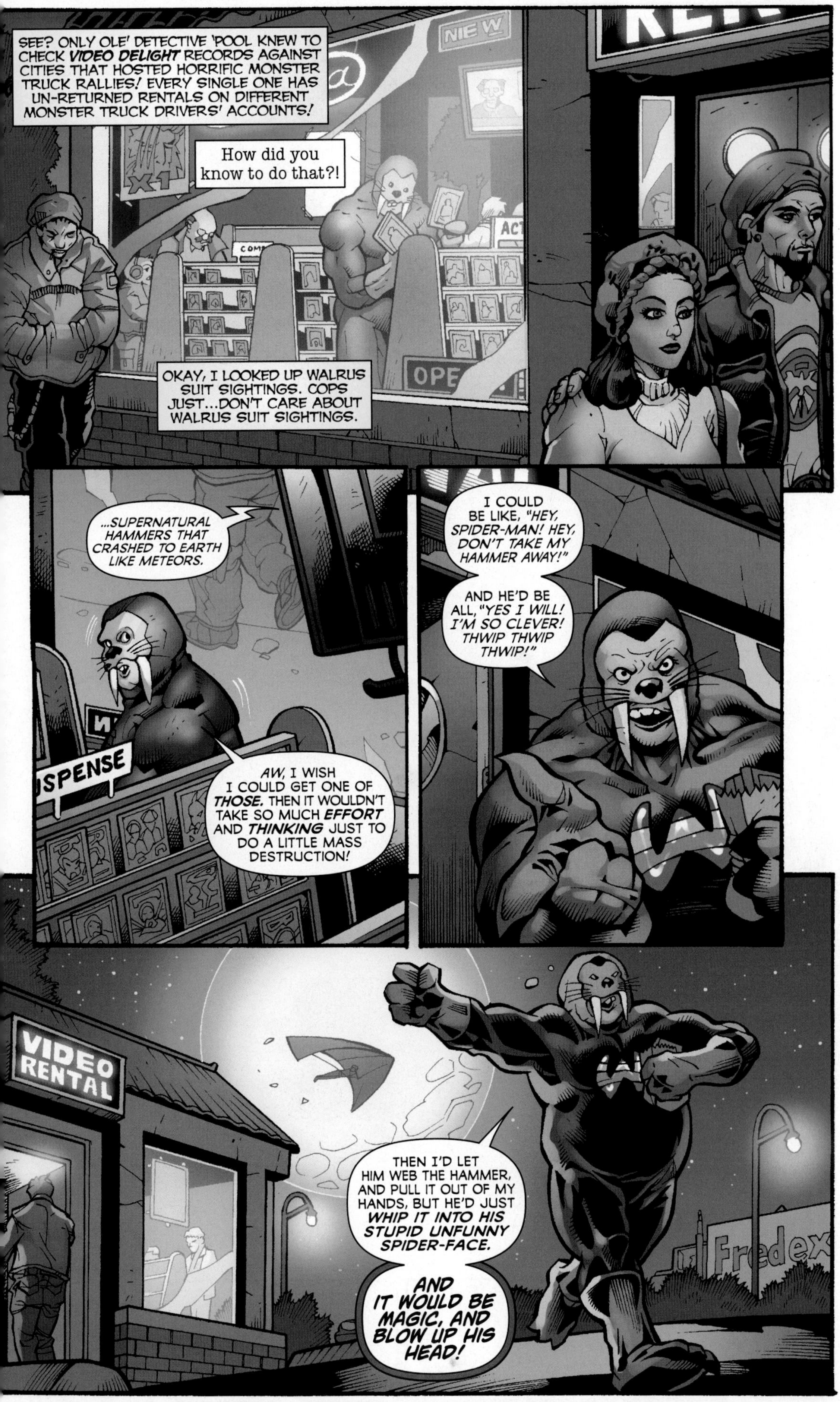
SEE? ONLY OLE' DETECTIVE 'POOL KNEW TO CHECK VIDEO DELIGHT RECORDS AGAINST CITIES THAT HOSTED HORRIFIC MONSTER TRUCK RALLIES! EVERY SINGLE ONE HAS UN-RETURNED RENTALS ON DIFFERENT MONSTER TRUCK DRIVERS' ACCOUNTS!
How did you know to do that?!
OKAY, I LOOKED UP WALRUS SUIT SIGHTINGS. COPS JUST...DON'T CARE ABOUT WALRUS SUIT SIGHTINGS.
...SUPERNATURAL HAMMERS THAT CRASHED TO EARTH LIKE METEORS.
SUSPENSE
AW, I WISH I COULD GET ONE OF THOSE. THEN IT WOULDN'T TAKE SO MUCH EFFORT AND THINKING JUST TO DO A LITTLE MASS DESTRUCTION!
I COULD BE LIKE, "HEY, SPIDER-MAN! HEY, DON'T TAKE MY HAMMER AWAY!"
AND HE'D BE ALL, "YES I WILL! I'M SO CLEVER! THWIP THWIP THWIP!"
VIDEO RENTAL
THEN I'D LET HIM WEB THE HAMMER, AND PULL IT OUT OF MY HANDS, BUT HE'D JUST WHIP IT INTO HIS STUPID UNFUNNY SPIDER-FACE.
AND IT WOULD BE MAGIC, AND BLOW UP HIS HEAD!
Fredex

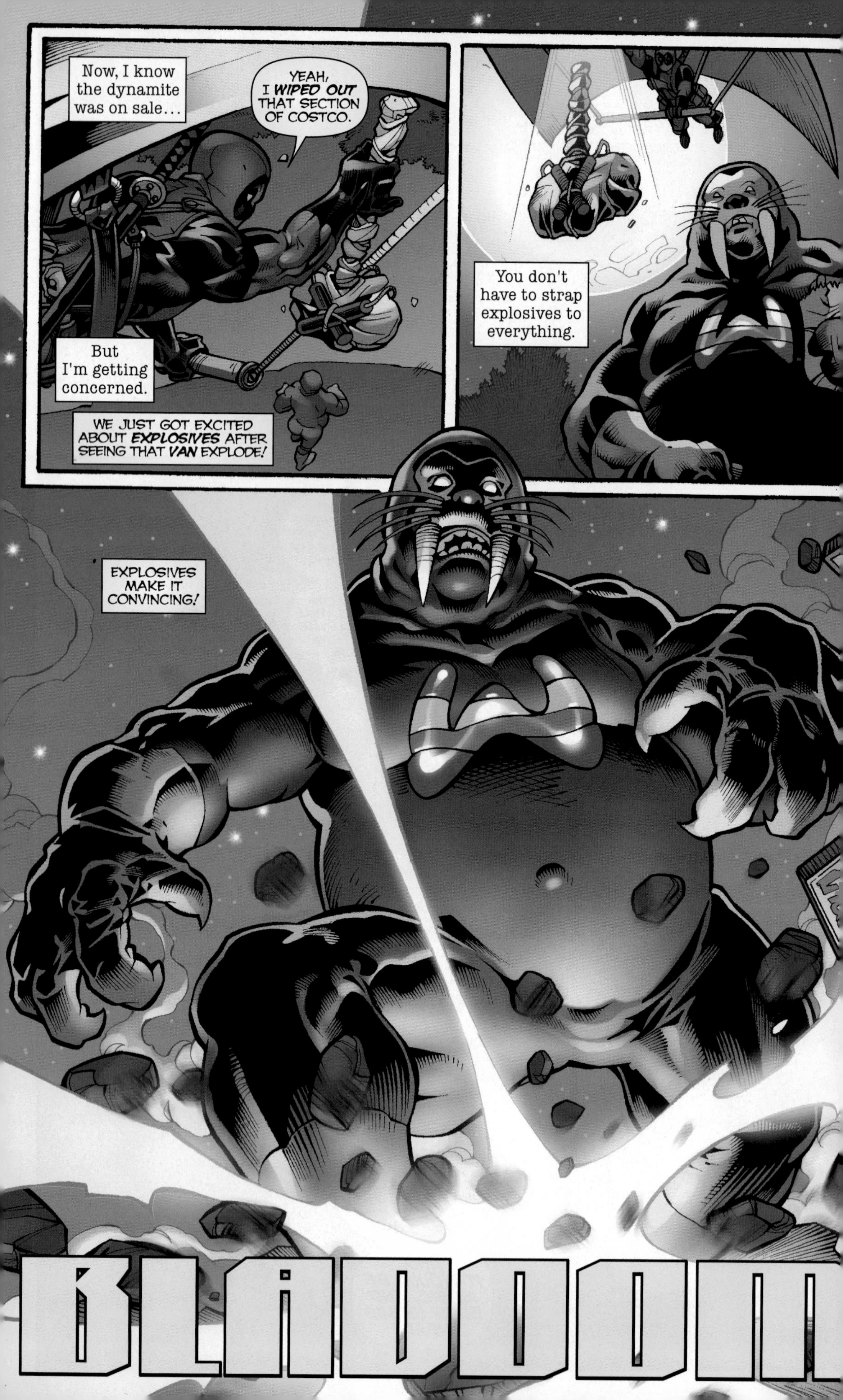

Now, I know the dynamite was on sale...
YEAH, I WIPED OUT THAT SECTION OF COSTCO.
But I'm getting concerned.
WE JUST GOT EXCITED ABOUT EXPLOSIVES AFTER SEEING THAT VAN EXPLODE!
You don't have to strap explosives to everything.
EXPLOSIVES MAKE IT CONVINCING!
BLAOOOM

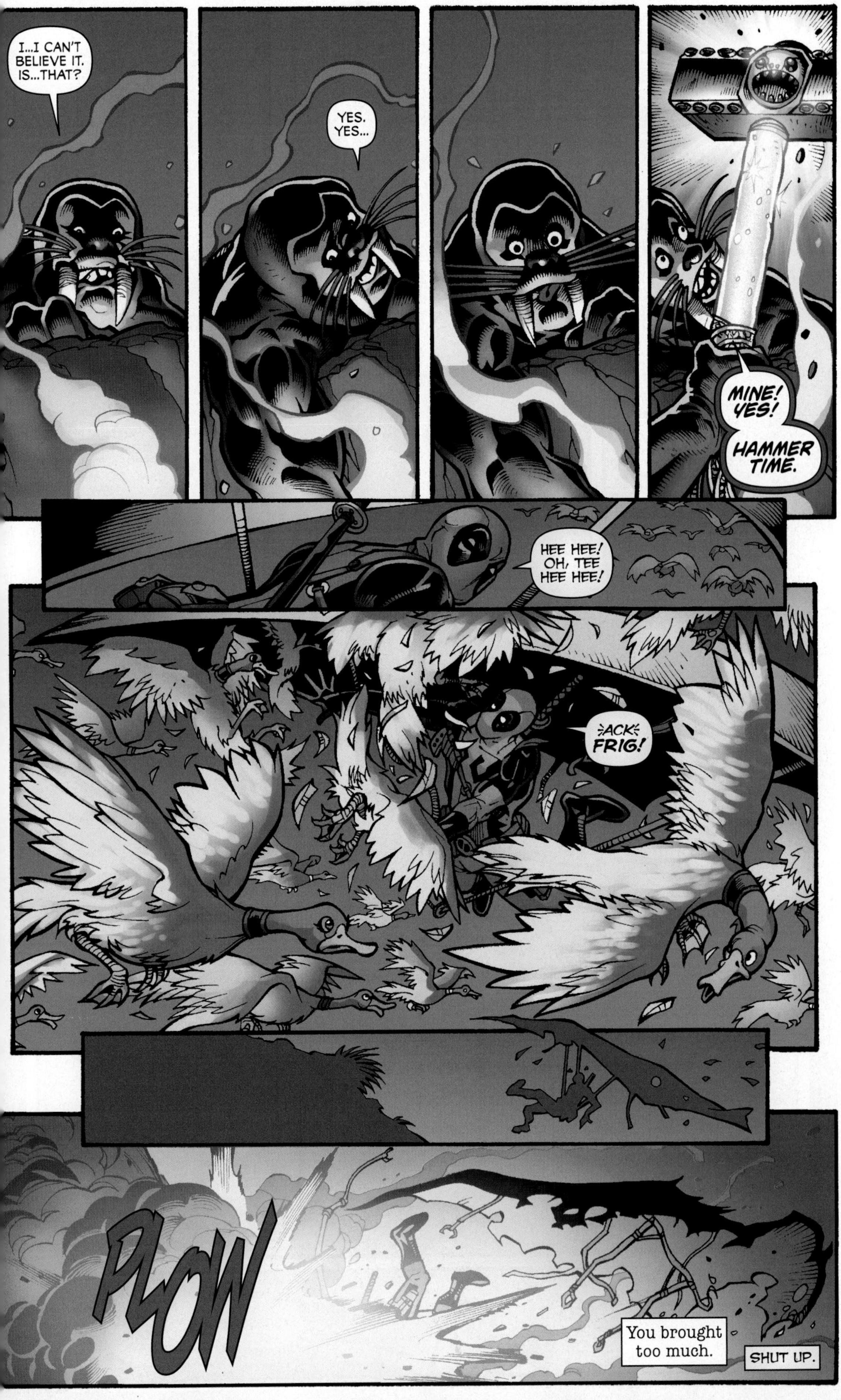
I...I CAN'T BELIEVE IT. IS...THAT?
YES. YES...
MINE! YES!
HAMMER TIME.
HEE HEE! OH, TEE HEE HEE!
ACK FRIG!
PLOW
You brought too much.
SHUT UP.

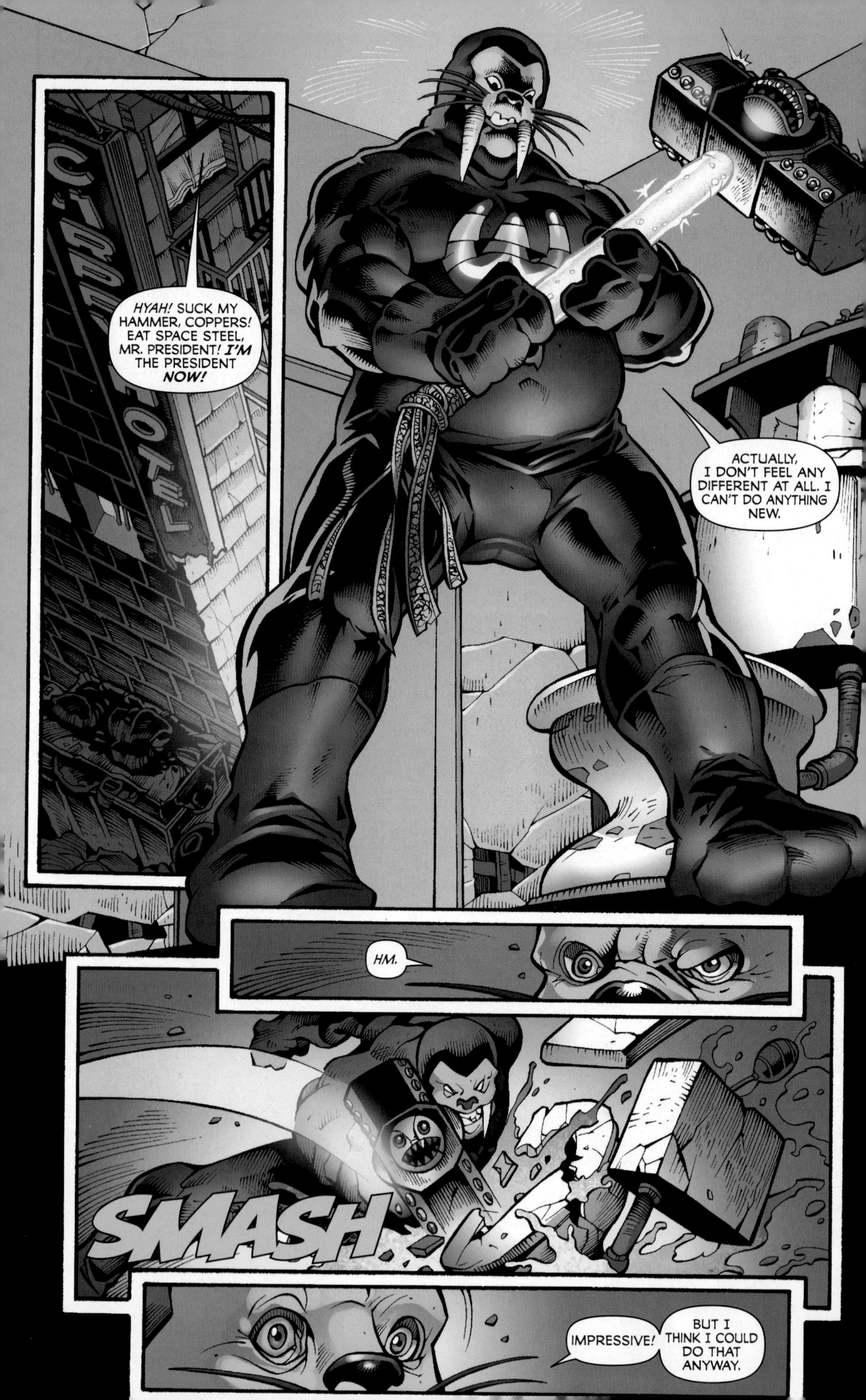

HYAH! SUCK MY HAMMER, COPPERS! EAT SPACE STEEL, MR. PRESIDENT! I'M THE PRESIDENT NOW!
ACTUALLY, I DON'T FEEL ANY DIFFERENT AT ALL. I CAN'T DO ANYTHING NEW.
HM.
SMASH
IMPRESSIVE!
BUT I THINK I COULD DO THAT ANYWAY.

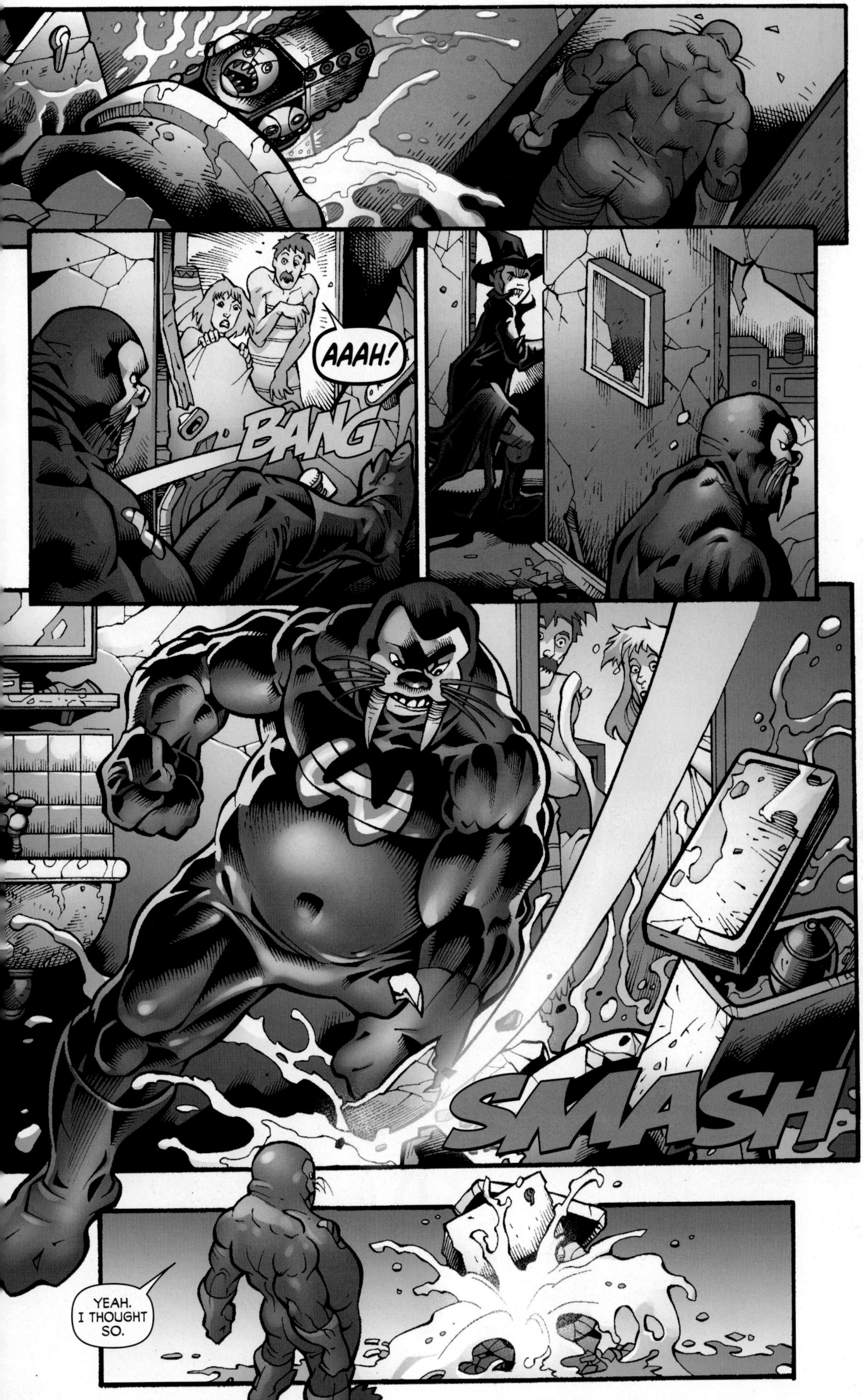
AAAH!
BANG
SMASH
YEAH. I THOUGHT SO.

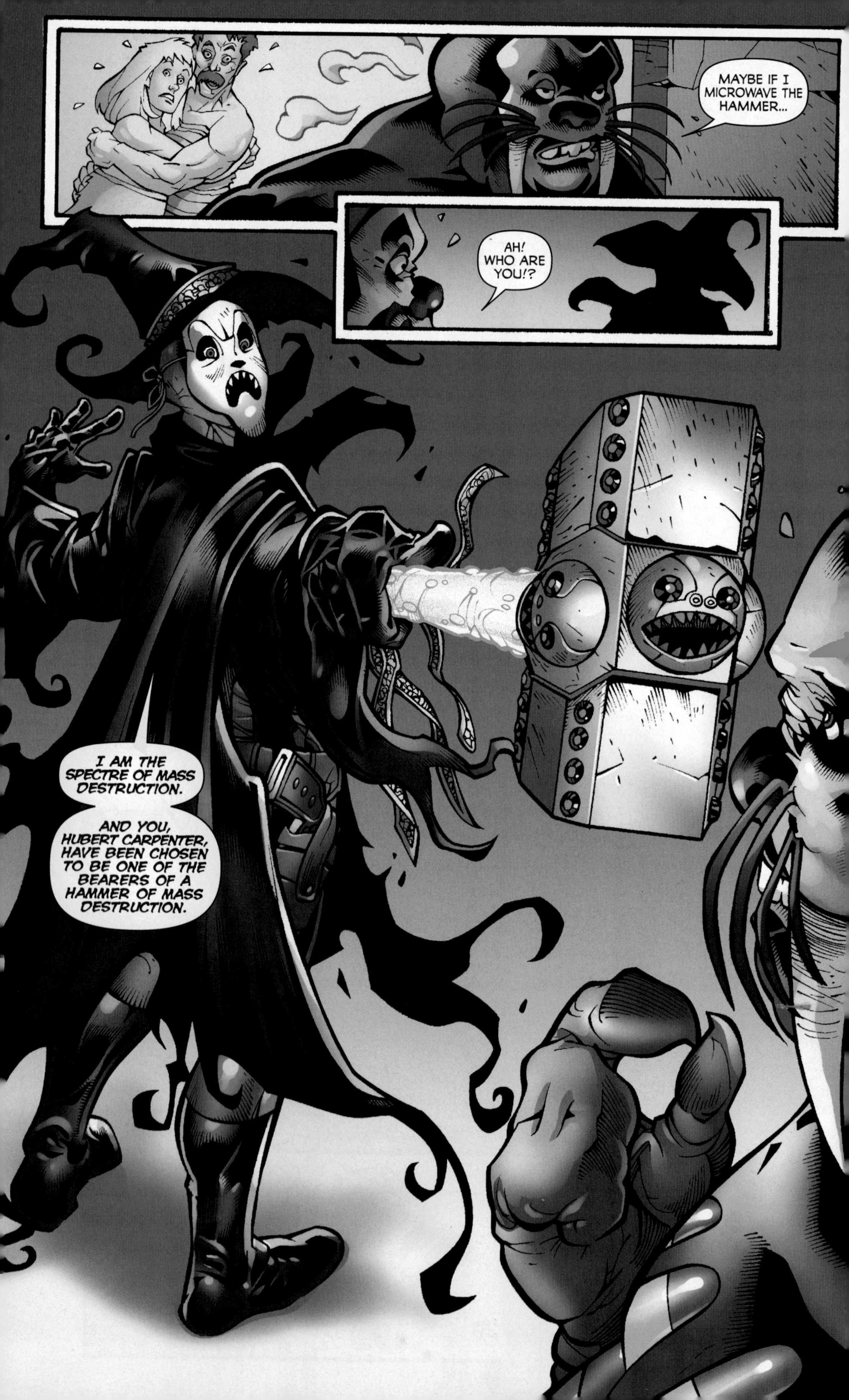

MAYBE IF I MICROWAVE THE HAMMER...
AH! WHO ARE YOU!?
I AM THE SPECTRE OF MASS DESTRUCTION.
AND YOU, HUBERT CARPENTER, HAVE BEEN CHOSEN TO BE ONE OF THE BEARERS OF A HAMMER OF MASS DESTRUCTION.

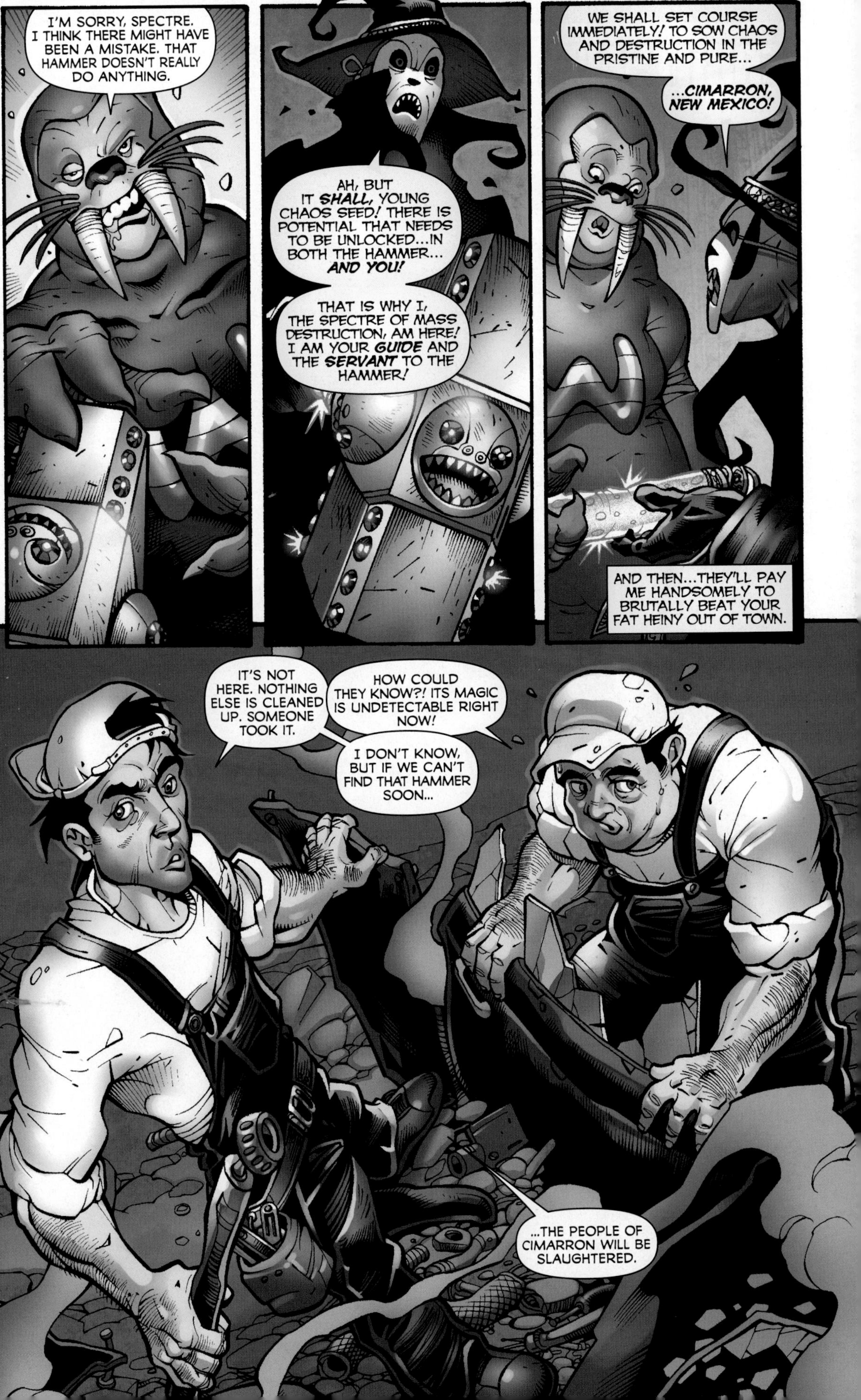
I'M SORRY, SPECTRE. I THINK THERE MIGHT HAVE BEEN A MISTAKE. THAT HAMMER DOESN'T REALLY DO ANYTHING.
AH, BUT IT **SHALL**, YOUNG CHAOS SEED! THERE IS POTENTIAL THAT NEEDS TO BE UNLOCKED...IN BOTH THE HAMMER... **AND YOU!**
THAT IS WHY I, THE SPECTRE OF MASS DESTRUCTION, AM HERE! I AM YOUR **GUIDE** AND THE **SERVANT** TO THE HAMMER!
WE SHALL SET COURSE IMMEDIATELY! TO SOW CHAOS AND DESTRUCTION IN THE PRISTINE AND PURE...
...CIMARRON, NEW MEXICO!
AND THEN...THEY'LL PAY ME HANDSOMELY TO BRUTALLY BEAT YOUR FAT HEINY OUT OF TOWN.
IT'S NOT HERE. NOTHING ELSE IS CLEANED UP. SOMEONE TOOK IT.
HOW COULD THEY KNOW?! ITS MAGIC IS UNDETECTABLE RIGHT NOW!
I DON'T KNOW, BUT IF WE CAN'T FIND THAT HAMMER SOON...
...THE PEOPLE OF CIMARRON WILL BE SLAUGHTERED.

FEAR ITSELF: DEADPOOL #2

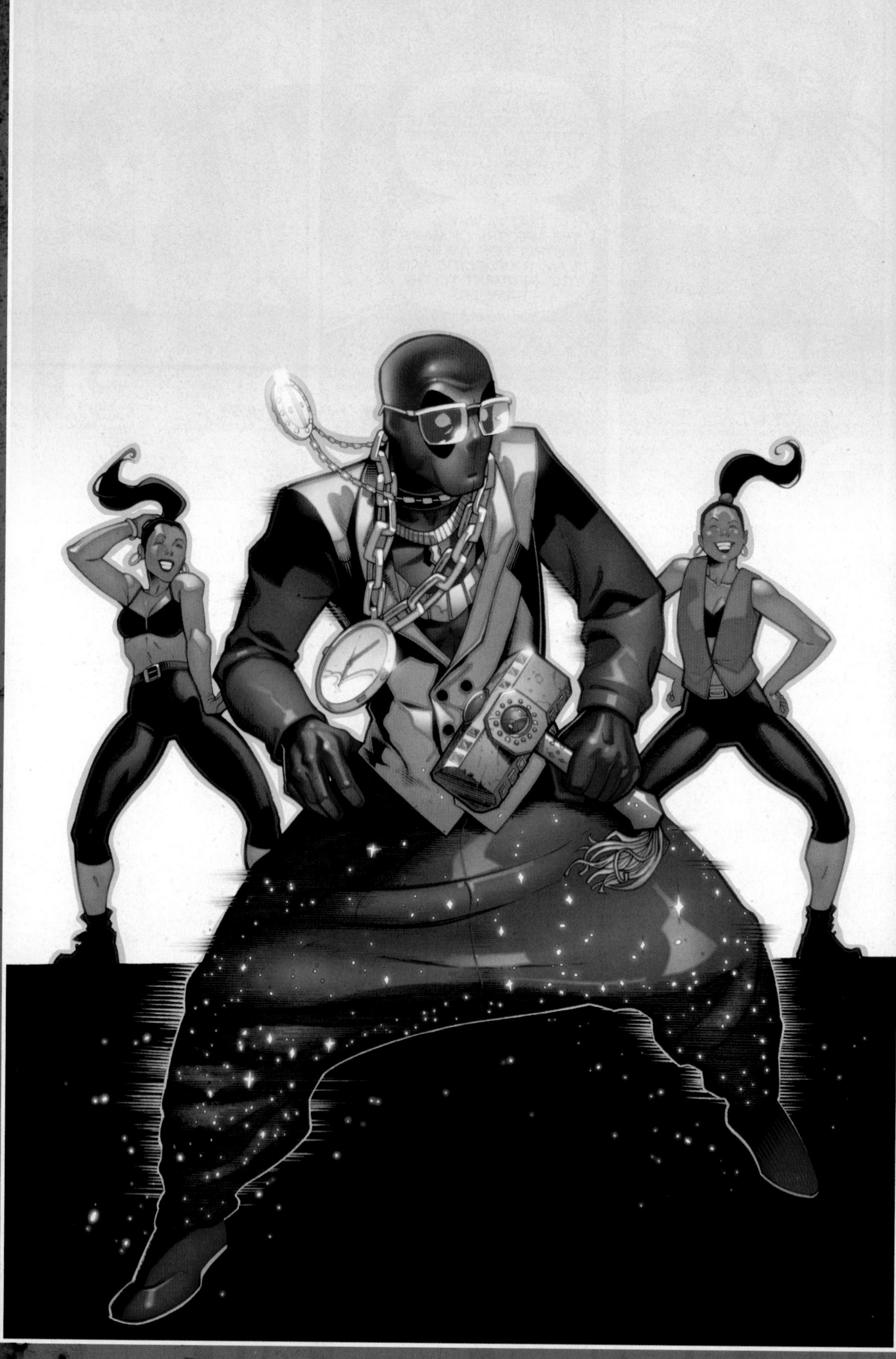

THUMP

≥SNORT≤ WHAUH! WHO'S THERE?!

MMMM... GO BACK TO SLEEP, SWEETIE. IT WAS PROBABLY NOTHING.

SORRY, HON. PROBABLY THOSE DAMNED RACCOONS AGAIN.

OR MAYBE...

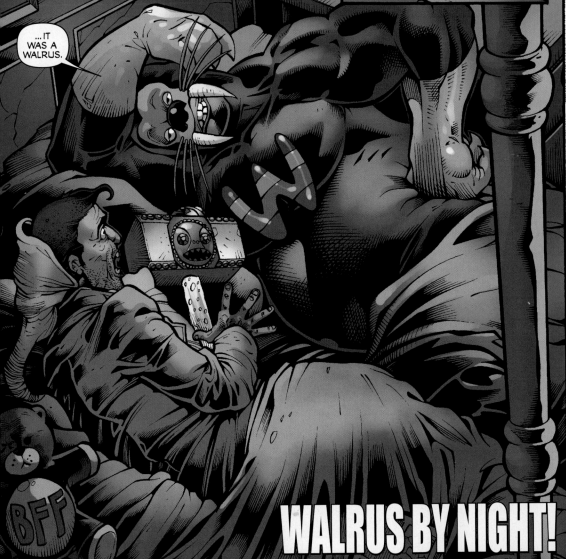

...IT WAS A WALRUS.

BFF

WALRUS BY NIGHT!

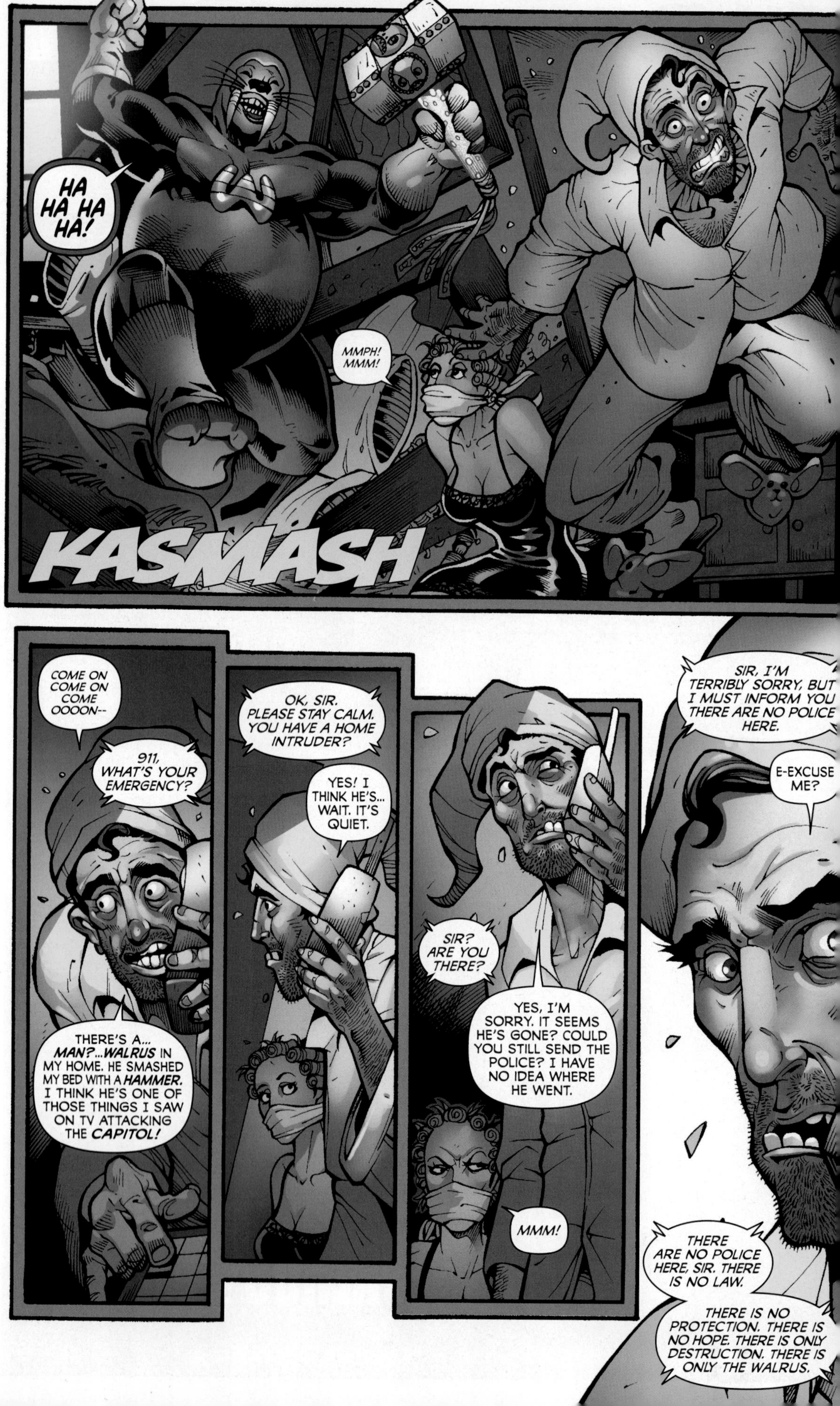
HA HA HA HA!
MMPH! MMM!
KASMASH
COME ON COME ON COME OOOON--
911, WHAT'S YOUR EMERGENCY?
THERE'S A... MAN?...WALRUS IN MY HOME. HE SMASHED MY BED WITH A HAMMER. I THINK HE'S ONE OF THOSE THINGS I SAW ON TV ATTACKING THE CAPITOL!
OK, SIR. PLEASE STAY CALM. YOU HAVE A HOME INTRUDER?
YES! I THINK HE'S... WAIT. IT'S QUIET.
SIR? ARE YOU THERE?
YES, I'M SORRY. IT SEEMS HE'S GONE? COULD YOU STILL SEND THE POLICE? I HAVE NO IDEA WHERE HE WENT.
MMM!
SIR, I'M TERRIBLY SORRY, BUT I MUST INFORM YOU THERE ARE NO POLICE HERE.
E-EXCUSE ME?
THERE ARE NO POLICE HERE, SIR. THERE IS NO LAW.
THERE IS NO PROTECTION. THERE IS NO HOPE. THERE IS ONLY DESTRUCTION. THERE IS ONLY THE WALRUS.

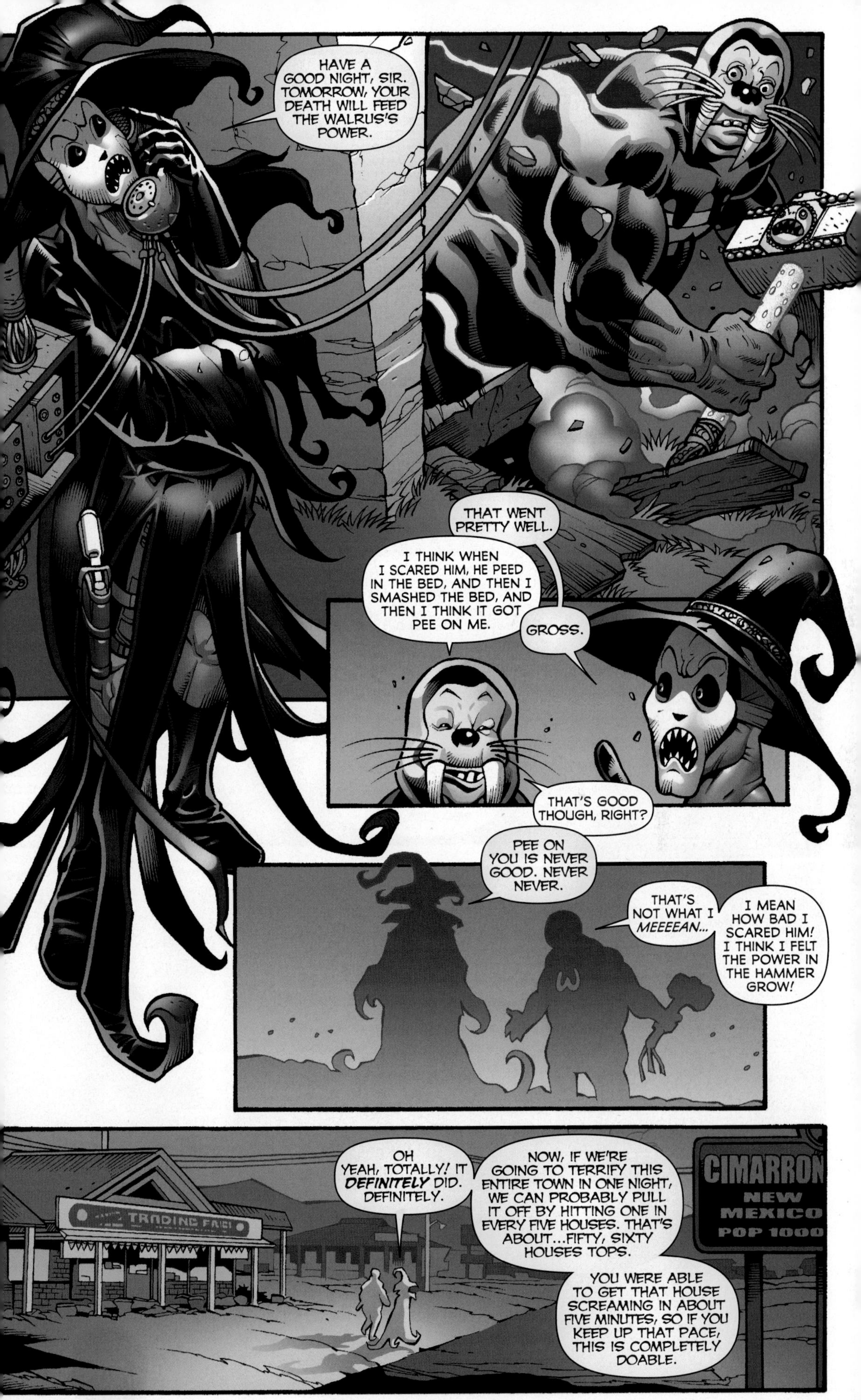
HAVE A GOOD NIGHT, SIR. TOMORROW, YOUR DEATH WILL FEED THE WALRUS'S POWER.
THAT WENT PRETTY WELL.
I THINK WHEN I SCARED HIM, HE PEED IN THE BED, AND THEN I SMASHED THE BED, AND THEN I THINK IT GOT PEE ON ME.
GROSS.
THAT'S GOOD THOUGH, RIGHT?
PEE ON YOU IS NEVER GOOD. NEVER NEVER.
THAT'S NOT WHAT I *MEEEEAN*...
I MEAN HOW BAD I SCARED HIM! I THINK I FELT THE POWER IN THE HAMMER GROW!
TRADING FACT
CIMARRON
NEW MEXICO
POP 1000
OH YEAH, TOTALLY! IT ***DEFINITELY*** DID. DEFINITELY.
NOW, IF WE'RE GOING TO TERRIFY THIS ENTIRE TOWN IN ONE NIGHT, WE CAN PROBABLY PULL IT OFF BY HITTING ONE IN EVERY FIVE HOUSES. THAT'S ABOUT...FIFTY, SIXTY HOUSES TOPS.
YOU WERE ABLE TO GET THAT HOUSE SCREAMING IN ABOUT FIVE MINUTES, SO IF YOU KEEP UP THAT PACE, THIS IS COMPLETELY DOABLE.

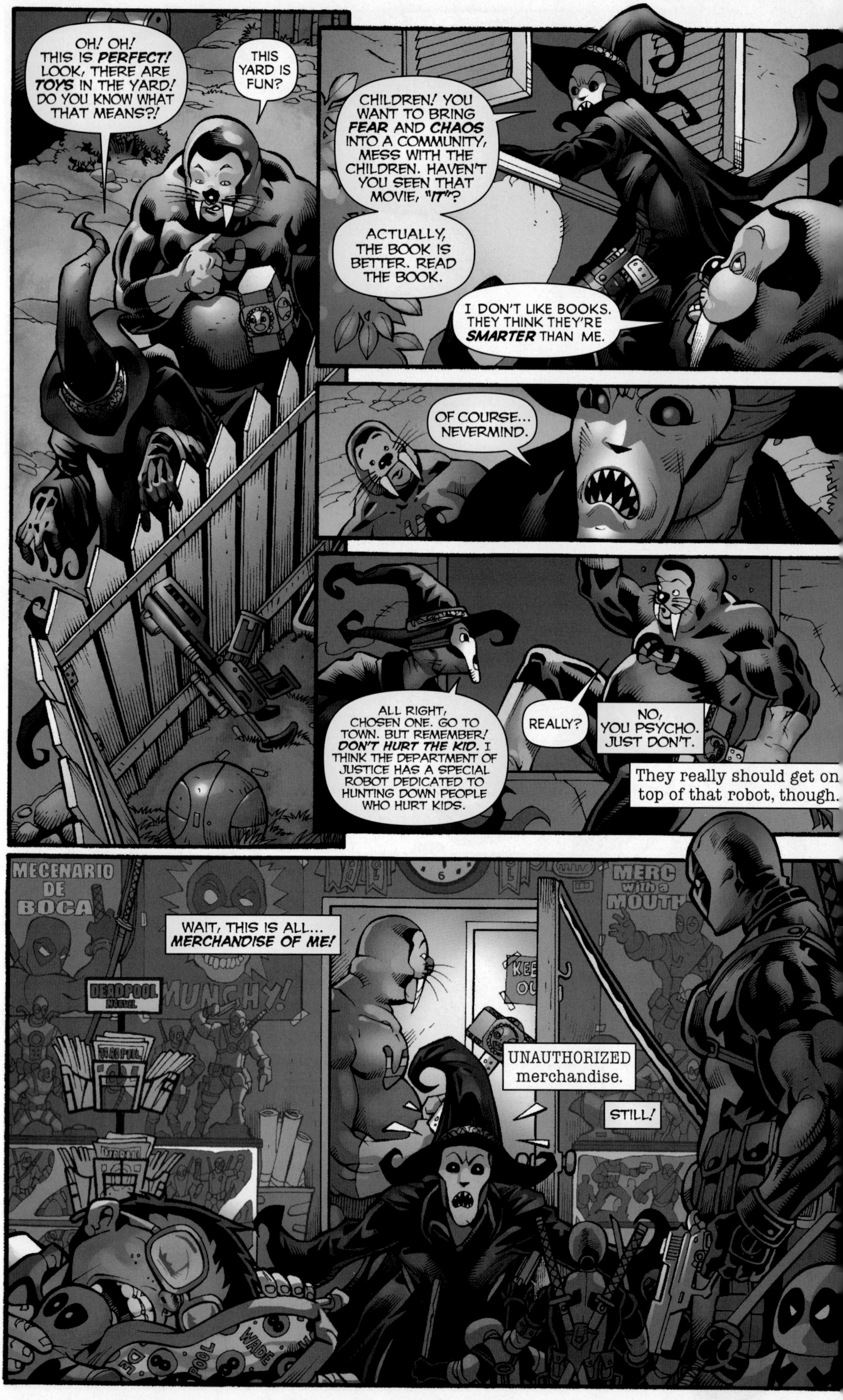
OH! OH! THIS IS PERFECT! LOOK, THERE ARE TOYS IN THE YARD! DO YOU KNOW WHAT THAT MEANS?!
THIS YARD IS FUN?
CHILDREN! YOU WANT TO BRING FEAR AND CHAOS INTO A COMMUNITY, MESS WITH THE CHILDREN. HAVEN'T YOU SEEN THAT MOVIE, "IT"?
ACTUALLY, THE BOOK IS BETTER. READ THE BOOK.
I DON'T LIKE BOOKS. THEY THINK THEY'RE SMARTER THAN ME.
OF COURSE... NEVERMIND.
ALL RIGHT, CHOSEN ONE. GO TO TOWN. BUT REMEMBER! DON'T HURT THE KID. I THINK THE DEPARTMENT OF JUSTICE HAS A SPECIAL ROBOT DEDICATED TO HUNTING DOWN PEOPLE WHO HURT KIDS.
REALLY?
NO, YOU PSYCHO. JUST DON'T.
They really should get on top of that robot, though.
MECENARIO DE BOCA
DEADPOOL
MUNCHY!
MERC with a MOUTH
WAIT, THIS IS ALL... MERCHANDISE OF ME!
UNAUTHORIZED merchandise.
STILL!
WADE
POOL

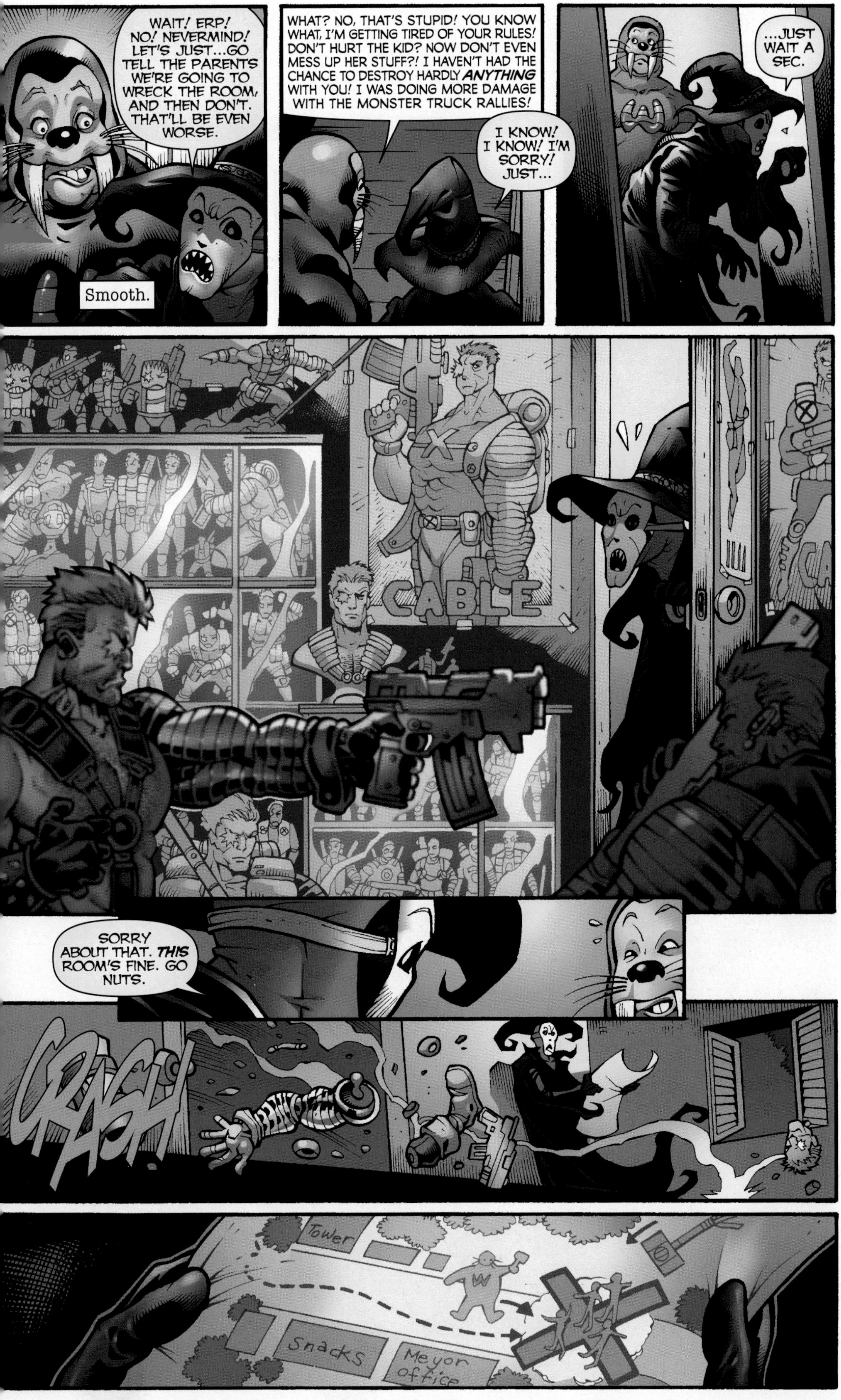
WAIT! ERP! NO! NEVERMIND! LET'S JUST...GO TELL THE PARENTS WE'RE GOING TO WRECK THE ROOM, AND THEN DON'T. THAT'LL BE EVEN WORSE.
Smooth.
WHAT? NO, THAT'S STUPID! YOU KNOW WHAT, I'M GETTING TIRED OF YOUR RULES! DON'T HURT THE KID? NOW DON'T EVEN MESS UP HER STUFF?! I HAVEN'T HAD THE CHANCE TO DESTROY HARDLY ANYTHING WITH YOU! I WAS DOING MORE DAMAGE WITH THE MONSTER TRUCK RALLIES!
I KNOW! I KNOW! I'M SORRY! JUST...
...JUST WAIT A SEC.
CABLE
SORRY ABOUT THAT. THIS ROOM'S FINE. GO NUTS.
CRASH
Tower
Snacks
Meyor office

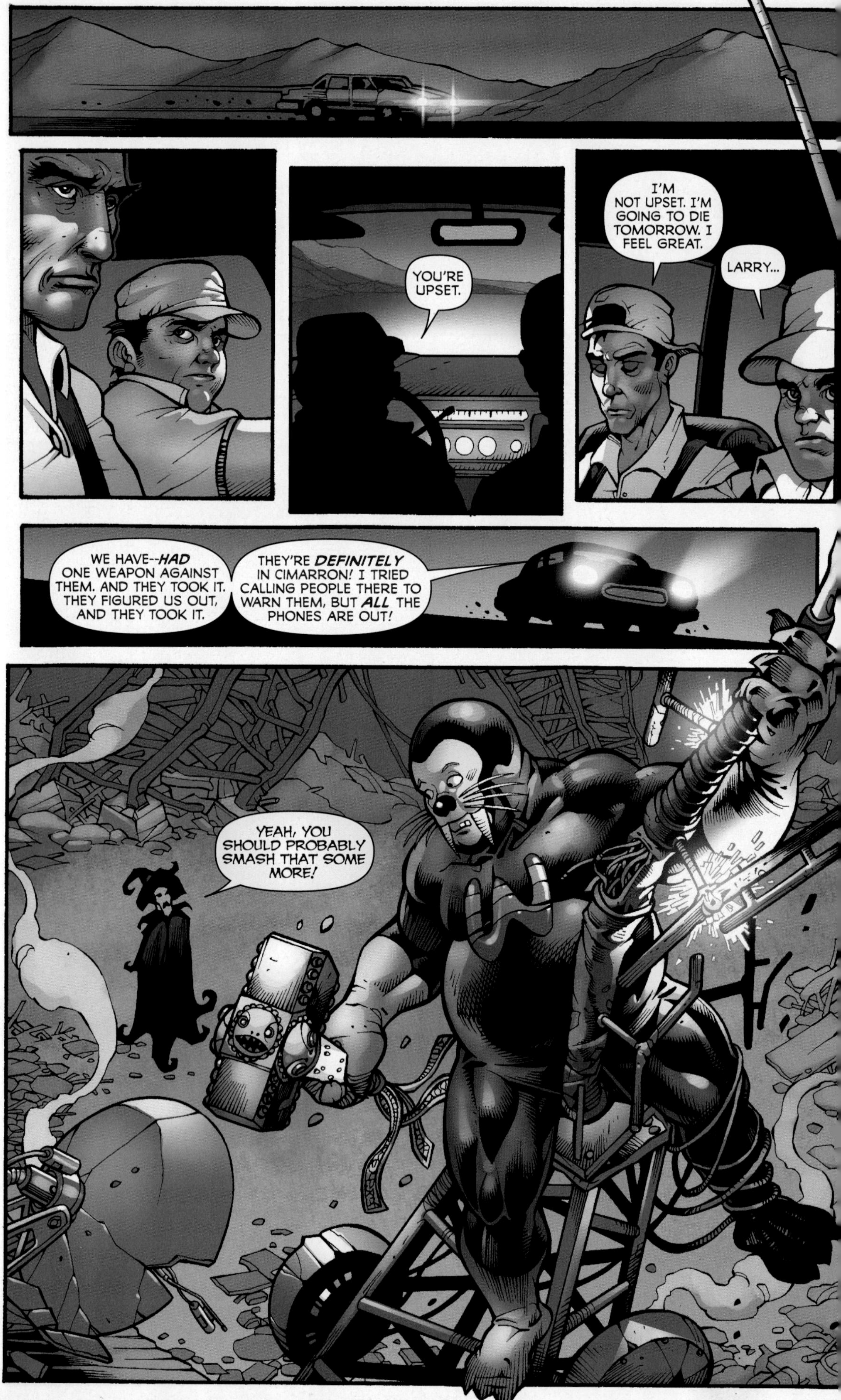
YOU'RE UPSET.
I'M NOT UPSET. I'M GOING TO DIE TOMORROW. I FEEL GREAT.
LARRY...
WE HAVE--*HAD* ONE WEAPON AGAINST THEM. AND THEY TOOK IT. THEY FIGURED US OUT, AND THEY TOOK IT.
THEY'RE *DEFINITELY* IN CIMARRON! I TRIED CALLING PEOPLE THERE TO WARN THEM, BUT *ALL* THE PHONES ARE OUT!
YEAH, YOU SHOULD PROBABLY SMASH THAT SOME MORE!

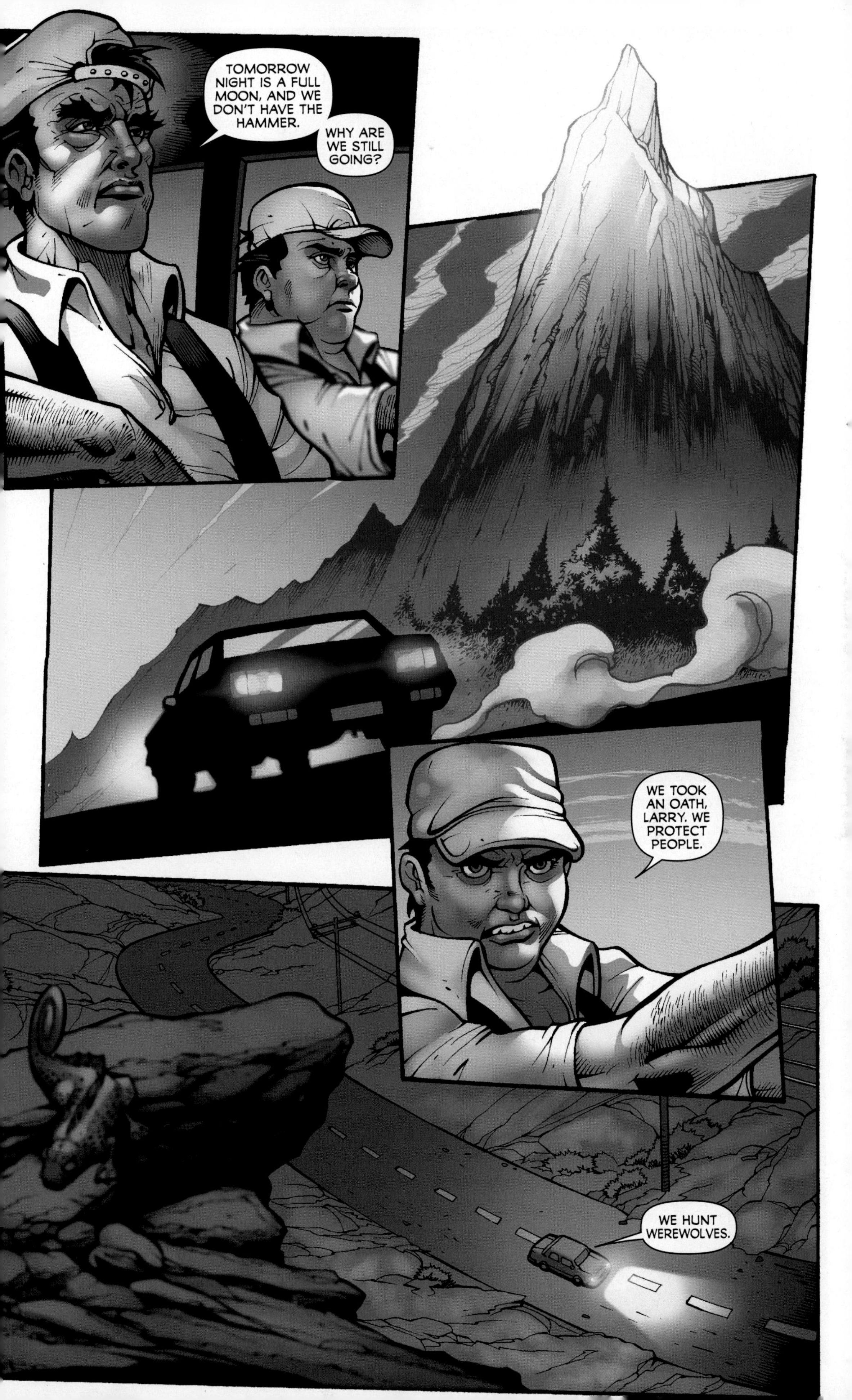
TOMORROW NIGHT IS A FULL MOON, AND WE DON'T HAVE THE HAMMER.
WHY ARE WE STILL GOING?
WE TOOK AN OATH, LARRY. WE PROTECT PEOPLE.
WE HUNT WEREWOLVES.

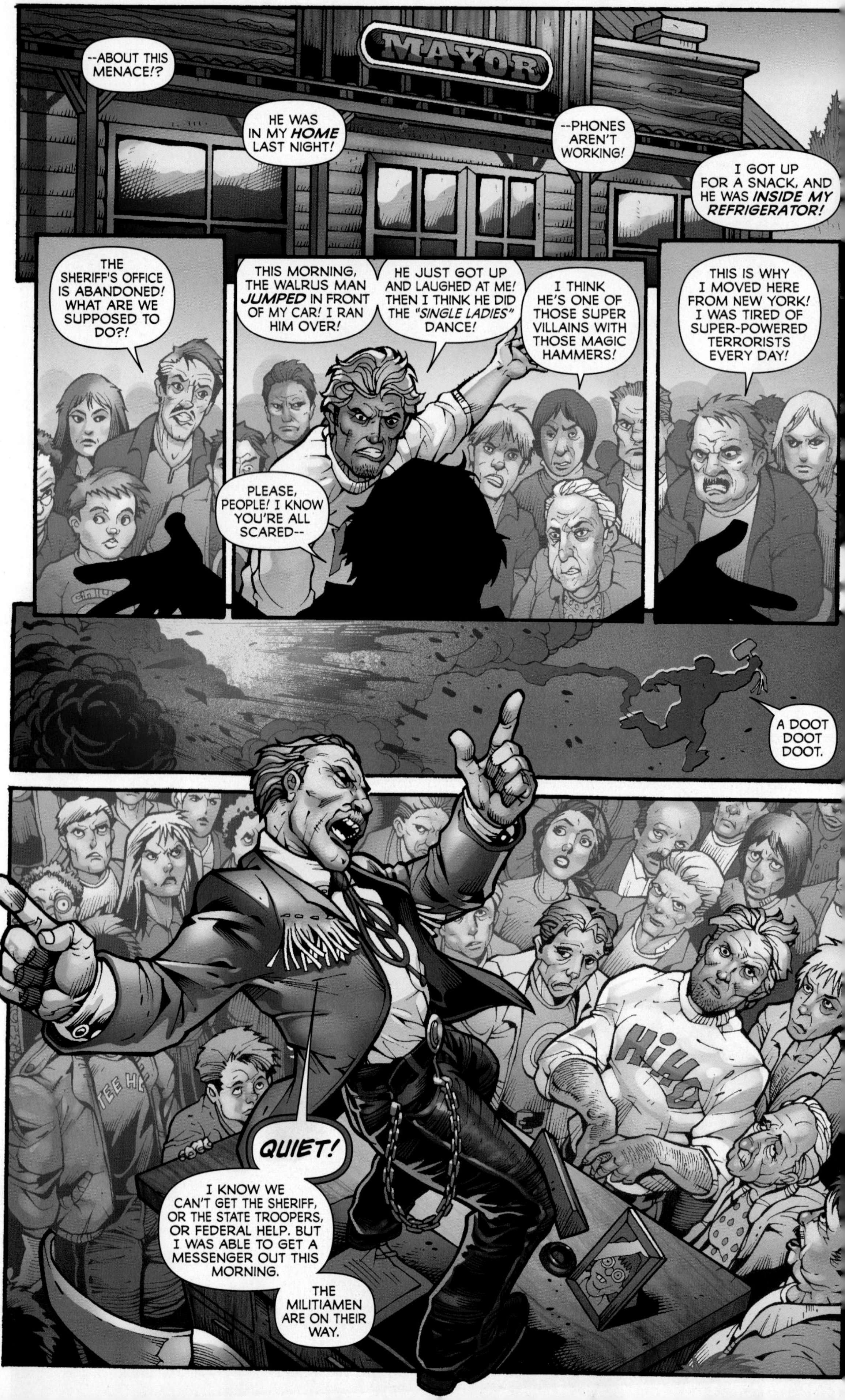

--ABOUT THIS MENACE!?
MAYOR
HE WAS IN MY *HOME* LAST NIGHT!
--PHONES AREN'T WORKING!
I GOT UP FOR A SNACK, AND HE WAS ***INSIDE MY REFRIGERATOR!***
THE SHERIFF'S OFFICE IS ABANDONED! WHAT ARE WE SUPPOSED TO DO?!
THIS MORNING, THE WALRUS MAN ***JUMPED*** IN FRONT OF MY CAR! I RAN HIM OVER!
HE JUST GOT UP AND LAUGHED AT ME! THEN I THINK HE DID THE *"SINGLE LADIES"* DANCE!
I THINK HE'S ONE OF THOSE SUPER VILLAINS WITH THOSE MAGIC HAMMERS!
THIS IS WHY I MOVED HERE FROM NEW YORK! I WAS TIRED OF SUPER-POWERED TERRORISTS EVERY DAY!
PLEASE, PEOPLE! I KNOW YOU'RE ALL SCARED--
A DOOT DOOT DOOT.
QUIET!
I KNOW WE CAN'T GET THE SHERIFF, OR THE STATE TROOPERS, OR FEDERAL HELP. BUT I WAS ABLE TO GET A MESSENGER OUT THIS MORNING.
THE MILITIAMEN ARE ON THEIR WAY.

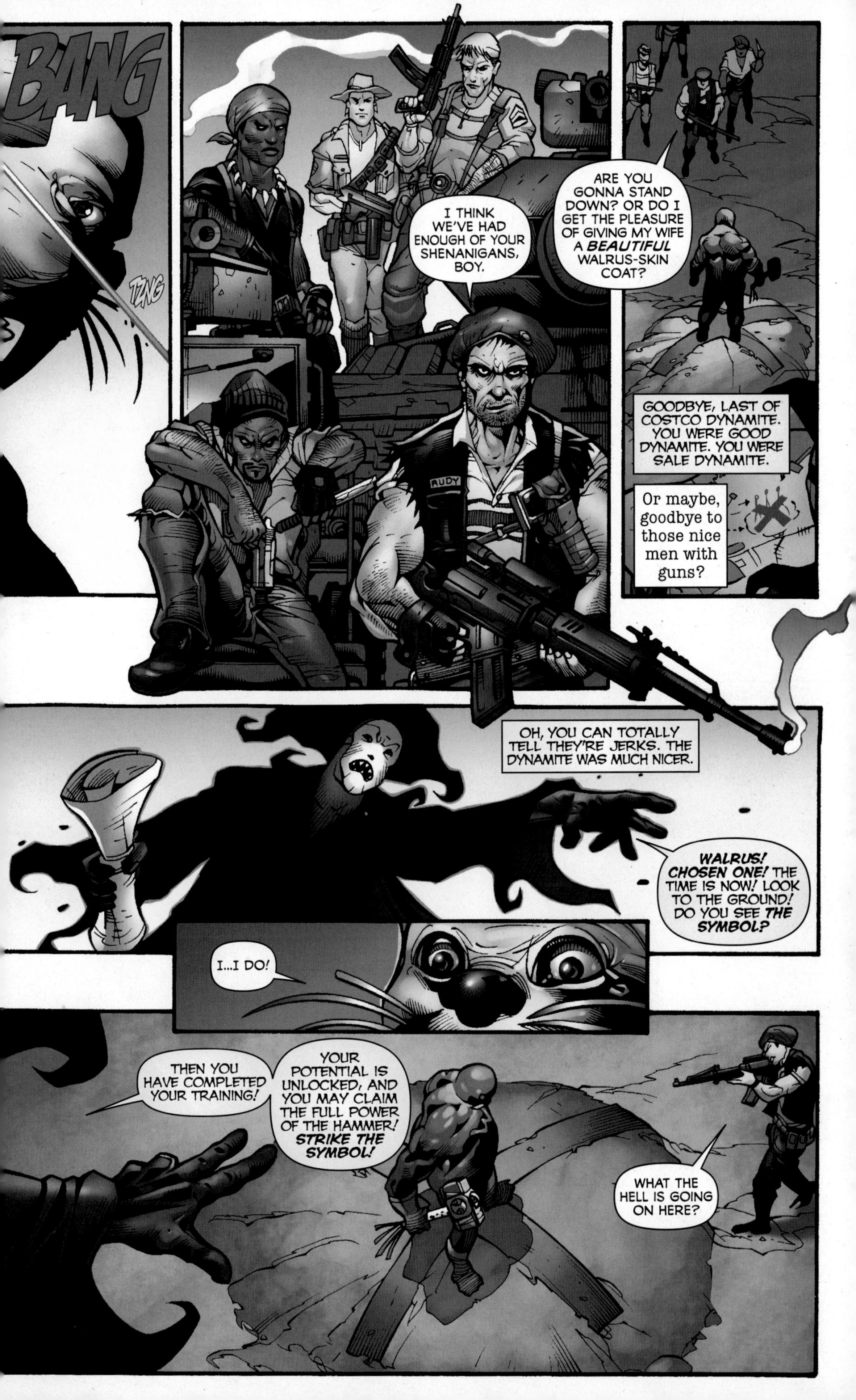
BANG
TZNG
I THINK WE'VE HAD ENOUGH OF YOUR SHENANIGANS, BOY.
ARE YOU GONNA STAND DOWN? OR DO I GET THE PLEASURE OF GIVING MY WIFE A BEAUTIFUL WALRUS-SKIN COAT?
RUDY
GOODBYE, LAST OF COSTCO DYNAMITE. YOU WERE GOOD DYNAMITE. YOU WERE SALE DYNAMITE.
Or maybe, goodbye to those nice men with guns?
OH, YOU CAN TOTALLY TELL THEY'RE JERKS. THE DYNAMITE WAS MUCH NICER.
WALRUS! CHOSEN ONE! THE TIME IS NOW! LOOK TO THE GROUND! DO YOU SEE THE SYMBOL?
I...I DO!
THEN YOU HAVE COMPLETED YOUR TRAINING!
YOUR POTENTIAL IS UNLOCKED, AND YOU MAY CLAIM THE FULL POWER OF THE HAMMER! STRIKE THE SYMBOL!
WHAT THE HELL IS GOING ON HERE?

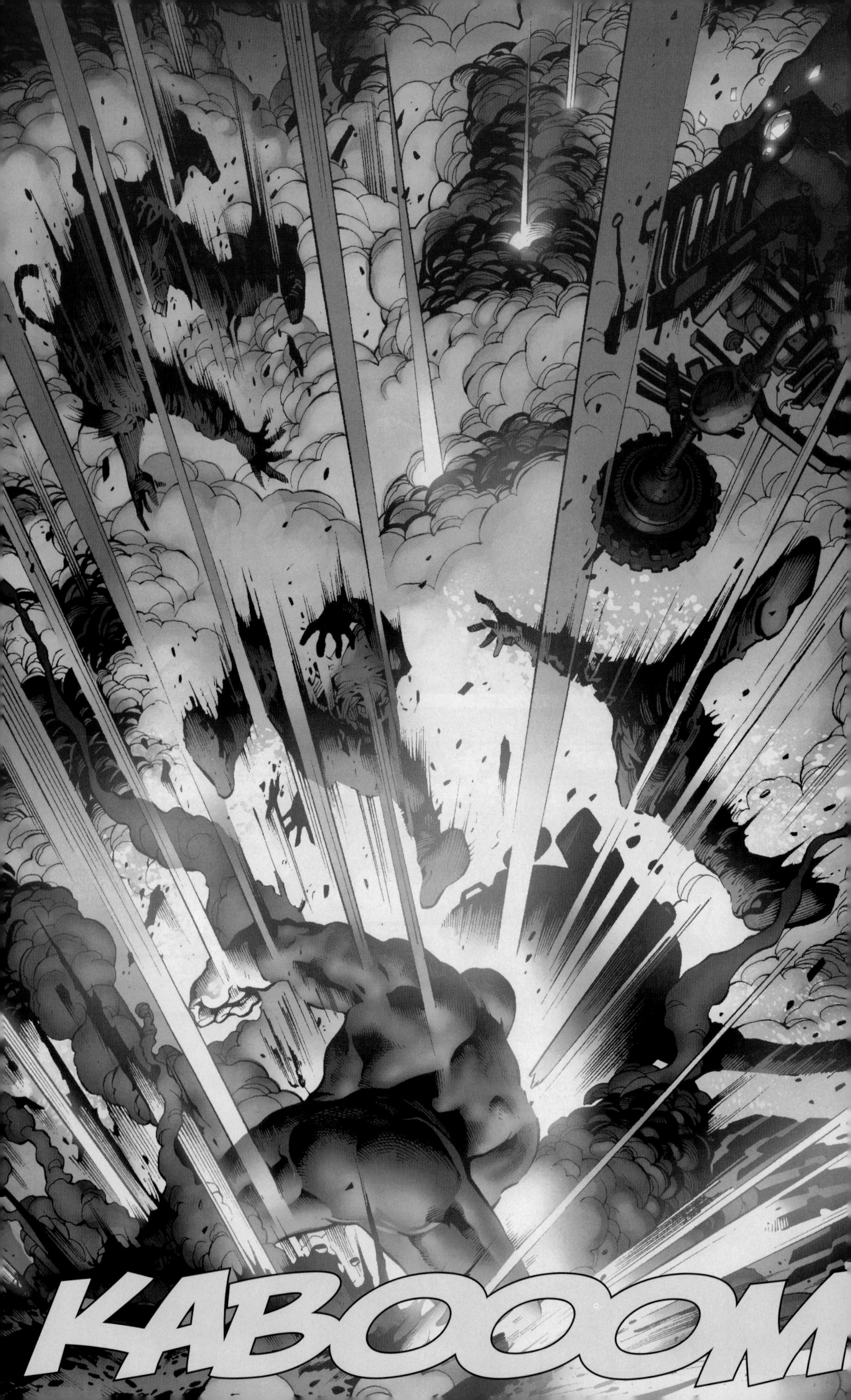
KABOOOM

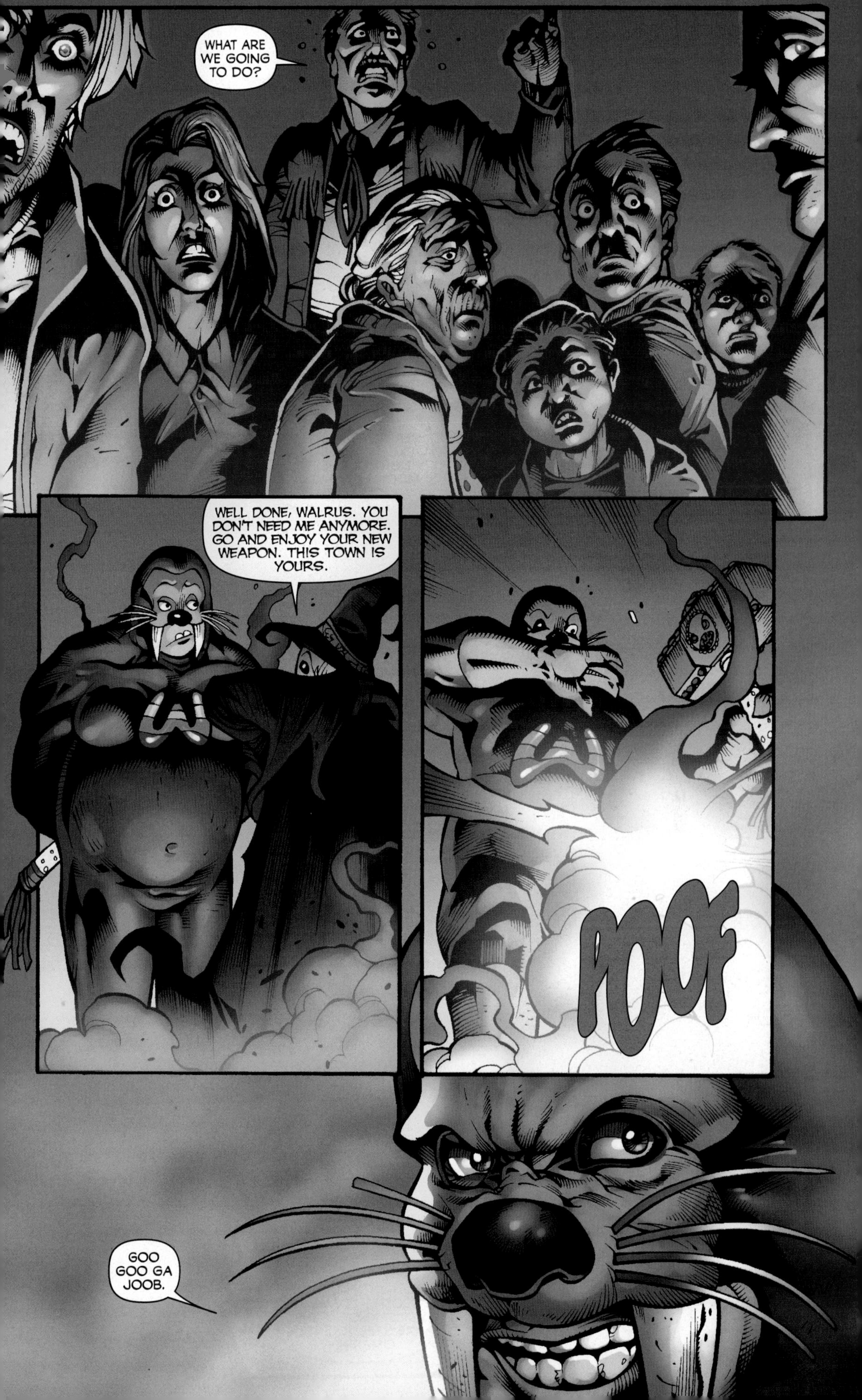
WHAT ARE WE GOING TO DO?
WELL DONE, WALRUS. YOU DON'T NEED ME ANYMORE. GO AND ENJOY YOUR NEW WEAPON. THIS TOWN IS YOURS.
POOF
GOO GOO GA JOOB.

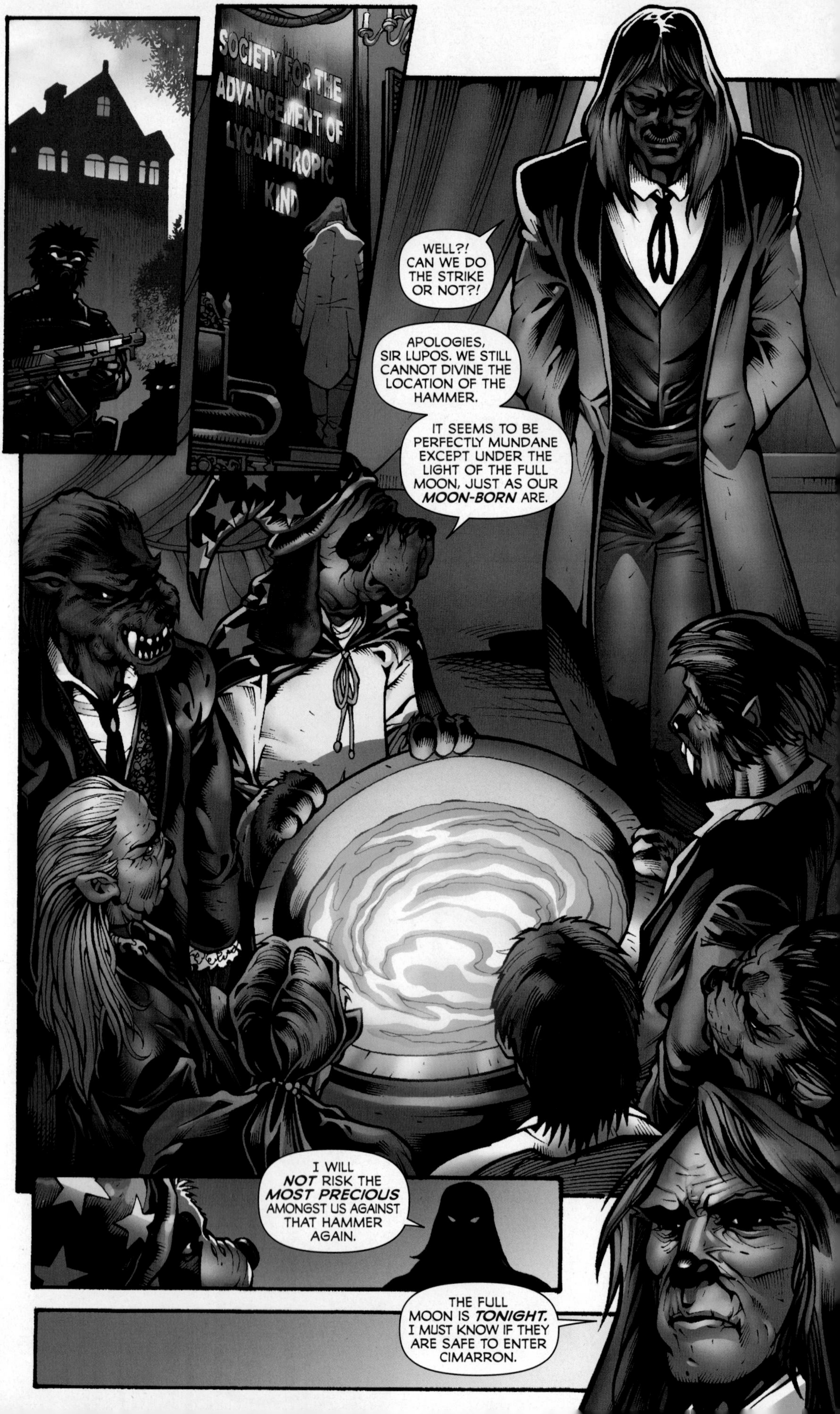
SOCIETY FOR THE ADVANCEMENT OF LYCANTHROPIC KIND
WELL?! CAN WE DO THE STRIKE OR NOT?!
APOLOGIES, SIR LUPOS. WE STILL CANNOT DIVINE THE LOCATION OF THE HAMMER.
IT SEEMS TO BE PERFECTLY MUNDANE EXCEPT UNDER THE LIGHT OF THE FULL MOON, JUST AS OUR *MOON-BORN* ARE.
I WILL ***NOT*** RISK THE ***MOST PRECIOUS*** AMONGST US AGAINST THAT HAMMER AGAIN.
THE FULL MOON IS ***TONIGHT.*** I MUST KNOW IF THEY ARE SAFE TO ENTER CIMARRON.

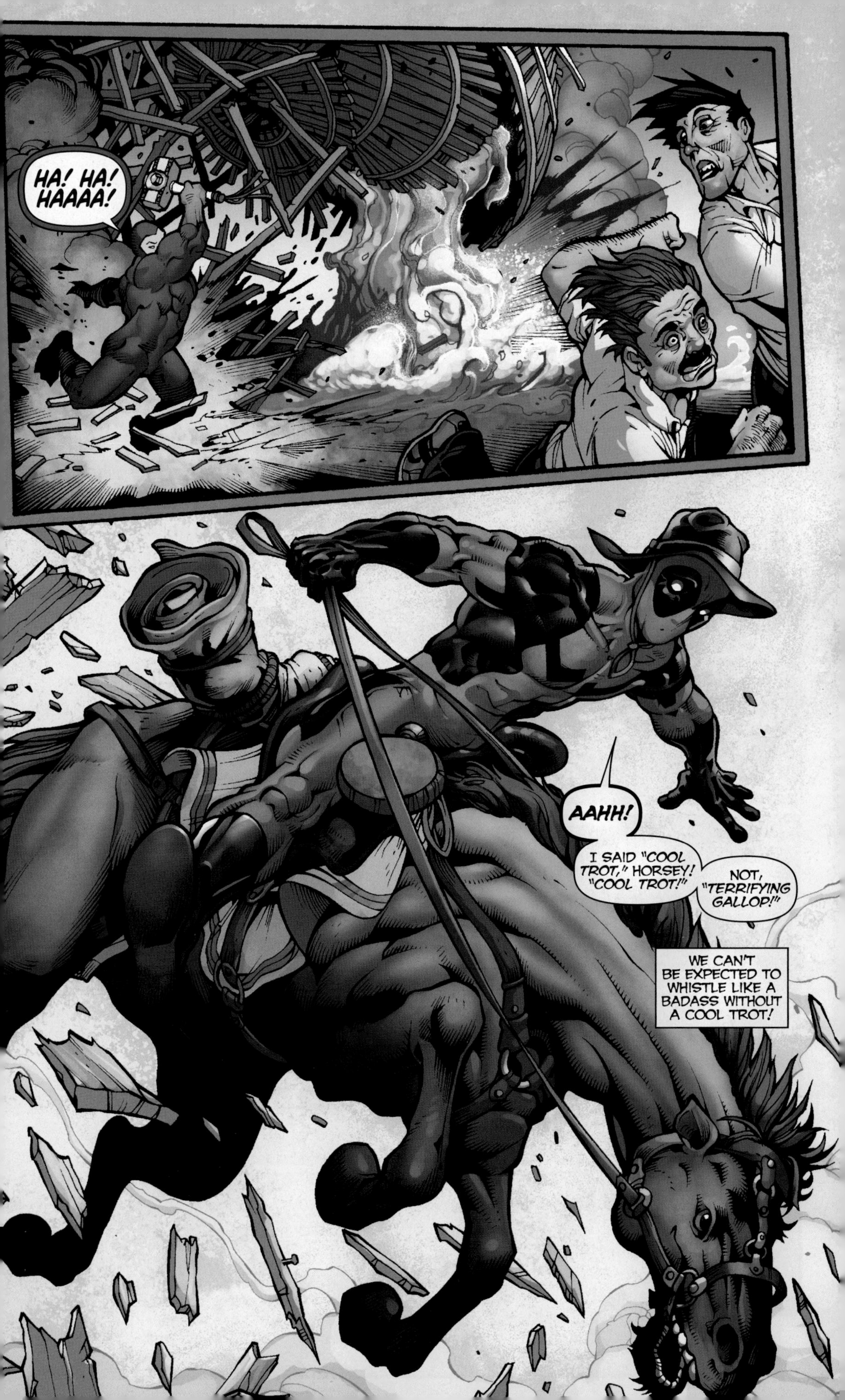
HA! HA! HAAAA!
AAHH!
I SAID "COOL TROT," HORSEY! "COOL TROT!"
NOT, "TERRIFYING GALLOP!"
WE CAN'T BE EXPECTED TO WHISTLE LIKE A BADASS WITHOUT A COOL TROT!

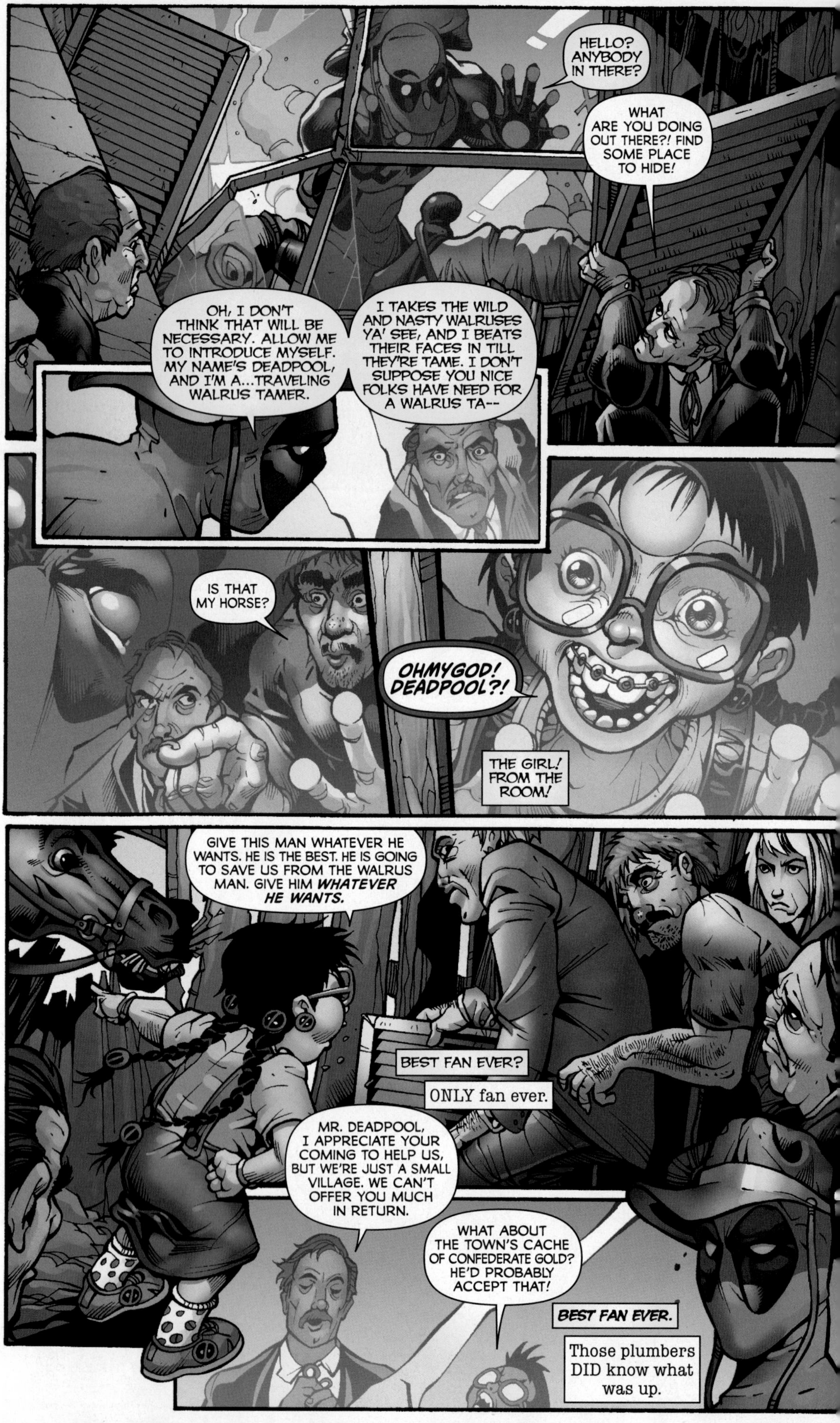
HELLO? ANYBODY IN THERE?
WHAT ARE YOU DOING OUT THERE?! FIND SOME PLACE TO HIDE!
OH, I DON'T THINK THAT WILL BE NECESSARY. ALLOW ME TO INTRODUCE MYSELF. MY NAME'S DEADPOOL, AND I'M A...TRAVELING WALRUS TAMER.
I TAKES THE WILD AND NASTY WALRUSES YA' SEE, AND I BEATS THEIR FACES IN TILL THEY'RE TAME. I DON'T SUPPOSE YOU NICE FOLKS HAVE NEED FOR A WALRUS TA--
IS THAT MY HORSE?
OHMYGOD! DEADPOOL?!
THE GIRL! FROM THE ROOM!
GIVE THIS MAN WHATEVER HE WANTS. HE IS THE BEST. HE IS GOING TO SAVE US FROM THE WALRUS MAN. GIVE HIM WHATEVER HE WANTS.
BEST FAN EVER?
ONLY fan ever.
MR. DEADPOOL, I APPRECIATE YOUR COMING TO HELP US, BUT WE'RE JUST A SMALL VILLAGE. WE CAN'T OFFER YOU MUCH IN RETURN.
WHAT ABOUT THE TOWN'S CACHE OF CONFEDERATE GOLD? HE'D PROBABLY ACCEPT THAT!
BEST FAN EVER.
Those plumbers DID know what was up.

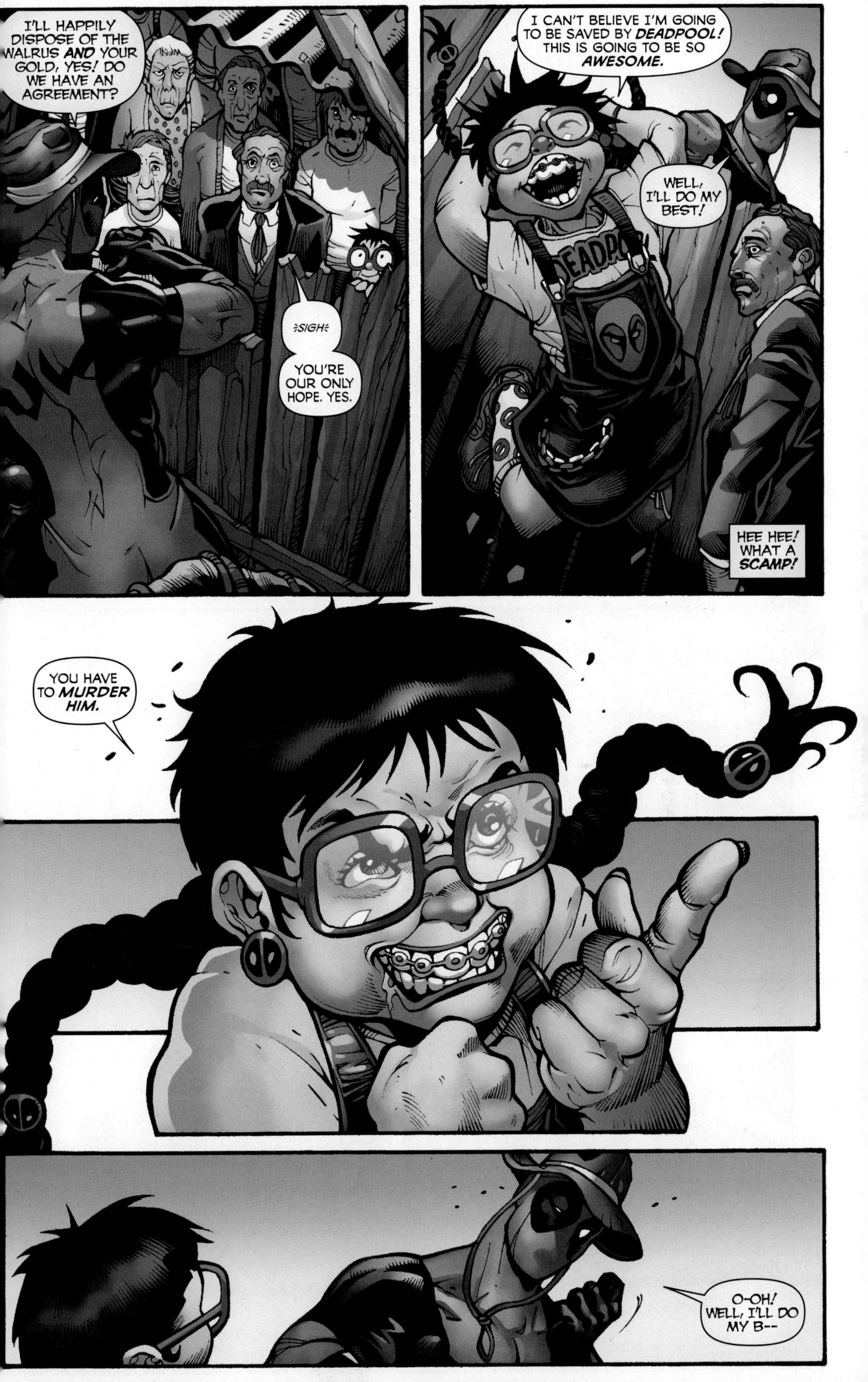
I'LL HAPPILY DISPOSE OF THE WALRUS AND YOUR GOLD, YES! DO WE HAVE AN AGREEMENT?
SIGH
YOU'RE OUR ONLY HOPE. YES.
I CAN'T BELIEVE I'M GOING TO BE SAVED BY DEADPOOL! THIS IS GOING TO BE SO AWESOME.
WELL, I'LL DO MY BEST!
HEE HEE! WHAT A SCAMP!
YOU HAVE TO MURDER HIM.
O-OH! WELL, I'LL DO MY B--

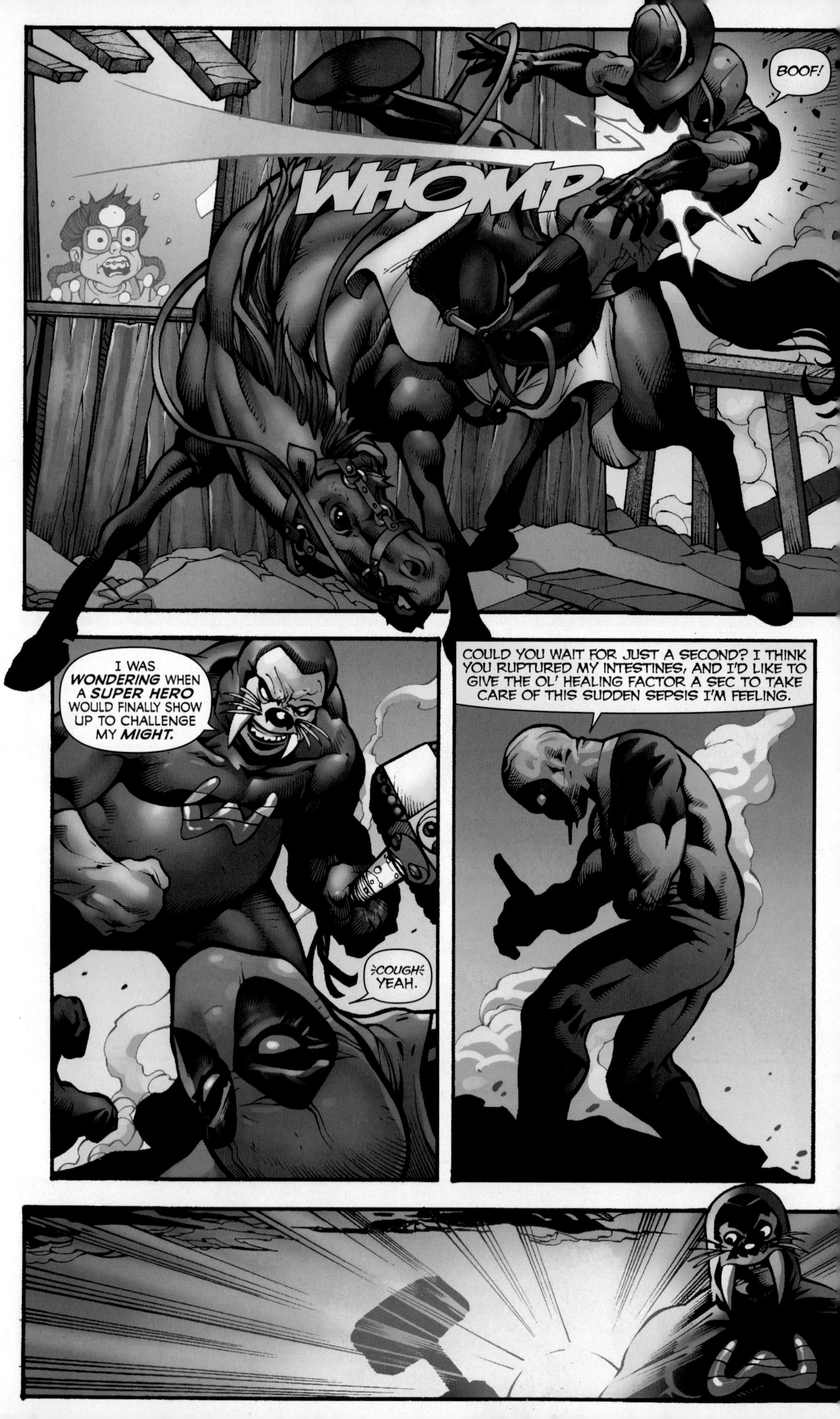
BOOF!
WHOMP
I WAS WONDERING WHEN A SUPER HERO WOULD FINALLY SHOW UP TO CHALLENGE MY MIGHT.
COUGH YEAH.
COULD YOU WAIT FOR JUST A SECOND? I THINK YOU RUPTURED MY INTESTINES, AND I'D LIKE TO GIVE THE OL' HEALING FACTOR A SEC TO TAKE CARE OF THIS SUDDEN SEPSIS I'M FEELING.

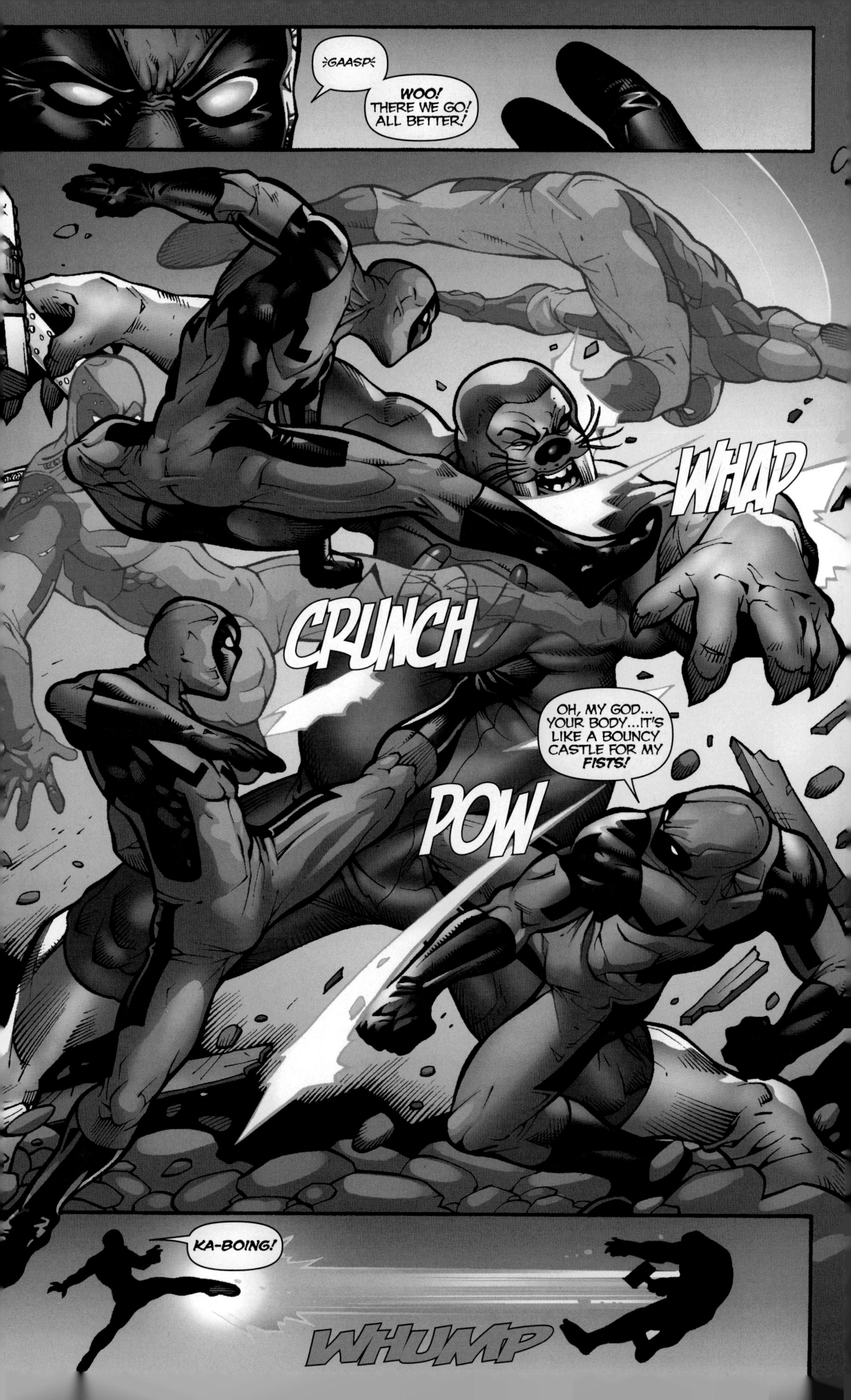

GAASP
WOO! THERE WE GO! ALL BETTER!
WHAP
CRUNCH
OH, MY GOD... YOUR BODY...IT'S LIKE A BOUNCY CASTLE FOR MY FISTS!
POW
KA-BOING!
WHUMP

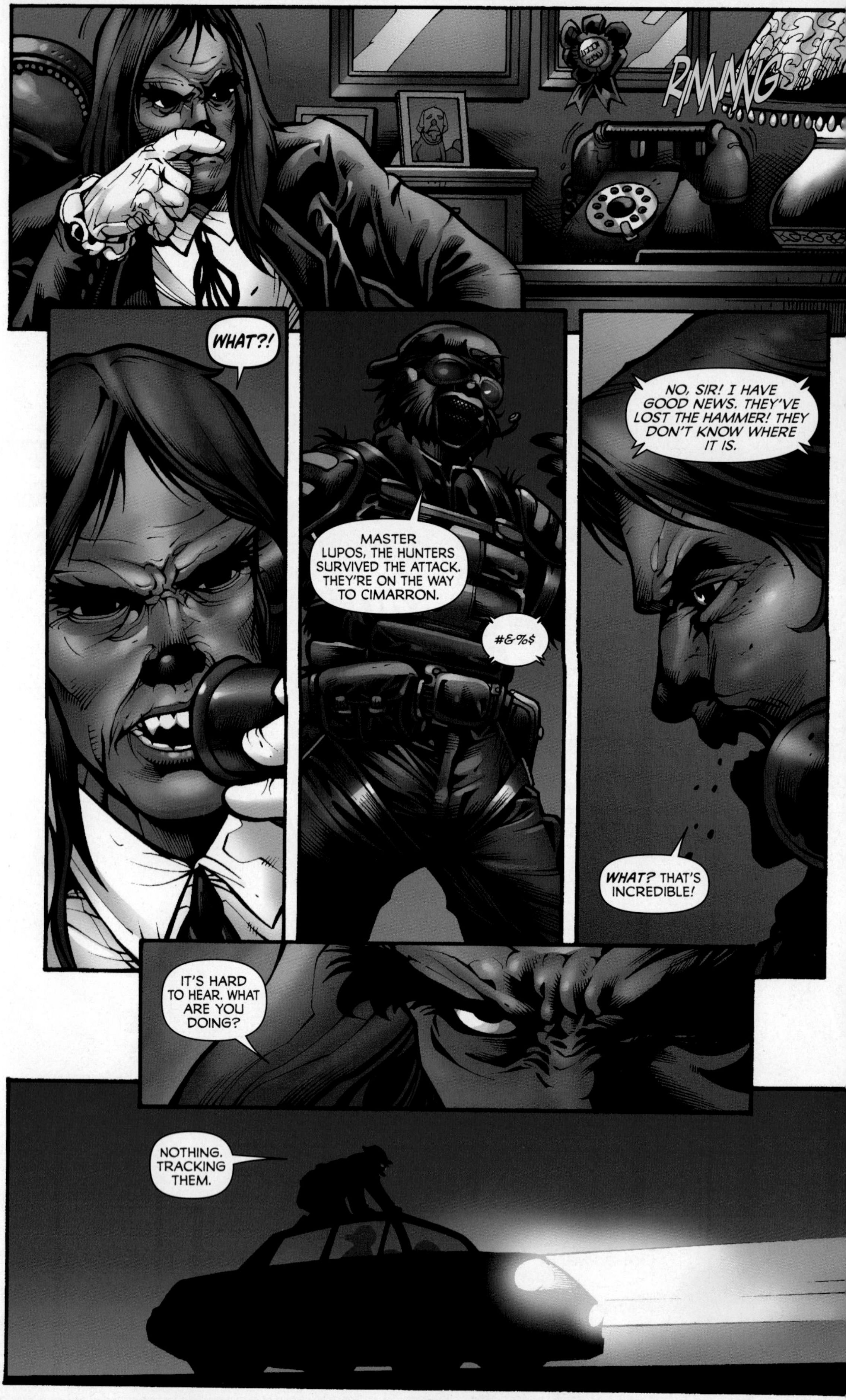
RINNNG
WHAT?!
MASTER LUPOS, THE HUNTERS SURVIVED THE ATTACK. THEY'RE ON THE WAY TO CIMARRON.
#&%$
NO, SIR! I HAVE GOOD NEWS. THEY'VE LOST THE HAMMER! THEY DON'T KNOW WHERE IT IS.
WHAT? THAT'S INCREDIBLE!
IT'S HARD TO HEAR. WHAT ARE YOU DOING?
NOTHING. TRACKING THEM.

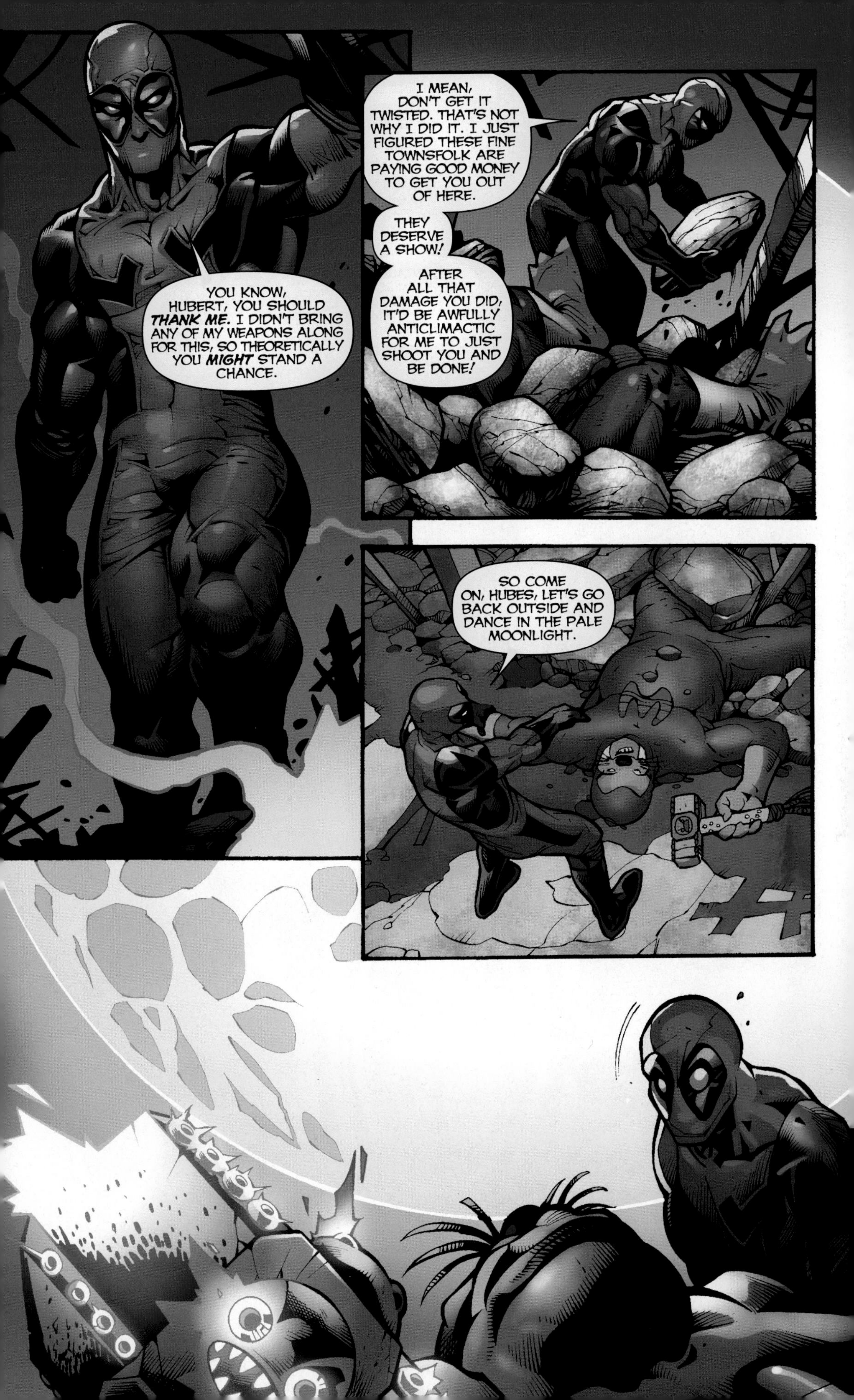
YOU KNOW, HUBERT, YOU SHOULD *THANK ME.* I DIDN'T BRING ANY OF MY WEAPONS ALONG FOR THIS, SO THEORETICALLY YOU *MIGHT* STAND A CHANCE.
I MEAN, DON'T GET IT TWISTED. THAT'S NOT WHY I DID IT. I JUST FIGURED THESE FINE TOWNSFOLK ARE PAYING GOOD MONEY TO GET YOU OUT OF HERE.
THEY DESERVE A SHOW!
AFTER ALL THAT DAMAGE YOU DID, IT'D BE AWFULLY ANTICLIMACTIC FOR ME TO JUST SHOOT YOU AND BE DONE!
SO COME ON, HUBES, LET'S GO BACK OUTSIDE AND DANCE IN THE PALE MOONLIGHT.

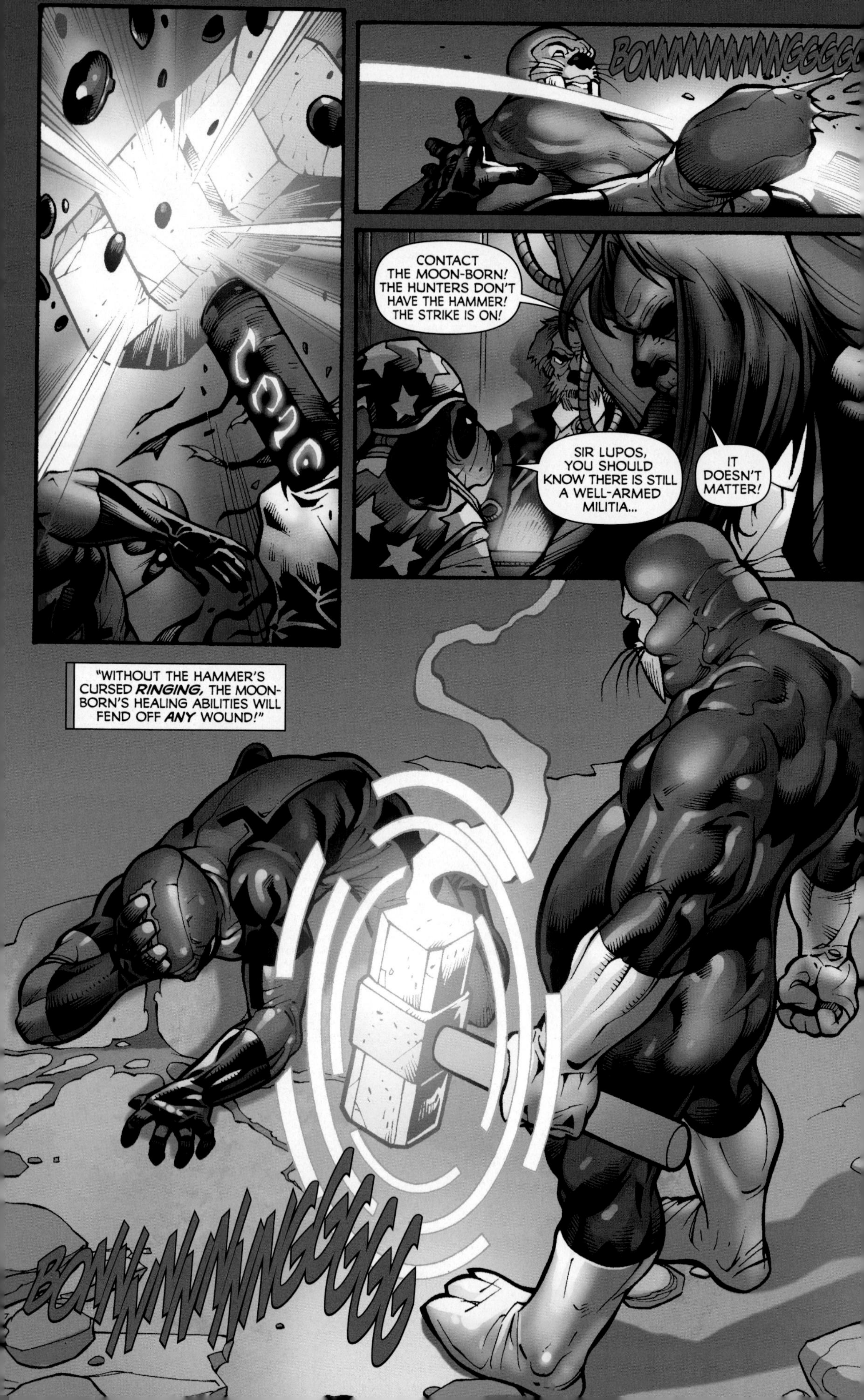
BONNNNNNNNGGGGG
CONTACT THE MOON-BORN! THE HUNTERS DON'T HAVE THE HAMMER! THE STRIKE IS ON!
SIR LUPOS, YOU SHOULD KNOW THERE IS STILL A WELL-ARMED MILITIA...
IT DOESN'T MATTER!
"WITHOUT THE HAMMER'S CURSED *RINGING,* THE MOON-BORN'S HEALING ABILITIES WILL FEND OFF *ANY* WOUND!"
BONNNNNNNGGGGG

FEAR ITSELF: DEADPOOL #3

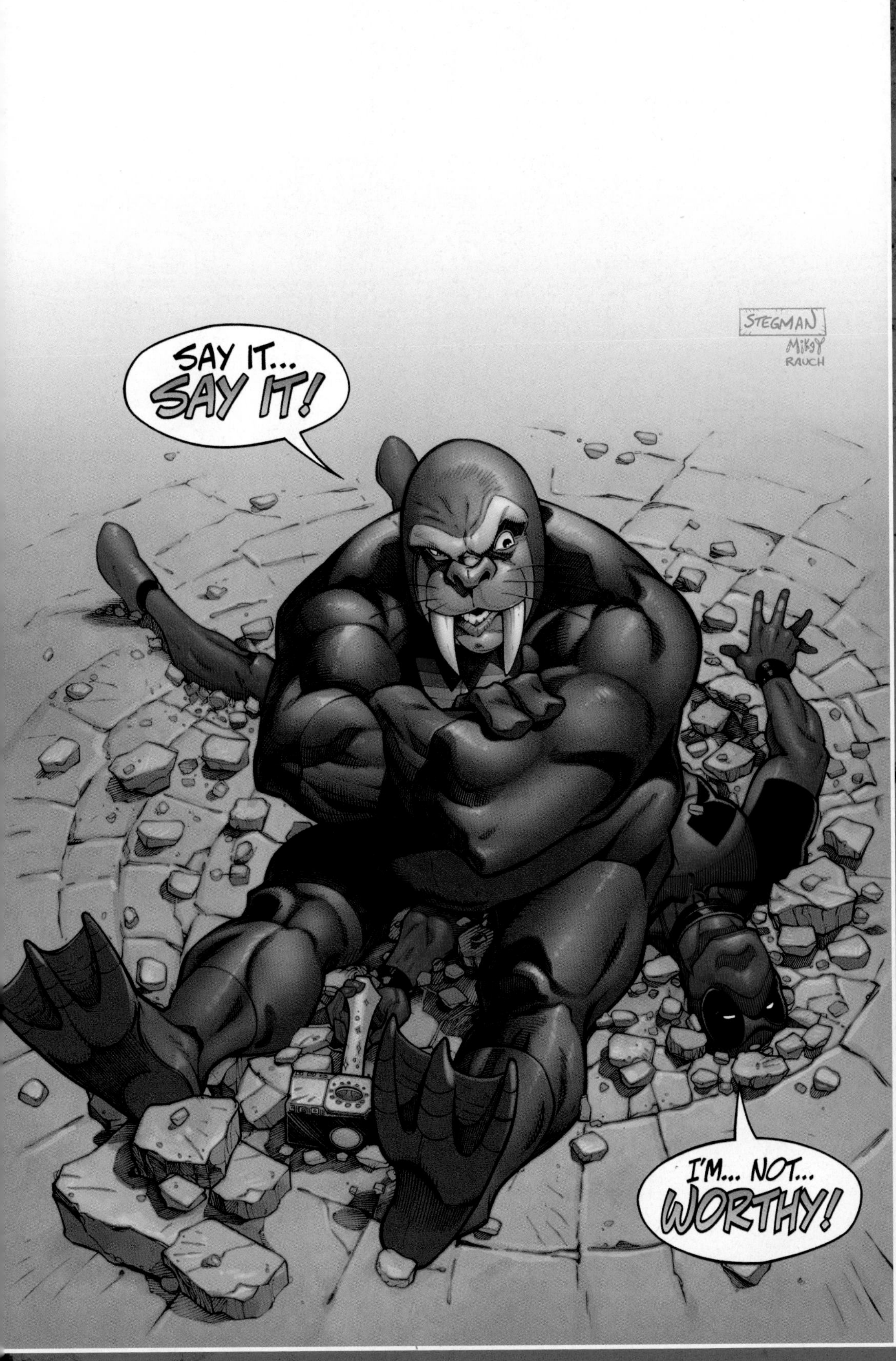
STEGMAN
Mikey
RAUCH
SAY IT... SAY IT!
I'M... NOT... WORTHY!

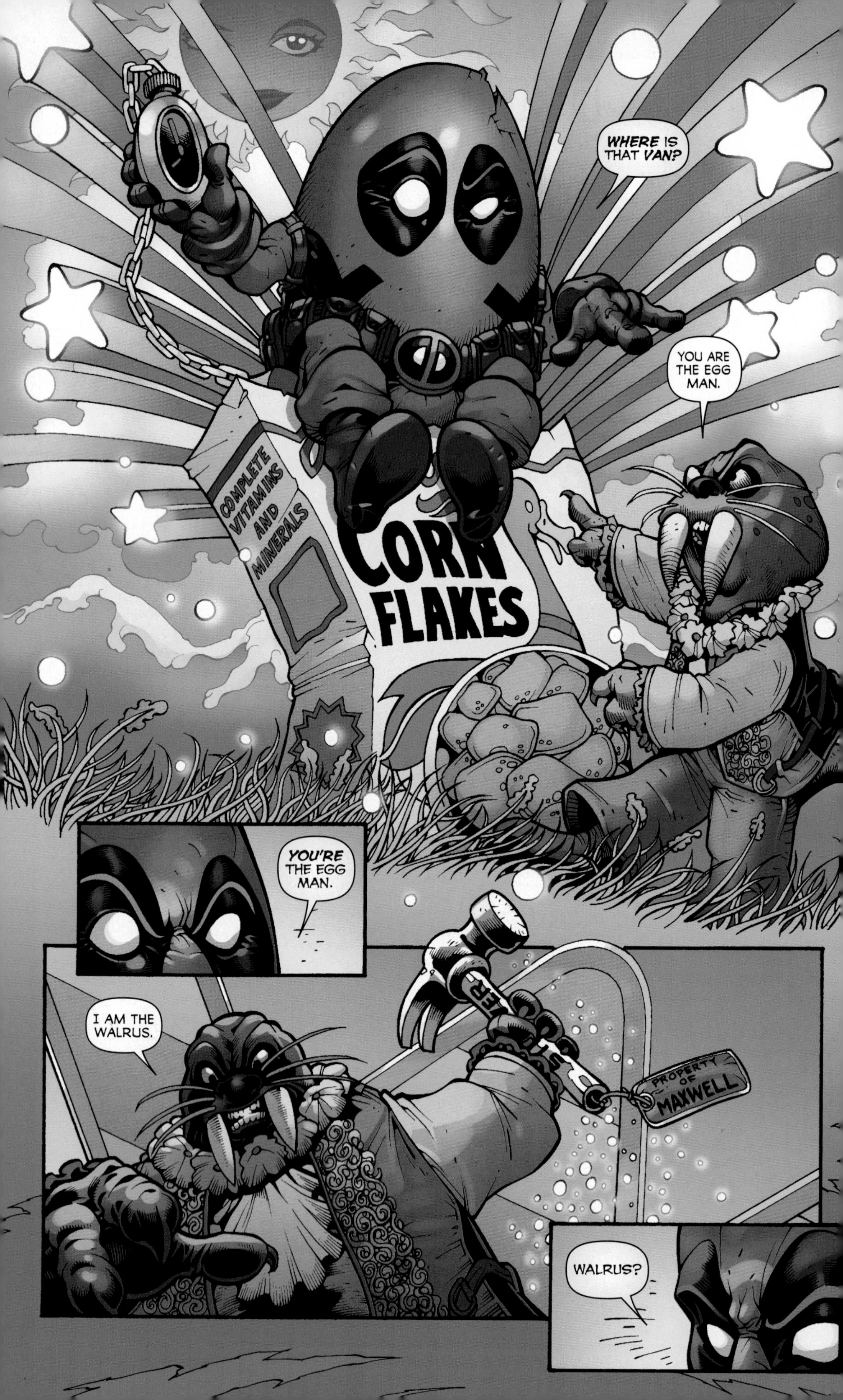

WHERE IS THAT VAN?
YOU ARE THE EGG MAN.
COMPLETE VITAMINS AND MINERALS
CORN FLAKES
YOU'RE THE EGG MAN.
I AM THE WALRUS.
PROPERTY OF MAXWELL
WALRUS?

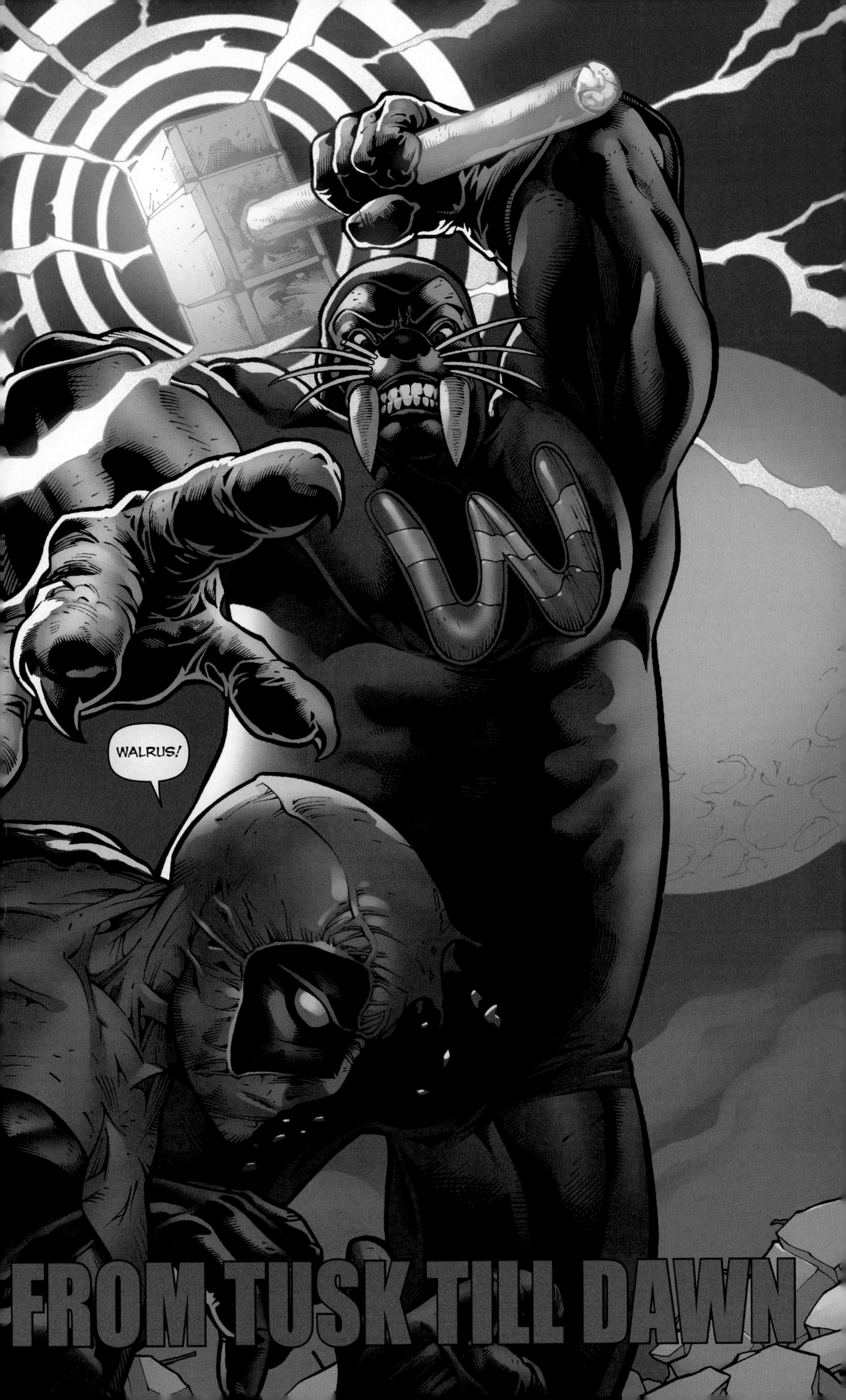
WALRUS!
FROM TUSK TILL DAWN

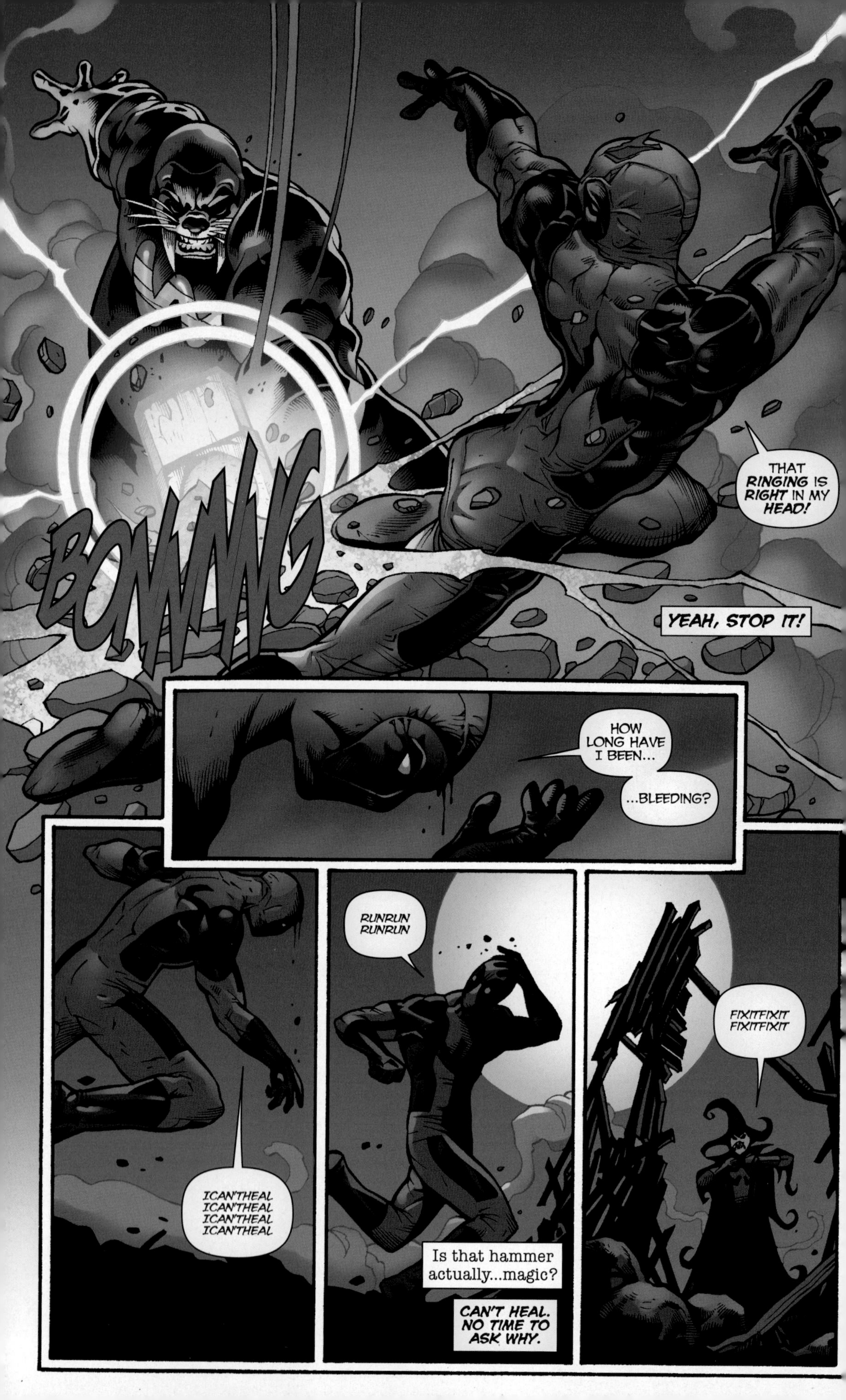
BONNNG
THAT RINGING IS RIGHT IN MY HEAD!
YEAH, STOP IT!
HOW LONG HAVE I BEEN...
...BLEEDING?
ICAN'THEAL ICAN'THEAL ICAN'THEAL ICAN'THEAL
RUNRUN RUNRUN
Is that hammer actually...magic?
CAN'T HEAL. NO TIME TO ASK WHY.
FIXITFIXIT FIXITFIXIT

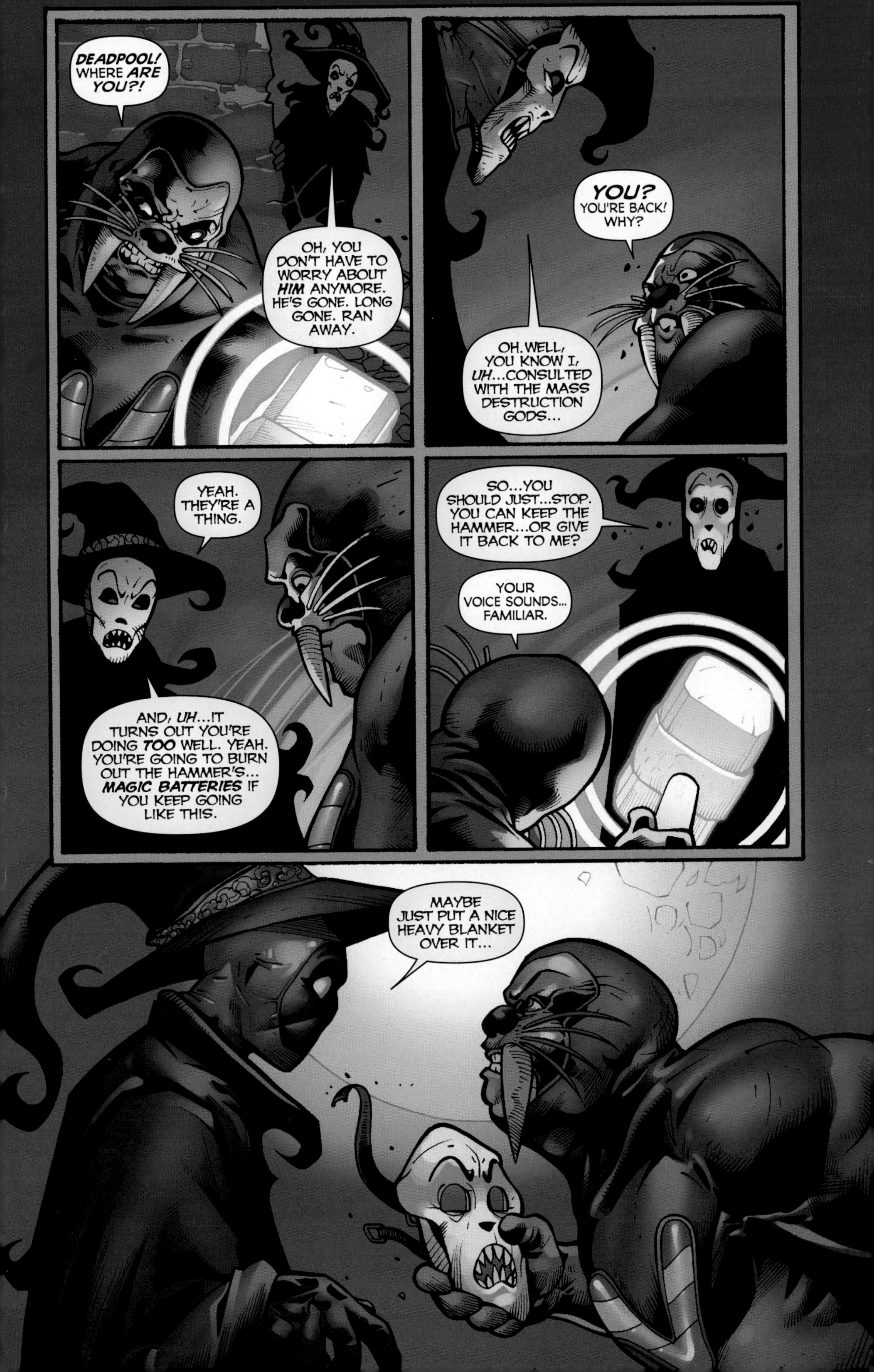
DEADPOOL! WHERE ARE YOU?!
OH, YOU DON'T HAVE TO WORRY ABOUT HIM ANYMORE. HE'S GONE. LONG GONE. RAN AWAY.
YOU? YOU'RE BACK! WHY?
OH. WELL, YOU KNOW I, UH...CONSULTED WITH THE MASS DESTRUCTION GODS...
YEAH. THEY'RE A THING.
AND, UH...IT TURNS OUT YOU'RE DOING TOO WELL. YEAH. YOU'RE GOING TO BURN OUT THE HAMMER'S... MAGIC BATTERIES IF YOU KEEP GOING LIKE THIS.
SO...YOU SHOULD JUST...STOP. YOU CAN KEEP THE HAMMER...OR GIVE IT BACK TO ME?
YOUR VOICE SOUNDS... FAMILIAR.
MAYBE JUST PUT A NICE HEAVY BLANKET OVER IT...

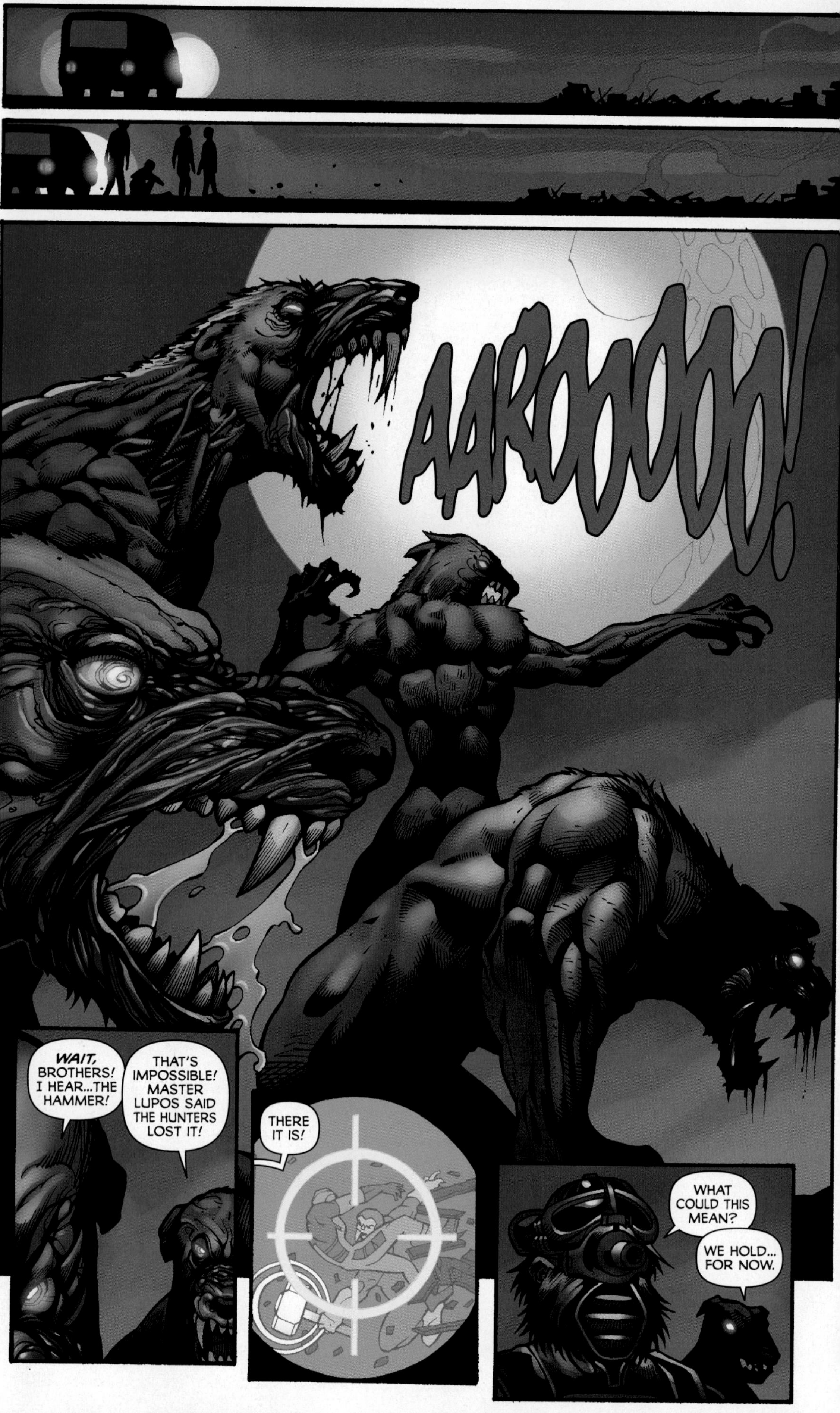
AAROOOOO!
WAIT, BROTHERS! I HEAR...THE HAMMER!
THAT'S IMPOSSIBLE! MASTER LUPOS SAID THE HUNTERS LOST IT!
THERE IT IS!
WHAT COULD THIS MEAN?
WE HOLD... FOR NOW.

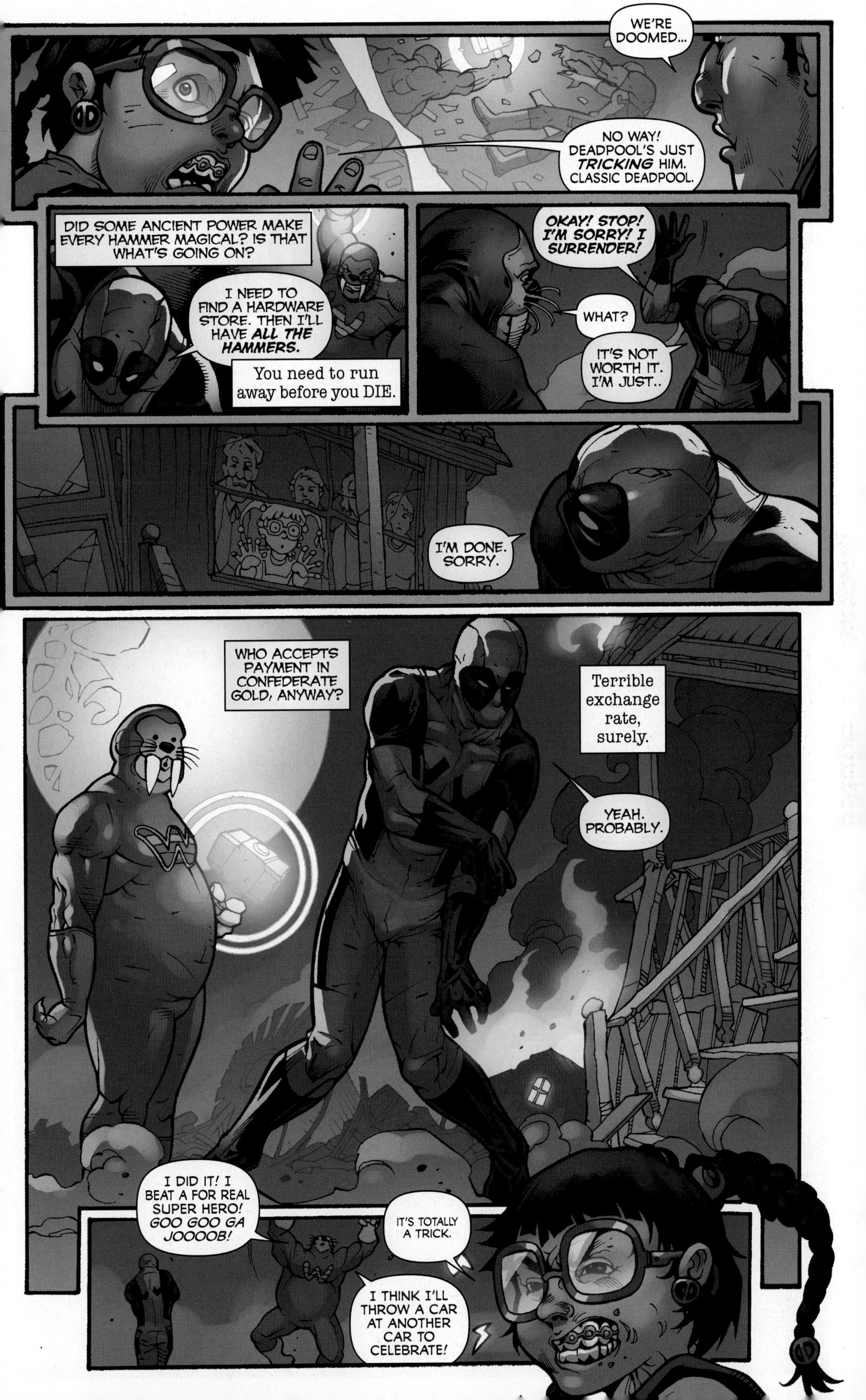
WE'RE DOOMED...
NO WAY! DEADPOOL'S JUST TRICKING HIM. CLASSIC DEADPOOL.
DID SOME ANCIENT POWER MAKE EVERY HAMMER MAGICAL? IS THAT WHAT'S GOING ON?
I NEED TO FIND A HARDWARE STORE. THEN I'LL HAVE ALL THE HAMMERS.
You need to run away before you DIE.
OKAY! STOP! I'M SORRY! I SURRENDER!
WHAT?
IT'S NOT WORTH IT. I'M JUST..
I'M DONE. SORRY.
WHO ACCEPTS PAYMENT IN CONFEDERATE GOLD, ANYWAY?
Terrible exchange rate, surely.
YEAH. PROBABLY.
I DID IT! I BEAT A FOR REAL SUPER HERO! GOO GOO GA JOOOOB!
IT'S TOTALLY A TRICK.
I THINK I'LL THROW A CAR AT ANOTHER CAR TO CELEBRATE!

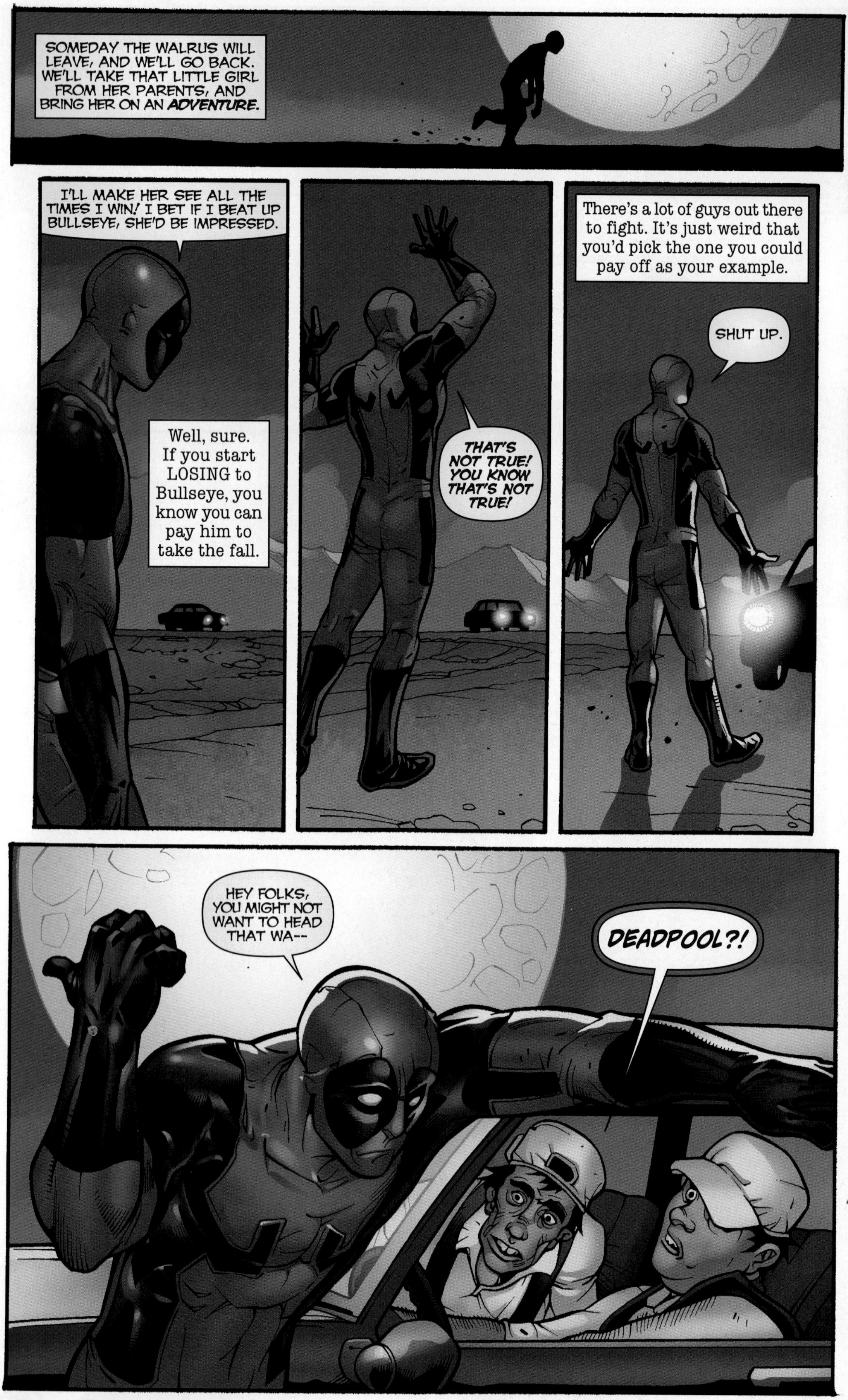
SOMEDAY THE WALRUS WILL LEAVE, AND WE'LL GO BACK. WE'LL TAKE THAT LITTLE GIRL FROM HER PARENTS, AND BRING HER ON AN *ADVENTURE*.
I'LL MAKE HER SEE ALL THE TIMES I WIN! I BET IF I BEAT UP BULLSEYE, SHE'D BE IMPRESSED.
Well, sure. If you start LOSING to Bullseye, you know you can pay him to take the fall.
THAT'S NOT TRUE! YOU KNOW THAT'S NOT TRUE!
There's a lot of guys out there to fight. It's just weird that you'd pick the one you could pay off as your example.
SHUT UP.
HEY FOLKS, YOU MIGHT NOT WANT TO HEAD THAT WA--
DEADPOOL?!

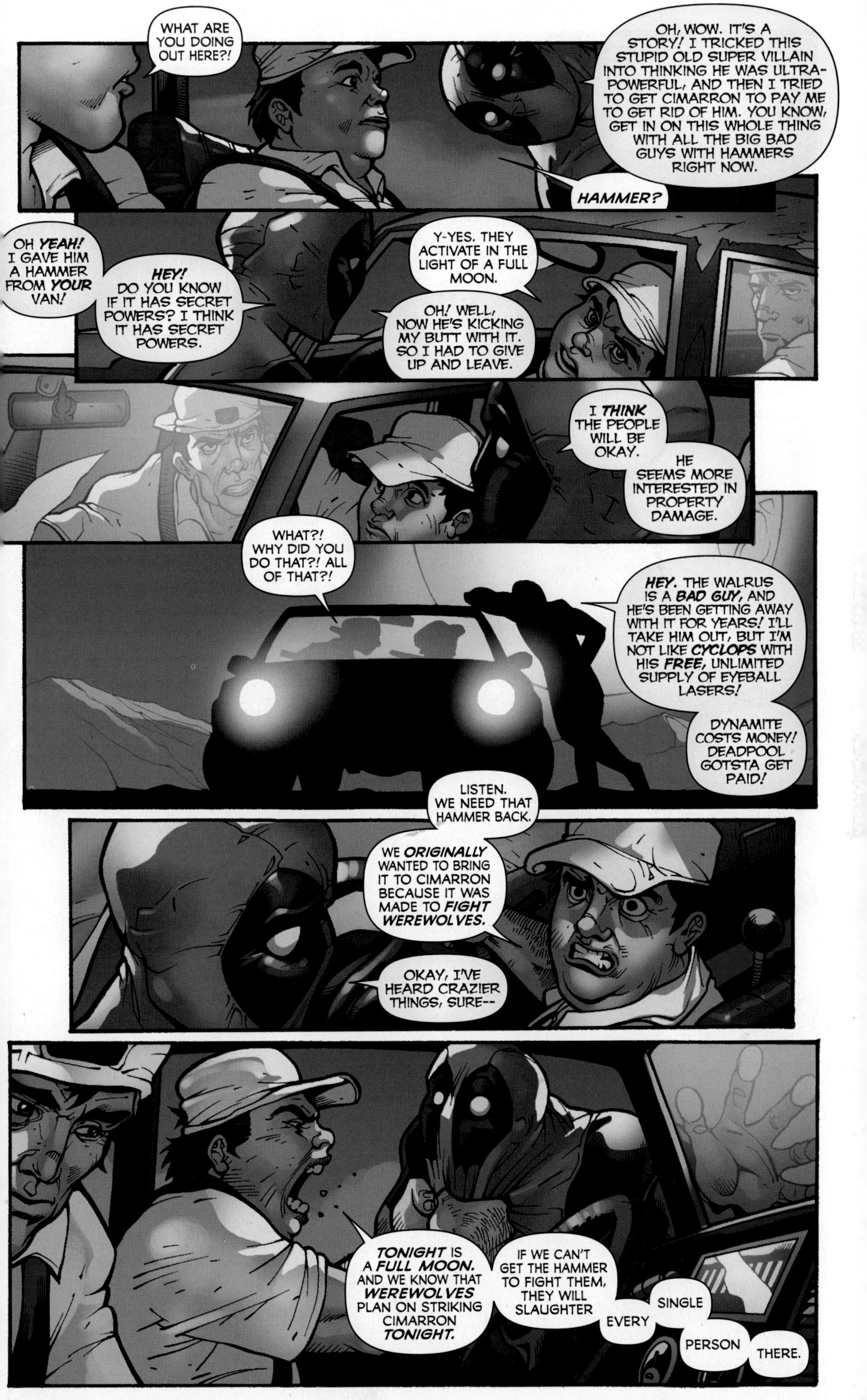
WHAT ARE YOU DOING OUT HERE?!
OH, WOW. IT'S A STORY! I TRICKED THIS STUPID OLD SUPER VILLAIN INTO THINKING HE WAS ULTRA-POWERFUL, AND THEN I TRIED TO GET CIMARRON TO PAY ME TO GET RID OF HIM. YOU KNOW, GET IN ON THIS WHOLE THING WITH ALL THE BIG BAD GUYS WITH HAMMERS RIGHT NOW.
HAMMER?
OH YEAH! I GAVE HIM A HAMMER FROM YOUR VAN!
HEY! DO YOU KNOW IF IT HAS SECRET POWERS? I THINK IT HAS SECRET POWERS.
Y-YES. THEY ACTIVATE IN THE LIGHT OF A FULL MOON.
OH! WELL, NOW HE'S KICKING MY BUTT WITH IT. SO I HAD TO GIVE UP AND LEAVE.
I THINK THE PEOPLE WILL BE OKAY.
HE SEEMS MORE INTERESTED IN PROPERTY DAMAGE.
WHAT?! WHY DID YOU DO THAT?! ALL OF THAT?!
HEY. THE WALRUS IS A BAD GUY, AND HE'S BEEN GETTING AWAY WITH IT FOR YEARS! I'LL TAKE HIM OUT, BUT I'M NOT LIKE CYCLOPS WITH HIS FREE, UNLIMITED SUPPLY OF EYEBALL LASERS!
DYNAMITE COSTS MONEY! DEADPOOL GOTSTA GET PAID!
LISTEN. WE NEED THAT HAMMER BACK.
WE ORIGINALLY WANTED TO BRING IT TO CIMARRON BECAUSE IT WAS MADE TO FIGHT WEREWOLVES.
OKAY, I'VE HEARD CRAZIER THINGS, SURE--
TONIGHT IS A FULL MOON. AND WE KNOW THAT WEREWOLVES PLAN ON STRIKING CIMARRON TONIGHT.
IF WE CAN'T GET THE HAMMER TO FIGHT THEM, THEY WILL SLAUGHTER
EVERY
SINGLE
PERSON
THERE.

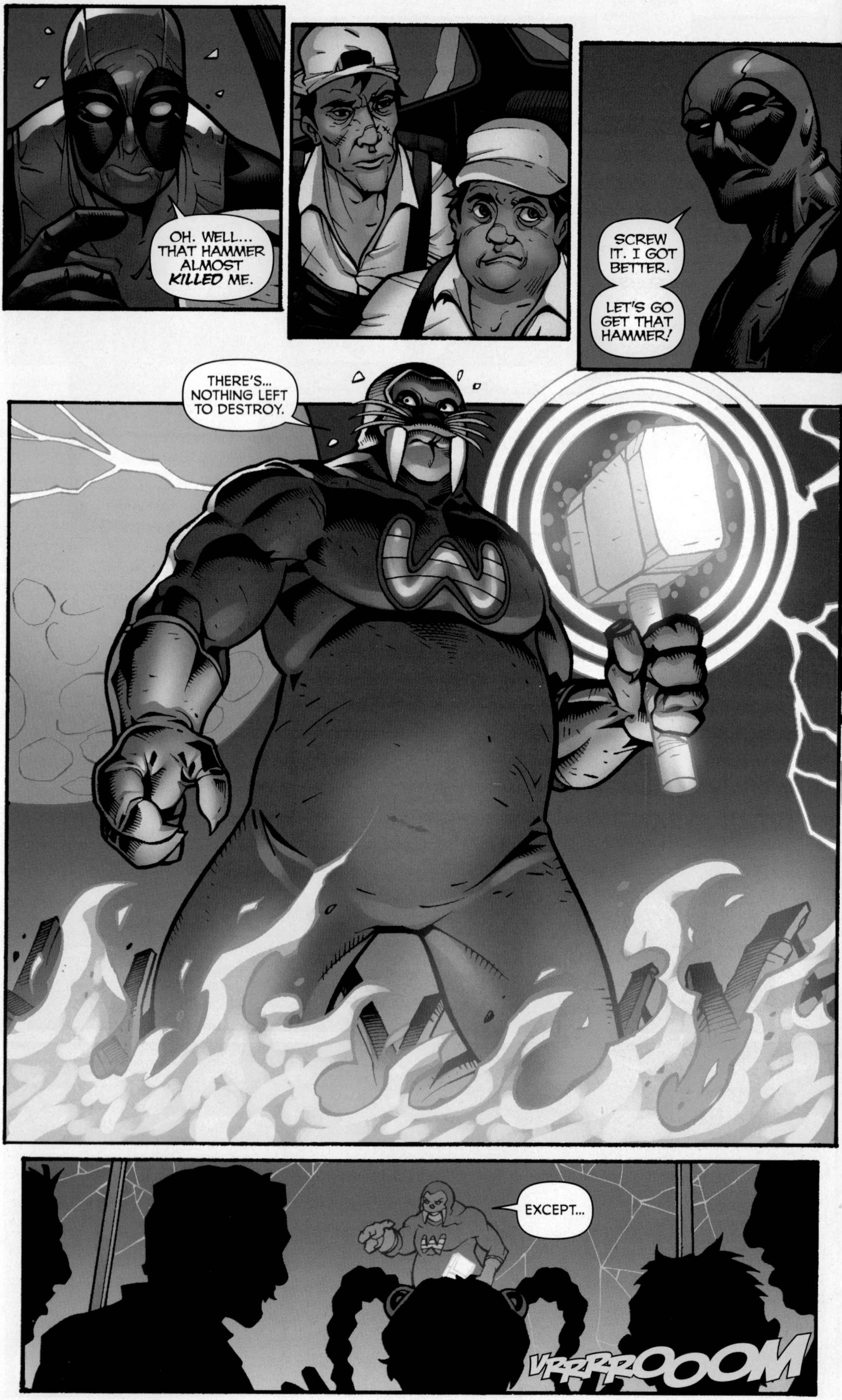
OH. WELL... THAT HAMMER ALMOST KILLED ME.
SCREW IT. I GOT BETTER.
LET'S GO GET THAT HAMMER!
THERE'S... NOTHING LEFT TO DESTROY.
EXCEPT...
VRRRROOOOM

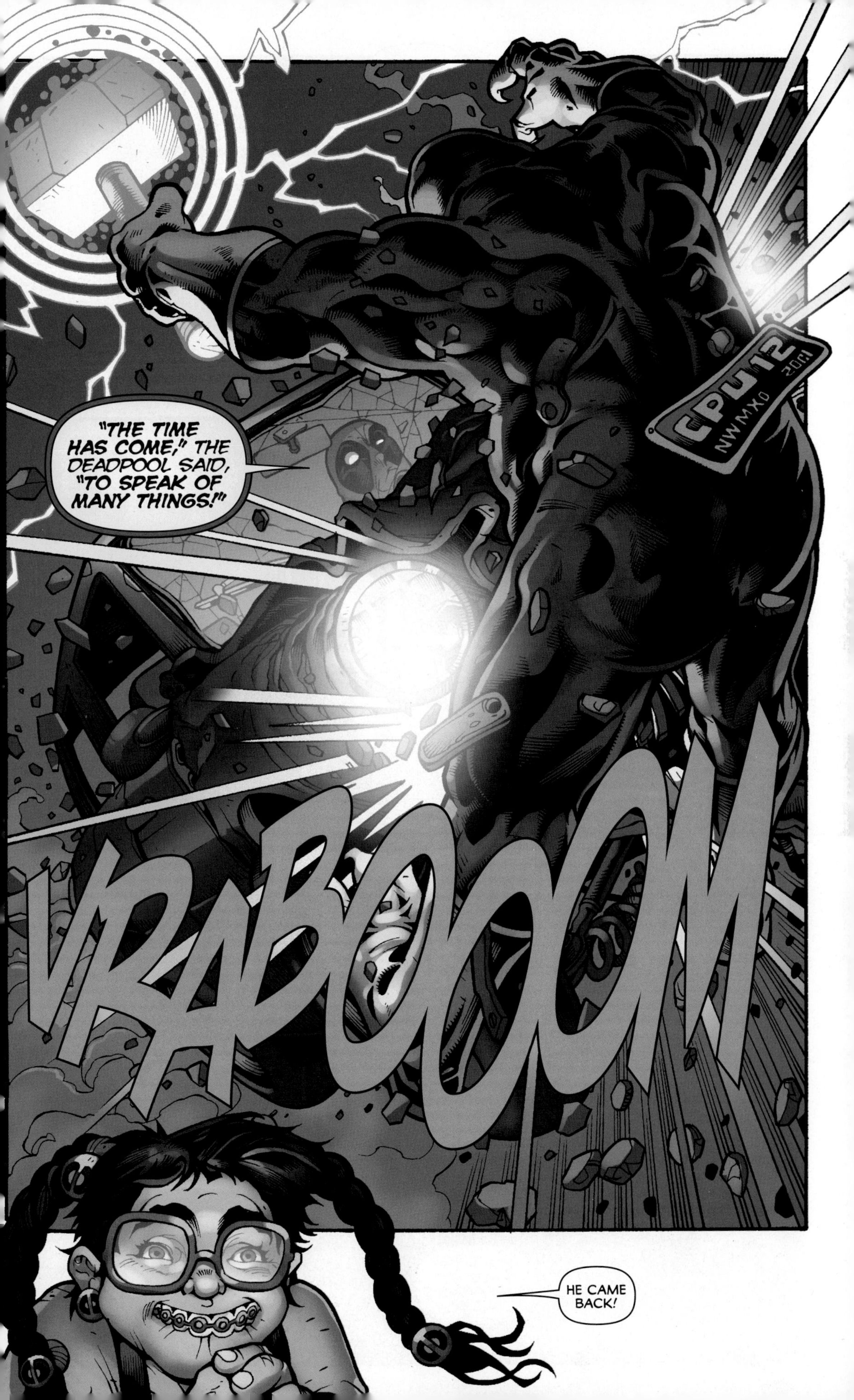
"THE TIME HAS COME," THE DEADPOOL SAID, "TO SPEAK OF MANY THINGS!"
CPU 12
NWMXO 2011
VRABOOOM
HE CAME BACK!

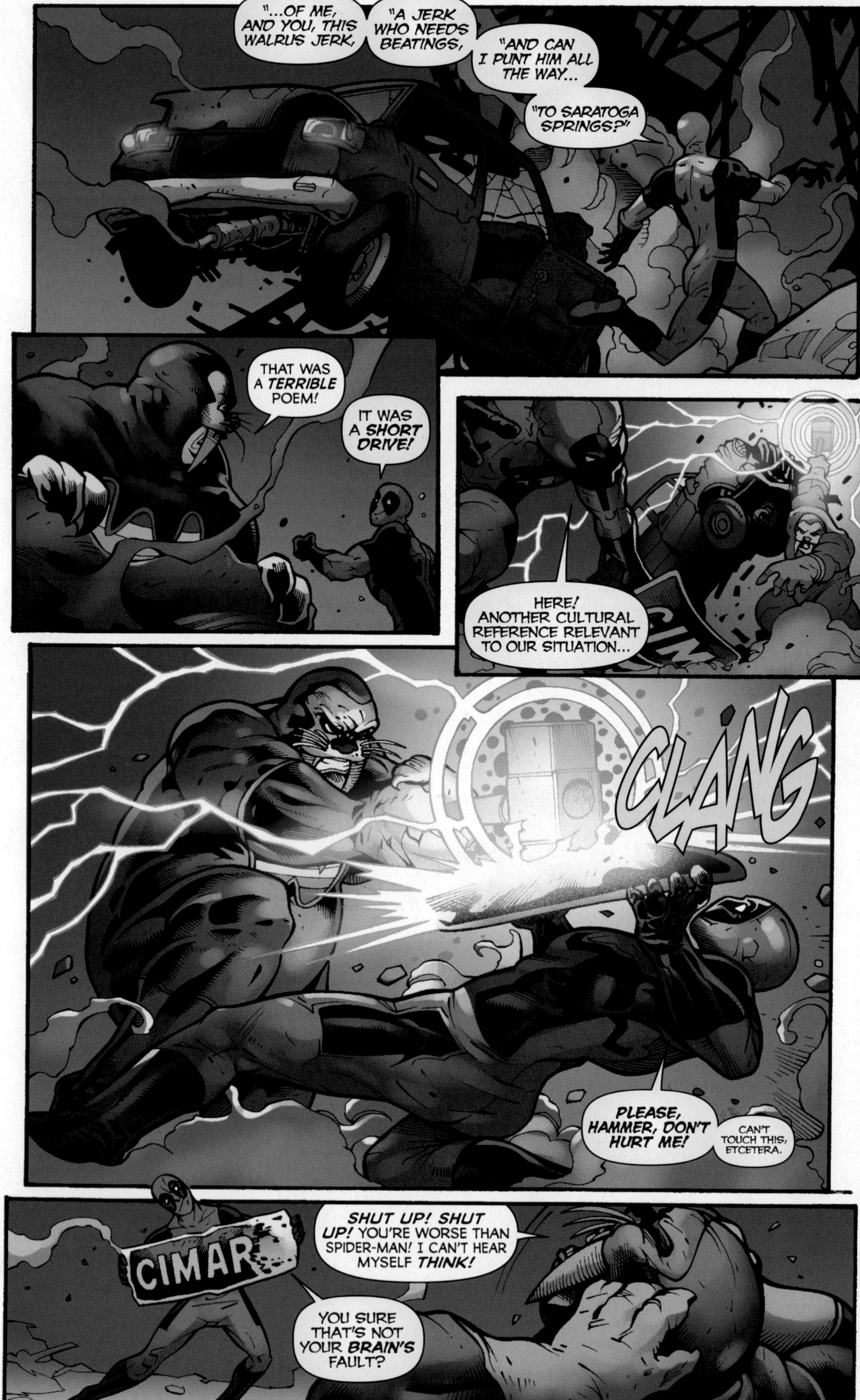
"...OF ME, AND YOU, THIS WALRUS JERK,
"A JERK WHO NEEDS BEATINGS,
"AND CAN I PUNT HIM ALL THE WAY...
"TO SARATOGA SPRINGS?"
THAT WAS A *TERRIBLE* POEM!
IT WAS A *SHORT DRIVE!*
HERE! ANOTHER CULTURAL REFERENCE RELEVANT TO OUR SITUATION...
CLANG
PLEASE, HAMMER, DON'T HURT ME!
CAN'T TOUCH THIS, ETCETERA.
SHUT UP! SHUT UP! YOU'RE WORSE THAN SPIDER-MAN! I CAN'T HEAR MYSELF *THINK!*
CIMAR
YOU SURE THAT'S NOT YOUR *BRAIN'S* FAULT?

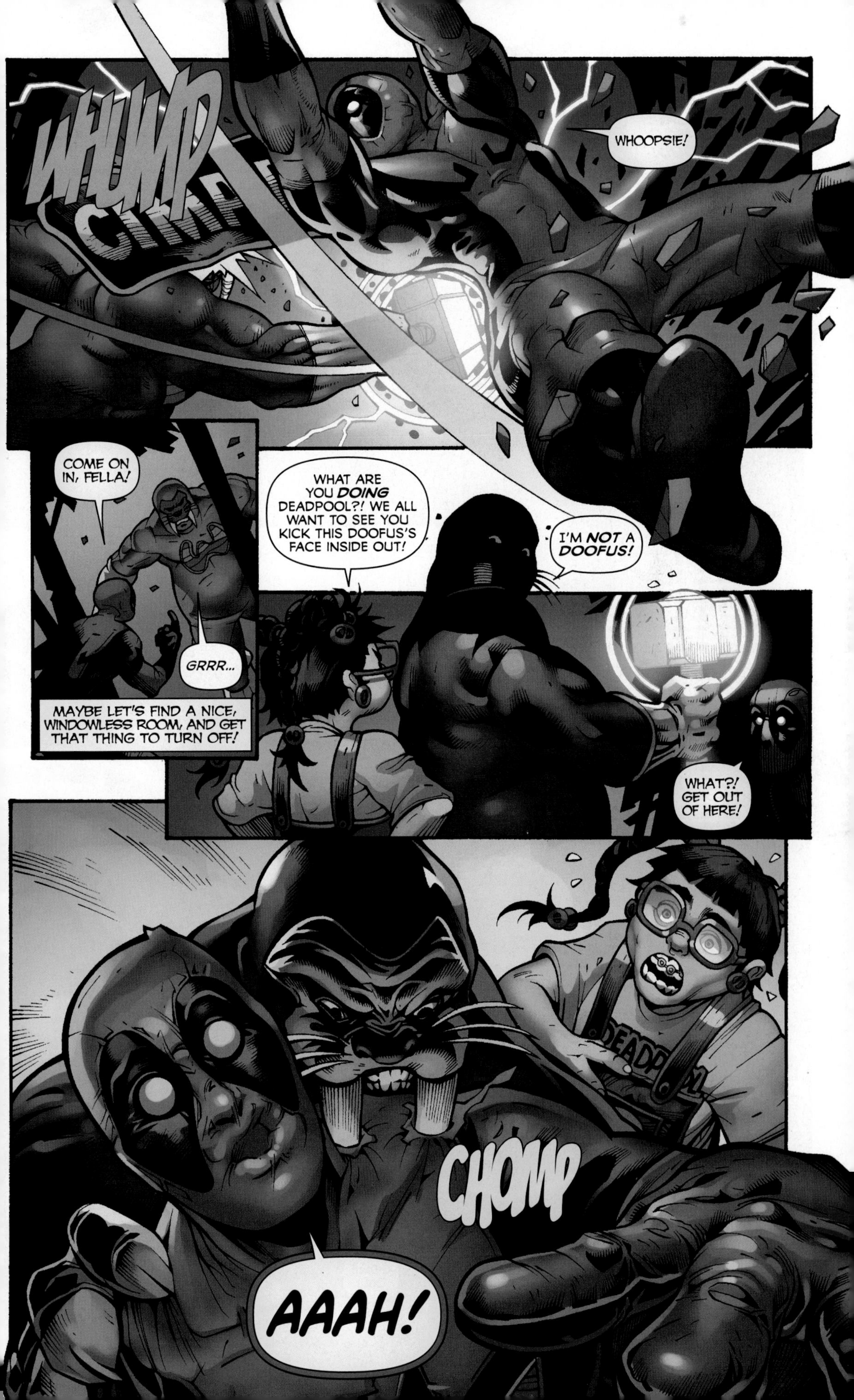
WHUMP
CLIMP
WHOOPSIE!
COME ON IN, FELLA!
GRRR...
MAYBE LET'S FIND A NICE, WINDOWLESS ROOM, AND GET THAT THING TO TURN OFF!
WHAT ARE YOU DOING DEADPOOL?! WE ALL WANT TO SEE YOU KICK THIS DOOFUS'S FACE INSIDE OUT!
I'M NOT A DOOFUS!
WHAT?! GET OUT OF HERE!
DEADPOOL
CHOMP
AAAH!

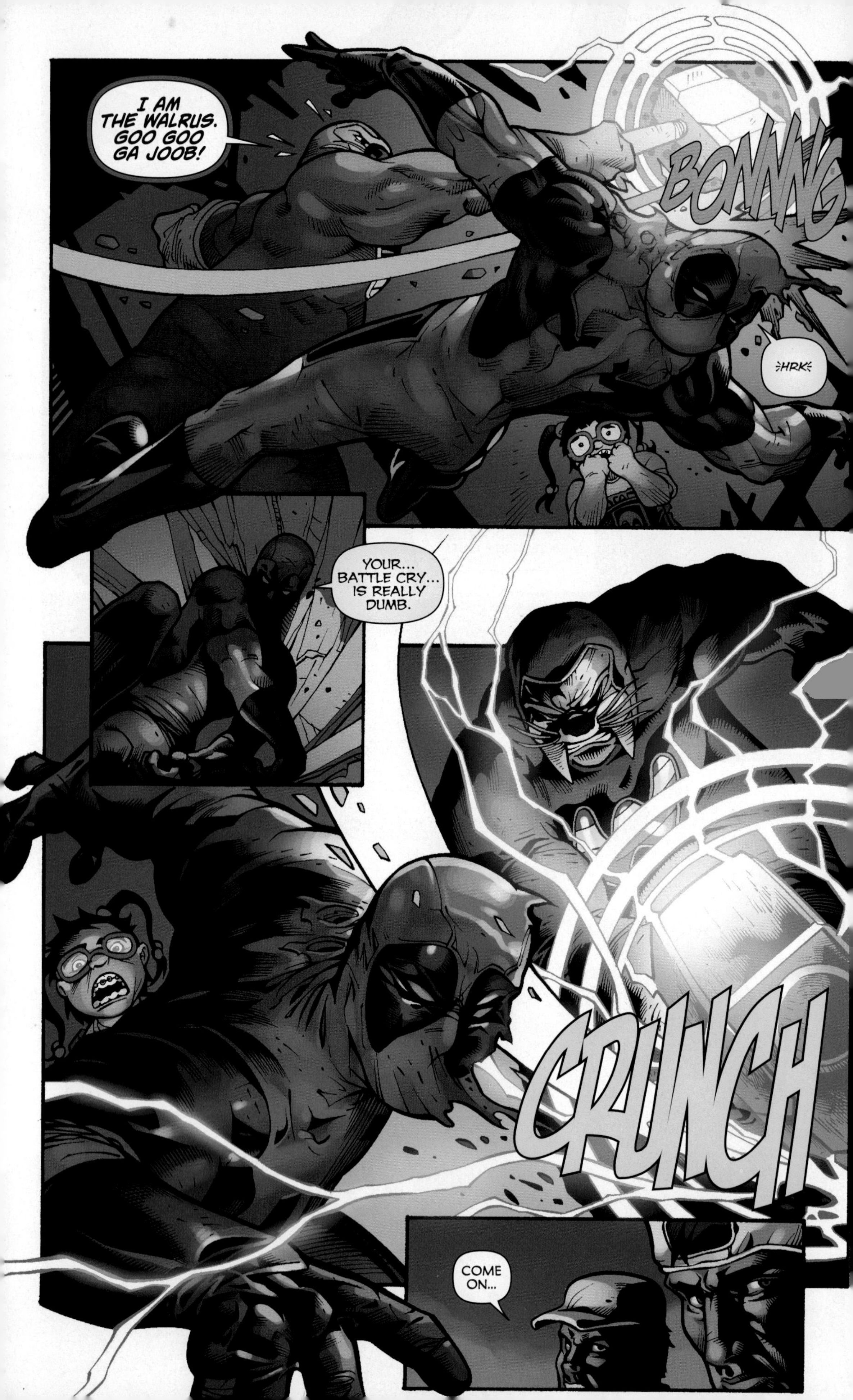
I AM THE WALRUS. GOO GOO GA JOOB!
BONNNG
HRK
YOUR... BATTLE CRY... IS REALLY DUMB.
CRUNCH
COME ON...

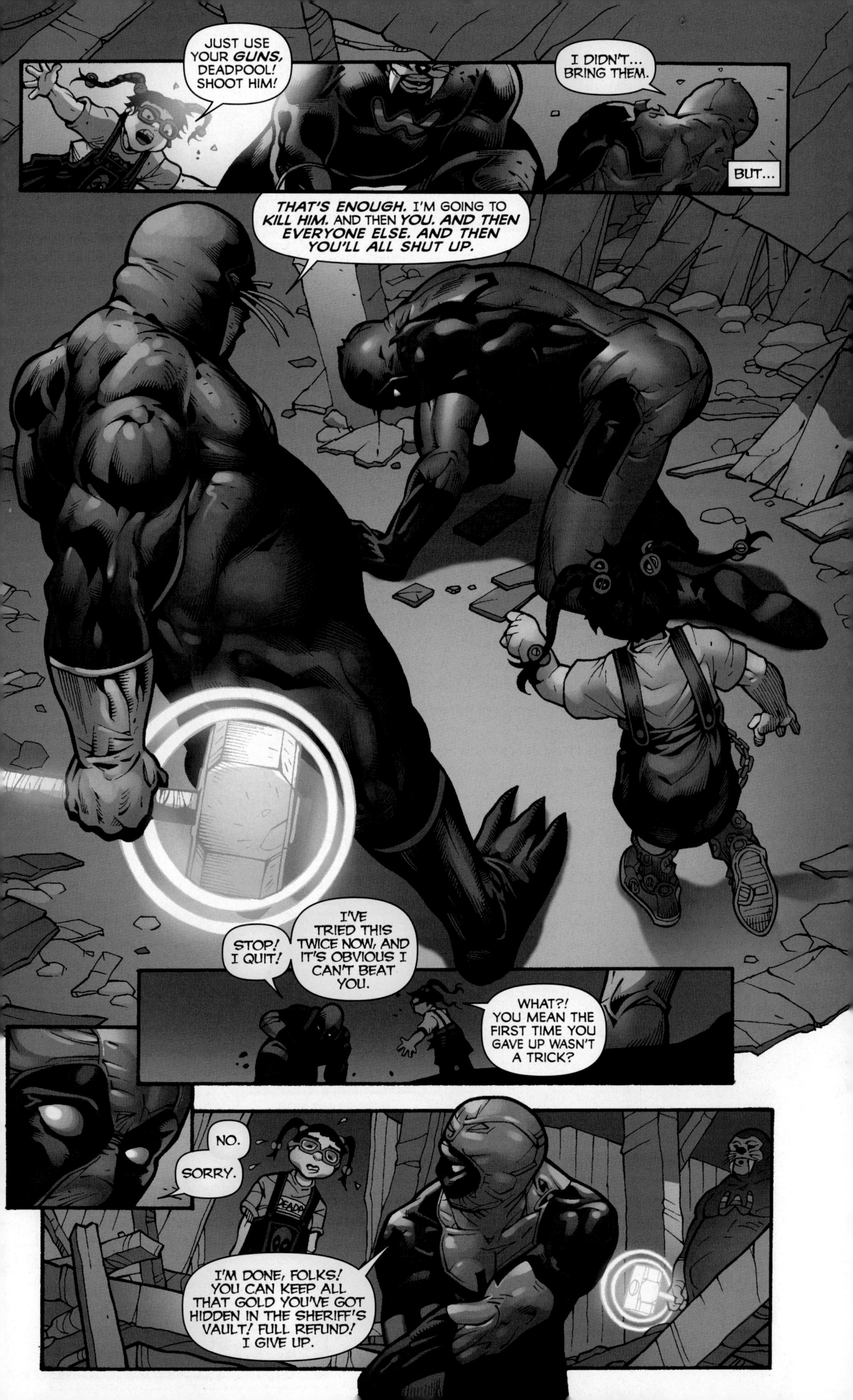
JUST USE YOUR *GUNS,* DEADPOOL! SHOOT HIM!
I DIDN'T... BRING THEM.
BUT...
THAT'S ENOUGH. I'M GOING TO *KILL HIM.* AND THEN *YOU. AND THEN EVERYONE ELSE. AND THEN YOU'LL ALL SHUT UP.*
STOP! I QUIT!
I'VE TRIED THIS TWICE NOW, AND IT'S OBVIOUS I CAN'T BEAT YOU.
WHAT?! YOU MEAN THE FIRST TIME YOU GAVE UP WASN'T A TRICK?
NO.
SORRY.
I'M DONE, FOLKS! YOU CAN KEEP ALL THAT GOLD YOU'VE GOT HIDDEN IN THE SHERIFF'S VAULT! FULL REFUND! I GIVE UP.

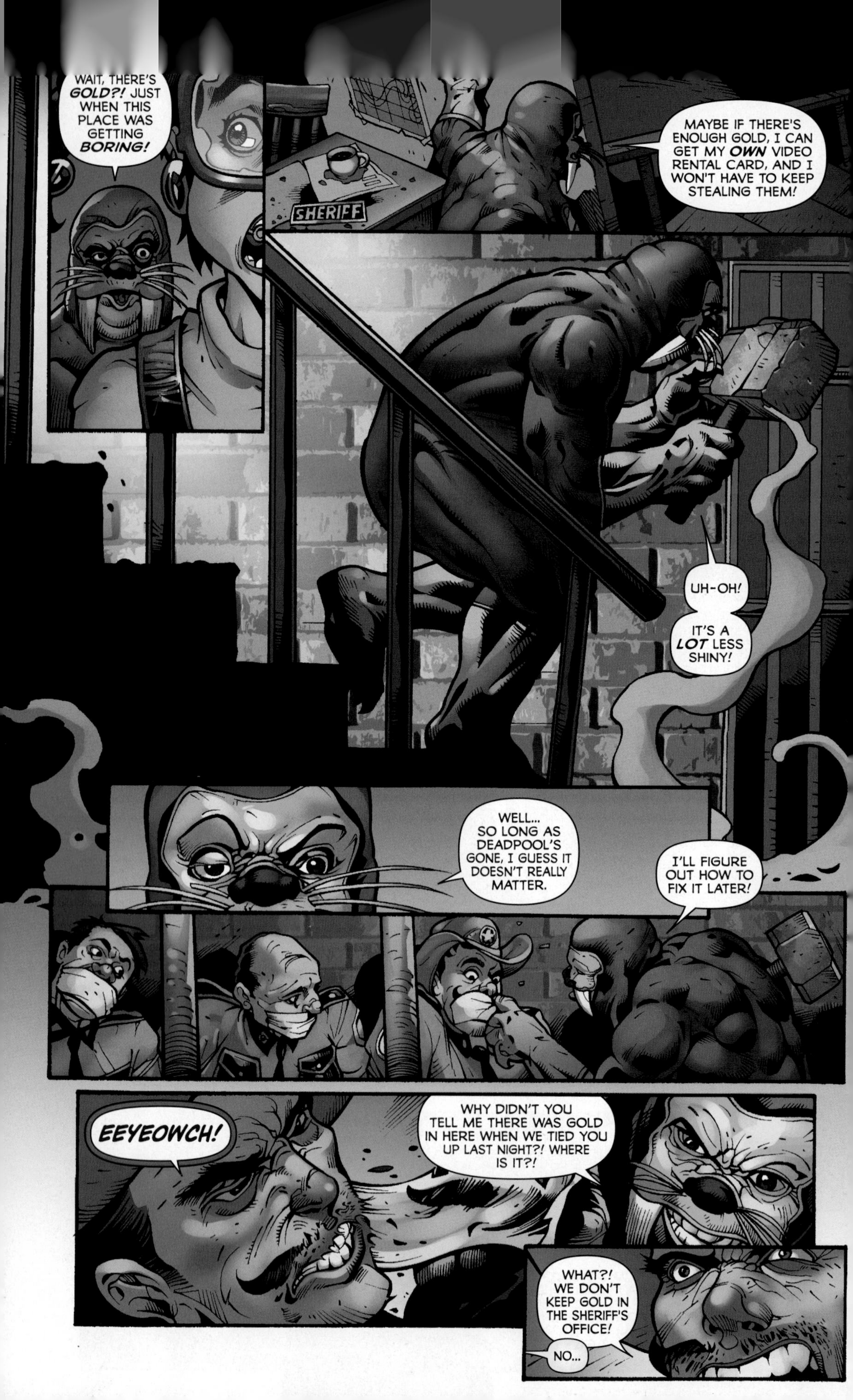
WAIT, THERE'S GOLD?! JUST WHEN THIS PLACE WAS GETTING BORING!
SHERIFF
MAYBE IF THERE'S ENOUGH GOLD, I CAN GET MY OWN VIDEO RENTAL CARD, AND I WON'T HAVE TO KEEP STEALING THEM!
UH-OH!
IT'S A LOT LESS SHINY!
WELL... SO LONG AS DEADPOOL'S GONE, I GUESS IT DOESN'T REALLY MATTER.
I'LL FIGURE OUT HOW TO FIX IT LATER!
EEYEOWCH!
WHY DIDN'T YOU TELL ME THERE WAS GOLD IN HERE WHEN WE TIED YOU UP LAST NIGHT?! WHERE IS IT?!
WHAT?! WE DON'T KEEP GOLD IN THE SHERIFF'S OFFICE!
NO...

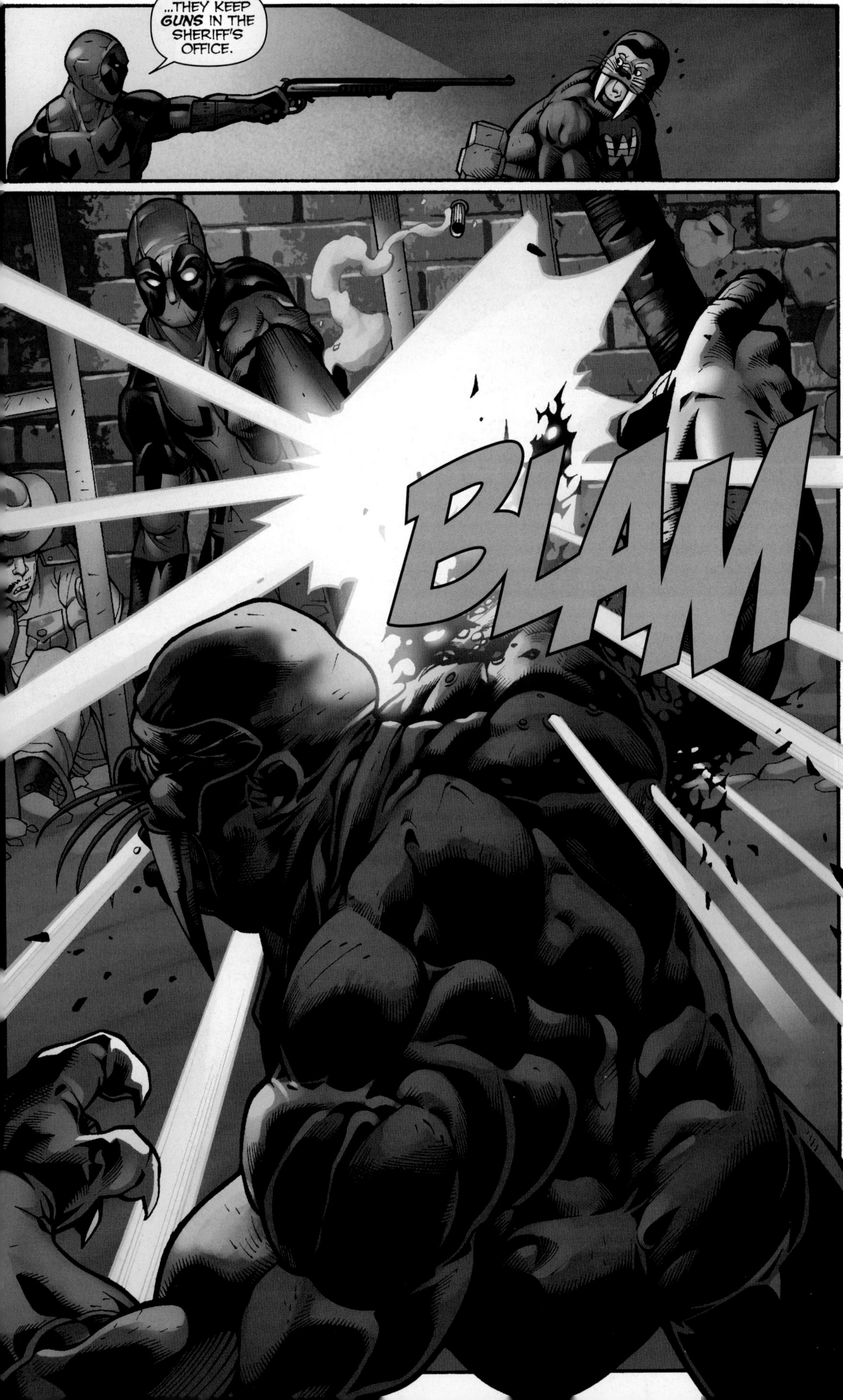
...THEY KEEP GUNS IN THE SHERIFF'S OFFICE.
BLAM

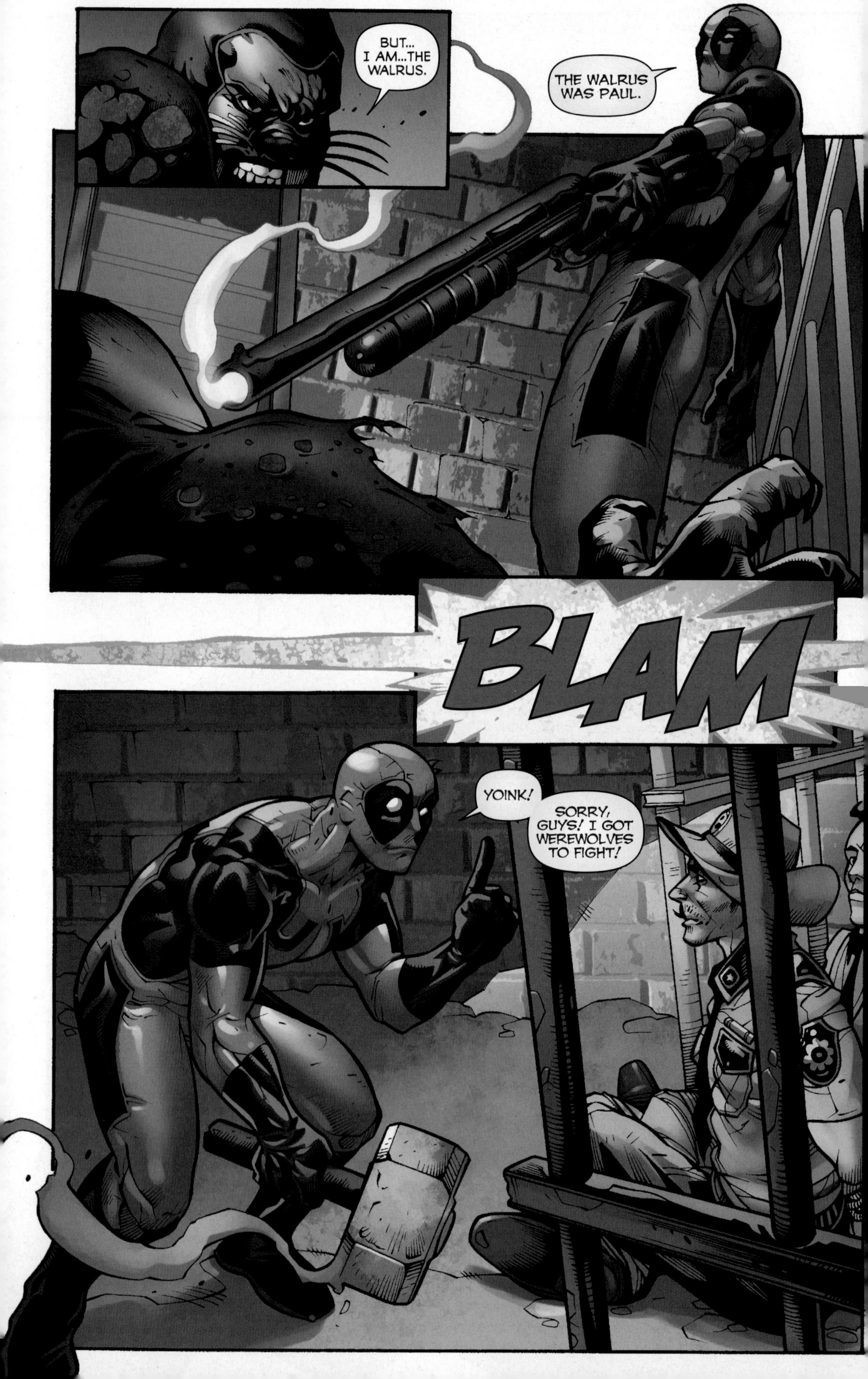
BUT... I AM...THE WALRUS.
THE WALRUS WAS PAUL.
BLAM
YOINK!
SORRY, GUYS! I GOT WEREWOLVES TO FIGHT!

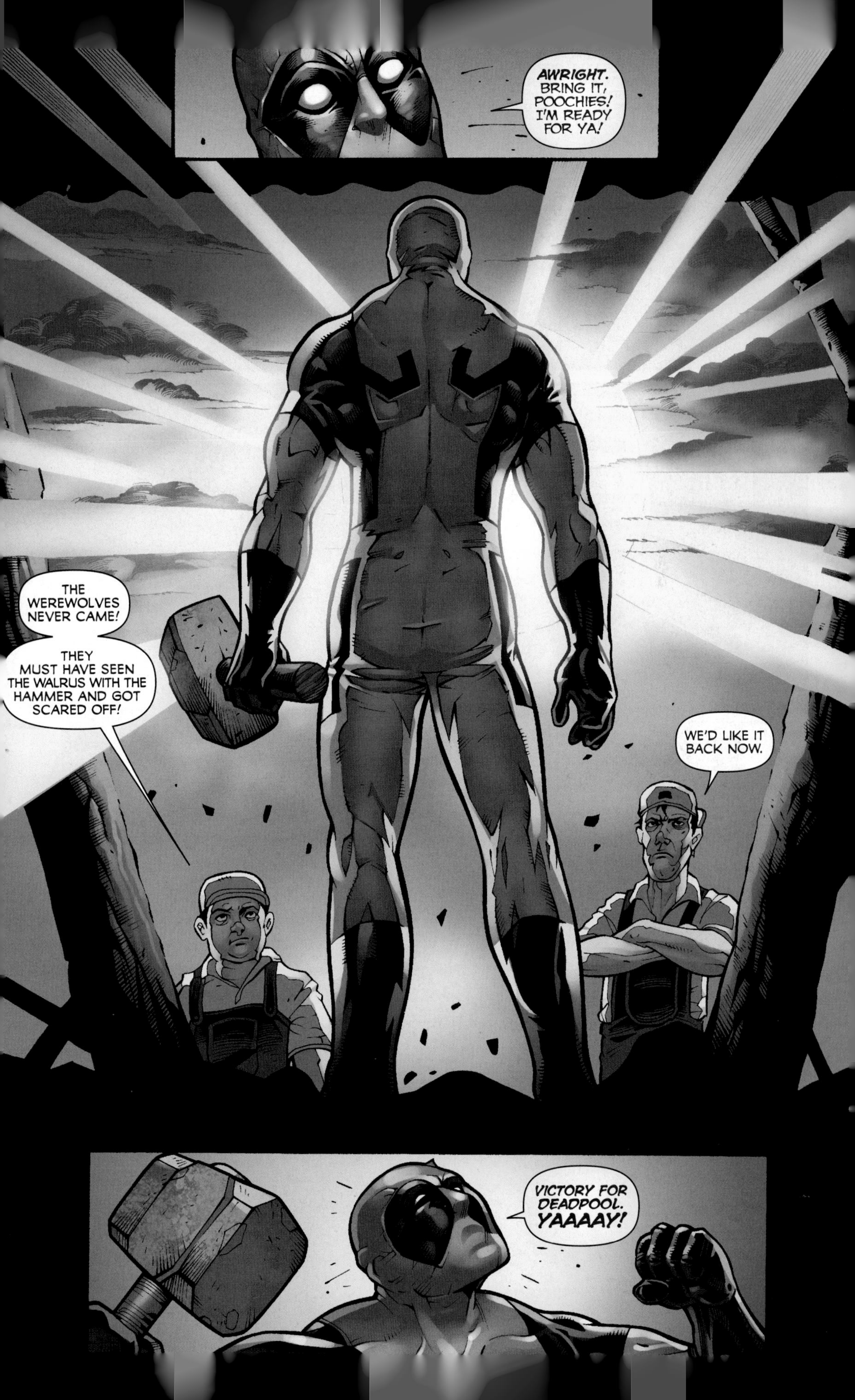
AWRIGHT. BRING IT, POOCHIES! I'M READY FOR YA!
THE WEREWOLVES NEVER CAME!
THEY MUST HAVE SEEN THE WALRUS WITH THE HAMMER AND GOT SCARED OFF!
WE'D LIKE IT BACK NOW.
VICTORY FOR DEADPOOL. YAAAAY!

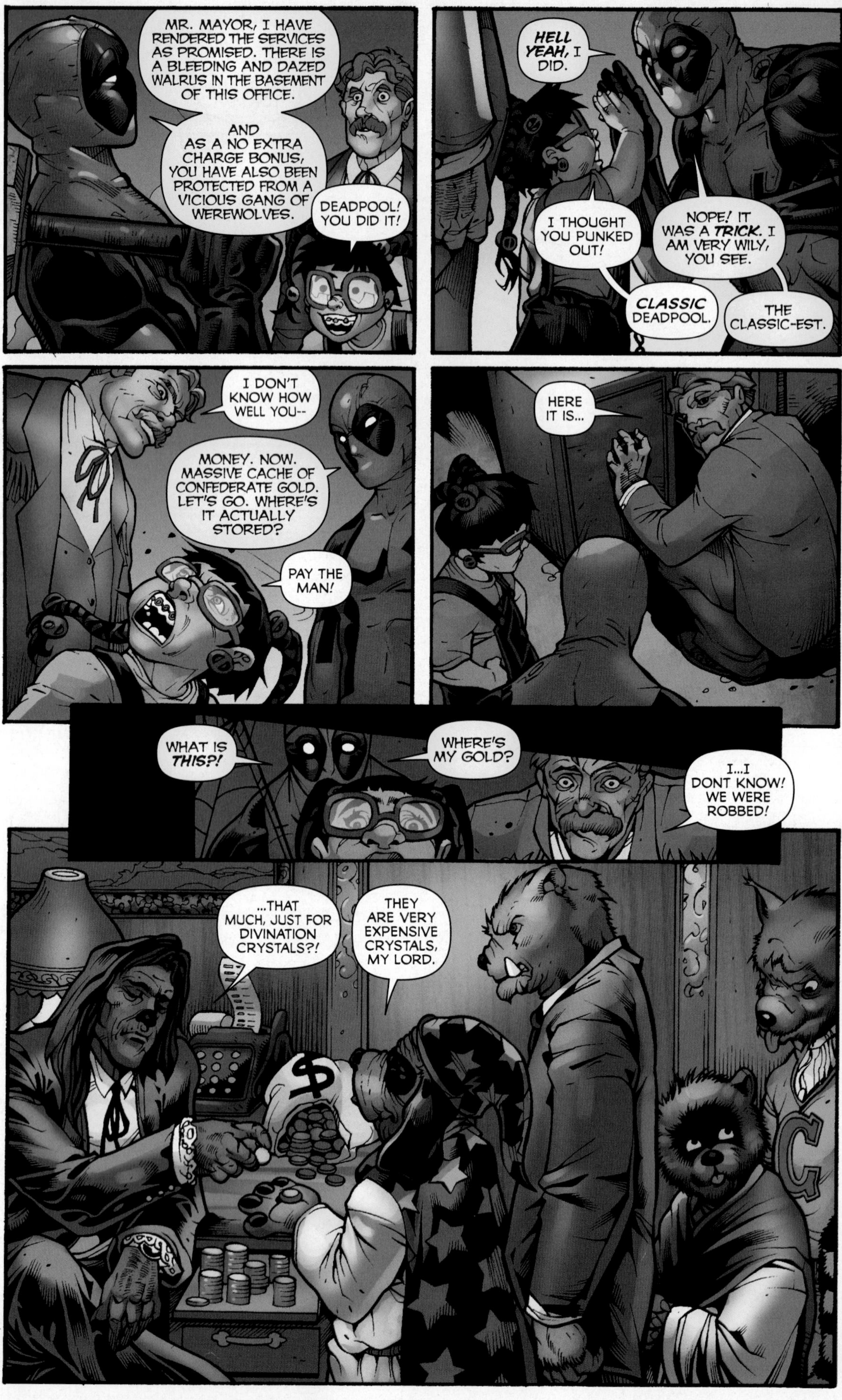
MR. MAYOR, I HAVE RENDERED THE SERVICES AS PROMISED. THERE IS A BLEEDING AND DAZED WALRUS IN THE BASEMENT OF THIS OFFICE.
AND AS A NO EXTRA CHARGE BONUS, YOU HAVE ALSO BEEN PROTECTED FROM A VICIOUS GANG OF WEREWOLVES.
DEADPOOL! YOU DID IT!
HELL YEAH, I DID.
I THOUGHT YOU PUNKED OUT!
NOPE! IT WAS A TRICK. I AM VERY WILY, YOU SEE.
CLASSIC DEADPOOL.
THE CLASSIC-EST.
I DON'T KNOW HOW WELL YOU--
MONEY. NOW. MASSIVE CACHE OF CONFEDERATE GOLD. LET'S GO. WHERE'S IT ACTUALLY STORED?
PAY THE MAN!
HERE IT IS...
WHAT IS THIS?!
WHERE'S MY GOLD?
I...I DONT KNOW! WE WERE ROBBED!
...THAT MUCH, JUST FOR DIVINATION CRYSTALS?!
THEY ARE VERY EXPENSIVE CRYSTALS, MY LORD.

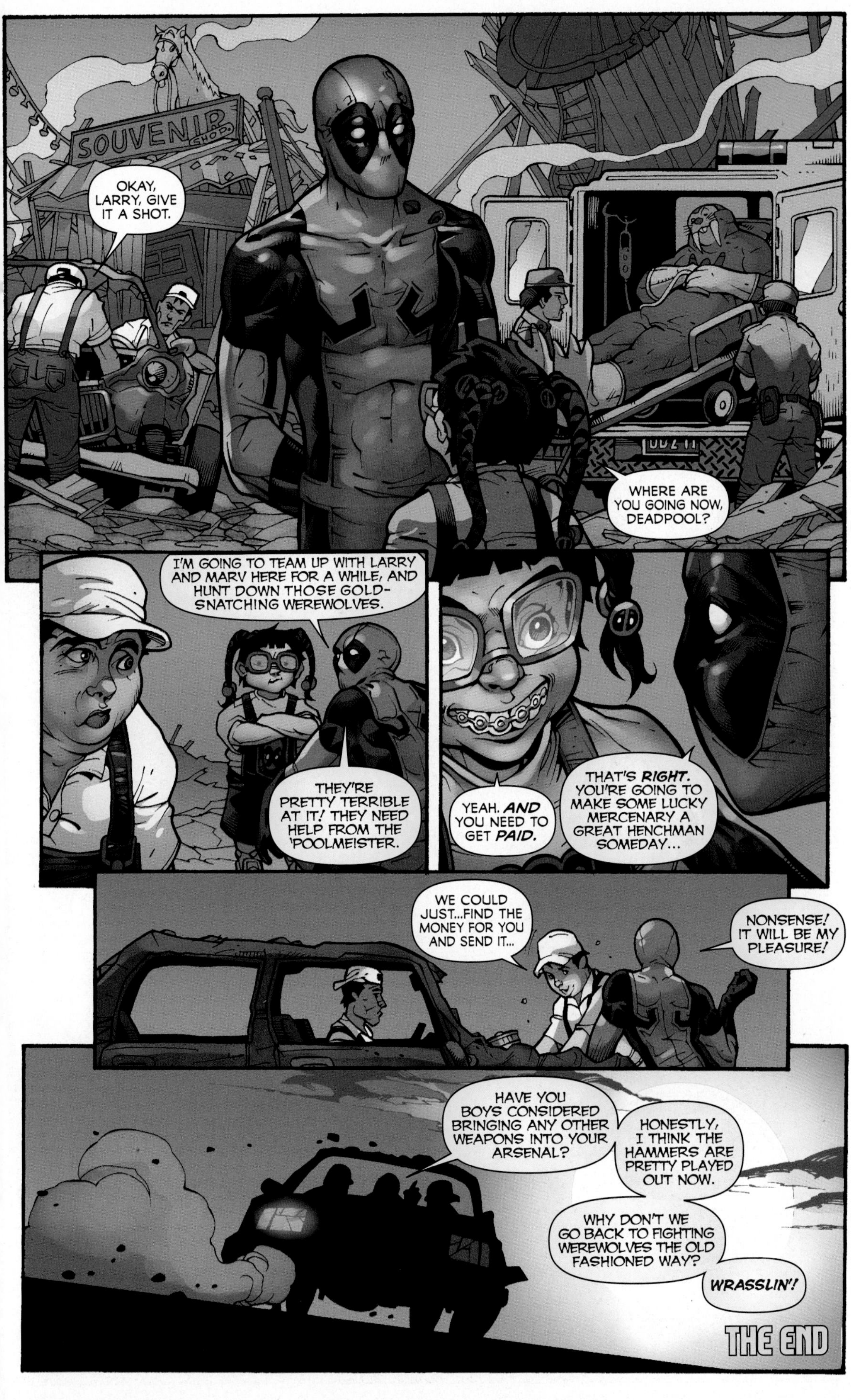
SOUVENIR SHOP
OKAY, LARRY, GIVE IT A SHOT.
WHERE ARE YOU GOING NOW, DEADPOOL?
I'M GOING TO TEAM UP WITH LARRY AND MARV HERE FOR A WHILE, AND HUNT DOWN THOSE GOLD-SNATCHING WEREWOLVES.
THEY'RE PRETTY TERRIBLE AT IT! THEY NEED HELP FROM THE 'POOLMEISTER.
YEAH. AND YOU NEED TO GET PAID.
THAT'S RIGHT. YOU'RE GOING TO MAKE SOME LUCKY MERCENARY A GREAT HENCHMAN SOMEDAY...
WE COULD JUST...FIND THE MONEY FOR YOU AND SEND IT...
NONSENSE! IT WILL BE MY PLEASURE!
HAVE YOU BOYS CONSIDERED BRINGING ANY OTHER WEAPONS INTO YOUR ARSENAL?
HONESTLY, I THINK THE HAMMERS ARE PRETTY PLAYED OUT NOW.
WHY DON'T WE GO BACK TO FIGHTING WEREWOLVES THE OLD FASHIONED WAY?
WRASSLIN'!
THE END

DEADPOOL CORPS: RANK AND FOUL

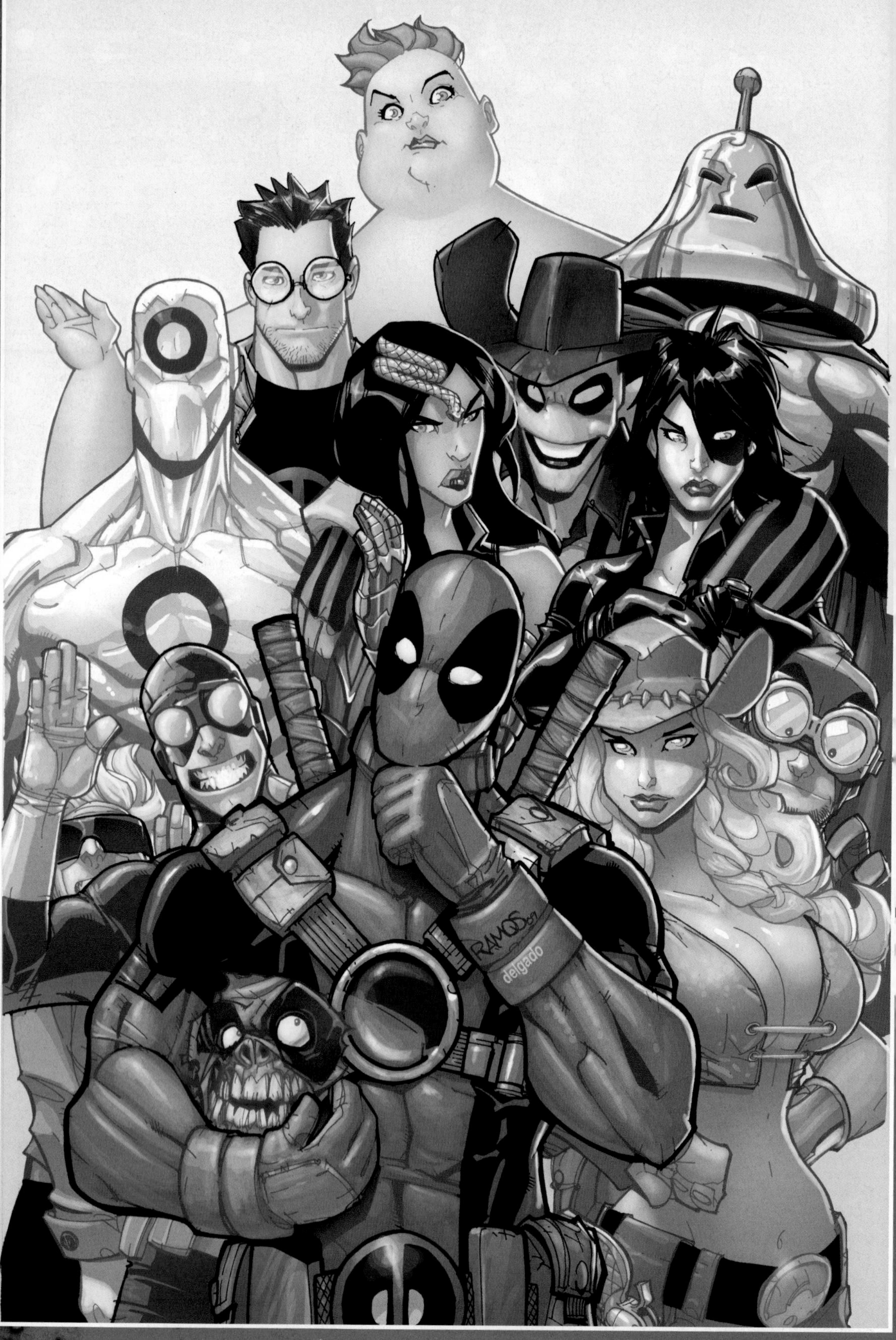
RAMOS
delgado

AJAX

HISTORY: A longtime government operative, Francis underwent cybernetic enhancement by Dr. Emrys Killebrew in Canada's Weapon X Program, where he was psychologically twisted to obey orders. Too sadistic to be trusted in the field, he was reassigned to the Hospice to treat ailing Weapon X subjects, but actually used to help Killebrew's inhumane experiments. As the Attending, Francis gleefully assisted the doctor. Killebrew took special interest in "Wade Wilson," who Francis helped torture in Killebrew's Workshop. Seeking death to escape suffering, Wilson repeatedly defied Francis, who subjected him to additional torture but failed to break his spirit. Wilson's example gave the other patients hope, reducing their fear. Francis, wanting to kill Wilson for insolence, complained to Killebrew, who deemed Wilson too valuable a subject to lose. Advised to make the patients fear him again, Francis chose a method to obtain both goals. Binding Wilson's friend, fellow patient Charles "Worm" Cunningham, within a torture device, Francis offered to release him if Wilson showed respect. Urged on by Worm, who correctly suspected Francis would torture him anyway, Wilson refused, and Francis lobotomized Worm. As Francis had known he would, Wilson killed Worm, who lingered on the earthly plane as a ghost, to end his suffering. Per Killebrew's rules, any patient who killed another earned a death sentence, and as Wilson furiously vowed to kill Francis for his crimes, Francis pulled out Wilson's heart. The trauma jump-started Wilson's failed healing factor, restoring him to life and driving him insane. Wilson, self-dubbed Deadpool shot Francis multiple times at point-blank range. In the ensuing chaos, Killebrew, Wilson, and several patients escaped, but Wilson made the same error as Francis, departing before confirming death. Recovered by Weapon X personnel, Francis was eventually rebuilt by Killebrew into a more powerful cyborg form as Ajax.

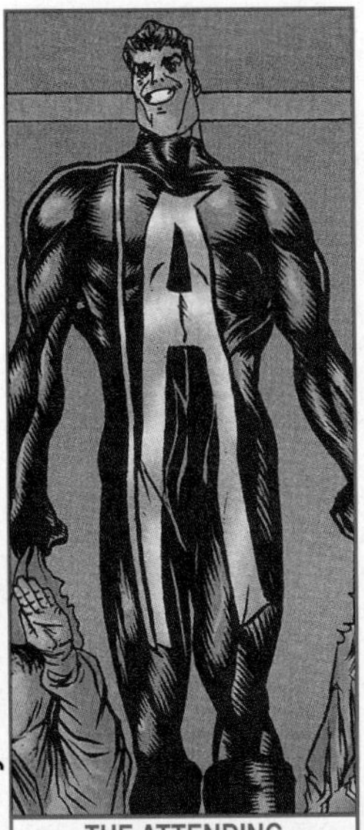

THE ATTENDING

Art by Steve Harris

HEIGHT: 6'4"
WEIGHT: 200 lbs.
EYES: Brown
HAIR: Black

ABILITIES/ACCESSORIES: As the Attending, Ajax possessed enhanced strength (lifting at least one ton), speed, durability and intuitive capacity to better predict opponents' moves. His nerves were altered to make him immune to all but the most excruciating pain levels, although he could be rendered immobile by a remotely activated spinal implant. As Ajax, he was even stronger (Class 10 or higher) and faster, enabling him to create "sonic micro booms" by snapping his fingers, rub his hands together so rapidly that they burst into flame, and literally boil an opponent alive via friction heat. He wore titanium-laced body armor with enhanced optical sensors, enabling him to perceive an opponent's skeleton and nervous system; he carried a metal shield with unrevealed properties.

POWER GRID	1	2	3	4	5	6	7
INTELLIGENCE	■	■	■				
STRENGTH	■	■	■	■			
SPEED	■	■	■				
DURABILITY	■	■	■	■	■	■	
ENERGY PROJECTION	■	■					
FIGHTING SKILLS	■	■	■	■			

REAL NAME: Francis (surname unrevealed)
ALIASES: "Frankie," the A-Man, the Attending
IDENTITY: Secret
OCCUPATION: Vengeance-seeker; former hospice attendant, government operative
CITIZENSHIP: Canada
PLACE OF BIRTH: Unrevealed
KNOWN RELATIVES: Unidentified mother
GROUP AFFILIATION: Formerly Weapon X (Canada)
EDUCATION: Unrevealed
FIRST APPEARANCE: Deadpool #14 (1998)

In recent years, Ajax, presumably under his own initiative, recruited over a dozen armored soldiers to kill Weapon X escapees, hoping to eventually locate Deadpool. In Montreal, he killed conjoined Jacques and Steve Soto, now mechanics. Days later, he attacked cyborg Todd Harris, now a lumberjack, who, already aware of Jacques and Steve's deaths, directed Ajax to mercenary hangout Hellhouse, which Deadpool frequented. After slaying Todd, Ajax visited Hellhouse, whose manager Patch (Bob Stirrat), nursing a grudge against Deadpool, provided his personal file. Ajax learned his quarry had recently been lured to Switzerland by Killebrew, now a recluse. Ajax tortured Killebrew into teleporting Deadpool to their location, then knocked Deadpool off a cliff to seemingly perish in the fall. As Deadpool's healing factor slowly restored him, the ghosts of Ajax's victims, including Worm, appeared, claiming that Deadpool and Ajax's intense mutual hatred and Deadpool's long-ago vow to kill Ajax had bound them to Earth and only Ajax's death would free them. Deadpool led Ajax on a chase, luring him into using his super-speed on ice to send him sliding into ice-cold water. Deadpool snapped Ajax's neck, although this did not give rest to his victims' ghosts, who realized they were bound to Earth by their own hatred.

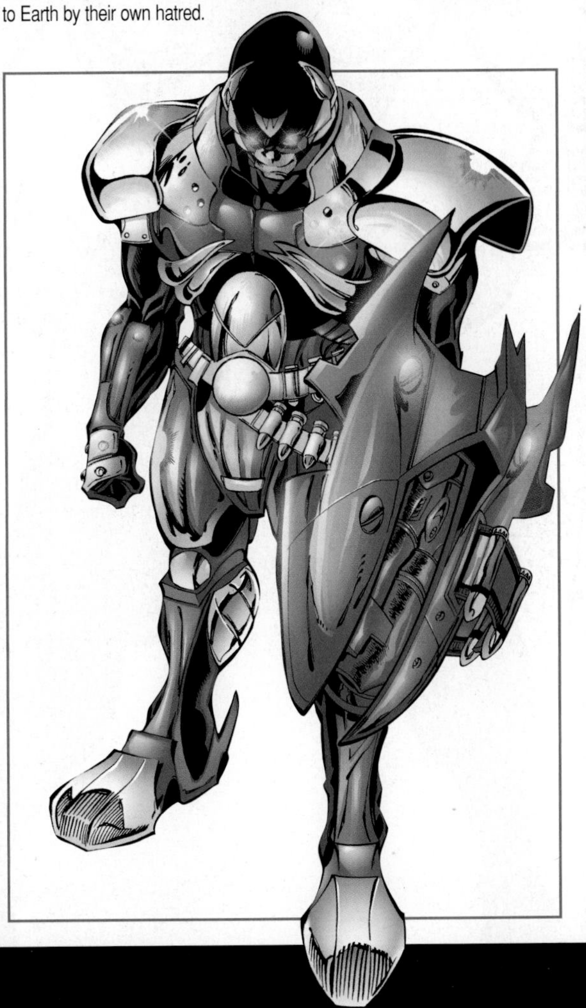

Art by Walter McDaniel

ANACONDA

REAL NAME: Blanche Sitznski
ALIASES: Ana, "Blondie"
IDENTITY: Known to authorities
OCCUPATION: Professional criminal; former physical trainer, steelworker
CITIZENSHIP: USA, with a criminal record
PLACE OF BIRTH: Pittsburgh, Pennsylvania
KNOWN RELATIVES: None
GROUP AFFILIATION: Formerly SHIELD's Six Pack, Serpent Society, Superia's Femizons, Legion Accursed, Sidewinder (Seth Voelker)'s Serpent Squad
EDUCATION: High school dropout
FIRST APPEARANCE: Marvel Two-in-One #64 (1980)

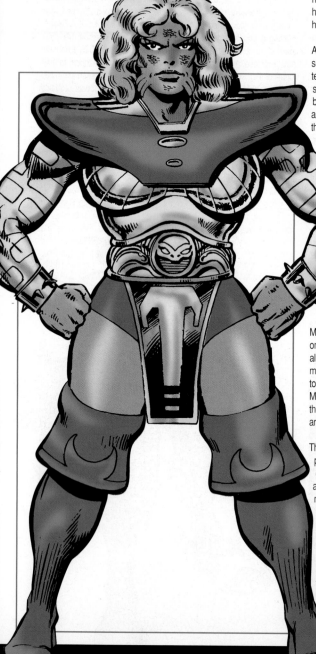

HISTORY: Originally a steelworker, Blanche Sitznski became a trainer for the Taskmaster's Academy, developing fighting techniques for thugs and would-be super criminals. Students at the Academy during Blanche's tenure included Rachel Leighton, who would later become Diamondback. Blanche's work came to the attention of Roxxon Oil's Brand Corporation, who imbued her with anaconda-like superhuman powers to serve in the Serpent Squad. Alongside team organizer Sidewinder (Seth Voelker), Black Mamba (Tanya Sealy) and Death Adder (Roland Burroughs), Anaconda joined the Serpent Squad and Roxxon President Hugh Jones dispatched the squad to retrieve the Serpent Crown, an ancient mystical artifact (powered by the Elder God Set) which had been lost in the Pacific Ocean. Causing underwater explosions to bring the buried Crown to the surface, the Serpent Squad drew the attention of super heroes Stingray (Walter Newell) and the Thing (Ben Grimm), as well as the Inhumans' Triton. The Squad made an adequate showing against the heroes, and Anaconda nearly incapacitated the Thing before Stingray's blast dropped her. Obtaining the Crown, Sidewinder set off depth charges to slow the heroes' pursuit and buried his comrades in the resulting blast, after which he delivered the Crown to Jones.

Anaconda, Black Mamba and Death Adder survived Sidewinder's seeming treachery and, after Anaconda released her remaining teammates, the trio continued to work as the Serpent Squad. Hired to steal a microprocessor from Stark International, the trio was opposed by Iron Man (Tony Stark), who bested them, defeating Anaconda with an electrical current as she tried to crush him. Evading the authorities, the trio finally caught up to Sidewinder and demanded payment for the Serpent Crown affair. Sidewinder not only complied, but offered to accept them as co-founders of his new Serpent Society, a professional criminal organization using trade union policies. At the Society's first official meeting, the Constrictor (Frank Payne) scorned the group's plans and walked out. To pass their initiation, Anaconda, Cobra (Klaus Voorhees) and Rattler (Gustav Krueger) had to steal devices from the Brand Corporation which had empowered Anaconda, but Captain America (Steve Rogers) was tipped off to the robbery by Constrictor and foiled the attempt. Realizing Constrictor had betrayed them, Anaconda hunted him down and gave him a vicious beating, ensuring he would remain silent about the Society in the future.

Anaconda was one of 99 super villains briefly recruited by the demon Mephisto into his Legion Accursed, intending to claim the power of the omnipotent Beyonder by forging the device Beyondersbane, which would allow any member of the Legion to transfer the Beyonder's power to the machine by touching him; however, none of the super villains were able to complete this simple task because the Thing, his power increased by Mephisto in order detain the Beyonder, instead single-handedly defeated the Legion Accursed. Anaconda was released from Mephisto's contract and returned to the Serpent Society.

The Society soon attracted underworld clients, and the team's first prestigious assignment was to assassinate MODOK on behalf of AIM (Advanced Idea Mechanics). Captain America again interfered, but although MODOK bested Anaconda, her teammates completed the mission. When AIM demanded MODOK's corpse before payment, Anaconda carried it from the morgue herself, defying her comrades' squeamishness. After a Scourge of the Underworld killed Death Adder, Anconda joined teammate Asp (Cleo Nefertiti) in searching for the killer, investigating the Circus of Crime for a possible motive. Eventually, the Serpent Society allowed a quartet of newcomers to join their ranks, but they proved to be agents of the Viper (Ophelia Sarkissian), who used them in a Trojan Horse operation so she could take over the Society. Anaconda joined most of the Society members in defecting to the Viper's rule and aiding her nihilist plot to poison drinking water with snake venom. When teammate Diamondback

(Rachel Leighton) returned to the Society with the Captain (a temporary alias of Steve Rogers when he surrendered his Captain America identity to the US government) and other heroes to stop the Viper, Anaconda fought her former ally, but Diamondback defeated her. The Viper was ultimately removed from the Society, but Sidewinder stepped down, transferring leadership to Cobra, who soon became King Cobra; the rest of the Society, including the four infiltrators and other former Viper agents, made peace and continued working together.

The Deviant priest-lord Ghaur and his Lemurian ally Llyra later hired the Society to retrieve various mystical artifacts around the globe. Anaconda joined a team of Society members in pursuing a Native American artifact at Lima, Ohio, but the X-Men opposed them and Colossus (Peter Rasputin) bested her in battle. Anaconda soon became romantically involved with her teammate Puff Adder. When it was learned that Diamondback had become involved with Captain America, she was deemed a risk and placed on trial, with most of the Society (including Anaconda) demanding her death. Asp and Black Mamba opposed the Society and helped Captain America and super-mercenary Paladin bring them down to save Diamondback, but Anaconda, Puff Adder and Rock Python remained at large. After Asp, Black Mamba and Diamondback became the freelance team BAD Girls, Inc., Anaconda, Puff Adder and Rock Python raided the trio's apartment and took them prisoner; however, MODAM suddenly joined the fight on behalf of the extreme feminist Superia. MODAM forced Anaconda, Asp, Black Mamba and Diamondback to accompany her to a cruise ship where a veritable army of superhuman women were being shipped to Superia's island Femizonia to join her Femizons, intending that they would help her establish a female-dominated society. During the cruise, Anaconda engaged in a bout with fellow passenger Quicksand and helped capture Captain America and Paladin when they invaded the ship.

Superia's plot came to naught and Anaconda departed Femizonia, reuniting with Puff Adder. The couple visited AIM Island during the AIM Weapons Expo and clashed briefly with Captain America when he investigated the facility. Anaconda and Puff Adder finally returned to the revived Serpent Society, now based in Arizona, where local hero Jack Flag feigned wanting to join their ranks so he could bring the organization down. Jack Flag's operation caught the attention of Captain America and his then-sidekick Free Spirit, who helped battle the Serpent Society, although the criminal team was finally broken up by the heroic Force Works, who had the entire organization arrested. Eventually returning to her life of crime, Anaconda journeyed to Madripoor to participate in the Bloodsport competition among various infamous superhumans and skilled fighters. In her first round, Anaconda fought and seemingly slew the mutant terrorist Forearm (Michael McCain), but in her second round she was bested by Puma. The Serpent Society re-formed yet again and sought revenge upon Captain America and Diamondback, taking both prisoner so they could ransom them to the Captain's rogues gallery, but they did not realize the "Diamondback" they had captured was an LMD imposter. Captain America escaped confinement and defeated the Society, turning them over to SHIELD.

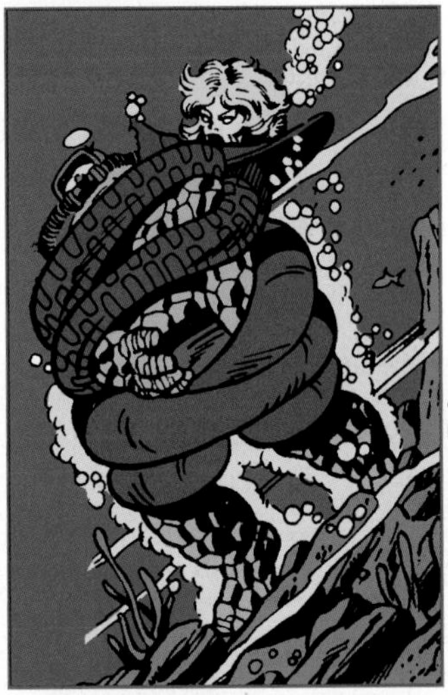
Art by George Pérez

Anaconda was released from SHIELD on the condition that she join GW Bridge's Six Pack on a mission to assess the mutant Cable (Nathan Summers), whose powers had grown to a godlike state, resulting in his forming the hovering island Providence. Anaconda made a poor showing against Cable, who teleported her into the Chrysler Building mid-combat. The Six Pack was defeated, and Anaconda was convinced to switch sides and work for Cable, helping him defend Providence when it was invaded by the X-Men. When Cable's power level was reduced, his ally Deadpool ("Wade Wilson") hid him at a Switzerland safe house. The Six Pack regrouped and tracked Cable to the location, only to be caught in a telepathic booby trap which threatened to kill them if Cable's mind died. Deadpool restored Cable's faculties, and the Six Pack were let go. The Six Pack (now joined by Deadpool) joined forces again when Cable took over the European nation Rumekistan. To discredit Cable's regime, the Six Pack shut down the country's electrical power, and Deadpool nearly killed Cable in an ambush. Cable survived and exposed the Six Pack as US agents, solidifying his hold over Rumekistan. Resuming her criminal career, Anaconda was quickly caught and left for the police by members of the New Warriors. Returning to the Serpent Society, Anaconda and the others were unnerved by the Skrull invasion masterminded by Queen Veranke. Panicking, the team took hostages at a complex in Danzig, Ohio, but they were routed and arrested by members of the Nova Corps, who freed the hostages. Anaconda later joined the Serpent Society in a battle against Luke Cage's Avengers in New York.

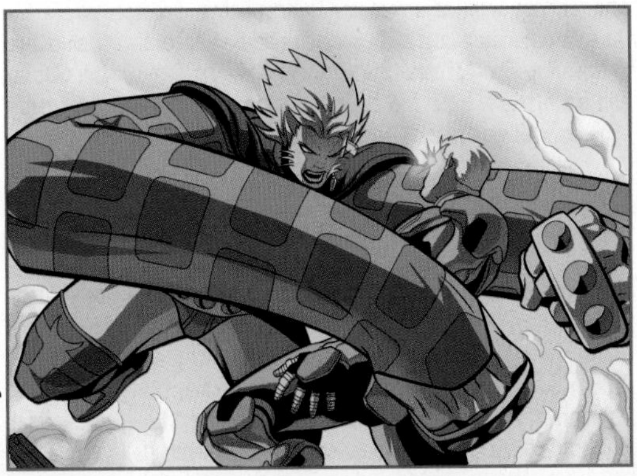
Art by Patrick Zircher

HEIGHT: 6'2"
WEIGHT: 222 lbs.
EYES: Green
HAIR: Blonde

ABILITIES/ACCESSORIES: Bionic implants in Anaconda's arms and legs allow her to elongate them, generally one-and-a-half times but up to twice their normal length. When elongated, her limbs swell with blood, granting them the appearance of unarticulated snakes. Anaconda can use her limbs to constrict enemies with enough force to incapacitate and kill most human beings, even superhumanly strong ones. She has enhanced strength (lifting 2 tons), durability, stamina and healing powers, allowing her to rapidly regenerate from most wounds. The bones in her arms and legs have been reinforced with Adamantium alloy to support her implants. Anaconda also has gills enabling her to breathe underwater, as well as tiny scales on her face, neck, chest and back, plus small fins on her lower cheeks. Able to swim at slightly superhuman speeds, she is an undisciplined but capable street fighter.

POWER GRID	1	2	3	4	5	6	7
INTELLIGENCE	■	■					
STRENGTH	■	■	■	■			
SPEED	■	■					
DURABILITY	■	■	■	■			
ENERGY PROJECTION	■						
FIGHTING SKILLS	■	■	■				

ASP

REAL NAME: Cleo Nefertiti
ALIASES: The Temptress
IDENTITY: Known to authorities
OCCUPATION: Licensed super hero, exotic dancer; former professional criminal, mercenary
CITIZENSHIP: Egypt
PLACE OF BIRTH: Tanta, Egypt
KNOWN RELATIVES: None
GROUP AFFILIATION: Initiative, Women Warriors; formerly BAD Girls, Inc., "Secret Avengers," Serpent Society
EDUCATION: Unrevealed
FIRST APPEARANCE: (Photo) Captain America #308 (1985); (full) Captain America #310 (1985)

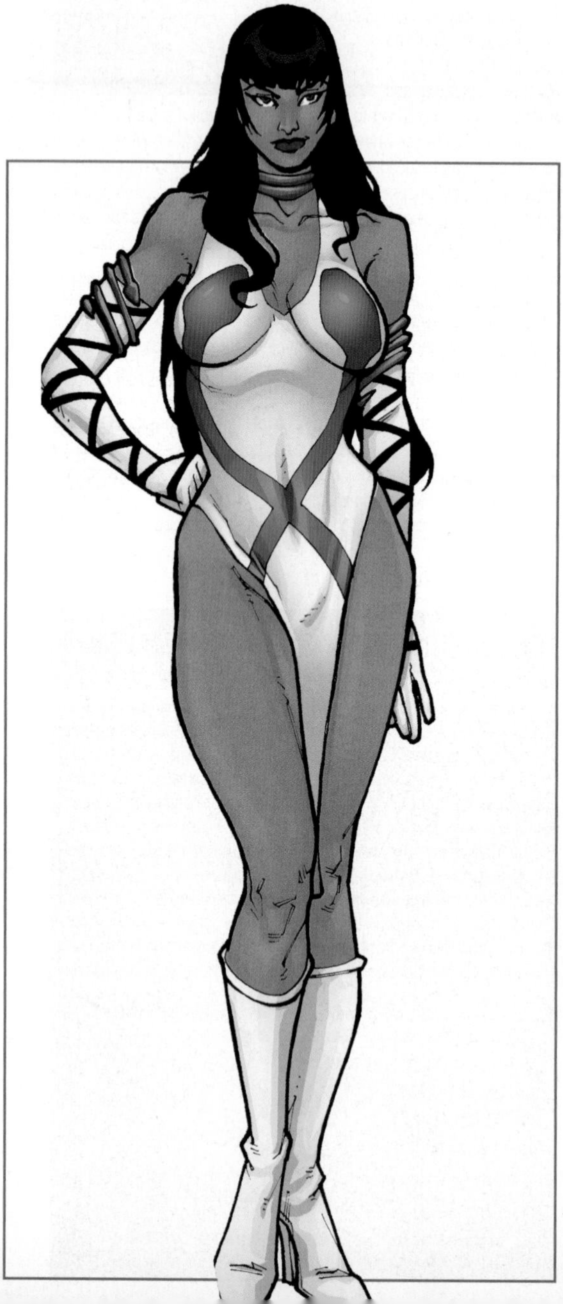

HISTORY: While the source of her superhuman abilities remains unrevealed, the Asp worked as an exotic dancer called "the Temptress" for some time, performing at New York City's Pink Flamingo lounge. After Sidewinder (Seth Voelker) recruited her as a founding member of the Serpent Society, a snake-themed mercenary group, Asp helped spread word of their existence through the underworld, visiting the Kingpin (Wilson Fisk) for future consideration of their services. The Serpent Society soon received their first assignment from AIM (Advanced Idea Mechanics), who hired them to assassinate their then-fugitive master MODOK. Asp and other Serpent Society members hunted MODOK, finally trapping him in a shopping mall, but they were attacked by Captain America (Steve Rogers), who had Asp and several others arrested; Sidewinder used his teleportation powers to rescue Asp and their teammates from prison. Although other Society members had successfully killed MODOK, AIM required his body to authorize payment, and Asp was among those retrieving MODOK's corpse from the morgue. When a Scourge of the Underworld vigilante slew their teammate Death Adder (Roland Burroughs), Asp joined Anaconda in interrogating the Circus of Crime, who had seen Burroughs before his death, but found they were uninvolved.

Asp became a close friend to fellow Society members Diamondback (Rachel Leighton) and Black Mamba (Tanya Sealy). After Sidewinder recruited members of a new Serpent Squad into the Society, they proved to be double agents serving the Viper (Ophelia Sarkissian, aka Madame Hydra), who took over the Society. Asp was among the few Society members who refused to serve Viper and was injected with a potentially fatal dose of Viper's snake venom, but Diamondback brought the Captain (formerly Captain America) to their aid and gave Asp the antitoxin in time to save her. Sidewinder regained control over the Society but soon resigned, promoting Cobra (Klaus Voorhees) to leadership. Asp joined the team on a mission for the Deviant priestlord Ghaur and Llyra, a Lemurian priestess of the Elder Gog Set, to recover a mystic artifact from the Savage Land, but Wolverine (Logan/James Howlett) and Dazzler (Alison Blaire) of the X-Men thwarted them. Asp and fellow super-criminals Nekra, the Owl (Leland Owlsley) and Scorpion (Mac Gargan) fell under the influence of Llan the Sorcerer and were compelled to journey across the border into Canada and fight his enemies Alpha Flight in Winnipeg, Manitoba. Asp was ultimately beaten by Gamma Flight's Witchfire and sent to prison, but the Society retrieved her.

When Diamondback, who had left the Society, went on a date with Steve Rogers, Asp and Black Mamba helped ensure that the evening went without incident, unaware that Diamondback's date was Captain America. In the course of the evening, Asp helped defeat Rogers' old foe Gamecock while he was in a showdown with the police. When the Society realized Diamondback was working with Captain America, King Cobra had her placed on trial. Although Asp and Black Mamba defended her, she was sentenced to death. Asp and Mamba arranged for Sidewinder to save her, but in so doing placed themselves at risk. King Cobra captured them and used them as bait to bring back Diamondback, who returned with the mercenary Paladin only to be captured. Finally, Captain America came to their rescue and, in spite of his reluctance to trust Asp and Mamba, helped them break up the Serpent Society and place nearly all of the organization behind bars, with the notable exceptions of Asp, Black Mamba and Diamondback.

Diamondback, Asp and Mamba formed their own team of mercenary adventurers as BAD Girls, Inc. (playing off the first letters of Black Mamba, Asp and Diamondback), but before they could find work, the still-at-large Society members Anaconda, Puff-Adder and Rock Python attacked them. They were narrowly saved by MODAM, who brought them to the island Femizonia to join Superia's Femizons, a would-be ruling class of superhuman women. During the cruise they befriended Impala, but Diamondback was nearly killed by Snapdragon (Sheoke Sanada), which made her want to give up costumed adventuring. When Paladin

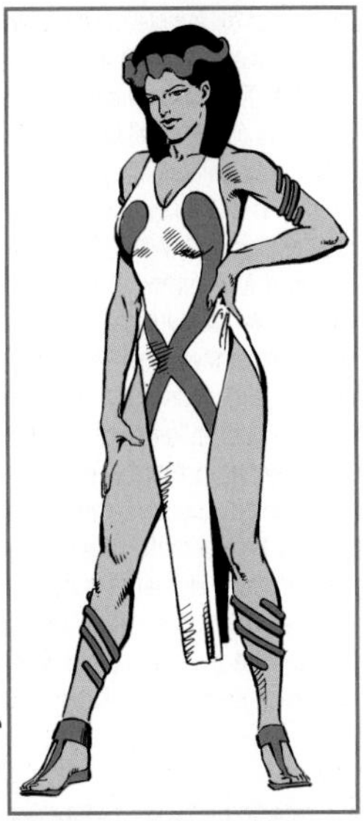

Art by Carl Potts

and Captain America infiltrated the Femizons' cruise ship en route to the island, they were defeated by the Femizons, and Superia planned to transform them into women. Fearing that Superia planned to transform all men into women, Asp and Mamba decided to help Paladin and the Captain, rescuing them from Superia. With the male heroes deprived of their clothes, Asp temporarily loaned her costume to Paladin as they escaped the Femizons and departed Femizonia with Diamondback. Back in the USA, Asp and Mamba searched for Snapdragon to help Diamondback overcome her fears, beginning at one of the criminal-friendly Bars With No Name, only to be threatened by Superia's lackeys Battleaxe (Anita Ehren), Golddigger (Angela Golden) and Steel Wind (Ruriko Tsumura); Impala came to the duo's aid and wound up joining BAD Girls as Diamondback's replacement. While trying to take custody of a Serpent Society saucer vehicle, the BAD Girls were confronted by the Avenger Sersi, who briefly transformed the trio into snakes, but they proved they were Captain America's allies and departed with the craft. They sought Snapdragon at the AIM Weapons Expo, but Diamondback had by now resumed her costumed life and secretly killed Snapdragon herself.

When Captain America unwittingly became involved with a Diamondback LMD used by the Red Skull (Johann Shmidt) in a plan against his old enemy, the real Diamondback noticed the deception and encouraged Asp and Mamba to rejoin the Serpent Society and have them investigate the Diamondback imposter. The Society captured Captain America and the LMD, but Cap escaped them and defeated the Society; the LMD was ultimately exposed. Diamondback, Asp and Mamba reformed BAD Girls, Inc. and took an assignment from an unidentified employer (secretly Cable/Nathan Summers) who hired them to steal a hard drive called the Dominus Objective from the Dominus Corporation in La Jolla, California. Deadpool ("Wade Wilson") had also been unknowingly hired by Cable to retrieve the device and fought the BAD Girls, only to find it had already been taken by Cat (Shen Kuei) on behalf of the Black Box. The BAD Girls traced Cat to a Rand-Meachum plant in Long Island with Deadpool in pursuit. There, they discovered Deadpool's mercenary ally Weasel (Jack Hammer) was involved and clashed with Iron Fist (Daniel Rand), Luke Cage and Cable on the premises. Asp hacked into Rand-Meachum's security feed and found evidence of Cat's theft; avoiding the other involved parties, they pursued the Cat to Hong Kong. Black Box used the Dominus Objective to gain power over all information stored electronically, but Cat revealed that Cable was his

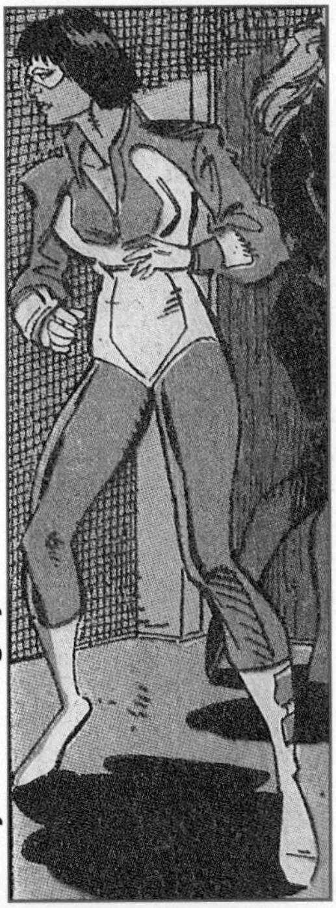

Art by Mark Bagley

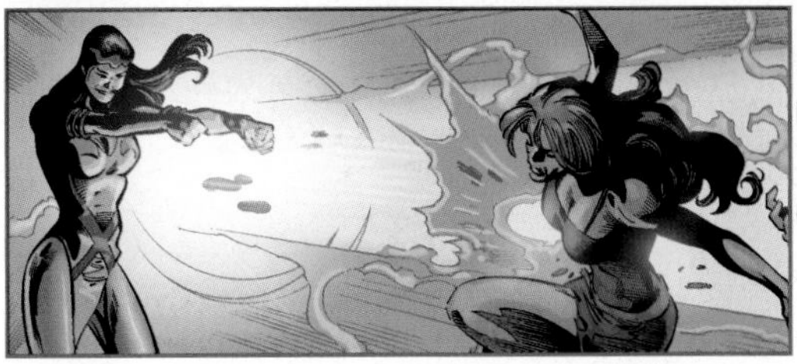

Art by Scot Eaton

true employer, with the BAD Girls and Deadpool serving as Cable's back-ups in case Cat had failed. The BAD Girls and Cat journeyed to Black Box's New Delhi, India base and aided Deadpool and Cable against Black Box's Executive Elite but the battle ended when Cable convinced Black Box to work for him.

When the superhuman community was divided over the US government's controversial new Superhuman Registration Act (SHRA), Diamondback recruited Asp and Mamba into Captain America's rebel "Secret Avengers" to oppose pro-SHRA forces, and they tried to recruit super-criminals into the resistance's ranks such as Goldbug and the Plunderer (actually the Plunderer's lackey, David Kivlin), but the vigilante Punisher (Frank Castle) killed both men, ending such plans. Captain America ultimately surrendered to the authorities and the Secret Avengers broke up, with many of them gaining amnesty by joining the government's new Fifty State Initiative organization of licensed super heroes. The BAD Girls, however, refused to surrender and later fought licensed Avengers members Ms. Marvel (Carol Danvers), Wasp (Janet Van Dyne) and Black Widow (Natasha Romanoff). When unstable politician Norman Osborn (formerly the super-criminal Green Goblin) became the Initiative's new director, aided by criminal lieutenants such as the Hood (Parker Robbins) and Taskmaster, the increasingly corrupt Initiative rapidly expanded by recruiting many criminals and ex-criminals, only a few of whom were truly reformed or rehabilitated. Black Mamba and the Asp joined the organization and were assigned to the Women Warriors, Delaware's official super-hero team, under Diamondback's leadership. Asp has since served the Initiative in missions such as the defense of Baltimore-Washington International Airport from the terrorists RAID. The Women Warriors were also on the front lines of Norman Osborn's siege of Asgard.

HEIGHT: 5'9"
EYES: Brown
WEIGHT: 115 lbs.
HAIR: Black

ABILITIES/ACCESSORIES: Asp can generate and project "venom bolts" of an unrevealed form of radiant energy from her hands. Asp can adjust her venom's strength to either temporarily paralyze or kill her victims. Her venom bolts only affect living organisms. Asp's body also secretes the venom through her skin pores, rendering prolonged physical contact with her potentially fatal. After repeated use of the venom bolts, Asp must rest to recharge her abilities. She generally rebuilds her energy levels by making swaying and undulating motions with her torso and arms; an accomplished dancer with superb muscular control, the Asp moves in a manner that is almost hypnotic in its provocativeness. Engaging in her "snake-dance," the Asp can regenerate her energy to peak capacity within ten minutes. A skilled aircraft pilot and computer hacker, she also carries a handgun.

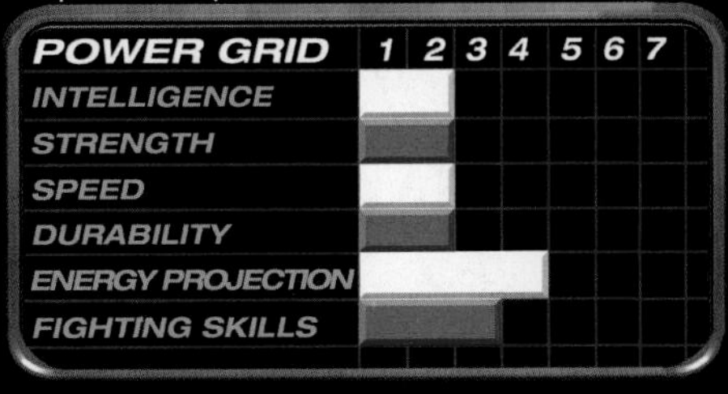
POWER GRID
1
2
3
4
5
6
7
INTELLIGENCE
STRENGTH
SPEED
DURABILITY
ENERGY PROJECTION
FIGHTING SKILLS

BIG BERTHA

REAL NAME: Ashley Crawford
ALIASES: Ample Amazon
IDENTITY: Known to authorities
OCCUPATION: Licensed super hero, fashion model
CITIZENSHIP: USA
PLACE OF BIRTH: Marshfield, Wisconsin
KNOWN RELATIVES: None
GROUP AFFILIATION: Great Lakes Initiative, Initiative; formerly Great Lakes Champions, Great Lakes X-Men, Great Lakes Avengers, Lightning Rods
EDUCATION: Unrevealed
FIRST APPEARANCE: West Coast Avengers #46 (1989)

HISTORY: With her in-born mutant ability to reshape her body, Ashley Crawford gave herself the perfect figure, allowing her to pursue a successful career as a world-renowned international fashion model. She also used her power to become the superhumanly obese crime fighter Big Bertha in her home state of Wisconsin, although she frequently met with revulsion and horror from those she saved. When she saw a newspaper ad placed by fellow wannabe hero Mr. Immortal (Craig Hollis) seeking costumed adventurers with special talents, she and fellow Wisconsinite heroes Dinah Soar, Doorman (DeMarr Davis) and Flatman (Val Ventura) signed up, becoming the Great Lakes Avengers, an unauthorized, self-declared Midwestern branch of the celebrated Avengers super-hero team; leather fetishist Leather Boy (Gene Lorrene) also mistakenly signed up, having misinterpreted the ad's intent, but was let go soon afterwards when the others learned he lacked super-powers. With her modeling fortune, Ashley paid the team's expenses and let them use her house as their headquarters.

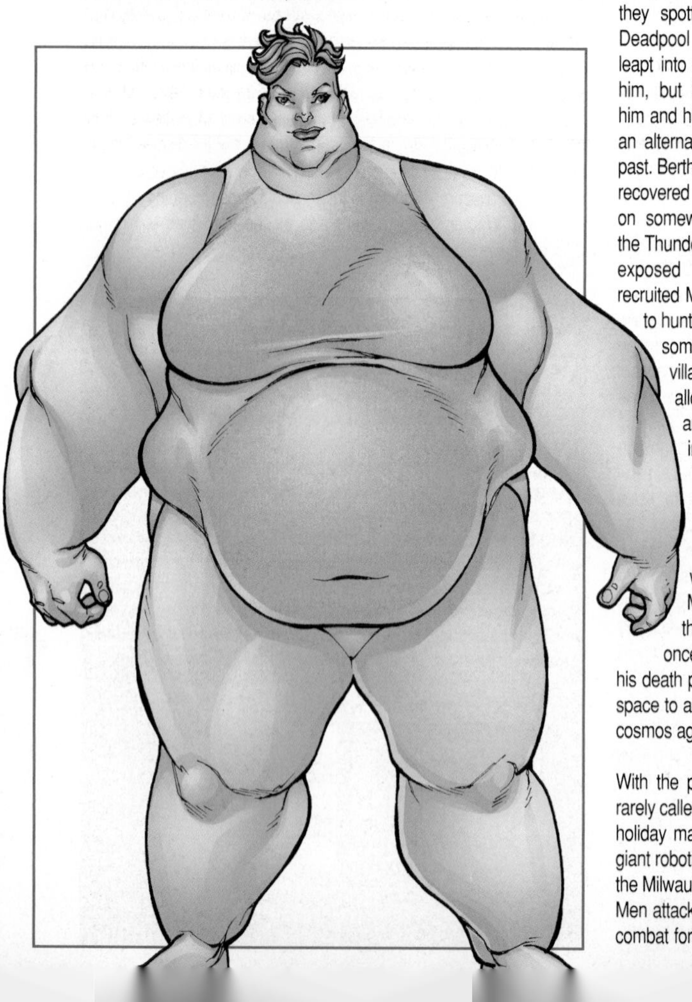

The GLA's activities soon caught the attention of ex-Avengers Hawkeye (Clint Barton) and Mockingbird (Bobbi Barton); after a tense first meeting, the two agreed to train the inexperienced GLA. The nascent team faced its first true test when they received an Avengers distress call from Texas' Absolom College. Ashley flew them to Texas in her private jet, where they fought the ancient collective intelligence That Which Endures and its human pawns. Bertha held her own against the That Which Endures-possessed She-Hulk (Jennifer Walters) while Mr. Immortal foiled the entity's plans. Bertha and the GLA trained intensively with Hawkeye and Mockingbird; Hawkeye eventually left to rejoin the official Avengers, leaving Mockingbird in command of the Great Lakes team. She led them into battle with the colossal alien Terminus in St. Louis, keeping the giant occupied until the actual Avengers could arrive and defeat the monster. Later, a fake distress call from Cytorrak gem-empowered preteen Stevie Wojciehowicz led Bertha and the GLA to a theme park, where they mistook Captain America (Steve Rogers) and the Human Torch (Jim Hammond) for imposters. After a brief battle, Cap foiled Stevie's plan to steal his shield and convinced the GLA that he and Hammond were legitimate, although not before they crammed Bertha into Doorman. Following this, Mockingbird too left the team.

When the Avengers were seemingly killed by the malevolent psychic entity Onslaught, the GLA renamed themselves the Lightning Rods to mimic Citizen V (Helmut Zemo)'s popular new Thunderbolts, who were then operating as super heroes. While on a trip to the aquarium, they spotted homicidal mercenary Deadpool ("Wade Wilson"); they leapt into action, hoping to capture him, but instead accidentally sent him and his companion Blind Al into an alternate timeline (Earth-9712)'s past. Bertha and the team eventually recovered the pair, and they parted on somewhat friendly terms. After the Thunderbolts were subsequently exposed as criminals, SHIELD recruited Mr. Immortal and his team to hunt them down; hoping to get some good publicity, they agreed. Once they located the fugitive villains, the Rods initially held their own but were soon defeated, allowing the Thunderbolts to steal the Lightning Rods' costumes and evade SHIELD in disguise. Bertha and the team revived in time to face the megalomaniacal Graviton alongside the Thunderbolts; after they were beaten soundly by the gravity-manipulating villain, the Rods could do little more than stand by as the Thunderbolts talked Graviton into relenting and escaped. After saving the people of Medina, Ohio from violent weather caused by the Crimson Cowl (Justine Hammer)'s Masters of Evil and their weather control device, Bertha and the team (now calling themselves the Great Lakes Avengers once more) attended Deadpool's funeral (although reports of his death proved to be exaggerated) and were pulled through time and space to assist the Avengers and a league of champions from a distant cosmos against a mad cosmic scholar.

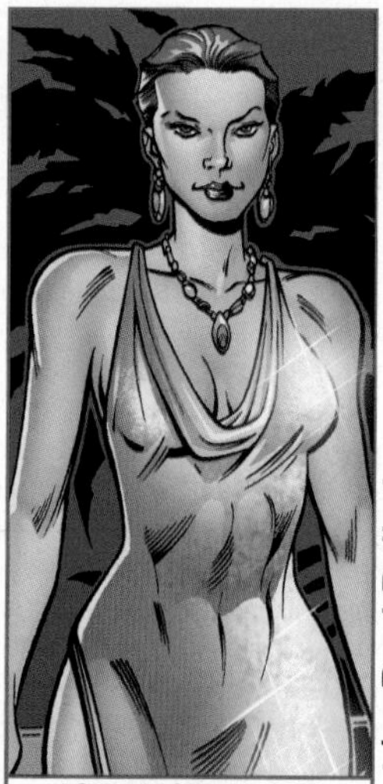

ASHLEY CRAWFORD

Art by Paul Pelletier

With the paucity of superhuman threats in Wisconsin, the GLA was rarely called into action; however, they made local headlines by defeating holiday madman Dr. Tannenbaum, and Bertha personally crushed his giant robotic snowman. When Ashley was modeling for a photo shoot at the Milwaukee convention center, the villainous animal-rights activist Ani-Men attacked the building; while she alerted the GLA and shifted to her combat form, the real Avengers arrived and quelled the threat, advising

Art by Kieron Dwyer

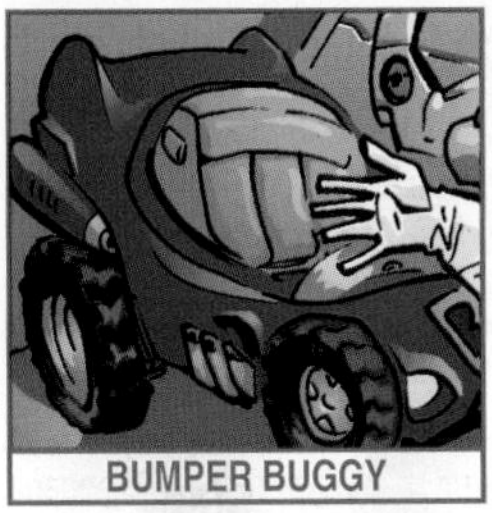

BUMPER BUGGY

Bertha and her teammates to "sit this one out". Shortly afterwards, the team learned that the Avengers had disbanded in the wake of a battle with the deranged Scarlet Witch (Wanda Maximoff). Now the sole remaining "Avengers" team, the GLA responded to a distress call from the University of Wisconsin, where the Inhuman/Deviant hybrid Maelstrom was stealing a chronal accelerator so he could build a machine to destroy the universe. Despite the GLA's best efforts, Maelstrom killed Dinah Soar and made off with the device.

While Flatman and Doorman sought new members, eventually recruiting Squirrel Girl (Doreen Green) and her squirrel partner Monkey Joe, Ashley's agent informed her that her career was stagnating as long as she stayed in Wisconsin; she was briefly tempted to relocate, but reconsidered, remembering how loyal and accepting her GLA friends were regardless of her appearance. Enraged that the GLA had accepted a squirrel after rejecting him, Leather Boy killed Monkey Joe, but Bertha captured Leather Boy by sitting on him. Shortly thereafter, the GLA set out to foil Maelstrom's doomsday plot, battling Maelstrom and his mercenary henchmen Batroc's Brigade. Maelstrom activated his device despite the GLA's interference, creating a massive vortex that began sucking in everything in the surrounding area. Mr. Immortal ultimately tricked Maelstrom into committing suicide, Bertha saved the lightweight Flatman from being sucked into Maelstrom's device, and Mr. Immortal deactivated it.

The original Avengers had always tolerated the GLA's unauthorized use of their name, partly because of their ties to Hawkeye and Mockingbird; but with the real Avengers disbanded and the GLA briefly monopolizing the Avengers name, the charitable Maria Stark Foundation managing the Avengers' business affairs threatened to sue if the GLA kept calling themselves Avengers. Giving in to the foundation's demands and realizing that most of their members were mutants, the former GLA redubbed itself the Great Lakes X-Men and donned new costumes based on the actual X-Men's outfits, although they promptly abandoned them when they learned that Leather Boy had designed them.

Bertha and the GLX crashed the Thing (Ben Grimm)'s super hero poker tournament, where the real X-Men's Marvel Girl (Rachel Grey)

GLX COSTUME

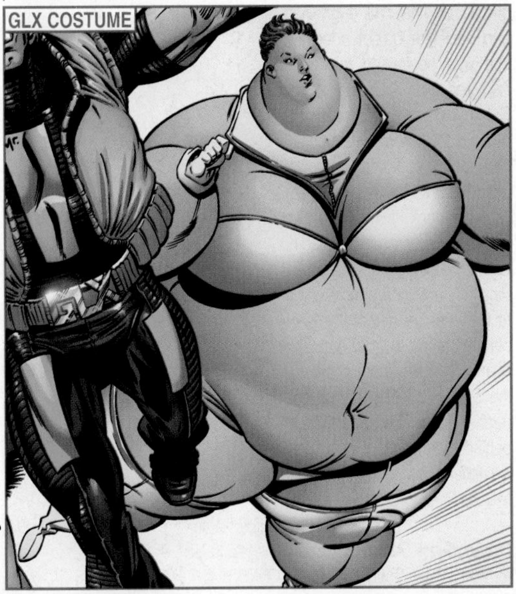

Art by Paul Pelletier

telepathically influenced them to change their team name; they first rechristened themselves the Great Lakes Defenders until Dr. Stephen Strange of the original Defenders mystically compelled Mr. Immortal to drop that name, but they ultimately settled on becoming the Great Lakes Champions, adopting the name of a long-disbanded Los Angeles super-team after winning the poker tournament. When the US government's new Super-Human Registration Act (SHRA) became law, the GLC registered immediately, unbeknownst to Deadpool, who intended to kick off his career as a bounty hunter of unregistered heroes by capturing some easy targets. He held off most of the GLC until Bertha enveloped him in her folds; she released him once it became clear that he was enjoying the experience, but Squirrel Girl soon beat him into submission and he left after learning the GLC were registered heroes. The GLC became Wisconsin's official Fifty-State Initiative team, and accordingly redubbed themselves the Great Lakes Initiative.

When the subversive organization AIM abducted the Olympian god Dionysus and used him to build a superhuman-targeted inebriation ray, they neglected to target Bertha and her teammates, who teamed up with Deadpool (immune to the ray because of his healing factor) to thwart AIM's plans. After Bertha crushed AIM's device, the GLI awarded Deadpool reserve membership; the mercenary took this as his cue to move into GLI HQ and refuse to leave. Remembering Deadpool's previous interest in her, Bertha's teammates pressured her to ask him on a date. He accepted, but was disappointed when she showed up as the svelte Ashley Crawford. When their date was interrupted by an attempted Maggia hit, Ashley assumed her superhuman form, sparking Deadpool's interest. Realizing Deadpool was a "chubby chaser" aroused by fat women, an offended Bertha told him he was just as shallow as the people who prized Crawford's supermodel looks. Hoping she could look past surface appearances the way she wanted him to, a smitten Deadpool unmasked, prompting Bertha to vomit at the sight of his gruesome visage. Squirrel Girl ultimately had to evict Deadpool from the GLI's base. Later, Bertha and her GLI teammates battled a Skrull who had infiltrated their group as Grasshopper during the Skrulls' "secret invasion," then welcomed new leader Gravity (Greg Willis) to the GLI.

HEIGHT: (Ashley) 6'1" (Bertha) 7'4"
WEIGHT: (Ashley) 120 lbs. (Bertha) 750 lbs.
EYES: Blue
HAIR: Reddish-blonde

ABILITIES/ACCESSORIES: Ashley Crawford can shape her body's adipose tissues, allowing her to assume and maintain an ideal physique. She can also instantly summon several hundred pounds of additional fat from an unrevealed source to transform into a super-obese form; during this process, she gains the enhanced skeletal and muscular structures needed to adequately support the extra mass. In this form, Ashley has superhuman strength (lifting 50 tons) and durability. Her skin is also highly durable and elastic, allowing it to repel small-arms fire. She can envelop opponents in her bulk, immobilizing them. She is surprisingly nimble and acrobatic in this form, and frequently leaps on top of opponents or obstacles, crushing them with her bulk. To return to her normal form, Ashley must vomit up her extra mass. A formidable unarmed combatant trained by Hawkeye and Mockingbird, Ashley is also a skilled pilot and card player.

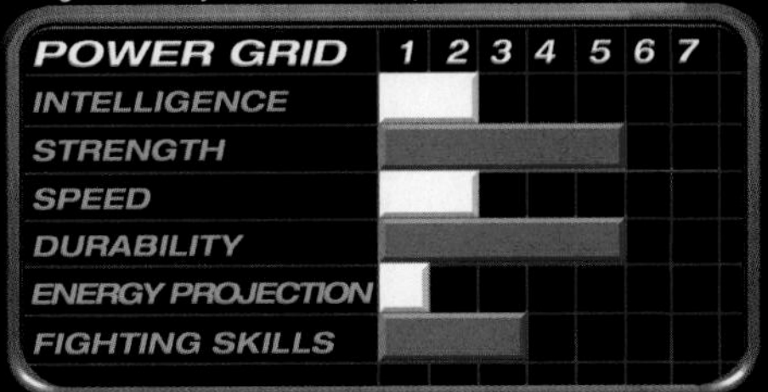
POWER GRID
1 2 3 4 5 6 7
INTELLIGENCE
STRENGTH
SPEED
DURABILITY
ENERGY PROJECTION
FIGHTING SKILLS

BLACK MAMBA

REAL NAME: Tanya Sealy
ALIASES: Tanya Sweet
IDENTITY: Known to authorities
OCCUPATION: Licensed super hero; former professional criminal, mercenary, fashion model, call girl
CITIZENSHIP: USA with a criminal record
PLACE OF BIRTH: Chicago, Illinois
KNOWN RELATIVES: None
GROUP AFFILIATION: Initiative, Women Warriors; formerly Serpent Society, "Secret Avengers," BAD Girls, Inc., Crimson Cowl (Justine Hammer)'s Masters of Evil, Sidewinder (Seth Voelker)'s Serpent Squad
EDUCATION: Unrevealed
FIRST APPEARANCE: Marvel Two-in-One #64 (1980)

HISTORY: Tanya Sealy was a call girl hired by the Roxxon Oil Corporation for experiments to transform her into a superhuman operative. She was sent to their Brand Corporation division, where a component was planted inside her brain that allowed her to tap into the Darkforce Dimension and wield its substance offensively. Dubbed Black Mamba, she joined the Serpent Squad, a team of snake-themed criminals led by Sidewinder (Seth Voelker), all of whom had been granted abilities via Roxxon's scientists. Roxxon sent the squad to retrieve the Serpent Crown, an ancient Lemurian mystical artifact drawing power from the Elder God Set. Following a battle with heroic interlopers the Thing (Ben Grimm), Stingray (Walter Newell) and the Inhumans' Triton, the squad's Black Mamba, Death Adder (Roland Burroughs) and Anaconda were trapped in an underwater landslide and Sidewinder left them behind, delivering the Serpent Crown and accepting full payment. Recovering, the Serpent Squad (sans Sidewinder) were later hired to steal a microscanner from Stark International, but Iron Man (Tony Stark) thwarted them. When the squad confronted Sidewinder about the money that he owed them, he not only paid up, but suggested that they form a new organization, the Serpent Society, in which they and other snake-themed criminals could operate like a trade union.

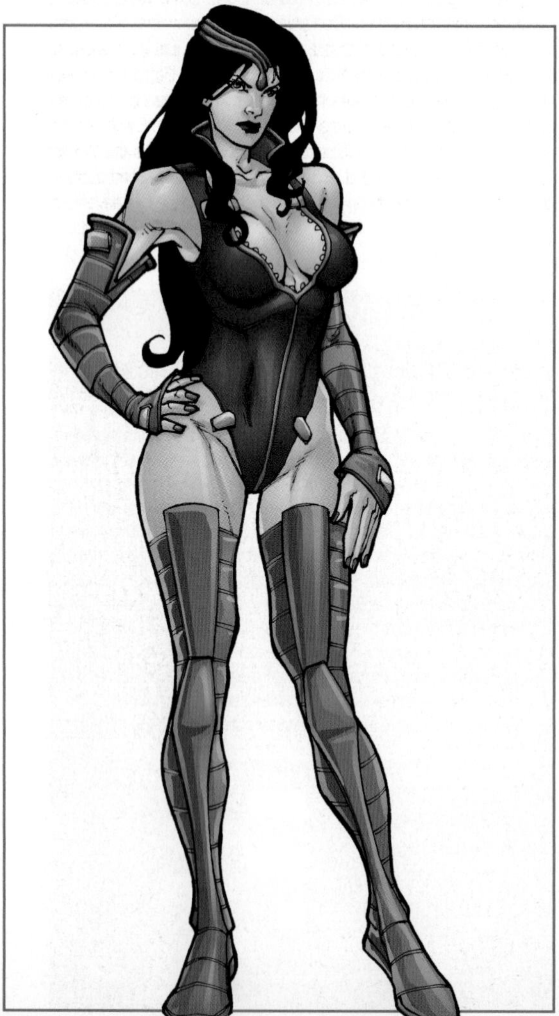

AIM (Advanced Idea Mechanics) hired the Serpent Society for its first assignment to assassinate AIM's then-fugitive master MODOK. Black Mamba joined the Serpent Society in the hunt for MODOK, finally trapping him in a shopping mall, but they were attacked by Captain America (Steve Rogers), who had Mamba and several others arrested; Sidewinder used his teleportation powers to rescue Mamba and the others from prison. Although other Society members had successfully killed MODOK, AIM required his body to authorize payment; Mamba joined other serpents in retrieving MODOK's corpse from the morgue. When a Scourge of the Underworld vigilante slew Death Adder (Roland Burroughs), the society sought the killer and Mamba interrogated Death Adder's parents, but to no avail. Mamba was once hired in her role as a call girl by Baron (Helmut) Zemo to romance Hercules (Heracles) and intoxicate him, thereby aiding Zemo's Masters of Evil when they ambushed Hercules and savagely battered him.

Black Mamba became a close friend to fellow serpents Diamondback (Rachel Leighton) and Asp (Cleo Nefertiti) and developed a romantic liaison with Sidewinder. After Sidewinder recruited members of a new Serpent Squad into the society, they proved to be double agents serving the Viper (Ophelia Sarkissian, aka Madame Hydra), who took over the Society. Mamba was among the few serpents who refused to serve Viper and was injected with a potentially fatal dose of Viper's snake venom, but Diamondback brought Captain America to their aid and gave Mamba the antitoxin in time to save her. After Sidewinder left the society, promoting Cobra (Klaus Voorhees) to leadership, Black Mamba joined the team on a mission for Deviant priestlord Ghaur and Lemurian Priestess of Set Llyra to recover a totem from Lima, Ohio, but the X-Men thwarted them. When Diamondback, by now no longer in the Society, went on a date with Steve Rogers, Asp and Black Mamba helped ensure that the evening went without incident, unaware that Diamondback's date was Captain America. In the course of the evening, Black Mamba helped drive away the costumed criminal Trump. When the Society realized Diamondback was working with Captain America, Voorhees (now King Cobra) had her placed on trial. Although Asp and Black Mamba defended her, she was sentenced to death. Asp and Mamba arranged for Sidewinder to save her, but in so doing placed themselves at risk. King Cobra captured them and used them as bait to bring back Diamondback, who returned with the mercenary Paladin, only to be captured themselves. Finally, Captain America came to their rescue and, in spite of his reluctance to trust Asp and Mamba, helped them break up the Serpent Society and place nearly all of the organization behind bars, with the notable exceptions of Asp and Black Mamba.

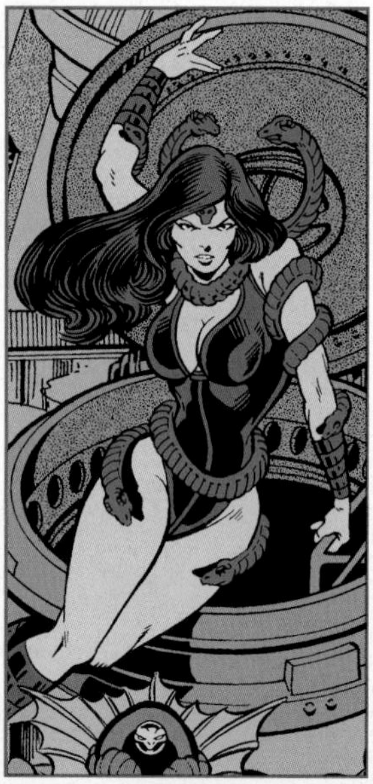

Art by George Pérez

Diamondback, Asp and Mamba formed their own team of

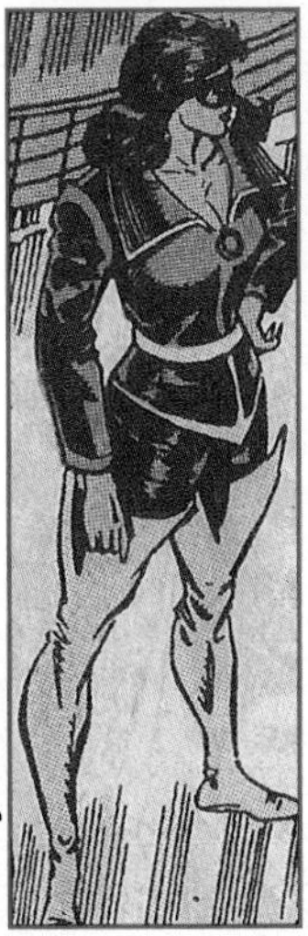

Art by Rik Levins

mercenary adventurers as BAD Girls, Inc., but before they could find work, still-at-large society members Anaconda, Puff Adder and Rock Python attacked them. They were narrowly saved by MODAM, who brought them to the island Femizonia to join Superia's Femizons, a would-be ruling class of superhuman women. During the cruise they befriended Impala, but Diamondback was nearly killed by Snapdragon (Sheoke Sanada), which made her want to give up costumed adventuring. When Paladin and Captain America infiltrated the Femizons' cruise ship en route to the island, they were defeated by the Femizons and Superia planned to transform them into women. Fearing that Superia planned to transform all men into women, Asp and Mamba decided to help Paladin and the Captain. As they fought their way through Femizonia, Mamba learned from Captain America how to manipulate her Darkforce around a person without injuring them, enabling him to briefly impersonate Superia. Eventually, the four and Diamondback escaped the Femizons and exited Femizonia. Back in the USA, Asp and Mamba searched for Snapdragon to help Diamondback overcome her fears, beginning at one of the criminal-friendly Bars With No Name, only to be threatened by Superia's lackeys Battleaxe (Anita Ehren), Golddigger (Angela Golden) and Steel Wind (Ruriko Tsumura); Impala came to the duo's aid and wound up joining BAD Girls as Diamondback's replacement. While trying to take custody of a Serpent Society saucer vehicle, the BAD Girls were confronted by the Avenger Sersi, but proved they were Captain America's allies and departed with the craft. They sought Snapdragon at the AIM Weapons Expo, but Diamondback had by now resumed her costumed life and secretly killed Snapdragon herself. Mamba was among the Darkforce wielders who fell under the Darkling (Henrique Gallant)'s control, but the New Warriors helped release her and Darkling's other victims from his thrall. Mamba became a fashion model and went on a date with Deathlok (John Truman), which was interrupted when Puff Adder asked her to rejoin the Serpent Society; Deathlok and Puff Adder came to blows, but Mamba ended the fight by refusing Puff Adder's invitation.

Black Mamba joined the Crimson Cowl (Justine Hammer)'s Masters of Evil, aiding in her plot to control a biotoxin that Justin Hammer had subjected most super-criminals to and which would place them at the Cowl's mercy, but they were thwarted by the villains turned heroes known as the Thunderbolts. When Captain America became involved with a Diamondback LMD used by the Red Skull (Johann Shmidt) in a plan against his old enemy, the real Diamondback noticed the deception and encouraged Asp and Mamba to rejoin the Serpent Society and have them investigate the Diamondback imposter. The Society captured Captain America and the LMD, but Cap escaped them and defeated the society; the LMD was ultimately exposed. Diamondback, Asp and Mamba re-formed BAD Girls, Inc. and a mysterious employer (secretly Cable) hired them to steal a hard drive called the Dominus Objective from the Dominus Corporation in La Jolla, California. Deadpool ("Wade Wilson") had also been unknowingly hired by Cable to retrieve the device and fought

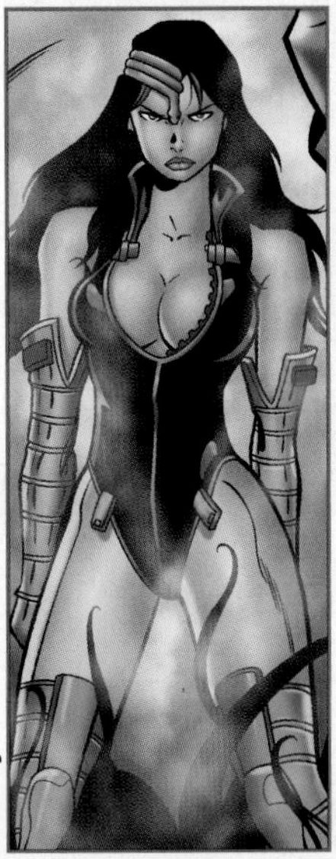

Art by Patrick Zircher

the BAD Girls, only to find it had already been taken by Cat (Shen Kuei) on behalf of the Black Box. The BAD Girls traced Cat to a Rand-Meachum plant in Long Island with Deadpool in pursuit. There, they discovered Deadpool's mercenary ally Weasel (Jack Hammer) was involved and clashed with Iron Fist (Daniel Rand), Luke Cage and Cable on the premises. Asp found evidence of Cat's theft; avoiding the other involved parties, they pursued the Cat to Hong Kong. Black Box used the Dominus Objective to gain power over all information stored electronically, but Cat revealed that Cable was his true employer, who had hired the BAD Girls and Deadpool as back-ups in case Cat had failed. The BAD Girls and Cat journeyed to Black Box's New Delhi, India base and aided Deadpool and Cable against Black Box's Executive Elite, but the battle ended when Cable convinced Black Box to work for him.

When the superhuman community was divided over the US government's controversial new Superhuman Registration Act (SHRA), Diamondback recruited Asp and Mamba into Captain America's rebel "Secret Avengers" to oppose pro-SHRA forces and they tried to recruit super-criminals into the resistance's ranks such as Goldbug and the Plunderer, but the vigilante Punisher (Frank Castle) killed both men, ending such plans. Captain America ultimately surrendered to the authorities and the Secret Avengers broke up, with many of them gaining amnesty by joining the government's new Fifty State Initiative organization of licensed super heroes. The BAD Girls, however, refused to surrender and later fought with Ms. Marvel (Carol Danvers), the Wasp (Janet van Dyne) and Black Widow (Natasha Romanoff) of the Avengers. After the Earth was invaded by Queen Veranke and her Skrull armies, Black Mamba rejoined the Serpent Society, who were panicked by the invasion. They seized hostages in Danzig, Ohio and barricaded themselves within a compound, only to be routed by Nova (Richard Rider) and the Nova Corps, who turned them over to the authorities. With the Initiative now operating under corrupt politician Norman Osborn's guidance, Black Mamba and the Asp joined the organization and were assigned to the Women Warriors, Delaware's official super-hero team, under Diamondback's leadership. Black Mamba has since aided the Initiative in adventures such as the defense of Baltimore-Washington International Airport from the terrorists RAID. The Women Warriors were also on the front lines of Norman Osborn's siege of Asgard.

HEIGHT: 5'7" **EYES:** Green
WEIGHT: 115 lbs. **HAIR:** Black

ABILITIES/ACCESSORIES: Black Mamba can tap into the Darkforce Dimension's black energies. She manifests this energy as an inky black cloud that surrounds her targets. People enveloped by her cloud are entranced by visions of someone they love, or they witness their greatest fantasies. While they are in this state, Black Mamba constricts the Darkforce around them, slowly suffocating them; even the Thing could not resist the Darkforce's physical constriction. The Cat is the only person known to have fully resisted her powers' effects. Her powers are limited by her range, which is line of sight. Black Mamba can also surround someone with her Darkforce and project the likeness of another person over them without suffocating her target; in this manner, she can create illusionary disguises. She can also breathe underwater and is a capable aircraft pilot.

POWER GRID	1	2	3	4	5	6	7
INTELLIGENCE	■	■					
STRENGTH	■	■					
SPEED	■	■					
DURABILITY	■	■					
ENERGY PROJECTION	■	■	■				
FIGHTING SKILLS	■	■	■				

BLACK SWAN

REAL NAME: Unrevealed
ALIASES: Swan, "Fritzie," "Sparrow," "Fancy Feast," "Swan-boy," Mr. Black, Schwarzer Schwan (name in German)
IDENTITY: Secret
OCCUPATION: Assassin, mercenary
CITIZENSHIP: Germany
PLACE OF BIRTH: Unrevealed; possibly Bavaria, Germany
KNOWN RELATIVES: None
GROUP AFFILIATION: None
EDUCATION: Unrevealed
FIRST APPEARANCE: Deadpool #65 (2002)

HISTORY: The mutant Black Swan was raised in the Bavarian Alps as an assassin, his aristocratic family's profession for roughly 300 years. The Swan gained a reputation as a top gentleman assassin, and a snob intolerant of rudeness. Hired alongside Taskmaster and Canadian mercenary Tyrell Farsa to take down revolutionaries in Zaire, the Swan took care of his part of the assignment before returning to the drop point. Angered by Farsa soiling one of his silk handkerchiefs, the Swan used his powers to damage Farsa's mind, leaving him permanently unable to take care of himself.

The Swan accepted a contract he intended to use as his "swan song" to cap his career. However, the hit was accidently interrupted by the

mercenary Deadpool ("Wade Wilson"), who was publicly given credit for the kill. Desiring revenge for this, The Swan teamed with Nijo, brother of one killed in the hit, to destroy Deadpool's reputation permanently. Tricking Deadpool into entering his German castle, the Swan implanted a psonic "virus" in his brain, causing Deadpool to allow himself to be beaten almost to death by the Swan before returning him to America with his memory of the last several hours wiped. Using Nijo to monitor Deadpool's activities, the Swan was increasingly angered to learn that his mind virus was not destroying Deadpool's career as quickly as he hoped. Relearning who had attacked him, a mentally deteriorating Deadpool confronted Nijo and the Black Swan in his castle, watching Swan kill Nijo during a confrontation before Deadpool used a bomb threat to force Swan to cure his schizophrenic assistant Ratbag (Erik Nicieza). Swan fought Deadpool, ransacking his mind to gain the bomb's deactivation codes. However, the Swan pushed his powers beyond their previous limit, enabling Deadpool to access his mind as easily as he accessed Deadpool's, who then overpowered the Swan and threw him into a fireplace grill before the bomb went off, seemingly killing both men.

Surviving by instinctively copying Deadpool's healing factor into himself, Black Swan soon realized his powers had also scrambled the abilities of himself, Deadpool, and the dead Nijo, merging them and his facial scarring into Nijo's revived corpse and leaving Deadpool a seeming shell of his former self. Swan found himself unhappily burdened with Nijo's strict sense of honor, while Nijo, taking the name Agent X/Alex Hayden, had Swan's marksman skills, and violent intolerance for rudeness. Tracking Hayden to Los Angeles, the Swan arrived with Deadpool in tow, intending to switch everyone's abilities back to their rightful owners. Linking all three minds together, the Swan restored everyone's rightful abilities, but then absorbed everyone's powers into himself, greatly increasing his own abilities. Drunk on his newfound power, the Swan briefly held his own against Agent X, Deadpool, Outlaw (Inez Temple), business associate Sandi Brandenberg, and Taskmaster, before they overwhelmed him. Agent X forced the wounded Swan to reabsorb his scarred face before the others shot him to death. Fearful that the Swan's healing factor could kick in once more and resurrect him, the five had the Swan's corpse stuffed, and then took it on vacation with them.

HEIGHT: 6'2"			**EYES:** Light brown	
WEIGHT: 210 lbs.			**HAIR:** Dark brown, with graying temples	

ABILITIES/ACCESSORIES: The Black Swan had telepathy that he visualized as akin to a hacker invading a computer, using it to alter a target's perception of him, allowing him to "hide" in plain sight before killing. He could create psonic "viruses" in others that could delete memories, impair motor skills, and corrupt basic bodily functions, sometimes permanently. He could also "rewire" brains to cure mental illnesses such as schizophrenia. He could transfer and/or copy skills and powers to and from himself. With Deadpool's healing powers enhancing his own abilities, the Swan could regenerate missing body parts, fully function with a hole in his spine, levitate, create bulletproof shields around himself with concentration, and cause aneurisms from hundreds of yards away. The Swan had several silver-topped canes, including some sword canes, he used to incapacitate foes. He was an expert marksman and swordsman, and could speak fluent English.

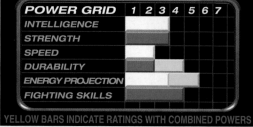

POWER GRID	1	2	3	4	5	6	7
INTELLIGENCE							
STRENGTH							
SPEED							
DURABILITY							
ENERGY PROJECTION							
FIGHTING SKILLS							

YELLOW BARS INDICATE RATINGS WITH COMBINED POWERS

HISTORY: Often too scared to sleep as a child, Althea became more courageous and eventually learned how to make grown men cry. Fighting alongside Captain America (Steve Rogers) in World War II, she became one of his closest associates in Europe; she reminded him what it meant to be a hero. Before they parted in Moscow, Rogers gave her a medal to thank her. Blinded under unrevealed circumstances, Al eventually joined the mysterious Union and later caused trouble worldwide, even for the Vatican. Eventually Deadpool ("Wade Wilson") was hired by a Middle Eastern agency to assassinate her, but he spared her life in Zaire and instead killed everyone else at the British Shadows Ops installation where she was stationed. At some point, Al took secret retribution on him in a way that made her feel guilty for many years. Though unaware of what she did, Deadpool later kidnapped her, imprisoning her at his San Francisco home — the Deadhut. Deadpool built the Box, a chamber filled with moving and/or sharp objects, and forced Al inside it each time she misbehaved. Al initially tried to escape and nearly got away two years into her imprisonment when Deadpool was working in Guadalajara. She traveled to meet her old Union colleague Tommy Mulroom in Maine, but Deadpool was already waiting there. With Tommy viciously beaten, Al accepted her situation and stopped trying to escape; upon realizing this, Deadpool stopped locking the doors. Al eventually developed a strange friendship with Deadpool and played along with his cruel games.

Al mocked Deadpool when he started seeing Siryn, though she secretly hoped the girl would bring out the best in Deadpool and often tricked him into meeting her. When Landau, Luckman & Lake offered Deadpool the chance to become a hero, Al encouraged him to comply. Getting her first real visitor in years when Deadpool's arms supplier Weasel (Jack Hammer) teleported to the Deadhut to warn Deadpool about T-Ray, Al was scared of the consequences and tried to hide his arrival. A short time later, Al got Deuce, Daredevil (Matt Murdock)'s former dog, from Deadpool after Weasel had won the dog from "Foggy" Nelson in a poker game. Not happy about having a dog, Al saw it as further torture. Leaving the house for five minutes with Deuce, she met Weasel again and they became friends, after which Weasel often visited Al to discuss Deadpool.

At a road trip to the Aquarium, Deadpool offered Al freedom. Al tried to get away with Deuce's help at first, but when the dog abandoned her she gave up. Picking her up during a fight against the Great Lakes Avengers, Deadpool tried to teleport back to the Deadhut, but his teleportation belt interacted with Doorman (DeMarr Davis)'s teleportation ability, sending Al and Deadpool back in time, diverging Reality-9712 when they dropped on an unsuspecting May Parker. Posing as May and her nephew Peter, Al had to deal with an annoyingly helpful Anna Watson and her niece Mary Jane, while Deadpool met Weasel's younger self to repair his teleportation belt; Al and Deadpool returned to their era and the Deadhut.

When Deadpool learned Weasel had been visiting Al, Deadpool tossed

REAL NAME: Althea (last name unrevealed)
ALIASES: Blind Alfred
IDENTITY: Secret
OCCUPATION: Unrevealed
CITIZENSHIP: UK
PLACE OF BIRTH: Unrevealed
KNOWN RELATIVES: None
GROUP AFFILIATION: Formerly the Union
EDUCATION: Unrevealed
FIRST APPEARANCE: Deadpool #1 (1997)

them both into the Box, after which Al punished Deadpool by not playing his games anymore. This worked, and after closing the Box, Wade released Al. Still feeling guilty over what she did in the past, Al stayed and convinced Deadpool to finish his job with LL&L even though they asked him to kill once again. She even planned to tell Deadpool what she had done to him years ago, but after nearly being blown up by LL&L's Overboss Dixon and being tricked by Gerry LeQuare into encouraging Deadpool to kill the Messiah, Al finally left Deadpool despite him needing her help to deal with his guilt over killing the Messiah. Al and Weasel attended Deadpool's funeral after he had been seemingly killed by Weapon X. Later, Deadpool proved that he could find Al at any time when he met with her to get validation for a crazy scheme to improve his reputation by beating Taskmaster.

HEIGHT: 5'3"
WEIGHT: 143 lbs.
EYES: Pink opacity over sclera (original unrevealed)
HAIR: White

ABILITIES/ACCESSORIES: An elderly, blind woman, Al maintained her quick wit despite her years-long imprisonment. It is assumed she went through combat training in the past.

POWER GRID	1	2	3	4	5	6	7
INTELLIGENCE							
STRENGTH							
SPEED							
DURABILITY							
ENERGY PROJECTION							
FIGHTING SKILLS							

YELLOW BARS INDICATE RATINGS AT YOUNGER AGE

BOB

REAL NAME: Bob (full name unrevealed)
ALIASES: None
IDENTITY: No dual identity
OCCUPATION: Mercenary, janitor; former pirate, terrorist
CITIZENSHIP: USA
PLACE OF BIRTH: Unrevealed
KNOWN RELATIVES: Allison (wife), Terry, Howie (sons), Herm (cousin)
GROUP AFFILIATION: Formerly Agency X, Hydra
EDUCATION: Unrevealed
FIRST APPEARANCE: Cable & Deadpool #38 (2007)

HISTORY: Bob was searching for employment in a career that would impress his wife and provide him with health insurance. His cousin Herm recommended he join Hydra's ranks and Bob complied, but although he received a 42,000 dollar salary, he soon learned Hydra had no dental plan. In Hydra training, Bob was terrified by the stories he heard of the organization's enemies, particularly Captain America (Steve Rogers), Elektra Natchios and Wolverine (Logan/James Howlett). He claimed that his courses included "Tactics of Retreat 101," "Advanced Tactics of Surrender" and "Hiding Places 301." Herm once gave Bob access to a Hydra jet's cockpit, but Herm was eventually captured after an altercation with the Avengers. Bob was assigned to a Hydra weapons research facility near Hyberadad, Pakistan and began keeping a blog about his ordeals. After the facility's agents captured Agent X (Alex Hayden)

AS PARROT

when he raided the base, Agency X hired Deadpool ("Wade Wilson") to rescue their boss. Deadpool's ally Weasel (Jack Hammer) performed reconnaissance on the base using Bob's blog and Deadpool took Bob hostage to access Agent X's cell. Under Deadpool's coercion, Bob helped Agent X and Deadpool escape the facility by piloting a Hydra jet, accidentally leaving Weasel behind.

Bob remained with Deadpool as he continued working with Agency X, accompanying him to a fight with T-Ray (which Bob kept out of) and flew Deadpool to Providence to aid his friend Cable. When Deadpool returned to Pakistan to stop Wolverine from slaughtering the staff of the same Hydra base Bob hailed from, he brought Bob with him in the hopes of exchanging him for Weasel. They discovered that Weasel was the new base commander as the "Penetraitor" and Wolverine decapitated Deadpool, but Bob reattached his head, and Weasel betrayed Hydra. However, Weasel's new teleportation technology accidentally sent Deadpool and Bob back in time, first appearing in the 1940s where they fought alongside Captain America and Bucky (James Barnes) against Arnim Zola, then to the early days of the Fantastic Four, who, with the help of the Fantastic Four of their own era, helped return them to the present. Bob also accompanied Deadpool as Dr. Stephen Strange and Brother Voodoo (Jericho Drumm) led him to revive his enemy T-Ray, journeyed to the Savage Land to remove Brainchild's energy generator so it could be used by the nation Rumekistan and fought an army of symbiote-infected dinosaurs that Deadpool accidentally sent to Manhattan with Weasel's teleportation technology. One of the dinosaurs snared Bob with a tendril and, as he tried to pull himself free, he accidentally pulled an electrical sign on the beast, killing it. The scene was captured on television and he was declared a hero; his wife was impressed.

After Norman Osborn slew Skrull invasion leader Veranke, he hired Bob and Tiger Shark to assassinate Deadpool to cover-up the aid Deadpool rendered him against Veranke. However, Bob double-crossed Tiger Shark and aided Deadpool instead. Deadpool eventually received a payout from Osborn's lieutenant Bullseye and used it to purchase a boat so that he could become a pirate. Bob was brought aboard the ship as Deadpool's pet parrot, forced to wear a parrot costume and speak in a parrot-like voice when addressing Deadpool. The two attempted to foment piracy at the island Jallarka, only to find other pirates in the territory who stole their boat. With their blind navigator Kalani's help they recovered the boat. Quickly tiring of piracy, Deadpool sent Bob home.

HEIGHT: 5'10"   EYES: Brown
WEIGHT: 183 lbs.   HAIR: Brown

ABILITIES/ACCESSORIES: Bob received standard Hydra training in armed and unarmed combat. However, as a marksman he is almost incapable of hitting a live target and usually hides during violent outbreaks ("strategic invisibility") and believes that if he cannot see his enemies, they will not be able to see him. He is unable to resist threats of torture and in moments of stress will shout the Hydra motto ("Hail Hydra! Immortal Hydra! We shall never be destroyed! Cut off a limb and two more shall take its place!"). He is also a competent (albeit self-taught) pilot. He usually carries a cell phone, rifle or handgun.

POWER GRID	1	2	3	4	5	6	7
INTELLIGENCE							
STRENGTH							
SPEED							
DURABILITY							
ENERGY PROJECTION							
FIGHTING SKILLS							

SANDI BRANDENBERG

HISTORY: As a child, Sandi would take in stray animals and keep them even if they attacked her, believing that she couldn't let them go once they knew who she was. As an adult, Sandi became a dancer and while on vacation at a casino in Las Vegas met the mercenary Taskmaster while he was posing as "Tony Masters." Taskmaster impressed Sandi with his ability dice-rolling abilities and convinced her to go on a date with him. Summoned to business in New York, Taskmaster brought Sandi to him with his private jet and arranged a romantic balcony dinner so that he could observe the destruction of a building owned by the Triad gangs, who had crossed him during his assignment. However, members of the Triads traced Taskmaster to his suite and began a firefight, during which Taskmaster revealed his masked identity to Sandi. Unfortunately, one of the Triads shot Sandi in the back during the altercation. Sandi survived her injury and ended her relationship with Taskmaster, although he remained obsessed with her.

Remaining in New York, Sandi went to work for Deadpool ("Wade Wilson") when, flush with money from having seemingly slain the heads of the Four Winds, he established the offices of Deadpool, Inc. As Deadpool's personal secretary, Sandi managed his assignments. When rival mercenary Black Swan began a ploy for revenge on Deadpool for stealing his credit for assassinating the Four Winds, Sandi contacted Taskmaster, who shared what he knew of the Black Swan with Deadpool. At this time, Sandi was in an abusive relationship with her latest boyfriend that finally ended with her being hospitalized from her injuries. Sandi made Deadpool promise that he wouldn't kill her boyfriend, but Taskmaster made no such promise and executed him. That same day, Deadpool engaged in a showdown with Black Swan and was lost and presumed dead after detonating explosives in Swan's castle base.

Shortly afterward, Sandi was sought out by the amnesiac Agent X (Alex Hayden) who hoped to become a mercenary and wanted Sandi's help. Wondering if he might be Deadpool, Sandi arranged for Taskmaster and Outlaw (Inez Temple) to begin training him, and she maintained his clients much as she had for Deadpool. When Agent X obtained the Alpine Amusement Park and planned to set up Agency X there, the Four Winds crime cartel's Higashi threatened violence against him if he did not sell the land; Sandi helped drive the Four Winds away from the park using an elephant left behind by the previous owner, and Higashi was impressed with her courage. He began to make romantic gestures to Sandi, much to Hayden and Taskmaster's consternation. Higashi's lieutenant Saguri ordered the deaths of Agent X and all of his friends when she believed him to be Deadpool, but Higashi protected Sandi, and Agent X ended hostilities by killing Saguri. After Agency X was finally set up, Sandi took on an assignment, pitting herself against the invulnerable Fight-Man to impress Hayden. Sandi's ploy worked and she wound up sleeping with Hayden. Sandi still went on a date with Higashi to a Four Winds conference, but remained in love with Hayden. When the Black Swan and Deadpool returned, revealing that they and Agent X were each made up from pieces of each other, Sandi helped them sort themselves out and defeat Black Swan, then had him stuffed to prevent his return.

HEIGHT: 5'6" **EYES:** Brown
WEIGHT: 126 lbs. **HAIR:** Brown

ABILITIES/ACCESSORIES: Sandi is a competent hand-to-hand combatant and keeps a handgun as her sidearm.

POWER GRID	1	2	3	4	5	6	7
INTELLIGENCE	■	■					
STRENGTH	■	■					
SPEED	■	■					
DURABILITY	■	■					
ENERGY PROJECTION	■						
FIGHTING SKILLS	■	■	■				

REAL NAME: Sondra "Sandi" Brandenberg
ALIASES: None
IDENTITY: No dual identity
OCCUPATION: Secretary; former dancer
CITIZENSHIP: USA
PLACE OF BIRTH: Columbus, Ohio
KNOWN RELATIVES: Unidentified mother
GROUP AFFILIATION: Agency X
EDUCATION: High school graduate
FIRST APPEARANCE: Taskmaster #1 (2002)

Taskmaster made one last attempt at convincing Sandi of his feelings for her, but she rejected him again. Sandi and Outlaw later hired Deadpool to rescue Agent X from a Hydra base in Pakistan, unfortunately finding that Hydra had afflicted Hayden with an eating disorder that transformed him into an obese glutton. Sandi and Outlaw's association with Deadpool led to them being targeted by his nemesis T-Ray, but Deadpool rescued them. Deadpool and his sidekick Bob, agent of Hydra worked for Agency X for a brief period to make up for Hayden's incapacitation and Sandi and Outlaw joined them for a fight against symbiote-infected dinosaurs, which finally led Agent X back into battle. Sandi and Outlaw placed Hayden on a diet to help him regain his old physique.

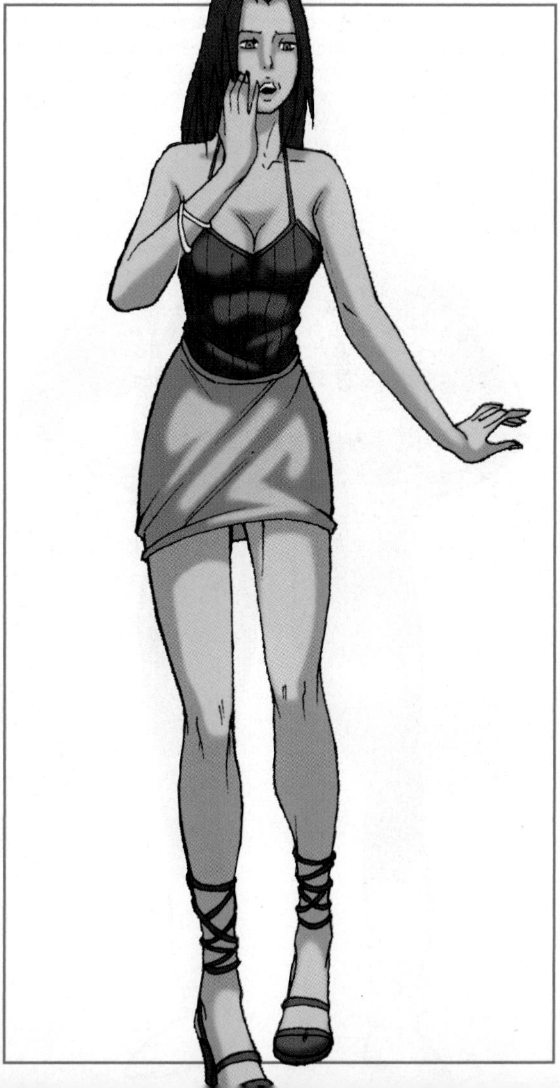

G.W. BRIDGE

REAL NAME: George Washington Bridge
ALIASES: None
IDENTITY: No dual identity
OCCUPATION: Espionage agent; former director of SHIELD, mercenary
CITIZENSHIP: USA
PLACE OF BIRTH: Unrevealed
KNOWN RELATIVES: Sandy (wife, deceased), Tyler (stepson)
GROUP AFFILIATION: SHIELD, Six Pack/Wild Pack, Weapon: PRIME
EDUCATION: Unrevealed
FIRST APPEARANCE: X-Force #1 (1991)

HISTORY: George Washington Bridge was a founding member of the Wild Pack, a six-person mercenary strike force which included Cable, Domino (Neena Thurman), Grizzly (Theodore Wincester), Hammer (Eisenhower Canty) and Garrison Kane. Cable was a mystery man to the rest of the Wild Pack, who did not suspect that he had traveled from Earth-4935's future, hoping to change the past. On one assignment, the Wild Pack were hired by AIM to steal a fiber ionic fibrillator from Hydra, only to learn later that AIM allowed the theft to discover how far along Hydra's experiments were. On another mission, the Pack clashed with the Mandarin. Many of the Wild Pack's assignments came from the mysterious Mr. Tolliver (actually Cable's son, Tyler Summers). After destroying a corporate building in Tehran, Iran, Tolliver's people suggested the Wild Pack change their name to avoid litigation from Symkaria's Wild Pack, leading to their new name: Six Pack. While on a mission in Afghanistan, the Six Pack came across a facility run by the mutant terrorist Stryfe (secretly Cable's clone), who revealed he was also working for Tolliver. Cable was determined to battle Stryfe, forcing the Six Pack to join him on his mission. Although Stryfe escaped in Afghanistan, they clashed again in Uruguay, but the mission went disastrously wrong when Stryfe captured Kane to force Hammer into turning over data he stole from Stryfe's computers. Cable shot Hammer in the back in a futile attempt to stop him and when the facility exploded, Kane was caught in the blast and lost both his arms. Cable only saved himself from the blast, and the Six Pack were demoralized by his betrayal and the grievous injuries Kane and Hammer suffered; they went their separate ways.

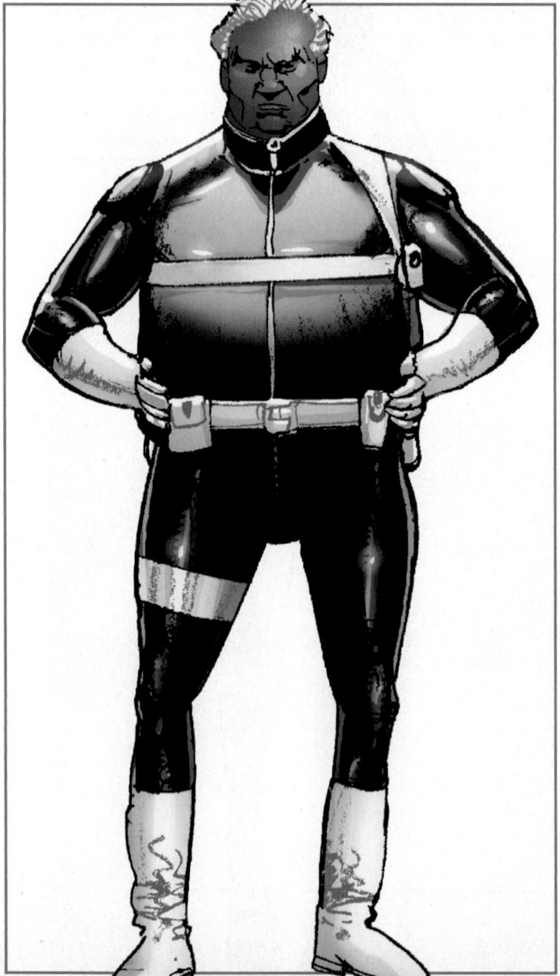

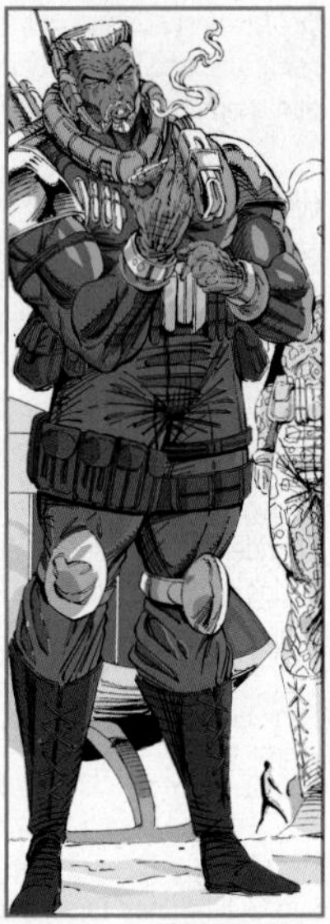

Art by Rob Liefeld

Bridge joined SHIELD and rose to the rank of commander. After Cable was sighted leading the mutant heroes X-Force against Stryfe's Mutant Liberation Front (MLF), SHIELD Director Nick Fury gave Bridge the assignment to deal with him. At the same time, Bridge was manipulated by Psi-Borg (Fionna Wyman), a Hydra psychic who altered his memories so that he would recruit her and Hydra agents Knockabout (Jarno Sprague) and Violence (Violet Pinkerton) into SHIELD's Super Agent program. At the time, SHIELD's Helicarrier had been commandeered by Mad Dog (Robert Baxter), and Fury was desperate for aid in retaking the vessel. When Bridge offered the Super Agents, Fury accepted them with few reservations. With additional resources from Canada's Department K, Bridge gathered Weapon: PRIME (PRototype Induced Mutation Echelon), which included Kane (now Weapon X) and Grizzly along with Rictor, Tigerstrike and Yeti (Wendigo). Weapon: PRIME found X-Force's base in the Adirondack Mountains and clashed with X-Force, during which Cable wounded Bridge. Cable destroyed the headquarters, again saving himself, but abandoning X-Force; to Bridge, it justified his earlier sense of betrayal. With his injuries, Bridge was unable to prevent X-Force from stealing the SHIELD Personnel Armed Carrier Weapon: PRIME had used, or stop Rictor from defecting to X-Force. The failure of Weapon: PRIME injured Bridge's reputation, causing him to quit SHIELD, but he soon rejoined to explore the appearance of Graymalkin, Cable's space station. Bridge lost the opportunity to use the station to find Cable when SHIELD and War Machine (James Rhodes) clashed with X-Force aboard the station, which was destroyed.

Bridge was finally probed by SHIELD ESPer Network Nina, who discovered what Psi-Borg had done to him, exposing the Super Agents as Hydra agents. Bridge also joined SHIELD and the Externals' Gideon and Crule against Hydra and participated in the SHIELD assault on Hydra's Iceland base. The entire Six Pack were soon reunited and Cable tried to make amends with his former allies, and while Bridge no longer saw Cable as an enemy, he could not see him as a friend. When Danielle Moonstar infiltrated the MLF, Bridge served as one of her SHIELD contacts. After Nick Fury was seemingly killed by the Punisher (Frank Castle) while under the influence of psychoactive drugs and memory-altering regression therapy, Bridge became SHIELD's new director and kept tabs on the Punisher's activities. As anti-mutant pressure from the agency Operation: Zero Tolerance began to grow, Cyclops (Scott Summers) was framed for an attack on Senator Robert Kelly's life and placed in SHIELD custody under Bridge's watch, but Cable led X-Force in rescuing Cyclops. When the psychic entity Onslaught sent a wave of Sentinels to attack Manhattan, the SHIELD Helicarrier was knocked from the sky, and the Punisher came to SHIELD's assistance. Bridge made a deal with the Punisher, sending him to defend pro-mutant Reverend

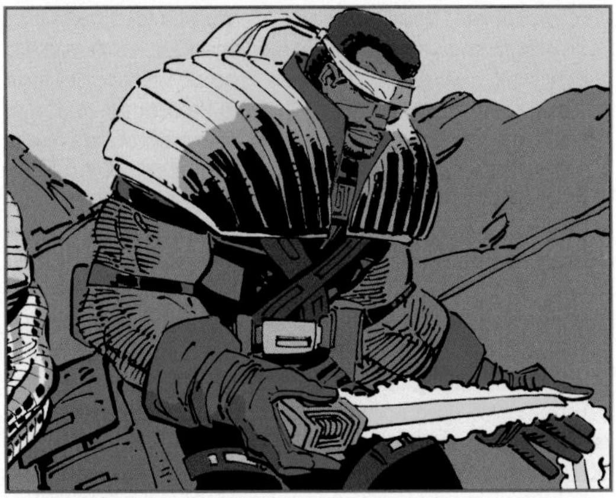

Art by John Romita Jr.

William Conover from a new MLF. As Zero Tolerance continued to grow in power, Bridge sent Domino to aid Moonstar, whose cover in the MLF was finally broken. After Zero Tolerance's leader Bastion surrendered, Bridge helped round up the parties culpable for its practices. As the new team of heroes called Thunderbolts became popular in Manhattan, Bridge found himself under pressure from their leader Citizen V (secretly Helmut Zemo) to release the Avengers' files to assist them. When New York was besieged by the Elements of Doom, Bridge finally acquiesced to the Thunderbolts, but shortly thereafter Zemo exposed the Thunderbolts to Bridge as the Masters of Evil, having completed the work necessary to their deception.

Fury was at last revealed to be alive and resumed leadership of SHIELD while Bridge took charge of hunting the Thunderbolts, whose remaining members had become heroes, but were still fugitives. Bridge employed the Lightning Rods (formerly Great Lakes Avengers) against the Thunderbolts, but they met with a quick defeat. Bridge found himself beset by office politics when fellow agent Clay Quartermain reassigned him to the Washington DC bureau, forcing him to step down from fieldwork to a desk assignment. Placed under the command of Seth Waters, Bridge began to realize a conspiracy was at work within SHIELD and with the aid of reporter Irene Merryweather exposed the details to the Daily Bugle, revealing how SHIELD forces had captured Cable in order to seize samples of the techno-organic virus which afflicted him and weaponize it into their Nemesis robot program. The scandal brought down Waters, and Bridge returned to active duty. While investigating mutant empath Randall Shire, Bridge fell under Shire's domination; Shire, in turn, had been possessed by Semijan, one of the Undying, extraterrestrials in a competition to cause the most deaths. Semijan hoped to use Bridge's authority to launch a nuclear attack, but Cable rescued Bridge and drove out the Undying; Bridge was released from Shire's control when he accidentally used his own empathic powers to turn his followers against him. Bridge served as liaison with the Commission on Superhuman Activities' short-lived team the Redeemers, who briefly took the place of the Thunderbolts. However, Bridge again faced a transfer when he was targeted by General Deutsch, who accused him of covering up for Cable and threatened to reassign him to Alaska. When several of Bridge's friends were mysteriously killed, Bridge realized he was also targeted for death and, with the help of Merryweather and Cable, he exposed Deutsch as a pawn of the Dark Sisterhood cabal, who were routed by Cable.

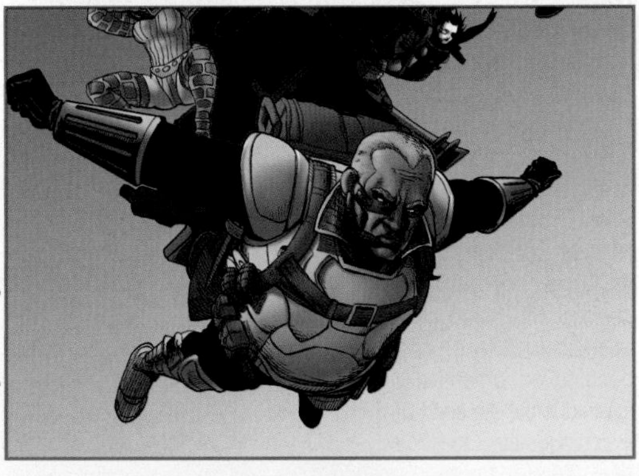

Art by Reilly Brown

When Cable realized the full potential of his mutant powers, the Earth's nations became concerned with how he would use that power. Fury authorized Bridge to assemble a new Six Pack, returning to duty with Domino and Hammer and joined by Anaconda, Constrictor and Solo (James Bourne). The Six Pack invaded Cable's island base Providence, but were no match for his advanced power. Regardless, their attempt helped SHIELD gauge Cable's power. Cable was stripped of his godlike power by his ally Deadpool ("Wade Wilson"), who rendered him comatose. When the Six Pack traced Cable to his Swiss chateau, they set off a telepathic security net which drew all of their minds into Cable's; the Six Pack were threatened with death if Cable's mind perished, but Deadpool was able to restore Cable in time. SHIELD let Cable continue operating Providence for the time now that his power had diminished.

SHIELD's Jasper Sitwell assigned Bridge to trace the Punisher and he began to track his movements, but also took a Six Pack assignment to Rumekistan in an attempt to destabilize the government Cable had established there. Although Constrictor had departed the Six Pack, Bridge surreptitiously recruited Deadpool to his side and Deadpool nearly killed Cable. Recovering, Cable took the Six Pack into custody, and Domino gave testimony against them, ultimately returning them to the USA in disgrace. Continuing with his assignment to capture the Punisher, Bridge assembled Domino, Silver Sable and Valentina de Fontaine (the latter actually a Skrull imposter). After finally succeeding in capturing the Punisher, their prison convoy was interrupted by the Punisher's arch-foe Jigsaw (Billy Russo) and the Wrecking Crew, but the Punisher helped defeat them and allowed himself to be incarcerated. Bridge quietly authorized the illegal execution of Jigsaw by SHIELD forces. The Punisher later escaped, but Bridge allowed him to remain at large. When SHIELD was dismantled Bridge retired from the service. Marrying a woman with a son named Tyler, Bridge attempted to enjoy his retirement, but as an ally of the Punisher he was targeted by Death-Adder (Roland Burroughs) and Basilisk (Basil Elks), villains resurrected by the Hood (Parker Robbins) to capture the Punisher. The criminals murdered Bridge's new wife and turned Bridge over to the Hood, who had Microchip execute him in a ritual to resurrect the Punisher's family.

HEIGHT: 6'1" **EYES:** Brown
WEIGHT: 230 lbs. **HAIR:** White, formerly black

ABILITIES/ACCESSORIES: GW Bridge was an experienced intelligence officer, leader, tactician, hand-to-hand combatant, marksman, commando, paratrooper and explosives handler. As an agent of SHIELD, he often wore a standard-issue jumpsuit made of flameproof, bulletproof Kevlar/beta cloth material; on special missions he would don additional body armor. He kept a SHIELD communicator (including a headset-mounted apparatus which relayed data to his right eye) and a SHIELD laser pistol on most missions, but also wielded a variety of conventional firearms and energy rifles.

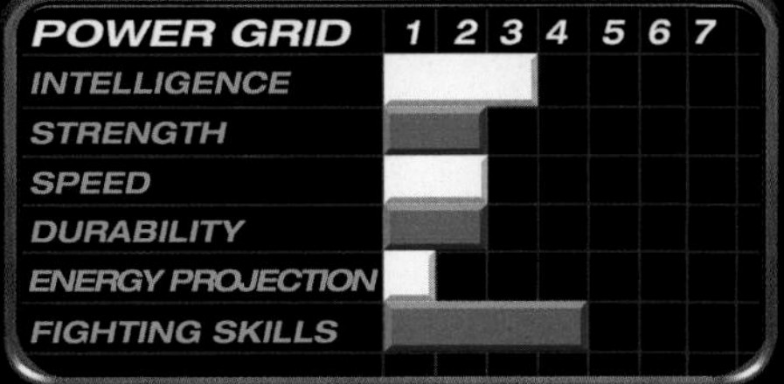
POWER GRID
1 2 3 4 5 6 7
INTELLIGENCE
STRENGTH
SPEED
DURABILITY
ENERGY PROJECTION
FIGHTING SKILLS

CAT

REAL NAME: Shen Kuei
ALIASES: None
IDENTITY: Known to authorities
OCCUPATION: Freelance espionage operative
CITIZENSHIP: People's Republic of China
PLACE OF BIRTH: Unrevealed
KNOWN RELATIVES: Unidentified son, unidentified brother (deceased)
GROUP AFFILIATION: Formerly Oracle Inc.'s Heroes for Hire, Silver Sable's Wild Pack
EDUCATION: Unrevealed
FIRST APPEARANCE: Master of Kung Fu #38 (1976)

HISTORY: Shen Kuei is one of the world's most formidable martial artists, having trained since the age of four. He became known in Hong Kong's underworld as "Cat" and recognizable by the black cat tattoo on

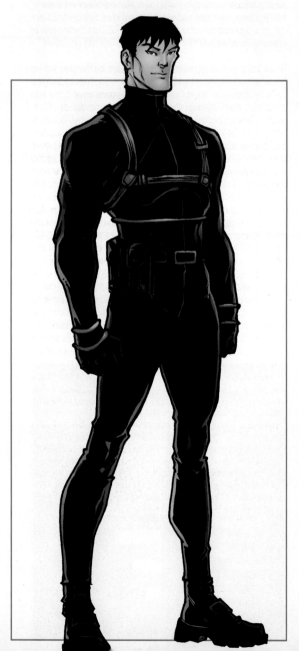

his chest. Cat hired himself as a freelance espionage agent, taking most of his assignments from the Chinese government. His brother operated a Hong Kong nightclub called the Jade Peacock, which ran an illegal gambling den from a secret room. The Jade Peacock attracted many figures from Hong Kong's criminal underworld, but fear of Cat's abilities prevented any serious attempts to dethrone him. Cat's activities drew the attention of British intelligence, who sent MI6 agent Juliette Jeunet to spy on him, taking work as a torch singer in the Jade Peacock. Juliette grew close to Cat and became his lover, although he suspected she was a spy.

MI6's Sir Denis Nayland Smith sent his agent Shang-Chi to Hong Kong to retrieve papers from Cat which he said were stolen from MI6 and to protect Juliette. Shang found Juliette at the Jade Peacock, but she was reluctant to flee Hong Kong, having truly fallen in love with Cat. Cat learned of Shang's arrival and confronted him at the Jade Peacock, dubbing him "Britisher" for serving MI6. The two initially fought side-by-side against a street gang who had threatened Shang, but members of the underworld were displeased by the violence, fearing it would draw attention to the club's activities; Shang used the arrival of the gangsters as an opportunity to flee with Juliette and recover the stolen documents, only to find they were not "stolen" at all. Shang discarded the papers but still had to contend with Cat, who considered Shang to have turned his back on China and been corrupted by the western world. Shang and Cat fought almost evenly until Juliette struck herself with a dagger to prove to Cat that she loved him. Eager to rush Juliette to a doctor, Cat had to turn his back to Shang, who was armed with a knife; Shang did not seize the opportunity and allowed Juliette and Cat to depart in peace.

Cat later took a new assignment for China, smuggling hashish bricks that each contained a microdot bearing plans for a neutron bomb. At first Cat took the pirate Kogar as his partner, but the two soon fell out. By this time, Juliette had separated from Cat, disapproving of his work for China. Cat took the whip-wielding mercenary Pavane as his new lover while Juliette became involved with Cat's own lieutenant Skull-Crusher. Juliette also made an alliance with Kogar to help him steal the hashish from Cat, although Juliette did not know what secret the bricks concealed. Skull-Crusher proved to be a constant irritant to Cat's careful operation, particularly when he journeyed to London to start a fight with Shang-

Chi, setting Shang on a collision course with Cat's plans. Juliette intercepted a shipment of hashish meant for the Jade Peacock and substituted it with a barrel from Kogar, not knowing he had planted a bomb inside. The bomb killed Cat's brother, but when Shang-Chi came on the scene to aid Juliette, Kogar informed Cat that Shang was his brother's killer. The ploy succeeded, tricking Cat and Shang into another fight, but in his eagerness Kogar gave away too much detail of Cat's brother's death, making Cat realize Shang was innocent. Most of the hashish was destroyed by Juliette, ending the smuggling operation. Shang had become romantically inclined to Juliette and Cat encouraged them to follow

Art by John Romita Jr.

their hearts, but Juliette remained bound to Skull-Crusher so Shang left her. Cat soon ended his relationship with Pavane.

As a free agent, Cat learned of a sunken ship near Hong Kong which contained plans and materials for a particle beam weapon, lost since the vessel was bombed beneath the waves. Aware that the world's governments would want such a weapon, Cat assembled a crew to raise the ship for the sole purpose of destroying the parts and plans, bringing Juliette back to him, but strictly as an operative. Shang-Chi was now an agent of Freelance Restorations, and his own lover, Leiko Wu, came to investigate Cat's operation, ultimately choosing to aid him and falling in love with him, although Cat realized he still loved Juliette. Shang pursued Leiko and soon met up with Juliette. Cat succeeded in destroying the plans and parts for the weapon, but when he was confronted by Shang he assumed Shang was there to oppose him. To end the fight, Juliette and Leiko drew their weapons on each other and threatened to shoot; Cat and Shang's fight ended, and Cat returned to Juliette. When Razor-Fist (William Scott) came to Hong Kong searching for Shang-Chi, Cat and Juliette learned of this and sent a warning to Freelance Restorations. At some point, Cat and Juliette had a son and Cat also trained the spy Agent (Rick Mason).

After Leiko Wu was captured by the terrorist cooperative called the Red Wolves, Shang turned to Cat for help, relying on his past love for Leiko. Cat agreed to aid him and his comrades Clive Reston and Black Jack Tarr. Cat and Shang were sent to impersonate a pair of Yakuza gangsters scheduled to purchase weaponry bound for the Red Wolves' training camp. By working their way from drug dealers to the top of the Yakuza, Cat and Shang found Ryohei Hashioka was in league with the Red Wolves' organizer Brian Argus and traced Hashioka to Argus' island near Hong Kong. Cat, Shang, Reston and Tarr raided the base, but while Leiko was rescued by Shang, Cat vanished during the battle; finding no trace of his body, Shang was certain he still lived. By this time Juliette had again left Cat to raise their son away from him, concerned that the evil she had seen in him would reflect upon their child. Cat came to Manhattan to visit them, but Cat's son was kidnapped by Shockwave (Lancaster Sneed) and Razor-Fist (Douglas Scott) on behalf of an unidentified opponent of Cat who was afraid Cat was after his criminal enterprises in Manhattan. Cat went to rescue his son and was aided by Spider-Man (Peter Parker), together saving the child while besting both kidnappers, and Cat informed them that while he had no interest in their employer's transactions, he would remain in Manhattan as long as he wished. Cat was later hired on a mission in Symkaria by Silver Sable to join her Wild Pack in defending geneticist Wolfgang Hessler from his former employer the Master of the World (Eshu). The Heroes for Hire came to liberate Hessler, unaware they were aiding the Master's plans, and Cat sparred with their leader Iron Fist (Daniel Rand), ultimately besting him when the hero was distracted by Cat's teammate Paladin defeating Iron Fist's girlfriend Misty Knight. Soon after, Cat was hired by Heroes for Hire and served alongside Iron Fist and Shang-Chi on a mission to Madripoor to investigate the pirate Lionmane, who sought to become a modern-day warlord in what he considered was an inevitable collapse of the present Chinese government. Lionmane hired Cat away from Heroes for Hire, making him betray his teammates, but in a fight with Lionmane's forces Iron Fist defeated Cat and Lionmane. Cat subsequently joined the Bloodsport competition held in Madripoor with the world's elite hand-to-hand combatants in a winner-take-all tournament, but he lost to Taskmaster.

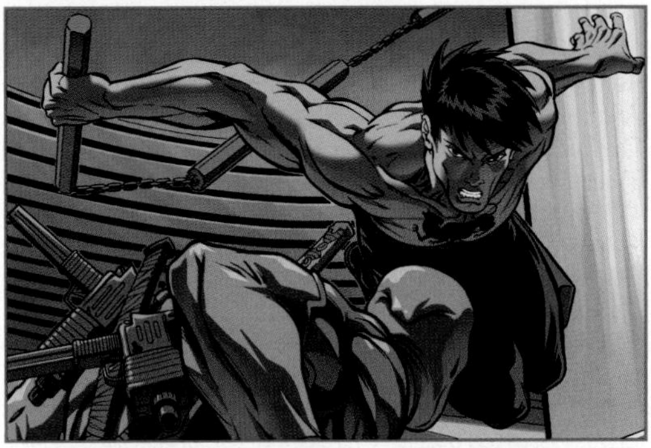

Art by Patrick Zircher

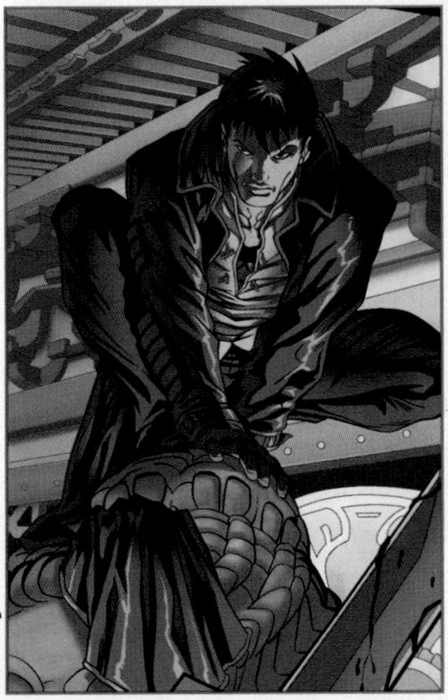

Art by Patrick Zircher

When the mutant Cable's powers became vastly enhanced, many of the Earth's nations feared what he might accomplish and began plotting his downfall. Cat was hired by China to retrieve several components from his former base Graymalkin which, when assembled, would strip Cable of his powers. To facilitate the operation, Cat was aided by the Roxxon International Research facility in Tokyo, Japan. Cat found himself at odds with Deadpool ("Wade Wilson"), who had been hired by the X-Men to perform the same operation; Deadpool was excited to be pit against Cat, revealing that he worshipped him as a fellow mercenary. Deadpool seemingly stole all of the pieces Cat had gathered in Tokyo, but he secretly kept one part to himself. From Deadpool's ally Weasel (Jack Hammer), Cat learned Deadpool's location on Providence, the artificial island Cable had created, and provided the missing component, allowing Deadpool the opportunity he needed to shut down Cable's mind with the device. Some time later, Cat was asked by the Black Box (Garebed Bashur) to steal a hard drive from the Dominus Corporation called the "Dominus Objective," which would grant Black Box mastery over all electronically stored information. Cat was uncertain of the assignment, but Cable, who wanted Black Box to achieve his goals so to gain his abilities for his own side, secretly hired Cat to take the job; Cable also secretly hired Deadpool and BAD Girls, Inc., in case Cat failed at his mission. Cat successfully stole the item, avoiding Deadpool and the BAD Girls, as well as Iron Fist, Luke Cage, Weasel and Cable himself. After Black Box activated the Dominus Objective, granting him immense powers through the "infonet," Cat contacted the BAD Girls and brought them to aid Cable and Deadpool against Black Box's Executive Elite, an army of cloned soldiers. Cat destroyed the cloning vats where the Executive Elite were created, forcing them to surrender.

HEIGHT: 5'9"
WEIGHT: 155 lbs.
EYES: Blue
HAIR: Black

ABILITIES/ACCESSORIES: The Cat is an extraordinary hand-to-hand combatant and one of the greatest living masters of the martial arts disciplines. He occasionally wields weapons such as knives, spears and shuriken.

POWER GRID	1 2 3 4 5 6 7
INTELLIGENCE	3
STRENGTH	2
SPEED	2
DURABILITY	2
ENERGY PROJECTION	1
FIGHTING SKILLS	6

CORPSE CORPS

MEMBERS: Proto-husk duplicates of Basilisk (Basil Elks), Bird-Man (Henry Hawk or Achille DiBacco), Brutacus, Bucky (James Buchanan, Fred Davis or James Monroe), Cheetah (Esteban Carracus), Cyclone (Andre Gerard), Egghead (Elihas Starr), Hydron, Kangaroo (Frank Oliver), Mirage (Desmond Charne), Porcupine (Alexander Gentry), Red Raven, Reptilla, Ringer (Anthony Davis), Thornn, Turner D. Century (Clifford Michaels), Vakume, Vamp/Animus (Denise Baranger), Whizzer (Robert Frank), presumably others
FIRST APPEARANCE: Deadpool #0 (1998)

HISTORY: Growing impatient with the length of time true cloning took, geneticist Arnim Zola sought new methods to create duplicates of other beings. Utilizing his experience creating artificial humanoids such as Primus and Doughboy, Zola developed a system using what he dubbed "proto-husks." Instead of the months or years needed to grow a true clone, proto-husks could be grown in hours and infused with the DNA of organic beings to create seemingly identical duplicates. These duplicates appeared to possess all of the superhuman powers of the originals (even abilities derived via technology), though it is unrevealed if this was something ingrained into each proto-husk's DNA, the result of further genetic tinkering by Zola, or if outside technology was employed to replicate these abilities. Zola preferred to imbue these proto-husks with the DNA of costumed heroes and villains who were at the time believed deceased, though several of them had their DNA samples covertly retrieved by Zola before their "deaths," such as Bucky, Red Raven and the five members of the Salem's Seven. After the Scourge of the Underworld murdered 18 super villains at the Bar with No Name in Ohio, Zola retrieved DNA samples and costume tech from several of the victims.

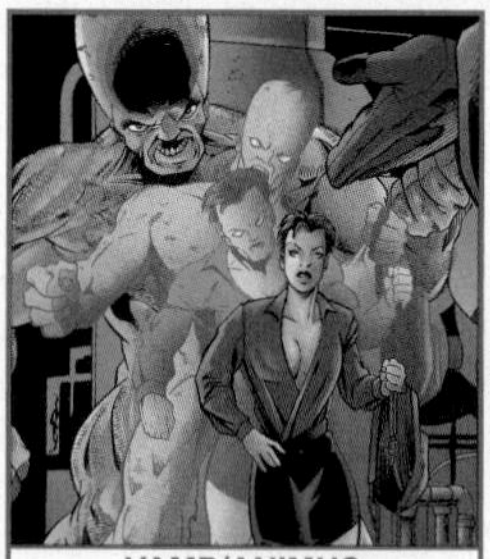

Art by Yancey Labat

VAMP/ANIMUS

Zola's prized member of this project was Vamp, who could transform into the monstrous Animus. While he cultivated the rest of what would become the Corpse Corps, he allowed Vamp to take on mercenary assignments, one of which brought her into conflict with Deadpool ("Wade Wilson") due to the convoluted machinations of Typhoid Mary (Mary Walker). As Animus throttled Deadpool, Deadpool's friend Weasel (Jack Hammer) crashed into the room with an ambulance, running over and destroying Vamp/Animus. Undeterred, Zola created a second Vamp/Animus proto-husk and sent it to retrieve the MacGuffin files from a Texas oil tycoon. However, at the same time Deadpool had been hired to recover the files as well and when Animus absconded with them, Deadpool followed him to Zola's lair. Once there, Deadpool shot this Vamp dead before harassing Zola, who released the Corpse Corps to stop him. Though outnumbered, Deadpool easily killed the team, partly due to their inexperience in their new forms. Zola bargained for his life with Deadpool, allowing the mercenary to take four Gwen Stacy proto-husks he had created as well as the MacGuffin files. The Stacy duplicates perished shortly afterwards in a plane crash. Presumably, Zola can create a new Corpse Corps provided he has the genetic material needed.

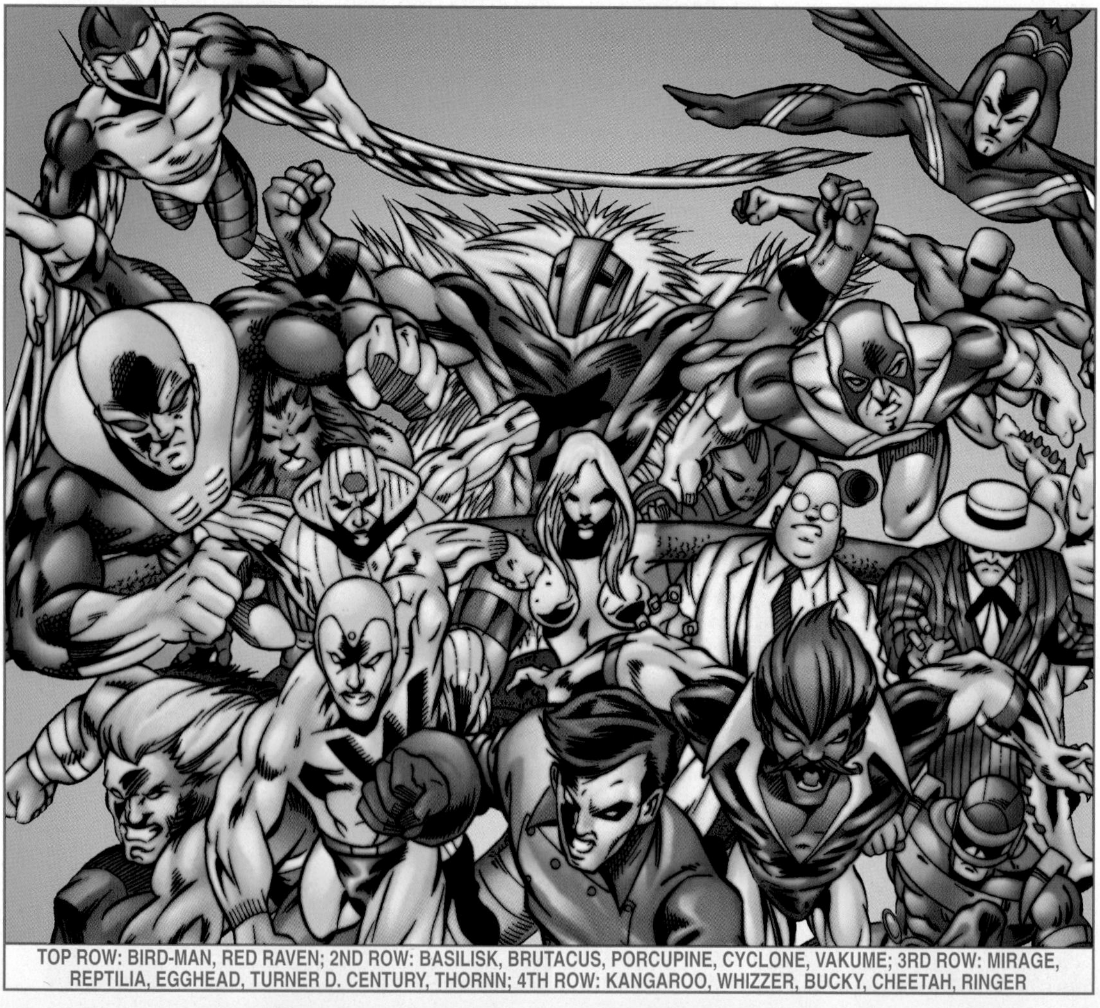

TOP ROW: BIRD-MAN, RED RAVEN; 2ND ROW: BASILISK, BRUTACUS, PORCUPINE, CYCLONE, VAKUME; 3RD ROW: MIRAGE, REPTILIA, EGGHEAD, TURNER D. CENTURY, THORNN; 4TH ROW: KANGAROO, WHIZZER, BUCKY, CHEETAH, RINGER

COURIER

HISTORY: Employed by his father's international delivery service International Infonet Inc., aka Gavin and Sons, the mutant Jacob Gavin Jr. traveled the world, working with and against many superhumans. Two years after encountering fellow shape changer Copycat (Vanessa Carlysle) in Thailand, Courier acted as middleman for Nyko Halfghanaghan, using data on arms merchant Tolliver (Tyler Dayspring), to hire the Executive Elite to assassinate Deadpool ("Wade Wilson"). Days later, Copycat extorted Courier into sharing the Tolliver data. Months later, following the firm's change to "Gavin and Son," Earth-9921's New Son, pursuing a complex plan to create a new world, hired Courier to, among other things, employ mutant dream therapist Fontanelle to profile New Son's Earth-616 counterpart Gambit (Remy LeBeau). Courier also visited the Savage Land to steal the High Evolutionary's terraforming schematics; when Fontanelle learned Gambit was stranded in Antarctica, New Son rescued him and sent him to assist Courier, who acted as intermediary when New Son employed Gambit to steal spaceship blueprints and mutant data files. When Courier met with Crew ASKEW's scientists to recruit their multi-science expertise, Gambit covertly observed. Technology smuggler Pelican interrupted to offer ASKEW a percentage in mass-producing will-sapping gas, and Gambit prevented mercenaries Greg and Stan Mengo from stealing it; encountering dimension-warping Quiet Bill, Courier recruited him for New Son as well. Later, when Gambit visited Millstone, Arizona, seeking information about X-Men enemy Mr. Sinister from former friend John Greycrow (aka Scalphunter), Courier unexpectedly used New Son's technology to teleport Gambit to their employer; Scalphunter knocked out Courier, fought the returning Gambit, then revealed only Sabretooth (Victor Creed) could provide the desired data. Courier reluctantly accompanied Gambit to recruit Sabretooth, who led them to Sinister's lab, where Gambit traded Courier's cell sample for technology to detect potential X-Men impostors; however, after Gambit and Courier departed, Courier remotely destroyed the sample.

Learning he and Courier were predestined to visit 1891, Gambit used Dr. Doom (Victor von Doom)'s time machine to travel back, pulling the unsuspecting Courier with him. Gambit persuaded Courier to assume female form as "Jacqueline Gavin," to investigate obstetrician Dr. Nathan Milbury, the future Mr. Sinister; realizing his "patient" was a mutant, Milbury drugged Courier, who reverted to a gelatinous form. In exchange for part of Courier's cellular structure, Milbury restored cohesion to Courier, whose default form was now the "Jacqueline" form. After returning to the present, Courier hired costumed mercenaries to attack Gambit and, per New Son's plans, force him to push his powers to their peak. However, Courier, who had by now befriended Gambit, also arranged for the Thieves' Guild to help Gambit. New Son imprisoned Courier, who, with Quiet Bill, was freed when the X-Men investigated New Son. Later, Courier impersonated Charles Xavier to access the FBI's Black Womb files, whose information might prove applicable to New Son; X-Men enemy Mystique held Courier hostage, but Gambit, his powers increased, easily rescued his friend. When New Son, who believed Gambit posed a threat to Earth-616, abducted Gambit to his native reality, Courier worked with Fontanelle and Quiet Bill to rescue Gambit, whose powers returned to normal. Courier presumably returned to Infonet, which was, perhaps, renamed "Gavin and Daughter." Whether Courier retained his powers following M-Day is unrevealed.

REAL NAME: Jacob "Jake" Gavin Jr.
ALIASES: Jacqueline "Jackie" Gavin Jr.
IDENTITY: Secret
OCCUPATION: Information broker, international courier
CITIZENSHIP: Unrevealed
PLACE OF BIRTH: Unrevealed
KNOWN RELATIVES: Jacob Gavin (father), unidentified mother, one or more unidentified brothers
GROUP AFFILIATION: None
EDUCATION: Unrevealed
FIRST APPEARANCE: Deadpool: The Circle Chase #1 (1993)

HEIGHT: 5'9" (variable; formerly 6'2") **EYES:** Blue (variable)
WEIGHT: 175 lbs. (variable) **HAIR:** Black (variable)

ABILITIES/ACCESSORIES: Due to a "photoreflexive malleable genetic imprint," Courier has absolute control of his entire cellular structure, down to individual cells, allowing him to change shape into anyone of his same basic height and mass, although the process takes hours; he can alter his retinal scan to become an exact match to another's, deceive most mechanical detection systems (including those which recognize his mutant nature), render himself immune to most poisons and survive gunshot wounds, even directly to the head, although he is unsure he could survive a beheading. He can regrow severed parts by redistributing his existing body mass, although repeated applications of this ability gradually results in a height decrease, and destroy detached parts from afar. He is an accomplished negotiator and a charismatic public speaker.

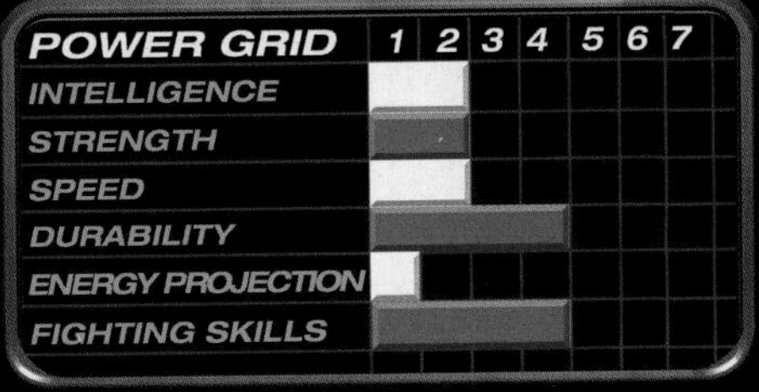

POWER GRID
1 2 3 4 5 6 7
INTELLIGENCE
STRENGTH
SPEED
DURABILITY
ENERGY PROJECTION
FIGHTING SKILLS

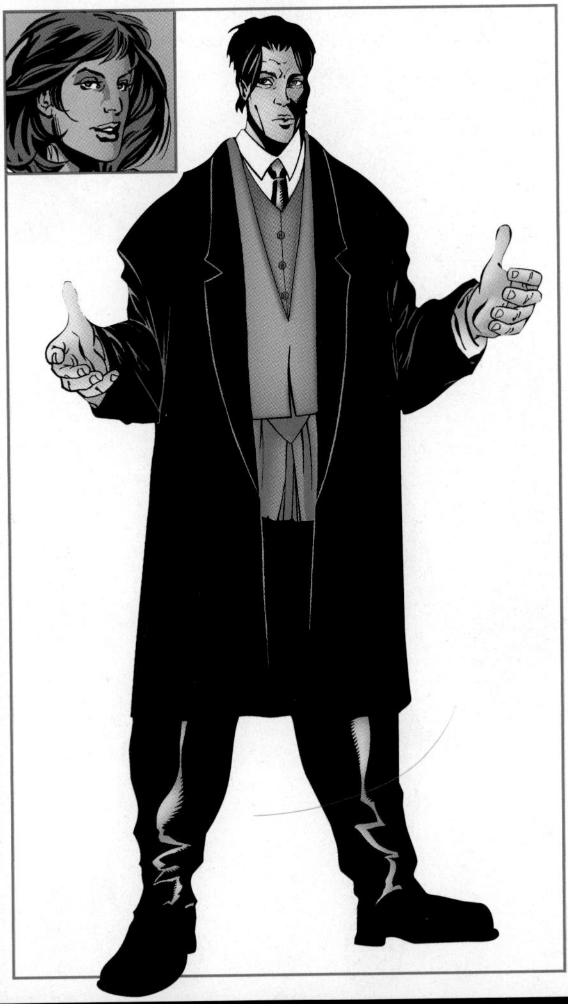

Art by Mat Broome with Yanick Paquette (inset)

ZOE CULLODEN

REAL NAME: Zoe Culloden; original name unrevealed
ALIASES: Expediter
IDENTITY: Secret
OCCUPATION: Currently unrevealed; former Overboss, Expediter, operative
CITIZENSHIP: Romania (presumed)
PLACE OF BIRTH: Presumably Romania
KNOWN RELATIVES: None
GROUP AFFILIATION: Formerly Landau, Luckman & Lake; Landau, Luckman, Lake and LeQuare
EDUCATION: Private education, LL&L training
FIRST APPEARANCE: Wolverine #79 (1994)

HISTORY: Nearly three decades ago, Chang, Expediter for intergalactic firm Landau, Luckman & Lake, sensed potential in a girl living under inhumane conditions in a Bucharest orphanage. Taking her as a protégé, he named her "Zoe Culloden." She joined the firm in adulthood, working with Noah DuBois, Dixon Mason and precognitive Montgomery Burns, suvpervised by Gerry LeQuare. Monty foretold of an alien Messiah (S'met'kth), its potential destroyer Tiamat and its potential protector Mithras. Monty eventually proclaimed mercenary "Wade Wilson" the predestined Mithras. Zoe studied Wilson's life, becoming obsessed with earning a promotion through the "Mithras Directive." Years later, after Dixon had become Overboss, Monty deemed Wilson increasingly unlikely to become Mithras, and Zoe investigated. She befriended Wilson's girlfriend Vanessa Carlysle (later Copycat) and developed sympathy for the unlikely couple. When Wilson failed an assignment, his client targeted Vanessa, but Zoe saved her life. She returned to LL&L, but Monty revealed that Wilson, having contracted cancer, would leave Vanessa. Soon afterward, Gerry LeQuare was reported dead,

but secretly kept the Mithras Directive under surveillance. Zoe became Expediter a few years later. When Wilson became Deadpool, and Zoe again championed him as Mithras.

In recent years, Chang was slain by Bloodscream and Roughhouse, but Zoe mistakenly believed Wolverine (Logan/James Howlett) was involved. She confronted him in Scotland, but was interrupted by Wolverine's longtime enemy Cyber, whom she helped Wolverine and his Excalibur allies defeat. Zoe and Noah observed Wolverine for weeks, ultimately steering him into battle with Genesis (Tyler Dayspring) to prevent revival of Apocalypse (En Sabah Nur). Meanwhile, the Messiah's arrival approached, and Zoe, convinced Deadpool's success as Mithras would earn her Overboss status, tried recruiting him, but was rebuffed. When Typhoid (Mary Walker) took interest in Deadpool, Zoe

Art by Adam Kubert

attempted to forestall her influence, but Typhoid stole Zoe's computer interface and used it to cruelly manipulate Deadpool. Zoe brought Deadpool to LL&L's extradimensional office to explain the Mithras Directive. Zoe convinced Deadpool the Mithras role would awaken heroic potential, but unknowingly disheartened him by revealing he was destined to kill Tiamat as he would any assassination target. After Noah and others perished in Arecibo, Puerto Rico, Zoe, via holographic interface, accompanied Deadpool to confront Noah's killer Tiamat. While Deadpool fought Tiamat, Zoe's connection was cut by Dixon. Tiamat defeated Deadpool, but Dixon used the fight to collect data. Zoe escaped, inadvertently teleporting to Deadpool's home, where Deadpool had already arrived. Dixon bombed Deadpool's home to kill them both, but LeQuare rescued them. He teleported Zoe to confront Dixon, but before the pair could battle, the Messiah arrived. Deadpool, having learned its true nature, slew it. Dixon underwent a breakdown, and Zoe became Overboss, but her superiors were displeased with the Mithras Directive's management. Weeks later, Deadpool brought a seriously injured Monty to LL&L, and Zoe detained them, thinking their forced service might earn her credit with LL&L. When she learned Monty was in love with her, however, she freed Deadpool, resigned as Overboss and departed with Monty. The couple later attended Deadpool's supposed funeral.

AS OVERBOSS

HEIGHT: 5'7"   **EYES:** Blue
WEIGHT: 100 lbs.   **HAIR:** Blond, sometimes dyed brown

ABILITIES/ACCESSORIES: Zoe Culloden is an accomplished strategist, athlete, hand-to-hand combatant and actress able to duplicate several accents/dialects. As Expediter, she wore a wrist-device interfaced with LL&L's computer system, allowing her to teleport, scan and analyze anything in her vicinity, communicate with fellow LL&L employees and erase a target's short-term memories. She used a cloaking device, aura-cloaked dampers, infrared shields and psi-suppressors to be undetectable by most perceptions. She carried a weapon which propelled bolos able to contain even superhuman targets and otherwise had access to LL&L's advanced technology. As Overboss, she wore a forehead gem which gave her direct mental and physical control of subordinates and enabled her to fire energy blasts capable of stunning even the rapid-healing Deadpool.

POWER GRID	1	2	3	4	5	6	7
INTELLIGENCE							
STRENGTH							
SPEED							
DURABILITY							
ENERGY PROJECTION							
FIGHTING SKILLS							

YELLOW BAR INDICATES CULLODEN IS A TELEPORTER

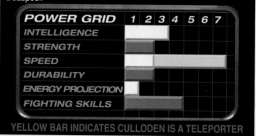

Art by Gus Vazquez with Pete Woods & David Brewer (inset)

HISTORY: Little is known about the man called Deadpool ("Wade Wilson")'s early life, not even his name. Although Deadpool believes his name is "Wade Wilson," it has been alleged he took it from another and his true name is "Jack," full name unrevealed. He once claimed that his father abandoned his mother while pregnant, who physically abused Deadpool as a youth, and who an adult Deadpool confronted and beat up in turn. He later claimed his mother died when he was five, a trauma which provoked a brutal streak in his personality, and that his father, a career military officer, was shot by one of his friends when he was 17. Possibly Deadpool had two sets of parents - his birth parents and a pair of adoptive parents, or perhaps a stepmother and stepfather from remarriages by his birth parents - partially explaining these discrepancies. Given Deadpool's perpetually erratic mental state, he may no longer remember the truth about his origins and could yet supply additional contradictory accounts.

In any event, following a brief stint in army black ops, from which he was supposedly discharged for being "too good," the future Deadpool began his mercenary career circa age 19. Accepting assassination jobs against people he felt warranted death, he habitually took new identities after failing assignments. After one such failure, he was injured fleeing his employers and collapsed into an icy river in Maine. He was found and nursed back to health by a young couple named, allegedly, Wade and Mercedes Wilson. Seeking his rescuer's identity as his own, the young mercenary attacked him and left him for dead, but accidentally killed his wife Mercedes as well. Unhinged over murdering an innocent woman, he became convinced that he was Mercedes' husband, Wade Wilson. Using that name, he resumed his mercenary activities, unaware Mercedes' husband survived and, sponsored by the mercenary's former employers, became sorcerer/assassin T-Ray. Further unaware he was being observed by interdimensional firm Landau, Luckman, Lake & LeQuare as a potential candidate for the Mithras Directive, through which a prophesied hero would protect an alien Messiah (S'met'kth) destined to bring Earth peace, the young mercenary Wilson next surfaced in Tangier, Morocco, where he romanced a woman named Francie. When this relationship ended, he traveled throughout Asia and, in Japan, a crime lord called the Boss hired him to infiltrate rival criminal Oyakata's sumo wrestling ring. Wilson spent three years as a wrestler under Oyakata's tutelage, becoming romantically involved with his daughter Sazae. When Boss ordered Oyakata's murder, Wilson reneged on his assignment, allegedly the first time he ever did so, and relocated to the USA. There he fell in love with teenage mutant prostitute Vanessa Carlysle, with whom he shared dreams of a better future. Hired by Middle Eastern interests to assassinate blind British government operative Althea (later Blind Al), at a Zaire base, Wilson inexplicably killed everyone there except for Al, who fled. Wilson's vengeful employers targeted Vanessa, who was rescued by LLL&L's Zoe Culloden, Wilson's "sponsor" in the Mithras Directive. Learning he had contracted cancer, Wilson left Vanessa, believing she could never find happiness with a terminally ill man.

In Canada, Wilson joined Department K, a Canadian government special weapons development branch. As a test subject in Department K's Weapon X Program, his cancer was temporarily regressed via a healing factor derived from Department K mutant operative Wolverine (Logan/James Howlett). As a potential Canadian super-operative, Wilson joined an unidentified unit, possibly an early incarnation of Weapon PRIME (PRototype Induced Mutation Echelon), training alongside near-invulnerable Sluggo and the cyborgs Garrison Kane and Slayback; he also reunited with Vanessa, who revealed her shape-shifting powers and joined as Copycat. During one mission or training session, Wilson seemingly killed Slayback for unrevealed reasons. When his healing factor malfunctioned, Wilson's health worsened and, his body horribly scarred, he was sent to the Hospice, where failed Weapon X subjects were supposedly treated or allowed to die with dignity. Apparently unknown to the Canadian government, the Hospice's patients served as experimental subjects for Dr. Emrys Killebrew and his sadistic assistant,

REAL NAME: Unrevealed
ALIASES: Wade Winston Wilson, Merc with a Mouth, Big Dee Pee, Captain Wilson, Johnny Salvini, Armando Khan, Mithras, Dr. Koffer, Takehiko Adachi, Chiyonosake ("the Wolf of the Rice Wine"), Wade T. Wilson, Jack, Rhodes, Corpus, Lopez, "Test-o-clees," others; impersonated Hobgoblin (Jason Macendale), others
IDENTITY: Known to authorities
OCCUPATION: Mercenary, adventurer; former pirate, mob enforcer, government operative, sumo wrestler, soldier, presumably others
CITIZENSHIP: Canada, with international criminal record
PLACE OF BIRTH: Unrevealed
KNOWN RELATIVES: Gretchen (ex-wife), unidentified parents (both possibly deceased)
GROUP AFFILIATION: Formerly Code Red, Agency X, Great Lakes Initiative, SHIELD's Six Pack, One World Church, Deadpool Inc., Weapon X, Team Deadpool, Heroes for Hire, Secret Defenders, Frightful Four, Department K, Oyakata's sumo stable, US Army; former operative of Commission on Superhuman Activities, Landau, Luckman & Lake, Tolliver, Taskmaster, Kingpin (Fisk), Dr. Druid, Yakuza and many others; Deadpool has often considered himself an X-Men member, but no one else does
EDUCATION: High school dropout, US Army Special Forces training, otherwise unrevealed
FIRST APPEARANCE: New Mutants #98 (1990)

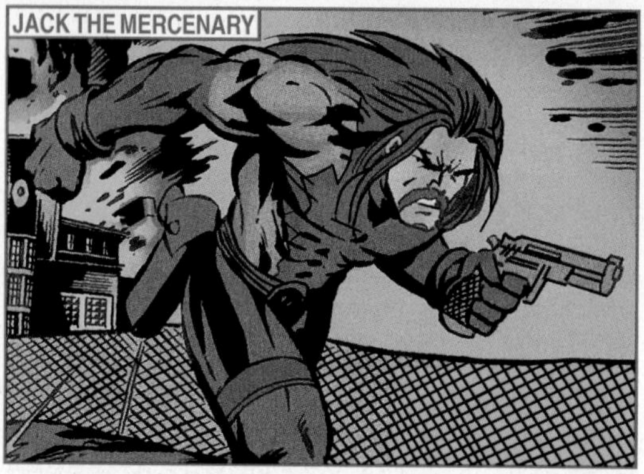
JACK THE MERCENARY

Art by David Brewer

the superhuman Attending, with so hopeless an atmosphere that patients placed bets in a "deadpool" on when they would die. Killebrew subjected Wilson to torturous experiments to learn why his healing factor failed and for his own twisted satisfaction. Trapped between life and death, perceived a manifestation of the cosmic entity Death, and formed a near-romantic relationship with her, but because Killebrew insistently kept him alive for future experimentation, he could not truly join her. Seeking death, Wilson repeatedly taunted the Attending, earning his fellow patients' respect; despite the Attending's rage, Killebrew forbade him to kill Wilson. The Attending instead lobotomized Wilson's friend, cyborg Charles "Worm" Cunningham, whom Wilson then mercifully killed. As the Attending knew, under Killebrew's rules, any patient who killed another earned execution, and Wilson, despite Killebrew's interest, proved no exception. The Attending tore out Wilson's heart, and Death insisted that he join her, but Wilson's thirst for vengeance was so strong that it jumpstarted his healing factor, regenerating his heart. However, this didn't cure his scarred body, and also rendered him insane, a condition which proved inherent in his mutation; curing his insanity would negate his healing factor. Wilson attacked the Attending, leaving him for dead in turn, and was ready to die, but Death abandoned him. Taking the name Deadpool, he escaped the Hospice with his fellow patients.

Following his escape, Deadpool, per his own account, spent time as a mob enforcer alongside surgically altered Maggia leader Hammerhead. He soon resumed freelance mercenary work, donning a costume to accompany his codename, and his constant irreverent banter in even the deadliest situations earned him the nickname "the Merc with a Mouth." At some point he worked with or against Wolverine, by then a spy for Canada's Department H, presumably neither aware they shared a bond via their healing factors; he also clashed with Cable (Nathan Summers) and other super-powered mercenaries during his checkered career. It was presumably during these years he, for reasons known only to himself, abducted Blind Al and kept her prisoner in his San Francisco base, the hologram-equipped "Deadhut," where he occasionally meted out punishment by locking Al in his private torture chamber, "the Box." Al's escape attempts only motivated Deadpool to kill anyone whose help she sought, leaving her resigned to captivity, even developing an odd friendship with her captor. Following Baron (Heinrich) Zemo's death during a confrontation with Captain America (Steve Rogers), Deadpool, presumably on assignment, visited the villain's grave in Bolivia, where he first met Bullseye (Lester), a less experienced but no less deadly mercenary. For whatever reason, the two fought, mutilating Zemo's corpse in the process, the first of many battles they waged over the years. Deadpool acquired a position as Kingpin (Wilson Fisk)'s personal assassin, although he apparently had little contact with the Kingpin's many Manhattan-based super hero enemies. Years after the Hospice escape, Deadpool apparently returned to Canada and, under Department H's auspices, received treatment from Dr. Walter Langkowski, aka Alpha Flight's Sasquatch, whose Department H tenure began long after Deadpool's ended. Eventually, Deadpool abandoned the treatment as abruptly as he had sought it and returned to the USA. Hired by criminal genius Wizard (born Bentley Wittman), Deadpool initially went to the wrong address and took a job impersonating up-and-coming super villain Hobgoblin (Roderick Kingsley). Re-connecting with Wizard, Deadpool joined him, Taskmaster, and Constrictor in a short-lived Frightful Four incarnation to battle the Thing (Ben Grimm). When this failed, Deadpool returned to Kingpin, but Bullseye upstaged him during an assignment and replaced him as Kingpin's assassin; the two again fought, with Bullseye keeping the job, but the pair eventually developed mutual respect and camaraderie, if not actual friendship. Deadpool nevertheless landed a one-time assignment from Kingpin, to kill the Beyonder, who easily defeated him. Eventually, Deadpool accepted assignments and camaraderie at the Chicago mercenary hangout Hellhouse, where diminutive Patch (Bob Stirrat) issued assignments in exchange for profit cuts. During this period, Deadpool developed a rivalry with fellow Hellhouse patron T-Ray, whom Deadpool, still believing himself Wade Wilson, blamed for Mercedes' death. He also recruited nonpowered but ingenious Weasel (Jack Hammer) as weapon supplier; the two became close friends and fellow employees under time-traveling arms merchant Tolliver (Tyler Dayspring), in whose service Deadpool occasionally worked with Sluggo and Copycat, among others.

In recent years, Tolliver sent Deadpool to assassinate his father, Cable, in whose company Copycat was impersonating longtime fellow mercenary Domino (Neena Thurman); ironically, although Deadpool quickly overcame Cable and his new charges, the New Mutants, he was defeated by Domino/Copycat, evidently unaware she was acting contrary to her employer's wishes, who put him in a crate and mailed it to Tolliver. When Cable reorganized his charges as X-Force, they worked with Spider-Man (Peter Parker) against Black Tom Cassidy and Juggernaut (Cain Marko), but Deadpool teleported both criminals to work with Tolliver. Tolliver then sent him to attack Domino, who revealed herself as Copycat, and Deadpool was defeated by Cable and the true Domino, who swore vengeance against Copycat. Deadpool next accompanied Tolliver to the "Dead Man's Hand" underworld summit in Las Vegas to divide up the fallen Kingpin's empire, where, following a chance battle with Nomad (Jack Monroe), Deadpool killed Troy Donahue, underling to Tolliver's rival Lotus Newmark. Tolliver seemingly perished battling X-Force, supposedly leaving behind a will that ceded advanced technology to whoever found it; his mercenaries, including Deadpool, searched the world for it, and Deadpool's quest led to a chance encounter and battle with Blood Wraith, whose Ebony Blade he absconded with before its owner reclaimed it in Bosnia. Erroneously believed to have confidential knowledge about the will, Deadpool's search was interrupted by Slayback, who, having reconstituted himself following his death, sought revenge. In the ensuing battle, Copycat intervened and was gravely injured, prompting Deadpool to partially transfer his healing ability, saving her life, but weakening his remaining power. After slaying sorceress Malachi while in Dr. Anthony Druid's Secret Defenders, Deadpool, employed by External Gideon, joined Juggernaut to abduct Professor X and other X-Men, with whom Gideon empowered the Psi-Ber Sentinel, but Deadpool withdrew from the proceedings before the X-Men defeated Gideon. Deadpool again clashed with Juggernaut and Black Tom, who had forced Killebrew into service and believed Deadpool's healing factor could cure Tom's ailment. With help from Tom's niece, X-Force

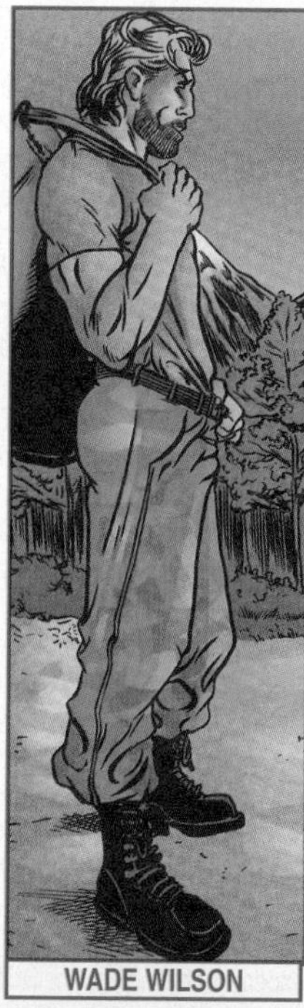
WADE WILSON

Art by Steve Harris

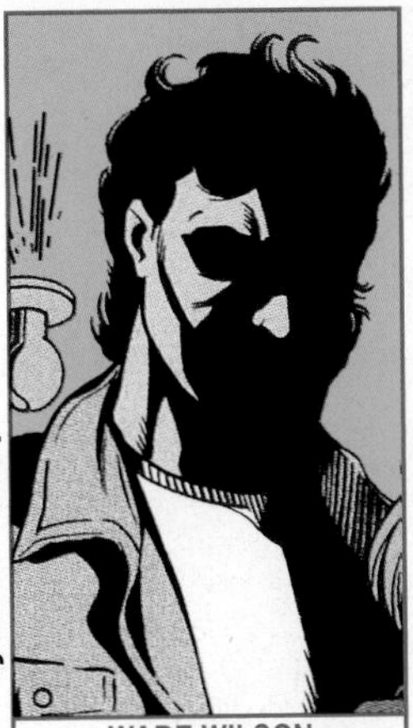

WADE WILSON

Art by Aaron Lopresit

member Siryn, Deadpool defeated the pair. Although he was strongly attracted to Siryn, she only partially returned his feelings; questioning his worthiness, he sought Copycat for advice but found her dating fellow Weapon X alumnus Kane. When Wolverine visited Kane for mutual friend Vindicator (James Hudson), Deadpool fought both men, exorcising longtime resentment. Unidentified information brokers, employing Slayback, abducted Deadpool in hope of his healing factor curing the Legacy virus, but Deadpool's power could not be adapted, and he was rescued by Wolverine and mutant mercenary Maverick (Christoph Nord). Deadpool in turn rescued Siryn when she was imprisoned by Gamesmaster (Jeremy Stevens). Deadpool's former employer the Boss hired him to protect Oyakata, now targeted by Boss' renegade assassin Widdle Wade, whom Deadpool slew. Learning Boss had created Wade from Deadpool's DNA, he killed Boss as well.

Deadpool was subsequently assigned to sabotage experimental gamma radiation facility Project Michelangelo, unaware Zoe Culloden and Noah DuBois of rechristened Landau, Luckman & Lake had arranged a core meltdown to test his heroic potential. When Deadpool risked his life containing the crisis, Zoe considered it proof he was the predestined Mithras, but Deadpool refused to believe he could accomplish anything heroic. As his healing factor waned, Deadpool received a supposed challenge from Black Tom; with Siryn accompanying him, he instead encountered atonement-seeking Killebrew, who, having realized Deadpool's failing powers would eventually leave him dead, had lured him to be treated. Using a sample of Hulk (Bruce Banner)'s blood, Killebrew restored Deadpool to health, but Deadpool still wanted him dead for his past crimes. Unwilling to murder him before Siryn, who believed Deadpool could transcend his violent past, Deadpool reluctantly let Killebrew live. Assigned to free a mental patient, Deadpool fought Arnim Zola's Vamp/Animus (Denise Baranger), who had been hired to kill him, and learned both assignments came from the patient, Typhoid (Mary Walker), former assassin for Kingpin. When she embarked on a Manhattan killing spree, Deadpool assisted Daredevil (Matt Murdock) in capturing her. Deadpool hoped he and Typhoid could help each other find redemption, but she instead undermined his self-improvement goals, provoking him into being as brutal as she. While unwinding at an aquarium, Deadpool met the Lightning Rods (aka the Great Lakes Avengers), a super-team whose dedication to heroism exceeded their capabilities. Inadvertently sent back in time several years into an alternate timeline (Reality-9712) during the encounter, he battled that reality's Kraven the Hunter (Sergei Kravinoff) and interacted with a younger Weasel before returning. Following a stint in Iron Fist (Daniel Rand)'s Heroes for Hire and fresh harassment from Zoe regarding the Mithras Directive, the increasingly troubled Deadpool sought comfort from Siryn, who seemingly drew him into a romantic interlude. However, she revealed herself as a disguised Typhoid, toying with him for amusement. Horrified, he returned to the Deadhut and discovered Weasel visiting Blind Al. Enraged that anyone, even a friend, had invaded his home without permission, Deadpool locked them in the Box, although they soon escaped. He met T-Ray for an intended duel to the death, but Deadpool's emotional turmoil distracted him, enabling T-Ray to defeat him. With nothing to lose, he wearily accompanied Zoe to LL&L, where she revealed the Mithras role's full extent. Appalled by being entrusted with such responsibility, Deadpool decided to rebuild his character more slowly, making peace with Blind Al, but the Attending, now called Ajax, teleported him away and seemingly killed him. Reviving under Death's administrations, he was confronted by the ghosts of Ajax's victims, including Worm Cunningham, who urged Deadpool to kill Ajax, believing this would free their earthbound souls. Although reluctant to again kill, Deadpool did so, never learning that the act failed to free the ghosts. Craving redemption, Deadpool accepted Culloden's offer; to his dismay, however, he learned the Mithras' destined role was to kill Tiamat, a potential threat to Messiah, rendering Deadpool's efforts to escape violence seemingly futile. Deadpool narrowly escaped death at Tiamat's hands, leading Tiamat to obsess over killing the Mithras over the Messiah, and Tiamat's Elders stripped him of his armor and granted it to Deadpool, showing him the Messiah brought not true peace, but only mindless bliss; protected from this bliss by Tiamat's armor, Deadpool apparently slew the Messiah.

When the alien Coterie gathered hundreds of super heroes for a "Contest of Champions," Deadpool was among the participants. Despite this seeming vindication of his heroic impulses, Deadpool was no longer optimistic about bettering himself; with LL&L ex-precognitive Montgomery as reluctant sidekick, he set up headquarters in Bolivia and resumed his mercenary career. Troubled by seeming hallucinations too intense for even his addled mind, he consulted deranged psychiatrist Dr. Bong, who suggested he exorcise frustrations by fighting Wolverine. The fight indeed cleared Deadpool's mind, but his psyche received a stunning blow when Mercedes Wilson, who he still believed was his wife, returned to life. Hoping to recapture his supposed loving relationship with her, he emotionally bonded with her, but the couple was teleported away by T-Ray, creator of Deadpool's hallucinations, who revealed himself as not only Mercedes' resurrector, but also her husband, proving Deadpool's hopes were based on lies. Yet the revelation did not break Deadpool's spirit as hoped, for Deadpool, robbed of the loving relationship with Mercedes he had deemed his only saving grace, declared his situation ludicrous and vowed to forget a past for which he could never atone, the better to improve in the future. Swearing further vengeance, T-Ray departed with Mercedes. Norse God Loki Laufeyson, claiming to be Deadpool's father, subsequently imprisoned Death to manipulate Deadpool into battle with his foster brother Thor Odinson. When Deadpool failed to meet Loki's expectations, the god revealed his deception and cursed him to resemble actor Thom Cruz; although long ashamed by disfigurement, Deadpool was even less content to wear another's face. Hired by the Council of Werewolves to assassinate lycanthropic author Duncan Vess, Deadpool's failed due to interference from Wolverine and the renegade werewolf Lycus. After a half-hearted attempt to earn the bounty placed on X-Man Gambit (Remy LeBeau) by the New Son, Deadpool made many attempts to re-disfigure his face, but Loki's curse foiled him. Seeking new quarters, he became roommates with Constrictor and Titania (actually Copycat posing as Mary MacPherran),in the "Deadlounge." Taskmaster hired the three to retrieve Baron (Helmut) Zemo's orbital platform, an assignment during which Deadpool briefly

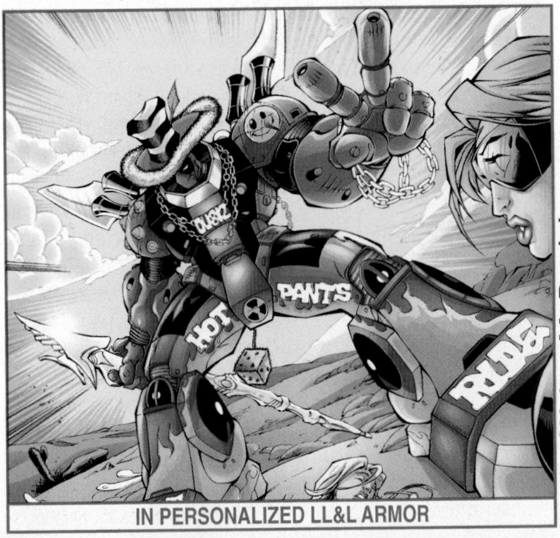
HOT
PANTS

IN PERSONALIZED LL&L ARMOR

Art by Walter McDaniel

IN TIATAMAT'S ARMOR

Art by Walter McDaniel

led Taskmaster trainees (Pyron/Deadair, Malovick/Deadend, Eclecta/Deadweight) as "Team Deadpool," but Taskmaster double-crossed Deadpool, leaving him stranded in space. Following adventures with interstellar outlaw Dirty Wolff and his Last Men gang, Deadpool returned to Earth, where madman Dr. Michael Achebe hired him and his roommates to steal Erik Killmonger's leopard Preyy. When this proved a pretext intended to manipulate Deadpool and Killmonger into killing each other, Deadpool lost patience with the ensuing debacle involving the Avengers, Wakandans, and others; Copycat subsequently revealed her imposture as part of Wizard and Taskmaster's vengeance scheme, which Deadpool easily survived. Loki's curse was broken shortly afterward. When Siryn was injured in an X-Force mission, Deadpool allied with the Watchtower group, capturing Wolverine in exchange for Siryn's treatment; Siryn was cured, while Wolverine, as Deadpool doubtlessly expected, defeated his captors. Alone again, Deadpool accepted corrupt police officer Fred Pierson's assignment to kill mob bosses, with tattoo artist Ananastasia assisting him. Deadpool fell in love with Ananastasia, who betrayed him following the assassinations. When Pierson reneged on her payment, Ananastasia killed Pierson and freed Deadpool, but despite her claims of love, the disbelieving Deadpool shot her. He subsequently dated several women in succession, not realizing all were Copycat, who still obsessed over him.

After failing to protect client John Cassera from mobster Maxy Millions, Deadpool trained Cassera's son Christopher as Kid Deadpool, aka Pool Boy, and together they killed Millions, although Christopher retained a grudge for Deadpool's failure to protect his father. After defeating mass murderer sisters Grace and Mary Mercy, Deadpool targeted the Punisher (Frank Castle) for Peter Gnucci, nephew of infamous Ma Gnucci, but although Deadpool nearly defeated Punisher, Gnucci himself died, rendering the assignments pointless. Feral mutant Sabretooth (Victor Creed) recruited Deadpool for a new USA-based anti-mutant Weapon X Program, which upgraded Deadpool's healing factor to unprecedented levels. Paired with longtime ally/rival Garrison Kane, Deadpool was shocked when Kane shot a mutant child in the back, proving himself more inhumane than Deadpool had ever been. When Weapon X targeted Copycat, Deadpool rescued her from Kane, but failed to stop Sabretooth from killing her. Confronting Weapon X's Director (Malcolm Colcord), Deadpool was gassed and lost physical cohesion, literally melting until only his right hand remained, cursing the Director to the last. Bodiless, Deadpool attended his own funeral as a ghost, but the Weapon X upgrade, possibly boosted by Thanos of Titan, who resented Death's fondness for Deadpool,

WEAPON X UNIFORM

Art by Barry Windsor-Smith

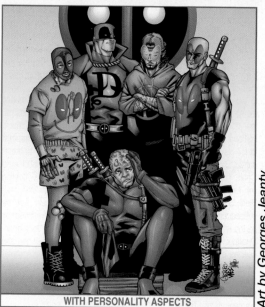

WITH PERSONALITY ASPECTS

Art by Georges Jeanty

resurrected him by rebuilding him from his severed hand, restoring his healing factor to its previous peak, but leaving him amnesiac. A chance encounter with Weasel restored his memory, and he discovered that four individuals had claimed the Deadpool name: "Heroic Deadpool," "Killer Deadpool," "Maniac Deadpool," and "Media Deadpool," personality aspects given form by T-Ray and the Gemini Star artifact. On Thanos' behalf, T-Ray intended to manifest and extinguish Deadpool's entire personality, leaving him an empty shell, but Deadpool damaged the Gemini Star, causing his personality fragments to enter T-Ray, rendering T-Ray amnesiac instead. Seemingly restored to his customary approximation of "normal," Deadpool irrationally claimed the incident's denouement "proved" he was the true Wade Wilson. Thanos cursed Deadpool to be unable to die, although Deadpool apparently remained unaware of this. Following an assignment against the Four Winds crime family, Deadpool, erroneously believed to have killed all four leaders, gained great status as a mercenary and formed Deadpool, Inc., aided by business partner Sandi Brandenberg. His success proved short-lived when Black Swan, the Four Winds' true killer, sought vengeance for stolen glory. Both were believed dead after an explosion, but Swan's telepathic power merged both men's memories and skills within underling Nijo. Believing the amnesiac Nijo to be Deadpool, Sandi helped him recover and become Agent X, and the two, with Taskmaster, formed a new mercenary endeavor, Agency X. Black Swan soon resurfaced, with Deadpool in tow, supposedly intending to restore all three to their previous states. During the transfer, the Swan instead absorbed Deadpool and Agent X's abilities, but Agent X, aided by his friends, broke through Swan's telepathic shield and killed him, reversing the transfer. Himself once more, Deadpool declined to join Agency X, returning to his solo career. In unrevealed circumstances, he married and divorced a woman named Gretchen; SHIELD agent Valerie Jessup recruited Deadpool's services for an off-the-books mission by promising information on Gretchen's whereabouts, which apparently never led Deadpool to her.

Deadpool was next hired by the One World Church to steal the Facade virus, with which the Church's leaders intended to transform Earth's populace into blue-skinned beings like themselves to eliminate racism. When Cable intervened, Deadpool, having briefly joined the Church, fought him, but the virus depowered both men, forcing Cable to merge their deteriorating bodies into one and then re-separate them in healthy form. The process created a DNA link between the two, allowing Deadpool to access Cable's teleportation technology and accompany him in his activities — with the disadvantage of merging the two every time the teleportation technology was used, requiring a painful separation. When Cable established the island community Providence in his long-term plan to improve the world, Deadpool became dedicated to his goals. When Cable threatened to destroy the world's weapons, the X-Men vowed to stop him; declaring himself an X-Man, much to their chagrin, Deadpool tagged along, but turned against the team to side with Cable, although he remained obsessed with supposed membership. Deadpool assisted Cable against SHIELD, Agent X, the monstrous Skornn and other enemies, but when he realized his irrationality and bloodlust could compromise Cable's goals, he resolved to foil his healing factor and commit suicide. He consulted information broker Black Box, who instead brainwashed him to kill the missing Cable. Deadpool tracked him through alternate realities via their DNA link, returned him to their native reality, shot himself in the head to break Black Box's control and soon recovered. With Deadpool's help, Cable subsequently took over the nation Rumekistan, but he and Deadpool parted ways regarding the USA's Superhuman Registration Act, which Deadpool, granted authority to capture unregistered superhumans, saw as a means to achieve the heroic status he had sought for so long. Assigned to apprehend Cable, Deadpool fought his friend, then took hostages, boasting his new status allowed him unlimited power, a statement which Cable broadcast to the world and which cost Deadpool his new status. Thinking turnabout was fair play, Deadpool joined the government-sanctioned Six Pack to discredit Cable, but the group's Rumekistan sabotage, when exposed, only furthered Cable's agenda. When Providence was destroyed following the Hecatomb's attack, Cable dropped from sight, and Deadpool joined Agency X, rescuing Agent X from Hydra and in the process taking a new sidekick, the hapless Bob, Agent of Hydra. When chance reunited him with the Great Lakes Avengers, now the Great Lakes Initiative, Deadpool became a reserve member after helping them defeat AIM; quickly becoming a nuisance, he was ejected by Squirrel Girl. Following a surreal adventure through time and space with Bob, Deadpool yet again revived his solo career, and his sanity further deteriorated, leaving him to hear two argumentative voices in his head and occasionally lapse into cartoon-like hallucinations. His skills unimpeded, he was anonymously hired to capture Wolverine by Winter Soldier, acting on Wolverine's instructions. After a prolonged and brutal battle, he succeeded, but Wolverine's son Daken, who wanted no one but himself to kill Wolverine, emerged from hiding to interfere. After Daken defeated Deadpool, Winter Soldier shot Daken, allowing Wolverine to depart with his son, the purpose of the entire exercise.

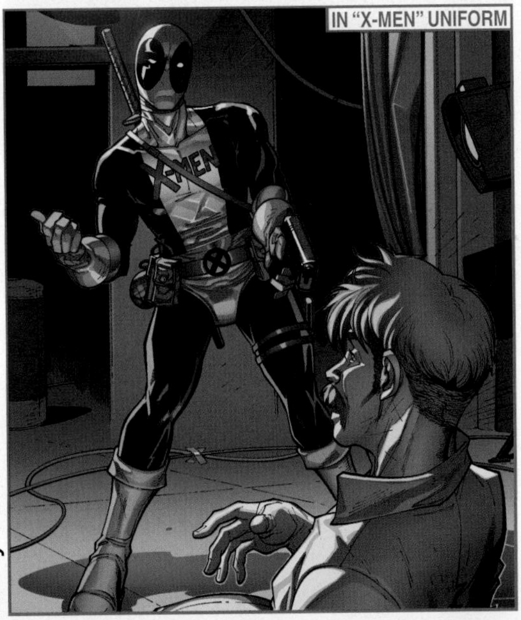

Deadpool recovered and took an assignment from ex-SHIELD Director Nick Fury during the Skrulls' "Secret Invasion." To access their computers, Deadpool publicly feigned cooperation with the aliens, earning a reputation as a traitor to Earth. He allowed the Skrulls to duplicate his healing factor in several soldiers, but because it was intended to counter his cancer, it induced fatal cellular overload in the subjects. His Skrull data transmission to Fury was intercepted by Norman Osborn, who used it to achieve a public victory during the invasion that won him unprecedented political power. Learning of Osborn's treachery, Deadpool attacked Osborn's Thunderbolts. Osborn sent his operative Hawkeye (actually Bullseye) to kill Deadpool. The two longtime associates embarked on a prolonged battle of weapons and warped wits, until Hawkeye, reluctant to kill his almost-friend, secretly paid Deadpool to end his vendetta. During an AIM assignment in the Savage Land, Deadpool met his Earth-2149 counterpart, a zombie reduced to a disembodied but equally deranged head who matched him wisecrack for wisecrack; back in the USA, Deadpool briefly joined the Red Hulk's Code Red team. During a brief stint as a pirate, Deadpool saved the island Jallarka from pirates. Fulfilled Fulfilled by the experience, which renewed his long-standing heroic impulses, he sought to join the X-Men, who hesitantly accepted him as an ally until Deadpool targeted X-Men critic Mark Kincaid, allowing the X-Men to garner good publicity by stopping him; which the X-Men learned was apparently Deadpool's intent all along.

HEIGHT: 6'2"	**EYES:** Brown
WEIGHT: 210 lbs.	**HAIR:** None (originally brown, then varied)

ABILITIES/ACCESSORIES: Deadpool's superhuman healing factor rapidly regenerates damaged or destroyed tissue. The speed at which this ability functions is directly proportionate to an injury's severity and partially affected by Deadpool's mental state, working most efficiently when he is awake, alert and in good spirits. Over the years, the power's efficiency has waxed and waned, since a single instance of overwhelming reconstruction can leave it weakened for weeks; at present, he can regrow severed hands within minutes and survive decapitation for about 12 minutes, at which point oxygen deprivation would affect his brain unless his head was reattached. Due to Thanos' curse, he is supposedly incapable of dying by any means. His healing factor also grants him virtual immunity to poisons and most drugs, as well as an extended life span and an enhanced resistance to diseases. Due to repeated brain injuries, he regenerates decaying brain cells at such a hyper accelerated rate that his sanity and memories suffer regular damage; his most frequent symptom is the belief he is a character in a comic book. Deadpool formerly could access Cable's bodysliding technology without use of machinery due to the two men's DNA mingling. Deadpool is an extraordinary athlete and hand-to-hand combatant, skilled in multiple unarmed combat techniques; his healing factor may contribute to his abilities, allowing him to undertake intensive exercise with minimal fatigue or aches. He is a master assassin, an excellent marksman, and an accomplished user of bladed weapons. He is fluent in Japanese, German and Spanish, among other languages. He employs a wide variety of weapons depending on his assignment or whim, but is virtually never without a combination of guns and knives; he customarily wears multiple pouches on his costume, containing mostly unrevealed paraphernalia. He wears a teleportation device in his belt and carries a holographic image inducer to disguise his true appearance as necessary.

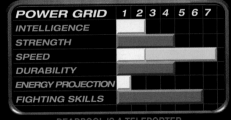

IN "X-MEN" UNIFORM

Art by Paco Medina

POWER GRID	1	2	3	4	5	6	7
INTELLIGENCE							
STRENGTH							
SPEED							
DURABILITY							
ENERGY PROJECTION							
FIGHTING SKILLS							

DEADPOOL IS A TELEPORTER

DEADPOOL (EARTH-2149)

REAL NAME: Possibly Wade Wilson
ALIASES: "Merc With Half a Mouth," "Merc With Only a Mouth," "Zombie Deadpool," "Z-Pool," "Headpool," "Shorty"
IDENTITY: Known to various government authorities
OCCUPATION: Zombie; former idol, mercenary
CITIZENSHIP: Canada (Earth-2149)
PLACE OF BIRTH: Unrevealed (Earth-2149)
KNOWN RELATIVES: None
GROUP AFFILIATION: Deadpool Corps
EDUCATION: Presumably military training
FIRST APPEARANCE: Marvel Zombies #1 (2006)

HISTORY: Earth-2149 fell victim to a virus that transformed many superhumans, including Deadpool, into flesh-eating zombie-like creatures that retained their intelligence. Though most zombies were destroyed, a few remained and, seeking new worlds to feed upon, located Earth-616 and sent Deadpool there through the Nexus of Realities. He set a trap to lure local super team the Command, but his body was destroyed when he was knocked into a swamp boat's roaring fan. His head survived and was taken to the Hollow, ARMOR's headquarters, where it convinced the Zombie (Simon Garth) to help it escape. No longer feeling the hunger due to losing his body, Deadpool accompanied Garth to the Black Talon (Samuel Barone)'s Taino island base en route zombifying a female Piranha and various Men-Fish. As Morbius' Midnight Sons tracked Deadpool, Black Talon offered the Hood (Parker Robbins) Deadpool as a weapon. Meanwhile, Deadpool infected a new zombie horde. and Morbius' efforts to destroy the zombie virus instead transformed the zombies into an airborne, flesh-devouring swarm/cloud. Forming a new host body, Deadpool took control of the zombie cloud, temporarily destroying the Man-Thing (Ted Sallis). After sorceress Jennifer Kale obliterated Deadpool's new body, Garth faked Deadpool's death and sent him away on a rowboat, while the remaining zombie virus-mind was trapped within Garth's virtually mindless form.

The rowboat eventually arrived in the Savage Land, where Deadpool became revered by a tribe of headhunters. Seeking the head as a weapon of mass destruction, AIM sent agents, including Earth-616's Deadpool and Dr. Betty, to retrieve it before Hydra could. Deadpool-2149 ordered his followers to behead Deadpool-616 so his head could be placed on the body, but when this plot failed, Deadpool-2149 teamed with his counterpart and Dr. Betty to escape Hydra as well as a zombified tyrannosaurus rex that Deadpool had infected. The trio fled in a stolen Hydra ship to an AIM space station. Deadpool-2149's head was turned over to AIM agents, but Deadpool-616 reconsidered and liberated it. Both Deadpools and Dr. Betty then traveled to South Florida, where Deadpool-616 sought the Nexus of Realities to send his counterpart home, en route encountering Man-Thing, who somehow recognized Deadpool-2149 from the Taino incident. After disposing of Hydra agent Lord Falcon, the group located the Nexus, and the two Deadpools entered it. Due to the two dimensional counterparts entering the Nexus at the same time, the portal's structure shifted and locked on to them as focal points, leading them to other worlds in which various Deadpools played important roles. The two Deadpools first arrived on Earth-6466, where they were briefly captured by SHIELD's Major Deadpool before escaping to Earth-3010, where they aided Lady Deadpool against that reality's Captain America, who was attempting to capture the rebel. Another jump through the Nexus landed the two Deadpools on Earth-1108, where Deadpool shot and apparently killed the cowboy Deadpool Kid. Finally returning to Earth-616, and Sorcerer Supreme Dr. Voodoo stabilized the Nexus, allowing the Deadpools to use it to reach Earth-2149. They were followed by Betty and Bill and swiftly attacked by superhuman zombies. until a small human survivor group found the quartet and led them to safety, Even though Voodoo's stabilization of the Nexus had by then worn off, leaving them stranded, Deadpool-2149 realized that they may have arrived at an earlier time period and suggested they replicate his original journey to Earth-616. Under undisclosed circumstances, "Headpool" found himself trapped in yet another dimension after his companions returned to their own reality, from which Deadpool-616 rescued him before recruiting him into the Deadpool Corps.

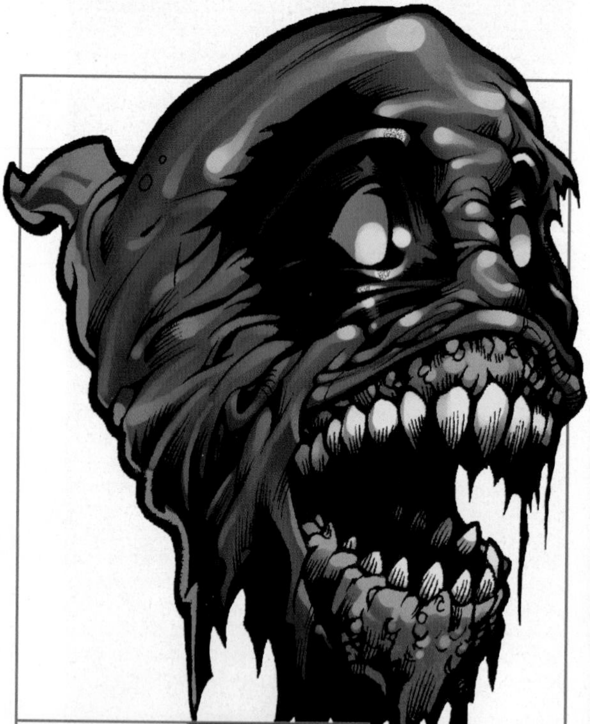

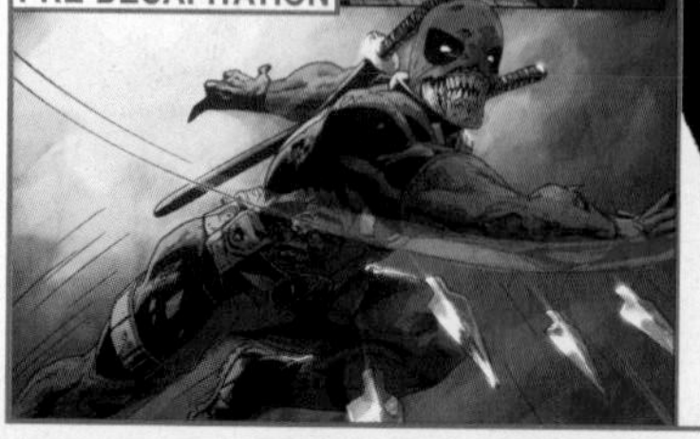

PRE-DECAPITATION

HEIGHT: 11" (originally 6'2")
WEIGHT: 10 lbs. (originally 210 lbs.)
EYES: White (originally brown)
HAIR: None (originally brown)

ABILITIES/ACCESSORIES: Before his infection, Deadpool had all the powers of his Earth-616 counterpart, including a rapid healing factor and peak human speed, and agility. The zombie virus eliminated his healing factor, although he was still highly durable, though unable to regenerate as before. As a head, Deadpool lacks any locomotion. While he no longer constantly feels the zombie hunger, he still does so out of habit and can transmit the virus via biting. It is uncertain how Deadpool's can speak and perform other functions without his body, though it is presumed that this ability is linked to the virus he is infected with.

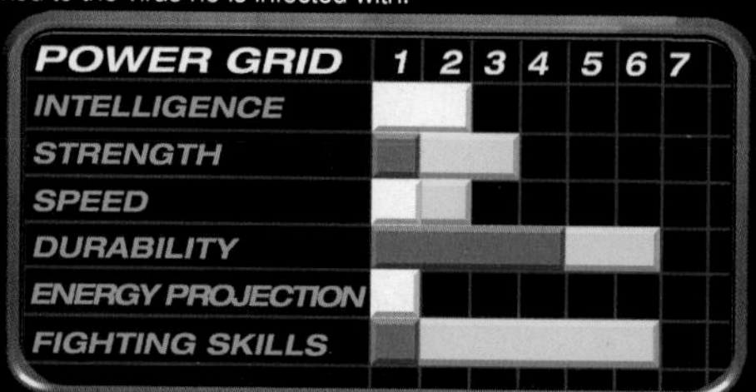

POWER GRID
1 2 3 4 5 6 7
INTELLIGENCE
STRENGTH
SPEED
DURABILITY
ENERGY PROJECTION
FIGHTING SKILLS

YELLOW BARS INDICATE RATINGS WITH PRE-BEHEADED LEVELS

DEADPOOL CORPS

HISTORY: One of the modern era's most erratic and dysfunctional super hero coalitions, the Deadpool Corps, consisting of Deadpool-616, Deadpool-2149 (aka Headpool) Lady Deadpool-3010, Deadpool-10330 (aka Kidpool), and Deadpool-103173 (aka Dogpool), have banded together to help save the Multiverse against a threat that could destroy everything in existence.

Hired by AIM to locate the zombified, disembodied head of Deadpool from Earth-2149 (aka "Headpool"), Deadpool-616 had a change of heart and decided to help return Headpool to his home dimension. Deadpool, Headpool, Dr. Betty Swanson (an AIM scientist and Deadpool-616's contact within the organization), and AIM agent Bill traveled to the Florida Everglades so Deadpool could use the Nexus of Realities, a focal point uniting all dimensions, to return Headpool to his dimension. However, two dimensional counterparts entering the Nexus at the same time caused a disruption in the Nexus, sending Deadpool and Headpool to various other dimensions, locking onto the location of that reality's Deadpool. The pair first traveled to Earth-6466 where they met Major Wilson, codenamed Deadpool, of SHIELD, who captured them believing that they were scouts sent from an invading force through the dimensional portal. Tricking Major Wilson into believing Headpool was a symbiote and the pair needed each other to survive, Deadpool-616 gained the upper hand and escaped with Headpool into the dimensional portal. The duo traveled next to Earth-3010, where the USA removed all alienable rights and liberties of its people, creating a fascist state enforced by Captain America (later General America), SHIELD, and the giant robotic Sentinels. While there, they encountered Lady Deadpool, who was battling General America. The Deadpool duo helped Lady Deadpool escape capture, and Deadpool-616 threw Headpool at Captain America, allowing him to bite Captain America's arm. In order to stop the spread of Zombie virus, Deadpool-616 cut Captain America's arm off. After a quick goodbye, the pair entered the dimensional portal again, taking the infected arm with them. The deadly duo next traveled to Earth-1108 where Deadpool-616 swiftly shot and apparently killed the cowboy Deadpool Kid. After they returned to Earth-616, Sorcerer Supreme Dr. Voodoo stabilized the Nexus to allow Deadpool to return Headpool to his home dimension. Deadpool and Headpool entered the portal, but once the Man-Thing (Ted Sallis), guardian of the Nexus, appeared, Dr. Swanson and Bill entered the portal as well to escape Man-Thing.

At some point Deadpool-616 was contacted by an Elder of the Universe to recruit a team of alternate dimension versions of himself to save the Multiverse. Having already come into contact with alternate versions of himself and generally getting along with "himself," Deadpool readily agreed. Deadpool first returned to Earth-3010 to recruit Lady Deadpool, who Deadpool once again helped escape from General America. Deadpool next traveled to Earth-10330, an Earth where the Xavier Institute became a boarding school for mutant boys like Cyclops, Wolverine, Colossus, Angel, and others, where he recruited Kidpool, who believed he was destined for bigger and better things than the rest of the other students. Deadpool finally traveled to Earth-103173, a reality where scientists Von Braun and Eigor conducted the Mascara-X Project, a process similar to Earth-616's Weapon X Program, on a dog in hopes to create a new process for the Babelline Cosmetics company that would give its customers eternal youth. Believed dead, the scientists discarded the dog's body, but it was discovered by a local circus who exploited the dog's power giving him the name "Deadpool, the Daredevil Dog," until Deadpool-616 recruited him for the Deadpool Corps.

Soon after his return home, Headpool was inadvertently transported to Earth-1058, where he was mistakenly believed to be a genetic anomaly and taken to Dr. Killcraven on Goat Skull Island for experimentation. Deadpool-616 then traveled to Earth-1058, rescued Headpool and recruited him. Returning to Earth-616, Deadpool introduced all the members of the Deadpool Corps as they prepared themselves for their suicide mission with hardcore training by playing the latest in Deadpool-616's video game collection.

CURRENT MEMBERS: Deadpool (Wade Wilson, Earth-616), Headpool (Wade Wilson, Earth-2149), Dogpool (Wade Wilson, Earth-103173), Kidpool (Wade Wilson, Earth-10330), Lady Deadpool (Wanda Wilson, Earth-3010)
BASE OF OPERATIONS: Deadpool-616's apartment
FIRST APPEARANCE: Prelude to the Deadpool Corps #4 (2010)

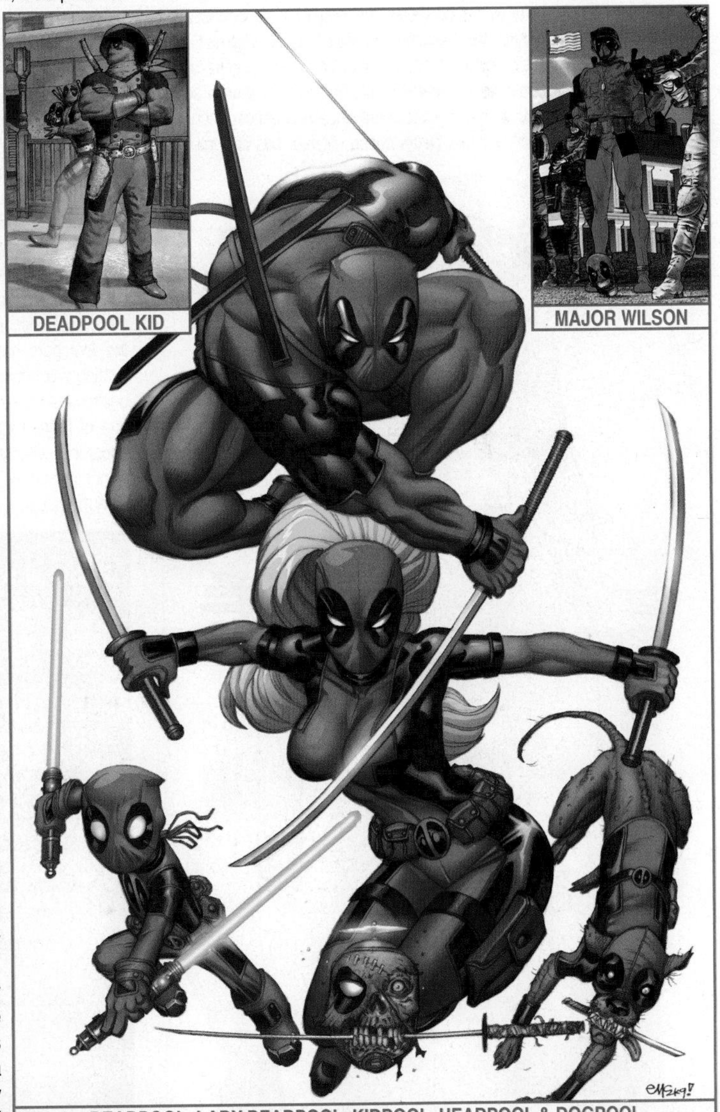
DEADPOOL KID

MAJOR WILSON

DEADPOOL, LADY DEADPOOL, KIDPOOL, HEADPOOL & DOGPOOL

DINAH SOAR

REAL NAME: Unrevealed
ALIASES: Wisconsin's Winged Wonder, Ms. Rodan '97
IDENTITY: Known to authorities
OCCUPATION: Adventurer
CITIZENSHIP: Unrevealed, possibly Savage Land
PLACE OF BIRTH: Unrevealed, possibly Savage Land
KNOWN RELATIVES: Unrevealed
GROUP AFFILIATION: Great Lakes Avengers; formerly Lightning Rods
EDUCATION: Unrevealed
FIRST APPEARANCE: West Coast Avengers #46 (1989)

HISTORY: A long-lived, pteranodon-like humanoid creature capable of flight, Dinah Soar had an inaudible hypersonic voice and claimed to come from an unidentified race of beings like herself. Little is known of their culture, though they believed dreams were best ignored. Dinah may be related to the Savage Land's similarly winged Nhu'ghari race, human derivatives mutated by radioactive properties. Somehow finding Mr. Immortal's personal ad seeking costumed heroes, she joined the group that would become the Great Lakes Avengers (GLA), and alongside them, Dinah protected the Midwestern US population from crime and superhuman threats. Shortly after the team's formation, a curious Dinah followed Mr. Immortal when he visited the gravesite of his deceased girlfriend on the Christmas following her death, observing him from a nearby tree. Initially annoyed by her intrusion upon his privacy, Mr. Immortal revealed he had received Dinah's name in the team's secret Santa gift exchange, and gave her a whistle so she could communicate with the team. Deeply moved, Dinah chose Mr. I as her life-mate, the one mortal she could bond with in her lifetime, granting him the ability to hear her special language. Over the next three years, Mr. I taught Dinah about human society and cultures while Dinah used her voice and presence to calm Mr. Immortal's periodic rages, ease his depression and soothe his pain when recovering from wounds. They became very close friends, then lovers.

Sometime during the team's early days, they prevented a bank robbery in Milwaukee, Wisconsin and were confronted by Avengers Hawkeye (Clint Baron) and Mockingbird (Bobbi Barton), who were investigating the GLA's unauthorized use of the Avengers name. After provoking a scuffle, Hawkeye decided the team could be shaped into a true fighting force through his leadership. During their training, Dinah saved Mr. Immortal after he got lost within the Darkforce dimension linked to their teammate Doorman. The GLA later rescued several of the real Avengers from That Which Endures, an unconscious collective sentience trying to eliminate humankind in favor of mutantkind. Sometime later, notified by Hawkeye (who had rejoined the original Avengers), Dinah and the team delayed the extraterrestrial Terminus' rampage in St. Louis, Missouri, until the Avengers arrived.

After the GLA briefly changed their name to the Lightning Rods, Dinah assisted in battles against Deadpool ("Wade Wilson"), the Thunderbolts, Graviton (Franklin Hall), Dr. Tannenbaum and his giant robot snowman and tornadoes caused by the Crimson Cowl (Justine Hammer) and her Masters of Evil. When the criminal Ani-Men attacked the Milwaukee Convention Center, Dinah and the GLA rushed to the scene by car, but arrived after the Avengers had stopped the attack. Deeply discouraged by being upstaged by the Avengers, Mr. Immortal decided to disband the GLA, but continue his relationship with Dinah; however, upon learning the Avengers had disbanded, Mr. Immortal eagerly led the GLA in fighting the Inhuman/Deviant geneticist Maelstrom, who was trying to destroy the universe. While using her voice to soothe Mr. Immortal after one of Maelstrom's "proto-natural" force bolts struck him, Dinah was apparently killed when another bolt tore through her abdomen. Dinah's spirit now spends time playing cards in the afterlife with other deceased GLA members.

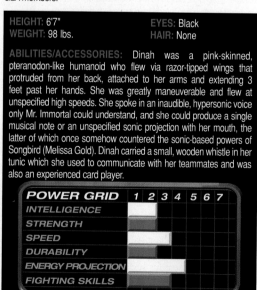

Art by John Byrne

HEIGHT: 6'7"
WEIGHT: 98 lbs.
EYES: Black
HAIR: None

ABILITIES/ACCESSORIES: Dinah was a pink-skinned, pteranodon-like humanoid who flew via razor-tipped wings that protruded from her back, attached to her arms and extending 3 feet past her hands. She was greatly maneuverable and flew at unspecified high speeds. She spoke in an inaudible, hypersonic voice only Mr. Immortal could understand, and she could produce a single musical note or an unspecified sonic projection with her mouth, the latter of which once somehow countered the sonic-based powers of Songbird (Melissa Gold). Dinah carried a small, wooden whistle in her tunic which she used to communicate with her teammates and was also an experienced card player.

POWER GRID	1	2	3	4	5	6	7
INTELLIGENCE							
STRENGTH							
SPEED							
DURABILITY							
ENERGY PROJECTION							
FIGHTING SKILLS							

HISTORY: Soldier Malcolm Colcord was naïve and excited to be assigned to guard a US/Canadian project (Weapon X), where he was looked after by the Professor (Truett Hudson), the project's director. A few days after his arrival, mutant subject Wolverine (Logan/James Howlett) escaped and brutalized Colcord with his newly created Adamantium claws, destroying an eye, pulping a cheekbone and disfiguring him beyond recognition. Colcord was saved, but refused plastic surgery, choosing to have a constant reminder to fuel his hatred of mutants. After recovering, the increasingly cruel Colcord was plagued by nightmares of mutants, his family left him and he was relegated to a secluded office for years, amassing extensive files on nearly all known mutants. Secretly sponsored by sentient bacterial colony John Sublime, who feared mutants threatened his genetic dominance, Colcord later gained the attention of military leaders and the US President when he proposed weaponizing mutants through the renewal of WX, under the guise of utilizing mutants for mankind's benefit. After WX was reinstated, Colcord, now called the Director, discovered neural implants in Wolverine that allowed him to control him. He sent him to eliminate former WX members now considered expendable, including Senator Drexel Walsh, who was preparing to reveal the workings of the original program. Walsh's videotaped murder was publicly released, resulting in Wolverine's eventual return to WX, where Colcord attempted to brainwash him. Freed by the spectral Shiver Man, Wolverine destroyed much of the complex before the Director set it to self-destruct.

Colcord recruited mutant operatives by offering them solutions to various personal problems, giving them implants that prevented them from harming or disobeying their superiors. He also gained SHIELD agent Brent Jackson as second-in-command, but never trusted or liked him. WX eliminated worldwide problems quietly, definitively and without morality, but Colcord faced insubordination early on, when Sabretooth stole his Wolverine files for his own personal vendetta, Jackson began challenging his decisions and leadership and the mentally unstable Aurora made passes at him. After he had WX rescue brainwashed mutant technomorph Madison Jeffries, Colcord manipulated him into creating a concentration camp for mutants called Neverland, where Colcord began secretly executing large numbers of mutants. He soon gave in to his longing for a woman's touch by kissing Aurora after Sabretooth similarly disfigured her. In an early move against Weapon X, Cable (Nathan Summers)'s Mutant Underground anonymously informed Colcord of his ex-wife's pending marriage. He attacked her and her fiancé, but his children prevented him from killing her. He kidnapped her fiancé and threatened her life if she were to ever remarry. Renewing contact with his nonmutant children affirmed his drive to eliminate mutants in a twisted bid to protect their futures and enabled him to begin a romance with Aurora, who convinced him to repair the damage to his face and let go of the past, becoming a kinder, gentler man. However, Jackson soon manipulated Colcord's mutant hatred to provoke him to viciously beat Aurora. Soon after, Jackson and the Underground overthrew him; during the coup, an unhinged Colcord used a mirror shard to disfigure his face once more. Moments away from execution, Colcord was saved by Jeffries, and escaped with Aurora, who later beat him in revenge. After turning to alcohol for a time, Colcord regained composure and purpose, using Jeffries to build a fleet of mutant-hunting Sentinels. Soon afterward, the "War of the Programs" began in earnest when Jackson, Colcord, and Sublime led their factions against each other – however, following the depowering of the majority of Earth's mutants on "M-Day," Colcord's location and activities are unrevealed.

REAL NAME: Malcolm Colcord
ALIASES: "Chief," "Herr Director"
IDENTITY: Known to authorities
OCCUPATION: Anti-mutant activist; former director of Weapon X, government employee, soldier
CITIZENSHIP: Unrevealed (US or Canada)
PLACE OF BIRTH: Unrevealed
KNOWN RELATIVES: Kathleen (ex-wife), Suzie (daughter), Jimmy (son)
GROUP AFFILIATION: Weapon X; formerly either US or Canadian Army
EDUCATION: Military and intelligence training
FIRST APPEARANCE: (Shadowed) Wolverine #160 (2001); (full) Weapon X #8 (2003)

HEIGHT: 5'11" **EYES:** Blue
WEIGHT: 165 lbs. **HAIR:** Black

ABILITIES/ACCESSORIES: The Director is a trained soldier and experienced administrator familiar with cutting-edge technology, including Weapon X's extensive array, teleportation devices, anti-mutant weaponry and computer networks. He is a highly skilled manipulator, torturer and has working knowledge of psychological warfare. The Director smokes occasionally.

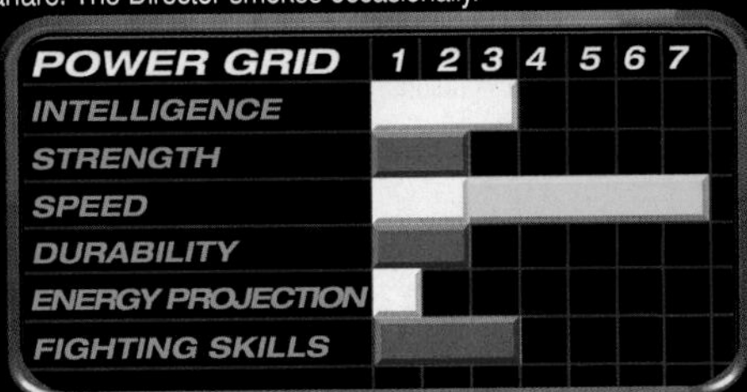
POWER GRID
1 2 3 4 5 6 7
INTELLIGENCE
STRENGTH
SPEED
DURABILITY
ENERGY PROJECTION
FIGHTING SKILLS

YELLOW BAR INDICATES THE DIRECTOR CAN TELEPORT

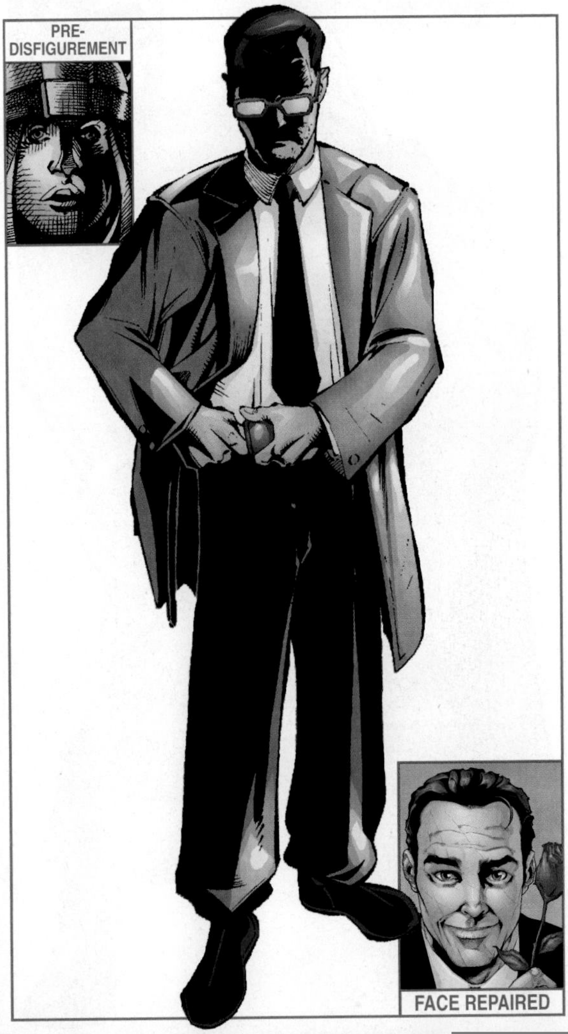
PRE-DISFIGUREMENT
FACE REPAIRED

DOCTOR BONG

REAL NAME: Lester Verde
ALIASES: Easter Bunny, "Dr. Bing"
IDENTITY: Publicly known
OCCUPATION: Entrepreneur, genetic engineer, psychologist; former journalist, music critic and performer
CITIZENSHIP: USA
PLACE OF BIRTH: Unrevealed
KNOWN RELATIVES: Lester Jr., Chester, Nestor, Fester and Howie (Bong Quintuplets, cloned "sons"), Stephanie Verde (mother), Beverly Switzler (ex-wife)
GROUP AFFILIATION: Chief executive officer of the Bellwether Media Group
EDUCATION: Ph.D.s in journalism and psychology; advanced training in acoustics, quantum mechanics and bioengineering
FIRST APPEARANCE: Howard the Duck #15 (1977)

HISTORY: A portly boy, Lester Verde was tormented by other children until he called the bullies "monkey-mouths." His mother told him he had a talent for words, so young Lester decided to become a writer, and a third-grade field trip to a newspaper printer helped focus that dream toward journalism. Verde was disappointed in college, however, when Professor Jim Furgen suggested he use journalism for moral ends. In retribution, Verde used a misleadingly-worded article to destroy Furgen's personal and professional life. In a later art class, Verde developed amorous feelings for life-drawing model Beverly Switzler. He worked up the nerve to ask her out after four such modeling sessions, but was shocked to learn that she was already dating a boy named David Schuster. Verde gained revenge by writing a suggestive letter that caused David's parents to separate the two lovers. David went against his parents' wishes to visit Beverly one fateful winter day, and died in a car crash en route, something for which Beverly later blamed Verde. Verde made a name for himself after college, hoping Beverly would notice his writing, first as a tabloid journalist then as a gonzo reporter for a rock magazine. He went on tour with bands, becoming not only a trusted associate, but part of the act. He even played the Easter Bunny in the violent stage show of Mildred Horowitz and his Band, a decision that cost him his left hand in a guillotine-based musical performance. Under unrevealed circumstances, Verde replaced his left hand with a metal ball and underwent advanced training. He eventually became the disfigured master geneticist and acoustician Dr. Bong and established an apparently mobile castle base (populated by various genetic creations). Verde vowed to reveal the circumstances that led to him becoming Dr. Bong only to the woman who agreed to be his mate.

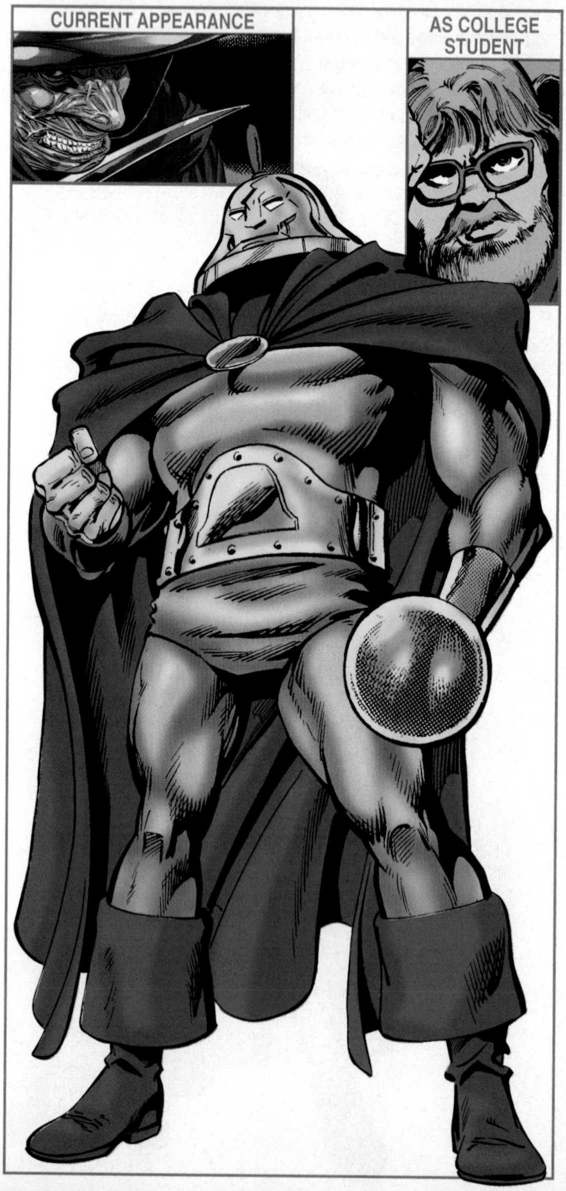
CURRENT APPEARANCE
AS COLLEGE STUDENT

Nine years after Beverly had rejected him in college, Bong found Beverly and her friend Howard the Duck aboard the SS Damned traveling through the Mediterranean. He attacked the ship with one of his genetic creations, a top hat-wearing sea serpent, and bombarded the ship with illusionary boulders, as well as a real, hollow boulder that housed a flying stone swan with which he transported Beverly (with Howard in tow) to his castle on a bell-shaped atoll. Removing the illusion from the Damned, Bong convinced passengers and crew to leave. He bonged Howard into unconsciousness and left the duck in the care of his creation Fifi, a French maid duck-woman, in the hopes they would mate. Apparently transporting his castle to the Himalayas at some point, Bong further hoped Beverly would agree to marry him after hearing his origin. She agreed to be Bong's bride if he spared Howard's life, but he neglected to mention his plan to alter Howard's genetic structure in his Evolvo-Chamber to facilitate his mating with Fifi. Beverly made a poorly thought out attempt to save Howard by flipping various switches on the chamber. Bong then teleported Beverly to a Russian trawler where he forced the captain to marry them, while Bev's manipulation soon caused Howard to turn into human form; Howard and Fifi fled Bong's castle in a bell-shaped "Flying Bonger" aircraft, but Fifi seemingly perished when the US Air Force shot down this UFO. Perhaps feeling Beverly would never be happy with him until Howard was out of the way, Bong confronted Howard anew shortly after he reverted to his standard, anatine (duck-like) form, but Howard eluded Bong with a well-placed pipe-to-the-bell, which teleported Bong back to his wife.

Although resigned to marriage, Beverly became frustrated with Bong's boring life. Her husband privately removed his helmet for her, but read Edgar Allen Poe's "The Bells," instead of consummating the marriage. She feigned love while Bong plotted Howard's end. Bong returned to his feathery nemesis months later and challenged him to mortal combat; if Howard resisted, Bong threatened to destroy him with misleading news articles. To oppose Bong, Howard wore his Iron Duck armor (as well as sonar dishes that nullified vibrations); the dishes proved effective initially,

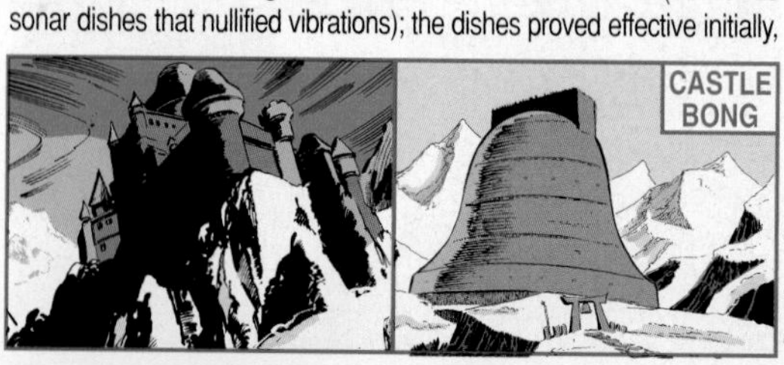
CASTLE BONG

Art by Gene Colan & John Byrne

but one battery-less dish ran out of power seconds later. Striking Bong's helmet with a hammer, Howard unwittingly teleported them to Bong's castle, where Bong swiftly destroyed Howard's armor. As their battle raged, Beverly worked with Bong's reptilian beasts to create the Bong Quintuplets from her husband's toenail clippings and force Bong to face his own medicine with the threat of a news article declaring him an unfit parent. Fearing public humiliation, Bong teleported Howard and Beverly back to Cleveland and became devoted to fatherhood.

A recovered Fifi eventually found her way back to Castle Bong, and her master found the perils of fatherhood included keeping his boys away from corrupting television shows. Via technology and his scientific expertise, Bong transformed television signals into a pocket dimension that he could enter and control using hypersonic vibrations generated by his helmet. Individuals using outdated ultrasound remote controls were accidentally drawn into the Bongvision™ dimension, including She-Hulk (Jennifer Walters) and several American families. She-Hulk fought her way to the real world and turned off Bong's machine, temporarily trapping Bong in the Bongvision™ world.

Continuing his education while his quintuplets matured, Bong earned a degree as a psychologist. Though working through his own megalomaniacal issues, Bong took Deadpool ("Wade Wilson") as his first client. Diagnosing Deadpool as having severe psychological damage, Bong prescribed a therapeutic hero-villain battle, something his patient achieved with Wolverine (James Howlett/Logan) while Bong held Kitty Pryde at bay. The session helped Deadpool unlock repressed memories, but damaged a relationship Bong was trying form with a woman named Barbara.

Bong later used his psychological knowledge to create a marketing firm and his Molecular Management™ techniques to genetically engineer perfect teen idols in the hope of guiding the next generation of voters to become malleable enough to vote his other clients into politics. With funding from transgender billionaire Kenneth Flogg, Bong created the Bellwether Media Group, including the Globally Branded Content Dot Com division. With his company established, he had his assistant

Peter Pitterpool hire Beverly as supervisor for the data collection department with five identical blondes (Heather, Tiffany, Britney, Jennifer and Kimberly) working under her. Beverly unwittingly helped Bong as he used morally questionable technology to determine the marketability of an artificially grown boy band called the Backdoor Boys. When potential band member "TJ" failed a focus group study, TJ escaped to avoid being "recycled" in the Evolvo-Chamber and asked Beverly and Howard for help. Bong showed off his technology and revealed his plans to Beverly and Howard. When TJ struck Bong over the head with a pipe, the resultant vibrations knocked Howard into one of his genetic vat. Abandoning his corporation in favor of revenge, Bong turned the dials into the red zone and fled before the vat exploded, leaving Howard unconscious on the floor in the form of a humanoid mouse. TJ was arrested following an explosion at the company headquarters and Bong, escaping in a Flying Bonger, called Beverly repeatedly over the next day hoping she would take him back. Feeling their marriage was never legal, Bev suggested he grow his own girlfriend. Determined to get revenge, Bong revealed Howard's location to government and Girl Scout officials, identifying him as a wanted terrorist. The subsequent arrest attempt destroyed Howard and Beverly's home. The pair ended up with Beverly's childhood friend Detective Suzi Pazuzu of the Cleveland Division of Police, and Bong turned to Flogg for aid. Flogg instead forced Bong to work with his submissive assassin Ian Whippingham to kill the women and duck and claim the ancient Amulet of Pazuzu from Suzi. Howard inadvertently gained the artifact instead, turning into the androgynous warrior Gub-gala-emegir (roughly translated as "Cleansing Blade") who slew Whippingham and then assaulted Bong. Bev saved Bong and removed the amulet, returning Howard to his mouse form, but made her lack of interest clear to Bong, who finally accepted that their relationship was over.

Without Beverly as the guiding focus in his life, Bong has become a frequent visitor of the "Bar with No Name." This brought him into brief conflict with the mercenary Daughters of the Dragon (Misty Knight and Colleen Wing) and later involved him in illegal bets on the outcome of superhuman battles.

HEIGHT: 6'2" (6'8" with helmet)
WEIGHT: 225 lbs. (260 lbs. with helmet and glove)
EYES: Blue
HAIR: Reddish blond

ABILITIES/ACCESSORIES: A genius in multiple fields, Dr. Bong has mastered acoustics, bioengineering, psychology, quantum mechanics and rhetoric. He can perform seemingly impossible feats with the proper application of sound, build up or destroy anyone's public life with a few well-chosen words, alter the nature of life, create and manipulate sapient minds and even apparently manipulate pocket dimensions. Dr. Bong wears a bell-shaped helmet on his head and a clapper-like mallet in place of his severed left hand to perform a wide variety of tintinnabulatory feats. Sonic vibrations created by striking mallet to helmet can be used to activate specially tuned devices, paralyze or kill living beings, create virtually impenetrable force barriers (effective even against intangible foes) and apparently allow for teleportation, although other sources have proposed the bell merely activates other technological devices. If struck incorrectly, the sound of his bell helmet can harm even Dr. Bong. He also carriers a clapper-like mace and wears a fireproof costume.

He maintains Castle Bong, a facility that seems to exist both on a bell-shaped Mediterranean atoll and on a high Himalayan peak. Whether the building teleports between locations, is in two separate locations joined by dimension-warping technology or whether the island is merely an illusion is unrevealed. The high-tech facility includes a bell-shaped temple, a castle with bell-shaped towers and vast arrays of complicated machinery intended primarily for show. Despite the elaborate scientific laboratories of other villains, Bong

prefers a minimalist approach to gadgetry. Aside from teleportation, Bong can travel using Flying Bongers, bell-shaped saucers that include devices for communicating with Castle Bong. Using his Evolvo-Chamber, Bong can create living creatures or alter the genetic structure of living beings. The creatures, whether human, animal or something in-between, possess near-human intelligence, but often have stunted verbal abilities. Bong outfits his creations with pleasure buttons that allow for easier control in case of emergency. His creations include several umbilicus (navel) lacking humans (including the Bong Quintuplets and the Backdoor Boys), at least two humanoid ducks (a muscular male and the female Fifi), a humanoid giraffe named Carlo, a cat-person, a gigantic top hat-wearing sea serpent and multiple reptilian servants (including Lassie and Greta).

Bong can apparently use sonic vibrations to create illusory rocks and flying rock swans, the temporary illusion of death and manipulate a pocket dimension within TV reruns dubbed Bongvision™. Within that dimension, all TV shows are recreated with an enhanced sense of realism, all controllable by Bong.

POWER GRID	1	2	3	4	5	6	7
INTELLIGENCE							
STRENGTH							
SPEED							
DURABILITY							
ENERGY PROJECTION							
FIGHTING SKILLS							

YELLOW BAR INDICATES DR. BONG CAN TELEPORT

DOMINO

REAL NAME: Neena Thurman
ALIASES: "Dom," Beatrice, Jessica Marie Costello, Luisa Mendoza, Samantha Wu, Elena Vladescu, Tamara Winter, Christina Elizabeth Alioso, Priscilla Sutherland, Hope Eldrige, others; impersonated Val Cooper
IDENTITY: Secret
OCCUPATION: Adventurer; former mercenary
CITIZENSHIP: USA
PLACE OF BIRTH: Project Armageddon base, Florida
KNOWN RELATIVES: Milo Thurman (husband, deceased), Beatrice (mother), Lazarus (brother), unidentified sister, many other unidentified siblings (deceased)
GROUP AFFILIATION: X-Men, X-Force (X-Men strike team); formerly SHIELD's Six Pack, X-Force (Cable-founded), Cable's Underground, X-Corporation, Six Pack/Wild Pack, NSA
EDUCATION: Unrevealed
FIRST APPEARANCE: X-Force #8 (1992)

HISTORY: The albino Neena was one of many children born to the US government's Project Armageddon, designed to genetically engineer the perfect weapon using a precognitive mutant named Beatrice as a surrogate. One of only two survivors from numerous attempts, Neena was taken by Beatrice's cult, the Armajesuits, and delivered to a Chicago priest, remaining in his care until her mutant powers manifested when she turned 13. Neena ran away and was arrested in Seattle for shoplifting, but escaped the juvenile authorities. Two years later, she became a combatant in the underground fighting arenas of Madripoor. Ultimately, she forged a distinguished career in many fields of covert activity, both as an agent of various organizations and governments and as a freelance mercenary. While a member of the National Security Agency (NSA), Neena was assigned to bodyguard Milo Thurman — whose highly-developed mind made him a prodigy in predicting world events – who coined her nickname "Domino" due to her power causing things to fall into place for her. She and Thurman fell in love and eventually married; however, their relationship was short-lived after a raid by AIM forced Thurman into even deeper government cover, and his superiors told him that Domino had been killed. Domino left the NSA and returned to her mercenary ways. On a mission in El Salvador, Domino disabled a prototype combat droid codenamed Jericho with an electromagnetic pulse, unaware that Jericho was being neurologically controlled by rogue CIA agent Ekatarina Gryaznova and that the resultant feedback left Gryaznova comatose. Later, Domino joined the Wild Pack (later renamed the Six Pack) led by the mutant soldier Cable (Nathan Summers). When a mission in Uruguay went awry after Cable was forced to place his own needs above those of the team, Domino and her teammates barely escaped with their lives.

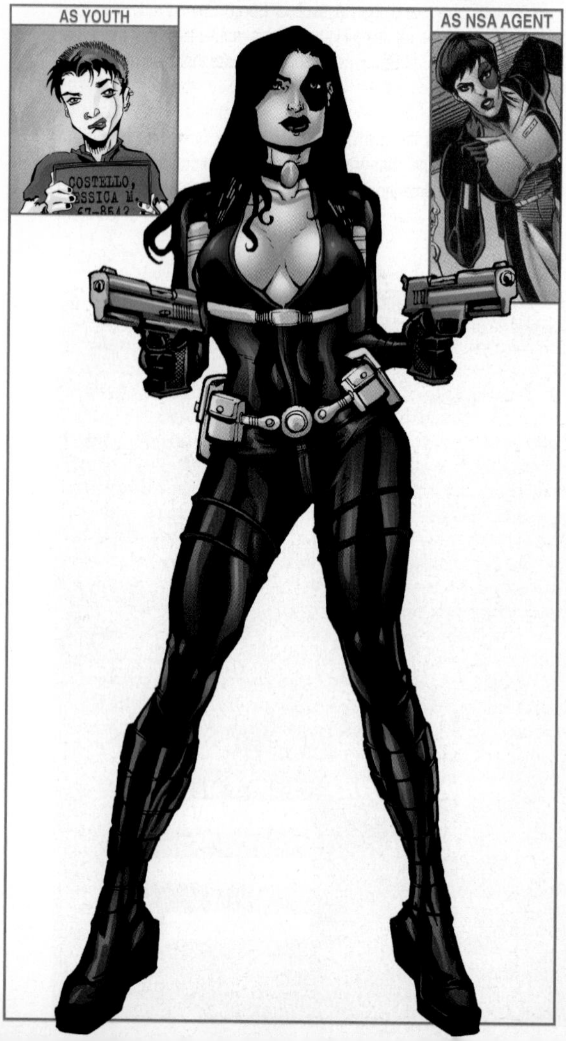
AS YOUTH
COSTELLO,
AS NSA AGENT

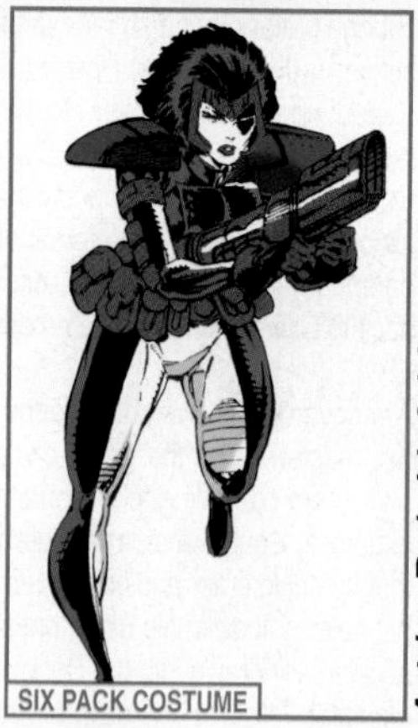
SIX PACK COSTUME

Art by Rob Liefeld

Some time later, Domino was captured by Tolliver, secretly Cable's estranged son Tyler, who had his agent Copycat (Vanessa Carlysle) impersonate Domino in Cable's new X-Force team. Held prisoner for more than a year, Domino was freed by Cable who tasked her with finding and protecting the then-missing X-Force. Domino sought help from her old Six Pack teammates Grizzly (Theodore Wincester) and Hammer (Eisenhower Canty), eventually reuniting with Cable (who had already found X-Force) and the remaining Six Pack, but all opted to not work with Cable again, whom they could not trust. Cable later asked Domino to help train X-Force, and she joined the team as co-leader. On the eve of Earth being overlapped with Reality-295 ("Age of Apocalypse"), Domino and Cable confessed their true feelings and kissed. After reality was restored, Domino helped Cable restructure X-Force before investigating a series of murders committed by a feral Grizzly, who forced her to kill him. Domino agreed to share a psionic link with Cable as a sign of their mutual trust. Later, Domino and Cable received a call for help from former Six Pack teammate Garrison Kane and discovered him with Copycat. The emotion-manipulating Psycho-Man made Domino attack Copycat, whom she already resented for her role in her year-long captivity, after which he kidnapped Copycat to the Microverse; Domino, Cable and Kane teamed with the Micronauts to oppose the Psycho-Man. Soon after, Domino learned Thurman was alive when Donald Pierce and his cyborg Reavers captured him to gain his alleged prophetic abilities through cybernetic conversion. Domino was forced to kill Thurman to defeat Pierce's plans. Domino was then asked by G.W. Bridge to help prevent SHIELD agent Danielle Moonstar from being exposed by the government's Operation: Zero Tolerance. Moonstar was undercover posing as a member of the Mutant Liberation Front (MLF) who had taken control of a medical research center they believed was engaged in anti-mutant research. Posing as a camera crew,

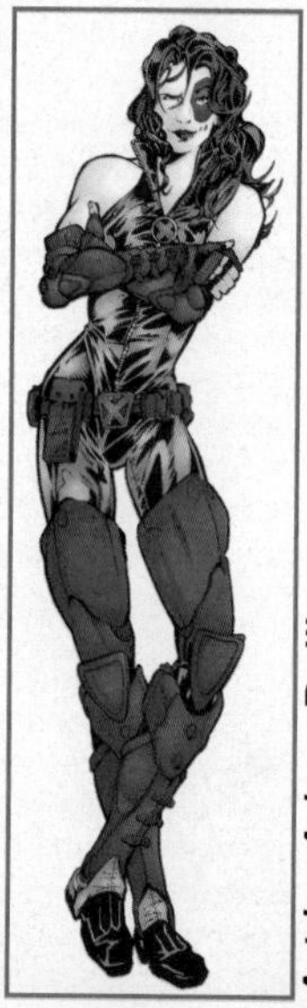
Art by Adam Pollina

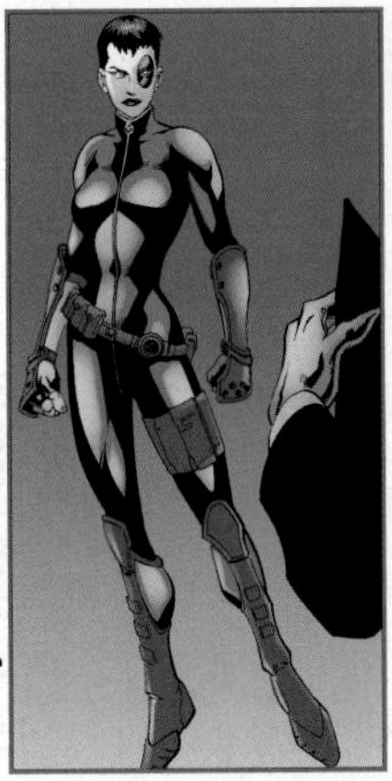

Art by Mike Miller

Domino, Sunspot (Roberto Da Costa) and Siryn infiltrated the center, unaware that Zero Tolerance forces had discerned their true identities. Assaulted by Prime Sentinels, Domino was captured by their commander, Ekatarina Gryaznova, who hated Domino, and implanted a neural inhibitor at the base of her skull that created a synaptical static which caused her reflex and reaction times to become increasingly erratic. Seeking to overcome the device's effects and reclaim her fighting prowess, Domino left X-Force, broke up with Cable, and returned to her mercenary ways. She was later contacted by mutant Jesse Aaronson, who sought her help finding his brother. In exchange, Aaronson offered to reveal Gryaznova's whereabouts, taking Domino to the Aguilar Institute in California where Domino was captured by Gryaznova, now calling herself Gryphon. Aaronson turned to X-Force for help rescuing her, and then used his technology disrupting power to deactivate Domino's implant, after which she defeated Gryaznova.

Subsequently rejoining X-Force, Domino quit when Pete Wisdom offered to turn X-Force into a proactive black ops unit. She was subsequently possessed by the Undying alien Aentaeros who sought to use her to kill its rival Undying Semijan; however, Cable intervened and forced Aentaeros to release Domino. She drifted back into freelance work and took an assignment that marked her as a target of mutant assassin Marcus Tsung, who apparently killed her. She was revived by alien technology grafts, then turned to X-Force for help in defeating Tsung. Wisdom's sister Romany had the alien tech removed from Domino to create a techno-organic world engine, then sent British mutant Corben to kill X-Force, but Corben failed, and X-Force confronted Romany. The engine was destroyed in an explosion that seemingly killed all of X-Force except Domino, though the others soon resurfaced. When Domino discovered Project Armageddon was still active, she infiltrated the base and was shocked to find that she had a younger brother Lazarus. Soon after, the Armajesuits led by Domino's mother, Beatrice, arrived to kill Lazarus to prevent his mutant emotion-controlling ability from being used to destroy civilization; however, Domino defeated them and left Lazarus with the same priest that had cared for her as a child. Domino soon joined Xavier's X-Corporation in its Hong Kong branch where, with the X-Men's help, she hindered John Sublime's Third Species mutant organ harvesting movement. After learning that mutants were being executed in a concentration camp by Malcolm Colcord's clandestine Weapon X program, Domino and Cable formed an Underground resistance, working with the traitorous Weapon X agent Brent Jackson to depose Colcord. Domino was later recruited by Bridge to join a new SHIELD incarnation of the Six Pack in investigating Cable after his powers increased markedly and he began affecting change on a global scale. After Cable lobotomized himself to control his powers, the Six Pack tracked him to a Swiss safehouse where they became trapped in his mind. After Cable was healed and the Six Pack freed, Domino helped him oppose and defeat the ancient mutant-devouring Skornn entity. Later, the Six Pack was hired by the Thin Man to determine the state of affairs in Rumekistan, which had been taken over by Flag-Smasher (Karl Morgenthau) and his anti-national terrorist ULTIMATUM group. Domino assassinated Flag-Smasher, allowing Cable to take control of the country. Fearing his return to messianic-like behavior, Domino confronted Cable, threatening to kill him if he spiraled out of control again.

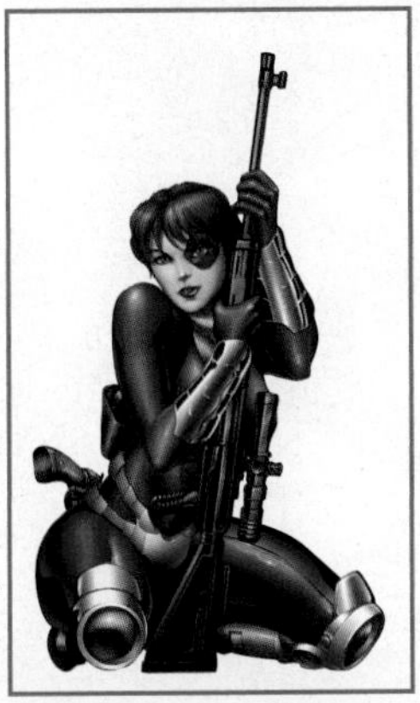

Art by Georges Jeanty

After an insane Scarlet Witch depowered the majority of mutants during "M-Day," Domino reformed X-Force with Shatterstar (Gavedra-Seven) and Caliban to liberate mutants sequestered by the Office of National Emergency (ONE). Later, the Six Pack was tasked with sabotaging both Rumekistan and Cable's island paradise Providence in an effort to tarnish Cable's international reputation, but ultimately failed. Domino publicly confessed her role in the mission, after which she joined the staff of Providence until the island was decimated in a battle between the X-Men and the alien Shi'ar weapon the Hecatomb. Domino was later recruited by Bridge to join a SHIELD strike team assembled to take down the Punisher (Frank Castle), instead aiding him against magical Hand assassins and the Wrecking Crew. Subsequently, Domino encountered Wolverine's X-Force strike team while tracking down mutant criminal Vanisher (Telford Porter), and joined the team. X-Force then clashed with the Red Hulk's Code Red team after Leonard Samson manipulated Domino into apparently learning the Red Hulk's true identity, then accompanied X-Force to the Reality-80521 to help Cable safeguard the first mutant born since "M-Day" from Lucas Bishop and Stryfe (Cable's clone). Returning to Reality-616, X-Force rescued mutants from the Leper Queen's Sapien League, then aided the X-Men in opposing Madelyne Pryor's Sisterhood, keeping an eye on a visiting Deadpool ("Wade Wilson") and battling Selene's zombie mutant army.

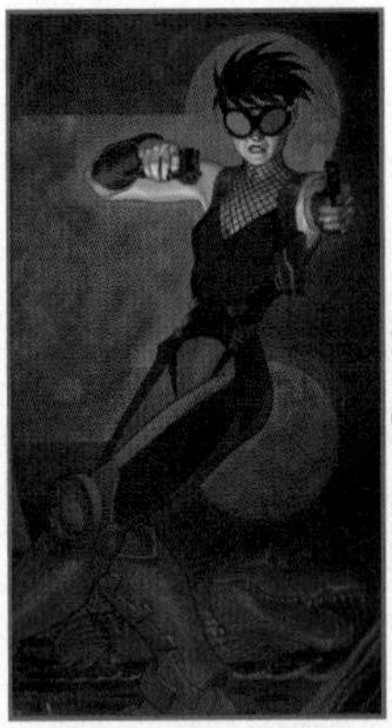

Art by Brian Stelfreeze

HEIGHT: 5'8" **EYES:** Blue
WEIGHT: 120 lbs. **HAIR:** Black

ABILITIES/ACCESSORIES: Domino subconsciously generates a psionic aura about herself that alters probabilities, causing her to receive "good luck" while her opponents suffer "bad luck." This causes improbable (but not impossible) things to occur within her line of sight, and can vary from having an enemy's equipment malfunction to hitting just the right button to shut down an overloading machine. While she cannot consciously control this ability, she can activate it by placing herself in a situation in which she could be harmed. Non-activity on her part will not trigger the effect. When engaging in an action that her power can affect, her cerebral cortex emits bioelectric pulses down her spine that instinctively guides her movements. This augments her natural reflexes and agility to near superhuman levels. As a by-product of her mutant ability, she can instinctively calculate the odds of virtually any event's occurrence. Domino has been extensively trained in various armed and unarmed combat techniques, as well as in covert operations and demolitions. She is a superb marskwoman, athlete and swimmer, and is fluent in several languages. She wears body armor, contacts that magnify her vision and shoot lasers, and wields conventional firearms and weapons.

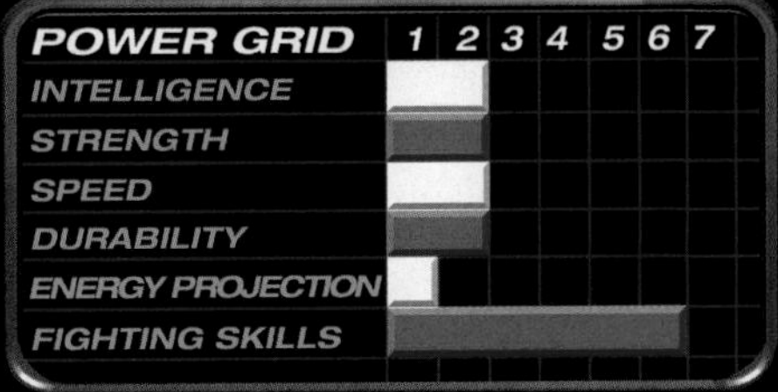
POWER GRID
1 2 3 4 5 6 7
INTELLIGENCE
STRENGTH
SPEED
DURABILITY
ENERGY PROJECTION
FIGHTING SKILLS

EXECUTIVE ELITE

MEMBERS: Black Box/Commcast (Garabed Bashur), Makeshift (Amie Zamborano), Rive (Anastasia Summit)
FIRST APPEARANCE: (Bashur as Commcast) Deadpool: The Circle Chase #2 (1993); (Makeshift & Rive) Deadpool: The Circle Chase #3 (1993); (Bashur as Black Box) Cable & Deadpool #15 (2005)

HISTORY: A mercenary organization formed by mutant cyberpath Garabed Bashur, the Executive Elite consisted of Bashur as Commcast, blade artist Rive, who wielded an energy sword and wore wrist-mounted spikes, and techno-construct assembler Makeshift, who could rapidly create technologically advanced weapons. With his knowledge of cloning, Bashur made copies of himself and his teammates, but a problem with the process ultimately prevented further duplication, leaving him one last ancillary body. When Nyko Halfghanaghan sought revenge for the murder of his brother Pico, he tasked the Courier (Jacob Gavin Jr.) with hiring the Executive Elite to eliminate the three main suspects – mercenary Deadpool ("Wade Wilson"), mutant soldier Cable (Nathan Summers), and mutant shape-shifter Copycat (Vanessa Carlysle). As payment, they were offered information on the will of arms dealer Tolliver (Tyler Dayspring), which would lead to a hidden cache of advanced technology. Realizing they needed information the Elite had, Deadpool and his friend Weasel (Jack Hammer) lured the Elite into the open by making Deadpool a target; clones of Bashur and his teammates ambushed Deadpool in Sarajevo, where he was rendered unconscious with a strong electrical charge. They took Deadpool to their mobile base dubbed "the Edsel," where they sought to learn more about Tolliver's will by using a device to tap into Deadpool's memories; however, Weasel rescued him. Bashur sought to escape, but was killed by Weasel while Deadpool killed Rive and Makeshift; Deadpool and Weasel gained the information they sought.

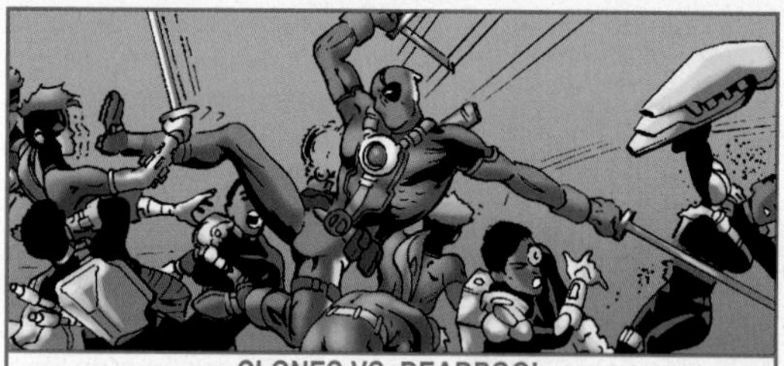
CLONES VS. DEADPOOL

Art by Patrick Zircher

Reviving in his last remaining cloned body, Bashur reinvented himself as information broker the Black Box. He sought to procure the Dominus Objective, a computer hard drive that, when linked to another system, processes all stored information and channels it to a single recipient in an orderly and filtered fashion. Bashur hired the Cat (Shen Kuei) to steal it; however, the Cat was reluctant to accept until Cable secretly paid him to take the assignment, to ensure Bashur received the Dominus Objective, so to become an invaluable resource in Cable's mission to prevent future apocalypse. Cable also secretly hired Deadpool and the mercenary BAD Girls, Inc. to steal it in the unlikely event the Cat failed. Succeeding, the Cat delivered the drive to Bashur who interfaced with it, granting him worldwide control of all electronically stored information, so to safeguard humanity. Cable and Deadpool confronted Bashur, but he set clones of Rive and Makeshift against them. While Cable clashed with Bashur, Deadpool slew the Rive and Makeshift clones; however, more clones kept coming until the Cat destroyed their cloning vats, leaving only four clones each of Rive and Makeshift. After Bashur was overwhelmed by learning of Cable's dystopian future, and his tireless work to prevent it, Bashur pledged his - and the Executive Elite's - service to Cable, to prepare mankind for that future. However, following Bashur's apparent death at the hands of Sabretooth (Victor Creed), the current activities and whereabouts of the Executive Elite are unrevealed.

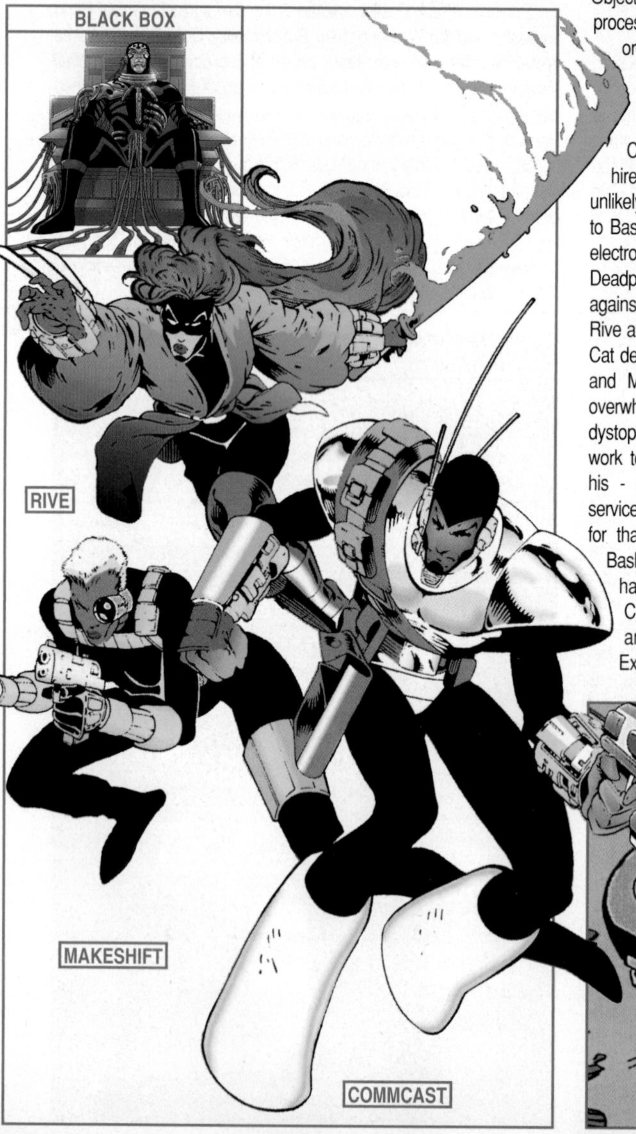
BLACK BOX
RIVE
MAKESHIFT
COMMCAST

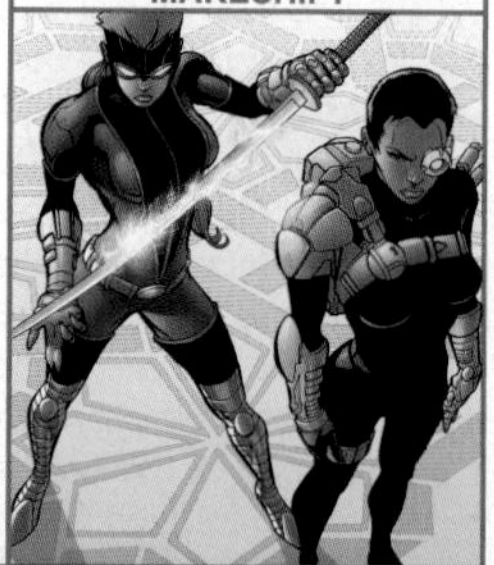
CLONED RIVE & MAKESHIFT

Art by Patrick Zircher

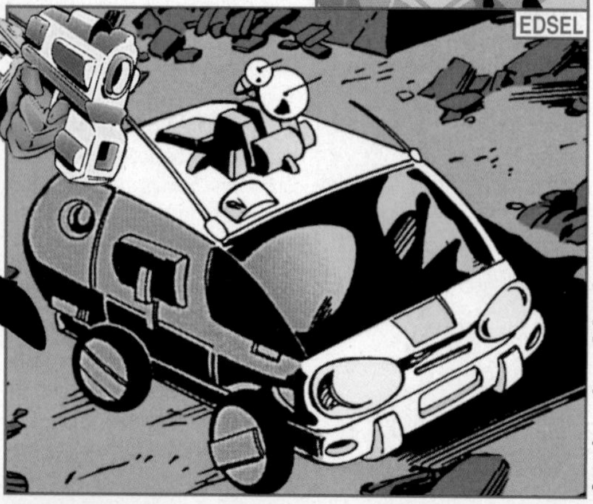
EDSEL

Art by Joe Madureira

HISTORY: A two-dimensional mutant and homosexual in denial, Val Ventura studied fashion in college, then earned a Ph.D in astrophysics, becoming an accomplished scientist, albeit often dismissed by his peers. Ventura eventually used his powers to become Flatman, an eager-to-please super hero who was sensitive when teased about his code name and whose naïveté could be exploited by clever criminals. Answering a personal ad seeking costumed adventurers, Flatman became the deputy leader of the group that became the "Great Lakes Avengers" (GLA), assisting Midwestern authorities in fighting crime. Following a scuffle while investigating the GLA's unauthorized use of the Avengers name, Avengers veterans Hawkeye (Clint Barton) and Mockingbird (Bobbi Barton) decided the GLA could be shaped into a true fighting force through proper training and leadership. While training under the Bartons, the GLA rescued several Avengers from That Which Endures, an unconscious collective sentience trying to eliminate humankind in favor of mutantkind. Later, after rejoining the Avengers, Hawkeye called in the GLA to help delay the extraterrestrial Terminus' rampage in St. Louis, Missouri, until the Avengers arrived.

After the GLA briefly changed their name to the "Lightning Rods" Flatman assisted in battles against Deadpool ("Wade Wilson"), the Thunderbolts, Graviton, Dr. Tannenbaum and his giant robot snowman and tornadoes caused by the Crimson Cowl (Justine Hammer) and her Masters of Evil. Sick of being upstaged by the real Avengers, Mr. Immortal was about to disband the GLA until he learned the original Avengers had just disbanded. Mr. Immortal then eagerly led the GLA against the Inhuman/Deviant geneticist Maelstrom, who was trying to destroy the universe, a battle that left teammate Dinah Soar dead and Mr. Immortal demoralized. Often mistaken for Mr. Fantastic (Reed Richards), Flatman temporarily assumed command of the GLA and undertook a membership drive in New York City, recruiting Squirrel Girl after she saved him from a mugging in Central Park, and Grasshopper (Doug Taggert), who was killed seconds later by Maelstrom-hired mercenaries Batroc's Brigade. Inspired by Avengers veteran Living Lightning (Miguel Santos)'s open homosexuality, Flatman came out of the closet, then helped the GLA locate Maelstrom's doomsday machine. Flatman's uniform was sucked into the universe-collapsing vortex created by the machine, but Mr. Immortal tricked Maelstrom into committing suicide and deactivated the device, saving Flatman, who stood sideways to conceal his nudity.

Forced by legal problems to drop the GLA name, the mostly mutant team rechristened themselves the "Great Lakes X-Men" (GLX) and defeated Dr. Tannenbaum's killer Christmas trees. While attending the Thing (Ben Grimm)'s poker competition, they were telepathically influenced by Marvel Girl (Rachel Grey) to stop using the X-Men name, dubbing themselves "Great Lakes Champions" after Flatman unexpectedly won the game. After the passage of the Superhuman Registration Act, the GLA registered as licensed super heroes, and after a brief misunderstanding and fight with Deadpool, the GLA became the Fifty State Initiative's Wisconsin team, renaming themselves the "Great Lakes Initiative." The team then stopped AIM (Advanced Idea Mechanics) from conquering the US using the Dionysus-powered "inebriation ray," fought an alien Skrull imposter disguised as the latest Grasshopper and welcomed Gravity as a new member.

HEIGHT: Variable **EYES:** Brown
WEIGHT: 98 lbs. **HAIR:** Brown

ABILITIES/ACCESSORIES: Flatman's approximately ½ inch thick body has a highly malleable, ribbon-like consistency. He can contort and compress his body into various shapes and stretch to an unrevealed length. He can slide through extremely narrow openings, wrap himself around a target to restrain it, and when standing sideways, cannot be seen, effectively disappearing. His malleable body is highly durable, and despite his extreme thinness, he can lift other people and objects well over his own weight. An excellent hand-to-hand combatant, he has mastered the deadly Origami-Fu fighting style. Flatman is an expert in astrophysics, knowledgeable in time travel theories, an experienced poker and video game player, and loves to knit.

POWER GRID	1	2	3	4	5	6	7
INTELLIGENCE	■	■	■				
STRENGTH	■	■	■				
SPEED	■	■					
DURABILITY	■	■	■	■	■		
ENERGY PROJECTION	■						
FIGHTING SKILLS	■	■	■	■	■		

REAL NAME: Val Ventura
ALIASES: "Flatso," "Shoelace," "Stretcho," "Doc," the 2-D Defender, "Flatty"
IDENTITY: Known to authorities
OCCUPATION: Licensed super hero, scientist
CITIZENSHIP: USA
PLACE OF BIRTH: Unrevealed
KNOWN RELATIVES: Unrevealed
GROUP AFFILIATION: Great Lakes Initiative; formerly Great Lakes Champions, Great Lakes X-Men, Great Lakes Avengers, Lightning Rods
EDUCATION: Ph.D in astrophysics, undergraduate degree in fashion
FIRST APPEARANCE: West Coast Avengers #46 (1989)

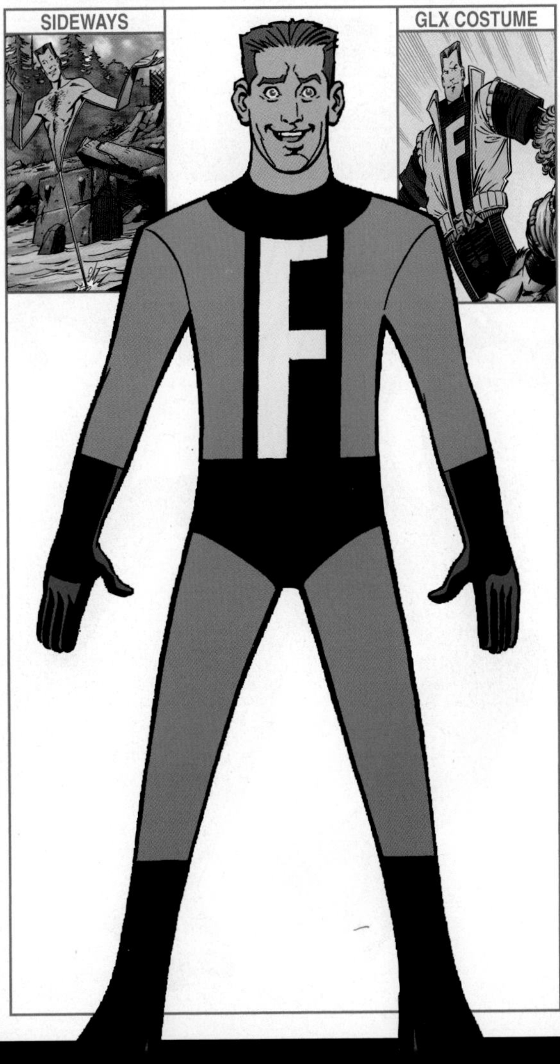
SIDEWAYS
GLX COSTUME

Art by Mike Wieringo

GRASSHOPPER

REAL NAME: Douglas "Doug" Taggert; Neil Shelton; others unrevealed
ALIASES: The Ever-Gregarious Grasshopper
IDENTITY: (All) Secret
OCCUPATION: (Taggert) Research scientist; (Shelton) security officer; (unidentified) unrevealed; (Skrull) warrior
CITIZENSHIP: (Taggert, Shelton, unidentified) USA; (Skrull) Skrull Empire
PLACE OF BIRTH: (All) Unrevealed
KNOWN RELATIVES: (Shelton) Cindy Shelton (sister); (others) none
GROUP AFFILIATION: (Taggert) Roxxon, Great Lakes Avengers; (Shelton) Roxxon; (unidentified) none; (Skrull) Great Lakes Initiative
EDUCATION: (All) Unrevealed
FIRST APPEARANCE: (Taggert) GLA #1 (2005); (in-story) GLA #2 (2005); (Shelton) GLX-Mas Special #1 (2006); (unidentified) Deadpool/GLI Summer Fun Spectacular #1 (2007); (Skrull) Avengers: The Initiative #19 (2009)

HISTORY: Roxxon Energy Corporation research scientist Doug Taggert either acquired or built an armored, insect-themed battle suit. Dubbing himself the Grasshopper, Taggert set out to protect Roxxon and do a little super heroing on the side. Two weeks later, things seemed to be looking up for him; he had been assigned to Cindy Shelton's research team, and he hoped to romance her or, at least, to discover her inexplicable animosity for his armored alter-ego. While patrolling one night, he detected mercenaries Batroc the Leaper, Machete (Mariano Lopez) and Maximillian Zaran robbing Roxxon's Manhattan labs, trying to steal the Atomic Inverter X-99 for their employer Maelstrom. Battling

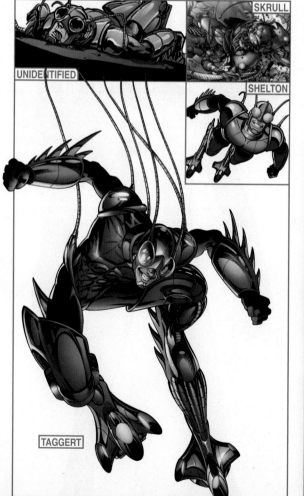

SKRULL

UNIDENTIFIED

SHELTON

TAGGERT

them, Grasshopper was soon joined by out-of-town heroes Flatman (Val Ventura) and Doorman (DeMarr Davis) and their newest Great Lakes Avengers recruit, Squirrel Girl (Doreen Green). During the battle, Doorman asked Grasshopper to join the GLA; unaware that it was not an official Avengers team, Doug agreed. Five point eight seconds later, Zaran threw a sai at Doorman; it passed right through Davis' Darkforce portal body and straight into Grasshopper's head, killing him instantly. Angel of death Deathurge escorted Taggert's indignant soul to the afterlife, where Doorman later saw him playing cards with other dead GLA members. Doorman offered his apologies, but Doug was unimpressed.

Cindy's long-lost brother Neil acquired the suit, becoming the next Grasshopper. His first outing in the suit pitted him against the criminal Killer Shrike (Simon Maddicks), who tried to steal Project Z from Roxxon's Manhattan lab on Christmas Day, assuming that Roxxon security had taken the day off. Surprised that Shelton (who was Jewish) was present, the Shrike was soon kicked into submission. Cindy, sensing that something was different about the Grasshopper, thanked him and asked him out, unaware that her would-be paramour was her brother. Fending off her advances, Shelton set his suit to "maximum jump" and leaped off; unfortunately for Shelton, the jump sent him into outer space, where he promptly suffocated. Doorman escorted the protesting Shelton's soul to the afterlife, then later watched as his body burned up as it re-entered Earth's atmosphere; Doorman's teammates mistook the flaming corpse for a "Christmas star."

A third Grasshopper acquired a replica of the suit and leaped from New York to Milwaukee; he may have been trying to follow in Taggert's footsteps by joining the GLA (now renamed the Great Lakes Initiative). Before he could reach their base, however, Deadpool ("Wade Wilson"), irate at having just been expelled from GLI HQ by Squirrel Girl, broke his neck, killing him. A Skrull impersonating Grasshopper later joined the GLI; he revealed himself during Queen Veranke's Skrull invasion of Earth (much to team leader Mr. Immortal's surprise), but the team, aided by Wisconsinite hero Gravity (Greg Willis) and Skrull Kill Krew member Catwalk (Kimberly Dee), defeated him.

HEIGHT: (Taggert) 5'8"; (Shelton) 5'9"; (unidentified) 5'7"; (Skrull) variable
WEIGHT: (Taggert) 145 lbs.; (Shelton) 153 lbs.; (unidentified) 148 lbs.; (Skrull) variable
EYES: (All) unrevealed
HAIR: (All) unrevealed

ABILITIES/ACCESSORIES: The Grasshopper battle suit's extremely powerful legs are primarily used to leap prodigious distances; the suit's maximum leap can propel it into outer space, although this is achieved with the aid of boot-jets. The legs can also deliver powerful kicks. The helmet has vision-enhancing zoom lenses built into the eyepieces and danger-detecting insectroid sensors. Several of the suit's functions are voice-activated. The suit is lightly armored, and provides little defense against even thrown projectiles. The Skrull Grasshopper possessed all of the Grasshopper's abilities, as well as the shape-shifting abilities inherent to his species; his version of the Grasshopper suit also incorporated several mechanical tentacles.

POWER GRID	1	2	3	4	5	6	7
INTELLIGENCE							
STRENGTH							
SPEED							
DURABILITY							
ENERGY PROJECTION							
FIGHTING SKILLS							

Art by Paul Pelletier with Tie Templeton, Kismer Brown & Vance Edling

HISTORY: Founded circa the late 1940s, the church housing Sister Margaret's School for Wayward Children underwent scandal in the 1950s when its directors were convicted of unspeakable crimes. Over time, the church was burned, condemned, demolished and rebuilt to serve its original purpose under such nuns as Sister Butchie. Less than a decade ago, fire severely damaged the church, and the school again closed. Ex-pornographer Patch acquired the building and converted it into a clearinghouse for mercenary assignments, whether legal or not, earning a percentage on every job successfully completed. Dubbed "Hellhouse," Patch's establishment provided mercenaries - many superhumans - with a place to drink and socialize as well as to find work. He entrusted some select patrons with pagers for easy contact. Domino (Neena Thurman), formerly of the Six Pack, was an early customer and over the years Hellhouse counted mutates, cyborgs, sorcerers, extraterrestrials, and others among its patronage. Regulars included malleable C.F., baseball-obsessed Fenway, and fast-healing Deadpool ("Wade Wilson"), whose prankish tendencies, which endeared him to some patrons, were matched only by his hostilities toward T-Ray (Wade Wilson), a mercenary sorcerer whose wife Deadpool had killed, though Deadpool had come to believe the victim had been his own wife, killed by T-Ray. Patch's rules against violence on the premises were often ignored by both men, whom he frequently threatened with expulsion.

In recent years, T-Ray, sensing Deadpool was approaching a nervous breakdown, cultivated a more menacing aura, intimidating even seasoned mercenaries by accepting an assignment to murder several children. When Deadpool returned from an unexpected absence, Patch threatened to put him on probation, but was dissuaded by a gift of obscene chocolates. Deadpool and partner Weasel accepted twin assignments to abduct and kill a mental patient, but target and clients alike proved to be Typhoid Mary, who could pay for neither assignment. Deadpool brought Typhoid to Hellhouse, hoping she could work off her debt in Patch's employ, but T-Ray attacked him, burning off his mask, exposing his hideously scarred face and causing him to flee. Furious, Patch placed T-Ray on a month's probation, but T-Ray challenged Patch's authority, with other mercs too frightened to even accept Patch's $10,000 offer to evict him. Days later, Deadpool returned and assaulted some mercs to re-establish his reputation. Soon afterward, Zoe Culloden of Landau, Luckman & Lake visited Hellhouse, attempted to steer Typhoid away from Deadpool, but Typhoid stole Culloden's computer interface and used it to find Deadpool, who she cruelly deceived. The following day, T-Ray won a duel with Deadpool; returning to Hellhouse, T-Ray pronounced Deadpool defeated, implying neither he nor his enemy would soon return. With both troublemakers gone, Patch did better business, although Deadpool's antics were missed by some.

Eventually T-Ray returned and intimidated many mercs into switching loyalties to him, giving him virtual control of Hellhouse, where superhuman underlings now loitered in public view. Patch's resentment culminated when his former ally Alestaire Grunch sought protection from T-Ray, on whose behalf he had manipulated Deadpool into encountering T-Ray's resurrected wife Mercedes Wilson. Patch summoned Deadpool to Hellhouse, where more than a dozen T-Ray loyalists fought him, nearly overpowering him until Patch, C.F., and Fenway entered the fray, taking Deadpool's side to reclaim Patch's authority. Although Grunch was killed before he could elaborate on T-Ray's plot, Deadpool soon after fought and defeated T-Ray. Deadpool returned to Hellhouse weeks later and found Patch, disgusted by recent events, had hired Scrunch to take over as dispatcher. Patch continued associating with Hellhouse patrons, however, as he, C.F., Fenway and other regulars attended Deadpool's supposed funeral months later. Hellhouse presumably remains in business, although with the 50 States Initiative team Spaceknights' arrival in Chicago, Patch's transactions are presumably more low-profile.

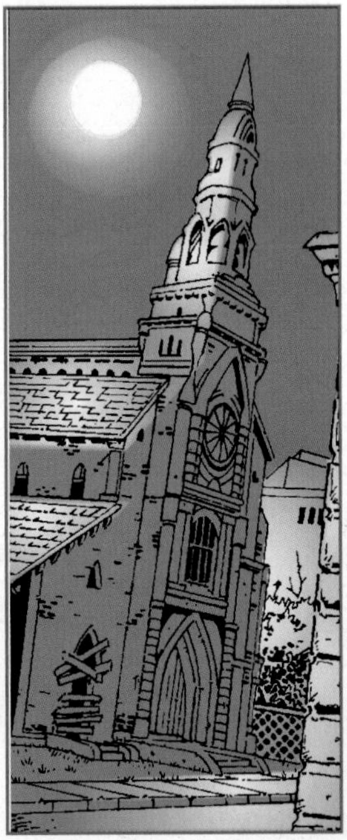

Art by Mike Wieringo

EMPLOYEES: Patch (Bob Stirrat, proprietor/dispatcher); Scrunch (Otis Matthews, dispatcher)
KNOWN PATRONS: C.F. (Steele Fitzpatrick), Cricket (Kevin Gill), Deadpool ("Wade Wilson"), Domino (Neena Thurman), Fenway (Homer Un), Hoover Tron (Jaime Zaid), Librarian (Adele Hawthorne), Roach (Richie-Bob Guinness), Scumson (Starko Schumzianaqo), T-Ray (Wade Wilson), Typhoid Mary (Mary Walker), Weasel (Jack Hammer), many others
LOCATION: Chicago, Illinois
FIRST APPEARANCE: Deadpool #1 (1997)

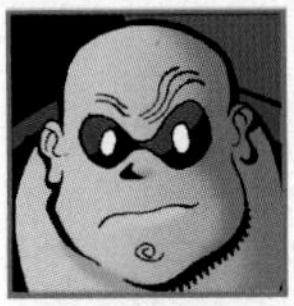

C.F.
Deadpool #1 (1997)

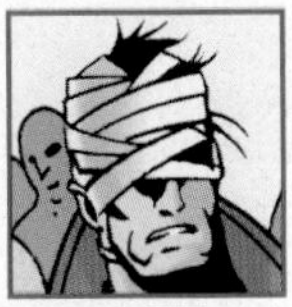

CRICKET
Deadpool #5 (1997)

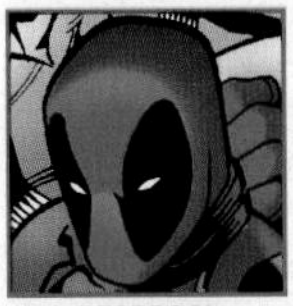

DEADPOOL
New Mutants #98 (1991)

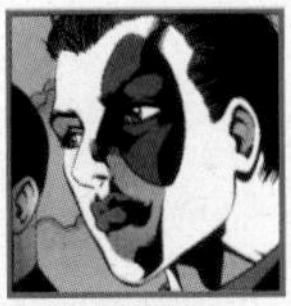

DOMINO
X-Force #8 (1992)

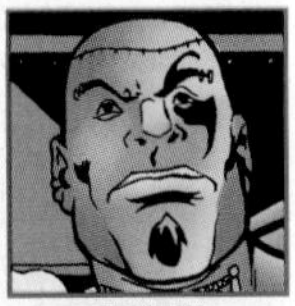

FENWAY
Deadpool #1 (1997)

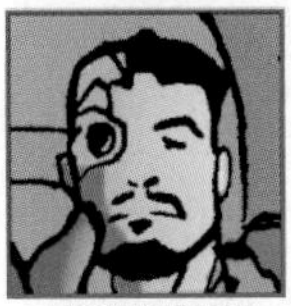

HOOVER TRON
Deadpool #30 (1999)

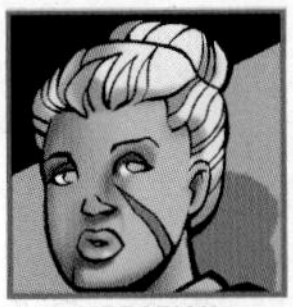

LIBRARIAN
Deadpool #7 (1997)

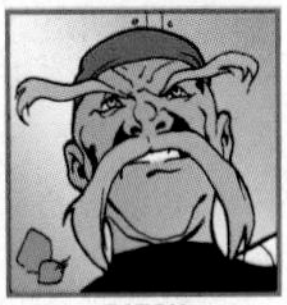

PATCH
Deadpool #1 (1997)

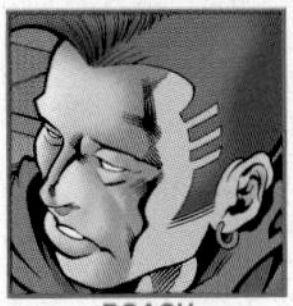

ROACH
Deadpool #5 (1997)

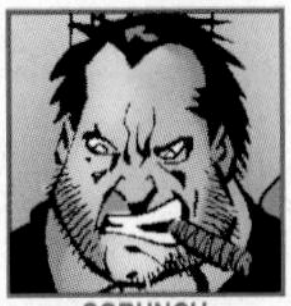

SCRUNCH
Deadpool #38 (2000)

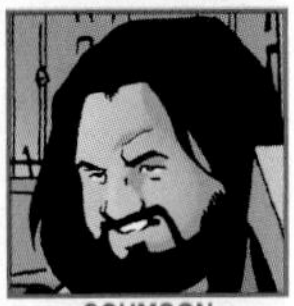

SCUMSON
Deadpool #30 (1999)

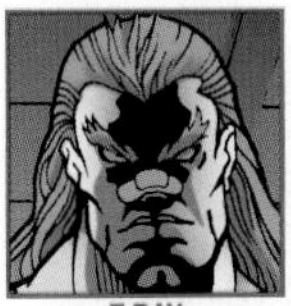

T-RAY
Deadpool #1 (1997)

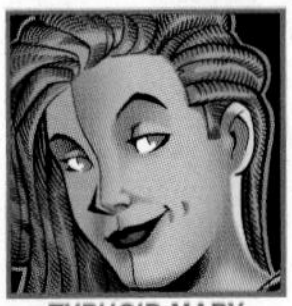

TYPHOID MARY
Daredevil #254 (1988)

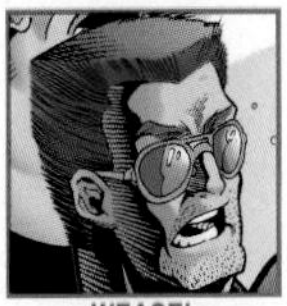

WEASEL
Deadpool: The Circle Chase #1 (1993)

HIT-MONKEY

REAL NAME: Presumably inapplicable
ALIASES: None
IDENTITY: Secret
OCCUPATION: Assassin
CITIZENSHIP: None
PLACE OF BIRTH: Unidentified mountain, Honshu, Japan
KNOWN RELATIVES: Unnamed macaque clan
GROUP AFFILIATION: Formerly a macaque clan
EDUCATION: Raised with macaque traditions, self-taught in martial arts
FIRST APPEARANCE: Hit-Monkey #1 (2010)

ADVANCED PEDAL DEXTERITY

Art by Carlo Barberi

HISTORY: A clan of macaque monkeys lived peacefully near volcanic hot springs in the mountains of northern Japan until the day they discovered an unconscious business-suit wearing assassin with a bag of weapons and money on the run from an unrevealed army. The monkeys took in the assassin and cared for him using the traditional healing herbs of their society, but one young male was threatened by the outsider and seemed to understand the blood on the man's hands was a warning of the capacity for violence in humans. He begrudgingly watched the clan accept the man and studied him practicing martial arts, copying the moves when no one was looking. When the human's health deteriorated, the dissenting macaque demanded they let the outsider die. He was exiled when he used martial arts against his clan to settle the disagreement. Two days later, he saw gun-toting humans approaching the mountain and returned to find the assassin surrounded by soldiers and the clan hidden in rock crevices. The assassin was gunned down, as were the rest of the clan when they moved to retaliate. The exiled survivor took the assassin's guns and shot back. Using his innate skills, the martial arts he copied from the human and the bag full of weapons,

he took revenge. That was the day the legend of Hit-Monkey was born. Hit-Monkey's reputation grew and he became something of a bogeyman among assassins: a hitman who hits hitmen. He was known for clean, efficient kills and a keen sense of style.

Hit-Monkey gained Spider-Man (Peter Parker)'s attention after hitting an illegal gambling ring and killing Mr. Cheng, a grocer once saved by the wall-crawler. Hit-Monkey spent the next night relaxing at a Manhattan night club with several lady friends while Spider-Man and Deadpool ("Wade Wilson") investigated the murder scene and deduced Deadpool would be on Hit-Monkey's hit list. Next, Hit-Monkey executed two corrupt members of the New York City Police Department. The following day he trailed Spider-Man to Deadpool's location. Despite the mercenary's disguise (a lady's dress), Hit-Monkey recognized and attacked his target, wounding Spider-Man in the process. Spider-Man and Deadpool eluded capture temporarily, and when Hit-Monkey found them again he saw in Spider-Man the potential for good, and decided to stop fighting. Deadpool, determined to kill his assailant, attacked the unarmed Hit-Monkey, only to be surprised when the simian assassin fired guns with his feet, seemingly killing Deadpool. Upon healing, Deadpool faked Spider-Man's death to draw a remorseful Hit-Monkey out and "arrest" him; a battle ensued and Hit-Monkey was apparently killed when his damaged gun exploded, but no body was found.

EXILED FROM MACAQUE CLAN

HEIGHT: 2'5"
WEIGHT: 31 lbs.

EYES: Amber
HAIR: Gray

ABILITIES/ACCESSORIES: As a Japanese macaque (Macaca fuscata, also known as the snow monkey), Hit-Monkey is proportionally stronger and faster than a human being, though he is not super powered. Like other macaques, he is adapted for cold weather, is an excellent swimmer, possesses advanced pedal dexterity enabling him to use his feet like hands and has an olfactory sense far greater than that of humans. He is smarter than the average macaque, understanding concepts of murder and revenge, and is able to copy fighting styles and firearms usage after observing them. He is one of the world's best paw-to-hand fighters and is skilled with a variety of weaponry. His signature style is a combination of Eastern martial arts and monkey agility, recognizable to experienced assassins. He is also trained in survival and the use of medicinal herbs native to northern Japan. Hit-Monkey has natural animal magnetism, making human females want to hang out with him. He has a 3" non-prehensile tail.

POWER GRID	1	2	3	4	5	6	7
INTELLIGENCE							
STRENGTH							
SPEED							
DURABILITY							
ENERGY PROJECTION							
FIGHTING SKILLS							

HISTORY: Dr. Edward Lansky, the popular Empire State University vice chancellor, secretly worked on a body suit capable of harnessing the power of light to stop New York City budget cuts for higher education. Donning the suit, Lansky hired Tarantula (Antonio Rodriquez) and his gang to stage his own kidnapping at an upcoming speech to the students about the budget cuts. Fortunately for Lansky, Spider-Man (Peter Parker) and the students failed to stop the kidnapping, allowing him to further his plans from behind the scenes. Spider-Man stayed a thorn in Lansky's side, however, saving Lansky's first target, the city's mayor, from Tarantula. Despite his failure, Lansky kept Tarantula employed, but hired Kraven (Sergei Kravinoff) to assist him in kidnapping school Chancellor Richard Gorman. Tarantula delivered Gorman while Spider-Man caught Kraven. Instead of paying Tarantula, Lansky knocked him out with a gas bomb and later tested his Lightmaster suit against the mercenary. Confident enough to continue with his plan on his own, Lightmaster tried to kidnap city controller Goldin, but Spider-Man got in Lightmaster's way once again. After blinding Spider-Man temporarily, Lightmaster kidnapped Goldin. Some investigative work at the Daily Bugle led Spider-Man to Lightmaster's identity and he visited Lansky's home equipped with special lenses in his mask to avoid getting blinded again. Spider-Man lured Lightmaster, whose hostages were still alive, into the city, and knowing about Lansky's theory that solid light was a conductor, tricked Lightmaster into shooting an energy relay. Lightmaster was electrocuted, but survived. Unfortunately, the electricity interacted with experimental components in his suit and Lansky slowly transformed into an unstable energy being in need to be surrounded by light at all time to survive.

During imprisonment, Lightmaster tried to determine Spider-Man's true identity to expose it to the public. Lightmaster escaped prison and hired the Enforcers (Fancy Dan, Montana, Ox/Ronald Bloch) to hold everyone at the Coffee Bean hostage to lure Spider-Man out of hiding. Watching the Enforcers get beaten by Spider-Man and then seeing Hector Ayala (aka the White Tiger) depart the building afterward, Lightmaster incorrectly deduced Hector Ayala to be Spider-Man. He kidnapped Ayala from the ESU campus, planning to expose his secret, but Parker attached a Spider-Tracer on Ayala's jacket. Spider-Man soon found Lightmaster and Ayala at the abandoned light-display sign factory Light Inc., where Ayala broke free and revealed himself to be the White Tiger in a live broadcast. The real Spider-Man joined the fight against Lightmaster, but the criminal wasn't easily beaten this time around and forced Spider-Man to flee into the factory's giant light bulb logo. Seeing an opportunity to burn the web-slinger alive, Lightmaster accidentally overloaded the city's power system and, when the lights went out, Lightmaster seemingly faded into nothingness.

In truth, Lightmaster was banished to what he later termed the "Light dimension." Subsequently, Dazzler (Alison Blaire)'s concerts and light-based powers inadvertently affected Lightmaster within the "Light dimension" and he gathered enough psychic strength to return to Earth as a light globe and then target Dazzler as his new power source. With Spider-Man's help, Dazzler escaped the first attempt, but Lightmaster soon caught her, weakened from the hunt, off-guard in a dark alley and absorbed enough of her energy to rebuild his own light body. Spider-Man tried to save Dazzler, but was knocked out by Lightmaster, who took Dazzler to his hidden ESU lab to examine and absorb her powers. When Spider-Man arrived, Lansky pulled the lever to transfer his energy form into Dazzler's body. Taking

ORIGINAL SUIT

Art by Keith Pollard

REAL NAME: Edward Lansky
ALIASES: None
IDENTITY: Publicly known
OCCUPATION: Criminal; former physics professor, vice chancellor
CITIZENSHIP: USA, with a criminal record
PLACE OF BIRTH: New York City, New York
KNOWN RELATIVES: None
GROUP AFFILIATION: Hood's army; formerly One World Church, Empire State University
EDUCATION: Ph.D. in physics
FIRST APPEARANCE: (Lansky) Spectacular Spider-Man #1 (1976); (Lightmaster) Spectacular Spider-Man #3 (1977)

control of her, he fought Spider-Man, but the hero ultimately webbed up the possessed Dazzler and reversed the process with Lansky's machines, stranding Lightmaster once again in the "Light dimension."

Feeling a disturbance at ESU, the Quantum Band-wielding hero Quasar (Wendell Vaughn) found Lansky's abandoned lab and became Lightmaster's new entry point to Earth. Lightmaster absorbed the

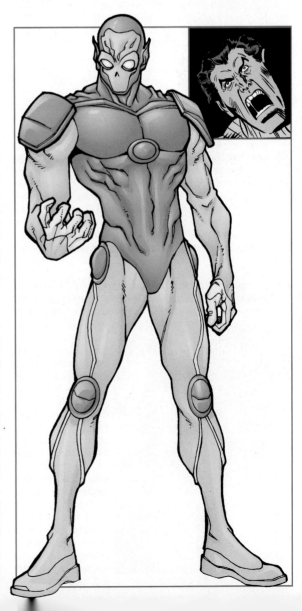

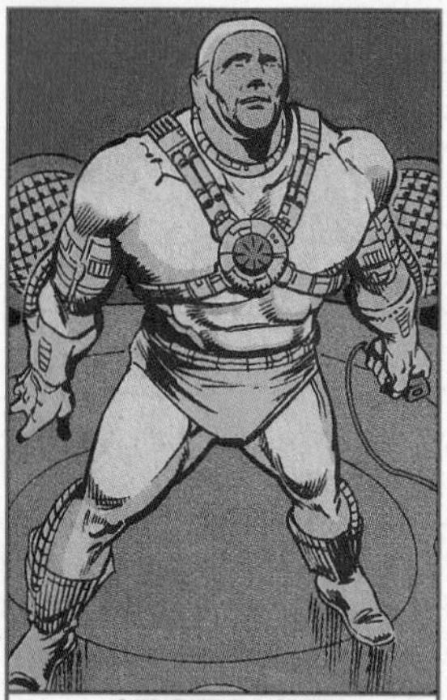

GENETECH SUIT

Art by Vince Evans

Quantum Bands' energies until he was powerful enough to encase Quasar in his light form. Drawn to the scene by his danger-warning "spider-sense," Spider-Man was easily knocked away by Lightmaster, who left him alive as he was more interested in regaining his organic form than killing his nemesis. In control of the Quantum Bands and Quasar, Lightmaster returned to his empty Light Inc. hideout. In need of his machinery to re-enter his old Lightmaster suit, he started stealing the equipment, but Spider-Man interfered once again and when Quasar deactivated the Quantum Bands Lightmaster lost his power source and his energy form drifted apart. Realizing Lightmaster just wanted to become human again, Quasar and Spider-Man worked together to grant Lightmaster his wish. Back in human form, Lightmaster immediately tried to betray them, but Spider-Man easily knocked him out, and Quasar turned him over to the authorities.

Soon thereafter, the criminal lawyer Bono hired Lightmaster and other criminals to recover hidden evidence against Bono's future self, but She-Hulk (Jennifer Walters) and Freelance Peacekeeping Agent Death's Head retrieved the evidence before them. Incarcerated once again, Lansky got his prison sentence shortened by becoming a test subject for Genetech, who accidentally turned him into living light again. Using a containment suit designed by Genetech to escape, Lightmaster went after Cloak (Tyrone Johnson) and Dagger (Tandy Bowen) to turn the latter into his new power source. Determined to save Dagger, Cloak stole a Genetech rifle created to sap Lightmaster's energy, but a design flaw instead made Lightmaster more powerful by turning him into a giant. Lightmaster nonetheless was beaten when Cloak drew him into the Darkforce dimension, absorbing his light until only Lansky's withered husk was left behind. Genetech and their specially equipped Light Brigade regenerated Lightmaster by putting him in a Light Molecular Recombinator.

Still trapped in his light form and seeking direction in his life, Lightmaster joined the One World Church, who planned to eliminate racial strife by turning humanity blue via the Sunic Pharmacopoeia-created Façade virus. Lightmaster was hired by Sunic and became their Singapore facility's protector. Aware that Lightmaster worked for the OWC, Cable redirected him into the OWC's recalibrated Façade virus transmitter. Lightmaster's light enabled the machine to transmit the virus through optic lines all over the world, but due to Cable (Nathan Summers)'s tinkering it turned everyone temporarily pink instead of permanently blue. A weakened Lightmaster returned to Manhattan and became a regular at the local Bar With No Name, donning his original suit. Though Quasimodo recommended him to Norman Osborn for his scientific knowledge on solid light, Lightmaster hooked up with the Hood (Parker Robbins)'s army to gain some underworld recognition. Along with other criminals, the Hood sent Lightmaster after rival crime lord Mr. Negative, but various circumstances, including a Mr. Negative-corrupted Spider-Man, Hammerhead making a deal with Norman Osborn on Negative's behalf and the Spot's (Jonathan Ohnn) betrayal, screwed up their plan to take out Mr. Negative, leaving Lightmaster in the lower, less-respected ranks in Hood's army. Donning his original suit, a motivated Lightmaster was quickly captured by Spider-Man.

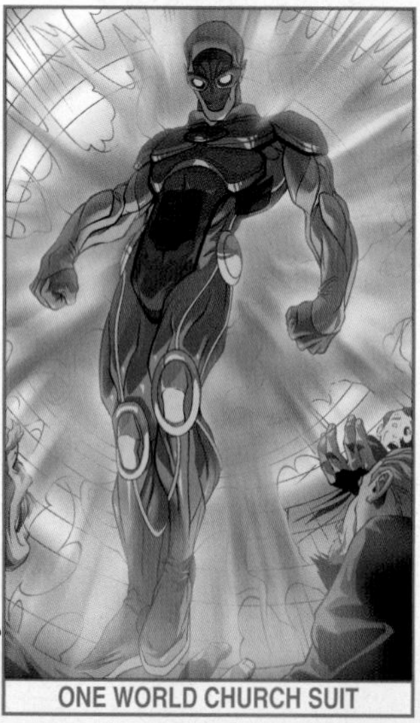

ONE WORLD CHURCH SUIT

Art by Patrick Zircher

HEIGHT: 5'11" **EYES:** Brown
WEIGHT: 175 lbs. **HAIR:** Brown

ABILITIES/ACCESSORIES: Lightmaster wears a high-tech body suit with a padded inner lining to enhance his average physique's appearance. It contains special circuitry using a high-density light-switch computer (which uses photons instead of electrons) linked to his brain which enable him to control photons for a variety of effects on different wavelengths. He can project low-mass light beams from his hands as concussive force powerful enough to deform 1" thick steel and propel a human being standing 10 feet from him about 15 feet. He can emit photons as gamma rays on a nearly lethal radioactive level and as concentrated laser light hot enough to burn human flesh. Lightmaster can overload the power grid of an area as big as Manhattan's Chinatown with a photon-based electromagnetic pulse. Though Lightmaster's current suit allows him to perform powerful feats, it needs a few seconds to change between wavelengths.

At various points in the past, Lightmaster consisted of pure light. In his light form, Lightmaster requires being surrounded by light to survive. In light form, Lightmaster's mental patterns were hard for telepaths to lock down, and he could survive in outer space unsupported. Each time he was turned into light, Lansky possessed varying powers due to the different suits he wore and other factors. He always possessed his basic powers to control photons, but as a being of pure light his control over photons was natural and didn't depend on technology. Consisting of pure light during his tenure with the One World Church, he wore a suit that kept him stable and enabled him to mentally morph his appendages into solid light weapons and shift his body out of sync to become pure light, allowing him to avoid attacks and imprisonment. He could fly nearly as fast as light. Mutated by a Genetech weapon, Lightmaster could grow to giant proportions by absorbing light. At one point, Lightmaster could take possession of beings or items with light-based powers. During one of those instances Lightmaster gained control over the Quantum Bands, which temporarily enhanced his powers exponentially.

Lightmaster's original suit allowed him to bind photons to create solid objects, according to pre-programmed responses within his controlling computer, which determined form, size and relative velocity of these objects. He could also project light blasts from his hand as concussive force as powerful as in later years. He could fly at up to 140 mph by surrounding himself in an aerodynamic nimbus of light to which he attached a complex solid light spiral which rotated at several hundred revolutions per second like a propeller. The nimbus of light protected him from friction and wind. In flight, he could carry any load he could lift in his arms.

POWER GRID	1 2 3 4 5 6 7
INTELLIGENCE	5
STRENGTH	2
SPEED	6
DURABILITY	7
ENERGY PROJECTION	6
FIGHTING SKILLS	2

HISTORY: The man who would become Madcap was a devout Christian on the way home from a church field trip when the group's bus was struck by an AIM (Advanced Idea Mechanics) tanker truck carrying the experimental Compound X07. While he was thrown clear of the wreckage, his parents and sister were killed. His skin absorbed the spilled Compound X07, mutating his body. When he awoke in the hospital to the news of his family's demise, he attempted suicide in his despair. Throwing himself in front of a moving vehicle, he discovered not only did he not feel pain, but all his wounds instantaneously healed. The last remaining vestiges of his sanity gone, he decided life was a joke and he was going to prove it to the rest of the world. He soon realized that he could cause delusional hallucinations in those around him through eye contact. Stealing a costume and a prop bubble-blowing gun (his "Fun Gun," which he used to make people look at him so that he could establish eye contact and use his new mind-altering psionic abilities) from Ace Costume Shop, he became Madcap.

Spreading temporary insanity to all he saw throughout Manhattan, New York, Madcap even affected Nomad (Jack Monroe) when the hero saw the chaos Madcap was causing and tried to apprehend him. Nomad broke Madcap's jaw with a single punch, but Madcap simply snapped the bones back into place, sprayed Nomad with his Fun Gun, rendered him temporarily insane and escaped. After recovering, Nomad — wanting to prove himself a hero in his own right — neglected to ask his mentor Captain America (Steve Rogers) for aid in tracking down Madcap, and instead investigated him alone, tracking him down to a small apartment around Coney Island. Nomad convinced Madcap he wanted to learn his philosophy and join his crusade, and he accompanied Madcap for a time, going along with his craziness, but when Madcap caused a woman with a baby in a stroller to go insane, Nomad ended the charade and again attempted to capture the madman. During their fight atop a roller coaster, Nomad, having learned Madcap's gaze actually transmitted the madness, covered his head and then bound him.

Though he was remanded to Bellevue Hospital, Madcap quickly escaped and, after disrupting the Rose (Richard Fisk)'s thugs' gun-smuggling operations, was recruited by cable access television host Dollar Bill (Aaron Tagma English), who witnessed the incident and hoped to turn Madcap into a celebrity. Madcap's on-air antics led the vengeful Rose back to him, and Madcap was kidnapped by more of the Rose's men, who intended to torture and kill him. Daredevil (Matt Murdock) attempted to rescue Madcap, but a fire broke out after the Rose's agents threw Molotov cocktails into the room. Daredevil had to choose between saving a bound Madcap, who was making no attempt to save himself, and Max the Ax, one of the Rose's men who had been rendered unconscious during the fight. Choosing to save Max, Daredevil was unable to return in time to save Madcap, who seemingly burned to death. However, Madcap survived after regenerating in the morgue and returned to a shocked and flustered Dollar Bill's home, suggesting new ideas for their show, changing the name to the Madcap Mystery Hour. Finding Madcap hilarious, Power Pack's young Starstreak (Katie Power) and Tattletale (Franklin Richards) located and began going on adventures with him through Manhattan's streets until realizing how dangerous Madcap truly was. They tried to make him realize his responsibilities as an adult, but to no avail, as Madcap simply grew bored and wandered away to cause more havoc.

Madcap's antics later enraged She-Hulk (Jennifer Walters) during one of his publicity stunts at a zoo, who shattered his bones, though when he fully healed seconds later, she departed, seeing further conflict pointless. Dr. Karl Malus had his strength-augmented Power Tools agents kidnap Madcap to learn more about his powers, and they brutally beat Dollar Bill in the process. Hospitalized, Bill sought Daredevil's help, but instead Hawkeye (Clint Barton) responded to Bill's plea. Seeking leads, Hawkeye stumbled upon Malus' lair where Madcap was being held. Power Tools member Handsaw cut off one of Madcap's arms before

REAL NAME: Unrevealed
ALIASES: Impersonated Nomad (Jack Monroe)
IDENTITY: Known to authorities
OCCUPATION: Prankster, absurdist philosopher; former television host
CITIZENSHIP: USA
PLACE OF BIRTH: Unrevealed
KNOWN RELATIVES: Unidentified parents (deceased), Katy (sister, deceased)
GROUP AFFILIATION: Ghost Rider Assassination League; former agent of Hydra, Wild Pack
EDUCATION: Unrevealed
FIRST APPEARANCE: Captain America #307 (1985)

being driven insane by him, causing her to attack her own teammates. Hawkeye and Madcap evacuated the lair before Malus could destroy it, but Madcap rushed back in to retrieve his missing limb and was caught in the explosion. To Hawkeye's surprise, Madcap emerged alive and, after reattaching his severed arm, fruitlessly sought Malus anew; having felt tactile sensations via the energies released when Malus' machinery exploded, Madcap hoped Malus could help him regain his sense of feeling again.

When the Impossible Woman ("Impet") brought her relatively serious child Impia to Earth in hopes of having Reed Richards "cure" her so she would be "fun," the two aliens witnessed Madcap dive from a tall building, smack into the concrete below, and then pick himself back up and introduce himself to them. Impet asked Madcap to show Impia how to have fun, and Madcap agreed in exchange for 20 hen's lips. The unwitting Impet left to go find some non-existant hen's lips, leaving Impia with Madcap. After Madcap sent the cosmic hero Quasar (Wendell Vaughn) on a crazed rampage, Impia instead calmed Quasar down, and Madcap, feeling Impia to be hopeless, departed down a sewer manhole. Madcap was later present in one of the Bar With No Name establishment when an employee dressed as the Scourge of the Underworld shot at everyone to get the bar cleared for the night. Noting they could have just stopped serving drinks, Madcap happily dug some bullets out of his chest and departed.

Realizing that by maintaining his Madcap Comedy Hour show, he wasn't fully showing humanity the joke of life. He went to Grand Central Station, where he performed atop an information booth. After a security guard Madcap zapped fired wildly into a crowd, Ghost Rider (Dan Ketch) tried to stop him and even broke Madcap's neck during their fight by accidentally hanging him with his chain. Recovering, Madcap was subjected to Ghost Rider's penance stare, which caused Madcap true pain for the first time since his accident. Madcap vowed further mayhem to gain further such treatment, but apparently lost interest. Instead, a disillusioned Madcap tried to commit suicide by blowing himself up in Central Park, though his efforts were stopped by rookie heroes Jack Flag (Jack Harrison) and Free Spirit (Cathy Webster). Jack Flag managed to set the explosives off without injuring civilians, and Flag's quick recovery from the injury infuriated Madcap, who accused the hero of stealing his gimmick. Imprisoned in the Vault, Madcap unsuccessfully tried to escape during a breakout caused by the newly-formed Thunderbolts as a diversion to recover their ally Moonstone (Karla Sofen) from the prison; Madcap was personally subdued by Citizen V (Helmut Zemo). Later escaping under unrevealed circumstance, Madcap decided to impersonate Nomad for no particular reason, and was unwittingly hired by Silver Sable's Wild Pack for a mission to protect biotechnician Professor Wolfgang Hessler. This brought the Wild Pack into conflict with the Heroes for Hire, including mercenary Deadpool ("Wade Wilson"). Even after giving up his ruse, Madcap continued the mission, spending much of it fighting Deadpool, who used his holographic image inducer to impersonate Madcap during the struggle. Deadpool snapped Madcap's neck at one point, but their respective healing factors left them at a standstill. During the fight, Hessler was abducted by Luke Cage, who had been brainwashed by the Master of the World, and Madcap left the team afterward.

Madcap's unique physiology spared him when Hydra chose him as part of their plot to murder and resurrect superhumans to employ in a brainwashed army, though Madcap played along and aided in their assault on a SHIELD Helicarrier until being "killed" again by Wolverine (James Howlett/Logan) during the assault. Never truly dead either time, Madcap simply left the carnage eventually. For reasons unrevealed, he sought legal council from Goodman, Lieber, Kurtzberg & Holliway shortly after. He was later among those recruited by the Lilin Blackout to help keep the Ghost Riders (Ketch and Johnny Blaze) from the angel Zadkiel and to find Kid Blackheart. Paired with Scarecrow (Ebenezer Laughton), Madcap was sent to the Jasper County fairgrounds, where they encountered the Son of Satan (Daimon Hellstrom) and Jaine Cutter, who were seeking to protect Kid Blackheart. When Madcap used his insanity power on both Hellstrom and Cutter, Cutter shot Hellstrom with her mystical Breathing Gun, while Hellstrom blasted Cutter with Hellfire. Regaining coherence via the pain of these attacks, Hellstrom turned his hellfire trident on Madcap, who was overwhelmed with the pleasure of feeling pain, while Cutter took out Scarecrow. As Hellstrom and Cutter departed, Madcap begged for more.

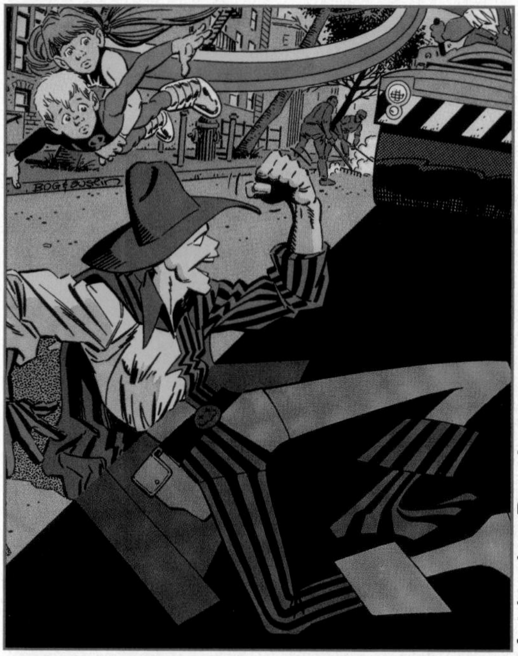

Art by Jon Bogdanove

HEIGHT: 5'9" **EYES:** Blue
WEIGHT: 145 lbs. **HAIR:** Brown (sometimes dyed blond)

ABILITIES/ACCESSORIES: Madcap has nearly-limitless regenerative abilities enabling him to rapidly heal to his flesh, bones, and internal organs. He can heal within seconds from penetrating wounds, fractures, third-degree burns and being flattened by a trash compactor; he is even able to move and function while in a flattened state. He can expel bullets or other objects that penetrate his flesh but don't pass the whole way through his body. Body parts which become separated from his body can be simply reattached by contacting the two cut portions. He is unable to feel physical pain and has limited tactile sensation, though he can feel pain via injury to his soul.

Additionally, Madcap can psionically manipulate other beings' minds, temporarily lowering their inhibitions and causing them to behave in a variety of outlandish, euphoric and sometimes violent fashions. He cannot control exactly what type of behavior his targets exhibit; this may be dictated by the subjects own psyches. Madcap's victims have generally appeared to act crazily for 15 to 30 minutes after a single treatment. He generally must establish eye contact with another being to affect them. He has gymnast-level athletic prowess and is extraordinarily flexible.

POWER GRID	Rank (1–7)
INTELLIGENCE	2
STRENGTH	2
SPEED	2
DURABILITY	6
ENERGY PROJECTION	3
FIGHTING SKILLS	2

MESSIAH

HISTORY: For untold millennia, S'met'kth traveled the universe, using its vast psychic power to bring peace and utter bliss to thousands of planets by depriving their inhabitants of free will. More than 3,000 years ago, an unidentified race's Council of Elders prophesied S'met'kth's eventual arrival on their world; while many beings saw S'met'kth as a benevolent Messiah, the Council considered it the Ultimate Destroyer for eliminating all-important free will. The Council sent a Champion (gifted with technology to render him immune to S'met'kth's bliss power) to Earth to stop S'met'kth's arrival in the 21st century AD, before it could reach the Council's homeworld. In recent decades, the shadowy Landau, Luckman, Lake & LeQuare organization's precog, Montgomery Burns, foresaw S'met'kth's arrival heralding a golden age of peace. Burns also foresaw the alien Champion (whom LLL&L dubbed Tiamat), as well as a human agent, the Mithras, who would protect S'met'kth from Tiamat. The Council, too, predicted the Mithras, and their Champion trained to defeat him. LLL&L's Gerry LeQuare faked his death to secretly guide the Mithras, prophesied to be Deadpool ("Wade Wilson"), to discover and end S'met'kth's true threat.

S'met'kth, meanwhile, continued bringing bliss to many more races, including the Dr'azim and portions of the Skrull and Shi'ar Empires. As S'met'kth approached, Mithras Directive overboss Mason Dixon sought to replace Deadpool with Captain America (Steve Rogers) as Mithras due to visions predicting Deadpool's defeat. Dixon further used planetwide jammer units to prevent detection of S'met'kth's approach. As foreseen, Tiamat defeated Deadpool, who narrowly escaped death, and traveled to Egypt to confront the arriving S'met'kth, who was detected by NASA after bliss-incapacitating a space shuttle crew. As Captain America confronted Tiamat, US Air Force fighter planes attacked S'met'kth who turned their missiles back on them, destroying them. Distracted by this attack, Captain America fell before Tiamat. S'met'kth judged Earth; noting pollution, greed, confusion, anger, and pain, it began to replace these worldwide with pleasure, peace and bliss. When Deadpool attacked anew, Tiamat obsessed about destroying the Mithras, neglecting S'met'kth. Noting Tiamat's obsession was risking everything, the Council stripped him of his weapons and granted them to Deadpool, telepathically informing him of S'met'kth's true intent.

S'met'kth took control of Captain America and physically battled Deadpool while arguing the value of peace, and the pain that free will, decisions, guilt and doubt brought. Eventually realizing that peace without free will was no life at all, Deadpool dropped Captain America with a gonad-crushing kick, then used the Council's weapons against S'met'kth. The would-be Messiah fell from the skies, apparently deceased, though its body was never recovered, at least in any official records. Across the universe, those affected by S'met'kth regained their free will; some were joyous, some furious about having lost the bliss, while violence, hatred, hope, and achievement continued anew.

REAL NAME: S'met'kth
ALIASES: Destroyer, Ultimate Destroyer
IDENTITY: Existence unknown to Earth's general populace; publicly known by many races
OCCUPATION: Eliminator of free will, bringer of bliss and harmony
CITIZENSHIP: Unrevealed
PLACE OF BIRTH: Unrevealed
KNOWN RELATIVES: None
GROUP AFFILIATION: None
EDUCATION: Unrevealed
FIRST APPEARANCE: (Mentioned) Deadpool #21 (1998); (partial) Deadpool #23 (1998); (full) Deadpool #24 (January, 1999)

HEIGHT: Unrevealed **EYES:** Multiple, variously colored
WEIGHT: Unrevealed **HAIR:** None

ABILITIES/ACCESSORIES: According to Uatu, S'met'kth had power to rival Galactus. It could shift entire planets' populations into a state of transcendental bliss, uniting their minds in perfect harmony, but at the same time robbing them of independent thought and free will. S'met'kth needed to be within the planet's atmosphere to cause the change, but once a planet is affected, its inhabitants remained in that state until S'met'kth was incapacitated (or possibly only if he was slain). S'met'kth could travel through space unaided and achieve intergalactic distances in days. It is unharmed by the heat and friction of atmospheric re-entry and can survive indefinitely without heat, air, or conventional forms of sustenance; it may survive by feeding off the psychic energies drained from others when it removes their free will. Its presence within an atmosphere causes significant environmental turmoil, such as the formation of tornados and flame-red clouds. It can almost effortlessly turn most attacks back on their wielders. It is believed that it can use its immense energies to bolster its physical abilities as needed. An unspecified alien life form (the serpentine skeletal headdress-like creature formerly worn by Tiamat) can bond with and render its wearer immune to S'met'kth's power. Additionally, something specific to Tiamat's weapons or energies transmitted by his race's Council of Elders proved lethal to S'met'kth.

POWER GRID	1 2 3 4 5 6 7
INTELLIGENCE	3
STRENGTH	7
SPEED	7
DURABILITY	6
ENERGY PROJECTION	7
FIGHTING SKILLS	1

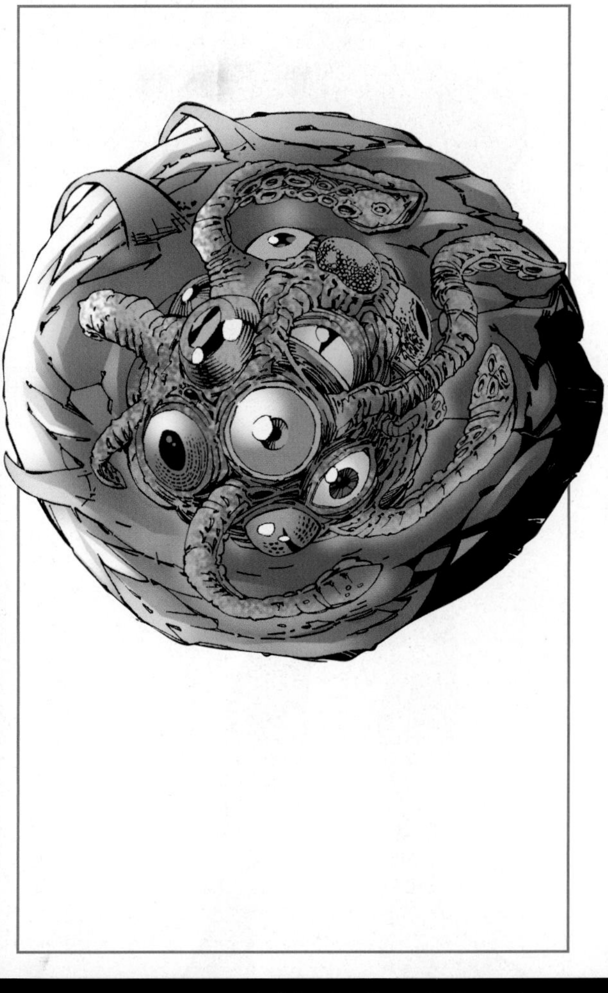

Art by Walter McDaniel

MR. IMMORTAL

REAL NAME: Craig Hollis
ALIASES: "Mr. I", "Immy"
IDENTITY: Known to authorities
OCCUPATION: Licensed super hero; former fast-food employee
CITIZENSHIP: USA
PLACE OF BIRTH: Sheboygan, Wisconsin
KNOWN RELATIVES: Audrey & Edward Hollis (parents, deceased), Mr. O'Doughan (foster father), Terri O'Doughan (foster sister, deceased)
GROUP AFFILIATION: Great Lakes Initiative, Initiative; formerly Great Lakes Champions, Great Lakes X-Men, Great Lakes Avengers, Lightning Rods
EDUCATION: Unrevealed
FIRST APPEARANCE: West Coast Avengers #46 (1989)

HISTORY: Craig Hollis was born the first and apparently only member of the species Homo supreme, allegedly the ultimate evolution of mankind, a man evolved beyond death. Cosmic entity Oblivion sent his minion Deathurge, the embodiment of man's self-destructive instincts, to monitor him, as Craig is apparently destined to be the last living thing in the universe. Hollis' mother Audrey died giving birth to him. As he took her spirit away, Deathurge promised to watch over her son. Deathurge (whom Craig dubbed D'urge) constantly encouraged the boy to risk

his life through dangerous play. Only Craig could see "D'urge," so his father assumed that he was an imaginary friend. On Craig's eighth birthday, Deathurge convinced Craig to play with matches, starting a fire that killed Craig's father. Orphaned, Craig was sent to live with a foster family. His foster father Mr. O'Doughan was violently abusive, but Craig soon befriended his daughter, Terri. He eventually moved away from the O'Doughan house with Terri, who had become his lover. Happy in his real life for the first time, Craig stopped playing with Deathurge and assumed he had simply outgrown his "imaginary" friend, though Deathurge continued observing him. Working in a fast food joint, Craig eked out a living in Milwaukee until Terri, haunted by her memories of abuse, killed herself. Craig could only watch as Deathurge took her to the afterlife, stunned to realize his old friend was real and wishing he could go with them. Wanting to join Terri, Craig leapt to his death off a high-rise, but revived moments later. Undaunted, he killed himself several more times before realizing that he was unable to die. Designing a costume and dubbing himself "Mr. Immortal," he vowed to fight crime. In his first outing, he tried to stop a convenience store robbery, but was shot in the head. While he revived, the robbers escaped.

Deciding his powers would work better in a team, Craig placed a classified ad looking for fellow costumed heroes in the Wisconsin area. The ad netted him the two-dimensional Flatman (Val Ventura), the massive Big Bertha (Ashley Crawford), the teleporting Doorman (DeMarr Davis) and the pteranodon-like humanoid Dinah Soar; the ad also attracted Leather Boy (Gene Lorrene), a non-powered leather fetishist who had misinterpreted Craig's ad. Together (minus Lorrene), they formed the Great Lakes Avengers, although they lacked official Avengers sanction. Mr. Immortal served as team leader despite his emotional instability, with Flatman as his deputy leader. On his first Christmas without Terri, Craig held vigil at her grave, and was visited by Dinah Soar. Although he initially objected to her presence, he relented and gave Dinah her Christmas gift, a whistle she could use to communicate with the rest of the GLA. When she thanked him, Craig was astonished to find that he could suddenly hear and understand Dinah's inaudible subsonic speech; she explained that her extremely long-lived people could only bond with a chosen mortal once within their lifetime, and she had chosen to bond with Craig. The two became close friends, with Craig serving as Dinah's guide to human culture while her unique voice soothed his emotional turmoil.

The GLA's activities soon caught the attention of ex-Avengers Hawkeye (Clint Barton) and Mockingbird (Bobbi Barton); after a tense first meeting, the two agreed to train the inexperienced GLA. While Mr. Immortal initially resented Hawkeye taking over the GLA's leadership, he went along with it for the good of the team. Training intensively under the Bartons, the GLA received their first true test when they responded to an Avengers distress call from Texas, where Avengers She-Hulk (Jen Walters) and Scarlet Witch (Wanda Maximoff) had fallen under the control of ancient collective entity That Which Endures. The collective intended to spread its influence to mutants using the Assimilator device; while his teammates battled That Which Endures' minions, Craig shut down the Assimilator, absorbing a lethal dose of radiation in the process. Hawkeye later quit to rejoin the original Avengers, leaving Mockingbird in charge of the team. She led them into battle against the colossal alien Terminus in St. Louis. Mr. I allowed the alien to crush him, giving his teammates time to distract it until the actual Avengers could arrive and defeat the monster. The GLA were next lured into action by Stevie Wojciehowicz, a Cyttorak gem-empowered child who fooled them into attacking Captain America (Steve Rogers) and the Human Torch (Jim Hammond); while Rogers foiled Stevie's attempt to steal his shield, Mr. I was incinerated by the Torch twice. Shortly afterward, Mockingbird quit, leaving Mr. I in command.

The GLA later renamed themselves the Lightning Rods to mimic the Thunderbolts, then-popular heroes. Spotting homicidal mercenary Deadpool ("Wade Wilson") during a trip to the aquarium, they tried to

Art by Gus Vazquez with Paul Pelletier (inset)

capture him, but instead accidentally sent him and his companion Blind Al into an alternate past (Earth-9712). When the Rods rescued both of them, Deadpool thanked them by blowing up Mr. I with a bandolier of grenades. After the Thunderbolts were exposed as criminals, elite intelligence agency SHIELD recruited Mr. I and his team to hunt them down. Upon locating the fugitives, the Rods held their own at first but were soon defeated, allowing the Thunderbolts to steal the Lightning Rods' costumes and evade SHIELD in disguise. Mr. I and his team revived in time to face the megalomaniacal Graviton alongside the Thunderbolts; after the team was battered (and Mr. I was crushed) by the gravity-manipulating villain, the Rods watched as the Thunderbolts talked Graviton into relenting and escaped. After saving the people of Medina, Ohio, from violent weather caused by the Crimson Cowl (Justine Hammer)'s Masters of Evil, Mr. I and his team (once more calling themselves the GLA) attended Deadpool's funeral (although reports of his death proved to be exaggerated) and were pulled through time and space to assist the Avengers and a league of champions from a distant cosmos against a mad cosmic scholar.

By this time, Craig had Dinah had become lovers, but while their relationship flourished, the GLA stagnated. Superhuman threats were rare in Wisconsin, though the team saved Muskego from Christmas-themed maniac Dr. Tannenbaum and his giant robot snowman. The group spent most of their time sitting around their base playing cards. Craig grew increasingly frustrated with the GLA's dubious reputation; the final straw came when they were upstaged by the Avengers in a battle with the militant animal-rights activist Ani-Men in Milwaukee. Craig intended to dissolve the GLA, but then learned that the Avengers had disbanded in the wake of a battle with the deranged Scarlet Witch. With his group the only remaining team of "Avengers," Craig gleefully responded to a distress call at the University of Wisconsin, where the Inhuman/Deviant hybrid Maelstrom was stealing a chronal accelerator, with which he intended to build a machine to destroy the universe. Struck down by Maelstrom, Craig was comforted by Dinah as he revived, until Maelstrom pierced her heart with a bolt of proto-natural force. Craig could only rage impotently as Deathurge claimed her soul.

Consumed with grief, Craig started wearing Dinah's costume and spent the next few weeks in a drunken haze, leaving deputy leader Flatman in charge. Flatman eventually recruited replacement members Squirrel Girl (Doreen Green) and her squirrel partner Monkey Joe, enraging the embittered Leather Boy, who invaded GLA HQ, broke Craig's neck and killed Monkey Joe. When Deathurge (in the form of a squirrel) came for Monkey Joe's soul, Craig captured and interrogated him, learning of his own origins and of Maelstrom's plans. Newly inspired, Craig led the GLA to Maelstrom's Lake Michigan base. While his teammates fought their way through Maelstrom's minions Batroc the Leaper, Maximillian Zaran and Machete (Mariano Lopez), Doorman teleported Craig through the dome at the cost of his own life (although Oblivion soon resurrected him as Deathurge's replacement). Once inside, Craig convinced Maelstrom that once the universe ended, only loneliness would remain, and that they should commit suicide. After Craig shot himself with Machete's gun, Maelstrom blew his own head off; Craig revived moments later and shut off Maelstrom's device, saving the universe.

When the Maria Stark Foundation which managed the Avengers' legal affairs ordered the GLA to stop using the Avengers name, Craig's team complied. Upon discovering that his teammates were all mutants, too, Craig redubbed the team the Great Lakes X-Men, complete with new leather costumes, which they abandoned upon learning that Leather Boy had designed them. Already dreading a Christmas without Dinah, Mr. I led his team into battle with Tannenbaum again, defeating his monstrous Christmas trees by weighing them down with decoration. Later that day, he accidentally tripped all the deathtraps Deathurge (still trapped in squirrel form) had set for Squirrel Girl's new partner, Tippy-Toe, but revived in time to celebrate Christmas with his friends. The GLX

crashed the Thing (Ben Grimm)'s super hero poker tournament, where the X-Men's Marvel Girl (Rachel Grey) telepathically influenced them to abandon their team name; they switched to "Great Lakes Defenders" until original Defenders founder Dr. Stephen Strange mystically compelled them to drop that name, then declared themselves the Great Lakes Champions after winning the tournament.

When the US government adopted the Superhuman Registration Act, the GLC registered immediately, becoming licensed government super heroes; unaware of this, Deadpool invaded GLC HQ in the hopes of launching a career as a bounty hunter of unregistered heroes, briefly killing Mr. I before Squirrel Girl trounced him. Now Wisconsin's official super-hero team as part of the federal Initiative, the team soon rechristened themselves the Great Lakes Initiative (GLI). When subversive organization AIM abducted the Olympian god Dionysus and used him to power their superhuman-

GLX COSTUME

targeted inebriation ray, they neglected to target the GLA, who teamed up with Deadpool (whose healing factor rendered him immune to the ray) to destroy the device. After this victory, the team awarded Deadpool reserve GLI membership, and the mercenary started living in their base. Mr. I's attempts to get Deadpool to leave typically ended with Craig dying violently, and Bertha's and Flatman's efforts fared no better. Luckily, Craig's future counterpart on Earth-2992 told the visiting Squirrel Girl that she was needed in her home reality, and she returned to kick Deadpool out. During the Skrull invasion, Craig was shocked to discover his new teammate Grasshopper was a Skrull imposter, and battled him alongside Skrull-hunters Gravity (Greg Willis) and Catwalk (Kimberly Dee). When corrupt megalomaniac Norman Osborn was given control of the Initiative, he reassigned Wisconsinite hero Gravity to lead the GLI; despite losing his leadership position, Craig enthusiastically welcomed Willis to the team.

HEIGHT: 6'2"	EYES: Blond
WEIGHT: 156 lbs.	HAIR: Blue

ABILITIES/ACCESSORIES: Once he reaches the point of death, Hollis regenerates from any and all injuries, often returning to life almost immediately. When non-fatally injured, he heals at a normal human rate; those injuries will rapidly heal the next time he dies, however. He has recovered from being shot, stabbed, drowned, crushed, exploded, poisoned, decapitated, irradiated and incinerated. Upon reviving, he is often extremely enraged due to the pain of death; before her death, Dinah Soar's voice could bring him out of this state. He has also apparently stopped aging. Hollis is highly athletic and acrobatic, and is a skilled card player.

POWER GRID	1	2	3	4	5	6	7
INTELLIGENCE							
STRENGTH							
SPEED							
DURABILITY							
ENERGY PROJECTION							
FIGHTING SKILLS							

OUTLAW

REAL NAME: Inez Temple
ALIASES: "Crazy Inez"
IDENTITY: Known in the criminal underworld
OCCUPATION: Mercenary
CITIZENSHIP: USA
PLACE OF BIRTH: Harlingen, Texas
KNOWN RELATIVES: Douglas R. Temple (father, deceased), Lance Temple (Outlaw Kid), "Hoot" Temple, Belle Temple, Luke Temple Jr. (ancestors, deceased)
GROUP AFFILIATION: Agency X; formerly the 198
EDUCATION: High school graduate
FIRST APPEARANCE: Deadpool #65 (2002)

HISTORY: Descended from the heroic 19th century hero the Outlaw Kid, Inez Temple was a feisty child, fighting with other children, who nicknamed her "Crazy Inez." Inez eventually discovered she was a mutant with superhuman strength and went to work as a mercenary; evidently concerned about her appearance, she received breast implants and donned a blonde wig to become Outlaw. While at the Merc Works gym, Outlaw met the notorious mercenary Deadpool ("Wade Wilson") and soon encountered him again when she declined a job bodyguarding the Dazzler (Alison Blaire), which Deadpool took in her stead. After Deadpool disappeared in an explosion while battling the Black Swan, an amnesiac man called Agent X (Alex Hayden) appeared and befriended Deadpool's former secretary Sandi Brandenberg. Agent X asked Sandi to help him become a mercenary, and she hired Taskmaster and Outlaw to help train him. Testing Agent X's marksmanship, Outlaw discovered he was ambidextrous, convincing her he was not Deadpool as Sandi felt.

Agent X and Outlaw were among the mercenaries who accepted an offer from the Culver Sport and Gun Club to obtain the Punisher (Frank Castle)'s custom .45 handguns. After defeating their competitors, Agent X and Outlaw fought each other, but then decided to work together. After amusing themselves at a bar and spending an evening together at Outlaw's apartment, the duo found the Punisher's weapons, only to end up face-to-face with the Punisher. After begging for their lives, they convinced him to spare them and instead gave up their employers; the Punisher settled for humiliating them by removing their clothes and abandoning them in a phone booth. When Hayden was targeted for death by the Four Winds, who hired a multitude of killers, Outlaw and Taskmaster fought alongside him, during which Outlaw bested Crossfire in a showdown. The altercation with the Four Winds finally ended when Agent X threatened the Four Winds' families. Hayden offered Outlaw a place in his Agency X organization but she declined in order to return home and see to her recently deceased father's funeral arrangements.

When Outlaw returned, she was chagrined to find that Hayden and Sandi had slept together. She caught up with Agent X, Sandi and Taskmaster just as they confronted the revived Black Swan and Deadpool and helped the others defeat Black Swan, ultimately having him stuffed to prevent his return. Outlaw joined Agency X on their vacation, bringing Black Swan's remains with them. When most of Earth's mutants lost their powers due to the Scarlet Witch (Wanda Maximoff)'s altering reality on "M-Day," Outlaw was one of the relatively few who retained their abilities. Outlaw and fellow mutant Peepers sought out the Xavier Institute for protection from the X-Men as remaining mutants found themselves threatened by forces such as the Leper Queen and her Sapien League. Outlaw joined the refugee camp of mutants called "the 198," who were watched over by the O*N*E government defense agency. During the tumult of the Superhuman Registration Act, the 198 fled the Xavier Institute and hid out in a Nevada desert military base, but O*N*E director General Lazer tried to have them killed, a fate they escaped thanks to Cyclops (Scott Summers), Lucas Bishop and Iron Man (Tony Stark). Outlaw returned to Agency X and, with Sandi, hired Deadpool to save Agent X from Hydra's clutches. Deadpool returned with Hayden, who had become morbidly obese due to Hydra giving him an eating disorder. Outlaw was disgusted with his indulgent appetite and finally wounded his pride by comparing his laziness to the heroism of Deadpool against an army of symbiote-infected dinosaurs. Hayden wound up rescuing Sandi and Outlaw in battle with the dinosaurs and afterward the two women placed him on a diet. When Deadpool was framed for destroying an apartment building by Tombstone, Outlaw helped shelter him from the Punisher's attempts to assassinate him. Although Outlaw's apartment was wrecked by the resulting battles, Deadpool refurnished it for her and she slept with him as a show of gratitude.

HEIGHT: 5'11"   **EYES:** Light brown
WEIGHT: 142 lbs.   **HAIR:** Brown (with blond wig)

ABILITIES/ACCESSORIES: Outlaw possesses superhuman strength (lifting 2 tons) and durability. Outlaw is a champion lariat thrower, excellent hand-to-hand combatant and remarkable sharpshooter. She usually wields two Colt .44 revolvers and occasionally uses a lariat or sniper rifle as the situation merits.

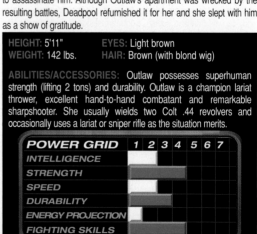

POWER GRID	1	2	3	4	5	6	7
INTELLIGENCE							
STRENGTH							
SPEED							
DURABILITY							
ENERGY PROJECTION							
FIGHTING SKILLS							

HISTORY: After many of Earth's mightiest heroes seemingly sacrificed themselves to end the threat of the psionic Onslaught, mutant prodigy Franklin Richards created a pocket dimension accessed via a blue ball with its own Earth to keep the heroes safe. Some formed a new group of Avengers, along with natives of this world like Swordsman, to battle enemies like the Super-Adaptoid and the Hulk, who broke Swordsman's back. Over the next year, that world's Norse god Loki learned he was in an artificial pocket dimension and gained access to blue balls of energy that were tied to the false world. Using that power, he captured many villains and heroes, including the recovering Swordsman and the time-traveling Mantis, who shared an unrevealed connection with Swordsman. The superhumans were released when the Avengers defeated Loki, but soon after the true Earth's heroes returned to their own world. Swordsman decided the remnants of the heroic age could be forged into a new team. Unfortunately, he was diagnosed with cancer, and although an experimental treatment using the DNA of a deceased Canadian genetic aberration was being tested, he wanted a team that could function without him.

When Avengers' janitor Ernest Sanger donned the Ant-Man armor left behind by Hank Pym, Swordsman asked him to lead the new team. Ernest, now Mant, was directed toward other individuals affected by the missing heroes, including the Super-Adaptoid, now called Amazo-Maxi-Woman and possessing the personality and body of a teenage girl; Panther Cub, the son of a Wakandan valet who had claimed the missing Black Panther's vestments; Miss Thing, who had slain the Canadian aberration and donned its Adamantium claws and bones; and Sterling, the cosmic waste left behind after the Silver Surfer abandoned that Earth, now in human form and with the basest of desires. Swordsman, now calling himself Deadpool, trained the group before leaving to complete his treatments. Like Loki before him, Deadpool came to understand his world's true nature, and he too gained access to the blue balls of energy. Knowing he was created by a child's imagination, Deadpool's mind snapped; he gained an eating disorder and the desire to destroy all reality. He started by stealing a SHIELD helicarrier and defacing the Sphinx in Egypt. Gaining dozens of pounds due to overeating, Deadpool at some point adopted a sidekick named Tim.

CURRENT MEMBERS: Mant (Ernest Sanger, leader), Miss Thing (Mary Rina), Panther Cub (T'Dogo), Amazo-Maxi-Woman (Super-Adaptoid), Sterling
FORMER MEMBERS: Deadpool (formerly Swordsman)
BASE OF OPERATIONS: Avengers Mansion (Franklin Richard's Counter-Earth)
FIRST APPEARANCE: Heroes Reborn: Remnants #1 (2000)

The team continued without him, and their public relations campaign caught the attention of SHIELD's General Darlegung who asked them to hunt down their former trainer. Begrudgingly accepting the mission, the team was given a disused Fantasticar and tracked down the absconded helicarrier. Despite getting in each other's way, struggling with inappropriate costumes and ignoring Mant, the group fought waves of LMDs before finding Deadpool and his sidekick Tim. After revealing their world's nature, Deadpool aimed nuclear missiles at the Watcher's base on the moon. Mant, tired of being stepped on by the other team members, took command of the group, naming them the Remnants and inspiring them to battle. Having begun the launch sequence by the time his speech had ended, Deadpool gave the team a book of rules for existing in a fictional universe, then rode a missile to the Blue Area of the moon. After the explosion, the Remnants saw the image of the Celestial Ashema asserting her control over the world and they believed Deadpool had torn a hole in the universe. Thanks in part to the efforts of true Earth's Dr. Doom (Victor von Doom), Ashema's efforts were successful and stabilized the artificial world. The Remnants' subsequent activities are unrevealed.

NOTE: It is unrevealed whether the Remnants founder Swordsman is connected to the Swordsman present in the altered reality caused by the temporary merging of Franklin Richards' first pocket realm and another alternate Earth reality. Additionally, it is unrevealed whether the Swordsman of a second Franklin Richards-created pocket realm (created to escape the reborn Onslaught) is a duplicate of the Remnants founder or whether he is patterned after true Earth's Swordsman Jacques DuQuesne.

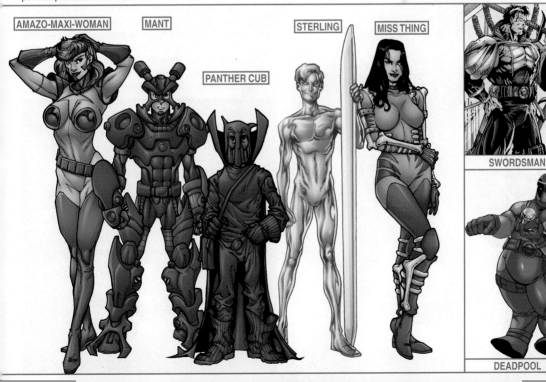

AMAZO-MAXI-WOMAN | MANT | PANTHER CUB | STERLING | MISS THING | SWORDSMAN | DEADPOOL

SKORNN

REAL NAME: Skornn
ALIASES: None
IDENTITY: No dual identity
OCCUPATION: Predator
CITIZENSHIP: Unrevealed
PLACE OF BIRTH: Unrevealed
KNOWN RELATIVES: None
GROUP AFFILIATION: None
EDUCATION: Unrevealed
FIRST APPEARANCE: X-Force #1 (2004)

HISTORY: The Skornn is a member of a vicious, ancient - possibly alien or demonic - race also called the Skornn. At some point, they encountered the Shi'ar. On Earth, the Skornn terrorized Macedonia and other areas between periods of slumber, feasting on the energy signatures of the few mutants they could find. During one such slumber, a group of powerful mutants, including En Sabah Nur (later Apocalypse) and Garbha Hsien (later Saul), created the Five Fingers of Annihilation blade to destroy the Skornn. Later, in the city of Karanada (80 miles south of modern-day Plovdiv, Bulgaria), the local priests threatened to awaken the Skornn, prompting the Council of Nirinthia to seek out the Traveler (Nathan Summers, later Cable), for aid. His arrival came too late, as he found the Skornn had awakened, slaughtering the entire town including the council and priests. Allied with mutant priestess D'narda, Traveler confronted the Skornn, but was only able to defeat it when D'narda

sacrificed herself, allowing the Five Fingers to pierce her body as it plunged into the Skornn, sending it back into slumber. During his time travels, Traveler/Cable would again encounter the Skornn on Earth-5013, where he failed to save that reality's counterparts of his X-Force team.

In his own Earth-4935 future, Cable was warned of the efforts of the anti-mutant Order of the Five Blades and their genetically-modified human agents the Helix, to find and awaken more Skornn. Once again returning to Earth-616, Cable began preparing for the inevitable revival of the Skornn, which came when members of the Helix arrived from the future and sacrificed themselves to awaken the Skornn. During this time, Cable recovered the Five

Art by Rob Liefeld

Fingers of Annihilation from a temple on Mt. Xixabangma, between Tibet and Nepal, where the monk Zed had kept it hidden. The Helix tried to steal the blade, but failed, though they murdered Zed in the process. Reforming the original members of his X-Force team to stop the threat, Cable discovered one member, Caliban, being used as a "bloodhound" by the anti-mutant project Watchtower, led by the Administrator, who wanted to use mutants as pawns to defeat the Skornn. Helix members took the Skornn to Manhattan, where it disrupted a debutante ball at the Hellfire Club, killing and feeding upon young mutants. This rampage caught the attention of the Human Torch (Johnny Storm) and the Thing (Ben Grimm), who futilely battled the creature until Cable arrived, along with X-Force, Wolverine (James Howlett/Logan), Deadpool ("Wade Wilson") and the Mutant Liberation Front (led by Stryfe/Domino of Earth-5014, which diverged from Earth-5013 when Domino survived the Skornn's assault). As the heroes battled the Skornn and Helix members (all the while being observed by the Shi'ar, who had gathered their Imperial Guard near Earth to battle the Skornn), Cable realized that to stop the creature without sacrificing his allies, he had to do so himself. Spilling his blood on the Five Fingers, Cable plunged the ancient sword into the Skornn, causing a temporal explosion that sent the Skornn to an unrevealed time and location. While Cable was also assumed dead in the incident, he soon turned up again unharmed. Presumably, there are still other Skornn slumbering, waiting to be awakened.

HEIGHT: Variable (originally 9'4")   **EYES:** Blue
WEIGHT: Variable   **HAIR:** None

ABILITIES/ACCESSORIES: The Skornn feeds on the energy of mutants and other superhuman beings, including those mutated by cosmic radiation. As it feeds, it grows, the limits of which are unrevealed. It possesses superhuman strength (lifting at least 75 tons), though the limits are also unrevealed. It is nearly invulnerable, capable of withstanding almost any physical or psionic attack. The Skornn's only known weakness is the Five Fingers of Annihilation, a blade containing the combined partial power of numerous mutants.

POWER GRID	1	2	3	4	5	6	7
INTELLIGENCE							
STRENGTH							
SPEED							
DURABILITY							
ENERGY PROJECTION							
FIGHTING SKILLS							

TIAMAT

HISTORY: Long ago, an unidentified race's telepathic, precognitive Council of Elders learned of S'met'kth, a powerful being that brought peace and bliss to planets by robbing free will, leaving inhabitants in an inert stupor. Believing free will critically important, the Council plotted to slay S'met'kth before he could reach their world. Over 3000 years ago, the Council identified an infant as their Champion and sent him and other children to Earth aboard a living starship, where they foresaw he would meet his final destiny in the 21st century AD. The Champion and other children waited, grew and changed, the others becoming a steed and living armor or weapons to aid the Champion. Via the Council's visions, the Champion trained himself to combat S'met'kth, but also the Mithras, a human who would defend S'met'kth. Less than 20 years before its arrival, the human organization Landau, Luckman, Lake, & LeQuare's precognitive Montgomery Burns foresaw S'met'kth, followed by another vision of the being (whom they dubbed Tiamat) who would destroy S'met'kth unless protected by the Mithras. Agents Zoe Culloden, Dixon Mason and Noah DuBois resolved to keep these events secret even from their employers. Dixon organized the Mithras Directive to groom and prepare the Mithras, whom Montgomery's visions showed to be Deadpool ("Wade Wilson"). After Monty prophesied Deadpool's defeat against Tiamat, Dixon mindwiped Monty and kept this secret, planning to use Captain America (Steve Rogers) as the back-up Mithras.

WITH STEED

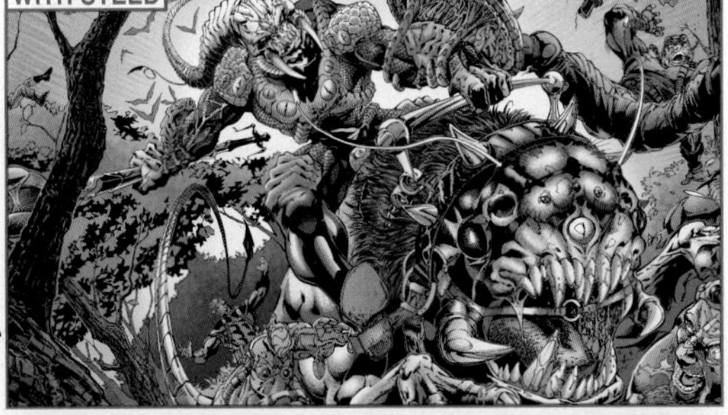

Art by Walter McDaniel

HEIGHT: 7'1"
WEIGHT: 540 lbs.
EYES: Solid white (presumably translucent membranes; no visible pupil or iris)
HAIR: None

ABILITIES/ACCESSORIES: Tiamat is superhumanly strong (Class 10), can swiftly recover from penetrating wounds and is amphibious, though he prefers water. He has exceptional speed, agility and reflexes, and may be precognitive; but his prophecies may come from the Council of Elders. He is a master combatant, killing opponents instantly with surgical precision or painlessly. He can understand (and speak a few words in) English, but generally speaks a dialect resembling gurgling. Tiamat's armor, weaponry, ship and other technology were all living creatures. His chest harness was a radially symmetric star-fish like creature, which extruded fanged tentacles able to tear through and/or bite others. The helmet was a serpentine skeletal being that shielded its wearer from S'met'kth's control. Tiamat rode a monstrous, amphibious steed that chewed through metal. He utilized small insectoid drones that transmitted images to him via a glowing green globe, plus larger, bee-like warrior drones.

POWER GRID	1	2	3	4	5	6	7
INTELLIGENCE	■	■	■				
STRENGTH	■	■	■	■			
SPEED	■	■					
DURABILITY	■	■	■	■			
ENERGY PROJECTION	■						
FIGHTING SKILLS	■	■	■	■	■	■	

REAL NAME: Unrevealed, possibly Champion (or a translation thereof)
ALIASES: Champion, Ultimate Chaos, Undoing of the World as We Know It
IDENTITY: Secret
OCCUPATION: Warrior, assassin
CITIZENSHIP: Unidentified extraterrestrial race
PLACE OF BIRTH: Unidentified planet
KNOWN RELATIVES: None
GROUP AFFILIATION: None
EDUCATION: Unspecified combat training
FIRST APPEARANCE: (Pictured, identified) Deadpool #21 (1998); (full) Deadpool #23 (1998)

Preparing for S'met'kth's arrival, the Champion/Tiamat burrowed his ship through the bedrock below the SETI (Search for ExtraTerrestrial Intelligence) radio telescope in Arecibo, Puerto Rico. To prevent S'met'kth's detection, Dixon jammed space scanning equipment across Earth, but Tiamat, following the visions, destroyed the 83 agents sent to place the SETI jammer and slew DuBois and others who investigated. Deadpool, as Mithras, was sent there, but Tiamat's visions' enabled him to anticipate the exact moment he could impale Deadpool through the chest. Surviving, Deadpool teleported away. The Council of Elders criticized their Champion for failing to confirm the Mithras' death, and Tiamat vowed to destroy Deadpool. Tiamat traveled to Egypt shortly before S'met'kth's arrival and defeated the Dixon-sent Captain America. When Deadpool arrived and slew his steed, Tiamat, now-obsessed with destroying the Mithras, attacked him, ignoring S'met'kth as it arrived. Losing faith in their Champion, the Council stripped Tiamat of his armor and weapons, and gave them to Deadpool, whom they convinced of S'met'kth's threat. Deadpool then apparently slew S'met'kth, while Tiamat, distraught over having had his destiny usurped, wandered into the desert.

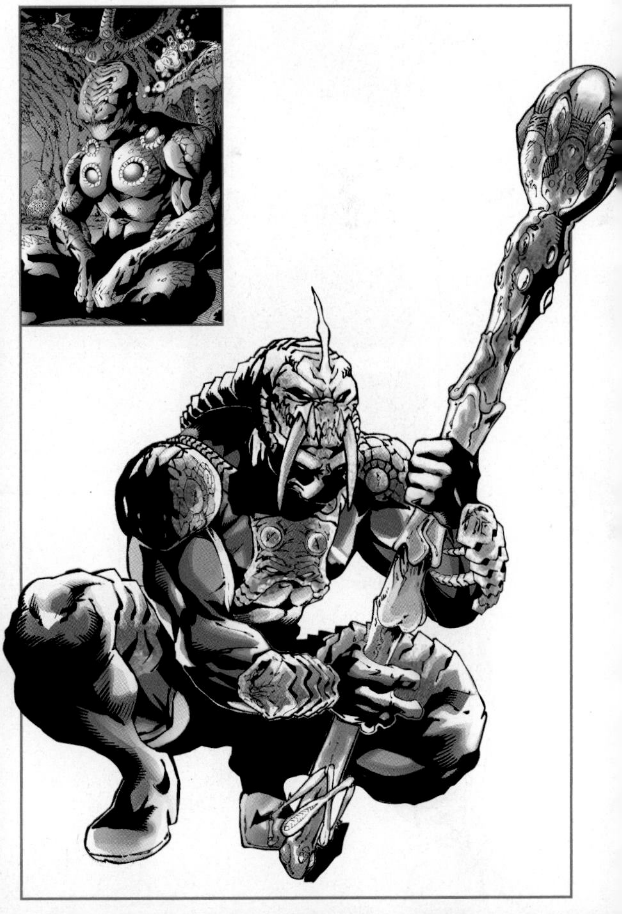

ULTIMATUM

CURRENT MEMBERS: Anarchy, Lynette Cole, Flag-Smasher (Guy Thierrault), Michael Straka, Ultimator
FORMER MEMBERS: Flag-Smasher (Karl Morgenthau), Vladimir Korda, Vladimir Krantz, Red Skull (Johann Shmidt), Toler Weil
BASE OF OPERATIONS: Rumekistan; formerly a warehouse in Paris, France, a warehouse in Manhattan, New York, a ski lodge on the Symkarian-Latverian border, a base in the Arctic Circle, an abandoned Hydra base in the Swiss Alps
FIRST APPEARANCE: Captain America #321 (1986)

HISTORY: ULTIMATUM (Underground Liberated Totally Integrated Mobile Army to Unite Mankind) is a terrorist organization devoted to bringing about the end of all nations, thereby enabling the establishment of a world government and ending wars and strife between nations. It was the brainchild of Flag-Smasher (Karl Morgenthau), who believed violent action was necessary to achieving his goals. Unknown to the Flag-Smasher, major funding for the organization came from the Red Skull (Johann Shmidt) who at the time was believed deceased. At the time of their founding, groups such as Hydra were waning, enabling Flag-Smasher to recruit from other terrorist organizations; ULTIMATUM agents included men from Canada, China, Germany, Israel, Poland, South Africa and the USA. The standard ULTIMATUM weapon is an Uzi submachine gun, and they possess rocket-propelled jet skis with electromagnetic grips as well as a variety of explosives. They have also acquired many military-grade vehicles such as tanks, submarines and attack helicopters.

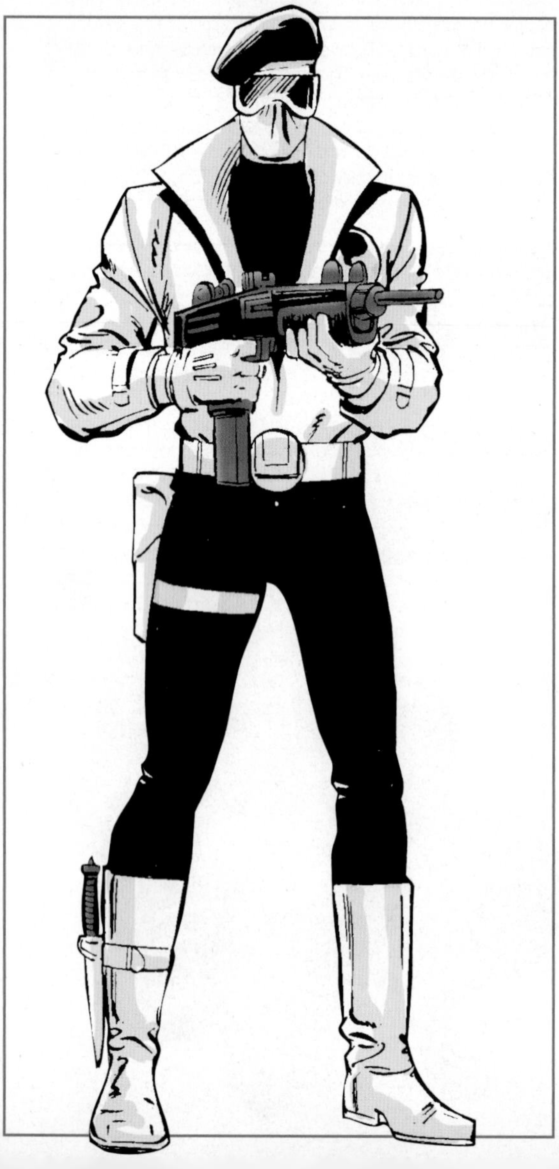

In ULTIMATUM's earliest known overt action, Flag-Smasher led them in sky-jacking an airplane near London, England, and holding the passengers hostage. The hostages were brought to a monastery in the Swiss Alps while Flag-Smasher sent a message to Captain America (Steve Rogers, who had previously defeated him) to surrender himself in exchange for their release. Captain America found the monastery and disguised himself as an ULTIMATUM agent, but when Cap tried to rescue the hostages, Vladimir Korda opened fire, killing at least four of them. Captain America killed Korda and joined SHIELD forces led by Jerry Hunt in a raid of ULTIMATUM's base in the Swiss Alps, a facility formerly run by Hydra's Count Otto Vermis; several dozen agents were captured, including Flag-Smasher

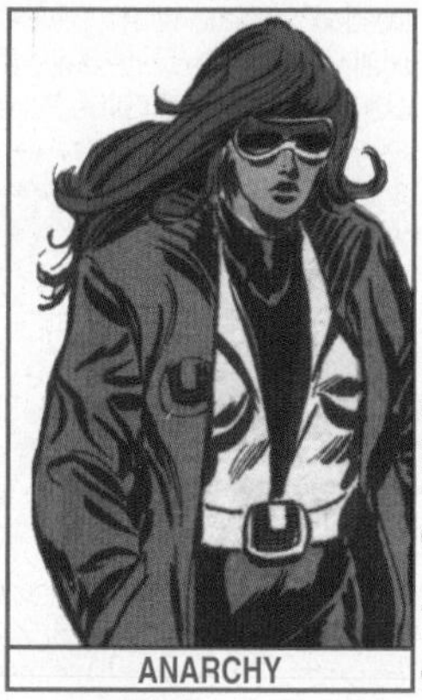

ANARCHY

Art by Sal Velluto

ULTIMATUM next plotted to use an electromagnetic pulse generator near the North Pole to shut down all devices on Earth, sending civilization to a pre-industrial state, enabling the group to unite mankind. However, Flag-Smasher then learned that the Red Skull was his financier and turned against the operation. Flag-Smasher found himself pitted against his own ULTIMATUM forces loyal to the Skull and he called on Captain America, knowing he could trust his old foe for help. However, the Captain America who responded was John Walker, the government-appointed replacement, and Flag-Smasher bested him in combat and demanded that his partner Battlestar (Lemar Hoskins) bring him the "real" Captain America. Battlestar returned with "the Captain" (Steve Rogers' temporary alias) and Demolition-Man (Dennis Dunphy, aka D-Man). The Captain helped Flag-Smasher fight ULTIMATUM and destroy the electromagnetic pulse generator, although Demolition-Man was believed dead after his Quinjet crashed into the building housing the generator. Subsequently, the Skull pit an ULTIMATUM agent against John Walker in Washington, DC, but the agent was beaten badly.

Next, the Red Skull masterminded a plot to destabilize relations between the USA and Symkaria and start a war. ULTIMATUM forces led by Major Toler Weil and supported by the Life Foundation made a deal with Symkaria's Prime Minister Klaus Limka to assassinate Symkaria's King Stefan. ULTIMATUM also hired the mutant assassin Sabretooth (Victor Creed) to kill Limka and plant evidence implicating the CIA. The ULTIMATUM attempt on Stefan's life failed, although his Queen Vivian was killed. The anti-terrorist rogue Solo (James Bourne) broke up an ULTIMATUM effort to destroy the Arc de Triomphe in Paris, France, and

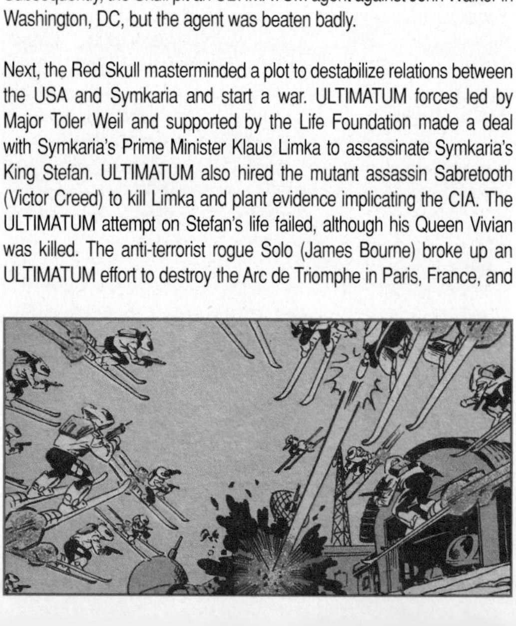

Art by Kieron Dwyer

Art by Lewis LaRosa

1ST FLAG-SMASHER

ULTIMATOR

Art by Leonardo Manco

used intelligence gained there to track Major Weil to a ski lodge on the Symkarian-Latverian border where Symkaria's Silver Sable had joined Captain America and Spider-Man (Peter Parker) in the pursuit. Weil escaped the four heroes, but other ULTIMATUM agents were captured. Next, ULTIMATUM attempted to destroy Ellis Island in New York, but Solo and Spider-Man halted the operation and Spider-Man eventually took Weil prisoner. To find Weil's leader, Spider-Man impersonated an ULTIMATUM agent and freed Weil from prison, following him to Washington's National Archives where he found the Red Skull and prevented ULTIMATUM's attempted destruction of the Archives and recorded evidence proving the Skull was behind the Symkarian-USA tensions.

Flag-Smasher finally retained mastery over ULTIMATUM and purged their ranks of agents loyal to the Red Skull. While Manhattan was engulfed by fights between superhumans due to the "Acts of Vengeance" plot, Flag-Smasher and his lieutenant Anarchy masterminded a mass theft of munitions to rearm ULTIMATUM and overthrow the US government. However, the Punisher (Frank Castle) and Moon Knight (Marc Spector) intervened and destroyed the weaponry. Soon after, ULTIMATUM distributed weapons to teenagers in New York so they could destroy all of Manhattan's banks, destabilizing the world economy. This time, the Punisher was aided by Ghost Rider (Daniel Ketch) in halting Flag-Smasher's plans. ULTIMATUM attempted to rob the World Unity Council as they transported delegates aboard a cruise ship to Italy, using film actress Lynette Cole as an undercover agent aboard the ship, but SHIELD's Nick Fury and Alpha Flight's Weapon Omega (Kyle Gibney) prevented the theft and caught Cole. Flag-Smasher reclaimed the remains of the Arctic base and when his men discovered Demolition-Man was still alive, Flag-Smasher used him as a hostage to again try to capture Captain America, but this time the call was answered by the USAgent (John Walker's new identity) and the Falcon (Sam Wilson), who rescued Demolition-Man. ULTIMATUM attempted to assassinate Japanese delegate Takao Kuroto when he visited the USA, but they were thwarted by Solo and Spider-Man. An ULTIMATUM base in Paris was broken up by Deathlok (Michael Collins), Silver Sable and the Wild Pack as they searched for a lead on Harlan Ryker's Cyberwarriors program, which had offered its services to ULTIMATUM.

ULTIMATUM attempted a major assault on Washington DC, but were thwarted by Captain America and his allies Free Spirit (Cathy Webster), Jack Flag (Jack Harrison) and Zachary Moonhunter. As the European Union gained power, Flag-Smasher found himself in opposition to his own minions as ULTIMATUM sought to destroy the Channel Tunnel from England to France, while Flag-Smasher saw the growing bonds in Europe as a validation of his anti-nationalist views. Flag-Smasher wound up aiding Spider-Man and the Sandman (William Baker) against his own men, although he still made an attempt to destroy Buckingham Palace. An ULTIMATUM agent called the Ultimator threatened the life of Carnelia's Prime Minister Maurus Vasilyev when his nation made a

treaty with Trebekistan, but the Avengers rescued Vasilyev and arrested the Ultimator. ULTIMATUM set a fake bomb in New York's subway tunnels as a diversion while Flag-Smasher set a bomb to destroy their true target, Wall Street, but the X-Men intervened and Marrow realized the deception, stopping the real bomb in time.

With the support of Marduk, an Annunaki (Mesopotamian) god posing as Oracle, Inc. CEO Nestor Zoltan, ULTIMATUM launched an assault on multiple countries to overthrow their governments, thus enhancing Marduk's godly power when the souls of those slain were claimed by his "Genesis Well." While Flag-Smasher led ULTIMATUM in Rumekistan, additional forces battled Alpha Flight in Greenland, the Avengers in Cuba and the Winter Guard in Novosibirsk, Russia. However, Citizen V (John Watkins III) of the V-Battalion struck a deal with Flag-Smasher and used technology the V-Battalion had appropriated to control the Collective Man, using his powers to put all the people of Rumekistan to sleep. Flag-Smasher was thus able to conquer the country without additional fighting, and Citizen V promised to let him alone provided he recall ULTIMATUM's other forces. Under Flag-Smasher's guidance, Rumekistan became a military state policed by ULTIMATUM and most laws were abolished in the name of personal freedom. However, the country also suffered economically and became a totalitarian regime. The would-be mutant messiah Cable (Nathan Summers) took an interest in Rumekistan's plight and sent Deadpool ("Wade Wilson") to injure Flag-Smasher during a public address, but Domino (Neena Thurman) shot Flag-Smasher first, killing him. Cable stepped in and claimed control over Rumekistan and left ULTIMATUM in place to ensure a peaceful transition of power. Cable quickly set to work repairing the damage neglect and poor resources had wrecked on Rumekistan, aided by ULTIMATUM Captain Michael Straka. Although Cable was eventually lost and believed dead, Rumekistan thrived thanks to his actions. With Flag-Smasher's death, Canadian ULTIMATUM agent Guy Thierrault took up his uniform and became the organization's new leader, battling SHIELD and the Runaways in Santa Monica. Later, he led ULTIMATUM in an attempt to destroy the Liberty Bell in Philadelphia, but they were bested by the Initiative's Liberteens.

Art by Patrick Scherberger

2ND FLAG-SMASHER

WEASEL

REAL NAME: Jack Hammer
ALIASES: Weas, Penetraitor, Penetraitor, "Deadpool's Whipping Boy"
IDENTITY: Known to authorities
OCCUPATION: Information broker; former Hydra Sector Commander
CITIZENSHIP: USA, with a criminal record
PLACE OF BIRTH: Queens, New York
KNOWN RELATIVES: John Hammer (father), Virginia Hammer (mother), Juan (cousin)
GROUP AFFILIATION: Formerly Hydra
EDUCATION: Unrevealed degree from Empire State University, New York; claims to have attended Cal-Polytech
FIRST APPEARANCE: Deadpool: The Circle Chase #1 (1993)

HISTORY: Perpetually messy and girl crazy Jack Hammer, who claims his entire family is in jail, was a genius student who attended Empire State University, but lost his way through unrevealed circumstances, eventually becoming a wayward information broker and arms dealer named "Weasel," who killed a man at some point in unrevealed circumstances. Meeting mercenary Deadpool ("Wade Wilson"), the pair became friends, working together for time-traveling arms merchant, Tolliver (Tyler Dayspring), and sharing an unrevealed significant experience at Niagara Falls. While plying his trade in war-torn Sarajevo, Weasel helped Deadpool in his hunt for Tolliver's will, rescuing him from the Executive Elite before learning the location of Tolliver's vault in Nepal, where the cyborg Slayback sought revenge on Deadpool for past transgressions; Weasel activated the weapons-neutralizing Zero android, which ended the conflict. As his weapons supplier, Weasel often assisted Deadpool in his assignments from the Hellhouse, but was soon offered a full-time contract by the Taskmaster. Deadpool and Taskmaster fought for Weasel's services, Deadpool's unpredictability winning the bout, then

celebrating Weasel's return with a wedgie. Weasel later won Deuce "the Devil-Dog" from "Foggy" Nelson in a poker game, and soon began visiting Deadpool's housemate/prisoner Blind Al without Deadpool's knowledge. During a confrontation with the Great Lakes Avengers, Deadpool's teleportation belt interacted with Doorman (DeMarr Davis)'s teleportation ability, sending Al and Deadpool through time, diverging Reality-9712, where Deadpool (disguised as Peter Parker) had that reality's younger Weasel repair his teleportation belt, while Weasel worked with Flatman (Val Ventura) and Doorman in the present to eventually recover them. When he learned of Weasel's visits with Al, a furious Deadpool locked Weasel in a torture room. After escaping, Weasel went into hiding, returned to freelance work and began developing his own personal teleportation device.

Much later, Weasel encountered an amnesiac Deadpool, helping restore his memory before assisting him against Deadpool's nemesis T-Ray. Sometime later, Weasel was caught hacking Rand-Meachum's computer systems by Iron Fist (Daniel Rand) and Luke Cage. Deadpool initially defended Weasel, but after learning Weasel had lied to him about it, he refused to help; Weasel was arrested and sent to jail. After pleading a deal to be released after four months, Weasel was hired by the Rumekistan resistance movement to help liberate the country from the terrorist group ULTIMATUM's control. There, Weasel and Deadpool rekindled their friendship, with Weasel helping Deadpool regain his mercenary reputation, then tried to help Deadpool's subsequent attempt to become a super hero by provoking a tussle with the Rhino (Aleksei Sytsevich). They were then asked to rescue Agent X (Alex Hayden) from the terrorist organization Hydra. Though Deadpool succeeded in the mission, Weasel was captured. Joining Hydra as a new Sector Commander, Weasel used their resources to finish creating his teleportation device, dubbed the Penetrator, and donned a portable version himself as the "Penetraitor," spelled with an "i" because he planned to betray Hydra. After Deadpool and new ally (and Hydra agent) Bob arrived to rescue him, they were confronted by Wolverine (Logan/James Howlett) who sought to stop Hydra from having teleportation technology; however, Weasel revealed his secret plan when he had Hydra agents outfitted with Penetrator armor that teleported them all to Guantanamo Bay prison. Damaged during the fight with Wolverine, Weasel's armor malfunctioned and sent Deadpool and Bob back in time, forcing Weasel to turn to the Fantastic Four for help recovering them. Continuing to tinker with his Penetrator tech, Weasel transported himself, Deadpool and Bob to the Savage Land to procure advanced technology to aid Rumekistan. Clashing with the Savage Land Mutates, Deadpool tried to use Weasel's Penetrator tech, accidentally transporting dinosaurs to Manhattan, where they were infected by alien symbiotes. After the infected dinosaurs were stopped by a gathering of heroes, Weasel helped teleport the dinosaurs back to the Savage Land. Weasel continues to support Deadpool as his pal and weapons supplier.

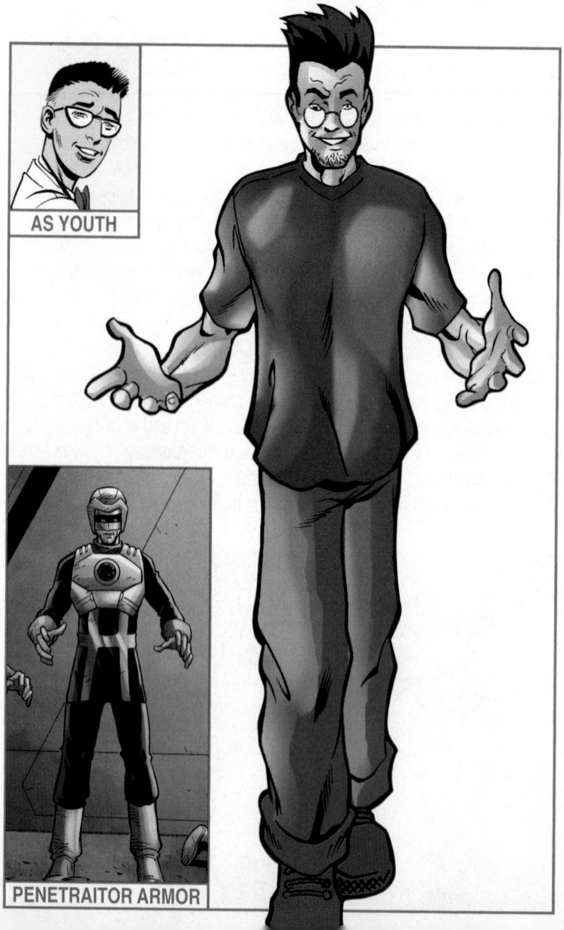

AS YOUTH

PENETRAITOR ARMOR

HEIGHT: 5'7"
WEIGHT: 130 lbs.
EYES: Brown
HAIR: Black

ABILITIES/ACCESSORIES: A talented information broker, Weasel is adept at operating and hacking computers. He is also a skilled designer and creator of advanced technological devices, such as his Penetrator teleportation armor, and has access to exotic weaponry, like Pym Particles. He is also a capable marksman, skilled in use of a variety of weaponry.

POWER GRID	1	2	3	4	5	6	7
INTELLIGENCE							
STRENGTH							
SPEED							
DURABILITY							
ENERGY PROJECTION							
FIGHTING SKILLS							

HISTORY: In Earth-4935's 38th century, Zero was the prototype android for Apocalypse (En Sabah Nur)'s series of 13 ADAM units meant to destroy all threats to Earth. After Apocalypse's apparent death, the High Lord's heir, Stryfe (Cable/Nathan Summers' clone) and his caretaker Ch'vayre located the ADAM production facility in what was once New Orleans. They activated Zero and programmed him to resurrect Apocalypse. The teenage Stryfe tasked Zero with reanimating dead soldiers first, but Zero guided Stryfe to locate the Askani's Madame Sanctity (Tanya Trask) to improve his mutant abilities. Zero was subsequently puzzled to watch Stryfe kill Ch'vayre for having negative thoughts about him. Stryfe became Sanctity's pupil, and the Askani believed Zero could herald an era of enlightenment. Under unrevealed circumstances, Zero was separated from Stryfe for years, during which time Stryfe amassed power while Cable gained followers, including ADAM Unit-11. Stryfe later reclaimed and reprogrammed Zero, rendering him mute to avoid perceived sarcasm.

Stryfe and Zero traveled back in time to modern day Earth-616, as did Cable. Over the next seven years Years Stryfe organized the Mutant Liberation Front, for which Zero served as primary transport. Stryfe also had Zero deliver the Legacy virus to Mr. Sinister under false pretenses. Soon after Stryfe seemingly died battling Cable, Zero was deactivated and found by agents of Tolliver. Tolliver faked his death and left a will offering the most powerful weapon – apparently Zero – to the mercenary that found it. Deadpool ("Wade Wilson"), Garrison Kane, Copycat, Slayback and Weasel (Jack Hammer) found Zero in a Nepalese monastery, and Weasel reactivated Zero with his original programming. Zero destroyed Slayback and hesitated before killing Deadpool, who convinced Zero some "weapons" could be beneficial. Zero left to investigate the methods and motives of Tyler (exposed as Tolliver's true identity), who revealed the presence of Sister Askani, having also traveled from Earth-4935. Zero captured Askani for Tyler, but witnessing Tyler torture her, Zero asked Cyclops (Scott Summers) and Jean Grey to confront Cyclops' son Cable (possessed by Stryfe) and grandson Tyler. After watching the family defeat Stryfe's psychic

REAL NAME: Ambient-Energy Dampening Actualization Module (ADAM) Unit Zero
ALIASES: Wavelength displacement unit, Algorithmic wavelength dampening ambient-energy absorbing modular unit, Zero Unit, Blank Man, "Neutered albino Schwarzenegger," "Clamoring container of synthetic cells and arteries"
IDENTITY: Publicly known
OCCUPATION: Peacekeeper; former terrorist agent
CITIZENSHIP: Earth-4935, late 38th century
PLACE OF BIRTH: Former site of New Orleans, Nor-Am Pact region, Earth-4935, late 38th century
KNOWN RELATIVES: ADAM Unit-Eleven, others in ADAM series
GROUP AFFILIATION: Formerly Stryfe (Cable's clone)'s Mutant Liberation Front
EDUCATION: Programmed with data from Apocalypse (En Sabah Nur), Stryfe and the Askani
FIRST APPEARANCE: New Mutants #86 (1990)

ghost, Zero departed. Attacked by droids programmed to destroy Stryfe's data, Zero took refuge in Maine and summoned Douglock (the Technarch Warlock); they were joined by a civilian family and the British team Excalibur. Zero transported everyone to Stryfe's base beneath the Pentagon to save them from droids, but accidentally activated the base's self-destruct mechanism and unlocked Legacy virus information in his memory. Shadowcat (Kitty Pryde) removed a destruct mechanism from Zero's body, and Zero forced Douglock to absorb his knowledge before saving Washington DC from the exploding base. Zero's damaged and memory-wiped body ended up in the Arkansas laboratory of geneticist Edwin Martynec, one of Stryfe's followers. After Martynec was defeated by Siryn and Warpath, the scientist and nonfunctioning android were placed in Emma Frost's custody.

HEIGHT: 6'	EYES: None
WEIGHT: 200 lbs.	HAIR: None

ABILITIES/ACCESSORIES: Zero can fly and create portals through space and time, using temporal monitors to pinpoint specific eras, locations and timelines. This energy manipulation allows him to keep peace by nullifying all technological and biological weapons. He automatically records all nearby energy signals and can control, contain, redirect or neutralize any energy signature in his database or create fields to detain even noncorporeal beings. He can create an EMP-like charge to deactivate nearby technology or destroy weapons from a distance with projected energy. He can store vast amounts of data, remotely reprogram other computer systems, create holograms, perform multiple levels of diagnostics for self-repair and send beacons to other techno-organic sentient beings. Zero is constructed of durable artificial metals, although repeated attacks by weapons from his own era will eventually injure him. When inert, the "zero" symbol disappears, reappearing when Zero absorbs energy. Under Stryfe's control, Zero was programmed not to talk and included an autonomous destructive device that could only be removed by an outside force.

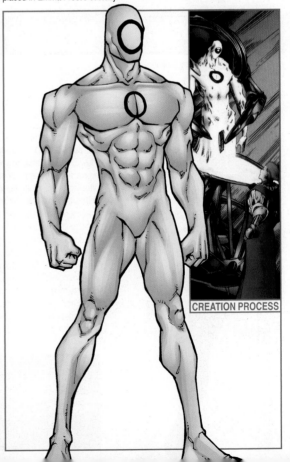

CREATION PROCESS

POWER GRID	1	2	3	4	5	6	7
INTELLIGENCE							
STRENGTH							
SPEED							
DURABILITY							
ENERGY PROJECTION							
FIGHTING SKILLS							

YELLOW BAR INDICATES ZERO CAN TELEPORT

ANANASTASIA

REAL NAME: Ananastasia "Anna" Rinaldi
ALIASES: None
IDENTITY: No dual identity
OCCUPATION: Tattoo artist; former dancer, security specialist
CITIZENSHIP: USA

PLACE OF BIRTH: Congers, New York
KNOWN RELATIVES: None
GROUP AFFILIATION: None
EDUCATION: Unrevealed
FIRST APPEARANCE: Deadpool #46 (2000)

HISTORY: Ananastasia dropped out of FBI training when she could not complete the psych training, which included handling Bellevue patients. After working as a security specialist in Miami, she was imprisoned for an undisclosed offense under an assumed name. Upon release, Anna was an exotic dancer before discovering a talent for tattoo art. Romanced by several mobsters, including Vincent Calabresse, Anna had a secret affair with Officer Fred Pierson. From Calabresse, Anna received full-time bodyguard Busta Bloodvessel, a former rapper who retired after a heart attack. Anna and Pierson plotted to use Deadpool ("Wade Wilson") to free her of her mobster lovers and cash in on a million dollar insurance policy on Pierson's wife. Ananastasia acted as a go-between for Pierson, who hired Deadpool to kill Anna's other lovers under the pretense that the mobsters had threatened his family over Pierson's undercover work.

Ananastasia's beauty soon entranced Deadpool, and Anna seemed genuinely attracted to him despite his disfigurements. Following Anna's murder of Pierson's wife, made to look like a mob hit, and Deadpool's botched hit on Calabresse (the sole survivor of Deadpool's efforts), Deadpool told Ananastasia his suspicions about Bloodvessel being in cahoots with the mobsters. Anna ambushed Deadpool, knocking him unconscious with a shovel, and she and Pierson buried Deadpool alive. When Pierson told Anna he received much less money than planned, Anna — knowing he was lying — tied up Pierson and returned to save Deadpool. When Pierson told Deadpool the double cross was Anna's idea, she murdered Pierson, as well as Busta's informant, Sandee Savage, with the same gun she used to kill Pierson's wife. Calabresse and Bloodvessel approached as Anna asked Deadpool to run away with her, and a furious Calabresse forced Busta to crash his car in an attempt to kill Anna. The resulting explosion killed Calabresse and left Bloodvessel unconscious. Anna tried to prove her sincerity and trust in Deadpool by giving him her gun, but Deadpool, noting she did not know him at all, apparently shot her.

HEIGHT: 5'6"   WEIGHT: 130 lbs.   EYES: Green   HAIR: Black

ABILITIES/ACCESSORIES: Ananastasia is a skilled street fighter, experienced with handguns, and a talented tattoo artist, exotic dancer, and manipulator.

INTELLIGENCE: 2 STRENGTH: 2 SPEED: 2 DURABILITY: 2
ENERGY PROJECTION: 1 FIGHTING SKILLS: 3

Art by Gus Vazquez

ILANEY BRÜKNER

REAL NAME: Ilaney Brükner
ALIASES: None
IDENTITY: No dual identity
OCCUPATION: Pilot
CITIZENSHIP: Germany

PLACE OF BIRTH: Unrevealed
KNOWN RELATIVES: None
GROUP AFFILIATION: Formerly German Army Aviation Corps
EDUCATION: Army Aviators School graduate
FIRST APPEARANCE: Deadpool #18 (1998)

HISTORY: German army pilot Ilaney Brükner quit after crashing a transport plane in the Swiss Alps. Survivor's guilt led her to retreat into bad relationships, heavy drinking and a secluded house in the Swiss Alps. One day, Deadpool ("Wade Wilson"), with injured Dr. Emrys Killebrew in tow, forced his way into her house. At first trying to shoot Deadpool, she soon realized that he was the lesser evil when Ajax (Francis) attacked them. Ilaney helped Killebrew escape while Deadpool caused an avalanche that buried her house and Ajax. With all her belongings lost, she accompanied Deadpool and Killebrew, but the surviving Ajax soon caught up with them. Nearly dying after Deadpool jumped with her into an icy cold lake, Ilaney decided she wanted her life back. Returning to her old home in Germany's Black Forest, she became Deadpool's personal pilot for mercenary jobs all over the globe. During T-Ray's revenge plot against Deadpool, Ilaney witnessed a resurrected Mercedes Wilson return to Deadpool's life and tried to befriend her. She joined Deadpool and Mercedes during their investigations and was arrested with them by interdimensional holding firm Landau, Luckman & Lake after returning injured precognitive Montgomery Burns to them. LL&L's Overboss Zoe Culloden soon released the trio, and they returned to Earth where T-Ray attacked them. T-Ray trapped Ilaney in an endless nightmare that made her relive the traumatic plane crash, but released her after Mercedes left with T-Ray, who claimed to be the real Wade Wilson.

HEIGHT: 5'7"   EYES: Blue   WEIGHT: 197 lbs.   HAIR: Blond

ABILITIES/ACCESSORIES: Ilaney was a capable pilot schooled in flying small passenger planes and helicopters. She quickly adapted to the use of firearms, including shotguns and energy rifles.

INTELLIGENCE: 3 STRENGTH: 1 SPEED: 2 DURABILITY: 2
ENERGY PROJECTION: 1 FIGHTING SKILLS: 3

Art by Gus Vazquez

DEATHTRAP

REAL NAME: Alistaire Augustus Armstrong
ALIASES: None
IDENTITY: Secret
OCCUPATION: Assassin
CITIZENSHIP: UK
PLACE OF BIRTH: London, England
KNOWN RELATIVES: None
GROUP AFFILIATION: None
EDUCATION: Three unspecified Ph.D.s, Oxford University, UK
FIRST APPEARANCE: Deadpool #9 (1997)

HISTORY: Sometime after attending Oxford, the Renaissance-obsessed Deathtrap became an assassin within high-class circles, flaunting a love for brandy and women, and boasting a death count of 3000 people. He eventually became bored with killing through the "usual implements", so began creating elaborate death traps to slay his victims, making it his mission to elevate death to an art form. During a lull in business, he selected the mercenary Deadpool ("Wade Wilson") as a target in this new direction. Using his preference for form over function and his desire for the spectacle of the kill, Deathtrap originally planned to run Deadpool through a deadly gauntlet, through tricking him into believing he was rescuing a princess. However, Deadpool's seemingly never-ending chatter inspired him to use the mercenary's inherent proclivities against him, choosing a pre-schooler motif for his traps that mirrored Deadpool's underdeveloped psyche. After imprisoning Deadpool in a device intended to suffocate him by lowering a three-ton teddy bear toward him whenever he spoke, Deathtrap found himself ill prepared for how much Deadpool actually spoke; the tenor of Deadpool's voice caused Deathtrap's device to lower the bear far more rapidly than Deathtrap intended, seemingly crushing Deadpool. Deadpool survived, however, by snapping both his wrists and ankles to escape before the bear struck, then threatened Deathtrap. Knocking Deadpool out with a hammer, Deathtrap departed, leaving a note for him that promised the start of a beautiful friendship.

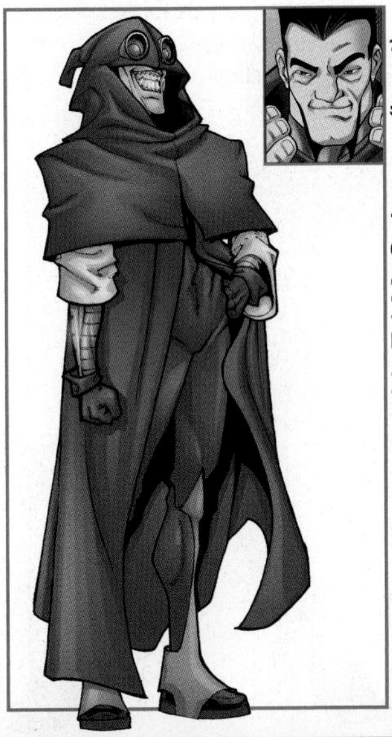
Art by Gus Vasquez with Ed McGuinness (inset)

HEIGHT: 6' **WEIGHT:** 149 lbs. **EYES:** Blue **HAIR:** Black

ABILITIES/ACCESSORIES: Deathtrap is a master assassin who is versed in all forms of torture. He is an extremely skilled technician and machinist, and exels at using these skills to create elaborate traps for his victims. He has extensive wealth, weaponry and resources at his disposal to create these traps, as well as at least two flying crafts. He wears an armor of unspecified capabilities underneath his cloak.

INTELLIGENCE: 4 **STRENGTH:** 2 **SPEED:** 2 **DURABILITY:** 2
ENERGY PROJECTION: 1 **FIGHTING SKILLS:** 3

DIRTY WOLFF

REAL NAME: Unrevealed
ALIASES: Daddy-Killer, Great Deathbringer, Mon-Tel, Violator of Worlds
IDENTITY: Secret
OCCUPATION: Plunderer
CITIZENSHIP: Benzwezil
PLACE OF BIRTH: Benzwezil
KNOWN RELATIVES: None
GROUP AFFILIATION: Leader of the Last Men
EDUCATION: Unrevealed
FIRST APPEARANCE: Deadpool #41 (2000)

HISTORY: Seemingly responsible for the destruction of his own race, Dirty Wolff at some point became leader of the Last Men, sole survivors of various races and most feared plunderers in 12 galaxies. For some time everything worked out fine, but then the galactic moral council known as the Code caught Dirty Wolff and sent him to their penal colony Damnation City, where he was imprisoned under the watchful eye of warden Lucifer Rasputin. Incidentally, the Last Men found Deadpool ("Wade Wilson") floating in space and after defeating their most feared member in combat they chose Deadpool to liberate Dirty Wolff from Damnation City. After infiltrating the penal colony dressed as a guard, Deadpool found Dirty Wolff chained up inside a cell in the bottom level. Deadpool released Dirty Wolff, who insisted on getting his bike before leaving. Damnation City's fuses got fried when Deadpool recharged the weakened Dirty Wolff on an electric chair, releasing all prisoners. A recharged Dirty Wolff and Deadpool fought the prisoners, but their situation was further complicated when the Last Men's ship was destroyed. Now forced to get to Dirty Wolff's bike, they continued to fight the prisoners while Lucifer evacuated the prison's staff, planning to self-destruct it. Deadpool and Dirty Wolff made it to the bike, but while Deadpool escaped, he accidentally left Dirty Wolff behind in Damnation City, which blew up a minute later, apparently killing him.

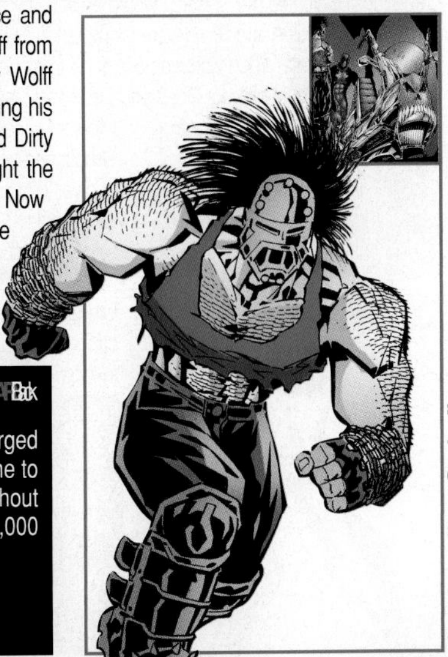
Art by Jim Calafiore

HEIGHT: 7'6" **WEIGHT:** 1640 lbs. **EYES:** Gray **HAIR:** Black

ABILITIES/ACCESSORIES: Dirty Wolff's powers were enhanced by electricity. Fully charged he possessed superhuman strength (lifting 75 tons) and durability, rendering him immune to bullets and most injuries. He could bite through metal and survive almost indefinitely without air. His bike was a rocket powered one-man vehicle that could reach speeds up to 10,000 mph.

INTELLIGENCE: 2 **STRENGTH:** 5 **SPEED:** 2 **DURABILITY:** 5
ENERGY PROJECTION: 1 **FIGHTING SKILLS:** 4

DOCTOR BETTY

REAL NAME: Betty Swanson
ALIASES: "Dr. Hotness"
IDENTITY: No dual identity
OCCUPATION: Biologist
CITIZENSHIP: USA

PLACE OF BIRTH: Unrevealed
KNOWN RELATIVES: None
GROUP AFFILIATION: AIM; formerly Hydra
EDUCATION: Ph.D in Biology from Cal Tech
FIRST APPEARANCE: Deadpool: Merc with a Mouth #1 (2009)

AIM UNIFORM

Art by Gus Vazquez with Bong Dazo (inset)

HISTORY: Betty Swanson is an agent of AIM (Advanced Idea Mechanics), assigned to go undercover with a Hydra science team sent to the Savage Land to search for undiscovered natural toxins that could be converted into bio-weapons. Hydra chanced upon the decapitated – but still sentient – head of the Earth-2149 ("Marvel Zombies") mercenary Deadpool, which could transmit a zombie virus. The head had been taken in by a group of native headhunters who worshipped it as a deity, so Hydra sent a heavily-armed retrieval team to recover it. In response, AIM hired Deadpool ("Wade Wilson") to recover the head first. Deadpool met with Swanson, then attacked the headhunters, resulting in both their captures, adding to Swanson's already great dislike of him. Recovering the head and escaping, they were confronted by the Hydra retrieval team, who had learned of Swanson's true leadership. During a subsequent battle between Hydra, the headhunters and the Savage Land's protector Ka-Zar (Kevin Plunder), and after an encounter with a zombie-fied Tyrannosaur, Deadpool and Swanson captured a Hydra ship and returned the head to AIM's space station. Swanson secured the head in the lab; however, Deadpool had a crisis of conscience and, after Hydra attacked the station, he stole the head, rescued Swanson from Hydra, commandeered Hydra's ship and Bill, Agent of AIM, then returned to Earth. Once in Florida, Dr. Voodoo (Jericho Drumm) helped stabilize the Nexus of All Realities, allowing Deadpool to journey to Earth-2149 to return the head. Frightened by the Nexus' guardian, Man-Thing (Ted Sallis), Swanson and Bill followed Deadpool through the Nexus, but became stranded on Earth-2149 and are seeking a way back to Earth-616.

HEIGHT: 5'8" **WEIGHT:** 142 lbs. **EYES:** Blue **HAIR:** Blond

ABILITIES/ACCESSORIES: Dr. Betty is a talented biologist who has experience as a double agent. She has space flight training, advanced AIM weaponry training, and wore a watch containing a GPS locator device.

INTELLIGENCE: 4 **STRENGTH:** 2 **SPEED:** 2 **DURABILITY:** 2
ENERGY PROJECTION: 1 **FIGHTING SKILLS:** 1

NOAH DUBOIS

REAL NAME: Noah DuBois
ALIASES: None
IDENTITY: No dual identity
OCCUPATION: Operative of Landau, Luckman & Lake; former Landau, Luckman, Lake & LeQuare operative, senatorial aide
CITIZENSHIP: Unrevealed

PLACE OF BIRTH: Unrevealed
KNOWN RELATIVES: None
GROUP AFFILIATION: Landau, Luckman & Lake
EDUCATION: LL&L training; otherwise unrevealed
FIRST APPEARANCE: Uncanny X-Men #299 (1993)

HISTORY: Early in his career with interdimensional firm Landau, Luckman & Lake, Noah DuBois worked with Zoe Culloden, Dixon Mason and Montgomery Burns to prepare for an alien "Messiah" predicted to initiate galaxywide peace - not realizing "peace" would be mindless bliss. Montgomery's predictions indicated the Messiah would be slain by monstrous Tiamat unless protected by the "Mithras." The four researched the "Mithras Directive" for years, and while Zoe and Dixon were promoted to Expediter and Overboss respectively, Noah preferred fieldwork. In recent years, Noah infiltrated Senator Robert Kelly's staff. When Zoe was assigned to guide Wolverine (Logan/James Howlett) through various crises, Noah sometimes accompanied her. As the Messiah's arrival neared, Noah and Zoe hired Deadpool ("Wade Wilson"), who Zoe believed to be the predestined Mithras, to sabotage the Antarctic Project Michelangelo facility. Deadpool disabled the facility designed to remove gamma radiation from the Earth's atmosphere, but after learning the damage would irradiate millions, risked his life to shut down Michelangelo's nuclear core, exhibiting the heroism required for the Mithras role. Overboss Dixon remained skeptical, as did Deadpool when he learned of the offer. Noah maintained surveillance of Deadpool for Dixon, who recommended him for Overboss training. When Dixon sent LL&L Black Out Troops to prevent the Messiah's detection, one unit was killed by Tiamat. Dixon instructed Noah to investigate, but he and other operatives were also killed. As Dixon intended, Noah's death motivated Deadpool to fight Tiamat ahead of schedule, enabling Dixon to record Tiamat's capabilities. Initially beaten, Deadpool subsequently defeated Tiamat and the Messiah, justifying Noah and Zoe's faith in him.

Art by Walter McDaniel with Brandon Peterson (inset)

HEIGHT: 6' **WEIGHT:** 180 lbs. **EYES:** Brown **HAIR:** Black (shaved)

ABILITIES/ACCESSORIES: Noah DuBois could telepathically communicate with others and intercept telepathic contact between others without their knowledge. His left glove contained an impulse weapon which fired energy bursts and he had access to LL&L teleportation, cloaking technology and other resources.

INTELLIGENCE: 3 **STRENGTH:** 2 **SPEED:** 2/7* **DURABILITY:** 2
ENERGY PROJECTION: 4 **FIGHTING SKILLS:** 4
*DuBOIS WAS A TELEPORTER

FOUR WINDS

CURRENT MEMBERS: Higashi (East Wind), Kita (North Wind), Manishi (West Wind), Minamiyori (South Wind), Kensuke Wei, others
FORMER MEMBERS: Ryoko Saguri, Gendo Sonoda
BASE OF OPERATIONS: Mobile, including Kenichi Building, New York and Kobe, Japan
FIRST APPEARANCE: Deadpool #65 (2002)

HISTORY: The Four Winds are a crime cartel with over 20,000 members, originating from Japan but globally based. Each crime family of the Four Winds maintains a rivalry with the other three, but all four will join forces against common enemies. During a summit of the four families in Kobe, Japan, one of the winds hired the mercenary Deadpool ("Wade Wilson") to assassinate another wind. However, as Deadpool fell through a skylight into the conference, the master assassin Black Swan killed all four winds; Deadpool mistakenly believed he was their killer and was held responsible by the Four Winds' followers. In each family a new wind rose to the rank of leadership, including Higashi, who faced considerable interference from his ambitious lieutenant Ryoko Saguri. When Higashi sought to obtain the site where the Alpine Amusement Park lay, he found the owner Agent X (Alex Hayden) unwilling to sell. Impressed by Hayden's secretary Sandi Brandenberg, Higashi began to romance her. When Taskmaster lyingly informed Higashi and Saguri that Agent X was actually Deadpool, Saguri hired a multitude of assassins to kill him and his allies, Sandi included. Although the

hired killers included the likes of Constrictor (Frank Payne), Rhino (Aleksei Sytsevich) and Crossfire (William Cross), Agent X held them at bay and left Sandi with Higashi for her safety. To end the hostilities, Agent X obtained information on the Four Winds' families and threatened their lives in return for his and his friends' protection. Secretly hired by Higashi, he then murdered Saguri, protecting Higashi's leadership. Higashi later hired Agent X and Taskmaster as his bodyguards for a Four Winds summit with Sandi as his date. Two assassins hired by Kita attacked them en route, but Agent X and Taskmaster defeated them. In gratitude, Higashi later loaned his forces to help Agent X, Taskmaster, Sandi and Deadpool against the Black Swan.

(FRONT, LEFT TO RIGHT) SAGURI, HIGASHI
(AROUND TABLE) MEMBERS OF EAST WIND

Art by UDON Studios

HALFGHANAGHAN BROTHERS

REAL NAME: Nyko & Pico Halfghanaghan
ALIASES: None
IDENTITY: No dual identities
OCCUPATION: (Nyko) unrevealed; (Pico) agent of Donald Pierce; former valet
CITIZENSHIP: Greece
PLACE OF BIRTH: Sparta, Greece
KNOWN RELATIVES: (Both) Mr. Halfghanaghan (father, deceased); (Nyko) Pico (brother); (Pico) Nyko (brother)
GROUP AFFILIATION: None
EDUCATION: Unrevealed
FIRST APPEARANCE: (Pico) X-Force #11 (1992); (Nyko) Deadpool: The Circle Chase #1 (1993)

HISTORY: Tolliver (Tyler Dayspring)'s right-hand man, midget Pico Halfghanaghan guarded and tortured the mercenary Domino (Neena Thurman), for more than a year while shape-shifter Copycat (Vanessa Carlyle) impersonated her to get close to Cable (Nathan Summers) for their boss. Eventually, after Domino was transferred from Tolliver's Austrian castle to his Sardinian villa, Cable and Copycat broke in looking for Tolliver, interrupting Pico torturing Domino with an electric whip. When Pico confronted the interlopers, Cable unceremoniously shot him in the head; Tolliver and Copycat's ex-boyfriend Deadpool ("Wade Wilson"), arrived moments later and in the ensuing conflict Pico was left for dead. Clinging to life, he was saved by Donald Pierce, who turned him into a cyborg. Soon afterward, Tolliver faked his death, leading mercenaries to target anyone who might have access to his will. Though not a former employee, Pico's brother Nyko was amongst those hunted, fighting off an attack in New Delhi, India, before meeting with middleman Courier (Jacob Gavin, Jr.) to hire the Executive Elite to assassinate Deadpool, whom Nyko blamed for his brother's seeming death. Some time later, Pierce sent Pico to kill Domino while she attended Rio de Janeiro's Carnival, but she swiftly overpowered him.

PICO

HEIGHT: (Nyko) 4'4"; (Pico) 4'6"
WEIGHT: (Nyko) 94lbs.; (Pico) 125 lbs.
EYES: (Both) unrevealed
HAIR: (Nyko) Gray; (Pico) white-blond

ABILITIES/ACCESSORIES: Pico has telescoping cybernetics legs that extend more than two stories in height and hands that act as energy whips, which can spin rapidly to deflect small missiles. Nyko, and Pico prior to cybernetic enhancement, carried twin high-caliber semiautomatic shotguns; both are excellent shots. Pico is also a capable gymnast, able to rapidly cartwheel and speaks fluent Portuguese.

Nyko/Pico **INTELLIGENCE:** 2/2 **STRENGTH:** 2/3 **SPEED:** 2/2
DURABILITY: 2/3 **ENERGY PROJECTION:** 1/2 **FIGHTING SKILLS:** 4/4

Art by Gus Vazquez with Marc Pacella (inset)

INVISIBLE MAN

REAL NAME: Darick Gallhager
ALIASES: "Electro," "Invisible Daddy," "Semi-Visible Man," "Inviso"
IDENTITY: Secret
OCCUPATION: Restaurant owner; former chemist
CITIZENSHIP: USA
PLACE OF BIRTH: Unrevealed location in USA

KNOWN RELATIVES: Unidentified wife (deceased), Christine (daughter, deceased)
GROUP AFFILIATION: None
EDUCATION: Ph.D. in chemistry
FIRST APPEARANCE: Agent X #8 (2003)

ORIGINAL APPEARANCE

Inset by Mitchell Breitweiser

HISTORY: Thirty years ago, US government chemist Dr. Darick Gallhager was working on a top-secret project when he discovered an invisibility formula. Planning to sell his formula to communist Russia and run away with his mistress, Gallhager was surprised when the US military raided his facility. Gallhager used the formula on himself to escape, but returned home to find it ablaze. Finding his wife dead, Darick located his daughter Christine, and the two escaped by using the formula on her as well, subsequently taking various false identities. Hating what her father had turned her into, Christine disguised her invisibility with makeup and used the remnants of Gallhager's research to build the Gal-Hag Cosmetics company while Gallhager became the owner of the Jose Lopez restaurant in Mexico as the Invisible Man. Feeling her father had robbed her of a childhood, Christine eventually hired the mercenary Agent X (Alex Hayden) to kill him. After Agent X tracked him to Little Italy, Gallhager eluded the mercenary via his invisibility and blasting his assailant with a stun gun every time he got close, all the while claiming innocence. Eventually captured and put into a dress to identify his location by Agent X, the Invisible Man was given an hour to explain his innocence. Upon hearing Gallhager's story, Agent X initially defended him when Christine came to kill him, but then escaped while Christine and the Invisible Man bickered. Agent X then tossed a grenade onto the Gal-Hag yacht, which exploded, apparently killing both Darick and Christine.

HEIGHT: 5'10"
WEIGHT: 158 lbs.
EYES: Invisible (originally brown)
HAIR: Invisible (originally black)

ABILITIES/ACCESSORIES: The Invisible Man's body was completely and irreversibly invisible. He was a brilliant chemist and carried an invisible 10,000 volt stun gun of his own design.

INTELLIGENCE: 4 STRENGTH: 2 SPEED: 2 DURABILITY: 2
ENERGY PROJECTION: 1 FIGHTING SKILLS: 2

BRENT JACKSON

REAL NAME: Brent Montgomery Jackson
ALIASES: Director Jackson, Agent Jackson, "Pooch-Meister," "Poochie"
IDENTITY: No dual identity
OCCUPATION: Director of Weapon X; former deputy director and recruiter for Weapon X, SHIELD special agent
CITIZENSHIP: USA

PLACE OF BIRTH: Unrevealed
KNOWN RELATIVES: None
GROUP AFFILIATION: Weapon X; formerly SHIELD
EDUCATION: SHIELD agent training
FIRST APPEARANCE: Wolverine #163 (2001)

HISTORY: Brash SHIELD agent Brent Jackson gained the notice of the Director (Malcolm Colcord) of the Weapon X (WX) program, and had him act as a mole within SHIELD, where in unrevealed circumstances, he betrayed a black ops team under his command. Jackson was later chosen to

Art by Sean Chen

capture Wolverine (Logan/James Howlett) for the murder of Senator Drexel Walsh. He captured Wolverine by using a Life Model Decoy of Wolverine's ally, former SHIELD director Nick Fury, clandestinely returning Wolverine to WX. Jackson recruited mutants for WX's ranks, but never gained the trust of the Director, who secretly implanted a chip that prohibited him from showing aggression toward a superior. Sent to find Sabretooth (Victor Creed) for a mission, Jackson, deeply disturbed by the carnage he found in his hotel room, saved a child Sabretooth was planning to murder. The confrontation left him with a deep hatred and fear of the mutant, which prompted him to arrogantly confront the Director, who beat Jackson, then suspended and imprisoned him briefly before reinstating him because of the usefulness of his devious nature. However, Jackson was secretly undermining the Director and gaining WX agents' loyalty. He also worked with the Mutant Underground to overthrow the Director, but also double-crossed them. Claiming mind-control for his dubious behavior, Jackson was questioned by the project's secret backers, then claimed directorship of WX, taking it underground before fighting a "War of the Programs" against Colton and his backer, John Sublime; Jackson's program presumably dissolved afterwards.

HEIGHT: 5'11"
WEIGHT: 185 lbs.
EYES: Blue
HAIR: Blond

ABILITIES/ACCESSORIES: Jackson is a trained SHIELD special agent, a proficient marksman and is familiar with cutting-edge technology, including Weapon X's extensive array, including teleportation devices, jetpacks, anti-mutant weaponry, motorcycles and computer networks.

INTELLIGENCE: 2 STRENGTH: 2 SPEED: 2/7* DURABILITY: 2
ENERGY PROJECTION: 1 FIGHTING SKILLS: 3
*AGENT JACKSON CAN TELEPORT

VALERIE JESSUP

REAL NAME: Valeria Toomes
ALIASES: Valeria Merrick
IDENTITY: Secret
OCCUPATION: Former SHIELD operative
CITIZENSHIP: USA
PLACE OF BIRTH: Flagstaff, Arizona
KNOWN RELATIVES: Unidentified son, Adrian Toomes (Vulture, father), Cheryl (mother), unidentified half-brother, unidentified grandparents (deceased), unidentified nephew, Malachi Toomes (cousin, deceased), Marcus Toomes (uncle), Ramona (sister-in-law)
GROUP AFFILIATION: Formerly SHIELD
EDUCATION: SHIELD agent training
FIRST APPEARANCE: Identity Disc #1 (2004)

HISTORY: When Valeria Toomes was a young girl, her mother, tired of her life on the run, took her away from her criminal father, Adrian. When she grew up, Valeria falsified her identity and joined SHIELD under the name Valerie Jessup. The subversive organization AIM discovered this, however, and contacted her, threatening to expose her identity unless she acted as their agent within SHIELD. Unwilling to betray SHIELD, Valeria turned to her long-lost father, now the super villain Vulture, to retrieve the disc containing her personal information. Posing as "Valeria Merrick," an agent of legendary crimelord Tristam Silver, Valeria gathered six super villains – Juggernaut (Cain Marko), Deadpool ("Wade Wilson"), Sabretooth (Victor Creed), Bullseye (Lester), Sandman (William Baker), and her father – to steal it from AIM under the pretense that the "Identity Disc" contained the identities of every costumed hero in the USA. After Sandman, who was in on the plan, faked his death to convince the others that "Merrick" meant business, the others investigated AIM front companies until they located the disc in AIM's subterranean Manhattan base. One by one, however, the Vulture secretly betrayed his colleagues until only he and the Juggernaut remained. After the Juggernaut retrieved the disk, Toomes knocked him out and destroyed it, but was captured while escaping from the base and taken into SHIELD custody. Valeria escorted her father from his interrogation session to a prison transport, giving her time to thank him. Skinhead Titus Purves threatened Valeria and her son to force Toomes to build a flying harness for him, but Toomes double-crossed and killed Purves.

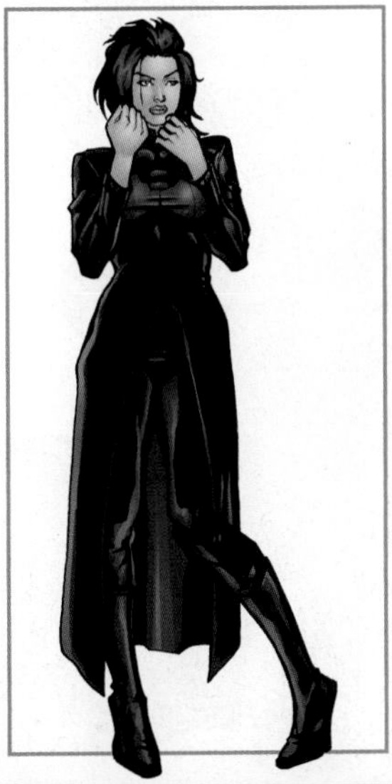

Art by Gus Vazquez

HEIGHT: 5'10" **WEIGHT:** 141 lbs. **EYES:** Brown **HAIR:** Red, dyed black

ABILITIES/ACCESSORIES: Valerie Jessup is a skilled planner and actress, and a fair unarmed combatant.

INTELLIGENCE: 3 **STRENGTH:** 2 **SPEED:** 2 **DURABILITY:** 2
ENERGY PROJECTION: 1 **FIGHTING SKILLS:** 3

KID DEADPOOL

REAL NAME: Christopher Cassera
ALIASES: Pool Boy, Christopher Hoisik
IDENTITY: Secret
OCCUPATION: Student
CITIZENSHIP: USA
PLACE OF BIRTH: Brooklyn, New York
KNOWN RELATIVES: John Cassera (father, deceased)
GROUP AFFILIATION: Former partner of Deadpool ("Wade Wilson")
EDUCATION: High school graduate, some undergraduate courses
FIRST APPEARANCE: Deadpool #50 (2001)

HISTORY: While Christopher Cassera was at the store, his father was set afire by mobster Maxy Millions and left for dead. Christopher returned to find Deadpool ("Wade Wilson"), who had been hired to kill Maxy and arrived too late to save John. As per John's dying wish, Deadpool took in Christopher, who demanded revenge for his father's death. Donning a spare costume and weaponry, Christopher became Kid Deadpool and helped Deadpool track Maxy Millions to downtown Brooklyn, where Christopher attacked Deadpool for being unable to save John. Upon running out of ammo, Christopher agreed to put aside his differences with Deadpool, and the duo soon tracked Maxy Millions to a nearby club, where Kid Deadpool slipped explosives into the mobster's pocket, detonating them when he tried to flee. Having avenged his father, Christopher was given half of Deadpool's fee for killing Maxy and used it for tuition to Oxford University under the false name Christopher Hoisik. As he left for Europe, Christopher attempted to destroy Deadpool's warehouse headquarters, but Deadpool found and disarmed the explosives. Returning from Europe, Kid Deadpool destroyed Deadpool's warehouse in his second attempt, finally coming to terms with Deadpool's role in his father's murder. Christopher then returned Deadpool's guns and detonator, keeping Deadpool's motorcycle and leaving to see the world with his new girlfriend Miki. Later attending Deadpool's funeral, he was possessed by Deadpool's spirit and forced to pinch the Juggernaut (Cain Marko)'s butt, resulting in a punch that launched him out of his boots and led to a fight amongst the other attendees.

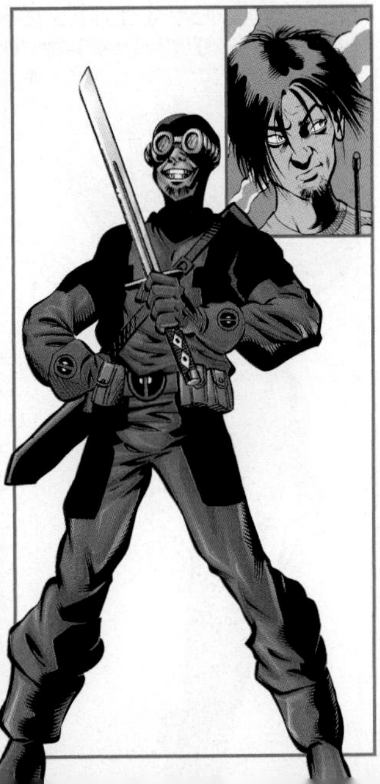

Art by Darick Robertson

HEIGHT: 5'10" **WEIGHT:** 154 lbs **EYES:** Blue **HAIR:** Black

ABILITIES/ACCESSORIES: Kid Deadpool is moderately skilled with firearms and other weapons, especially explosives. He typically uses a katana, night-vision goggles that allow him to see in total darkness and a motorcycle.

INTELLIGENCE: 3 **STRENGTH:** 2 **SPEED:** 2 **DURABILITY:** 2
ENERGY PROJECTION: 1 **FIGHTING SKILLS:** 2

EMRYS KILLEBREW

REAL NAME: Emrys Killebrew
ALIASES: Killbrew
IDENTITY: No dual identity
OCCUPATION: Recluse; former research scientist, pediatrician
CITIZENSHIP: Canada, possibly Switzerland
PLACE OF BIRTH: Unrevealed, presumably Canada
KNOWN RELATIVES: None
GROUP AFFILIATION: Formerly Weapon X (Canada)
EDUCATION: Ph.D.s in genetics, cybernetics, etc.
FIRST APPEARANCE: Deadpool #1 (1994)

HISTORY: Over a decade ago, Dr. Emrys Killebrew empowered super-operatives, including Francis (aka the Attending), for Canada's Weapon X. At the Hospice, intended to treat failed augmentation subjects, Killebrew, without his superiors' knowledge, conducted horrific experiments to gather scientific data and to amuse himself. One patient, "Wade Wilson," hoping to provoke Francis into killing him, took to humiliating him before the patients, but Killebrew considered Wilson too valuable a subject to kill. Francis instead lobotomized Wilson's friend Charles "Worm" Cunningham, prompting Wilson to grant Cunningham merciful death. To maintain order, Killebrew allowed Francis to kill Wilson, but Wilson survived and, as Deadpool, seemingly killed Francis. Killebrew fled but later reunited with Francis, augmenting him into the more powerful Ajax. In recent years, Killebrew, living in seclusion in the Swiss Alps, sought atonement and lured Deadpool to him. When Deadpool arrived with his friend Siryn, Killebrew, having discovered Deadpool's body chemistry was breaking down, offered to cure him. Although the trio acquired a sample of Hulk (Bruce Banner)'s blood as a cure, Deadpool intended to kill Killebrew for his crimes but was dissuaded by Siryn. Weeks later, Ajax located and tortured Killebrew into teleporting Deadpool to their location, where Ajax knocked him off a cliff. Recovering, Deadpool fled with Killebrew and bystander Ilaney Brükner. Killebrew tried to attack Ajax, allowing the other two to flee, but Ajax killed him. Although Deadpool apparently killed Ajax, Brükner suffered severe injury. Killebrew, now a ghost, healed Brükner and vanished into the afterlife, where punishment for his crimes awaited him.

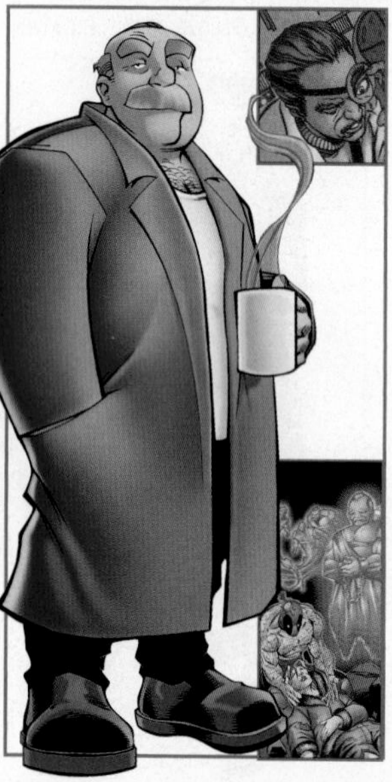

Art by Ed McGuiness with Steve Harris & Walter McDaniel (insets)

HEIGHT: 5'8"
WEIGHT: 300 lbs. (formerly 161 lbs.)
EYES: Blue
HAIR: Gray, formerly brown, sometimes dyed black

ABILITIES/ACCESSORIES: Dr. Killebrew was a brilliant geneticist and cyberneticist. As a ghost, his abilities are mostly unrevealed, although he restored a person near death to the peak of health with a single touch.

INTELLIGENCE: 5 **STRENGTH:** 2 **SPEED:** 2 **DURABILITY:** 2
ENERGY PROJECTION: 1 **FIGHTING SKILLS:** 2

MALACHI

REAL NAME: Malachi
ALIASES: None
IDENTITY: No dual identity
OCCUPATION: Sorceress
CITIZENSHIP: Unrevealed
PLACE OF BIRTH: Unrevealed
KNOWN RELATIVES: None
GROUP AFFILIATION: None
EDUCATION: Unrevealed
FIRST APPEARANCE: Secret Defenders #15 (1994)

HISTORY: Many millennia ago, the sorceress Malachi and her lover Korahn sought immortality in the form of the mystic Agamotto's Moebius Stone artifact. Agamotto's guardian eventually confronted and slew both Malachi and Korahn, fragmenting the Moebius Stone and scattering it across the world. Unbeknownst to Agamotto, Malachi survived via a Stone fragment, and she soon set out to obtain the other fragments. In recent years, Malachi located a Moebius Stone fragment within the hilt of a sword in the Chicago Museum of Art. Opposing and escaping Dr. Anthony Druid's Secret Defenders (Luke Cage, Deadpool/"Wade Wilson," Shadowoman), Malachi revitalized herself by draining the life energies of teenager Cody Fleischer and soon discovered the final Moebius Stone fragment in the ring of a corpse in a nearby graveyard. Despite opposition from the Secret Defenders and a resurrected Cody Fleischer (now Agamotto's servant Cadaver), Malachi retrieved the final fragment and restoring the Moebius Stone, causing worldwide aging and vitality fluctuations. Using the Stone to revive the long-dead Korahn, Malachi was shocked when Korahn preferred death to immortality. Taking advantage of the distraction, the Secret Defenders' Deadpool stabbed Malachi through the chest, and Dr. Druid destroyed the Moebius Stone before Dr. Stephen Strange's unstable "Strange" aspect could claim it.

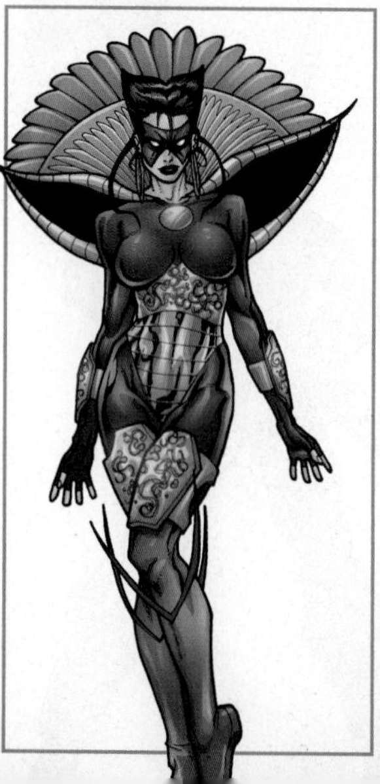

Art by Gus Vazquez

HEIGHT: 5'9"
WEIGHT: 140 lbs.
EYES: No visible irises
HAIR: Black

ABILITIES/ACCESSORIES: Malachi was an accomplished sorceress, capable of manipulating magical energy for a variety of effects including animating objects, projecting mystical energy blasts, controlling minds and flight. Possessing fragments of the Moebius Stone, Malachi could maintain her youth and vitality indefinitely by draining others' life forces. While using the complete Moebius Stone, Malachi could manipulate life forces across the planet, aging and de-aging others and even raising the dead. The complete Moebius Stone also made Malachi effectively immortal as she did not age, but she could still be killed by conventional means.

INTELLIGENCE: 3 **STRENGTH:** 2 **SPEED:** 2 **DURABILITY:** 2
ENERGY PROJECTION: 5 **FIGHTING SKILLS:** 2

MARY ZERO

REAL NAME: Unrevealed
ALIASES: None
IDENTITY: Secret
OCCUPATION: Thief
CITIZENSHIP: USA
PLACE OF BIRTH: Unrevealed
KNOWN RELATIVES: None
GROUP AFFILIATION: None
EDUCATION: Presumably a high school dropout
FIRST APPEARANCE: Agent X #3 (2002)

HISTORY: Possessing an unusual mutant ability which rendered her invisible and inaudible to most human beings, the self-named teenager Mary Zero became a thief, living unnoticed in people's homes and stealing food and goods from stores. On her birthday, Mary went to rob a jewelry store, coincidentally at the same time as a team of professional thieves. Riding along with them unnoticed in their car, they were pursued by Agent X (Alex Hayden), who forced the car off the road. Agent X stopped to see if Mary was injured and when she realized he could see, hear and remember her she was instantly smitten with him. Mary Zero accompanied Agent X as he clashed with assassins of the Four Winds; when a bullet that lodged in his throat nearly killed him, Mary was distraught at her inability to summon help, though he eventually recovered. To bring an end to the attempts on his life, Agent X had Mary walk into the Four Winds' offices and retrieve files on their members' families and mistresses, using the information to blackmail them. Hayden soon formed Agency X with his friends and Mary promised to stay with him. However, when the Scarlet Witch (Wanda Maximoff) warped reality, depriving many mutants of their powers, Mary Zero was among those affected; her abilities were made part of the being called the Collective.

HEIGHT: 5'
WEIGHT: 98 lbs.
EYES: Light brown
HAIR: Black

ABILITIES/ACCESSORIES: Mary Zero formerly existed outside the visible and audible perception of most humans. Those few people who did interact with Mary were typically affected by a shortterm memory loss which made them forget her. Animals were evidently able to perceive her. Agent X was the only human who seemed able to perceive and remember Mary.

INTELLIGENCE: 2 **STRENGTH:** 2 **SPEED:** 2 **DURABILITY:** 2
ENERGY PROJECTION: 1 **FIGHTING SKILLS:** 2

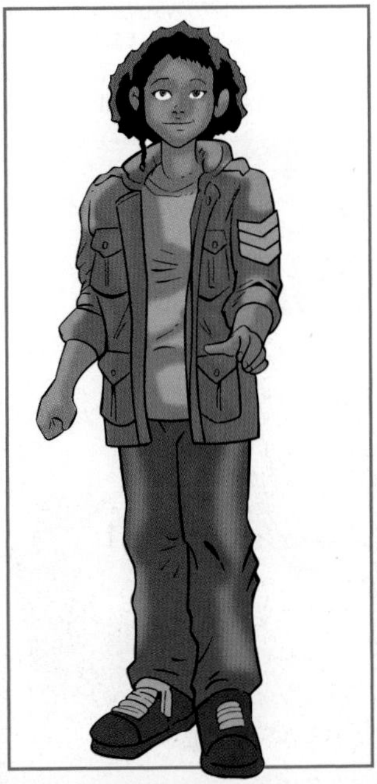

Art by UDON Studios

MERCY SISTERS

REAL NAME: Grace and Mary Mercy
ALIASES: "Switchblade Sisters," "Britney Spears Twins"
IDENTITY: No dual identity
OCCUPATION: Serial killers, students
CITIZENSHIP: USA
PLACE OF BIRTH: Long Island, New York
KNOWN RELATIVES: Unidentified parents (deceased)
GROUP AFFILIATION: None
EDUCATION: Unrevealed
FIRST APPEARANCE: (Shadowed; Grace identified) Deadpool #49 (2001); (Mary identified) Deadpool #50 (2001); (full) Deadpool #52 (2001)

HISTORY: The first victims of psychotic twin sisters Grace and Mary Mercy were their parents, whose bodies they hid in the downstairs storage bin of their apartment building. They continued killing, primarily those that upset them, such as a rival school's star soccer player and a nosey delivery boy who looked inside one of their deliveries, stashing the bodies in the barn of their family's Southampton summer residence. Their absence at school was noticed, however, and when school administrator Sarah Moreels came to investigate, Grace killed her with a hockey stick. The sisters killed again to obtain tickets to rock star Killer Dick's concert, whereupon they were invited backstage and ended up in his limousine. Upon learning that he was married with three children, however, they killed him. A substantial reward was offered for their arrest, which attracted mercenary Deadpool ("Wade Wilson")'s attention. Enamored by the prospect of killing a "super hero," the sisters crashed their cars into him simultaneously; however, Mary forgot to buckle her seatbelt and was mortally wounded. They fled to their summer home, where Mary euthanized Grace, and swore revenge on Deadpool. Though she challenged him to face her, Deadpool was still recuperating from his injuries and instead shot her in the face with a high-powered sniper rifle, apparently killing her.

HEIGHT: 5'6" **WEIGHT:** 133 lbs. **EYES:** Blue **HAIR:** Blond

ABILITIES/ACCESSORIES: The Mercy Sisters were ruthless, remorseless killers who used a variety of common items such as hockey sticks and hacksaws to kill and mutilate their victims. They were skilled with wielding knives and handguns.

INTELLIGENCE: 2 **STRENGTH:** 2 **SPEED:** 2 **DURABILITY:** 2
ENERGY PROJECTION: 1 **FIGHTING SKILLS:** 4

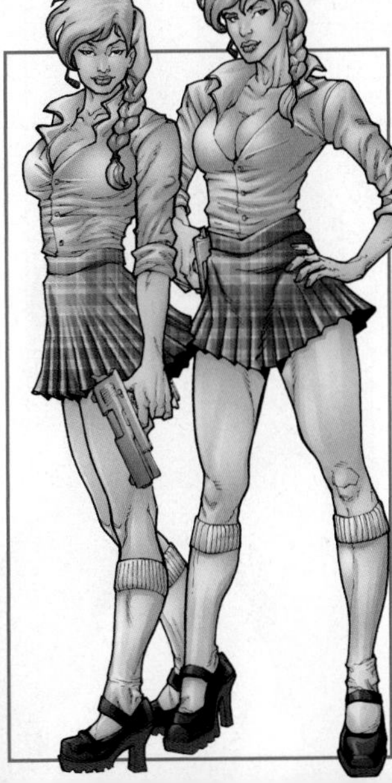

Art by Gus Vazquez

MONTGOMERY

REAL NAME: Montgomery "Monty" Burns
ALIASES: Consuela, Mon-Mon
IDENTITY: No dual identity
OCCUPATION: Former precognitive for Landau, Luckman & Lake
CITIZENSHIP: Unrevealed

PLACE OF BIRTH: Unrevealed
KNOWN RELATIVES: Unidentified mother
GROUP AFFILIATION: Formerly Landau, Luckman & Lake
EDUCATION: Unrevealed
FIRST APPEARANCE: Deadpool Minus-One (1997)

HISTORY: Recruited, voluntarily or not, for Landau, Luckman & Lake's Corporal Enhancement Division, aka Fleshwerks, Montgomery Burns, his precognition enhanced by LL&L's technology, foresaw an alien Messiah (S'met'kth) bringing peace to Earth, not realizing it would be mere mindless bliss. He further foresaw the Messiah's would-be killer, Tiamat, and protector, Mithras, determined to be Deadpool ("Wade Wilson"). Both Overboss Dixon Mason and fugitive LL&L executive Gerry LeQuare secretly consulted Monty, altering his memories afterward. The technology's repeated use eventually left him in a crippled, wasted state, and he became caregiver to fellow precogs. Monty secretly fell in love with Expediter Zoe Culloden. In recent years, Monty and other LL&L employees met with Deadpool, who rejected their claims; however, Monty's spontaneous reading of Deadpool's future guided Deadpool through other crises. To reciprocate, Deadpool took him to Monte Carlo, Monaco, for an adventure which restored the bitter precog's hopes. Dixon vindictively erased Monty's Monte Carlo memories. After killing the Messiah, Deadpool relocated to Bolivia, taking Monty, his powers gone, as reluctant confidante. When Mercedes Wilson, erroneously believed Deadpool's wife, was resurrected, Monty's research indicated her husband T-Ray (Wade Wilson) had resurrected her. After T-Ray tortured Monty, Deadpool returned Monty to LL&L for treatment, but Zoe, now Overboss, initially detained them as firm "property." After learning Monty was in love with her, however, she resigned from LL&L, allowing Deadpool to escape while she and the recovering Monty started life elsewhere. Months later, when Deadpool was believed dead, the couple attended his funeral.

Art by Gus Vazquez with Walter McDaniel (inset)

HEIGHT: 6'2"	WEIGHT: 85 lbs.	EYES: Brown	HAIR: Bald, formerly brown

ABILITIES/ACCESSORIES: Montgomery could predict future events up to several days in advance, although the details perceived varied. With enhancement, his range extended for years. He could receive telepathic impressions from others, even when observing them from afar electronically. A paraplegic, he is confined to a sophisticated wheelchair-like device.

INTELLIGENCE: 4 **STRENGTH:** 1 **SPEED:** 1 **DURABILITY:** 1
ENERGY PROJECTION: 1 **FIGHTING SKILLS:** 1

OYAKATA

REAL NAME: Unrevealed
ALIASES: Yokozuna (his sumo title)
IDENTITY: Secret
OCCUPATION: Oyakata, occasional hitman; former sumo wrestler
CITIZENSHIP: Japan

PLACE OF BIRTH: Tokyo, Japan
KNOWN RELATIVES: Unidentified wife (deceased), Sazae (daughter)
GROUP AFFILIATION: His own group of Rikishi
EDUCATION: Unrevealed
FIRST APPEARANCE: Deadpool Team-Up #1 (1998)

HISTORY: Many years ago, the man eventually known as the Oyakata was a rikishi (sumo wrestler) famous for his skilled hands. Considered unbeatable, the Oyakata retired to run his own heya (stable of wrestlers), where his daughter Sazae became chief. When the mercenary who would become Deadpool ("Wade Wilson") came to train at the heya, he was forbidden to join until he was able to defeat the Oyakata himself. After years of encouragement from the Oyakata, the man defeated him and was allowed to join the heya as Chiyonosake, soon becoming the heya's star wrestler. When Chiyonosake developed a relationship with Sazae, the Oyakata made him heir to his heya and fortune, but Chiyonosake left the heya soon after receiving the order to kill the Oyakata. In the following years, the Oyakata began secretly working as a hitman for the Yakuza, often using his skilled hands to kill his targets. Targeted by the diminutive Deadpool clone Widdle Wade, the Oyakata was saved by Deadpool, who the Oyakata recognized as Chiyonosake. Welcoming Deadpool back to the heya, the Oyakata was again attacked by Widdle Wade, who slaughtered nearly all of the Rikishi before Deadpool again intervened. Realizing that the Yakuza Boss had hired Widdle Wade to kill him, the Oyakata hired Deadpool to kill the Boss and asked Deadpool to either rejoin the heya or leave forever. Accepting his task, Deadpool left.

Art by Gus Vazquez

HEIGHT: 6'	WEIGHT: 205 lbs.	EYES: Brown	HAIR: Black

ABILITIES/ACCESSORIES: The Oyakata is an expert sumo wrestler, considered unbeatable in his heyday and using his talents as a hitman. His skilled hands can control whether delicate injuries, such as spinal trauma, are fatal and/or permanent.

INTELLIGENCE: 2 **STRENGTH:** 3 **SPEED:** 2 **DURABILITY:** 2
ENERGY PROJECTION: 1 **FIGHTING SKILLS:** 5

SACK

REAL NAME: Nelson Frank
ALIASES: None
IDENTITY: Secret
OCCUPATION: Criminal; former stadium janitor
CITIZENSHIP: USA
PLACE OF BIRTH: Brooklyn, New York
KNOWN RELATIVES: Unidentified mother (deceased)
GROUP AFFILIATION: Knights of Columbus
EDUCATION: High school dropout
FIRST APPEARANCE: Deadpool #46 (2000)

HISTORY: Nelson Frank was cleaning up after a game at Shea stadium when he happened upon a nondescript sack left in a men's room stall. Next to it was a pair of titanium gloves and the skeleton of a horned being. Not wanting to cause trouble, Nelson disposed of the skeleton and took the sack and gloves to his Brooklyn home where he left them in the living room. His mother knocked over the sack, allowing creatures from another dimension to escape a portal within the sack. The creatures ate his mother before Nelson figured out to put the gloves on and shove the "little bastards" back in. He used the creatures to get rid of a nosey neighbor, a nasty pizza deliveryman, a group of Girl Scouts and a couple of co-workers. He had a brainstorm to profit from the creatures and, as the Sack, he sought to rob Brooklyn First Federal Savings and Loan. Terrorizing the bank's patrons and guards with the creatures, the Sack ran afoul of the mercenary Deadpool ("Wade Wilson") during one of his heroic turns. Setting the creatures against Deadpool, they were repulsed by the mercenary's cancer-ridden skin. Deadpool foiled the Sack's robbery by throwing a knife in his shoulder, causing him to drop the sack. Quickly retrieving it, Deadpool put it over the Sack's head and shoulders, subjecting him to the creatures which quickly devoured him. The current location of the Sack's sack is unrevealed.

CREATURES

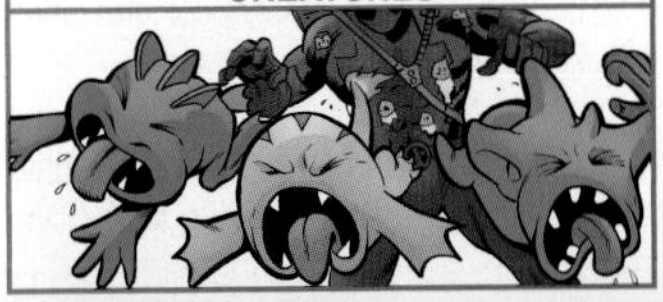

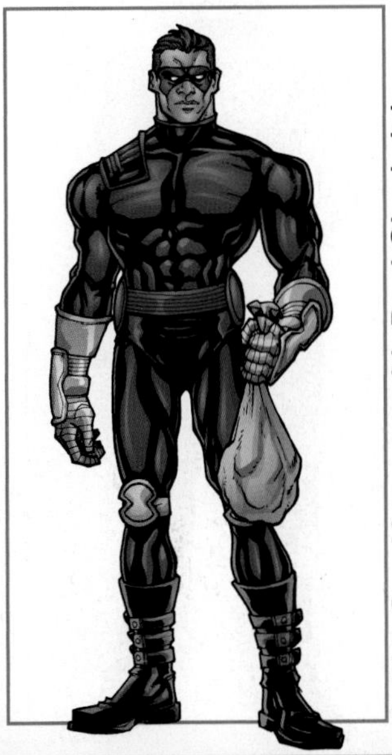

Art by Gus Vazquez with Paul Chadwick

HEIGHT: 5'10" **WEIGHT:** 161 lbs. **EYES:** Blue **HAIR:** Black

ABILITIES/ACCESSORIES: The Sack possessed a bag of unknown origin that contains a portal to a dimension populated by small, colorful, flesh-eating creatures with a variety of traits including fins, horns, pincers, tails and more. The Sack wore a pair of titanium gloves that allowed him to safely handle the creatures.

INTELLIGENCE: 2 **STRENGTH:** 2 **SPEED:** 2 **DURABILITY:** 2
ENERGY PROJECTION: 1 **FIGHTING SKILLS:** 2

SLUGGO

REAL NAME: Bernard Hoyster
ALIASES: None
IDENTITY: Secret
OCCUPATION: Mercenary; former government operative
CITIZENSHIP: Presumably Canada
PLACE OF BIRTH: Unrevealed
KNOWN RELATIVES: None
GROUP AFFILIATION: Formerly Weapon X (Canada), Department K
EDUCATION: Unrevealed
FIRST APPEARANCE: X-Force #22 (1993)

HISTORY: Mercenary Bernard Hoyster underwent mutation in Canada's Weapon X Program and, dubbed Sluggo, trained with fellow mercenaries Garrison Kane, Greg Terraerton and "Wade Wilson." After Wilson seemingly killed Terraerton (later called Slayback), their unit apparently disbanded. Finding work with crimelord Tolliver (Tyler Dayspring), Sluggo befriended Wilson's shape-shifting girlfriend Copycat (Vanessa Carlysle) and dated her friend Tina Valentino. Wilson, dubbed Deadpool, and Kane also worked for Tolliver, but Sluggo, increasingly disappointed by his life, lost touch with them. In recent years, following Tolliver's supposed death, Copycat, fleeing after being extorted into impersonating mercenary Domino (Neena Thurman), was pursued for information on Tolliver's will. She sought sanctuary with Tina, but both Deadpool and Sluggo tracked them to Boston. Sluggo impulsively shot Tina, killing her. Boston police reported the incident, drawing attention Domino, who sought revenge. Copycat fled to Tina's home in nearby Norwell; Sluggo and Deadpool followed, but Domino intervened, and she shot both men from behind. Desperate to avoid death, Copycat offered to lead her to X-Force, whom Domino had vowed to assist. Domino begrudgingly agreed and Copycat shot Sluggo and Deadpool in the heads to prolong unconsciousness. Weeks later, Sluggo, still seeking information, approached Copycat's mother, Dorothy Carlysle, but Copycat snared him with a rope. When questioned, Sluggo revealed Deadpool, also believed to possess relevant information, was in Bosnia-Herzegovina. Copycat threw Sluggo through the Carlysle home's picture window, advised her mother to have him arrested for breaking and entering and departed to assist Deadpool.

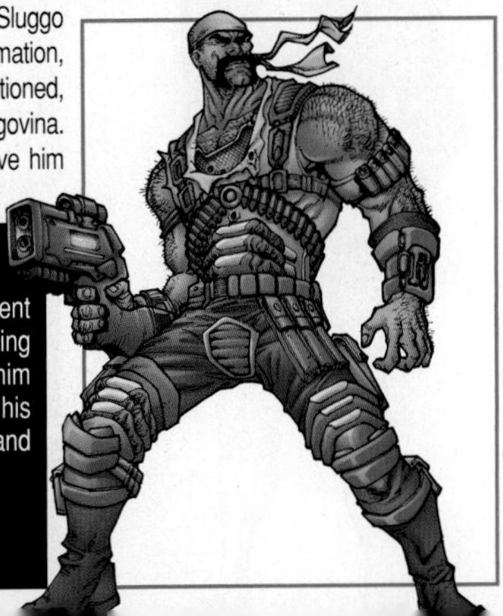

Art by Gus Vazquez

HEIGHT: 7'4" **WEIGHT:** 450 lbs. **EYES:** Blue **HAIR:** Black

ABILITIES/ACCESSORIES: Sluggo is virtually invulnerable to physical injury, to the extent he can breathe and speak even while being strangled. Energy blasts capable of rending holes through ordinary people cannot pierce his skin, although such blasts can render him unconscious. He customarily carries a large plasma gun, with various accessories in his belt and uniform. Although allegedly quite dim-witted, he is an experienced marksman and combatant.

INTELLIGENCE: 1 **STRENGTH:** 3 **SPEED:** 2 **DURABILITY:** 6
ENERGY PROJECTION: 4 **FIGHTING SKILLS:** 4

STREET SPEEDER

REAL NAME: Harrison Stavrou
ALIASES: None
IDENTITY: Secret
OCCUPATION: Public nuisance
CITIZENSHIP: USA

PLACE OF BIRTH: Brooklyn, New York
KNOWN RELATIVES: None
GROUP AFFILIATION: None
EDUCATION: BA in studio art
FIRST APPEARANCE: Deadpool #56 (2001)

Art by Gus Vazquez

HISTORY: An art school student, Harrison Stavrou was involved in a freak accident in which he inhaled a combination of various toxic paint fumes. Somehow gaining superhuman speed, Harrison quickly made a name for himself as the fun-loving, super-powered Street Speeder. Angry that he often rushed through the streets late at night, even after 9 pm, a group of elderly women held a bake sale, raising $21,025.73 toward having him killed. Upon learning that the Avengers did not kill for money, the women hired the mercenary Deadpool ("Wade Wilson"), who was known as a "conscience-free lowlife scum who felt no remorse about snuffing out a human life." Speeder easily avoided Deadpool's attempt to kill him with the Liefelder, a large gun given to him by the women. Using a pair of designer sneakers as bait, the wiley Deadpool planned to trap the Speeder in a net and drop a piano on him. Launching himself at the Street Speeder with a gigantic slingshot device, Deadpool missed and was struck by the piano after crashing into a wall. Seeing Deadpool's difficulty, the women attempted to get a refund, but Deadpool threatened to set them on fire and refused to give up. He next donned a rocket pack in an attempt to match the Street Speeder's quickness. Unfortunately, the Speeder simply stopped, causing Deadpool's velocity to send him into a fireworks factory. Shortly thereafter, Deadpool's former sidekick Kid Deadpool (Christopher Cassera) destroyed his warehouse apartment, and when the Street Speeder showed up to view the explosion, Deadpool shot him in the stomach, apparently killing him.

HEIGHT: 6'1"	**WEIGHT:** 164 lbs.	**EYES:** Blue	**HAIR:** Blond

ABILITIES/ACCESSORIES: The Street Speeder could move at superhuman speeds, nearing Mach 3. His running speed was sufficient to outrun a rocket-powered jetpack and even dodge gunfire at point-blank range. He could, however, be caught off guard when stationary.

INTELLIGENCE: 2 **STRENGTH:** 2 **SPEED:** 5 **DURABILITY:** 2
ENERGY PROJECTION: 1 **FIGHTING SKILLS:** 2

DUNCAN VESS

REAL NAME: Duncan Vess
ALIASES: None known
IDENTITY: Publicly known
OCCUPATION: Former author
CITIZENSHIP: Unrevealed

PLACE OF BIRTH: Unrevealed
KNOWN RELATIVES: None
GROUP AFFILIATION: None
EDUCATION: Unrevealed
FIRST APPEARANCE: Wolverine 1999 (1999)

HISTORY: Duncan Vess long ago forsook his werewolf heritage to live amongst humanity. In the 21st century, he was the author of the successful "Werewolf Chronicles" novel series, which brought him to the long-escaped attention of the Council of Werewolves. Angered at Vess' betrayal, the Council hired the mercenary Deadpool ("Wade Wilson") to kill him. Unaware of this, another werewolf, Lycus, targeted Vess for death. When

Art by Gus Vazquez

Wolverine (Logan/James Howlett) tried to get Vess to sign a copy of his newest novel, "Blood Moon," for his teammate Kitty Pryde, both men recognized the other's feral nature. Departing rapidly, Vess was ambushed in his home by Lycus while Wolverine, trailing Vess, encountered Deadpool as he prepared to break into Vess' home. While Wolverine battled Lycus, Deadpool used a silver dagger to goad Vess into trying to access his long disused werewolf self, to limited success. Lycus temporarily stunned Wolverine and Deadpool and cornered Vess. The arriving Council of Werewolves halted Lycus, revealing their reasons for hiring Deadpool and accusing Lycus of losing touch with his human side before turning him fully into a wolf, which fled into the New York streets. They prepared to destroy Vess for having forsaken his wolf side, but Wolverine stepped between them. As dawn approached, the Council teleported away, warning Vess to be long gone before the next full moon and that they would hunt him forever. Unable to live in werewolf tribes and forbidden to return to his chosen life, Vess resolved to disappear in a remote town where he could simply… be.

HEIGHT: 5'9" (possibly larger in werewolf form)	**WEIGHT:** 165 lbs.	**EYES:** Brown **HAIR:** Black

ABILITIES/ACCESSORIES: Vess is a talented writer. He previously adopted werewolf form, presumably with the standard werewolf strengths (enhanced strength, speed, senses, agility, reflexes, and healing) and vulnerabilities (silver, wolfsbane, magic, requiring moonlight to remain in wolf form). It is unclear whether he is can still adopt werewolf form.

INTELLIGENCE: 2/3* **STRENGTH:** 2/4* **SPEED:** 2/3* **DURABILITY:** 2/4*
ENERGY PROJECTION: 1 **FIGHTING SKILLS:** 2
*AS WEREWOLF

WIDDLE WADE

REAL NAME: Wade
ALIASES: None
IDENTITY: No dual identity
OCCUPATION: Hit man
CITIZENSHIP: Unrevealed, if applicable
PLACE OF CREATION: Tokyo, Japan
KNOWN RELATIVES: Deadpool ("Wade Wilson," genetic progenitor)
GROUP AFFILIATION: Yakuza
EDUCATION: Unrevealed
FIRST APPEARANCE: Deadpool #6 (1997)

HISTORY: Cloned by the Yakuza mob from Deadpool ("Wade Wilson")'s DNA, Widdle Wade was created to assassinate the Yakuza's sometime employee the Oyakata. After years of electroshock to focus his anger towards the Oyakata and being given their most difficult missions, Widdle Wade was informed that the Yakuza no longer wished the Oyakata dead. Refusing to stop until he was dead, Widdle Wade liberated the dog Daruma and soon found the Oyakata at a Tokyo night club. Attempting to kill him, Widdle Wade was halted by Deadpool, who had been hired to protect the Oyakata. The two briefly fought until Widdle Wade was hit and carried away by a passing truck. Returning to finish the job, Widdle Wade started a fire in the Oyakata's heya, where he killed nearly all of the Rikishi. Deadpool once again intervened and led Widdle Wade into the Dohyo, where the two battled again. After Widdle Wade broke Deadpool's sword in half, Deadpool impaled Widdle Wade with the sword fragment. As he apparently died, Widdle Wade revealed his face to Deadpool, who was shocked to see that Widdle Wade had not inherited his scars.

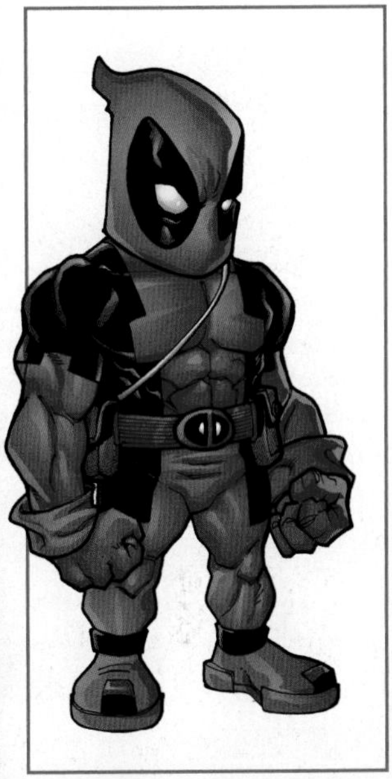

Art by Gus Vazquez

HEIGHT: 3'1" **WEIGHT:** 80 lbs. **EYES:** Brown **HAIR:** Unrevealed

ABILITIES/ACCESSORIES: Widdle Wade possessed the same abilities as his progenitor, Deadpool, including a superhuman healing factor that allowed him to regenerate damaged cells much faster than a normal human being. The healing factor granted Widdle Wade immunity to most poisons, drugs and diseases, and even extremely slowed his aging processes. His strength, stamina and reflexes were also enhanced during the cloning process, reflecting the physical attributes of someone twice his height. Widdle Wade was fluent in Japanese and was a skilled assassin, having mastered numerous fighting styles, bladed weapons and firearms.

INTELLIGENCE: 2 **STRENGTH:** 3 **SPEED:** 2 **DURABILITY:** 4
ENERGY PROJECTION: 1 **FIGHTING SKILLS:** 6

MERCEDES WILSON

REAL NAME: Mercedes Wilson
ALIASES: Angel with a dirty halo, Angel
IDENTITY: No dual identity
OCCUPATION: Former teacher
CITIZENSHIP: Possibly USA or Canada
PLACE OF BIRTH: Unrevealed
KNOWN RELATIVES: Wade Wilson (husband), unidentified parents
GROUP AFFILIATION: None
EDUCATION: Teaching degree at unidentified university
FIRST APPEARANCE: (Hallucination) Deadpool #26 (1999); (physical) Deadpool #27; (identified) Deadpool #28 (1999)

HISTORY: One winter, newlywed teachers Wade and Mercedes Wilson saved the drowning "Jack," unaware he was a mercenary who had botched a job. To hide, Jack tried to usurp Wade's identity, but the couple fought back; Jack accidentally slew Mercedes and seemingly killed Wade. Years later, mystical mercenary T-Ray, apparently the true Wade Wilson, initiated his revenge plot against Deadpool (who also believed himself "Wade Wilson"), who T-Ray believed was Jack. T-Ray planned to have Deadpool fall in love with Mercedes and try to become a better man before destroying him by revealing the truth. T-Ray instilled Deadpool with Mercedes-centered hallucinations, resurrected her with no memory of how she died and then tricked Deadpool into rescuing her. Mercedes adjusted to her new life while helping Deadpool learn who revived her. Mercedes chose to seek a peaceful life with her supposed husband instead of pursuing revenge on T-Ray, but T-Ray made Mercedes watch his battles with Deadpool at places and times important to the Wilsons', sowing doubt in her when Deadpool didn't recognize these. After summoning ghosts of Deadpool's victims and restoring Mercedes' death memories and transforming her into a mystic albino like himself, T-Ray claimed he was the true Wade Wilson and convinced Mercedes that Deadpool was Jack. However, to T-Ray's dismay, Deadpool found the whole situation ludicrous instead of spirit-crushing. Apologizing to Mercedes for his supposed actions, Deadpool asked that she not become a monster as he and T-Ray were. Disgusted she was resurrected solely for T-Ray's revenge scheme, Mercedes gave Deadpool some of her new power to take T-Ray down, but reclaimed it before Deadpool could kill him. Uncertain what she wanted in her new life, Mercedes left with T-Ray while vengefully leaving Deadpool to face the ghosts, though she likely left T-Ray soon after.

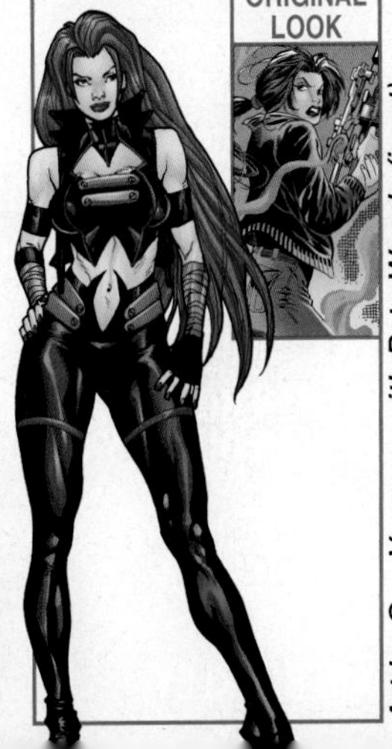

ORIGINAL LOOK

Art by Gus Vazquez with Pete Woods (inset)

HEIGHT: 5'7" **WEIGHT:** 140 lbs. **EYES:** Light amber; (originally brown) **HAIR:** Red; (originally black)

ABILITIES/ACCESSORIES: Her mystical powers largely unrevealed, Mercedes could temporarily transfer power to another person and may have enhanced endurance and strength. Mercedes has some knowledge of philosophy and classic literature.

INTELLIGENCE: 2 **STRENGTH:** 2 **SPEED:** 2 **DURABILITY:** 2
ENERGY PROJECTION: 3 **FIGHTING SKILLS:** 2

DEADPOOL
CORPS
RANK and FOUL

Head Writer/Coordinator
JEFF CHRISTIANSEN

Writing/Coordination Assistants
Mike O'Sullivan, Markus Raymond & Mike Fichera

Writers
MICHAEL HOSKIN, RONALD BYRD, MIKE O'SULLIVAN, JACOB ROUGEMONT, MADISON CARTER, MARKUS RAYMOND, KEVIN GARCIA, STUART VANDAL, CHRIS BIGGS, ROB LONDON, SEAN MCQUAID, DAVID WILTFONG, ERIC J. MOREELS & MIKE GAGNON

Select Character Artwork
GUS VAZQUEZ & TOM CHU

Cover Artists
HUMBERTO RAMOS & EDGAR DELGADO

Cover Design
SPRING HOTELING

Art Reconstruction
POND SCUM, NELSON RIBEIRO, MIKE FICHERA & JERRY KALINOWSKI

Select Coloring
TOM SMITH

Editor
JEFF YOUNGQUIST

Editors, Special Projects
JENNIFER GRÜNWALD & MARK D. BEAZLEY

Associate Editor
JOHN DENNING

Assistant Editor
ALEX STARBUCK

Copy Editors
BRIAN OVERTON & TED KUTT

Senior Vice President of Sales
DAVID GABRIEL

Production
NELSON RIBEIRO, JERRY KALINOWSKI, JERRON QUALITY COLOR & RYAN DEVALL

Editor in Chief
JOE QUESADA

Publisher
DAN BUCKLEY

Executive Producer

Special thanks to Tom Brevoort, Christos Gage, Joe Kelly, Shane McNichols, Doug Moench, Fabian Nicieza, Jimmy Palmiotti, Rob Rodi, Buddy Scalera, Jim Sharpe, Gail Simone, Kevin Lawrence Smith, Fred Van Lente, Mark O'English, www.g-mart.com and the guys at the Appendix (www.marvunapp.com).

For the appendixes to the OHotMU (pre-published and new additions — plus data corrections, Frequently Asked Questions and Power Grid legends), see www.marvunapp.com/ohotmu/appendixes.htm

In the Marvel Universe Handbook style, this one-shot has everything you need to make sense of Deadpool! (Is that even possible?) In this issue, there are more *all-new* profiles than 'Pool has voices in his head — from "allies" (Outlaw, Weasel, Zombie Deadpool), to enemies (Ajax, Lightmaster, Madcap), to the hotties (Dr. Betty, Blind Al, Big Bertha) and the sheer awesomeness of the Sack! How could you pass this up? You know at least one of your personalities will love it! Featuring *new art* for dozens of characters! More fun than a barrel of gun-wielding monkeys!

Ajax (Francis)
Anaconda
Ananastasia
Asp (Cleo Nefertiti)
Big Bertha
Black Mamba
Black Swan
Blind Al
Bob, Agent of Hydra
Sandi Brandenberg
G.W. Bridge
Ilaney Brükner
Cat (Shen Kuei)
Corpse Corps
Courier (Jacob Gavin)
Zoe Culloden
Deadpool ("Wade Wilson")
Deadpool (Earth-2149)
Deadpool Corps
Deathtrap
Dinah Soar
Director (Malcolm Colcord)
Dirty Wolff
Doctor Betty
Doctor Bong
Domino (Neena Thurman)
Noah DuBois
Executive Elite
Flatman
Four Winds
Grasshopper
Halfghanaghan Brothers
Hellhouse
Hit-Monkey
Invisible Man (Darick Gallhager)
Brent Jackson
Valerie Jessup
Kid Deadpool (Cassera)
Dr. Emrys Killebrew
Lightmaster (Lansky)
Malachi
Madcap
Mary Zero
Mercy Sisters
Messiah (S'met'kth)
Montgomery
Mr. Immortal
Outlaw (Inez Temple)
Oyakata
Remnants
Sack (Frank)
Skornn
Sluggo
Street Speeder
Tiamat (alien champion)
ULTIMATUM
Duncan Vess
Weasel (Jack Hammer)
Widdle Wade
Mercedes Wilson
Zero (ADAM Unit Zero)

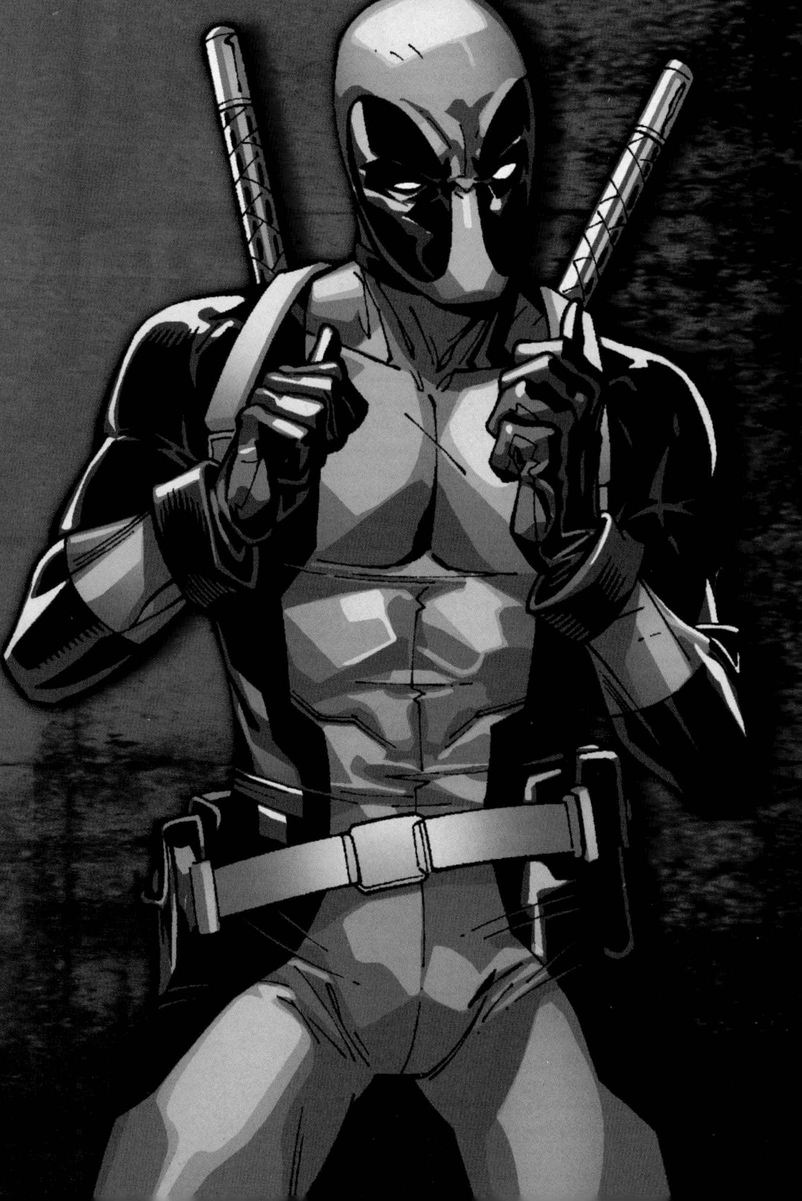

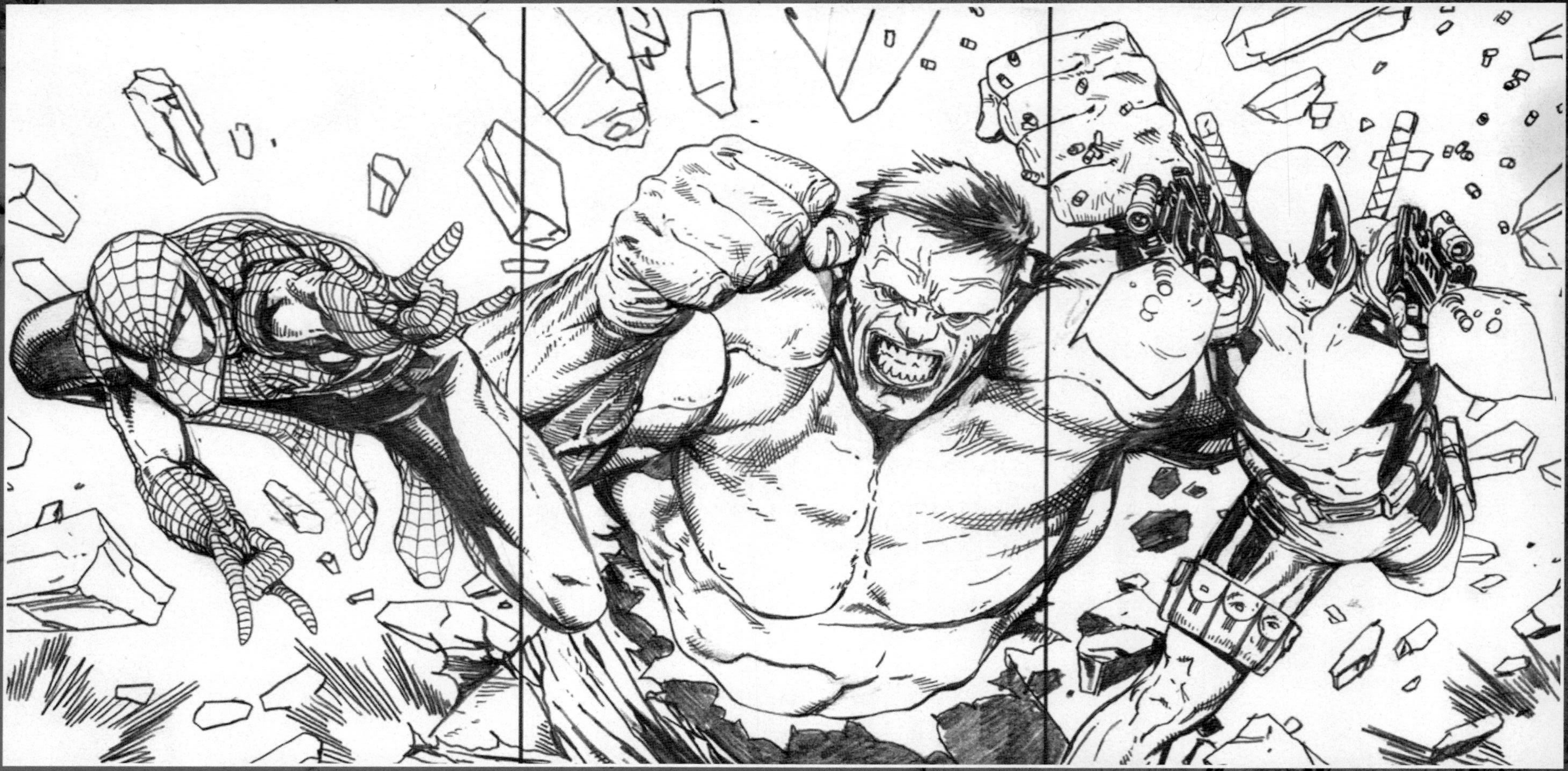

IDENTITY WARS COMBINED COVER SKETCH BY STEVE MCNIVEN

IDENTITY WARS COMBINED COVER PENCILS BY STEVE MCNIVEN

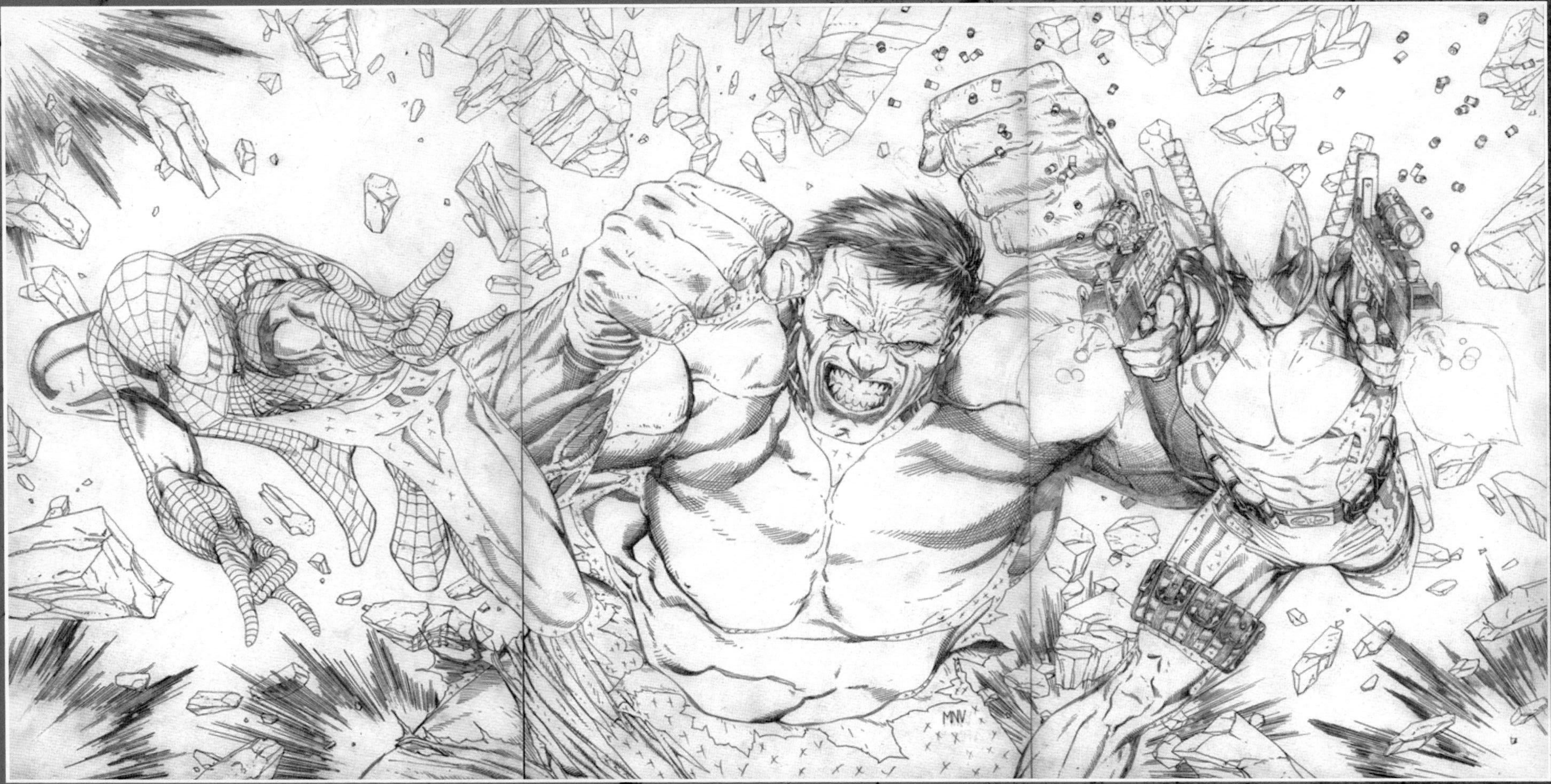
MNV

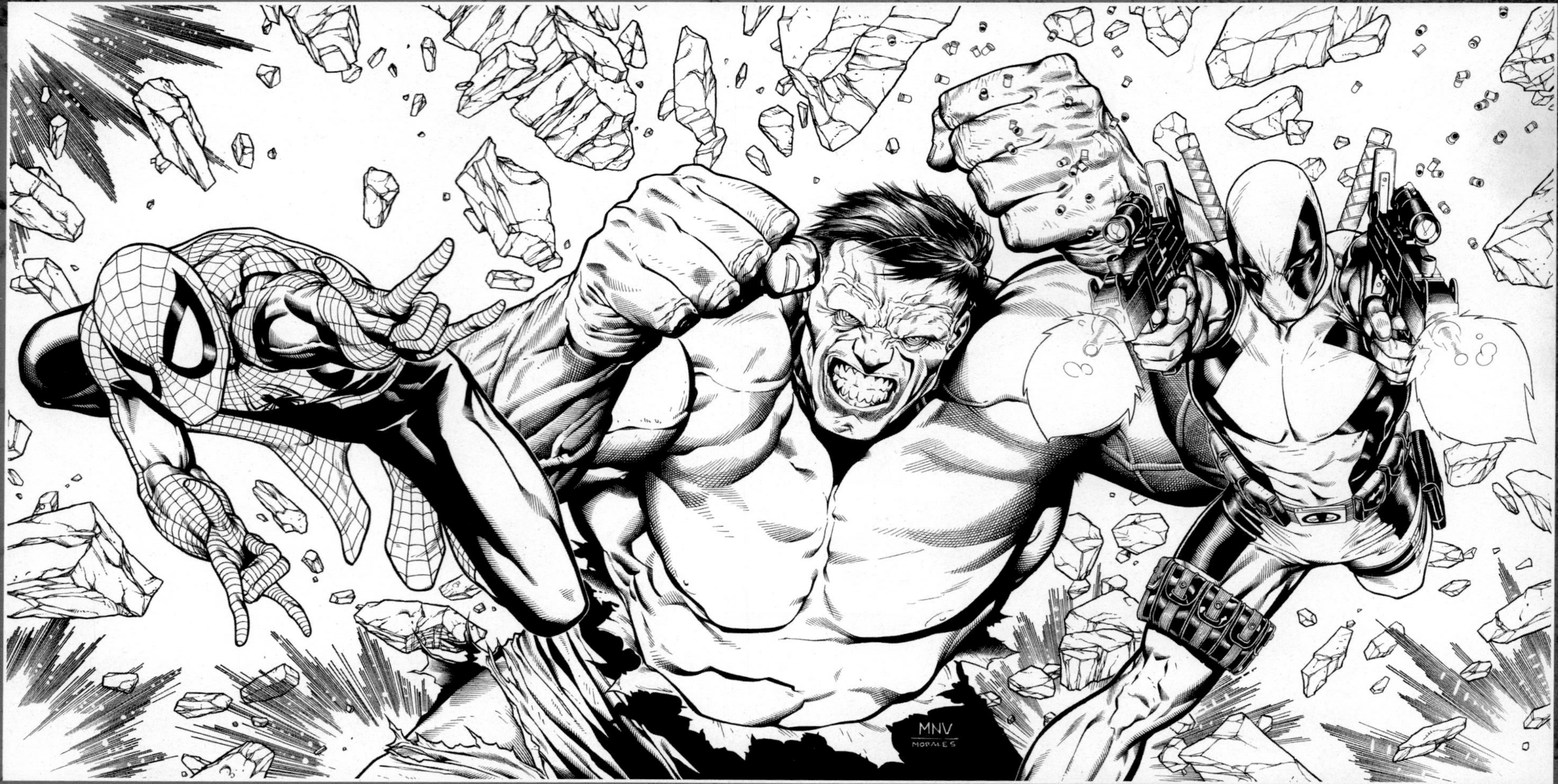
MNV
MORALES

IDENTITY WARS COMBINED COVER INKS BY MARK MORALES

IDENTITY WARS COMBINED COVER COLORS BY MARTE GRACIA

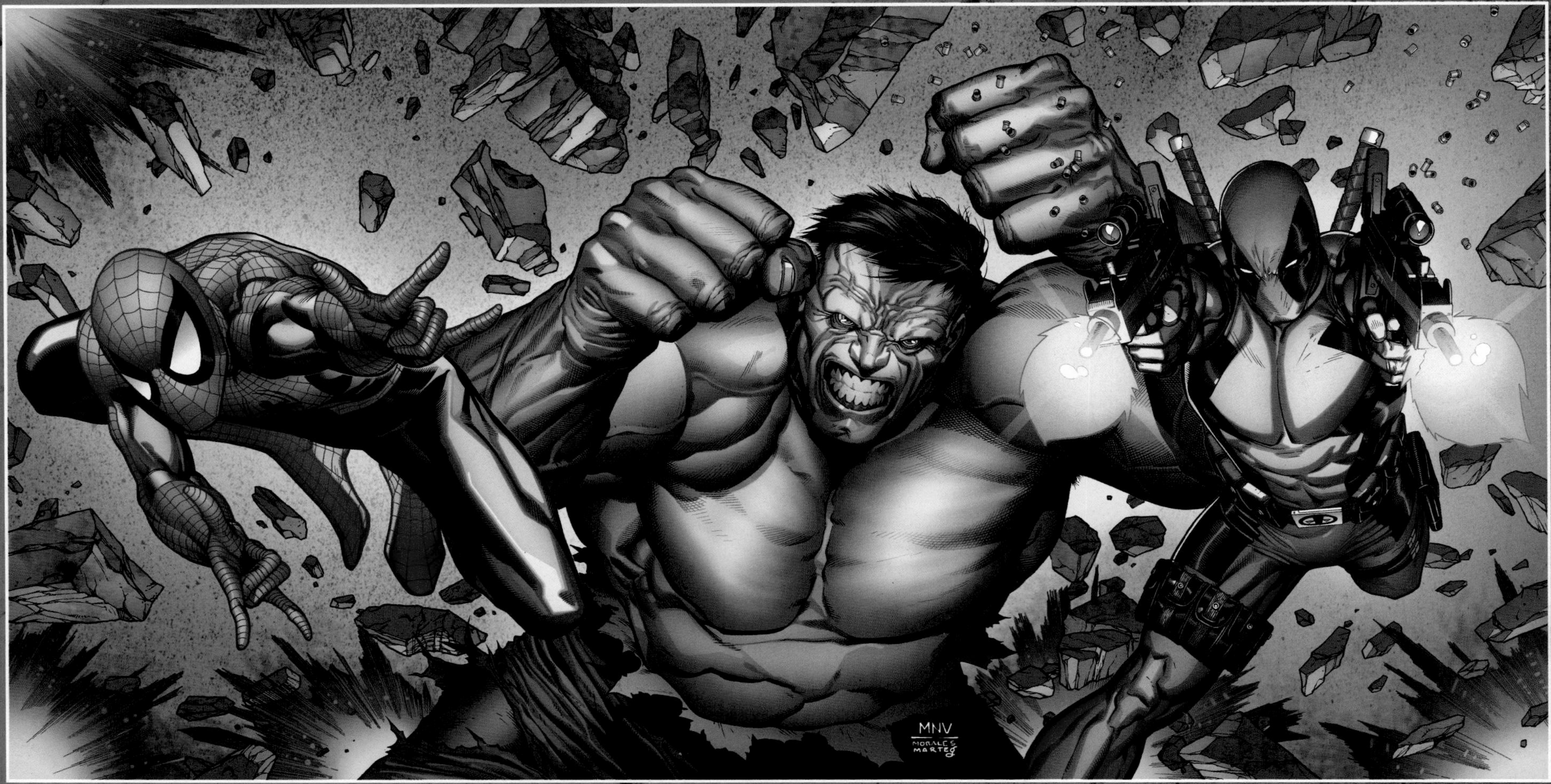
MNV
MORALES
MARTE G

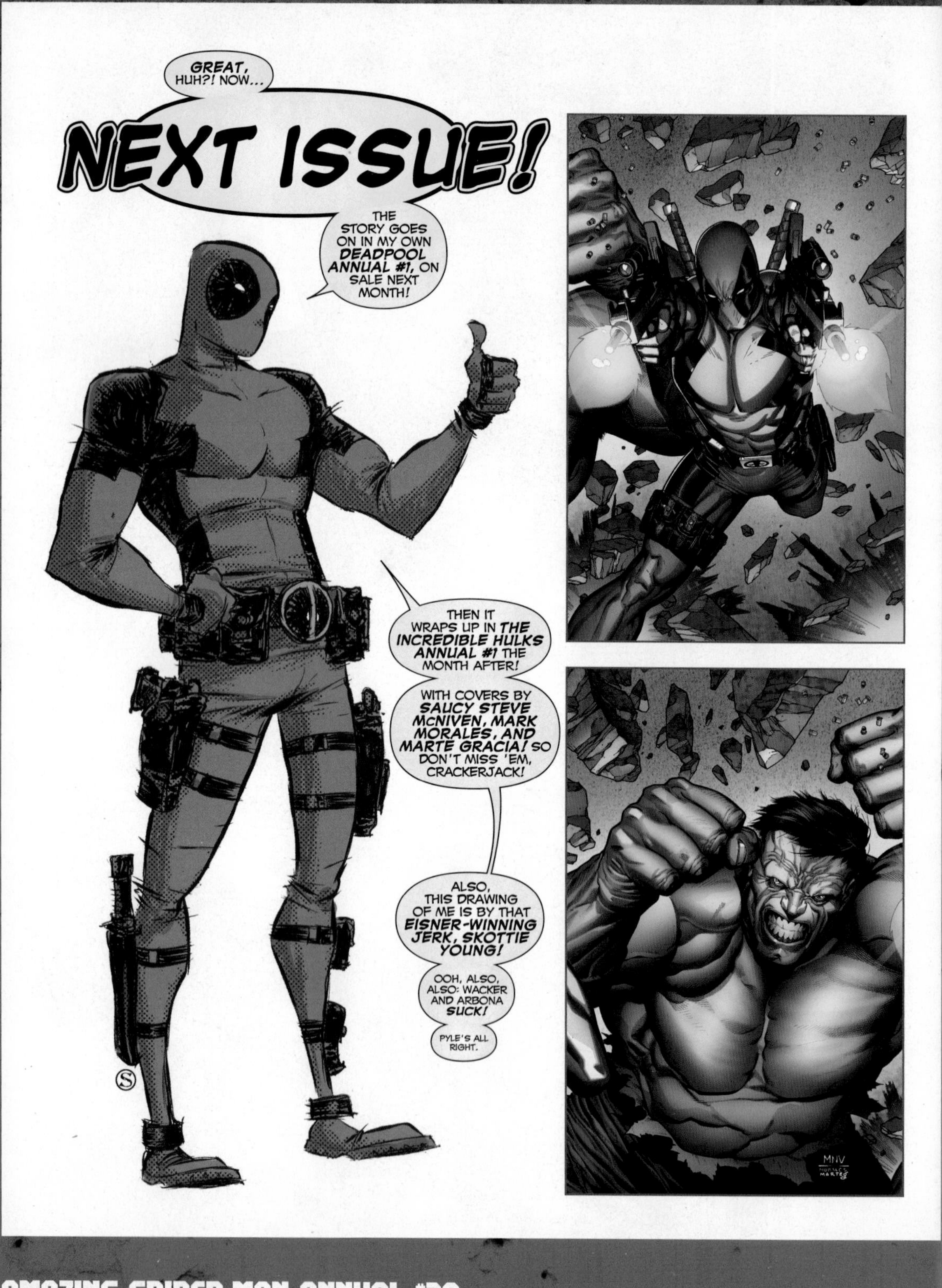
GREAT, HUH?! NOW...
NEXT ISSUE!
THE STORY GOES ON IN MY OWN DEADPOOL ANNUAL #1, ON SALE NEXT MONTH!
THEN IT WRAPS UP IN THE INCREDIBLE HULKS ANNUAL #1 THE MONTH AFTER!
WITH COVERS BY SAUCY STEVE McNIVEN, MARK MORALES, AND MARTE GRACIA! SO DON'T MISS 'EM, CRACKERJACK!
ALSO, THIS DRAWING OF ME IS BY THAT EISNER-WINNING JERK, SKOTTIE YOUNG!
OOH, ALSO, ALSO: WACKER AND ARBONA SUCK!
PYLE'S ALL RIGHT.

AMAZING SPIDER-MAN ANNUAL #38
"NEXT ISSUE" PAGE